ACCA

Applied Skills

Financial Management (FM)

EXAM KIT

PUBLISHING

British Library Cataloguing-in-Publication Data

A catalogue record for this book is available from the British Library.

Published by:

Kaplan Publishing UK

Unit 2 The Business Centre

Molly Millar's Lane

Wokingham

Berkshire

RG41 2QZ

ISBN: 978-1-78740-617-9

Acknowledgements

These materials are reviewed by the ACCA examining team. The objective of the review is to ensure that the material properly covers the syllabus and study guide outcomes, used by the examining team in setting the exams, in the appropriate breadth and depth. The review does not ensure that every eventuality, combination or application of examinable topics is addressed by the ACCA Approved Content. Nor does the review comprise a detailed technical check of the content as the Approved Content Provider has its own quality assurance processes in place in this respect.

The past ACCA examination questions are the copyright of the Association of Chartered Certified Accountants. The original answers to the questions from June 1994 onwards were produced by the examiners themselves and have been adapted by Kaplan Publishing.

We are grateful to the Chartered Institute of Management Accountants and the Institute of Chartered Accountants in England and Wales for permission to reproduce past examination questions. The answers have been prepared by Kaplan Publishing.

CONTENTS

Section

Key features in this edition

In addition to providing a wide ranging bank of real past exam questions, we have also included in this edition:

- An analysis of all of the recent examinations.

- Exam-specific information and advice on exam technique.

- Our recommended approach to make your revision for this particular subject as effective as possible.

- This includes step-by-step guidance on how best to use our Kaplan material (Study text, pocket notes and exam kit) at this stage in your studies.

- Enhanced tutorial answers packed with specific key answer tips, technical tutorial notes and exam technique tips from our experienced tutors.

- Complementary online resources including full tutor debriefs to point you in the right direction when you get stuck.

You will find a wealth of other resources to help you with your studies on the following sites:

www.mykaplan.co.uk

www.kaplan.co.uk/insights/study-tips

www.**acca**global.com/students/

Quality and accuracy are of the utmost importance to us so if you spot an error in any of our products, please send an email to mykaplanreporting@kaplan.com with full details, or follow the link to the feedback form in MyKaplan.

Our Quality Co-ordinator will work with our technical team to verify the error and take action to ensure it is corrected in future editions.

INDEX TO QUESTIONS AND ANSWERS

INTRODUCTION

Following the introduction of the revised exam format, all previous ACCA constructed response (long) exam questions within this kit have been adapted.

The specimen exam is included at the end of the kit.

KEY TO THE INDEX

EXAM ENHANCEMENTS

We have added the following enhancements to the answers in this exam kit:

Key answer tips

All answers include key answer tips to help your understanding of each question.

Tutorial note

Many answers include more tutorial notes to explain some of the technical points in more detail.

Top tutor tips

For selected questions, we 'walk through the answer' giving guidance on how to approach the questions with helpful 'tips from a top tutor', together with technical tutor notes.

These answers are indicated with the 'footsteps' icon in the index.

Within the questions in the exam kit you will see the following icons, shown in the question requirements:

🖥 = word processing

▦ = spreadsheet

The icons highlighting the constructed response workspace tool alongside some of the questions are for guidance only – it is important to recognise that each question is different and that the answer space provided by ACCA in the exam is determined by both the technical content of the question as well as the quality assurance processes ACCA undertakes to ensure the student is provided with the most appropriate type of workspace.

ONLINE ENHANCEMENTS

 Question debrief

For selected questions, we recommend that they are to be completed in full exam conditions (i.e. properly timed in a closed book environment).

In addition to the examiner's technical answer, enhanced with key answer tips and tutorial notes in this exam kit, online you can find an answer debrief by a top tutor that:

- works through the question in full

- points out how to approach the question

- shows how to ensure that the easy marks are obtained as quickly as possible, and

- emphasises how to tackle exam questions and exam technique.

These questions are indicated with the 'clock' icon in the index.

Online answer debriefs will be available on MyKaplan at:

www.MyKaplan.co.uk

ANALYSIS OF PAST EXAMS

The table below summarises the key topics that have been tested within the constructed response questions in the examinations to date. A much wider range of topics will now be examined following the introduction of objective test questions. Commencing September 2015, only selected questions will be released by ACCA every six months. The September 2016 exam was, however, released in full.

	M16/ J16	S16	D16	M17/ J17	S17/ D17	M18/ J18	S18/ D18	M19/ J19	S19/ D19
Financial management function									
Nature and purpose of financial management									
Financial objectives and corporate strategy									
Stakeholders and their impact on corporate strategy								✓	
Not for profits									
Financial management environment									
Economic environment									
Financial markets and institutions									
Working capital management									
Elements and importance (including cash operating cycle)				✓					
Overtrading	✓								
Inventories		✓							✓
Receivables		✓		✓			✓		
Payables		✓							
Cash									
Working capital needs and funding strategies							✓		✓
Investment appraisal									
Appraisal process									
Non-discounted techniques									
NPV with tax	✓								
NPV with tax and inflation		✓	✓	✓	✓			✓	
IRR							✓		
Risk and uncertainty	✓		✓	✓		✓			
Lease or buy							✓		✓
Asset replacement							✓		
Capital rationing			✓						✓

	M16/ J16	S16	D16	M17/ J17	S17/ D17	M18/ J18	S18/ D18	M19/ J19	S19/ D19
Business finance and cost of capital									
Sources of short term finance									
Sources of long term finance			✓		✓			✓	
Internal sources and dividend policy									
Gearing and capital structure									
Small & medium enterprises									
Islamic financing	✓					✓			
Sources and relative costs	✓								
Estimating cost of equity									
CAPM		✓	✓						
Cost of debt									
Overall cost of capital	✓		✓		✓			✓	
Gearing theories									
Impact of cost of capital on investments									
Forecasting after capital issue						✓			
Business valuations									
Nature and purpose of valuation									
Models for valuing shares	✓								
Valuing debt and other financial assets	✓								
Efficient markets hypothesis									
Risk management									
Foreign exchange risk	✓								
Interest rate risk	✓								
Forward contracts									
Money market hedge									
Futures									
Hedging for interest rate risk									

EXAM TECHNIQUE

GENERAL COMMENTS

- Read the examination questions carefully.

- **Divide the time** you spend on questions in proportion to the marks on offer:

  - one suggestion for this examination is to allocate 1.8 minutes to each mark available, so a 20 mark question should be completed in approximately 36 minutes.

  - within that, try to allow time at the end of each question to review your answer and address any obvious issues.

  Whatever happens, always keep your eye on the clock and **do not over run on any part of any question!**

- If you **get completely stuck** with a question:

  - flag the question and

  - **return to it later**.

- Stick to the question and **tailor your answer** to what you are asked.

  - Pay particular attention to the verbs in the question.

  - Try to apply your comments to the scenario where possible.

- If you do not understand what a question is asking, **state your assumptions**.

  Even if you do not answer in precisely the way the examiner hoped, you should be given some credit, if your assumptions are reasonable.

- You should do everything you can to make things easy for the marker.

  The marker will find it easier to identify the points you have made if your **answers are well laid out and well labelled, with references made to workings for calculation questions**.

OBJECTIVE TEST QUESTIONS

- Decide whether you want to attempt these at the start of the exam or at the end.

- No credit for working will be given in these questions, the answers will either be correct (2 marks) or incorrect (0 marks).

- Read the question carefully, as any alternative answer choices will be given based on common mistakes that could be made in attempting the question.

- If a question looks particularly difficult or time consuming, then miss it out first time through (make sure you flag it) and come back to it later. You may wish to enter a guess on the first run through in case you don't get time to return to the question.

CONSTRUCTED RESPONSE (LONG) QUESTIONS

- **Written elements**:

  Your answer should have:

  - a clear structure

  - a brief introduction, a main section and a conclusion.

  Be concise.

  It is better to write a little about a lot of different points than a great deal about one or two points.

  Where possible, try to relate comments to the specific context given rather than your answer looking like it was simply copied out of the textbook.

- **Computations**:

  It is essential to include all your workings in your answers.

COMPUTER-BASED EXAMS – ADDITIONAL TIPS

- Do not attempt a CBE until you have **completed all study material** relating to it.

- On the ACCA website there is a CBE demonstration. It is **ESSENTIAL** that you attempt this before your real CBE. You will become familiar with how to move around the CBE screens and the way that questions are formatted, increasing your confidence and speed in the actual exam.

- Be sure you understand how to use the **software** before you start the exam. If in doubt, ask the assessment centre staff to explain it to you.

- Questions are **displayed on the screen** and answers are entered using keyboard and mouse.

- In addition to the traditional multiple choice question type, CBEs will also contain other types of questions, such as number entry questions, formulae entry questions, multiple correct answers (select two or more), matching labels to targets, stem questions with multiple parts and written questions requiring text entry.

- You need to be sure you **know how to answer questions** of these types before you sit the exam, through practise.

EXAM-SPECIFIC INFORMATION

THE EXAM

FORMAT OF THE EXAM

The exam will be in **THREE sections**, and will be a mix of narrative and computational answers. All questions are compulsory.

		Number of marks
Section A:	Fifteen objective test questions of 2 marks each	30
Section B:	Three objective test case studies	
	– five questions per case study of 2 marks each	30
Section C:	Two constructed response (long) questions, mainly from the syllabus areas of working capital management, investment appraisal and business finance:	
	Question 1	20
	Question 2	20
		———
		100
		———

Total time allowed: 3 hours (plus 10 minutes to read the exam instructions).

Note that:

- the Financial Management exam will have both a discursive and computational element. The objective test questions and the objective test case study questions will therefore include a mix of calculation-based and explanation-based questions.

- there is likely to be a discussion element included in the constructed response questions in Section C.

PASS MARK

The pass mark for all ACCA Qualification examination exams is 50%.

APPROACH TO THIS EXAM

Financial Management is divided into three different sections, requiring the application of different skills to be successful.

Section A

Stick to the timing principle of 1.8 minutes per mark. This means that the 15 OT questions in section A (30 marks) should take 54 minutes.

Work steadily. Rushing leads to careless mistakes and the OT questions are designed to include answers which result from careless mistakes.

If you don't know the answer, eliminate those options you know are incorrect and see if the answer becomes more obvious.

Remember that there is no negative marking for an incorrect answer. After you have eliminated the options that you know to be wrong, if you are still unsure, guess.

Section B

There is likely to be a significant amount of information to read through for each case. You should begin by reading the OT questions that relate to the case, so that when you read through the information for the first time, you know what it is that you are required to do.

Each OT question is worth two marks. Therefore you have 18 minutes (1.8 minutes per mark) to answer the five OT questions relating to each case. It is likely that all of the cases will take the same length of time to answer, although some of the OT questions within a case may be quicker than other OT questions within that same case.

Once you have read through the information, you should first answer any of the OT questions that do not require workings and can be quickly answered. You should then attempt the OT questions that require workings utilising the remaining time for that case.

All of the tips for section A are equally applicable to each section B question.

Section C

The constructed response questions in section C will require a written response rather than being OT questions. Therefore, different techniques need to be used to score well.

Unless you know exactly how to answer the question, spend some time planning your answer. Stick to the question and tailor your answer to what you are asked. Pay particular attention to the verbs in the question e.g. 'Calculate', 'State', 'Explain'.

As stated earlier, if you **get completely stuck** with a question, leave space in your answer and return to it later.

If you do not understand what a question is asking, state your assumptions. Even if you do not answer in precisely the way the examining team hoped, you should be given some credit, provided that your assumptions are reasonable.

You should do everything you can to make things easy for the marker. The marker will find it easier to identify the points you have made if your answers are well laid out.

Computations: It is essential to include all your workings in your answers. Many computational questions require the use of a standard format. Be sure you know these formats thoroughly before the examination and use the layouts that you see in the answers given in this book and in model answers.

Adopt a logical approach and cross reference workings to the main computation to keep your answers tidy and make it easier for the marker to find your calculations.

All sections

Don't skip parts of the syllabus. The FM exam has 32 different questions so the examination can cover a very broad selection of the syllabus each sitting.

Spend time learning the rules and definitions.

Practise plenty of questions to improve your ability to apply the techniques and perform the calculations.

Spend the last five minutes reading through your answers and making any additions or corrections.

 Always keep your eye on the clock and do not over run on any part of any question!

DETAILED SYLLABUS, STUDY GUIDE AND CBE SPECIMEN EXAM

The detailed syllabus and study guide written by the ACCA, along with the specimen exam, can be found at:

www.accaglobal.com/financial-management

KAPLAN'S RECOMMENDED REVISION APPROACH

QUESTION PRACTICE IS THE KEY TO SUCCESS

Success in professional examinations relies upon you acquiring a firm grasp of the required knowledge at the tuition phase. In order to be able to do the questions, knowledge is essential.

However, the difference between success and failure often hinges on your exam technique on the day and making the most of the revision phase of your studies.

The **Kaplan Study Text** is the starting point, designed to provide the underpinning knowledge to tackle all questions. However, in the revision phase, poring over text books is not the answer.

MyKaplan knowledge check tests help you consolidate your knowledge and understanding and are a useful tool to check whether you can remember key topic areas.

Kaplan pocket notes are designed to help you quickly revise a topic area, however you then need to practise questions. There is a need to progress to full exam standard questions as soon as possible, and to tie your exam technique and technical knowledge together.

The importance of question practice cannot be over-emphasised.

The recommended approach below is designed by expert tutors in the field, in conjunction with their knowledge of the examiner and their recent real exams.

The approach taken for the fundamental exams is to revise by topic area. However, with the professional stage exams, a multi topic approach is required to answer the scenario based questions.

You need to practise as many questions as possible in the time you have left.

OUR AIM

Our aim is to get you to the stage where you can attempt exam standard questions confidently, to time, in a closed book environment, with no supplementary help (i.e. to simulate the real examination experience).

Practising your exam technique on real past examination questions, in timed conditions, is also vitally important for you to assess your progress and identify areas of weakness that may need more attention in the final run up to the examination.

In order to achieve this we recognise that initially you may feel the need to practise some questions with open book help and exceed the required time.

The approach below shows you which questions you should use to build up to coping with exam standard question practice, and references to the sources of information available should you need to revisit a topic area in more detail.

Remember that in the real examination, all you have to do is:

- attempt all questions required by the exam

- only spend the allotted time on each question, and

- get them at least 50% right!

Try and practise this approach on every question you attempt from now to the real exam.

Previously, the exam focus meant that students were able to attempt some form of 'question spotting' as there are a few large topic areas. Following the introduction of objective test questions, this will no longer be the case and to pass FM, students will need to understand information from the wide range of topics across the syllabus.

EXAMINER COMMENTS

We have included the examiner's comments to the specific new syllabus examination questions in this kit for you to see the main pitfalls that students fall into with regard to technical content.

However, too many times in the general section of the report, the examiner comments that students had failed due to:

- 'misallocation of time'

- 'running out of time' and

- showing signs of 'spending too much time on earlier questions and clearly rushing the answer to a subsequent question'.

Good exam technique is vital.

ACCA SUPPORT

For additional support with your studies please also refer to the ACCA Global website.

THE KAPLAN FINANCIAL MANAGEMENT REVISION PLAN

Stage 1: Assess areas of strengths and weaknesses

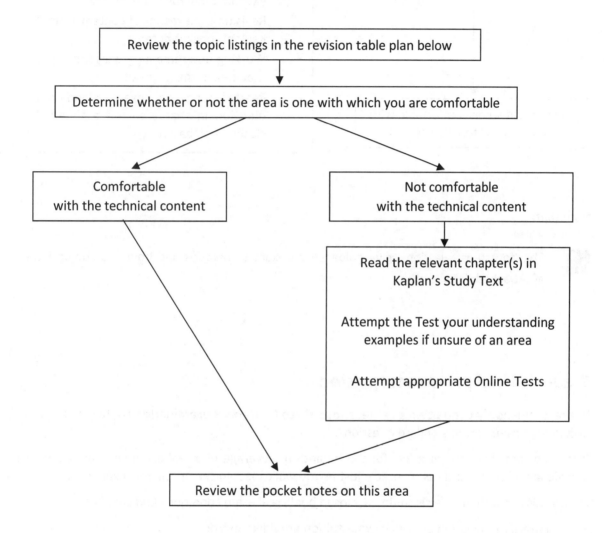

Review the topic listings in the revision table plan below

Determine whether or not the area is one with which you are comfortable

Comfortable with the technical content

Not comfortable with the technical content

Read the relevant chapter(s) in Kaplan's Study Text

Attempt the Test your understanding examples if unsure of an area

Attempt appropriate Online Tests

Review the pocket notes on this area

Stage 2: Practice questions

Follow the order of revision of topics as recommended in the revision table plan below and attempt the questions in the order suggested.

Try to avoid referring to text books and notes and the model answer until you have completed your attempt.

Try to answer the question in the allotted time.

Review your attempt with the model answer and assess how much of the answer you achieved in the allocated exam time.

Fill in the self-assessment box below and decide on your best course of action.

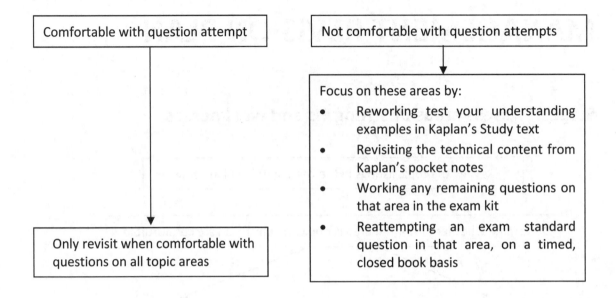

Note that:

 The 'footsteps questions' give guidance on exam techniques and how you should have approached the question.

Stage 3: Final pre-exam revision

We recommend that you **attempt at least one three hour mock examination** containing a set of previously unseen exam standard questions.

It is important that you get a feel for the breadth of coverage of a real exam without advanced knowledge of the topic areas covered – just as you will expect to see on the real exam day.

Ideally this mock should be sat in timed, closed book, real exam conditions and could be:

- a mock examination offered by your tuition provider, and/or

- the specimen exam in the back of this exam kit, and/or

- the last real examination (available shortly afterwards on MyKaplan with 'enhanced walk through answers' and a full 'tutor debrief').

THE KAPLAN FINANCIAL MANAGEMENT REVISION PLAN

Topic	Study Text Chapter	Pocket note Chapter	Questions to attempt	Tutor guidance	Date attempted	Self-assessment
Investment appraisal	2 & 3	2 & 3	Section C 24 & 39	Start with the basics – remind yourself of the four techniques and ensure you can compare and contrast between them. Start with question 24 before attempting question 39 as an example of a recent past exam question in this area.		
– Further aspects of discounted cash flows	4	4	Section C 39 & 28	A popular exam topic, guaranteed to form part of the exam. There are many questions on this area. Start with questions 39 and 28 which are basic warm up questions. Build up to questions 25 and 26 which are slightly more complex questions on this area.		
– Risk and uncertainty	6	6	Section C 27 & 23	This is an aspect that is often examined alongside the more complex areas of discounted cash flow techniques.		
– Asset investment decisions and capital rationing	5	5	Section C 31 & 32	This is an area that has not been widely examined within the recent exam diets. Despite this, it is worth having a quick recap of the techniques using these two questions.		

Topic	Study Text Chapter	Pocket note Chapter	Questions to attempt	Tutor guidance	Date attempted	Self-assessment
Working capital management	7	7	–	Begin by recapping on the key ratio calculations relating to working capital management and the calculation of the cash operating cycle.		
– Receivables and payables	9	9	Section C 14	Questions on working capital management will often draw upon several different elements.		
– Inventory	8	8	Section C 17	This question covers many aspects of working capital management and is a good illustration of the way the examiner tends to tackle this topic.		
– Cash and funding strategies	10	10	Section C 13 & 12	Question 13 contains good coverage of this chapter. Question 12 covers an area that has not been widely examined.		
Financial management function	1	1	Section A questions	Now is a good point to visit some of the less widely examined areas of the syllabus. Use the questions on this area in section A to revise the topic area.		

Topic	Study Text Chapter	Pocket note Chapter	Questions to attempt	Tutor guidance	Date attempted	Self-assessment
The economic environment for business	11	11	Section B 2	Question 2 reflects how this topic could be examined.		
Financial markets and the treasury function	12	12	Section A questions	Use the questions on this area in section A to revise the topic area.		
Sources of finance	15	15	49	Question 49, taken from the June 07 exam, is an excellent illustration of the way the examiner will often pull from more than one syllabus area within his questions.		
Financial ratios	19	19	50	Questions involving the calculation and interpretation of financial ratios are very common. You must be able to calculate each of the key ratios as well as appreciate how they interrelate with each other.		
The cost of capital	17	17	48	This is another popular exam topic. As well as reviewing the Study Text and the pocket notes, ensure you download and review the examiner's series of articles relating to CAPM.		

Topic	Study Text Chapter	Pocket note Chapter	Questions to attempt	Tutor guidance	Date attempted	Self-assessment
Capital structure	18	18	53	This is a tricky topic. Be sure to work carefully through the pocket notes, perhaps attempting the test your understandings within the Study Text before attempting the exam standard questions.		
Business valuations and market efficiency	20	20	Section B 23, 25 & 27	This is another popular exam topic and one which can be easily linked with other areas of the syllabus. You must be able to apply each of the main methods of business valuation and consider the impact that financing may have on a company's valuation.		
Dividend policy	16	16	46	This small topic is often examined alongside business valuations or sources of finance.		
Foreign exchange risk	13	13	Section B 31 & 32	Another topic that students often find difficult. This area won't be tested in a section C question but the understanding gained from this type of question practise will help in sections A and B.		
Interest rate risk	14	14	Section B 34	This area won't be tested in a section C question but the understanding gained from this type of question practise will help in sections A and B.		

Note that not all of the questions are referred to in the programme above. We have recommended an approach to build up from the basic to exam standard questions.

The remaining questions are available in the kit for extra practise for those who require more questions on some areas.

KAPLAN PUBLISHING

MATHEMATICAL TABLES AND FORMULAE SHEET

Economic order quantity

$$= \sqrt{\frac{2C_oD}{C_H}}$$

Miller-Orr Model

$$\text{Return point} = \text{Lower limit} + \left(\frac{1}{3} \times \text{spread}\right)$$

$$\text{Spread} = 3\left[\frac{\frac{3}{4} \times \text{Transaction cost} \times \text{Variance of cash flows}}{\text{Interest rate}}\right]^{\frac{1}{3}}$$

The Capital Asset Pricing Model

$$E(r)_j = R_f + \beta_j\,(E(r_m) - R_f)$$

The asset beta formula

$$\beta_a = \left(\frac{V_e}{(V_e + V_d(1-T))}\,\beta_e\right) + \left(\frac{V_d(1-T)}{(V_e + V_d(1-T))}\,\beta_d\right)$$

The Growth Model

$$P_0 = \frac{D_0(1+g)}{(r_e - g)} \qquad r_e = \frac{D_0(1+g)}{(P_0)} + g$$

Gordon's growth approximation

$$g = br_e$$

The weighted average cost of capital

$$\text{WACC} = \left(\frac{V_e}{V_e + V_d}\right)k_e + \left(\frac{V_d}{V_e + V_d}\right)k_d(1-T)$$

The Fisher formula

$$(1 + i) = (1 + r)(1 + h)$$

Purchasing power parity and interest rate parity

$$S_1 = S_0 \times \frac{(1+h_c)}{(1+h_b)} \qquad F_0 = S_0 \times \frac{(1+i_c)}{(1+i_b)}$$

Present Value Table

Present value of 1 i.e. $(1 + r)^{-n}$

Where   r = discount rate
         n = number of periods until payment

Periods (n)					Discount rates (r)						
	1%	2%	3%	4%	5%	6%	7%	8%	9%	10%	
1	0.990	0.980	0.971	0.962	0.952	0.943	0.935	0.926	0.917	0.909	1
2	0.980	0.961	0.943	0.925	0.907	0.890	0.873	0.857	0.842	0.826	2
3	0.971	0.942	0.915	0.889	0.864	0.840	0.816	0.794	0.772	0.751	3
4	0.961	0.924	0.888	0.855	0.823	0.792	0.763	0.735	0.708	0.683	4
5	0.951	0.906	0.863	0.822	0.784	0.747	0.713	0.681	0.650	0.621	5
6	0.942	0.888	0.837	0.790	0.746	0.705	0.666	0.630	0.596	0.564	6
7	0.933	0.871	0.813	0.760	0.711	0.665	0.623	0.583	0.547	0.513	7
8	0.923	0.853	0.789	0.731	0.677	0.627	0.582	0.540	0.502	0.467	8
9	0.914	0.837	0.766	0.703	0.645	0.592	0.544	0.500	0.460	0.424	9
10	0.905	0.820	0.744	0.676	0.614	0.558	0.508	0.463	0.422	0.386	10
11	0.896	0.804	0.722	0.650	0.585	0.527	0.475	0.429	0.388	0.350	11
12	0.887	0.788	0.701	0.625	0.557	0.497	0.444	0.397	0.356	0.319	12
13	0.879	0.773	0.681	0.601	0.530	0.469	0.415	0.368	0.326	0.290	13
14	0.870	0.758	0.661	0.577	0.505	0.442	0.388	0.340	0.299	0.263	14
15	0.861	0.743	0.642	0.555	0.481	0.417	0.362	0.315	0.275	0.239	15

(n)	11%	12%	13%	14%	15%	16%	17%	18%	19%	20%	
1	0.901	0.893	0.885	0.877	0.870	0.862	0.855	0.847	0.840	0.833	1
2	0.812	0.797	0.783	0.769	0.756	0.743	0.731	0.718	0.706	0.694	2
3	0.731	0.712	0.693	0.675	0.658	0.641	0.624	0.609	0.593	0.579	3
4	0.659	0.636	0.613	0.592	0.572	0.552	0.534	0.516	0.499	0.482	4
5	0.593	0.567	0.543	0.519	0.497	0.476	0.456	0.437	0.419	0.402	5
6	0.535	0.507	0.480	0.456	0.432	0.410	0.390	0.370	0.352	0.335	6
7	0.482	0.452	0.425	0.400	0.376	0.354	0.333	0.314	0.296	0.279	7
8	0.434	0.404	0.376	0.351	0.327	0.305	0.285	0.266	0.249	0.233	8
9	0.391	0.361	0.333	0.308	0.284	0.263	0.243	0.225	0.209	0.194	9
10	0.352	0.322	0.295	0.270	0.247	0.227	0.208	0.191	0.176	0.162	10
11	0.317	0.287	0.261	0.237	0.215	0.195	0.178	0.162	0.148	0.135	11
12	0.286	0.257	0.231	0.208	0.187	0.168	0.152	0.137	0.124	0.112	12
13	0.258	0.229	0.204	0.182	0.163	0.145	0.130	0.116	0.104	0.093	13
14	0.232	0.205	0.181	0.160	0.141	0.125	0.111	0.099	0.088	0.078	14
15	0.209	0.183	0.160	0.140	0.123	0.108	0.095	0.084	0.074	0.065	15

KAPLAN PUBLISHING

Annuity Table

Present value of an annuity of 1 i.e. $\dfrac{1-(1+r)^{-n}}{r}$

Where   r = discount rate
          n = number of periods

Periods   *Discount rates (r)*

(n)	1%	2%	3%	4%	5%	6%	7%	8%	9%	10%	
1	0.990	0.980	0.971	0.962	0.952	0.943	0.935	0.926	0.917	0.909	1
2	1.970	1.942	1.913	1.886	1.859	1.833	1.808	1.783	1.759	1.736	2
3	2.941	2.884	2.829	2.775	2.723	2.673	2.624	2.577	2.531	2.487	3
4	3.902	3.808	3.717	3.630	3.546	3.465	3.387	3.312	3.240	3.170	4
5	4.853	4.713	4.580	4.452	4.329	4.212	4.100	3.993	3.890	3.791	5
6	5.795	5.601	5.417	5.242	5.076	4.917	4.767	4.623	4.486	4.355	6
7	6.728	6.472	6.230	6.002	5.786	5.582	5.389	5.206	5.033	4.868	7
8	7.652	7.325	7.020	6.733	6.463	6.210	5.971	5.747	5.535	5.335	8
9	8.566	8.162	7.786	7.435	7.108	6.802	6.515	6.247	5.995	5.759	9
10	9.471	8.983	8.530	8.111	7.722	7.360	7.024	6.710	6.418	6.145	10
11	10.37	9.787	9.253	8.760	8.306	7.887	7.499	7.139	6.805	6.495	11
12	11.26	10.58	9.954	9.385	8.863	8.384	7.943	7.536	7.161	6.814	12
13	12.13	11.35	10.63	9.986	9.394	8.853	8.358	7.904	7.487	7.103	13
14	13.00	12.11	11.30	10.56	9.899	9.295	8.745	8.244	7.786	7.367	14
15	13.87	12.85	11.94	11.12	10.38	9.712	9.108	8.559	8.061	7.606	15

(n)	11%	12%	13%	14%	15%	16%	17%	18%	19%	20%	
1	0.901	0.893	0.885	0.877	0.870	0.862	0.855	0.847	0.840	0.833	1
2	1.713	1.690	1.668	1.647	1.626	1.605	1.585	1.566	1.547	1.528	2
3	2.444	2.402	2.361	2.322	2.283	2.246	2.210	2.174	2.140	2.106	3
4	3.102	3.037	2.974	2.914	2.855	2.798	2.743	2.690	2.639	2.589	4
5	3.696	3.605	3.517	3.433	3.352	3.274	3.199	3.127	3.058	2.991	5
6	4.231	4.111	3.998	3.889	3.784	3.685	3.589	3.498	3.410	3.326	6
7	4.712	4.564	4.423	4.288	4.160	4.039	3.922	3.812	3.706	3.605	7
8	5.146	4.968	4.799	4.639	4.487	4.344	4.207	4.078	3.954	3.837	8
9	5.537	5.328	5.132	4.946	4.772	4.607	4.451	4.303	4.163	4.031	9
10	5.889	5.650	5.426	5.216	5.019	4.833	4.659	4.494	4.339	4.192	10
11	6.207	5.938	5.687	5.453	5.234	5.029	4.836	4.656	4.486	4.327	11
12	6.492	6.194	5.918	5.660	5.421	5.197	4.988	4.793	4.611	4.439	12
13	6.750	6.424	6.122	5.842	5.583	5.342	5.118	4.910	4.715	4.533	13
14	6.982	6.628	6.302	6.002	5.724	5.468	5.229	5.008	4.802	4.611	14
15	7.191	6.811	6.462	6.142	5.847	5.575	5.324	5.092	4.876	4.675	15

Section A

OBJECTIVE TEST QUESTIONS

Each question is worth two marks.

FINANCIAL MANAGEMENT FUNCTION

1   In relation to the financial management of a company, which of the following provides the best definition of a firm's primary financial objective?

    A   To achieve long-term growth in earnings

    B   To maximise the level of annual dividends

    C   To maximise the wealth of its ordinary shareholder

    D   To maximise the level of annual profits

2   Indicate, by clicking in the relevant boxes, whether the following objectives are financial or non-financial objectives of a company.

Objective	Financial	Non-financial
Maximisation of market share		
Earnings growth		
Sales revenue growth		
Achieving a target level of customer satisfaction		
Achieving a target level of return on capital employed		

3   Which THREE of the following are the main types of decision facing the financial manager in a company?

    A   Income decision

    B   Investment decision

    C   Dividend decision

    D   Financing decision

    E   Appraisal decision

    F   Budget decision

4 **Which TWO of the following are examples of financial objectives that a company might choose to pursue?**

    A   Dealing honestly and fairly with customers on all occasions

    B   Provision of good working conditions and industrial relations

    C   Earning above a particular level of return on capital employed

    D   Producing environmentally friendly products

    E   Restricting the level of gearing to below a specified target level

5 Value for money is an important objective for not-for-profit organisations.

Which of the following actions is consistent with increasing value for money?

    A   Using a cheaper source of goods and thereby decreasing the quality of not-for-profit organisation services

    B   Searching for ways to diversify the finances of the not-for-profit organisation

    C   Decreasing waste in the provision of a service by the not-for-profit organisation

    D   Focusing on meeting the financial objectives of the not-for-profit organization

6 **Which of the following is LEAST likely to fall within financial management?**

    A   The dividend payment to shareholders is increased

    B   Funds are raised to finance an investment project

    C   Surplus assets are sold off

    D   Non-executive directors are appointed to the remuneration committee

7 **Indicate, by clicking in the relevant boxes, whether the following statements are true or false.**

Statement	True	False
Financial management is concerned with the long-term raising of finance and the allocation and control of resources		
Management accounting is concerned with providing information for the more day-to-day functions of control and decision-making		
Financial accounting is concerned with providing information about the historical results of past plans and decisions		

8 **Which of the following tasks would typically be carried out by a member of the financial management team?**

A   Evaluating proposed expansion plans

B   Review of overtime spending

C   Depreciation of non-current assets

D   Apportioning overheads to cost units

9 **Which TWO of the following are examples of internal stakeholders in a firm?**

A   Company directors

B   Customers

C   Suppliers

D   Employees

E   Finance providers

10 **What is the main purpose of corporate governance?**

A   To separate ownership and management control of organisations

B   To maximise shareholder value

C   To facilitate effective management of organisations and to make organisations more visibly accountable to a wider range of stakeholders

D   To ensure that regulatory frameworks are adhered to

11 The agency problem is a driving force behind the growing importance attached to sound corporate governance.

In this context, who are the agents?

A   Customers

B   Shareholders

C   Managers

D   Auditors

12 **Which TWO of the following statements are correct?**

1   Maximising market share is an example of a financial objective

2   Shareholder wealth maximisation is the primary financial objective for a company listed on a stock exchange

3   Financial objectives should be quantitative so that their achievement can be measured

4   Three E's are used as a performance measure to assess value of money in not for profit organisations. The three E's stand for economy, efficiency and environment

13 **Which TWO of the following are 'efficiency' targets that a not for profit organisation might put in place?**

A   Reduction of wastage of paper

B   Pay rates for staff of appropriate levels of qualification

C   Staff utilisation

D   Customer satisfaction ratings

14 Managerial reward schemes should help ensure managers take decisions that are consistent with the objectives of shareholders.

Which THREE of the following are characteristics of a carefully designed remuneration package?

A   Linking of rewards to changes in shareholder wealth

B   Matching of managers' time horizons to shareholders' time horizons

C   Possibility of manipulation by managers

D   Encouragement for managers to adopt the same attitudes to risk as shareholders

E   Motivational to primarily achieve short-term goals

15 **Indicate, by clicking in the relevant boxes, which of the following are typical criticisms of executive share option schemes (ESOPs)?**

Statement	Is a criticism	Is NOT a criticism
When directors exercise their options, they tend to sell the shares almost immediately to cash in on their profits		
If the share price falls when options have been awarded, and the options have no value, they cannot act as an incentive		
Directors may distort reported profits to protect the share price and the value of their share options		

16 The directors of Portico plc have recently engaged a firm of consultants to negotiate standard terms of trade for one of its strategic business units. This includes the agreement by Portico plc to pay a 5% penalty on any late invoice settlement.

This policy is an illustration of the company's concern for which major stakeholder?

A   Lenders

B   Suppliers

C   Customers

D   Trade unions

17   Under the terms of the UK Corporate Governance Code, what are the only type of directors permitted to sit on a company's audit committee?

    A   Independent non-executive directors

    B   Non-executive directors

    C   Executive directors

    D   Directors with financial experience

18   Which of the following would you expect to be the responsibility of financial management?

    A   Producing annual accounts

    B   Producing monthly management accounts

    C   Advising on investment in non-current assets

    D   Deciding pay rates for staff

19   Indicate, by clicking in the relevant boxes below, whether the following statements are true or false.

Statement	True	False
Value for money is usually taken to mean economy, efficiency and engagement		
Cum dividend means the buyer of the share is entitled to receive the dividend shortly to be paid		
The dividend payout ratio compares the dividend per share with the market price per share		
The agency problem means that shareholder wealth is not being maximised		

FINANCIAL MANAGEMENT ENVIRONMENT

20   Which of the following is/are among the elements of fiscal policy?

    1   Government actions to raise or lower taxes

    2   Government actions to raise or lower the size of the money supply

    3   Government actions to raise or lower the amount it spends

    A   1 only

    B   1 and 3 only

    C   2 and 3 only

    D   1, 2 and 3

21 **Which TWO of the following statements are correct?**

1   Securitisation is the conversion of illiquid assets into marketable securities

2   The reverse yield gap refers to equity yields being higher than debt yields

3   Disintermediation arises where borrowers deal directly with lending individuals

4   Demand-pull inflation will occur when there are increases in production costs independent to the state of demand

22 **Indicate, by clicking in the relevant boxes, whether the following statements are true or false.**

Statement	True	False
Coupon bearing securities have a fixed maturity and a specified rate of interest		
In the discount market, funds are raised by issuing bills at a discount to their eventual redemption or maturity value		

23 **The principal objectives of macroeconomic policy include which of the following?**

1   Full employment of resources

2   Price stability

3   Economic growth

4   Balancing the government budget

A   1 and 2 only

B   1 and 3 only

C   1, 2 and 3 only

D   1, 2, 3 and 4

24 Governments have a number of economic targets as part of their fiscal policy.

Which TWO of the following government actions relate predominantly to fiscal policy?

A   Decreasing interest rates in order to stimulate consumer spending

B   Reducing taxation while maintaining public spending

C   Using official foreign currency reserves to buy the domestic currency

D   Borrowing money from the capital markets and spending it on public works

E   Regulating foreign exchange rates

25   Which THREE of the following are key roles played by money markets?

A   Providing short-term liquidity to companies, banks and the public sector

B   Providing short term trade finance

C   Allowing an organisation to manage its exposure to foreign currency risk and interest rate risk

D   Dealing in long-term funds and transactions

E   Allowing companies to issue shares to raise money

26   Which of the following are money market instruments?

1   Certificates of deposit

2   Corporate bond

3   Commercial paper

4   Treasury bill

A   1, 2 and 4 only

B   1 and 3 only

C   1, 3 and 4 only

D   1, 2, 3 and 4

27   Which THREE of the following are common roles of the treasury function within a firm?

A   Short-term management of resources

B   Long-term maximisation of shareholder wealth

C   Long-term maximisation of market share

D   Risk management

E   Management of accounts receivable

F   Management of financial reporting

28   Which of the following is a difference between primary and secondary capital markets?

A   Primary capital markets relate to the sale of new securities, while secondary capital markets are where securities trade after their initial offering

B   Both primary and secondary capital markets relate to where securities are traded after their initial offering

C   Both primary and secondary capital markets relate to the sale of new securities

D   Primary markets are where stocks trade and secondary markets are where loan notes trade

29   Changes in monetary policy will influence which of the following factors?

   1   The level of exchange rates

   2   The cost of finance

   3   The level of consumer demand

   4   The level of inflation

   A   1 and 2 only

   B   2 and 3 only

   C   2, 3 and 4 only

   D   1, 2, 3 and 4

30   Which of the following is/are usually seen as forms of market failure where regulation may be a solution?

   1   Imperfect competition

   2   Social costs or externalities

   3   Imperfect information

   A   1 only

   B   1 and 2 only

   C   2 and 3 only

   D   1, 2 and 3

31   There are two main types of financial market: capital and money markets, and within each of these are primary and secondary markets.

   Which TWO of the following statements are true?

   A   Primary markets allow the realisation of investments before their maturity date by selling them to other investors

   B   Primary markets deal in new issues of loanable funds

   C   Capital markets consist of stock markets for shares and loan bond markets

   D   Money markets provide long-term debt finance and investment

32   **Indicate, by clicking in the relevant boxes, whether the following statements are true or false.**

Statement	True	False
Interest rate smoothing is the policy of some central banks to move official interest rates in a sequence of relatively small steps in the same direction, rather than waiting until making a single larger step		
If governments wish to influence the amount of money held in the economy or the demand for credit, they may attempt to influence the level of interest rates		

33   **A variety of Corporate Governance rules have been introduced in different countries but what are the principles, common to all, that they typically include?**

   1   The chairperson and chief executive officer should not be the same individual

   2   Non-executive directors on the board should prevent the board from being dominated by the executive directors

   3   The audit committee should consist solely of executive directors

   4   A remuneration committee should be established to decide on the remuneration of executive directors

   A   1 and 2 only

   B   1, 2 and 3 only

   C   1, 2 and 4 only

   D   1, 2, 3 and 4

34   **Which of the following statements is correct?**

   A   Direct taxes are levied on one set of individuals or organisations but may be partly or wholly passed on to others and are largely related to consumption not income

   B   Indirect taxes are levied directly on income receivers whether they are individuals or organisations

   C   A balanced budget occurs when total expenditure is matched by total taxation

   D   A deficit budget occurs when total expenditure is less than total taxation income

35 **Indicate, by clicking in the relevant boxes, whether the following statements are true or false.**

Statement	True	False
Demand-pull inflation might occur when excess aggregate monetary demand in the economy and hence demand for particular goods and services enable companies to raise prices and expand profit margins		
Cost-push inflation will occur when there are increases in production costs independent of the state of demand e.g. rising raw material costs or rising labour costs		

36 **Which THREE of the following are true, in relation to certificates of deposit?**

A   They are evidence of a deposit with an issuing bank

B   They are not negotiable and therefore unattractive to the depositor as they do not ensure instant liquidity

C   They provide the bank with a deposit for a fixed period at a fixed rate of interest

D   They are coupon-bearing securities

E   They are not tradeable

37 **Which of the following is least likely to be a reason for seeking a stock market listing?**

A   Enhancement of the company's image

B   Transfer of capital to other users

C   Improving existing owners' control over the business

D   Access to a wider pool of finance

38 **Which of the following is NOT typically a principal objective of macroeconomic policy?**

A   To achieve full employment of resources

B   To achieve economic growth

C   To achieve a balance of payments deficit

D   To achieve an appropriate distribution of income and wealth

39   Which **THREE** of the following are advantages of having a centralised treasury department in a large international group of companies?

A   No need for treasury skills to be duplicated throughout the group

B   Necessary borrowings can be arranged in bulk, at keener interest rates than for smaller amounts

C   The group's foreign currency risk can be managed much more effectively since they can appreciate the total exposure situation

D   Local operating units should have a better feel for local conditions than head office and can respond more quickly to local developments

E   Divisional managers will be motivated by having less responsibility for cash management

40   Investing in a small or medium sized business (SME) is inherently more risky than investing in a larger company due to lack of business history and a lower level of public scrutiny over accounts and records. What is the frequently used term to describe the difficulty SMEs can often face when raising finance?

A   Maturity gap

B   Funding gap

C   Duration gap

D   Equity gap

41   Indicate, by clicking in the relevant boxes, which market the following financial instruments would be traded on.

Statement	Money market	Stock market
Commercial paper		
Convertible loan notes		
Treasury bills		
Certificates of deposit		

42   Which of the following government actions would lead to an increase in aggregate demand?

1   Increasing taxation and keeping government expenditure the same

2   Decreasing taxation and increasing government expenditure

3   Decreasing money supply

4   Decreasing interest rates

A   1 only

B   1 and 3

C   2 and 4 only

D   2, 3 and 4

43 **Which TWO of the following activities are carried out by a financial intermediary?**

    A   Transforming interest rates

    B   Transforming foreign exchange

    C   Transforming maturity

    D   Transforming risk

44 **Indicate, by clicking in the relevant boxes, whether the following statements are true or false.**

Statement	True	False
A prospective merger would need to result in a company having a market share greater than 80% before it can be described as a monopoly		
A government may intervene to weaken its country's exchange rate in order to eliminate a balance of payments deficit		
A relatively high rate of domestic inflation will lead to a strengthening currency		
Government fiscal policy involves the management of interest rates		

WORKING CAPITAL MANAGEMENT

45 Thrifty plc's cash budget highlights a short-term surplus in the near future.

    Which of the following actions would be appropriate to make use of the surplus?

    A   Pay suppliers earlier to take advantage of any prompt payment discounts

    B   Buy back the company's shares

    C   Increase payables by delaying payment to suppliers

    D   Invest in a long term deposit bank account

46 **Indicate, by clicking in the relevant boxes, whether the following statements are true or false.**

Statement	True	False
Working capital should increase as sales increase		
An increase in the cash operating cycle will lead to an increase in working capital funding costs		
Overtrading is also known as under-capitalisation		

47 **Which of the following might be associated with a shortening working capital cycle?**

A   Lower net operating cash flow

B   Increasing tax-allowable depreciation expenditure

C   Slower inventory turnover

D   Taking longer to pay suppliers

48 The following information has been calculated for D Co:

Trade receivables collection period	10 weeks
Raw material inventory turnover period	6 weeks
Work in progress inventory turnover period	2 weeks
Trade payables payment period	7 weeks
Finished goods inventory turnover period	6 weeks

What is the length of the working capital cycle?

$\boxed{}$ weeks

49 A company sells inventory for cash to a customer, at a selling price which is below the cost of the inventory items.

How will this transaction affect the current ratio and the quick ratio immediately after the transaction? Indicate, by clicking in the relevant boxes, whether each ratio will increase or decrease.

Ratio	Increase	Decrease
Current ratio		
Quick ratio		

50 A company has the following summarised Statement of Financial Position at 31 December 20X4:

	$000	$000
Non-current assets		1,000
Current assets		
Inventories	200	
Receivables	150	
Cash	100	
	–––––	
	450	
Current liabilities		
Payables	200	
	–––––	
Net current assets		250
		–––––
		1,250
		–––––

Over the next year the company should double its sales. The company does not plan to invest in any new non-current assets, but inventories, receivables and payables should all move in line with sales.

What cash balance in one year's time would this imply if the non-current assets were all land, no new capital was raised and all profits were paid out as dividends?

A $100,000 cash in hand

B $200,000 cash in hand

C $50,000 overdraft

D $100,000 overdraft

51   Goldstar has an accounts receivables turnover of 10.5 times, an inventory turnover of 4 times and payables turnover of 8 times.

What is Goldstar's cash operating cycle to the nearest day (assume 365 days in a year)?

⬚ days

52   **The cash operating cycle is equal to which of the following?**

A   Receivables days plus inventory holding period minus payables days

B   Inventory holding period minus receivables days minus payables days

C   Receivables days plus inventory holding period plus payables days

D   Receivables days minus payables days minus inventory holding period

53   A company has annual credit sales of $27 million and related cost of sales of $15 million. The company has the following targets for the next year:

Trade receivables days   50 days

Inventory days   60 days

Trade payables   45 days

Assume there are 360 days in the year.

What is the net investment in working capital required for the next year?

A $8,125,000

B $4,375,000

C $2,875,000

D $6,375,000

54 A cash budget was drawn up as follows:

	October	November	December
	$	$	$
Receipts			
Credit Sales	20,000	11,000	14,500
Cash Sales	10,000	4,500	6,000
Payments			
Suppliers	13,000	4,200	7,800
Wages	4,600	2,300	3,000
Overheads	3,000	1,750	1,900
Opening cash	500		

What is the closing cash balance for December budgeted to be?

A $20,550 overdraft

B $21,050 overdraft

C $22,450 deposit

D $24,950 deposit

55 **Which TWO of the following would be key aspects of a company's accounts receivable credit policy?**

A Assessing creditworthiness

B Checking credit limits once a year

C Invoicing promptly and collecting overdue debts

D Delaying payments to obtain a 'free' source of finance

56 A company is preparing its cash flow forecast for the next financial period.

Which THREE of the following items should be included in the calculations?

A A corporation tax payment

B A dividend receipt from a short term investment

C The loss made on the disposal of an item of machinery

D A bad debt written off

E An increase in a provision

F The receipt of funding for the purchase of a new vehicle

57   For a retailer, let

S   = Sales

P   = Purchases

O   = Opening inventory

C   = Closing inventory

D   = Opening receivables

R   = Closing receivables

Which of the following is the best expression for receivables days at the period end?

A   [D + R]/P × 365

B   [D + R]/S × 365

C   R/S × 365

D   D/S × 365

58   **Which of the following is NOT usually associated with overtrading?**

A   An increase in the current ratio

B   A rapid increase in revenue

C   A rapid increase in the volume of current assets

D   Most of the increase in current assets being financed by credit

59   Generally, increasing payables days suggests advantage is being taken of available credit but there are risks involved.

Which of the following is unlikely to be one of the risks involved in increasing payables days?

A   Customer bargaining power increasing

B   Losing supplier goodwill

C   Losing prompt payment discounts

D   Suppliers increasing the price to compensate

60   **Which TWO of the following are aims of a Just in Time system of inventory control?**

A   Reduction in capital tied up in inventory

B   Creation of an inflexible production process

C   Elimination of all activities performed that do not add value

D   Lowering of inventory ordering costs

61   Although cash needs to be invested to earn returns, businesses need to keep a certain amount readily available.

Which TWO of the following are reasons for holding cash?

A   Movement motive

B   Transactions motive

C   Precautionary motive

D   Asset motive

62   Andrew Co is a large listed company financed by both equity and debt.

In which of the following areas of financial management will the impact of working capital management be smallest?

A   Liquidity management

B   Interest rate management

C   Management of relationship with the bank

D   Dividend policy

63   Crag Co has sales of $200m per year and the gross profit margin is 40%. Finished goods inventory days vary throughout the year within the following range:

	Maximum	Minimum
Inventory (days)	120	90

All purchases and sales are made on a cash basis and no inventory of raw materials or work in progress is carried. Crag Co intends to finance permanent current assets with equity and fluctuating current assets with its overdraft.

In relation to finished goods inventory and assuming a 360-day year, how much finance will be needed from the overdraft?

☐ million

64   Pop Co is switching from using mainly long-term fixed rate finance to fund its working capital to using mainly short-term variable rate finance.

Indicate, by clicking in the relevant boxes, whether each of the following items will increase, decrease or see no change with this change in working capital financing policy.

Ratio	Increase	Decrease	No change
Finance costs			
Re-financing risk			
Interest rate risk			
Overcapitalisation risk			

65 Which of the following is an advantage of implementing just-in-time inventory management?

   A   Quality control costs will be eliminated

   B   Monthly finance costs incurred in holding inventory will be kept constant

   C   The frequency of raw material deliveries is reduced

   D   The amount of obsolete inventory will be minimised

66 Max Co is a large multinational company which expects to have a $10m cash deficit in one month's time. The deficit is expected to last no more than two months. Max Co wishes to resolve its short-term liquidity problem by issuing an appropriate instrument on the money market.

   Which of the following instruments should Max Co issue?

   A   Commercial paper

   B   Interest rate futures

   C   Corporate loan notes

   D   Treasury bills

67 Mile Co is looking to change its working capital policy to match the rest of the industry. The following results are expected for the coming year:

	$000
Revenue	20,500
Cost of sales	(12,800)
Gross profit	7,700

Revenue and cost of sales can be assumed to be spread evenly throughout the year.

The working capital ratios of Mile Co, compared with the industry, are as follows:

	Mile Co	Industry
Receivable days	50	42
Inventory days	45	35
Payable days	40	35

Assume there are 365 days in each year.

If Mile Co matches its working capital cycle with the industry, what will be the decrease in its net working capital?

   A $624,600

   B $730,100

   C $835,600

   D $975,300

68 Swap Co is due to receive goods costing $2,500. The terms of trade state that payment must be received within three months. However, a discount of 1.5% will be given for payment within one month.

Which of the following is the annual percentage cost of ignoring the discount and paying within three months?

A   6.23%

B   9.34%

C   6.14%

D   9.49%

69 Will Co incurs costs of $65 every time it places an order with its raw materials supplier. It orders 300,000 units of product each year. The cost of holding one unit of inventory for a month is $2.50. Will Co keeps a buffer inventory at all times of 25,000 units of material.

Calculate the economic order quantity (EOQ) that will optimise the business's inventory costs to the nearest 10 units.

☐ units

70 **Which TWO of the following statements are true about cash management models?**

A   The Baumol model is more suitable when cash flows are steady and predictable

B   Both models assume that cash is either held in a current account or in long-term investments

C   In the Miller Orr model the upper limit for the current account balance is set by management

D   Both models take into account the transaction costs of switching between current accounts and investments

E   The Miller Orr model aims to keep cash balances as close to the return point at all times

71 A company has erratic daily cash movements with a standard deviation of $3,000 per day. It costs $25 to move cash between its current account and its short-term deposit account. The deposit account earns an interest rate of 7.3% per annum. There are 365 days in a year.

Calculate, to the nearest $000, the spread between the upper and lower limits that should be set for the current account using the Miller Orr cash management model.

$ ☐

72 A company has sales revenue of $30 million and its customers take an average of 75 days to pay. The company offers a 1% discount to customers who pay in 30 days.

Calculate, to the nearest hundred thousand dollars, the new anticipated receivables balance if 60% of customers take up the offer of the discount and the rest carry on paying in 75 days. Assume 360 days in a year.

$ ☐

INVESTMENT APPRAISAL

73 A company is considering investing in a two-year project. Machine set-up costs will be $125,000, payable immediately. Working capital of $4,000 is required at the beginning of the contract and will be released at the end.

Given a cost of capital of 10%, what is the minimum acceptable contract price (to the nearest thousand dollar) to be received at the end of the contract?

$[   ]

74 **Which TWO of the following statements are correct?**

A Tax allowable depreciation is a relevant cash flow when evaluating borrowing to buy compared to leasing as a financing choice

B Asset replacement decisions require relevant cash flows to be discounted by the after-tax cost of debt

C If capital is rationed, divisible investment projects can be ranked by the profitability index when determining the optimum investment schedule

D Government restrictions on bank lending are associated with hard capital rationing

75 A company has 31 December as its accounting year-end. On 1 January 20X5, a new machine costing $2,000,000 is purchased. The company expects to sell the machine on 31 December 20X6 for $350,000.

The rate of corporation tax for the company is 30%. Tax-allowable depreciation is obtained at 25% on the reducing balance basis, and a balancing allowance is available on disposal of the asset. The company makes sufficient profits to obtain relief for tax-allowable depreciation as soon as they arise.

If the company's cost of capital is 15% per annum, what is the present value of the tax savings from the tax-allowable depreciation at 1 January 20X5 (to the nearest thousand dollars)?

A $391,000

B $248,000

C $263,000

D $719,000

76 An investment project has a cost of $12,000, payable at the start of the first year of operation. The possible future cash flows arising from the investment project have the following present values and associated probabilities:

PV of Year 1 cash flow ($)	Probability	PV of Year 2 cash flow ($)	Probability
16,000	0.15	20,000	0.75
12,000	0.60	(2,000)	0.25
(4,000)	0.25		

What is the expected value (EV) of the net present value of the investment project?

$[   ]

77 A company has a 'money' cost of capital of 21% per annum. The inflation is currently estimated at 8% per annum.

What is the 'real' cost of capital (to the nearest whole number)?

[　　　　] %

78 A company is considering a project that has an initial outflow followed by several years of cash inflows, with a cash outflow in the final year.

How many internal rates of return could there be for this project?

A Either zero or two

B Either one or two

C Zero, one or two

D Only two

79 A project consists of a series of cash outflows in the first few years followed by a series of positive cash inflows. The total cash inflows exceed the total cash outflows. The project was originally evaluated assuming a zero rate of inflation.

If the project were re-evaluated on the assumption that the cash flows were subject to a positive rate of inflation, what would be the effect on the payback period and the internal rate of return? Indicate, by clicking in the relevant boxes, whether the payback period and internal rate of return would increase or decrease.

Method	Increase	Decrease
Payback period		
Internal rate of return		

80 **The lower risk of a project can be recognised by increasing which of the following?**

A The cost of the initial investment of the project

B The estimates of future cash inflows from the project

C The internal rate of return of the project

D The required rate of return of the project

81 A company has the following pattern of cash flow for a project:

Year	Cash flow $
0	(100,000)
1	40,000
2	20,000
3	30,000
4	5,000
5	40,000

The company uses a discount rate of 10%. In what year does discounted payback occur?

Year [　　　　]

82 Sudan Co wishes to undertake a project requiring an investment of $732,000 which will generate equal annual inflows of $146,400 in perpetuity.

If the first inflow from the investment is a year after the initial investment, what is the IRR of the project?

A   20%

B   25%

C   400%

D   500%

83 **Which THREE of the following are advantages of the IRR?**

A   Considers the whole life of the project

B   Uses cash flows not profits

C   It is a measure of absolute return

D   It is an accurate calculation

E   It is useful when liquidity is poor

F   It considers the time value of money

84 Jones Ltd plans to spend $90,000 on an item of capital equipment on 1 January 20X2. The expenditure is eligible for 25% tax-allowable depreciation, and Jones pays corporation tax at 30%. Tax is paid at the end of the accounting period concerned. The equipment will produce savings of $30,000 per annum for its expected useful life deemed to be receivable every 31 December. The equipment will be sold for $25,000 on 31 December 20X5. Jones has a 31 December year-end and has a 10% post-tax cost of capital.

What is the present value at 1 January 20X2 of the tax savings that result from the tax-allowable depreciation?

A $13,170

B $15,828

C $16,018

D $19,827

85   Four projects, P, Q, R and S, are available to a company which is facing shortages of capital over the next year but expects capital to be freely available thereafter.

	P	Q	R	S
	$000	$000	$000	$000
Total capital required over life of project	20	30	40	50
Capital required in next year	20	10	30	40
Net present value of project at company's cost of capital	60	40	80	80

In what sequence should the projects be selected if the company wishes to maximise net present values?

A   P, R, S, Q

B   Q, P, R, S

C   Q, R, P, S

D   R, S, P, Q

86   Alicia is contemplating purchasing for $280,000 a machine that she will use to produce 50,000 units of a product per annum for five years. These products will be sold for $10 each and unit variable costs are expected to be $6. Incremental fixed costs will be $70,000 per annum for production costs and $25,000 per annum for selling and administration costs. Alicia has a required return of 10% per annum.

By how many units must the estimate of production and sales volume fall for the project to be regarded as not worthwhile?

[   ] units

87   **The payback period is the number of years that it takes a business to recover its original investment from net returns. Select the correct items from the drop down choices.**

It is calculated **before/after** depreciation and **before/after** taxation

88   Data of relevance to the evaluation of a particular project are given below.

Cost of capital in real terms	10% per annum
Expected inflation	8% per annum
Expected increase in the project's annual cash inflow	6% per annum
Expected increase in the project's annual cash outflow	4% per annum

Which of the following sets of adjustments will lead to the correct NPV being calculated?

	Cash inflow	Cash outflow	Discount percentage
A	Unadjusted	Unadjusted	10.0%
B	6% p.a. increase	4% p.a. increase	18.8%
C	6% p.a. increase	4% p.a. increase	10.0%
D	8% p.a. increase	8% p.a. increase	18.8%

89 Spotty Ltd plans to purchase a machine costing $18,000 to save labour costs through efficiency savings. Labour savings would be $9,000 in the first year and would increase in the second year by 10%. The estimated general annual rate of inflation is 8% and the company's real cost of capital is estimated at 12%. The machine has a two-year life with an estimated actual salvage value of £5,000 receivable at the end of year 2. All cash flows occur at the year-end.

What is the negative NPV (to the nearest $10) of the proposed investment?

A $50

B $270

C $380

D $650

90 A company buys a machine for $10,000 and sells it for $2,000 at time 3. Running costs of the machine are: time 1 = $3,000; time 2 = $5,000; time 3 = $7,000.

If a series of machines are bought, run and sold on an infinite cycle of replacements, what is the equivalent annual cost of the machine if the discount rate is 10%?

A $22,114

B $8,892

C $8,288

D $7,371

91 A company has four independent projects available:

	Capital needed at time 0	NPV
	$	$
Project 1	10,000	30,000
Project 2	8,000	25,000
Project 3	12,000	30,000
Project 4	16,000	36,000

If the company has $32,000 to invest at time 0, and each project is infinitely divisible, but none can be delayed, what is the maximum NPV that can be earned?

A $85,000

B $89,500

C $102,250

D $103,000

92 A project has an initial outflow at time 0 when an asset is bought, then a series of revenue inflows at the end of each year, and then finally sales proceeds from the sale of the asset. Its NPV is £12,000 when general inflation is zero % per year.

If general inflation were to rise to 7% per year, and all revenue inflows were subject to this rate of inflation but the initial expenditure and resale value of the asset were not subject to inflation, what would happen to the NPV?

A   The NPV would remain the same

B   The NPV would rise

C   The NPV would fall

D   The NPV could rise or fall

93 **Which TWO of the following statements about the accounting rate of return (ARR) method and the payback method are true?**

A   Both methods are affected by changes in the cost of capital

B   The ARR does not take account of returns over the entire life of the project

C   The payback method is based on the project's cash flows

D   A requirement for an early payback can increase a company's liquidity

94 **Indicate, by clicking in the relevant boxes, whether the following statements in relation to a simulation exercise are true or false.**

Method	True	False
It considers the effect of changing one variable at a time		
It considers the impact of many variables changing at the same time		
It points directly to the correct investment decision		
It assesses the likelihood of a variable changing		

95 **When considering standard deviation as a statistical measure, which of the following statements is true?**

A   Standard deviation is a measure of the variability of a distribution around its mean

B   The tighter the distribution, the higher the standard deviation will be

C   The wider the dispersion, the less risky the situation

D   Standard deviation is the weighted average of all the possible outcomes

96 **In relation to a long-term lease, which of the following statements is NOT correct?**

A   All the risks and rewards of ownership transfer to the lessee

B   The asset and lease obligation will be recorded in the statement of financial position

C   The lease period will cover almost all of the leased asset's useful economic life

D   The lessor will be responsible for repairs and maintenance of the leased asset

97 **Peach Co's latest results are as follows:**

	$000
Profit before interest and taxation	2,500
Profit before taxation	2,250
Profit after tax	1,400

In addition, extracts from its latest statement of financial position are as follows:

	$000
Equity	10,000
Non-current liabilities	2,500

What is Peach Co's return on capital employed (ROCE)?

☐ %

98 A company undertakes a project that involves purchasing machinery at a cost of $65,000. The machinery is used on the project for four years, generating operating cash inflows of $20,000 per year. It is sold at the end of the project for $10,000. Taxation is charged at a rate of 30%.

Calculate the initial return on capital employed (ROCE) for the project, to the nearest whole percentage.

☐ %

BUSINESS FINANCE AND COST OF CAPITAL

99 The equity shares of Nice plc have a beta value of 0.80. The risk free rate of return is 6% and the market risk premium is 4%. Corporation tax is 30%.

What is the required return on the shares of Nice plc (to one decimal place)?

☐ %

100   Which TWO of the following statements are correct?

A   A bonus issue can be used to raise new equity finance

B   A share repurchase scheme can increase both earnings per share and gearing

C   Miller and Modigliani argued that the financing decision is more important than the dividend decision

D   Shareholders usually have the power to increase dividends at annual general meetings of a company

E   Offering new shares for tender may mean that not enough funding is raised from the share issue

101   Four companies are identical in all respects, except for their capital structures, which are as follows:

	A plc	B plc	C plc	D plc
	%	%	%	%
Equity as a proportion of total market capitalisation	70	20	65	40
Debt as a proportion of total market capitalisation	30	80	35	60

The equity beta of A plc is 0.89 and the equity beta of D plc is 1.22.

Within which ranges will the equity betas of B plc and C plc lie?

A   The beta of B plc and the beta of C plc are both higher than 1.22

B   The beta of B plc is below 0.89 and the beta of C plc is in the range 0.89 to 1.22

C   The beta of B plc is above 1.22 and the beta of C plc is in the range 0.89 to 1.22

D   The beta of B plc is in the range 0.89 to 1.22 and the beta of C plc is higher than 1.22

102   Which TWO of the following statements concerning profit are correct?

1   Accounting profit is not the same as economic profit

2   Profit takes account of risk

3   Accounting profit can be manipulated by managers

4   Gross profit margin is calculated as gross profit divided by shareholder's funds

103   A company issued its 12% irredeemable loan notes at 95. The current market price is 92. The company is paying corporation tax at a rate of 30%.

What is the current net cost of capital per annum of these loan notes (to one decimal place)?

[   ] %

104 **Ingham plc's capital structure is as follows:**

	$m
50c ordinary shares	12
8% $1 preference shares	6
12.5% loan notes 20X6	8
	26

The loan notes are redeemable at nominal value in 20X6. The current market prices of the company's securities are as follows.

50c ordinary shares	250c
8% $1 preference shares	92c
12.5% loan notes 20X6	$100

The company is paying corporation tax at the rate of 30%. The cost of the company's ordinary equity capital has been estimated at 18% pa.

What is the company's weighted average cost of capital for capital investment appraisal purposes?

A   9.71%

B   13.53%

C   16.29%

D   16.73%

105 **Indicate, by clicking in the relevant boxes, whether the following statements are true or false.**

	True	False
An increase in the cost of equity leads to a fall in share price		
Investors faced with increased risk will expect increased return as compensation		
The cost of debt is usually lower than the cost of preference shares		

106 A company has just declared an ordinary dividend of 25.6p per share; the cum-div market price of an ordinary share is 280p.

Assuming a dividend growth rate of 16% per annum, what is the company's cost of equity capital (to one decimal place)?

[   ] %

107 **Which TWO of the following would be implied by a decrease in a company's operating gearing ratio?**

   A   The company is less profitable

   B   The company is less risky

   C   The company has a lower proportion of costs that are variable

   D   The company has profits which are less sensitive to changes in sales volume

108 **Which of the following statements is part of the traditional theory of gearing?**

   A   There must be taxes

   B   There must exist a minimum WACC

   C   Cost of debt increases as gearing decreases

   D   Cost of equity increases as gearing decreases

109 **Which of the following statements is true of a scrip issue with perfect information?**

   A   Decreases earnings per share

   B   Decreases the debt/equity ratio (calculated on a market value basis) of the company

   C   Increases individual shareholder wealth

   D   Increases the market price of the share

110 A company incorporates increasing amounts of debt finance into its capital structure, while leaving its operating risk unchanged.

   Assuming that a perfect capital market exists, with corporation tax (but without personal tax), which of the following correctly describes the effect on the company's costs of capital and total market value? Indicate, by clicking in the relevant boxes, whether the cost of equity, weighted average cost of capital and total market value would increase, decrease or be unaffected.

	Increase	Decrease	Unaffected
Cost of equity			
Weighted average cost of capital			
Total market value			

111 **If, for a given level of activity, a firm's ratio of variable costs to fixed costs were to fall and, at the same time, its ratio of debt to equity were also to fall, what would be the effect on the firm's financial and operating risk? Indicate, by clicking in the relevant boxes, whether financial risk and operating risk would increase or decrease.**

	Increase	Decrease
Financial risk		
Operating risk		

112 A security's required return can be predicted using the CAPM using the formula:

$r_i = r_f + \beta_i (r_m - r_f)$

Security X has a beta value of 1.6 and provides a return of 12.0%

Security Y has a beta value of 0.9 and provides a return of 13.0%

Security Z has a beta value of 1.2 and provides a return of 13.2%

Security Z is correctly priced.

The risk free return is 6%.

What does this information indicate about the pricing of securities X, Y? Fill in the gaps in the statements below.

Security X is ....

Security Y is ....

Choose from the following:

underpriced

overpriced

113 The following are extracts from the statement of financial position of a company:

	$000	$000
Equity		
Ordinary shares	8,000	
Reserves	20,000	
		28,000
Non-current liabilities		
Bonds	4,000	
Bank loans	6,200	
Preference shares	2,000	
		12,200
Current liabilities		
Overdraft	1,000	
Trade payables	1,500	
		2,500
Total equity and liabilities		42,700

The ordinary shares have a nominal value of 50 cents per share and are trading at $5.00 per share. The preference shares have a nominal value of $1.00 per share and are trading at 80 cents per share. The bonds have a nominal value of $100 and are trading at $105 per bond.

What is the market value based gearing of the company, defined as prior charge capital/equity?

A   15.0%

B   13.0%

C   11.8%

D   7.3%

114   Fill in the gaps in the statements below.

Risk that cannot be diversified away can be described as ....

Risk that increases as a company gears up is described as ....

Choose from the following:

Business risk

Financial risk

Systematic risk

Unsystematic risk

115   An all equity company issues some irredeemable loan notes to finance a project that has the same risk as existing projects. The company operates in a tax-free environment under conditions of perfect capital markets. Indicate, by clicking in the relevant boxes, whether the following statements are true for the company.

	True	False
The cost of equity will fall		
The weighted average cost of capital will rise		

116   Which TWO of the following are most likely to result in a company's financial gearing being high?

A   Low taxable profits

B   High tax rates

C   Inexpensive share issue costs

D   Intangible assets being a low proportion of total assets

117   Compared to ordinary secured loan notes, which of the following statements is true when considering convertible secured loan notes?

A   Likely to be more expensive to service because of their equity component

B   Likely to be less expensive to service because of their equity component

C   Likely to be more expensive to service because converting to equity requires the holders to make additional payments

D   Likely to be less expensive to service because they must rank after ordinary secured loan stock

118 Which of the following is the best statement of the conclusion of Modigliani and Miller on the relevance of dividend policy?

    A   All shareholders are indifferent between receiving dividend income and capital gains

    B   Increase in retentions results in a higher growth rate

    C   Discounting the dividends is not an appropriate way to value the firm's equity

    D   The value of the shareholders' equity is determined solely by the firm's investment selection criteria

119 A company is going to take on a project using a mix of equity and debt finance in an economy where the corporation tax rate is 30%.

Assuming perfect markets, other than tax, which of the following statements is true about the project?

    A $\beta e > \beta a$; WACC < Cost of equity calculated using βa; WACC < Cost of equity calculated using βe

    B $\beta e < \beta a$; WACC > Cost of equity calculated using βa; WACC > Cost of equity calculated using βe

    C $\beta e > \beta a$; WACC < Cost of equity calculated using βa; WACC > Cost of equity calculated using βe

    D $\beta e < \beta a$; WACC > Cost of equity calculated using βa; WACC < Cost of equity calculated using βe

120 If a company that currently pays its workforce on a piece rate system were to automate its production line, which of the following responses would it expect of operating gearing?

    A   Decrease

    B   Increase

    C   Remain the same

    D   Increase or decrease depending on the nature of the production process

121 If a geared company's asset beta is used in the CAPM formula ($ri = rf + \beta i (rm - rf)$) what will ri represent?

    A   The WACC of the company

    B   The ungeared cost of equity

    C   The geared cost of equity

    D   The market premium

122 Which of the following does NOT directly affect a company's cost of equity?

    A   Return on assets

    B   Expected market return

    C   Risk-free rate of return

    D   The company's beta

123 **Which of the following ratios is used to measure a company's liquidity?**

A   Current ratio

B   Interest cover

C   Gross profit margin

D   Return on capital employed

124 **An analyst gathered the following data about a company:**

	$
Current liabilities	300
Total debt	900
Working capital	200
Capital expenditure	250
Total assets	2,000
Cash flow from operations	400

Fill in the gaps in the statements below. If the company would like a current ratio of 2, it could .... current assets by 100 or .... current liabilities by 50

Choose from the following:

increase

decrease

125 **In relation to preference shares as a source of capital for a company, fill in the gaps below to complete the sentence.**

Preference shares are a form of .... capital which carry .... risk from the company point of view than ordinary shares.

Choose from the following:

equity

loan

lower

higher

126 **What is the dividend cover ratio a measure of?**

A   How many times the company's earnings could pay the dividend

B   The interest or coupon rate expressed as a percentage of the market price

C   The returns to the investor by taking about of dividend income and capital growth

D   How much of the overall dividend pay-out the individual shareholders are entitled to

127 In relation to long-term leases, which TWO of the following statements are true?

A   The lease agreement cannot be cancelled

B   Many leases can be offered in sequence to cover the whole of useful life of the asset

C   The lessor retains the risks and rewards of ownership

D   The lessee is responsible for repairs and maintenance

128 In relation to an irredeemable security paying a fixed rate of interest, which of the following statements is correct?

A   As risk rises, the market value of the security will fall to ensure that investors receive an increased yield

B   As risk rises, the market value of the security will fall to ensure that investors receive a reduced yield

C   As risk rises, the market value of the security will rise to ensure that investors receive an increased yield

D   As risk rises, the market value of the security will rise to ensure that investors receive a reduced yield

129 Drumlin Co has $5m of $0.50 nominal value ordinary shares in issue. It recently announced a 1 for 4 rights issue at $6 per share. Its share price on the announcement of the rights issue was $8 per share.

What is the theoretical value of a right per existing share?

A $1.60

B $0.40

C $0.50

D $1.50

130 Small and medium-sized entities (SMEs) can have difficulty raising finance due to the maturity gap.

Which of the following is the best explanation of the maturity gap?

A   The lack of available funds from shareholders

B   Venture capitalists need an exit route for their investment within a specific time period

C   The business finds it difficult to obtain short-term funding but easier to obtain long-term funding secured against its non-current assets

D   The lack of business history makes borrowing more risky for lenders

131 Frost Co is planning a 1 for 4 rights issue with an issue price at a 10% discount to the current share price.

The EPS is currently $0.50 and the shares of Frost Co are trading on a price/earnings ratio of 20 times. The market capitalisation of the company is $50m.

What is the theoretical ex rights price per share (to two decimal places)?

$ [   ]

132 **Select the correct term to complete the below sentence.**

Small and medium-sized entities (SMEs) have restricted access to capital markets. The difference between the finance required to operate an SME and the amount obtained is known as the

A   Forecasted gap

B   Maturity gap

C   Funding gap

D   Asset gap

133 Green Co, a listed company, had the following share prices during the year ended 31 December 20X5:

At start of 20X5	$2.50
Highest price in the year	$3.15
Lowest price in the year	$2.40
At end of 20X5	$3.00

During the year, Green Co paid a total dividend of $0.15 per share.

What is the total shareholder return for 20X5?

A   26%

B   22%

C   32%

D   36%

134 Carp Co has announced that it will pay an annual dividend equal to 55% of earnings. Its earnings per share is $0.80 and it has ten million shares in issue. The return on equity of Carp Co is 20% and its current cum dividend share price is $4.60.

What is the cost of equity of Carp Co?

A   19.4%

B   20.5%

C   28.0%

D   22.7%

135 The following are extracts from the statement of profit or loss for Champ Co:

	$
Sales income	180,000
Cost of sales	(100,000)
Profit before interest and tax	80,000
Interest	(25,000)
Profit before tax	55,000
Tax	(15,000)
Profit after tax	40,000

70% of the cost of sale is variable costs.

What is the operational gearing of Champ Co to one decimal place?

[_____] **times**

BUSINESS VALUATIONS

136 Mrs Mays has been left $30,000 which she plans to invest on the Stock Exchange in order to have a source of capital should she decide to start her own business in a few years' time. A friend of hers who works in the City of London has told her that the London Stock Exchange shows strong form market efficiency.

If this is the case, which of the following investment strategies should Mrs Mays follow?

A   Study the company reports in the press and try to spot under-valued shares in which to invest

B   Invest in two or three blue chip companies and hold the shares for as long as possible

C   Build up a good spread of shares in different industry sectors

D   Study the company reports in the press and try to spot strongly growing companies in which to invest

137 A company has 7% loan notes in issue which are redeemable in seven years' time at a 5% premium to their nominal value of $100 per loan note. The before-tax cost of debt of the company is 9% and the after-tax cost of debt of the company is 6%.

What is the current market value of each loan note (to two decimal places)?

$[_____]

138 TKQ Co has just paid a dividend of 21 cents per share and its share price one year ago was $3.10 per share. The total shareholder return for the year was 19.7%.

What is the current share price (to two decimal places)?

$[_____]

139 Compton plc has announced a 1 for 4 rights issue at a subscription price of $2.50. The current cum-rights price of the shares is $4.10.

What is the new ex-div market value of the shares?

A $3.78

B $2.82

C $3.55

D $1.32

140 An investor believes that they can make abnormal returns by studying past share price movements.

In terms of capital market efficiency, to which of the following does the investor's belief relate?

A   Fundamental analysis

B   Operational efficiency

C   Technical analysis

D   Semi-strong form efficiency

141 Supa plc has 50 million shares in issue, and its capital structure has been unchanged for many years.

Its dividend payments in the years 20X1 to 20X5 were as follows.

End of year	Dividends
	$000
20X1	2,200
20X2	2,578
20X3	3,108
20X4	3,560
20X5	4,236

Dividends are expected to grow at the same average rate into the future.

According to the dividend valuation model, what should be the market price per share at the start of 20X6 if the required return on the shares is 25% per annum?

$ ☐

142 The following data relates to an all equity financed company.

Dividend just paid	$50m
Earnings retained and invested	70%
Return on investments	15%
Cost of equity	25%

What is the market value of the company (to the nearest million dollars)?

A $381m

B $200m

C $221m

D $218m

143 The following information relates to two companies, Alpha plc and Beta plc.

	Alpha plc	*Beta plc*
Earnings after tax	$210,000	$900,000
P/E ratio	16	21

Beta plc's management estimate that if they were to acquire Alpha plc they could save $100,000 annually after tax on administrative costs in running the new joint company. Additionally, they estimate that the P/E ratio of the new company would be 18.

On the basis of these estimates, what is the maximum that the shareholders of Beta plc should pay for the entire share capital of Alpha plc?

A $1.1m

B $2.9m

C $4.2m

D $2.0m

144 The shares of Fencer plc are currently valued on a P/E ratio of 8. The company is considering a takeover bid for Seed Limited, but the shareholders of Seed have indicated that they would not accept an offer unless it values their shares on a P/E multiple of at least 10.

Which TWO of the following are reasons which might justify an offer by Fencer plc for the shares of Seed on a higher P/E multiple?

A   Fencer has better growth prospects than Seed

B   Seed has better-quality assets than Fencer

C   Seed has a higher gearing ratio than Fencer

D   Seed is in a different country from Fencer, where average P/E ratios are higher

145 **Fill in the gap at the end of the following sentence.**

An investor, who bases all his investment decisions on information he has gathered from published statements and comments on company plans and performance, is acting as if he believed that the maximum level of efficiency of the capital market is …………… form efficient.

Choose from the following:

Strong

Semi-strong

Weak

Zero

146 The following data relate to an all-equity financed company.

Dividend just paid	$200,000
Earnings retained and invested	40%
Return on investments	15%
Cost of equity	23%

What is the market value (to the nearest $1,000)?

$ [   ]

147 **Indicate, by clicking in the relevant boxes, whether the following statements are true or false.**

Statement	True	False
The existence of projects with positive expected net present values contradicts the idea that the stock market is strong-form efficient		
The existence of information content in dividends contradicts the idea that the stock market is strong-form efficient		

148 Peter plc has made an offer of one of its shares for every three of Baker plc. Synergistic benefits from the merger would result in an increase in after-tax earnings of $4m per annum. Extracts from the latest accounts of both companies are as follows:

	Peter plc	Baker plc
Profit after tax	$120m	$35m
Number of shares	400 million	90 million
Market price of shares	250p	120p

Assume that the price of Peter plc's shares rises by 50c after the merger and that Peter issues new shares as consideration.

What will be the price-earnings ratio of the group?

A   6.76

B   8.11

C   9.07

D   10.75

149 Spanner Co has paid the following dividends per share in recent years:

Year	20X3	20X2	20X1	20X0
Dividend (cents per share)	36.0	33.8	32.8	31.1

The dividend for 20X3 has just been paid and SKV Co has a cost of equity of 16%.

Using the historical dividend growth rate and the dividend growth model, what is the market price of Spanner Co shares to the nearest cent on an ex dividend basis?

$ ☐

150 **Asset-based business valuations using net realisable values are useful in which of the following situations?**

A   When the company is being bought for the earnings/cash flow that all of its assets can produce in the future

B   For asset stripping

C   To identify a maximum price in a takeover

D   When the company has a highly-skilled workforce

151 For a company, let

EPS = Earnings per share

PPS = Price per share

VPS = Value per share

EY = Earnings yield

TE = Total earnings

Which of the following is the best expression for the value of the company?

A TE × [1/EY]

B EPS × [1/EY]

C EPS/PPS

D PPS/EPS

152 A company has just paid an ordinary share dividend of 32.0 cents and is expected to pay a dividend of 33.6 cents in one year's time. The company has a cost of equity of 13%.

What is the market price of the company's shares to the nearest cent on an ex dividend basis?

$

153 Toggle Co has in issue 6% loan notes which are redeemable at their nominal value of $100 in three years' time. Alternatively, each loan may be converted on that date into 30 ordinary shares of the company.

The current ordinary share price of Toggle Co is $3.50 and this is expected to grow at 4% per year for the foreseeable future.

Toggle Co has a pre-tax cost of debt of 5% per year.

What is the current market value of each $100 convertible loan note?

A $102.12

B $107.06

C $115.74

D $118.46

154 The owners of a private company wish to dispose of their entire investment in the company. The company has an issued share capital of $1m of $0.50 nominal value ordinary shares. The owners have made the following valuations of the company's assets and liabilities.

Non-current assets (book value)	$30m
Current assets	$18m
Non-current liabilities	$12m
Current liabilities	$10m

The net realisable value of the non-current assets exceeds their book value by $4m. The current assets include $2m of accounts receivable, which are thought to be irrecoverable.

What is the minimum price per share that the owners should accept for the company?

$ ☐

155 A company has annual after-tax operating cash flows of $2 million per year that are expected to continue in perpetuity. The company has a cost of equity of 10%, a before-tax cost of debt of 5% and an after-tax weighted average cost of capital of 8% per year. Corporation tax is 20%.

What is the theoretical value of the company?

A $20m

B $40m

C $50m

D $25m

156 Lane Co has in issue 3% convertible loan notes, which are redeemable in five years' time at their nominal value of $100 per loan note. Alternatively, each loan note can be converted in five years' time into 25 Lane Co ordinary shares.

The current share price of Lane Co is $3.60 per share and future share price growth is expected to be 5% per year. The before-tax cost of debt of these loan notes is 10% and corporation tax is 30%.

What is the current market value of a Lane Co convertible loan note, to the nearest whole $?

$ ☐

157 Indicate, by clicking on the relevant boxes, whether the following statements are true or false in relation to business valuation.

Statement	True	False
The earnings yield method and the dividend growth model should give similar values for a company		
Market capitalisation represents the maximum value for a company		
The price/earnings ratio is the reciprocal of the earnings yield		
The price/earnings ratio should be increased if the company being valued is riskier than the valuing company		

158 In relation to capital markets, which of the following statements is true?

A The return from investing in larger companies has been shown to be greater than the average return from all companies

B Weak form efficiency arises when investors tend not to make rational investment decisions

C Allocative efficiency means that transaction costs are kept to a minimum

D Research has shown that, over time, share prices appear to follow a random walk

159 In relation to behavioural finance, which TWO of the following are terms used to explain why investors in shares do not always make rational decisions?

A Herding

B Fishing

C Simulation

D Noise traders

E Bubble

160 In relation to behavioural finance, which of the following is an explanation of the market paradox?

A Rising share prices may lead to a continued rise in prices

B Shares that have performed poorly are bought by speculative investors

C Unethical insider trading in shares can boost the efficiency of the stock market

D Investors must believe that stock markets are inefficient in order for the markets to act in an efficient manner

RISK MANAGEMENT

161 **What does the term 'matching' refer to?**

A   The coupling of two simple financial instruments to create a more complex one

B   The mechanism whereby a company balances its foreign currency inflows and outflows

C   The adjustment of credit terms between companies

D   Contracts not yet offset by futures contracts or fulfilled by delivery

162 A company whose home currency is the dollar ($) expects to receive 500,000 pesos in six months' time from a customer in a foreign country. The following interest rates and exchange rates are available to the company:

Spot rate   15.00 peso per $

Six-month forward rate   15.30 peso per $

	Home country	Foreign country
Borrowing interest rate	4% per year	8% per year
Deposit interest rate	3% per year	6% per year

Working to the nearest $100, what is the six-month dollar value of the expected receipt using a money-market hedge?

A $32,500

B $33,700

C $31,800

D $31,900

163 Edted plc has to pay a Spanish supplier 100,000 euros in three months' time. The company's Finance Director wishes to avoid exchange rate exposure, and is looking at four options.

Indicate, by clicking in the relevant boxes, whether the following would provide cover or not against the exchange rate exposure that Edted would otherwise suffer.

Statement	Would provide cover	Would not provide cover
Do nothing for three months and then buy euros at the spot rate		
Pay in full now, buying euros at today's spot rate		
Buy euros now, put them on deposit for three months, and pay the debt with these euros plus accumulated interest		
Arrange a forward exchange contract to buy the euros in three months' time		

164 Indicate, by clicking in the relevant boxes, whether the following statements concerning currency risk are true or false.

Statement	True	False
Lagging is a method of hedging transaction exposure		
Matching receipts and payments is a method of hedging translation exposure		

165 A UK company has just despatched a shipment of goods to Sweden. The sale will be invoiced in Swedish kroner, and payment is to be made in three months' time. Neither the UK exporter nor the Swedish importer uses the forward foreign exchange market to cover exchange risk.

If the pound sterling were to weaken substantially against the Swedish kroner, what would be the foreign exchange gain or loss effects upon the UK exporter and the Swedish importer? Indicate, by clicking in the relevant boxes, which effect would be seen.

	Gain	Loss	No effect
UK exporter			
Swedish importer			

166 A UK company will purchase new machinery in three months' time for $7.5m. The forward exchange rate is $2.0383 − 2.0390/£.

What is the appropriate three-month forward rate at which the company should hedge this transaction (to four decimal places)?

[   ] $/£

167 The current spot exchange rate between sterling and the euro is €1.4415/£. The sterling annual interest rate is 5.75% pa and the euro annual interest rate is 4.75% pa.

What should the three month €/£ forward rate be (to four decimal places)?

[   ] €/£

168 Fill in the gap in the sentence below.

The difference between the price of a futures contract and the spot price on a given date is known as ....

Choose from the following:

the initial margin

basis

hedge efficiency

the premium

169 **Which of the following statements is correct?**

A   Once purchased, currency futures have a range of close-out dates

B   Currency swaps can be used to hedge exchange rate risk over longer periods than the forward market

C   Banks will allow forward exchange contracts to lapse if they are not used by a company

D   Currency options are paid for when they are exercised

170 The following options are held by Frances plc at their expiry date:

(1)   A call option on £500,000 in exchange for US$ at an exercise price of £1 = $1.90.

The exchange rate at the expiry date is £1 = $1.95.

(2)   A put option on £400,000 in exchange for Singapore $ at an exercise price of £1 = $2.90.

The exchange rate at the expiry date is £1 = $2.95.

Indicate, by clicking in the relevant boxes, which choice should be undertaken by the company for each option.

	Exercise	Let it lapse
Call option		
Put option		

171 Eady plc is a UK company that imports furniture from a Canadian supplier and sells it throughout Europe. Eady plc has just received a shipment of furniture, invoiced in Canadian dollars, for which payment is to be made in two months' time. Neither Eady plc nor the Canadian supplier use hedging techniques to cover their exchange risk.

If the pound sterling were to weaken substantially against the Canadian dollar, what would be the foreign exchange gain or loss effects upon Eady plc and the Canadian supplier? Indicate the effect by clicking in the relevant boxes.

	Gain	Loss	No effect
Eady plc			
Canadian supplier			

172 **Indicate, by clicking in the relevant boxes, whether the following statements are true or false about the impact of a fall in the value of a country's currency.**

Statement	True	False
Exports will be given a stimulus		
The rate of domestic inflation with rise		

173 **Which of the following statements is true of a put option?**

A   It is the right to sell an asset at a fixed price

B   It is an obligation to sell an asset at a fixed price

C   It is the right to buy an asset at a fixed price

D   It is an obligation to buy an asset at a fixed price

174 **The following statements refer to interest rate risk. Are each of the following statements true or false?**

Statement 1: The aim of a forward rate agreement (FRA) is to lock the company into a target interest rate and hedge both adverse and favourable interest rate movements.

Statement 2: An interest rate guarantees (IRG) is more expensive than an FRA as one has to pay for the flexibility to be able to take advantage of favourable interest rate movements.

	Statement 1	*Statement 2*
A	True	True
B	False	True
C	True	False
D	False	False

175 **The following statements refer to interest rate futures. Are each of the following statements true or false?**

Statement 1: If you sell a futures contract you have a contract to lend money.

Statement 2: Each contract is for a standardised amount with a set maturity date. A whole number of contracts must be dealt with.

	Statement 1	*Statement 2*
A	True	True
B	False	True
C	True	False
D	False	False

176 The shape of the yield curve at any point in time is the result of three theories acting together.

Which of the following theories does NOT influence the yield curve?

A   Liquidity preference theory

B   Expectations theory

C   Flat yield theory

D   Market segmentation theory

177 **Which of the following is shown by a yield curve?**

A   The relationship between liquidity and bond interest rates

B   The relationship between time to maturity and bond interest rates

C   The relationship between risk and bond interest rates

D   The relationship between bond interest rates and bond prices

178 **Which of the following measures will allow a UK company to enjoy the benefits of a favourable change in exchange rates for their Euro receivables contract while protecting them from unfavourable exchange rate movements?**

A   A forward exchange contract

B   A put option for Euros

C   A call option for Euros

D   A money market hedge

179 **Which of the following statements is correct?**

A   Governments may choose to raise interest rates so that the level of general expenditure in the economy will increase

B   The normal yield curve slopes upward to reflect increasing compensation to investors for being unable to use their cash now

C   The yield on long-term loan notes is lower than the yield on short-term loan notes because long-term debt is less risky for a company than short-term debt

D   Expectations theory states that future interest rates reflect expectations of future inflation rate movements

180 Interest Rate Parity Theory generally holds true in practice. However, it suffers from several limitations.

Which of the following is NOT a limitation of Interest Rate Parity Theory?

A   Government controls on capital markets

B   Controls on currency trading

C   Intervention in foreign exchange markets

D   Future inflation rates are only estimates

181   **Which of the following are descriptions of basis risk?**

1   It is the difference between the spot exchange rate and currency futures exchange rate

2   It is the possibility that the movements in the currency futures price and spot price will be different

3   It is the difference between fixed and floating interest rates

4   It is one of the reasons for an imperfect currency futures hedge

A   1 only

B   1 and 3

C   2 and 4 only

D   2, 3 and 4

182   Country X uses the dollar as its currency and country Y uses the dinar.

Country X's expected inflation rate is 5% per year, compared to 2% per year in country Y. Country Y's nominal interest rate is 4% per year and the current spot exchange rate between the two countries is 1.5000 dinar per $1.

According to the four-way equivalence model, which of the following statements is/are true?

1   Country X's nominal interest rate should be 7.06% per year

2   The future (expected) spot rate after one year should be 1.4571 dinar per $1

3   Country X's real interest rate should be higher than that of country Y

A   1 only

B   1 and 2 only

C   2 and 3 only

D   1, 2 and 3

183   The following data is available:

Country Y currency	Dollar
Country X currency	Peso
Country Y interest rate	1% per year
Country X interest rate	3% per year
Country X expected inflation rate	2% per year
Spot exchange rate in Country Y	1.60 peso per $1

What is the current six-month forward exchange rate in Country Y (to two decimal places)?

[   ]   **peso per $1**

184 Indicate, by clicking in the relevant boxes, whether the following statements about interest rate risk hedging are correct or incorrect.

Statement	Correct	Incorrect
An interest rate floor can be used to hedge an expected increase in interest rates		
The cost of an interest rate floor is higher than the cost of an interest rate collar		
The premium on an interest rate option is payable when it is exercised		
The standardised nature of interest rate futures means that over- and under-hedging can be avoided		

185 Brass Co has produced a cash forecast that predicts a cash shortage of 5 months, starting in 4 months' time. It has noted the following forward rate agreements available from its bank:

3-8 FRA 3.8% – 4.0%

4-5 FRA 3.8% – 4.0%

5-9 FRA 3.8% – 4.0%

4-9 FRA 3.8% – 4.0%

Indicate which FRA would be used and which rate would be fixed if Brass Co took on the most appropriate FRA to cover its position.

	3-8	4-5	5-9	4-9
FRA used				
	3.8%	4.0%	3.9%	7.8%
Rate fixed				

186 Plum Co, a company based in New Zealand, has entered into a contract with a Japanese company to purchase an item of machinery. The cost in Japanese Yen, is Yen 400,000 and is due to be paid in six months. Plum Co decides to enter into a forward exchange contract with its bank, who has offered a contract at the following six-month rates:

Japanese yen 77.2 – 78.2 = 1 New Zealand dollar

Calculate, to the nearest dollar, the value of New Zealand dollars that would be needed to settle the purchase invoice if the forward exchange contract is used.

| | NZD

Section B

OBJECTIVE TEST CASE STUDY QUESTIONS

Each objective test case question is worth 10 marks.

FINANCIAL MANAGEMENT FUNCTION AND ENVIRONMENT

1   The following are extracts from the last Board meeting at Y plc, a quoted high street retailer based in Country A. Y plc sources some products, such as food and clothing, from third party suppliers but also makes some of its own products, such as furniture. The context of the discussion is a plan to close a domestic furniture factory and build a new one in a cheaper country.

CEO: I think we should be more cautious about going ahead with plans to build a new factory in Country B as I've looked at their forecast inflation rates and they are higher than expected. This would send our costs sky high when the reason we want to build it is to save money. However, if we cannot boost profits, then I fear we will have to cut the next dividend, something that will be disastrous for our shareholders who will then sell our shares en masse.

Director A: Surely the exchange rate will move to compensate for the difference in inflation, so it won't make a huge difference?

Director B: I think the key issue is improving reported profit – that is the main way we can keep our shareholders happy, which is, after all, our job. Sacking people in Country A will only result in a boost to the share price due to the cost savings – as long as we keep shareholders informed, that is.

Director C: I think we should be more worried about what is happening in our own country – the Government is talking about restricting the money supply to control excessive cost-push inflation.

Director D: I have some good news – the government has blocked a proposed merger between W plc and X plc (two rivals of Y plc) on competition grounds.

(a) **Which TWO dividend concepts/theories are consistent with the CEO's fears over the cut in dividend?**

A   Modigliani and Miller dividend irrelevancy

B   Clientele effect

C   Residual theory

D   Dividend signalling

(b) **What theory is consistent with Director A's view on exchange rates?**

A   Interest rate parity

B   Purchasing power parity

C   Liquidity preference theory

D   Market segmentation theory

(c) **Which TWO statements concerning Director B's comments are true?**

A   Increasing profit is always in shareholders' best interests

B   Directors have a fiduciary duty to put shareholder interests first

C   Sacking staff will have no impact on the share price other than as a result of the cost savings that result

D   In a semi-strong market the share price of Y plc will react when news about the new factory and any redundancies is made public

(d) **Which of the following statements concerning Director C's comments is/are true?**

(i)   Restricting growth in the money supply will have more impact on 'demand pull' inflation than 'cost-push'.

(ii)   Restricting the money supply may result in smaller businesses struggling to raise finance.

(iii) Restricting the money supply is part of a government's fiscal policy.

A   (i), (ii) and (iii)

B   (i) and (ii) only

C   (ii) and (iii) only

D   (ii) only

(e) **Which of the following is NOT a reason governments seek to limit monopoly power of companies?**

A   Output is produced at a higher price than necessary

B   Reduced incentive to innovate

C   Reduced price discrimination

D   High prices to limit new market entrants

2 The senior management team of Arkwright Co are concerned that an imminent general election will mean a change in government. The two primary political parties have quite different economic policies.

The CEO has stated:

"If the other party comes to power then there will be a shift from managing the economy using monetary policy to managing it via fiscal policy. Each policy uses quite different methods to manage the budget deficit that the country currently has. The new potential government has also stated that it will use taxation as a way of controlling externalities. We need to understand these policies in order to determine how Arkwright Co will be affected by any change."

In addition, the FD has stated:

"Our shareholders use common measures such as earnings per share and return on capital employed to evaluate the performance of the company. One major shareholder's only real concern is that we maintain a consistent rate of dividend growth. We need to make sure that we evaluate the effect of any political changes, particularly if the corporation tax rate rises under the new government."

Arkwright Co's dividends over the past five years have been as follows:

20X3	$0.15 per share
20X4	$0.16 per share
20X5	$0.18 per share
20X6	$0.19 per share
20X7	$0.21 per share

(a) Calculate the equivalent annual percentage growth rate in dividends over the past five years to one decimal place.

$\boxed{}$ %

(b) Which TWO of the following statements about monetary and fiscal policy are correct?

A   Monetary policy is solely concerned with controlling the economy using interest rates

B   Fiscal policy involves managing the economy using taxation and government spending

C   If a government feels that inflation is too high due to rising aggregate demand levels it may choose to lower interest rates to try and reduce demand

D   The use of increasing government borrowing to stimulate the economy can lead to 'crowding out' of private investment

(c)   **If a country's government budget deficit is increasing, which of the following could represent the situation?**

A   An increase in government spending has outweighed an increase in taxation income, leading to increased government borrowing

B   An increase in government spending has been outweighed by an increase in taxation income, leading to decreased government borrowing

C   An increase in interest rates leading to increased government borrowing

D   A decrease in interest rates lasing to decreased government borrowing

(d)   **If the new government chooses to increase the rate of corporate taxation levels, which TWO of the following would represent the initial direct effects on earnings per share (EPS) and return on capital employed (ROCE)?**

A   EPS would rise

B   EPS would fall

C   There would be no effect on EPS

D   ROCE would rise

E   ROCE would fall

F   There would be no effect on ROCE

(e)   **The following statements have been made about externalities.**

1   Externalities do not affect the consumer of the product that causes them.

2   The existence of externalities suggests that there is a misallocation of resources.

Which of these statements is/are correct?

A   1 only

B   Both 1 and 2

C   2 only

D   Neither 1 nor 2

WORKING CAPITAL MANAGEMENT

3   Green Co is a furniture manufacturer whose auditors have pointed out that its working capital position is far from satisfactory. The main problem is the high level of inventory, which has led to the company building up a larger and larger bank overdraft. Managers at Green Co have been to numerous public lectures discussing various types of inventory control systems and technologies, but have felt that most of them are impractical.

(a)   **Indicate, by clicking in the relevant boxes, whether the following are or are not assumptions behind the traditional economic order quantity formula,**

$EOQ = \sqrt{(2 \times C_o \times D \div C_h)}$.

Statement	Is an assumption	Is not an assumption
Constant demand		
Zero lead time		

(b)   The production manager has established the following information about a major inventory item.

Purchase price per unit	$480
Annual demand	4,000
Supplier's delivery costs per order	$10
Chief buyer's salary per annum	$30,000
Total number of orders placed per annum*	1,000
Annual storage costs per unit	$2
Cost of capital	10% per annum

*Relates to all product lines, not just this one.

What is the economic order quantity for this inventory item?

[   ] units

(c)   Assume that Green Co adopts the EOQ as its order quantity for that item of inventory and that it takes one week for an order to be delivered.

How much inventory will Green Co have on hand when the order is placed? Assume there are 52 weeks in a year.

[   ] units

(d) The following statements refer to different types of inventory control systems and procedures.

1 A just-in time system implies relatively low reorder costs.

2 Periodic review means ordering inventory when it falls below the designated safety inventory level.

3 Use of the economic order quantity model means that holding and ordering costs should be the same.

Which of the above statements is/are correct?

A 1 only

B 1 and 3 only

C 2 and 3 only

D 1, 2 and 3

(e) The following possible benefits have been attributed to just-in-time systems.

1 Reduced inventory levels

2 Less waste

3 Reduced production times

4 Improved quality of output

Which of these claims can be justified?

A 1 only

B 1 and 2

C 1, 2 and 3

D 1, 2, 3 and 4

4 Hall Co is a retail organisation that buys goods from abroad for cash and sells them locally to both individuals and businesses. It has grown rapidly since its formation on 1 January 20X1 with results summarised below.

Year	20X1	20X2	20X3	20X4	20X5 (forecast)
	$000	$000	$000	$000	$000
Sales	200	400	800	1,200	1,600
Cost of sales	(100)	(200)	(400)	(600)	(800)
Gross profit	100	200	400	600	800
Administration costs	(50)	(60)	(200)	(500)	(640)
Net profit ($000)	50	140	200	100	160

In the first year, sales were made on a purely cash basis, then credit sales were introduced for businesses. However Hall Co has now found that its working capital position has deteriorated as business customers take longer and longer to pay. When making decisions that affect the company's finances, a discount rate of 10% is used, which is the best estimate of the cost of capital. Assume credit sales equal business sales.

(a) Indicate, by clicking in the relevant boxes, whether the following would influence or would not influence Hall Co's credit policy for accounts receivable:

Statement	Would influence	Would not influence
Competitors' terms		
Risk of irrecoverable debts		
Financing costs		
Suppliers' terms		

(b) During the period up to and including 20X5, the expected receivables period has been maintained. However, by 20X5, the actual business proportion of sales has grown from 50% to 60%. Credit periods are as follows: 40% of customers take 1 month's credit, 40% of customers take 2 months' credit and 20% of customers take 3 months' credit.

What is the annual cost in $ of financing 20X5 receivables?

$ [   ]

(c) **If Hall were to offer customers 1.5% discount for payments within one month, what would be the annual cost of that in respect of receivables who currently take two months or three months to pay?**

	2-month receivables	*3-month receivables*
A	19.89%	9.49%
B	9.49%	4.64%
C	4.64%	9.49%
D	9.49%	19.89%

(d) Hall is considering the use of debt factoring or invoice discounting. The following statements have been made in relation to these services.

1   It is apparent in both instances that someone else is collecting your debts.

2   The debts remain an asset of Hall Co under factoring.

Which of these statements are correct?

A   1 only

B   Both 1 and 2

C   2 only

D   Neither 1 nor 2

(e) **Which of the following is NOT a function of a credit control department?**

A   Advising existing customers on payment terms

B   Determining whether to accept cash discounts

C   Giving credit references to third parties

D   Investigating potential customers' creditworthiness

5 Jeeps Co is concerned about its cash position and has taken to delaying payments to some suppliers in order to ease that problem. Each month the purchase ledger department splits the total value of invoices for that month into three categories, A, B and C depending on their importance.

Category A invoices, amounting to $2,000,000, are urgent and paid after 30 days

Category B invoices, amounting to $3,000,000, are less urgent and paid after 60 days; and

Category C invoices, amounting to $4,000,000, are least urgent and paid after 90 days.

Several suppliers have reacted to this by offering Jeeps Co a 2% cash discount if the accounts are settled within 15 days. Jeeps Co is currently considering whether or not to accept this. Another supplier, who Jeeps Co now waits 90 days to pay, has been threatening legal action over the $300,000 currently owed. Jeeps Co feels that some sort of compromise might be needed.

Jeeps Co's cost of capital is 12% per annum.

Assume that there are 30 days in a month and that purchases accrue evenly over the 360-day year.

(a) Jeeps Co is considering the advantage of the early settlement discount from those it currently pays after:

1   60 days

2   90 days

From which payables should Jeeps take the 2% cash discount?

A   1 only

B   Both 1 and 2

C   2 only

D   Neither 1 nor 2

(b) **What is Jeeps Co's payables period (to the nearest day)?**

☐☐☐ days

(c) **Which of the following is NOT a symptom of over-trading?**

A   Rapid increase in current assets

B   Increase in shareholders' funds

C   Increase in inventory and debtors receivables periods

D   Rapid increase in revenue

(d) To avoid a court action, Jeeps Co is thinking of offering to repay the creditor it owes $300,000 in instalments as follows (all figures in $000)

Now	1 month	2 months	3 months	4 months	5 months
75	45	45	45	45	45

How much will Jeeps Co save, in present value terms, if the creditor accepts the instalment offer instead of Jeeps having to pay in full immediately (to the nearest $00)?

$ ☐☐☐

(e) A company can make decisions that affect its level of working capital. These can be described as either aggressive or conservative policies.

Indicate, by clicking in the relevant boxes, whether the following policies are aggressive or conservative.

Statement	Aggressive	Conservative
Both fluctuating and permanent current assets financed by short-term funds		
Delay paying creditors (payables) for as long as possible		

6 King Co is a decentralised organisation whose different divisions have approached the matter of cash control in different ways, partly because of their different circumstances. Assume 365 days in a year.

The Western division is facing a two-year major capital investment programme for which significant funds need to be raised to meet the steady demand for cash. The division intends to use the 'Baumol model' to decide when to raise funds, which will be done by selling off investments currently earning 5% per annum. The transaction cost of these sales will be $500 per transaction and the total amount needed over the two years is $2,000,000.

The Alpine division has no significant investment plans but finds itself regularly having to either sell investments to make funds available or invest surplus cash. This is because of the considerable variation in daily cash inflows, which has been quantified as having a standard deviation of $7,000. As a result, the division uses the 'Miller-Orr model' to determine when to invest and when to make sales, using the same transaction cost and investment rate as the Western division.

The Southern division has just been created to manufacture a product used by other divisions but mainly sold to outside customers. The coming month, Month 1, will be spent converting and equipping existing corporate premises at a total cash cost of $800,000. Production will start in Month 2 and sales in Month 3. Planned sales volumes are as follows.

Month	3	4	5	6	7
Sales volume (000s)	10	11	13	16	20

The product will sell for $24 per unit. 20% of sales will be for cash. Of the credit sales, 25% of credit customers (including other divisions) pay in the month following the sale, 50% will pay one month later and 25% after another month.

(a) How much finance should the Western division raise in a single tranche according to the Baumol model?

A $14,142

B $20,000

C $141,421

D $200,000

(b)   **What does the Miller-Orr model suggest is the spread between the upper and lower limits of cash levels that the Alpine division should maintain?**

A $1,123

B $8,028

C $21,489

D $153,569

(c)   **What will be the Southern division's cash receipts from sales in Month 5?**

$ [   ]

(d)   **It is important to distinguish between a cash budget and a cash forecast. What is the validity of the following statements?**

Statement 1:   A cash forecast is an estimate of cash receipts and payments for a future period under existing conditions before taking account of possible actions to modify cash flows, raise new capital, or invest surplus funds.

Statement 2:   A cash budget is a commitment to a plan for cash receipts and payments for a future period after taking any action necessary to bring the preliminary cash forecast into conformity with the overall plan of the business.

Drag and drop the relevant statements to indicate whether they are true or false.

(e)   **Which of the following is NOT an advantage to King Co of having a centralised treasury function?**

A   Better foreign currency risk management

B   Borrowing can be made at more advantageous rates

C   Increases individual division's responsibility for cash

D   The treasury function can be run as a profit centre to raise additional profits

7   Grumpy Co sells stress-relieving toys and, surprisingly perhaps, is happy with the progress it is making financially as it is growing and is profitable. There are issues however about cash flow.

An extract from the accounting records for the most recent financial period (a year) is as follows:

	$
Credit sales	480,000
Cash sales	80,000
Trade receivables	85,000
Other receivables	12,000
Credit purchases	212,000
Cash purchases	21,000
Trade payables	30,000
Other payables including VAT	26,000
Finished goods inventory at start of year	45,000
Finished goods inventory at end of year	52,000

In one typical cycle of trade (cycle X), goods were ordered on 17/1/15 and delivered 21 days later, the supplier was paid on 25/2/15. The goods remained in inventory for 62 days. At which point these goods were sold on credit terms of 60 days. Grumpy was eventually paid 68 days after the sale was made. Assume there are 365 days in the year.

(a)   **What is the receivables period from the table data?**

    A   68 days

    B   65 days

    C   55 days

    D   74 days

(b)   **What is the payables period from the table data?**

    [   ] days

(c)   **What is the inventory holding period?**

    A   81 days

    B   84 days

    C   90 days

    D   73 days

(d)   **For cycle X, what is the cash operating cycle?**

    [   ] days

(e)   **Indicate, by clicking in the relevant boxes, whether the following statements about a cash operating cycle are true or false.**

Statement	True	False
A long operating cycle is more serious in a period of strong growth		
Operating cycles tend to be longer in brand new businesses compared to established businesses		

INVESTMENT APPRAISAL

8 Bell Co has decentralised and divisional managers are allowed to make their own investment decisions subject to confirmation by the main company board. Because each of the three divisions (Ding, Dong and Merrily) are subject to different levels of risk, it has been thought appropriate to use different discount rates in each division.

Ding has been told that its real discount rate is 5%. The general rate of inflation, based on an index that uses a very wide range of prices, is 2%. In the industry in which Ding operates, a number of prices are seen to be inflating at 3%.

Dong is assessing a project in which the first of four annual lease payments has been agreed at $120,000. This is payable in one year's time and subsequent payments will rise by 4% per annum. Dong's proper money cost of capital is 8%.

Merrily is considering investing $1,000,000 in a project, which will produce the following annual outflows and inflows.

Year	1	2	3
Outflows ($000)	1,800	2,500	1,500
Inflows ($000)	2,000	3,000	2,000

The cash flows, which arise at the end of each year, are stated in current year terms. It is expected that outflows will rise by 3% per annum and inflows by 2% per annum. The money cost of capital of the Merrily Division is 9%.

(a) **What is Ding's money discount rate?**

A   7.1%

B   4.0%

C   1.9%

D   1.1%

(b) **What is the present value of Dong's last payment that will be made in four years' time (to the nearest $000)?**

$ ☐ ,000

(c) **What is the net present value of Merrily's project (to the nearest $000)?**

A $252,000

B $(10,000)

C $(39,000)

D $(61,000)

(d)   **When considering risk in project appraisal, what is the main advantage of using simulations to assist the appraisal?**

A   A clear decision rule

B   More than one variable can change at a time

C   Statistically more accurate than other methods

D   Being diagrammatic is easier to understand

(e)   **Is it possible to have a negative real discount rate to apply to the cash flow estimates made in current terms when making investment decisions?**

From the below, select yes or no and then select your reason

Answer:

Yes

No

Reason:

The calculation of a present value won't work if the discount rate is negative

Negative interest rates never happen in the real world

It will happen in deflationary times

It will happen if the rate of inflation exceeds the money cost of capital

9   Care Co needs to replace a major piece of office equipment that is in constant use and for which there is expected to continue to be use for the foreseeable future. Two types of machine are available with different capital costs, useful lives, scrap values and annual running costs.

Machine 1 will initially cost $480,000, have a life of four years, scrap value of $60,000 and annual running costs of $72,000.

Machine 2 will initially cost $540,000, have a life of three years, scrap value of $120,000 and annual running costs of $47,000.

Care Co's cost of capital is 10%. Assume all cash flows, except the initial capital cost, occur at the end of the relevant year and assume that taxation and inflation can be ignored.

(a)   **What is the equivalent annual cost of machine 2 (to the nearest $000)?**

$[   ],000

(b)   **Drag and drop the relevant statements to indicate whether they are true or false.**

(1)   The equivalent annual cost calculation assumes the same type of machine is going to be used into the foreseeable future.

(2)   The equivalent annual cost calculation assumes the capabilities of Machine 1 and Machine 2 are identical.

(c) It is now felt that the final scrap value of the machines depends on two factors: whether or not a new supplier enters the market (which would reduce the likely scrap value) and the strength of the dollar against other currencies (since sales of used machines will be made abroad and invoiced in the foreign currency). Adverse effects will each reduce the scrap value by 10% of the figure used in the investment appraisal. The relevant probabilities are as follows.

New supplier	Probability	Strong $	Probability
Yes	0.4	Yes	0.3
No	0.6	No	0.7

What is now the expected value of the scrap proceeds from machine 2?

A $106,800

B $109,000

C $111,600

D $113,000

(d) To overcome the difficulties of incorporating probabilities into the investment appraisal calculations, Care Co could perform a simulation exercise to help reach a decision.

Drag and drop to indicate whether the following statements, relating to simulation, are true or false.

(1) It eliminates the effects of risk associated with various estimates.

(2) It requires probabilities of estimates subject to risk to be known.

(e) Which of the following statements about Care Co's replacement decision are true?

1 The decision between machine 1 and machine 2 could be found by calculating total NPV of each machine over a 12 year period.

2 The replacement analysis model assumes that Care Co replaces like with like each time it needs to replace an existing asset.

A 1 only

B Both 1 and 2

C 2 only

D Neither 1 nor 2

10   Easter Co is about to hold its annual strategic planning meeting and a number of capital investment projects will be discussed. A summary of the projects' cash flows is shown below.

Project	NPV	Investment
	$000	$000
A	4,900	3,200
B	7,400	9,300
C	5,900	7,300
D	7,500	5,200
E	9,000	5,600

The investment will need to be made at the start of the coming year; no projects can be delayed and none are divisible. The funds available for these projects are limited to $10,000,000.

(a)   **Indicate, by clicking in the relevant boxes, whether the following statements about capital rationing are true or false.**

Statement	True	False
Both hard and soft capital rationing are the result of external factors		
Both hard and soft capital rationing are the result of internal policies		
Hard rationing is the result of external factors, soft rationing is the result of internal policies		
Soft rationing is the result of external factors, hard rationing is the result of internal policies		

(b)   **From the list below, select which TWO projects should be accepted, based on the circumstances described?**

A   project A

B   project B

C   project C

D   project D

E   project E

(c)   **What projects would be accepted if it were found that projects A and E were mutually exclusive?**

A   A and D

B   A and E

C   A, D and E

D   D and E

(d)   **What projects, and fractions of projects, would be accepted if a partner could be found to invest in a proportion of one of the projects making them effectively infinitely divisible (ignoring the mutually exclusive limitation)?**

A   A, D and 2/7 E

B   A, E and 3/13 D

C   A, D and E

D   D and E

(e)   A sixth project, Project F, is causing considerable confusion, particularly among those members of the board of Easter Co whose sole means of appraising projects is to find an internal rate of return (IRR) using the spreadsheet function on their computers. The summarised cash flows of Project F are as follows.

Time 0	Invest	$4.00m
Time 1	Receive	$8.80m
Time 2	Spend	$4.83m

The spreadsheet function requires you to enter the cash flows of a project and also enter a guess for the IRR. The directors are struggling to guess the IRR for this sixth project.

Which TWO of the following statements represent likely causes of confusion over project F?

A   It has a negative NPV when undiscounted

B   It never earns a positive NPV

C   It has no real IRRs

D   It has one positive and one negative IRR

E   It may have more than one IRR

11   Ace Co is considering a new project. Ace currently installs burglar alarms, putting contact points on access portals and movement sensors in general areas of a property. The new project is in the fire alarm business, a business considered to be similar in many ways to what Ace currently does.

A junior member of the finance team has estimated the cash flows for the project as follows:

Time	Description	Cash flow $
0	Loose tools	(6,000)
1–4	Contribution	25,000
1–4	Allocated overheads	(8,000)
2–5	Tax @ 25% of profit	(4,250)

No tax-allowable depreciation is available for loose tools.

Ace is entirely equity financed with a cost of equity correctly calculated as 12%.

(a)   **What is the NPV of the above project to the nearest $100?**

   A $28,700

   B $53,000

   C $58,400

   D $34,100

(b)   **The IRR of the above project has been correctly calculated as 26%. Which of the following statements are true?**

   (1)   The IRR is not a measure of absolute profitability and linear interpolation provides only an estimate of the IRR.

   (2)   If the IRR of the project is higher than its cost of capital then the project is always acceptable regardless of the pattern of the cash flows.

   A   Both statements are true

   B   Both statements are false

   C   Statement (1) only

   D   Statement (2) only

(c)   **If the loose tools became allowable for tax-allowable depreciation which of the following statements would be true?**

   (1)   Reported profit before tax would rise.

   (2)   The NPV of the project would rise.

   (3)   Assuming that one of the answers to the NPV calculation above is correct then the decision to proceed would alter.

   A   (1) and (2)

   B   (2) and (3)

   C   (2) only

   D   (1) only

(d)   **One of the directors thinks that calculating the payback period would be a useful addition. What is the project's payback period in months to one decimal place?**

   [   ] months

(e)   **Indicate, by clicking in the relevant boxes, whether the following statements on the payback period are true or false.**

Statement	True	False
It normally ignores time value		
It is a risk-focussed approach in decision-making		
There is clear advice once it is calculated		

12 The following information relates to an investment project, which is being evaluated by the directors of Fence Co, a listed company. The initial investment, payable at the start of the first year of operation, is $3.9 million.

Year	1	2	3	4
Net operating cash flow ($000)	1,200	1,500	1,600	1,580
Scrap value ($000)				100

The directors believe that this investment project will increase shareholder wealth if it achieves a return on capital employed greater than 15%. As a matter of policy, the directors require all investment projects to be evaluated using both the payback and return on capital employed methods. Shareholders have recently criticised the directors for using these investment appraisal methods, claiming that Fence Co ought to be using the academically-preferred net present value method.

The directors have a remuneration package which includes a financial reward for achieving an annual return on capital employed greater than 15%. The remuneration package does not include a share option scheme.

(a) **What is the payback period of the investment project, in years to 2 decimal places?**

☐ years

(b) **Based on the average investment method, what is the percentage return on capital employed of the investment project, to one decimal place?**

☐ %

(c) **Which TWO of the following statements about investment appraisal methods are correct?**

A The return on capital employed method considers the time value of money

B Return on capital employed must be greater than the cost of equity if a project is to be accepted

C Riskier projects should be evaluated with shorter payback periods

D Payback period ignores the timing of cash flows within the payback period

(d) **Which of the following statements about Fence Co is/are correct?**

1   Managerial reward schemes of listed companies should encourage the achievement of stakeholder objectives.

2   Requiring investment projects to be evaluated with return on capital employed is an example of dysfunctional behaviour encouraged by performance-related pay.

3   Fence Co has an agency problem as the directors are not acting to maximise the wealth of shareholders.

A   1 and 2 only

B   1 only

C   2 and 3 only

D   1, 2 and 3

(e) **Which of the following statements about Fence Co directors' remuneration package is/are correct?**

1   Directors' remuneration should be determined by senior executive directors.

2   Introducing a share option scheme would help bring directors' objectives in line with shareholders' objectives.

3   Linking financial rewards to a target return on capital employed will encourage short-term profitability and discourage capital investment.

A   2 only

B   1 and 3 only

C   2 and 3 only

D   1, 2 and 3

13   Link Co has been prevented by the competition authorities from buying a competitor, Twist Co, on the basis that this prevents a monopoly arising. Link Co has therefore decided to expand existing business operations instead and as a result the finance director has prepared the following evaluation of a proposed investment project for the company.

	$000
Present value of sales revenue	6,657
Present value of variable costs	(2,777)
Present value of contribution	**3,880**
Present value of fixed costs	(1,569)
Present value of operating cash flow	**2,311**
initial capital investment	(1,800)
Net present value	**511**

The project life is expected to be four years and the finance director has used a discount rate of 10% in the evaluation. The investment project has no scrap value.

The finance director is considering financing the investment project by a new issue of debt.

(a) **What is the percentage change in sales volume which will make the NPV zero, calculated to one decimal place?**

☐ %

(b) **Which of the following statements relating to sensitivity analysis is/are correct?**

1 Although critical factors may be identified, the management of Link Co may have no control over them.

2 A weakness of sensitivity analysis is that it ignores interdependency between project variables.

3 Sensitivity analysis can be used by Link Co to assess the risk of an investment project.

A 1 and 2 only

B 1 only

C 2 and 3 only

D 1, 2 and 3

(c) **Using the average investment method and assuming operating cash flows of $729,000 per year, what is the return on capital employed of the investment project?**

A 16%

B 28%

C 31%

D 64%

(d) **Which of the following statements relating to debt finance is correct?**

A Link Co can issue long-term debt in the euro currency markets

B The interest rate which Link Co pays on its new issue of debt will depend on its weighted average cost of capital

C A new issue of loan notes by Link Co will take place in the primary market

D Link Co will not be able to issue new debt without offering non-current assets as security

(e) **Indicate, by clicking in the relevant boxes, whether the following statements relating to competition policy are correct or incorrect.**

Statement	Correct	Incorrect
Scale economies are an advantage of monopoly and oligopoly		
Social cost or externalities are an example of economic inefficiency arising from market failure		
Monopoly is discouraged because it can lead to inefficiency and excessive profits		

14   Gaimett Co has some surplus cash that it wishes to invest in long-term projects. The market it operates in is in recovery from a recession and more potential projects are becoming available on a regular basis.

The finance director wishes to ensure that the best use is made of the available cash. A list of potential projects currently available has been made. All projects are divisible and must be started immediately.

Project	NPV $000	Investment value $000
A	125	375
B	240	800
C	80	400
D	40	50
E	150	600

(a)   **If the surplus cash available is $1.5 million, calculate the optimum combination of projects that Gaimett Co should undertake.**

A   B, E and 26.7% of A

B   C, E and 62.5% of B

C   A, D, E, C and 9.4% of B

D   A, B, D and 45.8% of E

(b)   Before the decision on the projects is made, project A becomes unavailable and it is realised that the remaining projects are actually indivisible.

Under the new circumstances, calculate the optimum combination of projects that Gaimett Co should undertake.

A   B, C and D

B   C, D and E

C   B, D and E

D   B, C, D and E

(c)   **Which TWO of the following would be reasons why managers may reduce the amount that they are willing to invest as part of soft capital rationing?**

A   The company's bank has refused to provide available funds

B   A debt covenant forbids the issue of new shares to raise cash

C   Managers believe that better quality projects will shortly be available

D   The precautionary motive

E   A stock market crash discourages shareholders from investing further

(d) The managers have decided that they will hold on to $600,000 of the available investment cash for 3 months, as they know that another very good project will become available at that time.

Which TWO of the following investments would be suitable to make use of this cash over this period?

A   Certificates of deposit

B   Listed company shares

C   Unlisted company shares

D   Instant access bank deposit account

E   Listed company debt

(e) **Which of the following should NOT be included in a cash flow forecast?**

A   Payment of a one off dividend

B   Receipt from an insurance company to cover the value of stolen inventory

C   Tax allowable depreciation allowed in relation to a new asset purchase

D   Buy back of shares

BUSINESS FINANCE AND COST OF CAPITAL

15 Brash Co can buy a new piece of sophisticated machinery for $500,000 by borrowing under a secured loan at 8%. It has also researched the possibility of leasing the asset.

The company's finance director is a little rusty on leasing issues as the business has never leased before and he has worked in Brash Co for 20 years. He said 'I studied leasing years ago but I think leasing is cheaper than borrowing because the lease company has access to greater amounts of finance and so benefits from economies of scale on that front'.

The managing director is sceptical, arguing that leasing companies are commercial and so each deal must be assessed on its merits. He commented: 'We have to careful here, I know the lease companies are always responsible for the maintenance but that can't be free!'

The lease offer is as follows:

The lease will be over 5 years with lease payments of $146,000 annually in advance (at the start of each accounting period). Tax is payable 1 year after the accounting year-end and the corporation tax rate is 25%. Maintenance is payable by the lessor and costs $20,000 per annum payable at the end of each year, including the last year in preparation for sale. The residual value is expected to be $40,000 (the expected tax written down value at the end of the lease) and the lessor will retain that.

(a) **Indicate, by clicking in the relevant boxes, whether the statements made by the finance director and the managing director are true or false.**

Statement	True	False
Statement by the finance director		
Statement by the managing director		

(b) **In a calculation to compare the cost of leasing with cost of borrowing to buy the asset above, which TWO of the following items are not relevant?**

A The interest cash flows saved on borrowing

B The saving on maintenance

C The residual value

D The cash benefits arising from use of the machinery

E The tax-allowable depreciation

(c) **What is the present value of the maintenance cash flows, after tax?**

A $63,180

B $64,380

C $84,240

D $103,047

(d) **What is the present value of the tax relief on the lease payments, after tax, to the nearest $000?**

$ ☐

(e) **Indicate, by clicking in the relevant boxes, whether the following statements about the potential effects of taking on a lease are true.**

Statement	True	False
The use of leasing as opposed to purchasing an asset could turn a negative NPV project into a positive NPV one		
If shareholders see that there is a significant lease in place then they may perceive an increase in risk		

16 Kelvin Co is considering an extensive rights issue to raise new finance. It currently has 4 million shares and has been very successful over a prolonged period.

The terms of the deal are as follows:

- One new share for every 4 held at a price of 90% of the existing market value per share

- The existing market value is $20 per share (the cum rights price).

One of the directors is unhappy with offering any discounts to existing shareholders. He claims that the companies past success should be enough to encourage shareholders to increase their investment.

(a) **What is the theoretical ex rights price (TERP) per share in $?**

$ [   ]

(b) **What would be the effect on the TERP value if the new shares were offered at a 20% discount level whilst raising the same total amount of finance?**

A   The TERP value would not change since the total amount raised would be the same

B   The TERP would increase

C   The TERP would fall

D   The TERP would fall to a level unacceptable to existing shareholders

(c) **Indicate, by clicking in the relevant boxes, whether the following statements about discounts on a rights issue are true or false.**

Statement	True	False
The level of discount is simply not relevant to the wealth of a shareholder as long as they accept the right. It is ignorance of the theory that encourages the offer of a discount in most cases		
The bigger the discount the more likely a shareholder is to accept the rights offer in most cases		

(d) **Which of the following actions by shareholders would be the worst thing that they could do in relation to a rights issue as far as shareholder wealth is concerned?**

A   Accept the rights offer without negotiation

B   Renounce their rights and sell them on the open market

C   Save their investment and do nothing

D   Sell 50% of their rights on the open market whilst ignoring the rest

(e) **Which of the following actions will result in the least dilution of control for existing shareholders?**

A   Accept the rights offer without negotiation

B   Renounce their rights and sell them on the open market

C   Save their investment and do nothing

D   Sell 50% of their rights on the open market

17   Dominance Co is considering raising some new finance but there is disagreement at board level how best to proceed.

The managing director thinks that the company should retain control in the hands of the existing and loyal shareholders. The finance director feels that the gearing level should be allowed to increase to benefit from the tax relief allowed on interest.

The existing equity is quoted at $4.20 cum div with an imminent dividend of 16c due any day. The company earnings have grown at a fairly steady rate of 8% over recent years, but expectations are for growth to be 2% points better in the future.

The company's debt is 4% irredeemable bonds, which were issued at a 5% discount of $95%. They have a nominal value of $100 but are currently quoted at $80 with the interest having just been paid. The corporation tax rate is 25%.

(a) **Assuming the business wants to retain control in the hands of the existing shareholders, how should it seek to raise the new finance?**

A   A placing of new shares via a loyal broker

B   A further public offering of shares

C   A rights issue where it is expected that 95% of the existing shareholders will accept the offer

D   Issue new debt

(b) **Assuming the business wants to maximise the tax shield on the new finance, how should it raise the money?**

A   A placing of new shares and $10,000,000 of preference shares

B   Accepting a VC offer which includes $5,000,000 of 4% redeemable bonds and some shares

C   Sell redeemable debt with a market value $12,500,000 with interest at 5%. The redemption value will make up 25% of the market value

D   Sell $12,000,000 irredeemable debt with interest at 5.25%

(c) **What is the percentage cost of equity to one decimal place?**

     [＿＿＿＿＿] %

(d) **What is the after tax cost of debt, as a percentage to two decimal places?**

    ☐ %

(e) **The cost of equity for Dominance Co is significantly greater than the cost of debt. The main reason for this is:**

A   The total risk level in the business

B   The specific risk in the business

C   The tax shield

D   The level of systematic risk in the business

18 The board of Empire Co are discussing their dividend policy and there have been various statements made by the directors.

Director A: Our shareholders rely on the level of dividend we pay and we cannot ignore that. We must pay out a dividend as expected otherwise our shareholders will be forced to sell shares or invest elsewhere.

Director B: I know that when I was young that if I got a rise in my allowance in a particular week then I was more likely to get it again. It was expected. We must pay what is expected.

Director C: What matters is the underlying value of the projects that we are doing now and we will do in the future. We should stop wasting time discussing this.

Director D: What matters is what we can afford in cash. If we are short of money then it should be discussion over – less dividend will have to be paid. What we could then do is issue more shares instead – I think that is called a scrip dividend.

(a) **Which director supports the dividend irrelevancy theory?**

A   Director A

B   Director B

C   Director C

D   Director D

(b) **Which director supports the signalling effect of dividends?**

A   Director A

B   Director B

C   Director C

D   Director D

(c) **Which director supports the dividend dependency theory?**

A   Director A

B   Director B

C   Director C

D   Director D

(d) **Which director is more concerned about company liquidity than dividend policy?**

   A   Director A

   B   Director B

   C   Director C

   D   Director D

(e) **Once the discussion about dividend policy was finalised there was another discussion about scrip issues. Indicate, by clicking on the relevant boxes, whether the following statements are true or false.**

Statement	True	False
In a scrip issue a shareholder will end up with more shares, this means there will be a gain to them		
Scrip issues serve the purpose of reducing market values in return for more shares. This can make the shares more marketable		

19 The board of a major bank is discussing their investment appraisal methodology as they have a new project under consideration. They have agreed that using the CAPM approach is sensible as they feel it likely that most of their shareholders will have a well-diversified shareholding in the stock market as a whole.

There has been some dispute about which risks constitute specific risks in the bank and which risks are more systematic in nature partly driven by the nature of the banks operations. Equally, no one seems quite sure what the required return derived from the CAPM formula actually represents.

The finance director has produced the following data relating to the bank itself, the financial market and the new project it is considering:

Data

Required return on existing debt	6.0%
Cost of existing debt to the bank	4.8%
Return on short dated government securities	5.2%
Return in the stock market	12.8%
Equity beta of the bank	1.35
Beta of the new project	1.52
Asset beta of the bank	1.15

(a) **Which TWO of the following risks could be correctly described as systematic risks in this case?**

   A   The interest rates set by the bank

   B   The risk of default by the banks customers on loans made

   C   The recessionary pressures in the country in which the bank operates

   D   The demand for loans made to the bank

   E   A change in government after a general election

(b) **In the CAPM what would be the value to use for the risk free rate of return (Rf), from the data above?**

A   6.0%

B   4.8%

C   5.2%

D   4.16% (the after tax return on short dated government securities)

(c) In the CAPM formula R = Rf + βj(Rm − Rf) where βj represents the project beta, R represents **the cost of equity capital/the required return on the new project** and the market risk premium is represented by **(Rm − Rf)/Rm.**

Pick the correct answers to complete the sentences.

(d) **What is the percentage required return on the new project as derived from the CAPM formula above, to two decimal places?**

☐ %

(e) **What is the meaning of a beta value of 1?**

A   The investment is risk free

B   The investment has the same level of risk as the bank

C   The investments total risk is as risky as the market

D   The investment has the same level of systematic risk as the market

20 The board of Freedling Co are in discussion about the various risk types that face the business. It is evident that there is considerable confusion and disagreement.

Operating risk

Some of the directors feel that given the increasing volume of trade having fixed costs is the best thing to do. 'How can it be risky to have fixed costs when we know how much they are and that they don't change overly much from one year to the next' was one comment.

Gearing risk

The directors were more aware in this area, with some favouring a more traditional view of gearing and others remembering Modigliani and Miller (M&M) fondly from their studies.

(a) **Indicate, by clicking in the relevant boxes, whether the following statements on operating gearing are true or false?**

Statement	True	False
Given the level of fixed costs do not change considerably from one year to the next, having a lot of fixed cost in Freedling's cost structure would mean that they had low levels of operating risk		
Variable costs are risky because they change as volume changes. Given Freedling is growing the year on year variable cost level has changed a lot as well		

(b) **In relation to changing the gearing of Freedling, which of the following statements are true?**

    (1) As debt is more risky for the company, it is more expensive than equity and including a higher proportion of debt in the capital structure will therefore increase the WACC.

    (2) Equity holders respond to the increased risk when a company includes more debt in its capital structure by increasing the return they demand from the company.

    A   Both statements are true

    B   Both statements are false

    C   Only statement (1) is true

    D   Only statement (2) is true

(c) **Assuming the board were considering raising more debt, indicate, by clicking in the relevant boxes, whether the assertion that the WACC of the business would fall holds true or not in the following models.**

Statement	Holds true	Does not hold true
Under M&M no tax		
Under M&M with corporation tax		
At low levels of gearing under the traditional theory of gearing		

(d) **Under M&M no tax which of the following statements are true?**

    (1) It does not matter how a business raises finance.

    (2) Shareholders, given the M&M assumptions, will recognise the level of risk inherent in any extra debt and compensate themselves by a commensurate increase in required return to leave the company WACC unaltered and without any inherent gain.

    A   Both statements are true

    B   Both statements are false

    C   Only statement (1) is true

    D   Only statement (2) is true

(e) In traditional theory diagrams the cost of debt line is often drawn with a slight tail, arcing upwards at very high levels of gearing. Indicate, by clicking in the relevant boxes, whether the following statements are true or false.

Statement	True	False
The rising tail represents an increased risk to debt holders		
Tax exhaustion can increase the cost of borrowing at high levels of gearing		
In practice, businesses rarely reach this point as banks refuse to lend despite the high interests rates possible		

21 Tulip Co is a large company with an equity beta of 1.05. The company plans to expand existing business by acquiring a new factory at a cost of $20m. The finance for the expansion will be raised from an issue of 3% loan notes, issued at nominal value of $100 per loan note. These loan notes will be redeemable after five years at nominal value or convertible at that time into ordinary shares in Tulip Co with a value expected to be $115 per loan note.

The risk-free rate of return is 2.5% and the equity risk premium is 7.8%.

Tulip Co is seeking additional finance and is considering using Islamic finance and, in particular, would require a form which would be similar to equity financing.

(a) **What is the cost of equity of Tulip Co using the capital asset pricing model, calculated to 1 decimal place?**

| | %

(b) **Using estimates of 5% and 6%, what is the cost of debt of the convertible loan notes?**

A 3.0%

B 5.2%

C 6.9%

D 5.7%

(c) **In relation to using the capital asset pricing model to value Tulip Co, which of the following statements is correct?**

A The model assumes that all shareholders of Tulip Co have the same required rate of return

B The model assumes a constant share price and a constant dividend growth for Tulip Co

C The model assumes that capital markets are semi-strong form efficient

D The model assumes that Tulip Co's interim dividend is equal to the final dividend

(d) **Which TWO of the following statements about equity finance are correct?**

A   Equity finance reserves represent cash which is available to a company to invest

B   Additional equity finance can be raised by rights issues and bonus issues

C   Retained earnings are a source of equity finance

D   Equity finance includes both ordinary shares and preference shares

E   Cutting a dividend provides a source of equity finance

(e) **Regarding Tulip Co's interest in Islamic finance, which of the following statements is/are correct?**

1   Murabaha could be used to meet Tulip Co's financing needs

2   Mudaraba involves an investing partner and a managing or working partner

A   1 only

B   2 only

C   Both 1 and 2

D   Neither 1 nor 2

BUSINESS VALUATIONS

22 Kevin Dutton is an investor who specialises in buying corporate debt at discounted values and aims to make gains either by selling bonds at a higher value later or by receiving redemption payments. Kevin is currently evaluating the following investments:

Last year Kevin bought $1m nominal value of unquoted 5% bonds in Company A at a price of $500,000. The bonds are to be redeemed at nominal value in 5 years' time but **Company A** is showing signs of financial distress. To value the bonds Kevin has estimated that a return of 30% is appropriate here to compensate for the risks of non-payment.

Company B, a forestry company, is looking to raise $5 million through the issue of 6 year deep discounted zero coupon bonds. The issue price has been set at a 40% discount. Kevin may invest but is looking for a return of 10% per annum to do so.

Kevin also owns fixed rate bonds in **Company C**. These bonds are traded on major bond markets. Kevin is thinking of selling them now as he believes that interest rates are going to increase shortly resulting in a drop in the bond price.

All three companies mentioned pay tax at 25%.

(a) **What is the estimated current market value of Kevin's investment in the bonds in company A, to the nearest $1,000?**

    A $293,000

    B $360,000

    C $391,000

    D $500,000

(b) **Calculate the gross redemption yield on the deep discounted bonds. Give your answer as a percentage to 1 dp.**

    [   ] %

(c) **Calculate the minimum discount required so the deep discounted bonds give a return over 10%. Give your answer to the nearest whole percent.**

    A   40%

    B   42%

    C   44%

    D   46%

(d) **Indicate, by clicking in the relevant boxes, whether the following statements concerning deep discounted bonds are true or false.**

Statement	True	False
It is illegal for companies to issue bonds at a discount		
Deep discount bonds can help Company B's cash flow		
Investors' required returns will generally be lower with deep discounted bonds		

(e)   **Which TWO of the following statements concerning bond prices are true?**

A   The price of bonds with fixed coupon rates will not be affected by changes in interest rates

B   Changes in expected inflation levels will not affect bond prices

C   Changes in bond values will result in changes in the return required by investors in those bonds

D   Bond prices typically fall as interest rates rise

E   The market price of the bond may not be the same as the theoretical price

23   Loki plc is a growing company specialising in making accessories for mobile phones and tablets. The company is currently all-equity financed with 2 million ordinary shares in issue. The existing shareholders are mainly family members and friends. The directors of Loki need to raise finance to fund a new factory and are considering a range of options including flotation and venture capital. Future growth is anticipated to be the following:

Earnings next year = $0.25m, expected to grow at 7% pa

Dividend next year = $0.14m, expected to grow at 4% pa

Flotation

Q plc, a listed company with similar business activities to Loki has a P/E ratio of 9, an equity beta of 1.2 and gearing, measured as Debt:Equity of 1:2. Loki is expected to grow faster than Q plc, at least in the short term.

If flotation is approved, then the issue share price would be set at a 15% discount to fair value. The directors of Loki do not believe that an asset valuation is of much use here.

Venture capital

The directors of Loki have been in discussion with 4Ts, a listed venture capital company. As well as contributing equity, 4Ts would seek to spread the risk of their investment by also investing in the form of 4-year 5% secured redeemable bonds and also convertible preference shares. The risk adjusted return on similar bonds has been estimated at 6%.

Corporation tax is currently 30%.

(a)   **Which of the following statements, concerning the usefulness of asset based methods of business valuation, is correct?**

A   Replacement cost normally represents the minimum price that should be accepted for the sale of a business as a going concern.

B   Break-up value should provide a measure of the maximum amount that any purchaser should pay for the business.

C   Book value will normally be a meaningless figure as it will be based on historical costs.

D   Asset based methods give consideration to non statement of financial position intangible assets such as a highly skilled workforce and a strong management team.

(b)   **Calculate the value of Loki plc's equity beta to 2 dp.**

[   ]

(c) **Calculate the issue price of Loki shares to the nearest cent using the dividend valuation model with a cost of equity of 14%.**

A $0.60

B $0.70

C $1.19

D $1.24

(d) **What is the market value of the redeemable bonds, in $ to two decimal places?**

$ [   ]

(e) **Which TWO of the following statements concerning 4Ts' perspective are true?**

A   4Ts' investment in the preference shares will have the lowest risk out of the three methods of finance offered due to the option to convert

B   4Ts will accept a lower level of dividends on the convertible preference shares compared to normal preference shares

C   4Ts are likely to prefer to use CAPM in valuing Loki shares

D   The current shareholders of Loki would be willing to sell a majority equity stake to 4Ts

24   Davina McNabb is a fund manager within M Inc, a global investment company. She has recently identified the following potential acquisition targets:

Company A is an unquoted, property development company with a portfolio of over two hundred houses at various stages of renovation. It has been loss making for the last two years due to the economic downturn. Davina believes that new government legislation will bring a welcome boost to the housing market.

Company B is an unquoted shoe manufacturer. It has also suffered in the recent recession but the directors are confident that the company is past the worst and growth lies ahead:

- Earnings are expected to be $12.5 million next year and expected to grow at 2% per annum

- Dividends will be $5 million for each of the next three years and then expected to grow at 3% thereafter.

Davina has located a similar listed company that has an earnings yield of 12% and a cost of equity of 14%.

Company C is a quoted fashion retailer. Davina believes that the current share price of $2.58 undervalues the company significantly, making it a suitable target. She is also interested in Company C as she feels it would have a good fit with her existing fund portfolio and would diversify away some risk.

(a) **Which of the following valuation methods is most suitable for valuing Company A?**

A   P/E ratio × earnings

B   Dividend valuation model (DVM)

C   Net realisable value of assets

D   Market capitalisation

(b) Calculate the value of Company B by reference to its predicted earnings, in millions of dollars, to one decimal place.

$ [   ] m

(c) Calculate the value of company B using the dividend valuation model.

A $42.3m

B $43.2m

C $46.8m

D $47.3m

(d) Which of the following statements concerning Davina's opinion that Company C is undervalued is true?

A   Davina believes that the stock market is strong form efficient and she has access to secret inside information.

B   Davina believes that the stock market is semi-strong form efficient and she has access to secret inside information.

C   Davina believes that the stock market is semi-strong form efficient and she has analysed financial statements and press releases to form his opinion.

D   Davina believes that the stock market is weak form efficient and she has produced graphs of historic share prices to form her opinion.

(e) Indicate, by clicking in the relevant boxes, whether the following statements concerning whether Davina should buy Company C to diversify away portfolio risk are true or false.

Statement	True	False
The shareholders of M Inc. are unlikely to value such diversification		
Davina should always try to reduce the average beta of her portfolio		
Davina should seek to diversify away any systematic risk in her portfolio		

25   Pike plc, a listed conglomerate, is looking to buy Minnow Co, an advertising company owned and run by Freda Minnow. Freda has agreed to the sale and has insisted on cash consideration as she wishes to retire. Pike plc is considering issuing bonds to generate the cash required.

The following information is available:

Statement of financial position for Minnow Co

- Net book value of equity $10.3m

- Net realisable value $11.2m

- Replacement cost $15.3m

- Bank loan $2.5m

Statement of profit or loss

- Minnow Co made a profit after tax of $7m last year. This expected to grow by 3% per annum.

- Despite owning and running the company, Freda Minnow does not take a salary, preferring to take money out of the business via high dividends. Pike plc estimates that it will need to offer a salary of $100,000 to replace Freda when she leaves.

Cash flow

- Pike Co anticipates that, after making a number of changes, Minnow Co will generate free cash flow of $6m next year. This is expected to grow by 4% per annum thereafter.

Other information

- Trout and Co, a quoted advertising agency with similar gearing and growth prospects to Minnow Co, has a P/E ratio of 7, a WACC of 12% and a cost of equity of 15%.

- Minnow Co pays corporation tax at 30%.

(a) **Based on asset values, what is the minimum amount Freda should accept for the equity of Minnow Co?**

    A $8.7m

    B $10.3m

    C $11.2m

    D $15.3m

(b) **Calculate the market value of Minnow Co using earnings. Give your answer to the nearest $million.**

    $ ☐

(c) **Calculate the market value of the equity of Minnow Co using discounted cash flows.**

    A $72.5m

    B $75.0m

    C $75.5m

    D $78.0m

(d) **Which TWO of the following statements about the proposed acquisition are true?**

    A   Freda probably prefers to take dividends due to tax considerations.

    B   A major risk faced by Pike Co is that customers will be loyal to Freda rather than the company, so may leave when she retires.

    C   If the stock market that Pike Co is listed on is strong form efficient, then the share price of Pike plc will only react to the acquisition when the confirmation is published.

    D   The directors of Pike Co should only be concerned about the unsystematic risks of Minnow Co.

(e) **Which of the following statements concerning the use of different valuation methods for Minnow Co is true?**

   (i)   Asset valuations are unlikely to give a good indicator of market value.

   (ii)   Theoretically, discounted cash flow approaches are the best method.

   (iii)   Dividend valuation model using historic dividend information would give a fair market valuation for the company.

   A   (i), (ii) and (iii)

   B   (i) and (ii) only

   C   (i) only

   D   (iii) only

26   It is now 1/1/20X6. Predator Co is looking make a bid for entire share capital of Prey Co, a small family owned company that makes specialist gears for high performance racing bikes. Prey Co's products have had a niche but loyal customer base for many years but demand started to soar in late 20X3 when it was revealed that all the gold medal winners in the cycling events at the Olympics were using a new revolutionary gear type developed and patented by Prey Co. The sale has been agreed in principle but a valuation still needs to be agreed for Prey Co. The following information is available:

Prey Co – Statement of Financial Position

	Note	$000s
Non-current assets	1	400
Current assets	2	50
Total assets		**450**
Share capital (50 cent ords.)		100
Reserves		170
Bank Loans – repayable 20X8		140
Current liabilities		40
Total equity and liabilities		**450**

Note 1: Included in non-current assets is specialist machinery that has a NBV of $100,000, would cost $500,000 to replace but would only be able to be sold for scrap of $25,000 if disposed of.

Note 2: Current assets have a net realisable value of $40,000.

Prey Co – Summary statements of financial position

$000s	20X1 (audited)	20X2 (audited)	20X3 (audited)	20X4 (audited)	20X5 (unaudited)	20X6 (forecast)
Profit after tax	(10)	20	60	130	140	156
Dividends paid	–	10	30	65	70	78

A similar quoted company has been found that has a cost of equity of 15% and a quoted P/E ratio of 10.

(a) **Calculate the asset value of Prey Co's shares using net realisable value, in $s, to the nearest $000.**

$ [   ] ,000

(b)   Calculate the asset value of Prey Co's shares using replacement cost.

   A $270,000

   B $500,000

   C $670,000

   D $770,000

(c)   Indicate, by clicking in the relevant boxes, whether the following statements concerning the use of asset valuations for Prey Co with the information given are true or false.

Statement	True	False
The replacement cost valuation is a good indication of corporate value as Prey Co operates in a capital intensive industry		
The replacement cost valuation is likely to be a poor indication of corporate value as Prey Co's most valuable asset is likely to be its brand name		
Net book value is an indicator of the minimum amount the current owners will want for their company		

(d)   Calculate the share price of Prey Co using earnings

   A $7.00

   B $7.80

   C $14.00

   D $15.60

(e)   What growth rate should be used if estimating the value of Prey Co using the dividend valuation model? Give your answer as a percentage to 1 dp.

   ☐ %

27   Ring Co has in issue ordinary shares with a nominal value of $0.25 per share. These shares are traded on an efficient capital market. It is now 20X6 and the company has just paid a dividend of $0.450 per share. Recent dividends of the company are as follows:

Year	20X6	20X5	20X4	20X3	20X2
Dividend per share	$0.450	$0.428	$0.408	$0.389	$0.370

Ring Co also has in issue loan notes which are redeemable in seven years' time at their nominal value of $100 per loan note and which pay interest of 6% per year.

The finance director of Ring Co wishes to determine the value of the company.

Ring Co has a cost of equity of 10% per year and a before-tax cost of debt of 4% per year. The company pays corporation tax of 25% per year.

(a)   Using the dividend growth model, what is the market value of each ordinary share, in dollars, to two decimal places?

   $ ☐

(b) **What is the market value of each loan note?**

A $109.34

B $112.01

C $116.57

D $118.68

(c) The finance director of Ring Co has been advised to calculate the net asset value (NAV) of the company.

Which TWO of the following formulae calculate correctly the NAV of Ring Co?

A   Total assets less current liabilities

B   Non-current assets plus net current assets

C   Non-current assets plus current assets less total liabilities

D   Net current assets plus non-current assets less long-term liabilities

E   Non-current assets less net current assets less non-current liabilities

(d) **Which of the following statements about valuation methods is true?**

A   The earnings yield method multiplies earnings by the earnings yield

B   The equity market value is number of shares multiplied by share price, plus the market value of debt

C   The dividend valuation model makes the unreasonable assumption that average dividend growth is constant

D   The price/earnings ratio method divides earnings by the price/earnings ratio

(e) **Indicate, by clicking in the relevant boxes, whether the following statements about capital market efficiency are correct or incorrect.**

Statement	Correct	Incorrect
Insider information cannot be used to make abnormal gains in a strong form efficient capital market		
In a weak form efficient capital market, Ring Co's share price reacts to new information the day after it is announced		
Ring Co's share price reacts quickly and accurately to newly-released information in a semi-strong form efficient capital market		

28 The finance director of Coral Co has been asked to provide values for the company's equity and loan notes. Coral Co is a listed company and has the following long-term finance:

	$m
Ordinary shares	7.8
7% Convertible loan notes	8.0
	15.8

The ordinary shares of Coral Co have a nominal value of $0.25 per share and are currently trading on an ex dividend basis at $7.10 per share. An economic recovery has been forecast and so share prices are expected to grow by 8% per year for the foreseeable future.

The loan notes are redeemable after six years at their nominal value of $100 per loan note, or can be converted after six years into 10 ordinary shares of Coral Co per loan note. The loan notes are traded on the capital market.

The before-tax cost of debt of Coral Co is 5% and the company pays corporation tax of 20% per year.

(a) **What is the equity market value of Coral Co (to two decimal places)?**

$ [   ] m

(b) **Assuming conversion, what is the market value of each loan note of Coral Co?**

A $110.13

B $112.67

C $119.58

D $125.70

(c) **Which of the following statements about the equity market value of Coral Co is/are true?**

1 The equity market value will change frequently due to capital market forces.

2 If the capital market is semi-strong form efficient, the equity market value will not be affected by the release to the public of insider information.

3 Over time, the equity market value of Coral Co will follow a random walk.

A 1 only

B 1 and 3 only

C 2 and 3 only

D 1, 2 and 3

(d) **Indicate, by clicking in the relevant boxes, whether the following are assumptions that are made by the dividend growth model.**

Statement	Is an assumption	Is not an assumption
Investors make rational decisions		
Dividends show either constant growth or zero growth		
The dividend growth rate is less than the cost of equity		

(e) **Why might valuations of the equity and loan notes of Coral Co be necessary?**

1   The company is planning to go to the market for additional finance.

2   The securities need to be valued for corporate taxation purposes.

3   The company has received a takeover bid from a rival company.

A   1 and 2 only

B   1 and 3 only

C   3 only

D   1, 2 and 3

29 Extracts from the financial statements of Bluebell Co, a listed company, are as follows:

	$m
Profit before interest and tax	238
Finance costs	(24)
Profit before tax	214
Corporation tax	(64)
Profit after tax	150

	$m
Assets	
Non-current assets	
Property, plant and equipment	768
Goodwill (internally generated)	105
	873
Current assets	
Inventories	285
Trade receivables	192
	477
Total assets	1,350
Equity and liabilities	
Total equity	688
Non-current liabilities	
Long-term borrowings	250
Current liabilities	
Trade payables	312
Short-term borrowings	100
Total current liabilities	412
Total liabilities	662
Total equity and liabilities	1,350

A similar size competitor company has a price/earnings ratio of 12.5 times.

This competitor believes that if Bluebell Co were liquidated, property, plant and equipment would only realise $600m, while 10% of trade receivables would be irrecoverable and inventory would be sold at $30m less than its book value.

Separately, Bluebell Co is considering the acquisition of Dandelion Co, an unlisted company which is a supplier of Bluebell Co.

(a) **What is the value of Bluebell Co on a net realisable value basis?**

    A $140.8 million

    B $470.8 million

    C $365.8 million

    D $1,027.8 million

(b) **What is the value of Bluebell Co using the earnings yield method?**

$ [＿＿＿＿＿＿] million

(c) **When valuing Bluebell Co using asset-based valuations, which of the following statements is correct?**

    A   An asset-based valuation would be useful for an asset-stripping acquisition

    B   Bluebell Co's workforce can be valued as an intangible asset

    C   Asset-based valuations consider the present value of Bluebell Co's future income

    D   Replacement cost basis provides a deprival value for Bluebell Co

(d) **Which of the following is/are indicators of market imperfections?**

    1   Low volume of trading in shares of smaller companies

    2   Overreaction to unexpected news

    A   1 only

    B   2 only

    C   Both 1 and 2

    D   Neither 1 nor 2

(e) **Which TWO of the following statements are correct?**

    A   Dandelion Co is easier to value than Bluebell Co because a small number of shareholders own all the shares

    B   Bluebell Co will have to pay a higher price per share to take control of Dandelion Co than if it were buying a minority holding

    C   Scrip dividends decrease the liquidity of shares by retaining cash in a company

    D   Dandelion Co's shares will trade at a premium to similar listed shares because it will have a lower cost of equity

    E   If Bluebell's shares are traded on a market that is semi-strong form efficient, there will be opportunities for insider trading on the shares

30 GWW Co is a listed company which is seen as a potential target for acquisition by financial analysts. The value of the company has therefore been a matter of public debate in recent weeks and the following financial information is available:

Year	20X3	20X4	20X5	20X6
Profit before interest and tax ($m)	12.6	13.8	14.9	15.7
Profit after tax ($m)	8.5	8.9	9.7	10.1
Total dividends ($m)	5.0	5.2	5.6	6.0

Statement of financial position for 20X6:

	$m	$m
Non-current assets		91.0
Current assets:		
Inventory	3.8	
Trade receivables	4.5	8.3
Total assets		99.3
Equity finance:		
Ordinary shares	20.0	
Reserves	47.2	67.2
Non-current liabilities:		
8% bonds		25.0
Current liabilities		7.1
Total liabilities		99.3

The shares of GWW Co have a nominal (par) value of $0.50 per share and a market value of $4.00 per share. The cost of equity of the company is 9% per year. The business sector of GWW Co has an average price/earnings ratio of 17 times. The 8% bonds are redeemable at nominal (par) value of $100 per bond in seven years' time and the before-tax cost of debt of GWW Co is 6% per year.

The expected net realizable values of the non-current assets and inventory are $86.0m and $4.2m respectively. In the event of liquidation, only 80% of the trade receivables are expected to be collectible.

(a) Calculate the market capitalisation (equity market value) of GWW Co to the nearest $ million.

$ ☐ million

(b)   Calculate the value of GWW Co using a net asset value (liquidation) basis, in $ millions to one decimal place.

$ [   ] million

(c)   Calculate the value of GWW Co using the price/earnings ratio method?

A $90.9 million

B $141.3 million

C $171.7 million

D $266.9 million

(d)   Calculate the value of GWW Co using the dividend growth model with growth calculated using the average historic dividend growth rate, to the nearest $5 million.

$ [   ] million

(e)   Calculate the value of growth to be used in the dividend growth model using the Gordon's growth approximation. Use the figures from the most recent year in your calculations.

A   4.4%

B   6.1%

C   6.9%

D   8.9%

RISK MANAGEMENT

31 Mallett Co is an Australian firm currently manufacturing a large item of machinery, which is due to be exported shortly to the United States. The sale has been priced in US dollars, the client is expected to pay 850,000 USD.

This is Mallett Co's first sale to an American client since most of its exports normally go to Asia. The client has agreed to pay Mallett Co three months from now. The following relevant additional information is available.

Spot rate   0.7233 US dollars to the Australian dollar

US dollar interest rate   3.3% per annum
Australian dollar interest rate   2.9% per annum

(a) **What will be the Australian dollar receipt, to the nearest thousand dollars, if the transaction is hedged using the money market?**

|_____| **AUD**

(b) **Which of the following relationships suggests that current long-term interest rates can be used to predict future short-term interest rates?**

A   Expectations theory

B   Fisher effect

C   Interest rate parity

D   Purchasing power parity

(c) **What is the 3-month forward exchange rate, to four decimal places?**

|_____| **US dollars to the Australian dollar**

(d) One risk that a company which exports and imports may face is that of exchange losses when accounting results of its foreign branches or subsidiaries are converted into home currency.

What is the name usually given to this type of risk?

A   Economic risk

B   Political risk

C   Transaction risk

D   Translation risk

(e) **Why is a currency option a particularly suitable device to reduce exposure to currency movements when tendering for a contract priced in a foreign currency?**

A   Cheapest means of achieving a hedge

B   Least risky means of achieving a hedge

C   Least unfavourable effect in the published accounts

D   You may not get the contract and therefore the currency

32 Noon Co, a company based in Centreland whose home currency is the Centreland Colon (CC), has been regularly buying components from and selling finished products to businesses in Flyland, where the currency is the Flyland Franc (FF).

One particular payment of 3,000,000 Flyland Francs has to be made by Noon Co to a supplier in Flyland in three months' time. The following information is available.

Spot rate   6.170 – 6.210 Flyland Francs to the Centreland Colon

Three-month forward rate   6.321 – 6.362 Flyland Francs to the Centreland Colon

Interest rates that can be used by Noon Co are as follows.

	Borrow	Deposit
Flyland Franc interest rate	18.0% per annum	13.5% per annum
Centreland Colon interest rate	8.1% per annum	6.3% per annum

(a) **What is the cost in Centreland Colons of a forward market hedge?**

A   471,550 CC

B   474,608 CC

C   483,092 CC

D   486,224 CC

(b) **Which of the following relationships attempt to explain the difference between forward and spot rates of exchange between two currencies and the relative rates of interest in the countries of origin of the two currencies?**

A   Expectations theory

B   Fisher effect

C   Interest rate parity

D   Purchasing power parity

(c) **What is the cost in Centreland Colons of a money market hedge?**

A   428,391 CC

B   463,091 CC

C   470,349 CC

D   479,874 CC

(d) **Indicate, by clicking in the relevant boxes, whether the following statements on the characteristics of interest rate futures are true or false.**

Statement	True	False
Amounts and periods are standardised		
They are legally binding contracts		
They can be bought and sold on a secondary market		
They can be used both to hedge risks and to speculate on interest rate movements		

(e) **If inflation is currently running at 3.8% per annum in Centreland, what (to the nearest 1%) is the implied inflation rate in Flyland?**

[   ] %

33 PZK Co, whose home currency is the dollar, trades regularly with customers in a number of different countries. The company expects to receive €1,200,000 in six months' time from a foreign customer. Current exchange rates in the home country of PZK Co are as follows:

Spot exchange rate: 4.1780 – 4.2080 euros per $

Six-month forward exchange rate: 4.2302 – 4.2606 euros per $

Twelve-month forward exchange rate: 4.2825 – 4.3132 euros per $

The interest rate in the home country of PZK Co is 4% per year.

As well as considering the use of derivatives to hedge the risk exposure presented by the receipt, the treasurer of PZK is looking at 'internal' methods such as invoicing in dollars and leading and lagging.

(a) **What type of risk exposure is PZK Co exposed to due to the foreign receipt?**

    A   Transaction risk

    B   Economic risk

    C   Translation risk

    D   Political risk

(b) **Calculate, to the nearest dollar, the loss compared to its current dollar value which PZK Co will incur by taking out a forward exchange contract on the future euro receipt.**

    $ ▢

(c) **Calculate the annual interest rate in the foreign customer's country implied by the spot exchange rate and the twelve-month forward exchange rate.**

    A   1.5%

    B   3.9%

    C   4.1%

    D   6.6%

(d) **With reference to PZK making foreign currency purchases, which of the following statements concerning whether PZK Co should 'lead' or 'lag' in its management of the anticipated receipt is true?**

    A   The $ is expected to weaken against the €, so PZK should lead

    B   The $ is expected to weaken against the €, so PZK should lag

    C   The $ is expected to strengthen against the €, so PZK should lead

    D   The $ is expected to strengthen against the €, so PZK should lag

(e) **Indicate, by clicking in the relevant boxes, whether the following statements concerning whether PZK Co should invoice in dollars are true or false.**

Statement	True	False
Invoicing in dollars will eliminate all foreign exchange risk that PZK is exposed to		
Invoicing in dollars will pass exchange rate risk to the customer		
Invoicing in dollars may not be commercially acceptable to foreign customers		

34 H Company, a large manufacturer, is planning to sell an existing subsidiary and use the funds to buy land and build a new factory. The proceeds of the sale are likely to be delayed, so the directors have estimated that $10 million will be needed in 3 months' time for a period of 6 months. Given this, the directors have decided that a bank loan would be appropriate as a form of finance rather than equity sources.

After checking that interest rate yield curves in the financial press are normal rather than inverted, the treasurer is now looking to hedge the interest rate exposure. Traditionally H Company has used forward rate agreements (FRAs) for hedging interest rate risk exposure but the treasurer is now considering using interest rate futures, although she is concerned that futures will not be as good a hedge as the FRAs.

H Company's bank have offered an FRA on the following terms:

3v9 FRA 7.2 – 7.8%

(a) **Which TWO of the following are possible reasons why the Directors decided that a bank loan was preferable to equity in this case?**

    A   The factory will act as security on the loan

    B   They believe Modigliani and Miller's theory of gearing with taxation

    C   All equity sources have higher issue costs than the loan

    D   The servicing cost of the debt will be lower

(b) **Which of the following would NOT be a possible explanation for the normal yield curve observed?**

    A   Expectations theory

    B   Liquidity preference theory

    C   Market segmentation theory

    D   An expected rise in interest rates

(c) **Select, from the drop down list, which represents the payment/receipt payable on the FRA if the reference interest rate moves to 7.6% in 3 months' time?**

$10,000 payment / $10,000 receipt / $20,000 payment / $20,000 receipt

(d) **Which THREE of the following are reasons why futures are not always a perfect hedge?**

    A   Futures contracts are in standard sizes which may not coincide with how much H Company wants to borrow

    B   Futures have standardised contract dates, which may not coincide with when H Company wants to take out the loan

    C   Basis risk

    D   Interest rates are hard to predict

(e) **Which of the following statements concerning FRAs and interest rate futures is/are true?**

    (i)   In both cases Company H stills needs to borrow the money at the market rate in three months' time.

    (ii)   Both have standardised contract sizes.

    (iii)   Both result in a net gain or loss that can be offset against the loss or gain on the associated real world borrowing.

    A   (i), (ii) and (iii)

    B   (i) and (ii) only

    C   (i) and (iii) only

    D   (i) only

35   It is now the 31st of January. The treasurer of F Company is reviewing cash forecasts and funding requirements and has identified the need for the following transactions:

Transaction 1:

F Company will have a surplus of $1 million from 1st of May for 3 months, which will need to be deposited to earn additional interest. The treasurer has seen inverted interest rate yield curves in the financial press, so is considering using a 3v6 FRA quoted at 5% – 5.6% to hedge the interest rate risk exposure. He is also considering the use of interest rate options as an alternative strategy.

Transaction 2:

F Company also needs to borrow $20 million longer term debt to finance expansion. The treasurer would prefer to borrow at a floating rate but does not feel that the company can obtain competitive rates. He is thus considering the possibility of borrowing fixed and entering into a swap arrangement. F Company's advisors have identified G Company as a possible counter party. Details of the current borrowing rates that each company can achieve are as follows:

Company	Best fixed rate	Best variable rate
F	7%	LIBOR + 3%
G	6%	LIBOR + 1%

(a)   **Which TWO predictions are normally associated with an inverted yield curve?**

A   An expected fall in interest rates

B   An expected rise in interest rates

C   A fall in inflation

D   A downturn of the economy into a recession

(b)   **What is the payment/receipt payable on the FRA if the reference interest rate moves to 5.5% on the 1st May?**

$250 payment / $250 receipt / $1,250 payment / $1,250 receipt

(c)   **Which of the following best describes an interest rate option?**

A   A right but not an obligation to buy or sell interest rate futures

B   An obligation to obtain a loan at an agreed interest rate at a future date

C   A right but not an obligation to obtain a loan (or deposit) at a future date

D   A right but not an obligation to an agreed interest rate on a notional loan or deposit

(d)   **With reference to interest rate swaps, which of the following statements it true?**

A   It allows the company a period of time during which it has the option to buy a forward rate agreement at a set price

B   It locks the company into an effective interest rate

C   It is an agreement whereby the parties to the agreement exchange interest rate commitments

D   It involves the exchange of principle

(e)   **Indicate, by clicking in the relevant boxes, whether the following statements concerning the swap are true or false.**

Statement	True	False
G company has been offered lower interest rates due to having a better credit rating		
Under the swap loan principals are exchanged		
If G defaults on the loan it has taken out, then F would also be liable under the swap		

36   Herd Co is based in a country whose currency is the dollar ($). The company expects to receive €1,500,000 in six months' time from Find Co, a foreign customer. The finance director of Herd Co is concerned that the euro (€) may depreciate against the dollar before the foreign customer makes payment and she is looking at hedging the receipt.

Herd Co has in issue loan notes with a total nominal value of $4 million which can be redeemed in 10 years' time. The interest paid on the loan notes is at a variable rate linked to LIBOR. The finance director of Herd Co believes that interest rates may increase in the near future.

The spot exchange rate is €1.543 per $1. The domestic short-term interest rate is 2% per year, while the foreign short-term interest rate is 5% per year.

(a)   What is the six-month forward exchange rate predicted by interest rate parity?

€ [   ]   per $1

(b)   As regards the euro receipt, what is the primary nature of the risk faced by Herd Co?

A   Transaction risk

B   Economic risk

C   Translation risk

D   Business risk

(c)   Which TWO of the following hedging methods will NOT be suitable for hedging the euro receipt?

A   Forward exchange contract

B   Money market hedge

C   Currency futures

D   Forward rate agreement

E   Currency swap

(d)   Which of the following statements support the finance director's belief that the euro will depreciate against the dollar?

1   The dollar inflation rate is greater than the euro inflation rate.

2   The dollar nominal interest rate is less than the euro nominal interest rate.

A   1 only

B   2 only

C   Both 1 and 2

D   Neither 1 nor 2

(e)   As regards the interest rate risk faced by Herd Co, which TWO of the following statements are correct?

A   In exchange for a premium, Herd Co could hedge its interest rate risk by buying interest rate options.

B   Buying a floor will give Herd Co a hedge against interest rate increases.

C   Herd Co can hedge its interest rate risk by selling interest rate futures now in order to buy them back at a future date.

D   Taking out a variable rate overdraft will allow Herd Co to hedge the interest rate risk through matching.

37 Park Co is based in a country whose currency is the dollar ($). The company regularly imports goods denominated in Euro (€) and regularly sells goods denominated in dinars. Two of the future transactions of the company are as follows:

Three months:	Paying €650,000 for imported goods
Six months:	Receiving 12 million dinars for exported capital goods

Park Co has the following exchange rates and interest rates available to it:

	Bid	Offer
Spot exchange rate (dinars per $1):	57.31	57.52
Six-month forward rate (dinars per $1):	58.41	58.64
Spot exchange rate (€ per $1):	1.544	1.552
Three-month forward rate (€ per $1):	1.532	1.540

Six-month interest rates:

	Borrow	Deposit
Dinars	4.0%	2.0%
Dollars	2.0%	0.5%

The finance director of Park Co believes that the upward-sloping yield curve reported in the financial media means that the general level of interest rates will increase in the future, and therefore expects the reported six-month interest rates to increase.

(a) **What is the future dollar value of the dinar receipt using a money market hedge, in $, to the nearest $000?**

$ [   ] ,000

(b) **Indicate, by clicking in the relevant boxes, whether Park Co will find each of the following hedges to be effective or not effective in hedging the foreign currency risk of the two transactions.**

Statement	Effective	Not effective
Leading the euro payment on its imported goods		
Taking out a forward exchange contract on its future dinar receipt		
Buying a tailor-made currency option for its future euro payment		

(c) **Which hedging methods will assist Park Co in reducing its overall foreign currency risk?**

1 Taking out a long-term Euro denominated loan.

2 Taking out a dinar-denominated overdraft.

A 1 only

B 2 only

C Both 1 and 2

D Neither 1 nor 2

(d) **Indicate, by clicking in the relevant boxes, whether the following statements are correct or incorrect.**

Statement	Correct	Incorrect
Purchasing power parity can be used to predict the forward exchange rate		
The international Fisher effect van be used to predict the real interest rate		

(e) **Which of the following statements is consistent with an upward-sloping yield curve?**

A   The risk of borrowers defaulting on their loans increases with the duration of the lending.

B   Liquidity preference theory implies that short-term interest rates contain a premium over long-term interest rates to compensate for lost liquidity.

C   Banks are reluctant to lend short-term, while government debt repayments have significantly increased the amount of long-term funds available.

D   The government has increased short-term interest rates in order to combat rising inflation in the economy.

38   Peony Co's finance director is concerned about the effect of future interest rates on the company and has been looking at the yield curve.

Peony Co, whose domestic currency is the dollar ($), plans to take out a $100m loan in three months' time for a period of nine months. The company is concerned that interest rates might rise before the loan is taken out and its bank has offered a 3 v 12 forward rate agreement at 7.10–6.85.

The loan will be converted into pesos and invested in a nine-month project which is expected to generate income of 580m pesos, with 200m pesos being paid in six months' time (from today) and 380m pesos being paid in 12 months' time (from today). The current spot exchange rate is 5 pesos per $1.

The following information on current short-term interest rates is available:

Dollars   6.5% per year
Pesos   10.0% per year

As a result of the general uncertainty over interest rates, Peony Co is considering a variety of ways in which to manage its interest rate risk, including the use of derivatives.

(a) **In relation to the yield curve, which of the following statements is correct?**

A   Expectations theory suggests that deferred consumption requires increased compensation as maturity increases

B   An inverted yield curve can be caused by government action to increase its long-term borrowing

C   A kink (discontinuity) in the normal yield curve can be due to differing yields in different market segments

D   Basis risk can cause the corporate yield curve to rise more steeply than the government yield curve

(b) **If the interest rate on the loan is 6.5% when it is taken out, what is the nature of the compensatory payment under the forward rate agreement? Pick from each of the two drop down options.**

Payment is made **from Peony Co to the bank / from the bank to Peony Co** of **$262,500 / $450,000**

(c) **Using exchange rates based on interest rate parity, what is the dollar income received from the project, calculated in millions, to one decimal place?**

$ [   ] million

(d) **In respect of Peony Co managing its interest rate risk, which of the following statements is/are correct?**

(1)   Smoothing is an interest rate risk hedging technique which involves maintaining a balance between fixed-rate and floating-rate debt

(2)   Asset and liability management can hedge interest rate risk by matching the maturity of assets and liabilities

A   1 only

B   2 only

C   Both 1 and 2

D   Neither 1 nor 2

(e) **In relation to the use of derivatives by Peony Co, which of the following statements is correct?**

A   Interest rate options must be exercised on their expiry date, if they have not been exercised before then

B   Peony Co can hedge interest rate risk on borrowing by selling interest rate futures now and buying them back in the future

C   An interest rate swap is an agreement to exchange both principal and interest rate payments

D   Peony Co can hedge interest rate risk on borrowing by buying a floor and selling a cap

Section C

CONSTRUCTED RESPONSE (LONG) PRACTICE QUESTIONS

FINANCIAL MANAGEMENT FUNCTION AND ENVIRONMENT – PRACTICE QUESTIONS

1 UUL CO

UUL Co is a public water supply company, which was, privatised a number of years ago. As the deputy Finance Director, you are reviewing the draft financial statements, which contain the following statement by the chairperson:

'This company has delivered above average performance in fulfilment of our objective of maximising shareholder wealth. Earnings, dividends and the share price have all shown good growth. It is our intention to continue to deliver strong performance in the future'.

The following information has been extracted from the draft financial statements:

Year	20X6	20X2
Dividend per share	7.1c	4.2c
Earnings per share	41.3c	31.6c
Price/earnings ratio	22.0	17.0

You have obtained the following information regarding the water industry for the last 5 years:

Dividend growth	11% annually
Earnings growth	12% annually
Share price growth	18% annually

General inflation in the economy has averaged 2% per annum.

The number of shares in issue has remained unchanged over the last 5 years and the price/earnings ratios are calculated using year-end share prices.

Required:

(a) Calculate the equivalent annual growth in:

   (i)   Dividends per share

   (ii)   Earnings per share

   (iii) Share price

   Critically comment on the views expressed by the chairperson. ⊞   **(8 marks)**

(b) Other than shareholders and directors, identify three other key stakeholders in a company such as UUL Co. Identify what financial and other objectives the company should aim to follow in order to satisfy each of these stakeholders. 🖥   **(6 marks)**

(c) Identify what government intervention and other regulation UUL Co may suffer and how this will impact upon the company. 🖥   **(6 marks)**

(Total: 20 marks)

NB FOR REFERENCE

🖥 = word processing

⊞ = spreadsheet

2   CCC

(a) CCC is a local government entity. It is financed almost equally by a combination of central government funding and local taxation. The funding from central government is determined largely on a per capita (per head of population) basis, adjusted to reflect the scale of deprivation (or special needs) deemed to exist in CCC's region. A small percentage of its finance comes from the private sector, for example from renting out City Hall for private functions.

CCC's main objectives are:

*   to make the region economically prosperous and an attractive place to live

*   to provide service excellence in health and education for the local community.

DDD is a large listed entity with widespread commercial and geographical interests. For historic reasons, its headquarters are in CCC's region. This is something of an anomaly, as most entities of DDD's size would have their HQ in a capital city, or at least a city much larger than where it is.

DDD has one financial objective: To increase shareholder wealth by an average 10% per annum. It also has a series of non-financial objectives that deal with how the entity treats other stakeholders, including the local communities where it operates.

DDD has total net assets of $1.5 billion and a gearing ratio of 45% (debt to debt plus equity), which is typical for its industry. It is currently considering raising a substantial amount of capital to finance an acquisition.

Required:

Discuss the criteria that the two very different entities described above have to consider when setting objectives, recognising the needs of each of their main stakeholder groups. Make some reference in your answer to the consequences of each of them failing to meet its declared objectives. 🖥   **(10 marks)**

(b)   MS is a private entity in a computer-related industry. It has been trading for six years and is managed by its main shareholders, the original founders of the entity. Most of the employees are also shareholders, having been given shares as bonuses. None of the shareholders has attempted to sell shares in the entity, so the problem of placing a value on them has not arisen. Dividends have been paid every year at the rate of 60 cents per share, irrespective of profits. So far, profits have always been sufficient to cover the dividend at least once but never more than twice.

MS is all-equity financed at present although $15 million new finance is likely to be required in the near future to finance expansion. Total net assets as at the last statement of financial position date were $45 million.

Required:

Discuss and compare the relationship between dividend policy, investment policy and financing policy in the context of the small entity described above, MS, and DDD, the large listed entity described in part (a).   **(10 marks)**

(Total: 20 marks)

3   NEIGHBOURING COUNTRIES

> *Question debrief*

(a)   Two neighbouring countries have chosen to organise their electricity supply industries in different ways.

In Country A, electricity supplies are provided by a nationalised industry. In Country B, electricity supplies are provided by a number of private sector companies.

Required:

Explain how the objectives of the nationalised industry in Country A might differ from those of the private sector companies in Country B.

Briefly discuss whether investment planning and appraisal techniques are likely to differ in the nationalised industry and private sector companies.   **(10 marks)**

(b)   Whilst the financial plans of a business are based on a single objective, it can face a number of constraints that put pressure on the company to address more than one objective simultaneously.

Required:

What types of constraints might a company face when assessing its long-term plans? Specifically refer in your answer to:

(i)   responding to various stakeholder groups, and   **(5 marks)**

(ii)   the difficulties associated with managing organisations with multiple objectives.   **(5 marks)**

(Total: 20 marks)

> *Calculate your allowed time, allocate the time to the separate parts*

4   RZP CO

As assistant to the Finance Director of RZP Co, a company that has been listed on the London Stock Market for several years, you are reviewing the draft Annual Report of the company, which contains the following statement made by the chairperson:

'This company has consistently delivered above-average performance in fulfilment of our declared objective of creating value for our shareholders. Apart from 20X2, when our overall performance was hampered by a general market downturn, this company has delivered growth in dividends, earnings and ordinary share price. Our shareholders can rest assured that my directors and I will continue to deliver this performance in the future'.

The five-year summary in the draft Annual Report contains the following information:

Year	20X4	20X3	20X2	20X1	20X0
Dividend per share	2.8¢	2.3¢	2.2¢	2.2¢	1.7¢
Earnings per share	19.04¢	14.95¢	11.22¢	15.84¢	13.43¢
Price/earnings ratio	22.0	33.5	25.5	17.2	15.2
General price index	117	113	110	105	100

A recent article in the financial press reported the following information for the last five years for the business sector within which RZP Co operates:

Share price growth	average increase per year of 20%
Earnings growth	average increase per year of 10%
Nominal dividend growth	average increase per year of 10%
Real dividend growth	average increase per year of 9%

You may assume that the number of shares issued by RZP Co has been constant over the five-year period. All price/earnings ratios are based on end-of-year share prices.

Required:

(a)   **Analyse the information provided and comment on the views expressed by the chairperson in terms of:**

(i)   **growth in dividends per share**

(ii)   **share price growth**

(iii)   **growth in earnings per share.**

Your analysis should consider both arithmetic mean and equivalent annual growth rates. ▦   (12 marks)

(b)   **Calculate the total shareholder return (dividend yield plus capital growth) for 20X4 and comment on your findings.** ▦   (3 marks)

(c)   **Discuss FIVE factors that should be considered when deciding on a management remuneration package that will encourage the directors of RZP Co to maximise the wealth of shareholders. (Note: you do not have to give examples of management remuneration packages that might be appropriate for RZP Co.)** ▭   (5 marks)

(Total: 20 marks)

5 JJG CO (JUNE 09 – MODIFIED)

 Question debrief

JJG Co is planning to raise $15 million of new finance for a major expansion of existing business and is considering a rights issue, a placing or an issue of bonds. The corporate objectives of JJG Co, as stated in its Annual Report, are to maximise the wealth of its shareholders and to achieve continuous growth in earnings per share.

Recent financial information on JJG Co is as follows:

	20X8	20X7	20X6	20X5
Revenue ($m)	28.0	24.0	19.1	16.8
Profit before interest and tax ($m)	9.8	8.5	7.5	6.8
Earnings ($m)	5.5	4.7	4.1	3.6
Dividends ($m)	2.2	1.9	1.6	1.6
Ordinary shares ($m)	5.5	5.5	5.5	5.5
Reserves ($m)	13.7	10.4	7.6	5.1
8% Bonds, redeemable 20Y5 ($m)	20.0	20.0	20.0	20.0
Share price ($)	8.64	5.74	3.35	2.67

The nominal value of the shares of JJG Co is $1.00 per share. The general level of inflation has averaged 4% per year in the period under consideration. The bonds of JJG Co are currently trading at their nominal value of $100. The following values for the business sector of JJG Co are available:

Average return on capital employed	25%
Average return on shareholders' funds	20%
Average interest coverage ratio	20 times
Average debt/equity ratio (market value basis)	50%
Return predicted by the capital asset pricing model	14%

Required:

(a) **Evaluate the financial performance of JJG Co, and analyse and discuss the extent to which the company has achieved its stated corporate objectives of:**

(i) **Maximising the wealth of its shareholders**

(ii) **Achieving continuous growth in earnings per share.**

Note: up to 7 marks are available for financial analysis. **(13 marks)**

(b) **Analyse and discuss the relative merits of a rights issue, a placing and an issue of bonds as ways of raising the finance for the expansion.** **(7 marks)**

(Total: 20 marks)

 Calculate your allowed time, allocate the time to the separate parts

6   NEWS FOR YOU

News For You operates a chain of newsagents and confectioner's shops in the south of a Northern European country, and are considering the possibility of expanding their business across a wider geographical area. The business was started in 20X2 and annual revenue grew to $10 million by the end of 20X6. Between 20X6 and 20X9 revenue grew at an average rate of 2% per year.

The business still remains under family control, but the high cost of expansion via the purchase or building of new outlets would mean that the family would need to raise at least $2 million in equity or debt finance. One of the possible risks of expansion lies in the fact that both tobacco and newspaper sales are falling. New income is being generated by expanding the product range stocked by the stores, to include basic foodstuffs such as bread and milk. News For You purchases all of its products from a large wholesale distributor, which is convenient, but the wholesale prices leave News For You with a relatively small gross margin.

The key to profit growth for News For You lies in the ability to generate sales growth, but the company recognises that it faces stiff competition from large food retailers in respect of the prices that it charges for several of its products.

In planning its future, News For You was advised to look carefully at a number of external factors that may affect the business, including government economic policy and, in recent months, the following information has been published in respect of key economic data:

(i)   Bank base rate has been reduced from 5% to 4.5%, and the forecast is for a further 0.5% reduction within six months.

(ii)   The annual rate of inflation is now 1.2%, down from 1.3% in the previous quarter, and 1.7% 12 months ago. The rate is now at its lowest for 25 years, and no further falls in the rate are expected over the medium/long term.

(iii)   Personal and corporation tax rates are expected to remain unchanged for at least 12 months.

(iv)   Taxes on tobacco have been increased by 10% over the last 12 months, although no further increases are anticipated.

(v)   The government has initiated an investigation into the food retail sector focusing on the problems of 'excessive' profits on certain foodstuffs created by the high prices being charged for these goods by the large retail food stores.

Required:

(a)   **Explain the relevance of each of the items of economic data listed above to News For You.** 🖥   **(10 marks)**

(b)   **Explain whether News For You should continue with their expansion plans. Clearly justify your arguments for or against the expansion.** 🖥   **(10 marks)**

(Total: 20 marks)

WORKING CAPITAL MANAGEMENT – EXAM STYLE QUESTIONS

7   GORWA CO (DEC 08 – MODIFIED)

The following financial information related to Gorwa Co:

	20X7	20X6
	$000	$000
Sales (all on credit)	37,400	26,720
Cost of sales	34,408	23,781
Operating profit	2,992	2,939
Finance costs (interest payments)	355	274
Profit before taxation	2,637	2,665

		20X7		20X6
	$000	$000	$000	$000
Non-current assets		13,632		12,750
Current assets				
Inventory	4,600		2,400	
Trade receivables	4,600		2,200	
	9,200		4,600	
Current liabilities				
Trade payables	4,750		2,000	
Overdraft	3,225		1,600	
	7,975		3,600	
Net current assets		1,225		1,000
		14,857		13,750
8% Bonds		2,425		2,425
		12,432		11,325
Capital and reserves				
Share capital		6,000		6,000
Reserves		6,432		5,325
		12,432		11,325

The average variable overdraft interest rate in each year was 5%. The 8% bonds are redeemable in ten years' time.

Required:

(a)   **Discuss, with supporting calculations, the possible effects on Gorwa Co of an increase in interest rates and advise the company of steps it can take to protect itself against interest rate risk.** 🖥   **(9 marks)**

(b)   **Use the above financial information to discuss, with supporting calculations, whether or not Gorwa Co is overtrading.** 🖥   **(11 marks)**

(Total: 20 marks)

8 FLG CO (JUNE 08 – MODIFIED)

 Question debrief

FLG Co has annual credit sales of $4.2 million and cost of sales of $1.89 million. Current assets consist of inventory and accounts receivable. Current liabilities consist of accounts payable and an overdraft with an average interest rate of 7% per year. The company gives two months' credit to its customers and is allowed, on average, one month's credit by trade suppliers. It has an operating cycle of three months.

Other relevant information:

Current ratio of FLG Co	1.4
Cost of long-term finance of FLG Co	11%

Required:

(a) **Discuss the key factors which determine the level of investment in current assets.** 📖

(4 marks)

(b) **Briefly discuss the ways in which factoring can assist in the management of accounts receivable.** 📖 **(3 marks)**

(c) **Calculate the size of the overdraft of FLG Co, the net working capital of the company and the total cost of financing its current assets.** ⊞ **(6 marks)**

(d) FLG Co wishes to minimise its inventory costs. Annual demand for a raw material costing $12 per unit is 60,000 units per year. Inventory management costs for this raw material are as follows:

Ordering cost:	$6 per order
Holding cost:	$0.5 per unit per year

The supplier of this raw material has offered a bulk purchase discount of 1% for orders of 10,000 units or more. If bulk purchase orders are made regularly, it is expected that annual holding cost for this raw material will increase to $2 per unit per year.

Required:

(i) **Calculate the total cost of inventory for the raw material when using the economic order quantity.** ⊞ **(4 marks)**

(ii) **Determine whether accepting the discount offered by the supplier will minimise the total cost of inventory for the raw material.** ⊞ **(3 marks)**

(Total: 20 marks)

 Calculate your allowed time, allocate the time to the separate parts

9 PKA CO (DEC 07 – MODIFIED) *Walk in the footsteps of a top tutor*

PKA Co is a European company that sells goods solely within Europe. The recently-appointed financial manager of PKA Co has been investigating the working capital management of the company and has gathered the following information:

Inventory management

The current policy is to order 100,000 units when the inventory level falls to 35,000 units. Forecast demand to meet production requirements during the next year is 625,000 units. The cost of placing and processing an order is €250, while the cost of holding a unit in stores is €0.50 per unit per year. Both costs are expected to be constant during the next year. Orders are received two weeks after being placed with the supplier. You should assume a 50-week year and that demand is constant throughout the year.

Accounts receivable management

Domestic customers are allowed 30 days' credit, but the financial statements of PKA Co show that the average accounts receivable period in the last financial year was 75 days. The financial manager also noted that bad debts as a percentage of sales, which are all on credit, increased in the last financial year from 5% to 8%.

Accounts payable management

PKA Co has used a foreign supplier for the first time and must pay $250,000 to the supplier in six months' time. The financial manager is concerned that the cost of these supplies may rise in euro terms and has decided to hedge the currency risk of this account payable. The following information has been provided by the company's bank:

Spot rate ($ per €):   1.998 ± 0.002

Six months forward rate ($ per €):   1.979 ± 0.004

Money market rates available to PKA Co:

	Borrowing	Deposit
One year euro interest rates:	6.1%	5.4%
One year dollar interest rates:	4.0%	3.5%

Assume that it is now 1 December and that PKA Co has no surplus cash at the present time.

Required:

(a) Calculate the cost of the current ordering policy and determine the saving that could be made by using the economic order quantity model. ⊞ **(6 marks)**

(b) Discuss ways in which PKA Co could improve the management of domestic accounts receivable. ⌨ **(6 marks)**

(c) Evaluate whether a money market hedge, a forward market hedge or a lead payment should be used to hedge the foreign account payable. ⊞ **(8 marks)**

(Total: 20 marks)

10   KXP CO (DEC 12 – MODIFIED)

KXP Co is an e-business that trades solely over the internet. In the last year, the company had sales of $15 million. All sales were on 30 days' credit to commercial customers.

Extracts from the company's most recent statement of financial position relating to working capital are as follows:

	$000
Trade receivables	2,466
Trade payables	2,220
Overdraft	3,000

In order to encourage customers to pay on time, KXP Co proposes introducing an early settlement discount of 1% for payment within 30 days, while increasing its normal credit period to 45 days. It is expected that, on average, 50% of customers will take the discount and pay within 30 days, 30% of customers will pay after 45 days, and 20% of customers will not change their current paying behaviour.

KXP Co currently orders 15,000 units per month of Product Z, demand for which is constant. There is only one supplier of Product Z and the cost of Product Z purchases over the last year was $540,000. The supplier has offered a 2% discount for orders of Product Z of 30,000 units or more. Each order costs KXP Co $150 to place and the holding cost is 24 cents per unit per year.

KXP Co has an overdraft facility charging interest of 6% per year.

Required:

(a)   Calculate the net benefit or cost of the proposed changes in trade receivables policy and comment on your findings. ▦   **(6 marks)**

(b)   Calculate whether the bulk purchase discount offered by the supplier is financially acceptable and comment on the assumptions made by your calculation. ▦
(6 marks)

(c)   Critically discuss the similarities and differences between working capital policies in the following areas:

(i)   Working capital investment

(ii)   Working capital financing. 💻   **(8 marks)**

(Total: 20 marks)

11   ULNAD

Ulnad Co has annual sales revenue of $6 million and all sales are on 30 days' credit, although customers on average take ten days more than this to pay. Contribution represents 60% of sales and the company currently has no bad debts. Accounts receivable are financed by an overdraft at an annual interest rate of 7%.

Ulnad Co plans to offer an early settlement discount of 1.5% for payment within 15 days and to extend the maximum credit offered to 60 days. The company expects that these changes will increase annual credit sales by 5%, while also leading to additional incremental costs equal to 0.5% of sales revenue. The discount is expected to be taken by 30% of customers, with the remaining customers taking an average of 60 days to pay.

Required:

(a) Evaluate whether the proposed changes in credit policy will increase the profitability of Ulnad Co. ⊞ **(6 marks)**

(b) Renpec Co, a subsidiary of Ulnad Co, has set a minimum cash account balance of $7,500. The average cost to the company of making deposits or selling investments is $18 per transaction and the standard deviation of its cash flows was $1,000 per day during the last year. The average interest rate on investments is 5.11%.

Determine the spread, the upper limit and the return point for the cash account of Renpec Co using the Miller-Orr model and explain the relevance of these values for the cash management of the company. ⊞ **(6 marks)**

(c) Discuss the key factors to be considered when formulating a working capital funding policy. 💻 **(8 marks)**

(Total: 20 marks)

12 APX CO (DEC 09 – MODIFIED)

APX Co achieved revenue of $16 million in the year that has just ended and expects revenue growth of 8.4% in the next year. Cost of sales in the year that has just ended was $10.88 million and other expenses were $1.44 million.

The financial statements of APX Co for the year that has just ended contain the following statement of financial position:

	$m	$m
Non-current assets		22.0
Current assets		
Inventory	2.4	
Trade receivables	2.2	
	────	
		4.6
		────
Total assets		26.6
		────
Equity finance:		
	$m	$m
Ordinary shares	5.0	
Reserves	7.5	
	────	
		12.5
Long-term bank loan		10.0
		────
		22.5
Current liabilities		
Trade payables	1.9	
Overdraft	2.2	
	────	
		4.1
		────
Total liabilities		26.6
		────

The long-term bank loan has a fixed annual interest rate of 8% per year. APX Co pays taxation at an annual rate of 30% per year.

The following accounting ratios have been forecast for the next year:

Gross profit margin:	30%
Operating profit margin:	20%
Dividend payout ratio:	50%
Inventory turnover period:	110 days
Trade receivables period:	65 days
Trade payables period:	75 days

Overdraft interest in the next year is forecast to be $140,000. No change is expected in the level of non-current assets and depreciation should be ignored.

Required:

(a) Prepare the following forecast financial statements for APX Co using the information provided:

(i) a statement of profit or loss for the next year; and

(ii) a statement of financial position at the end of the next year. ⊞ (9 marks)

(b) Analyse and discuss the working capital financing policy of APX Co. ▭ (6 marks)

(c) Analyse and discuss the forecast financial performance of APX Co in terms of working capital management. ▭ (5 marks)

(Total: 20 marks)

13 HGR CO (JUNE 09 – MODIFIED)

🕐 *Question debrief*

The following financial information relates to HGR Co:

Statement of financial position at the current date (extracts)

	$000	$000	$000
Non-current assets			48,965
Current assets			
Inventory		8,160	
Accounts receivable		8,775	
		16,935	
Current liabilities			
Overdraft	3,800		
Accounts payable	10,200		
		14,000	
Net current assets			2,935
Total assets less current liabilities			51,900

Cash flow forecasts from the current date are as follows:

	Month 1	Month 2	Month 3
Cash operating receipts ($000)	4,220	4,350	3,808
Cash operating payments ($000)	3,950	4,100	3,750
Six-monthly interest on traded bonds ($000)		200	
Capital investment ($000)			2,000

The finance director has completed a review of accounts receivable management and has proposed staff training and operating procedure improvements, which she believes will reduce accounts receivable days to the average sector value of 53 days. This reduction would take six months to achieve from the current date, with an equal reduction in each month. She has also proposed changes to inventory management methods, which she hopes will reduce inventory days by two days per month each month over a three-month period from the current date. She does not expect any change in the current level of accounts payable.

HGR Co has an overdraft limit of $4,000,000. Overdraft interest is payable at an annual rate of 6.17% per year, with payments being made each month based on the opening balance at the start of that month. Credit sales for the year to the current date were $49,275,000 and cost of sales was $37,230,000. These levels of credit sales and cost of sales are expected to be maintained in the coming year. Assume that there are 365 working days in each year.

Required:

(a)   Discuss the working capital financing strategy of HGR Co.   **(6 marks)**

(b)   For HGR Co, calculate:

(i)   the bank balance in three months' time if no action is taken; and

(ii)   the bank balance in three months' time if the finance director's proposals are implemented.

Comment on the forecast cash flow position of HGR Co and recommend a suitable course of action. ⊞   **(9 marks)**

(c)   Discuss how risks arising from granting credit to foreign customers can be managed and reduced.   **(5 marks)**

               (Total: 20 marks)

🕐 *Calculate your allowed time, allocate the time to the separate parts*

---

14   ANJO

Extracts from the recent financial statements of Anjo Inc. are as follows:

Statement of profit or loss

	20X6	20X5
	$000	$000
Sales revenue	15,600	11,100
Cost of sales	9,300	6,600
Gross profit	6,300	4,500
Administration expenses	1,000	750
Profit before interest and tax	5,300	3,750
Interest	100	15
Profit before tax	5,200	3,735

Statements of financial position

		20X6		20X5
	$000	$000	$000	$000
Non-current assets		3,050		3,650
Current assets				
Inventory	3,000		1,300	
Receivables	3,800		1,850	
Cash	120		900	
		6,920		4,050
Total assets		10,770		7,700

		20X6		20X5
	$000	$000	$000	$000
Total equity		6,100		5,950
Current liabilities				
Trade payables	2,870		1,600	
Overdraft	1,000		150	
		3,870		1,750
Total equity and liabilities		9,970		7,700

All sales were on credit. Anjo Inc. has no long-term debt. Credit purchases in each year were 95% of cost of sales. Anjo Inc. pays interest on its overdraft at an annual rate of 8%. Current sector averages are as follows:

Inventory days: 90 days

Receivables days: 60 days

Payables days: 80 days

Required:

(a)   Calculate the following ratios for each year and comment on your findings.

   (i)   **Inventory days**

   (ii)   **Receivables days**

   (iii)   **Payables days.** ⊞   **(8 marks)**

(b)   **Calculate the length of the cash operating cycle (working capital cycle) for each year and explain its significance.** ⊞   **(4 marks)**

(c)   **A factor has offered to take over sales ledger administration and debt collection for an annual fee of 0.5% of credit sales. A condition of the offer is that the factor will advance Anjo Inc. 80% of the face value of its receivables at an interest rate 1% above the current overdraft rate. The factor claims that it would reduce outstanding receivables by 30% and reduce administration expenses by 2% per year if its offer were accepted.**

   Evaluate whether the factor's offer is financially acceptable, basing your answer on the financial information relating to 20X6. ⊞   **(8 marks)**

                                                                                                         (Total: 20 marks)

15   ZSE CO (JUNE 10 – MODIFIED)

ZSE Co is concerned about exceeding its overdraft limit of $2 million in the next two periods. It has been experiencing considerable volatility in cash flows in recent periods because of trading difficulties experienced by its customers, who have often settled their accounts after the agreed credit period of 60 days. ZSE has also experienced an increase in bad debts due to a small number of customers going into liquidation.

The company has prepared the following forecasts of net cash flows for the next two periods, together with their associated probabilities, in an attempt to anticipate liquidity and financing problems. These probabilities have been produced by a computer model that simulates a number of possible future economic scenarios. The computer model has been built with the aid of a firm of financial consultants.

Period 1 cash flow	Probability	Period 2 cash flow	Probability
$000		$000	
8,000	10%	7,000	30%
4,000	60%	3,000	50%
(2,000)	30%	(9,000)	20%

ZSE Co expects to be overdrawn at the start of period 1 by $500,000.

Required:

(a) Calculate the following values:

    (i)   the expected value of the period 1 closing balance

    (ii)   the expected value of the period 2 closing balance

    (iii)   the probability of a negative cash balance at the end of period 2

    (iv)   the probability of exceeding the overdraft limit at the end of period 2.

    Discuss whether the above analysis can assist the company in managing its cash flows. ⊞   **(12 marks)**

(b) Identify and discuss the factors to be considered in formulating a trade receivables management policy for ZSE Co. 💻   **(5 marks)**

(c) Discuss whether profitability or liquidity is the primary objective of working capital management. 💻   **(3 marks)**

                                                 (Total: 20 marks)

16 PNP PLC (JUNE 07 – MODIFIED)

The following financial information relates to PNP plc, a UK-based firm, for the year just ended.

	£000
Sales revenue	5,242.0
Variable cost of sales	3,145.0
Inventory	603.0
Receivables	744.5
Payables	574.5

Segmental analysis of receivables

	Balance	Average payment period	Discount	Irrecoverable
Class 1	£200,000	30 days	1.0%	None
Class 2	£252,000	60 days	Nil	£12,600
Class 3	£110,000	75 days	Nil	£11,000
Overseas	£182,500	90 days	Nil	£21,900
	£744,500			£45,500

The receivables balances given are before taking account of irrecoverable debts. All sales are on credit. Production and sales take place evenly throughout the year. Current sales for each class of receivables are in proportion to their relative year-end balances before irrecoverable debts.

It has been proposed that the discount for early payment be increased from 1.0% to 1.5% for settlement within 30 days.

It is expected that this will lead to 50% of existing Class 2 receivables becoming Class 1 receivables, as well as attracting new business worth £500,000 in revenue. The new business would be divided equally between Class 1 and Class 2 receivables. Fixed costs would not increase as a result of introducing the discount or by attracting new business. PNP finances receivables from an overdraft at an annual interest rate of 8%.

Required:

(a) Calculate the net benefit or cost of increasing the discount for early payment and comment on the acceptability of the proposal. ▦ **(9 marks)**

(b) Calculate the current cash operating cycle and the revised cash operating cycle caused by increasing the discount for early payment. ▦ **(4 marks)**

(c) Identify and explain the key elements of a receivables management system suitable for PNP plc. 🖳 **(7 marks)**

(Total: 20 marks)

17 PLOT CO (DEC 13 – MODIFIED)

Plot Co sells both Product P and Product Q, with sales of both products occurring evenly throughout the year.

Product P

The annual demand for Product P is 300,000 units and an order for new inventory is placed each month. Each order costs $267 to place. The cost of holding Product P in inventory is 10 cents per unit per year. Buffer inventory equal to 40% of one month's sales is maintained.

Product Q

The annual demand for Product Q is 456,000 units per year and Plot Co buys in this product at $1 per unit on 60 days credit. The supplier has offered an early settlement discount of 1% for settlement of invoices within 30 days.

Other information

Plot Co finances working capital with short-term finance costing 5% per year. Assume that there are 365 days in each year.

Required:

(a) Calculate the following values for Product P:

(i) The total cost of the current ordering policy ▦ **(3 marks)**

(ii) The total cost of an ordering policy using the economic order quantity. ▦ **(3 marks)**

(iii) The net cost or saving of introducing an ordering policy using the economic order quantity. ▦ **(1 mark)**

(b) Calculate the net value in dollars to Plot Co of accepting the early settlement discount for Product Q. ▦ **(5 marks)**

(c) Identify the objectives of working capital management and discuss the central role of working capital management in financial management. 🖳 **(8 marks)**

(Total: 20 marks)

18   WQZ CO (DEC 10 – MODIFIED)

WQZ Co is considering making the following changes in the area of working capital management:

Inventory management

It has been suggested that the order size for Product KN5 should be determined using the economic order quantity model (EOQ).

WQZ Co forecasts that demand for Product KN5 will be 160,000 units in the coming year and it has traditionally ordered 10% of annual demand per order. The ordering cost is expected to be $400 per order while the holding cost is expected to be $5.12 per unit per year. A buffer inventory of 5,000 units of Product KN5 will be maintained, whether orders are made by the traditional method or using the economic ordering quantity model.

Receivables management

WQZ Co could introduce an early settlement discount of 1% for customers who pay within 30 days and at the same time, through improved operational procedures, maintain a maximum average payment period of 60 days for credit customers who do not take the discount. It is expected that 25% of credit customers will take the discount if it were offered.

It is expected that administration and operating cost savings of $753,000 per year will be made after improving operational procedures and introducing the early settlement discount.

Credit sales of WQZ Co are currently $87.6 million per year and trade receivables are currently $18 million. Credit sales are not expected to change as a result of the changes in receivables management. The company has a cost of short-term finance of 5.5% per year.

Required:

(a)   Calculate the cost of the current ordering policy and the change in the costs of inventory management that will arise if the economic order quantity is used to determine the optimum order size for Product KN5. ▦   (6 marks)

(b)   Briefly describe the benefits of a just-in-time (JIT) procurement policy. 💻

(3 marks)

(c)   Calculate and comment on whether the proposed changes in receivables management will be acceptable. Assuming that only 25% of customers take the early settlement discount, what is the maximum early settlement discount that could be offered? ▦   (6 marks)

(d)   Discuss the factors that should be considered in formulating working capital policy on the management of trade receivables. 💻   (5 marks)

(Total: 20 marks)

19   FLIT CO (DEC 14 – MODIFIED)

 *Question debrief*

Flit Co is preparing a cash flow forecast for the three-month period from January to the end of March for one of its divisions. The following sales volumes have been forecast:

	December	January	February	March	April
Sales (units)	1,200	1,250	1,300	1,400	1,500

Notes:

(1)   The selling price per unit is $800 and a selling price increase of 5% will occur in February. Sales are all on one month's credit.

(2)   Production of goods for sale takes place one month before sales.

(3)   Each unit produced requires two units of raw materials, costing $200 per unit. No raw materials inventory is held. Raw material purchases are on one months' credit.

(4)   Variable overheads and wages equal to $100 per unit are incurred during production, and paid in the month of production.

(5)   The opening cash balance at 1 January is expected to be $40,000.

(6)   A long-term loan of $300,000 will be received at the beginning of March.

(7)   A machine costing $400,000 will be purchased for cash in March.

Required:

(a)   **Calculate the cash balance at the end of each month in the three-month period.** ▦
                                                                                        (5 marks)

(b)   **Calculate the forecast current ratio at the end of the three-month period.** ▦
                                                                                        (2 marks)

(c)   **Assuming that Flit Co expects to have a short-term cash surplus during the three-month period, discuss whether this should be invested in shares listed on a large stock market.** 🖥   **(3 marks)**

Flit Co currently has total income of $30 million per year, of which 80% is from credit sales, and a net profit margin of 10%. Due to fierce competition, Flit Co has lost market share and is looking for ways to win back former customers and to keep the loyalty of existing customers. The sales director has pointed out that a major competitor of Flit Co currently offers an early settlement discount of 0.5% for settlement within 30 days, while Flit Co itself does not offer an early settlement discount. He suggests that if Flit Co could match this early settlement discount, annual income from credit sales would increase by 20%.

Credit customers of Flit Co take an average of 51 days to settle invoices. Approximately 0.5% of the company's credit sales have historically become bad debts each year and written off as irrecoverable. The finance director has been advised that offering an early settlement discount of 0.5% for payment within 30 days would increase administration costs by $35,000 per year, while 75% of credit customers would be likely to take the discount. The credit controller believes that bad debts would fall to 0.375% of credit sales if the early settlement discount were introduced.

Flit Co has an average short-term cost of finance of 4% per year. Assume that there are 360 days in each year.

(d) **Evaluate whether Flit Co should offer the early settlement discount.** ⊞ **(6 marks)**

(e) **Discuss TWO ways in which a company could reduce the risk associated with foreign accounts receivable.** 💻 **(4 marks)**

(Total: 20 marks)

 Calculate your allowed time, allocate the time to the separate parts

20 NESUD CO (SEP 16)

Nesud Co has credit sales of $45 million per year and on average settles accounts with trade payables after 60 days. One of its suppliers has offered the company an early settlement discount of 0.5% for payment within 30 days. Administration costs will be increased by $500 per year if the early settlement discount is taken. Nesud Co buys components worth $1.5 million per year from this supplier.

From a different supplier, Nesud Co purchases $2.4 million per year of Component K at a price of $5 per component. Consumption of Component K can be assumed to be at a constant rate throughout the year. The company orders components at the start of each month in order to meet demand and the cost of placing each order is $248.44. The holding cost for Component K is $1.06 per unit per year.

The finance director of Nesud Co is concerned that approximately 1% of credit sales turn into irrecoverable debts. In addition, she has been advised that customers of the company take an average of 65 days to settle their accounts, even though Nesud Co requires settlement within 40 days.

Nesud Co finances working capital from an overdraft costing 4% per year. Assume there are 360 days in a year.

Required:

(a) **Evaluate whether Nesud Co should accept the early settlement discount offered by its supplier.** ⊞ **(4 marks)**

(b) **Evaluate whether Nesud Co should adopt an economic order quantity approach to ordering Component K.** ⊞ **(6 marks)**

(c) **Critically discuss how Nesud Co could improve the management of its trade receivables.** 💻 **(10 marks)**

(Total: 20 marks)

21   OSCAR CO (SEP/DEC 2018)

Oscar Co designs and produces tracking devices. The company is managed by its four founders, who lack business administration skills.

The company has revenue of $28m, and all sales are on 30 days' credit. Its major customers are large multinational car manufacturing companies that are often late in paying their invoices. Oscar Co is a rapidly growing company and revenue has doubled in the last four years. Oscar Co has focused in this time on product development and customer service, and managing trade receivables has been neglected.

Oscar Co's average trade receivables are currently $5.37m, and bad debts are 2% of credit sales revenue. Partly as a result of poor credit control, the company has suffered a shortage of cash and has recently reached its overdraft limit. The four founders have spent large amounts of time chasing customers for payment. In an attempt to improve trade receivables management, Oscar Co has approached a factoring company.

The factoring company has offered two possible options:

Option 1

Administration by the factor of Oscar Co's invoicing, sales accounting and receivables collection, on a full recourse basis. The factor would charge a service fee of 0.5% of credit sales revenue per year. Oscar Co estimates that this would result in savings of $30,000 per year in administration costs. Under this arrangement, the average trade receivables collection period would be 30 days.

Option 2

Administration by the factor of Oscar Co's invoicing, sales accounting and receivables collection on a non-recourse basis. The factor would charge a service fee of 1.5% of credit sales revenue per year. Administration cost savings and average trade receivables collection period would be as Option 1. Oscar Co would be required to accept an advance of 80% of credit sales when invoices are raised at an interest rate of 9% per year.

Oscar Co pays interest on its overdraft at a rate of 7% per year and the company operates for 365 days per year.

Required:

(a)   Calculate the costs and benefits of each of Option 1 and Option 2 and comment on your findings. ⊞   (8 marks)

(b)   Discuss reasons (other than costs and benefits already calculated) why Oscar Co may benefit from the services offered by the factoring company. ⌨   (6 marks)

(c)   Discuss THREE factors which determine the level of a company's investment in working capital. ⌨   (6 marks)

(Total: 20 marks)

INVESTMENT APPRAISAL – EXAM STYLE QUESTIONS

22 ARMCLIFF CO

 *Question debrief*

Armcliff Co is a division of Shevin Inc., which requires each of its divisions to achieve a rate of return on capital employed of at least 10% pa. For this purpose, capital employed is defined as fixed capital and investment in inventories. This rate of return is also applied as a hurdle rate for new investment projects. Divisions have limited borrowing powers and all capital projects are centrally funded.

The following is an extract from Armcliff's divisional accounts:

Statement of profit or loss for the year ended 31 December 20X4

	$m
Sales revenue	120
Cost of sales	(100)
Operating profit	20

Assets employed as at 31 December 20X4

	$m	$m
Non-current assets (NBV)		75
Current assets (including inventories $25m)	45	
Current liabilities	(32)	
		13
Net capital employed		88

Armcliff's production engineers wish to invest in a new computer-controlled press. The equipment cost is $14m. The residual value is expected to be $2m after four years operation, when the equipment will be shipped to a customer in South America.

The new machine is capable of improving the quality of the existing product and also of producing a higher volume. The firm's marketing team is confident of selling the increased volume by extending the credit period.

The expected additional sales are:

Year 1	2,000,000 units
Year 2	1,800,000 units
Year 3	1,600,000 units
Year 4	1,600,000 units

Sales volume is expected to fall over time due to emerging competitive pressures. Competition will also necessitate a reduction in price by $0.50 each year from the $5 per unit proposed in the first year. Operating costs are expected to be steady at $1 per unit, and allocation of overheads (none of which are affected by the new project) by the central finance department is set at $0.75 per unit.

Higher production levels will require additional investment in inventories of $0.5m, which would be held at this level until the final stages of operation of the project. Customers at present settle accounts after 90 days on average.

Required:

(a)   Determine whether the proposed capital investment is attractive to Armcliff, using the average rate of return on capital method, as defined as average profit-to-average capital employed, ignoring receivables and payables.

Note: Ignore taxes.   **(10 marks)**

(b)   (i)   Suggest three problems which arise with the use of the average return method for appraising new investment.   **(3 marks)**

      (ii) In view of the problems associated with the ARR method, why do companies continue to use it in project appraisal? 🖥️   **(3 marks)**

(c)   Briefly discuss the dangers of offering more generous credit. 🖥️   **(4 marks)**

                                                                                  (Total: 20 marks)

> 🕐 *Calculate your allowed time, allocate the time to the separate parts*

23   WARDEN CO (DEC 11 – MODIFIED)

> 🕐 *Question debrief*

Warden Co plans to buy a new machine. The cost of the machine, payable immediately, is $800,000 and the machine has an expected life of five years. Additional investment in working capital of $90,000 will be required at the start of the first year of operation. At the end of five years, the machine will be sold for scrap, with the scrap value expected to be 5% of the initial purchase cost of the machine. The machine will not be replaced.

Production and sales from the new machine are expected to be 100,000 units per year. Each unit can be sold for $16 per unit and will incur variable costs of $11 per unit. Incremental fixed costs arising from the operation of the machine will be $160,000 per year.

Warden Co has an after-tax cost of capital of 11%, which it uses as a discount rate in investment appraisal. The company pays profit tax one year in arrears at an annual rate of 30% per year. Tax allowable depreciation and inflation should be ignored.

Required:

(a) Calculate the net present value of investing in the new machine and advise whether the investment is financially acceptable. ⊞ **(7 marks)**

(b) Calculate the internal rate of return of investing in the new machine and advise whether the investment is financially acceptable. ⊞ **(4 marks)**

(c) (i) Explain briefly the meaning of the term 'sensitivity analysis' in the context of investment appraisal. ▭ **(2 marks)**

(ii) Calculate the sensitivity of the investment in the new machine to a change in selling price and to a change in discount rate, and comment on your findings. ⊞ **(7 marks)**

(Total: 20 marks)

 Calculate your allowed time, allocate the time to the separate parts

---

24 INVESTMENT APPRAISAL

(a) Explain and illustrate (using simple numerical examples) the Accounting Rate of Return and Payback approaches to investment appraisal, paying particular attention to the limitations of each approach. ▭ **(7 marks)**

(b) (i) Explain the differences between NPV and IRR as methods of Discounted Cash Flow analysis. ▭ **(5 marks)**

(ii) A company with a cost of capital of 14% is trying to determine the optimal replacement cycle for the laptop computers used by its sales team. The following information is relevant to the decision:

The cost of each laptop is $2,400. Maintenance costs are payable at the end of *each full year* of ownership, but not in the year of replacement, e.g. if the laptop is owned for two years, then the maintenance cost is payable at the end of year 1.

Interval between replacement (years)	Trade-in value ($)	Maintenance cost
1	1,200	Zero
2	800	$75 (payable at end of Year 1)
3	300	$150 (payable at end of Year 2)

Required:

Ignoring taxation, calculate the equivalent annual cost of the three different replacement cycles, and recommend which should be adopted. What other factors should the company take into account when determining the optimal cycle? ⊞ **(8 marks)**

(Total: 20 marks)

25 CHARM INC

Charm Inc., a software company, has developed a new game, 'Fingo', which it plans to launch in the near future. Sales of the new game are expected to be very strong, following a favourable review by a popular PC magazine. Charm Inc. has been informed that the review will give the game a 'Best Buy' recommendation. Sales volumes, production volumes and selling prices for 'Fingo' over its four-year life are expected to be as follows:

Year	1	2	3	4
Sales and production (units)	150,000	70,000	60,000	60,000
Selling price ($ per game)	$25	$24	$23	$22

Financial information on 'Fingo' for the first year of production is as follows:

Direct material cost	$5.40 per game
Other variable production cost	$6.00 per game
Fixed costs	$4.00 per game

Advertising costs to stimulate demand are expected to be $650,000 in the first year of production and $100,000 in the second year of production. No advertising costs are expected in the third and fourth years of production. Fixed costs represent incremental cash fixed production overheads. 'Fingo' will be produced on a new production machine costing $800,000. Tax allowable depreciation will be claimed on a reducing balance basis at a rate of 25%. The machine will have a useful life of four years at the end of which no scrap value is expected.

Charm Inc. pays tax on profit at a rate of 30% per year and tax liabilities are settled in the year in which they arise. Charm Inc. uses an after-tax discount rate of 10% when appraising new capital investments. Ignore inflation.

Required:

(a) Calculate the net present value of the proposed investment and comment on your findings. ⊞ **(11 marks)**

(b) Discuss the reasons why the net present value investment appraisal method is preferred to other investment appraisal methods such as payback, return on capital employed and internal rate of return. ▭ **(9 marks)**

(Total: 20 marks)

26 PLAY CO

Play Co manufactures safety surfacing for children's playgrounds. The main raw material required is rubber particles and these are currently purchased from an outside supplier for $3.50 per tonne. This price is contractually guaranteed for the next four years. If the contract is terminated within the next two years, Play Co will be charged an immediate termination penalty of $150,000, which will not be allowed as a tax-deductible expense.

The directors are considering investing in equipment that would allow Play Co to manufacture these particles in house by using recycled tyres.

The machine required to process the tyres will cost $400,000, and it is estimated that at the end of year four the machine will have a second-hand value of $50,000.

The costs associated with the new venture are as follows:

Variable costs (per tonne produced)	$0.80
Fixed costs (per annum)	$192,500

The additional fixed costs include maintenance costs of $40,000 and the additional depreciation charge (calculated on a straight-line basis over the life of the asset) relating to the machine.

All of the above are quoted in current price terms. Inflationary increases are expected as follows:

Variable costs:	3% per annum
Maintenance costs:	5% per annum
Other fixed costs:	2% per annum

The annual demand for the particles (based on the sales forecasts of the company) is:

	Year 1	Year 2	Year 3	Year 4
Demand (in tonnes)	100,000	110,000	130,000	160,000

Profit tax of 30% per year will be payable one year in arrears. Tax allowable depreciation on a 25% reducing balance basis could be claimed on the cost of the equipment, with a balancing allowance being claimed in the fourth year of operation when the machine is disposed of.

Required:

(a) **Using 15% as the after-tax discount rate, advise Play Co on the desirability of purchasing the equipment. (Your workings should be shown to the nearest $000)** ▦ **(12 marks)**

(b) **Identify and briefly discuss FOUR limitations of Net Present Value techniques when applied to investment appraisal.** 💻 **(4 marks)**

(c) **Comment on how the project would affect the different stakeholders of Play Co.** 💻 **(4 marks)**

(Total: 20 marks)

---

27 DUO CO (DEC 07 – MODIFIED) *Walk in the footsteps of a top tutor*

Duo Co needs to increase production capacity to meet increasing demand for an existing product, 'Quago', which is used in food processing. A new machine, with a useful life of four years and a maximum output of 600,000 kg of Quago per year, could be bought for $800,000, payable immediately. The scrap value of the machine after four years would be $30,000. Forecast demand and production of Quago over the next four years is as follows:

Year	1	2	3	4
Demand (kg)	1.4 million	1.5 million	1.6 million	1.7 million

Existing production capacity for Quago is limited to one million kilograms per year and the new machine would only be used for demand additional to this.

The current selling price of Quago is $8.00 per kilogram and the variable cost of materials is $5.00 per kilogram. Other variable costs of production are $1.90 per kilogram. Fixed costs of production associated with the new machine would be $240,000 in the first year of production, increasing by $20,000 per year in each subsequent year of operation.

Duo Co pays tax one year in arrears at an annual rate of 30% and can claim tax allowable depreciation (tax-allowable depreciation) on a 25% reducing balance basis. A balancing allowance is claimed in the final year of operation.

Duo Co uses its after-tax weighted average cost of capital when appraising investment projects. It has a cost of equity of 11% and a before-tax cost of debt of 8.6%. The long-term finance of the company, on a market-value basis, consists of 80% equity and 20% debt.

Required:

(a) Calculate the net present value of buying the new machine and advise on the acceptability of the proposed purchase (work to the nearest $1,000). ⌗

(13 marks)

(b) Explain the difference between risk and uncertainty in the context of investment appraisal, and describe how sensitivity analysis and probability analysis can be used to incorporate risk into the investment appraisal process. ⌨ (7 marks)

(Total: 20 marks)

28 OKM CO (JUNE 10 – MODIFIED)

The following draft appraisal of a proposed investment project has been prepared for the finance director of OKM Co by a trainee accountant. The project is consistent with the current business operations of OKM Co.

Year	1	2	3	4	5
Sales (units/yr)	250,000	400,000	500,000	250,000	
	$000	$000	$000	$000	$000
Contribution	1,330	2,128	2,660	1,330	
Fixed costs	(530)	(562)	(596)	(631)	
Depreciation	(438)	(438)	(437)	(437)	
Interest payments	(200)	(200)	(200)	(200)	
Taxable profit	162	928	1,427	62	
Taxation		(49)	(278)	(428)	(19)
Profit after tax	162	879	1,149	(366)	(19)
Scrap value				250	
After-tax cash flows	162	879	1,149	(116)	(19)
Discount at 10%	0.909	0.826	0.751	0.683	0.621
Present values	147	726	863	(79)	(12)

Net present value = 1,645,000 – 2,000,000 = ($355,000) so reject the project. The following information was included with the draft investment appraisal:

(1) The initial investment is $2 million.

(2) Selling price: $12/unit (current price terms), selling price inflation is 5% per year.

(3) Variable cost: $7/unit (current price terms), variable cost inflation is 4% per year.

(4) Fixed overhead costs: $500,000/year (current price terms), fixed cost inflation is 6% per year.

(5) $200,000/year of the fixed costs are development costs that have already been incurred and are being recovered by an annual charge to the project.

(6)   Investment financing is by a $2 million loan at a fixed interest rate of 10% per year.

(7)   OKM Co can claim 25% reducing balance tax allowable depreciation on this investment and pays taxation one year in arrears at a rate of 30% per year.

(8)   The scrap value of machinery at the end of the four-year project is $250,000.

(9)   The real weighted average cost of capital of OKM Co is 7% per year.

(10)   The general rate of inflation is expected to be 4.7% per year.

Required:

(a)   **Identify and comment on any errors in the investment appraisal prepared by the trainee accountant. 💻**   **(5 marks)**

(b)   **Prepare a revised calculation of the net present value of the proposed investment project and comment on the project's acceptability. ▦**   **(10 marks)**

(c)   **Discuss the problems faced when undertaking investment appraisal in the following areas and comment on how these problems can be overcome:**

    (i)   **an investment project has several internal rates of return**

    (ii)   **the business risk of an investment project is significantly different from the business risk of current operations. 💻**   **(5 marks)**

(Total: 20 marks)

29   BRT CO (JUNE 11 – MODIFIED)

BRT Co has developed a new confectionery line that can be sold for $5·00 per box and that is expected to have continuing popularity for many years. The Finance Director has proposed that investment in the new product should be evaluated over a four-year time-horizon, even though sales would continue after the fourth year, on the grounds that cash flows after four years are too uncertain to be included in the evaluation. The variable and fixed costs (both in current price terms) will depend on sales volume, as follows.

Sales volume (boxes)	less than 1 million	1–1.9 million	2–2.9 million	3–3.9 million
Variable cost ($ per box)	2.80	3.00	3.00	3.05
Total fixed costs ($)	1 million	1.8 million	2.8 million	3.8 million

Forecast sales volumes are as follows.

Year	1	2	3	4
Demand (boxes)	0.7 million	1.6 million	2.1 million	3.0 million

The production equipment for the new confectionery line would cost $2 million and an additional initial investment of $750,000 would be needed for working capital. Tax allowable depreciation (tax-allowable depreciation) on a 25% reducing balance basis could be claimed on the cost of equipment. Profit tax of 30% per year will be payable one year in arrears. A balancing allowance would be claimed in the fourth year of operation.

The average general level of inflation is expected to be 3% per year and selling price, variable costs, fixed costs and working capital would all experience inflation of this level. BRT Co uses a nominal after-tax cost of capital of 12% to appraise new investment projects.

Required:

(a) Assuming that production only lasts for four years, calculate the net present value of investing in the new product using a nominal terms approach and advise on its financial acceptability (work to the nearest $1,000). ⊞   **(13 marks)**

(b) Discuss THREE ways of incorporating risk into the investment appraisal process. 💻

(7 marks)

(Total: 20 marks)

30   BASRIL

Basril Inc. is reviewing investment proposals that have been submitted by divisional managers. The investment funds of the company are limited to $800,000 in the current year. Details of three possible investments, none of which can be delayed, are given below.

Project 1

An investment of $300,000 in work station assessments. Each assessment would be on an individual employee basis and would lead to savings in labour costs from increased efficiency and from reduced absenteeism due to work-related illness. Savings in labour costs from these assessments in money terms are expected to be as follows:

Year	1	2	3	4	5
Cash flows (£000)	85	90	95	100	95

Project 2

An investment of $450,000 in individual workstations for staff that is expected to reduce administration costs by $140,800 per annum in money terms for the next five years.

Project 3

An investment of $400,000 in new ticket machines. Net cash savings of $120,000 per annum are expected in current price terms and these are expected to increase by 3.6% per annum due to inflation during the five-year life of the machines.

Basril Inc. has a money cost of capital of 12% and taxation should be ignored.

Required:

(a) Determine the best way for Basril Inc. to invest the available funds and calculate the resultant NPV:

(i)   on the assumption that each of the three projects is divisible

(ii)   on the assumption that none of the projects are divisible. ⊞   **(10 marks)**

(b) Explain how the NPV investment appraisal method is applied in situations where capital is rationed. 💻   **(4 marks)**

(c) Discuss the reasons why capital rationing may arise. 💻   **(6 marks)**

(Total: 20 marks)

31 ASOP CO (DEC 09 – MODIFIED)

ASOP Co is considering an investment in new technology that will reduce operating costs through increasing energy efficiency and decreasing pollution. The new technology will cost $1 million and have a four-year life, at the end of which it will have a scrap value of $100,000.

A licence fee of $104,000 is payable at the end of the first year. This licence fee will increase by 4% per year in each subsequent year.

The new technology is expected to reduce operating costs by $5.80 per unit in current price terms. This reduction in operating costs is before taking account of expected inflation of 5% per year.

Forecast production volumes over the life of the new technology are expected to be as follows:

Year	1	2	3	4
Production (units per year)	60,000	75,000	95,000	80,000

If ASOP Co bought the new technology, it would finance the purchase through a four-year loan paying interest at an annual before-tax rate of 8.6% per year.

Alternatively, ASOP Co could lease the new technology. The company would pay four annual lease rentals of $380,000 per year, payable in advance at the start of each year. The annual lease rentals include the cost of the licence fee.

If ASOP Co buys the new technology, it can claim tax allowable depreciation on the investment on a 25% reducing balance basis. The company pays taxation one year in arrears at an annual rate of 30%. ASOP Co has an after-tax weighted average cost of capital of 11% per year.

Required:

(a) **Based on financing cash flows only, calculate and determine whether ASOP Co should lease or buy the new technology.** ⊞ **(11 marks)**

(b) **Using a nominal terms approach, calculate the net present value of buying the new technology and advise whether ASOP Co should undertake the proposed investment.** ⊞ **(6 marks)**

(c) **Discuss and illustrate how ASOP Co can use equivalent annual cost or equivalent annual benefit to choose between new technologies with different expected lives.** ⌨ **(3 marks)**

(Total: 20 marks)

32 DEGNIS CO (JUN 16 – MODIFIED)

Degnis Co is a company that installs kitchens and bathrooms to customer specifications. It is planning to invest $4,000,000 in a new facility to convert vans and trucks into motorhomes.

Each motorhome will be designed and built according to customer requirements. Degnis Co expects motorhome production and sales in the first four years of operation to be as follows.

Year	1	2	3	4
Motorhomes produced and sold	250	300	450	450

The selling price for a motorhome depends on the van or truck which is converted, the quality of the units installed and the extent of conversion work required. Degnis Co has undertaken research into likely sales and costs of different kinds of motorhomes which could be selected by customers, as follows:

Motorhome type	Basic	Standard	Deluxe
Probability of selection	20%	45%	35%
Selling price ($/unit)	30,000	42,000	72,000
Conversion cost ($/unit)	23,000	29,000	40,000

Fixed costs of the production facility are expected to depend on the volume of motorhome production as follows:

Production volume (units/year)	200–299	300–399	400–499
Fixed costs ($000/year)	4,000	5,000	5,500

Degnis Co pays corporation tax of 28% per year, with the tax liability being settled in the year in which it arises. The company can claim tax allowable depreciation on the cost of the investment on a straight-line basis over ten years. Degnis Co evaluates investment projects using an after-tax discount rate of 11%.

Required:

(a) Calculate the expected net present value of the planned investment for the first four years of operation. ⊞ **(7 marks)**

(b) After the fourth year of operation, Degnis Co expects to continue to produce and sell 450 motorhomes per year for the foreseeable future.

Required:

Calculate the effect on the expected net present value of the planned investment of continuing to produce and sell motorhomes beyond the first four years and comment on the financial acceptability of the planned investment. ⊞ **(3 marks)**

(c) Critically discuss the use of probability analysis in incorporating risk into investment appraisal. 💻 **(5 marks)**

(d) Discuss the reasons why investment finance may be limited, even when a company has attractive investment opportunities available to it. 💻 **(5 marks)**

(Total: 20 marks)

33 HRAXIN CO (JUN 15 – MODIFIED)

Hraxin Co is appraising an investment project which has an expected life of four years and which will not be repeated. The initial investment, payable at the start of the first year of operation, is $5 million. Scrap value of $500,000 is expected to arise at the end of four years.

There is some uncertainty about what price can be charged for the units produced by the investment project, as this is expected to depend on the future state of the economy. The following forecast of selling prices and their probabilities has been prepared:

Future economic state	Weak	Medium	Strong
Probability of future economic state	35%	50%	15%
Selling price in current price terms	$25 per unit	$30 per unit	$35 per unit

These selling prices are expected to be subject to annual inflation of 4% per year, regardless of which economic state prevails in the future.

Forecast sales and production volumes, and total nominal variable costs, have already been forecast, as follows:

Year	1	2	3	4
Sales and production (units)	150,000	250,000	400,000	300,000
Nominal variable cost ($000)	2,385	4,200	7,080	5,730

Incremental overheads of $400,000 per year in current price terms will arise as a result of undertaking the investment project. A large proportion of these overheads relate to energy costs, which are expected to increase sharply in the future because of energy supply shortages, so overhead inflation of 10% per year is expected.

The initial investment will attract tax-allowable depreciation on a straight-line basis over the four-year project life. The rate of corporation tax is 30% and tax liabilities are paid in the year in which they arise. Hraxin Co has traditionally used a nominal after-tax discount rate of 11% per year for investment appraisal.

Required:

(a) Calculate the expected net present value of the investment project and comment on its financial acceptability. ⊞ (9 marks)

(b) Critically discuss if sensitivity analysis will assist Hraxin Co in assessing the risk of the investment project. 💻 (6 marks)

(c) Describe the process that would be undertaken to decide whether to lease or buy an asset for a long-term investment. 💻 (5 marks)

(Total: 20 marks)

34 HEBAC CO (SEP 16)

Hebac Co is preparing to launch a new product in a new market which is outside its current business operations. The company has undertaken market research and test marketing at a cost of $500,000, as a result of which it expects the new product to be successful. Hebac Co plans to charge a lower selling price initially and then increase the selling price on the assumption that the new product will establish itself in the new market. Forecast sales volumes, selling prices and variable costs are as follows:

Year	1	2	3	4
Sales volume (units/year)	200,000	800,000	900,000	400,000
Selling price ($/unit)	15	18	22	22
Variable costs ($/unit)	9	9	9	9

Selling price and variable cost are given here in current price terms before taking account of forecast selling price inflation of 4% per year and variable cost inflation of 5% per year.

Incremental fixed costs of $500,000 per year in current price terms would arise as a result of producing the new product. Fixed cost inflation of 8% per year is expected.

The initial investment cost of production equipment for the new product will be $2.5 million, payable at the start of the first year of operation. Production will cease at the end of four years because the new product is expected to have become obsolete due to new technology. The production equipment would have a scrap value at the end of four years of $125,000 in future value terms.

Investment in working capital of $1.5 million will be required at the start of the first year of operation. Working capital inflation of 6% per year is expected and working capital will be recovered in full at the end of four years.

Hebac Co pays corporation tax of 20% per year, with the tax liability being settled in the year in which it arises. The company can claim tax-allowable depreciation on a 25% reducing balance basis on the initial investment cost, adjusted in the final year of operation for a balancing allowance or charge. Hebac Co currently has a nominal after-tax weighted average cost of capital (WACC) of 12% and a real after-tax WACC of 8.5%. The company uses its current WACC as the discount rate for all investment projects.

Required:

(a)   **Calculate the net present value of the investment project in nominal terms and comment on its financial acceptability.** ▦ **(12 marks)**

(b)   **Discuss how the capital asset pricing model can assist Hebac Co in making a better investment decision with respect to its new product launch.** 💻 **(8 marks)**

(Total: 20 marks)

35   VYXYN CO (MAR/JUNE 2017)

Vyxyn Co is evaluating a planned investment in a new product costing $20m, payable at the start of the first year of operation. The product will be produced for four years, at the end of which production will cease. The investment project will have a terminal value of zero. Financial information relating to the investment project is as follows:

Year	1	2	3	4
Sales volume (units/year)	440,000	550,000	720,000	400,000
Selling price ($/unit)	26.50	28.50	30.00	26.00
Fixed cost ($/year)	1,100,000	1,121,000	1,155,000	1,200,000

These selling prices have not yet been adjusted for selling price inflation, which is expected to be 3.5% per year. The annual fixed costs are given above in nominal terms.

Variable cost per unit depends on whether competition is maintained between key suppliers of components. The purchasing department has made the following forecast:

Competition	Strong	Moderate	Weak
Probability	45%	35%	20%
Variable cost ($/unit)	10.80	12.00	14.70

The variable costs in this forecast are before taking account of variable cost inflation of 4.0% per year.

Vyxyn Co can claim tax-allowable depreciation on a 25% per year reducing balance basis on the full investment cost of $20m and pays corporation tax of 28% one year in arrears.

It is planned to finance the investment project with an issue of 8% loan notes, redeemable in ten years' time. Vyxyn Co has a nominal after-tax weighted average cost of capital of 10%, a real after-tax weighted average cost of capital of 7% and a cost of equity of 11%.

Required:

(a) Discuss the difference between risk and uncertainty in relation to investment appraisal. 💻   (3 marks)

(b) Calculate the expected net present value of the investment project and comment on its financial acceptability and on the risk relating to variable cost. ⊞   (9 marks)

(c) Critically discuss how risk can be considered in the investment appraisal process. 💻
                                                                        (8 marks)

                                                                  (Total: 20 marks)

36 DYSXA CO (DEC 2016)

Dysxa Co is looking to expand the capacity of an existing factory in its Alpha Division by 850,000 units per year in order to meet increased demand for one of its products. The expansion will cost $3.2 million.

The selling price of the unit is $3.10 per unit and variable costs of production are $1.10 per unit, both in current price terms. Selling price inflation of 3% per year and variable cost inflation of 6% per year are expected. Nominal fixed costs of production have been forecast as follows:

Year	1	2	3	4
Fixed costs ($)	110,000	205,000	330,000	330,000

Dysxa Co has a nominal after-tax weighted average cost of capital of 10% and pays corporation tax of 20% per year one year in arrears. The company can claim 25% reducing balance tax-allowable depreciation on the full cost of the expansion, which you should assume is paid at the start of the first year of operation.

Dysxa Co evaluates all investment projects as though they have a project life of four years and assumes zero scrap value at the end of four years.

Dysxa Co has limited the capital investment funds in its Delta division to $7 million. The division has identified five possible investment projects, as follows:

Project	Initial investment	Net present value
A	$3,000,000	$6,000,000
B	$2,000,000	$3,200,000
C	$1,000,000	$1,700,000
D	$1,000,000	$2,100,000
E	$2,000,000	$3,600,000

These projects are divisible and cannot be deferred or repeated. Projects C and E are mutually exclusive.

Required:

(a) Calculate the net present value of the investment project and comment on its financial acceptability. ⊞   (8 marks)

(b) Determine the net present value of the optimum investment schedule for Delta division. ⊞   (3 marks)

(c) Discuss the reasons why hard and soft capital rationing occur. 💻   (5 marks)

(d) Discuss TWO ways in which the risk of a project can be assessed. 💻   (4 marks)

                                                                  (Total: 20 marks)

37   PELTA CO (SEP/DEC 2017)

The directors of Pelta Co are considering a planned investment project costing $25m, payable at the start of the first year of operation. The following information relates to the investment project:

	Year 1	Year 2	Year 3	Year 4
Sales volumes (units/year)	520,000	624,000	717,000	788,000
Selling price ($/unit)	30.00	30.00	30.00	30.00
Variable costs ($/unit)	10.00	10.20	10.61	10.93
Fixed costs ($/year)	700,000	735,000	779,000	841,000

This information needs adjusting to take account of selling price inflation of 4% per year and variable cost inflation of 3% per year. The fixed costs, which are incremental and related to the investment project, are in nominal terms. The year 4 sales volume is expected to continue for the foreseeable future.

Pelta Co pays corporation tax of 30% one year in arrears. The company can claim tax-allowable depreciation on a 25% reducing balance basis.

The views of the directors of Pelta Co are that all investment projects must be evaluated over four years of operations, with an assumed terminal value at the end of the fourth year of 5% of the initial investment cost. Both net present value and discounted payback must be used, with a maximum discounted payback period of two years. The real after-tax cost of capital of Pelta Co is 7% and its nominal after-tax cost of capital is 12%.

Required:

(a)   (i)   **Calculate the net present value of the planned investment project.** ▦

(9 marks)

   (ii)   **Calculate the discounted payback period of the planned investment project.** ▦

(2 marks)

(b)   **Discuss the financial acceptability of the investment project.** 💻   (3 marks)

(c)   **Critically discuss the views of the directors on Pelta Co's investment appraisal.** 💻

(6 marks)

(Total: 20 marks)

38   COPPER CO (MAR/JUN 2018)

Copper Co is concerned about the risk associated with a proposed investment and is looking for ways to incorporate risk into its investment appraisal process. The company has heard that probability analysis may be useful in this respect and so the following information relating to the proposed investment has been prepared:

Year 1		Year 2	
Cash flow ($)	Probability	Cash flow ($)	Probability
1,000,000	0.1	2,000,000	0.3
2,000,000	0.5	3,000,000	0.6
3,000,000	0.4	5,000,000	0.1

However, the company is not sure how to interpret the results of an investment appraisal based on probability analysis.

The proposed investment will cost $3.5m, payable in full at the start of the first year of operation. Copper Co uses a discount rate of 12% in investment appraisal.

Required:

(a)   Using a joint probability table:

    (i)   Calculate the mean (expected) NPV of the proposed investment ▦ (8 marks)

    (ii)   Calculate the probability of the investment having a negative NPV ▦

        (1 mark)

    (iii)   Calculate the NPV of the most likely outcome ▦   (1 mark)

    (iv)   Comment on the financial acceptability of the proposed investment. ▦

        (2 marks)

(b)   Discuss TWO of the following methods of adjusting for risk and uncertainty in investment appraisal:

    (i)   Simulation

    (ii)   Adjusted payback

    (iii)   Risk-adjusted discount rates. 💻   (8 marks)

(Total: 20 marks)

39   MELANIE CO (SEP/DEC 2018)

Melanie Co is considering the acquisition of a new machine with an operating life of three years. The new machine could be leased for three payments of $55,000, payable annually in advance.

Alternatively, the machine could be purchased for $160,000 using a bank loan at a cost of 8% per year. If the machine is purchased, Melanie Co will incur maintenance costs of $8,000 per year, payable at the end of each year of operation. The machine would have a residual value of $40,000 at the end of its three-year life.

Melanie Co's production manager estimates that if maintenance routines were upgraded, the new machine could be operated for a period of four years with maintenance costs increasing to $12,000 per year, payable at the end of each year of operation. If operated for four years, the machine's residual value would fall to $11,000.

Taxation should be ignored.

Required:

(a)   (i)   Assuming that the new machine is operated for a three-year period, evaluate whether Melanie Co should use leasing or borrowing as a source of finance. ▦

        (6 marks)

    (ii)   Using a discount rate of 10%, calculate the equivalent annual cost of purchasing and operating the machine for both three years and four years, and recommend which replacement interval should be adopted. ▦

        (6 marks)

(b)   Critically discuss FOUR reasons why NPV is regarded as superior to IRR as an investment appraisal technique. 💻   (8 marks)

(Total: 20 marks)

40   PINKS CO (MAR/JUN 2019)

Pinks Co is a large company listed on a major stock exchange. In recent years, the board of Pinks Co has been criticised for weak corporate governance and two of the company's non-executive directors have just resigned. A recent story in the financial media has criticised the performance of Pinks Co and claims that the company is failing to satisfy the objectives of its key stakeholders.

Pinks Co is appraising an investment project which it hopes will boost its performance. The project will cost $20m, payable in full at the start of the first year of operation. The project life is expected to be four years. Forecast sales volumes, selling price, variable cost and fixed costs are as follows:

Year	1	2	3	4
	$000	$000	$000	$000
Sales (units/year)	300,000	410,000	525,000	220,000
Selling price ($/unit)	125	130	140	120
Variable cost ($/unit)	71	71	71	71
Fixed costs ($000/year)	3,000	3,100	3,200	3,000

Selling price and cost information are in current price terms, before applying selling price inflation of 5% per year, variable cost inflation of 3.5% per year and fixed cost inflation of 6% per year.

Pinks Co pays corporation tax of 26%, with the tax liability being settled in the year in which it arises. The company can claim tax-allowable depreciation on the full initial investment of $20m on a 25% reducing balance basis. The investment project is expected to have zero residual value at the end of four years.

Pinks Co has a nominal after-tax cost of capital of 12% and a real after-tax cost of capital of 8%. The general rate of inflation is expected to be 3.7% per year for the foreseeable future.

Required:

(a)   (i)   Calculate the nominal net present value of Pinks Co's investment project. ▦

(8 marks)

(ii)   Calculate the real net present value of Pinks Co's investment project and comment on your findings. ▦   (4 marks)

(b)   Discuss FOUR ways to encourage managers to achieve stakeholder objectives. ⌨

(8 marks)

(Total: 20 marks)

BUSINESS FINANCE AND COST OF CAPITAL – EXAM STYLE QUESTIONS

41 FENCE CO (JUNE 14 – MODIFIED)

The equity beta of Fence Co is 0.9 and the company has issued 10 million ordinary shares. The market value of each ordinary share is $7.50. The company is also financed by 7% bonds with a nominal value of $100 per bond, which will be redeemed in seven years' time at nominal value. The bonds have a total nominal value of $14 million. Interest on the bonds has just been paid and the current market value of each bond is $107.14.

Fence Co plans to invest in a project that is different to its existing business operations and has identified a company in the same business area as the project, Hex Co. The equity beta of Hex Co is 1.2 and the company has an equity market value of $54 million. The market value of the debt of Hex Co is $12 million.

The risk-free rate of return is 4% per year and the average return on the stock market is 11% per year. Both companies pay corporation tax at a rate of 20% per year.

Required:

(a) Calculate the current weighted average cost of capital of Fence Co. ⊞ **(7 marks)**

(b) Calculate a cost of equity which could be used in appraising the new project. ⊞

(4 marks)

(c) Explain the difference between systematic and unsystematic risk in relation to portfolio theory and the capital asset pricing model. 💻 **(4 marks)**

(d) Discuss the significance of the efficient market hypothesis (EMH) for the financial manager. 💻 **(5 marks)**

(Total: 20 marks)

42 BAR CO (DEC 11 – MODIFIED)

Bar Co is a stock exchange listed company that is concerned by its current level of debt finance. It plans to make a rights issue and to use the funds raised to pay off some of its debt. The rights issue will be at a 20% discount to its current ex-dividend share price of $7.50 per share and Bar Co plans to raise $90 million. Bar Co believes that paying off some of its debt will not affect its price/earnings ratio, which is expected to remain constant.

Statement of profit or loss information

	$m
Revenue	472
Cost of sales	423
Profit before interest and tax	49
Interest	10
Profit before tax	39
Tax	12
Profit after tax	27

Statement of financial position information

	$m
Equity	
Ordinary shares ($1 nominal)	60
Reserves	80
	───
	140
Long-term liabilities	
8% bonds ($100 nominal)	125
	───
	265

The 8% bonds are currently trading at $112.50 per $100 bond and bondholders have agreed that they will allow Bar Co to buy back the bonds at this market value. Bar Co pays tax at a rate of 30% per year.

Required:

(a) Calculate the theoretical ex rights price per share of Bar Co following the rights issue. ⊞ **(3 marks)**

(b) Calculate and discuss whether using the cash raised by the rights issue to buy back bonds is likely to be financially acceptable to the shareholders of Bar Co, commenting in your answer on the belief that the current price/earnings ratio will remain constant. ⊞ **(7 marks)**

(c) Compare and contrast the financial objectives of a stock exchange listed company such as Bar Co and the financial objectives of a not-for-profit organisation such as a large charity. 🖥 **(10 marks)**

(Total: 20 marks)

43 NUGFER (DEC 10 – MODIFIED)

The following financial position statement as at 30 November 20X6 refers to Nugfer Co, a stock exchange-listed company, which wishes to raise $200m in cash in order to acquire a competitor.

	$m	$m	$m
Assets			
Non-current assets			300
Current assets			211
Total assets			511
Equity and liabilities			
Share capital		100	
Retained earnings		121	
Total equity			221
Non-current liabilities			
Long-term borrowings		100	
Current liabilities			
Trade payables	30		
Short-term borrowings	160		
Total current liabilities		190	
Total liabilities			290
Total equity and liabilities			511

The recent performance of Nugfer Co in profitability terms is as follows:

Year ending 30 November	20X3	20X4	20X5	20X6
	$m	$m	$m	$m
Revenue	122.6	127.3	156.6	189.3
Operating profit	41.7	43.3	50.1	56.7
Finance charges (interest)	6.0	6.2	12.5	18.8
Profit before tax	35.7	37.1	37.6	37.9
Profit after tax	25.0	26.0	26.3	26.5

Notes:

(1) The long-term borrowings are 6% bonds that are repayable in 20X8.

(2) The short-term borrowings consist of an overdraft at an annual interest rate of 8%.

(3) The current assets do not include any cash deposits.

(4) Nugfer Co has not paid any dividends in the last four years.

(5) The number of ordinary shares issued by the company has not changed in recent years.

(6) The target company has no debt finance and its forecast profit before interest and tax for 20X7 is $28 million.

Required:

(a) Evaluate suitable methods of raising the $200 million required by Nugfer Co, supporting your evaluation with both analysis and critical discussion.

(16 marks)

(b) Briefly explain the factors that will influence the rate of interest charged on a new issue of bonds.

(4 marks)

(Total: 20 marks)

44 SPOT CO (DEC 13 – MODIFIED)

Spot Co is considering how to finance the acquisition of a machine costing $750,000 with an operating life of five years. There are two financing options.

Option 1

The machine could be leased for an annual lease payment of $155,000 per year, payable at the start of each year.

Option 2

The machine could be bought for $750,000 using a bank loan charging interest at an annual rate of 7% per year. At the end of five years, the machine would have a scrap value of 10% of the purchase price. If the machine is bought, maintenance costs of $20,000 per year would be incurred.

Required:

(a) Evaluate whether Spot Co should use leasing or borrowing as a source of finance, explaining the evaluation method which you use. (Ignore taxation). (10 marks)

(b) Discuss the attractions of leasing as a source of both short-term and long-term finance. (5 marks)

(c) In Islamic finance, explain briefly the concept of riba (interest) and how returns are made by Islamic financial instruments. (5 marks)

(Total: 20 marks)

45 ECHO CO (DEC 07 – MODIFIED) *Walk in the footsteps of a top tutor*

The following financial information relates to Echo Co:

Statement of profit or loss information for the last year

	$m
Profit before interest and tax	12
Interest	3
Profit before tax	9
Income tax expense	3
Profit for the period	6
Dividends	2
Retained profit for the period	4

Statement of financial position information as at the end of the last year

	$m	$m
Ordinary shares, nominal value 50c	5	
Retained earnings	15	
	—	
Total equity		20
8% loan notes, redeemable in three years' time		30
		—
Total equity and non-current liabilities		50
		—

Average data on companies similar to Echo Co:

Interest coverage ratio	8 times
Long-term debt/equity (book value basis)	80%

The board of Echo Co is considering several proposals that have been made by its finance director. Each proposal is independent of any other proposal.

Proposal A

The current dividend per share should be increased by 20% in order to make the company more attractive to equity investors.

Proposal B

A bond issue should be made in order to raise $15 million of new debt capital. Although there are no investment opportunities currently available, the cash raised would be invested on a short-term basis until a suitable investment opportunity arose. The loan notes would pay interest at a rate of 10% per year and be redeemable in eight years' time at nominal value.

Proposal C

A 1 for 4 rights issue should be made at a 20% discount to the current share price of $2.30 per share in order to reduce gearing and the financial risk of the company.

Required:

(a)   Analyse and discuss Proposal A. ▦   (5 marks)

(b)   Evaluate and discuss Proposal B. ▦   (8 marks)

(c)   Calculate the theoretical ex rights price per share and the amount of finance that would be raised under Proposal C. Evaluate and discuss the proposal to use these funds to reduce gearing and financial risk. ▦   (7 marks)

(Total: 20 marks)

46   PAVLON

(a)   Pavlon Inc. has recently obtained a listing on the Stock Exchange. 90% of the company's shares were previously owned by members of one family but, since the listing, approximately 60% of the issued shares have been owned by other investors.

Pavlon's earnings and dividends for the five years prior to the listing are detailed below:

Years prior to listing	Profit after tax ($)	Dividend per share (cents)
5	1,800,000	3.6
4	2,400,000	4.8
3	3,850,000	6.16
2	4,100,000	6.56
1	4,450,000	7.12
Current year	5,500,000(estimate)	

The number of issued ordinary shares was increased by 25% three years prior to the listing and by 50% at the time of the listing. The company's authorised capital is currently $25,000,000 in 25¢ ordinary shares, of which 40,000,000 shares have been issued. The market value of the company's equity is $78,000,000.

The board of directors is discussing future dividend policy. An interim dividend of 3.16 cents per share was paid immediately prior to the listing and the finance director has suggested a final dividend of 2.34 cents per share.

The company's declared objective is to maximise shareholder wealth.

Required:

(i)   **Determine and comment upon the nature of the company's dividend policy prior to the listing and discuss whether such a policy is likely to be suitable for a company listed on the Stock Exchange.** ▦   **(5 marks)**

(ii)   **Discuss whether the proposed final dividend of 2.34 cents is likely to be an appropriate dividend:**

–   **If the majority of shares are owned by wealthy private individuals; and**

–   **If the majority of shares are owned by institutional investors.** ▭
                                                                                            (10 marks)

(b)   The company's profit after tax is generally expected to increase by 15% per year for three years, and 8% per year after that. Pavlon's cost of equity capital is estimated to be 12% per year. Dividends may be assumed to grow at the same rate as profits.

Required:

Use the dividend valuation model to give calculations to indicate whether Pavlon's shares are currently under- or over-valued. ▦   **(5 marks)**

(Total: 20 marks)

47 ARWIN

Arwin plans to raise $5m in order to expand its existing chain of retail outlets. It can raise the finance by issuing 10% loan stock redeemable in ten years' time, or by a rights issue at $4.00 per share. The current financial statements of Arwin are as follows:

Statement of profit or loss for the last year

	$000
Sales revenue	50,000
Cost of sales	30,000
	———
Gross profit	20,000
Administration costs	14,000
	———
Profit before interest and tax	6,000
Interest	300
	———
Profit before tax	5,700
Taxation at 30%	1,710
	———
Profit after tax	3,990
	———

Changes in equity

	$000
Dividends	2,394
Net change in equity (retained profits)	1,596

Statement of financial position

	$000
Net non-current assets	20,100
Net current assets	4,960
	———
	25,060
	———
Ordinary shares, nominal value 25¢	2,500
Retained profit	20,060
12% loan stock (redeemable in six years)	2,500
	———
	25,060
	———

The expansion of business is expected to increase sales revenue by 12% in the first year. Variable cost of sales makes up 85% of cost of sales. Administration costs will increase by 5% due to new staff appointments. Arwin has a policy of paying out 60% of profit after tax as dividends and has no overdraft.

Required:

(a)   For each financing proposal, prepare the forecast statement of profit or loss after one additional year of operation. ⊞   (5 marks)

(b)   Evaluate and comment on the effects of each financing proposal on the following:

   (i)   Financial gearing

   (ii)   Operational gearing

   (iii) Interest cover

   (iv)   Earnings per share. 🖵   (12 marks)

(c)   Comment on the view that businesses are unlikely to have high financial gearing and high operating gearing. 🖵   (3 marks)

(Total: 20 marks)

48   AMH CO (JUNE 13 MODIFIED)

 Question debrief

AMH Co wishes to calculate its current cost of capital for use as a discount rate in investment appraisal. The following financial information relates to AMH Co:

Financial position statement extracts as at 31 December 20X8

	$000	$000
Equity		
Ordinary shares (nominal value 50 cents)	4,000	
Reserves	18,000	22,000
	─────	
Long-term liabilities		
4% Preference shares (nominal value $1)	3,000	
7% Bonds redeemable after six years	3,000	
Long-term bank loan	1,000	7,000
	─────	─────
		29,000
		─────

The ordinary shares of AMH Co have an ex div market value of $4.70 per share and an ordinary dividend of 36.3 cents per share has just been paid. Historic dividend payments have been as follows:

Year	20X4	20X5	20X6	20X7
Dividends per share (cents)	30.9	32.2	33.6	35.0

The preference shares of AMH Co are not redeemable and have an ex div market value of $0.40 per share.

The 7% bonds are redeemable at a 5% premium to their nominal value of $100 per bond and have an ex interest market value of $104.50 per bond.

The bank loan has a variable interest rate that has averaged 4% per year in recent years.

AMH Co pays profit tax at an annual rate of 30% per year.

Required:

(a)   Calculate the market value weighted average cost of capital of AMH Co.

(12 marks)

(b)   Discuss how the capital asset pricing model can be used to calculate a project-specific cost of equity for AMH Co, referring in your discussion to the key concepts of systematic risk, business risk and financial risk.

(8 marks)

(Total: 20 marks)

🕐 *Calculate your allowed time, allocate the time to the separate parts*

---

49   GTK INC (JUNE 07 – MODIFIED) 👣 *Walk in the footsteps of a top tutor*

The finance director of GTK Inc. is preparing its capital budget for the forthcoming period and is examining a number of capital investment proposals that have been received from its subsidiaries. Details of these proposals are as follows:

Proposal 1

Division A has requested that it be allowed to invest $500,000 in solar panels, which would be fitted to the roof of its production facility, in order to reduce its dependency on oil as an energy source.

The solar panels would save energy costs of $700 per day but only on sunny days. The Division has estimated the following probabilities of sunny days in each year.

	Number of sunny days	Probability
Scenario 1	100	0.3
Scenario 2	125	0.6
Scenario 3	150	0.1

Each scenario is expected to persist indefinitely, i.e. if there are 100 sunny days in the first year, there will be 100 sunny days in every subsequent year. Maintenance costs for the solar panels are expected to be $2,000 per month for labour and replacement parts, irrespective of the number of sunny days per year. The solar panels are expected to be used indefinitely.

Proposal 2

Division C has requested approval and funding for a new product that it has been secretly developing, Product RPG. Product development and market research costs of $350,000 have already been incurred and are now due for payment. $300,000 is needed for new machinery, which will be a full-scale version of the current pilot plant. Advertising takes place in the first year only and would cost $100,000. Annual cash inflow of $100,000, net of all production costs but before taking account of advertising costs, is expected to be generated for a five-year period. After five years Product RPG would be retired and replaced with a more technologically advanced model. The machinery used for producing Product RPG would be sold for $30,000 at that time.

Other information

GTK Inc. is a profitable, listed company with several million dollars of shareholders' funds, a small overdraft and no long-term debt. For profit calculation purposes, GTK Inc. depreciates assets on a straight-line basis over their useful economic life. The company can claim tax-allowable depreciation on machinery on a 25% reducing balance basis and pays tax on profit at an annual rate of 30% in the year in which the liability arises. GTK Inc. has a before-tax cost of capital of 10%, an after-tax cost of capital of 8% and a target return on capital employed of 15%.

Required:

(a)   For the proposed investment in solar panels (Proposal 1), calculate:

   (i)   the net present value for each expected number of sunny days

   (ii)   the overall expected net present value of the proposal.

   Comment on your findings. Ignore taxation in this part of the question. ▦

(10 marks)

(b)   Assuming GTK Inc. wishes to raise $1.1 million, discuss how equity finance or traded debt (bonds) might be raised, clearly indicating which source of finance you recommend and the reasons for your recommendation. ⌨   (10 marks)

(Total: 20 marks)

50   TFR (JUNE 07 – MODIFIED)

TFR is a small, profitable, owner-managed company that is seeking finance for a planned expansion. A local bank has indicated that it may be prepared to offer a loan of $100,000 at a fixed annual rate of 9%. TFR would repay $25,000 of the capital each year for the next four years.

Annual interest would be calculated on the opening balance at the start of each year. Current financial information on TFR is as follows:

Current revenue:	$210,000
Net profit margin:	20%
Annual taxation rate:	25%
Average overdraft:	$20,000
Average interest on overdraft:	10% per year
Dividend payout ratio:	50%
Shareholders' funds:	$200,000
Market value of non-current assets	$180,000

As a result of the expansion, revenue would increase by $45,000 per year for each of the next four years, while net profit margin would remain unchanged. No tax allowable depreciation would arise from investment of the amount borrowed.

TFR currently has no other debt than the existing and continuing overdraft and has no cash or near-cash investments. The non-current assets consist largely of the building from which the company conducts its business. The current dividend payout ratio has been maintained for several years.

Required:

(a) Assuming that TFR is granted the loan, calculate the following ratios for TFR for each of the next five years:

    (i)   interest cover

    (ii)   medium to long-term debt/equity ratio

    (iii) return on equity

    (iv) return on capital employed. ⊞   **(12 marks)**

(b) Comment on the financial implications for TFR of accepting the bank loan on the terms indicated above. ⌨   **(8 marks)**

                                     (Total: 20 marks)

51 GXG CO (JUNE 13 – MODIFIED)

GXG Co is an e-business that designs and sells computer applications (apps) for mobile phones. The company needs to raise $3,200,000 for research and development and is considering two financing options.

Option 1

GXG Co could suspend dividends for two years, and then pay dividends of 25 cents per share from the end of the third year, increasing dividends annually by 4% per year in subsequent years. Dividends in recent years have grown by 3% per year.

Option 2

GXG Co could issue $3,200,000 of bonds paying annual interest of 6%, redeemable after ten years at nominal value.

Recent financial information relating to GXG Co is as follows:

	$000
Operating profit	3,450
Interest	200
Profit before taxation	3,250
Taxation	650
Profit after taxation	2,600
Dividends	1,600

	$000
Ordinary shares (nominal value 50 cents)	5,000

Under both options, the funds invested would earn a before-tax return of 18% per year.

The profit tax rate paid by the company is 20% per year.

GXG Co has a cost of equity of 9% per year, which is expected to remain constant.

Required:

(a)   Using the dividend valuation model, calculate the value of GXG Co under option 1, and advise whether option 1 will be acceptable to shareholders. ⊞   **(6 marks)**

(b)   Calculate the effect on earnings per share and interest cover of the proposal to raise finance by issuing new debt (option 2), and comment on your findings. ⊞

(5 marks)

(c)   Discuss the factors to be considered in choosing between traded bonds, new equity issued via a placing and venture capital as sources of finance. 💻   **(9 marks)**

(Total: 20 marks)

52   ILL COLLEAGUE

A colleague has been taken ill. Your managing director has asked you to take over from the colleague and to provide urgently needed estimates of the discount rate to be used in appraising a large new capital investment. You have been given your colleague's working notes, which you believe to be numerically accurate.

Working notes

Estimates for the next five years (annual averages)

Stock market total return on equity	16%
Own company dividend yield	7%
Own company share price rise	14%
Own company equity Beta	1.4
Growth rate of own company earnings	12%
Growth rate of own company dividends	11%
Growth rate of own company sales	13%
Treasury bill yield	12%

The company's gearing level (by market values) is 1:2 debt to equity, and after-tax earnings available to ordinary shareholders in the most recent year were $5,400,000, of which $2,140,000 was distributed as ordinary dividends. The company has 10 million issued ordinary shares, which are currently trading on the Stock Exchange at 321 cents. Corporate debt may be assumed to be risk-free. The company pays tax at 35% and personal taxation may be ignored.

Required:

(a)   Estimate the company's weighted average cost of capital using:

(i)   the dividend valuation model

(ii)   the capital asset pricing model.

State clearly any assumptions that you make.

Under what circumstances would these models be expected to produce similar values for the weighted average cost of capital? ⊞   **(9 marks)**

(b)   You are now informed that the proposed investment is a major diversification into a new industry, and are provided with the following information about the new industry:

Average industry gearing level (by market value)   1:3 debt to equity

Average β equity   1.50

Using any relevant information from parts (a) and (b), recommend which cost of equity should be used for the investment. Any relevant calculations not included in your answer to part (a) should form part of your answer. ▦   **(6 marks)**

(c)   Discuss the problems estimating the appropriate data inputs for using the capital asset pricing model in investment appraisal. 💻   **(5 marks)**

(Total: 20 marks)

53   CARD CO (DEC 13 – MODIFIED)

Card Co has in issue 8 million shares with an ex-dividend market value of $7.16 per share. A dividend of 62 cents per share for 20X3 has just been paid. The pattern of recent dividends is as follows:

Year	20X0	20X1	20X2	20X3
Dividends per share (cents)	55.1	57.9	59.1	62.0

Card Co also has in issue 8.5% bonds redeemable in five years' time with a total nominal value of $5 million. The market value of each $100 bond is $103.42. Redemption will be at nominal value.

Card Co is planning to invest a significant amount of money into a joint venture in a new business area. It has identified a proxy company with a similar business risk to the joint venture. The proxy company has an equity beta of 1.038 and is financed 75% by equity and 25% by debt, on a market value basis.

The current risk-free rate of return is 4% and the average equity risk premium is 5%. Card Co pays profit tax at a rate of 30% per year and has an equity beta of 1.6.

Required:

(a)   Calculate the cost of equity of Card Co using the dividend growth model. ▦
        (3 marks)

(b)   Discuss whether the dividend growth model or the capital asset pricing model should be used to calculate the cost of equity. 💻   **(5 marks)**

(c)   Calculate a project-specific cost of equity for Card Co for the planned joint venture. ▦
        (4 marks)

(d)   Discuss whether changing the capital structure of a company can lead to a reduction in its cost of capital and hence to an increase in the value of the company. 💻   **(8 marks)**

(Total: 20 marks)

54   DINLA CO (MAR 16 – MODIFIED)

Dinla Co has the following capital structure.

Equity and reserves	$000	$000
Ordinary shares	23,000	
Reserves	247,000	270,000
Non-current liabilities		
5% Preference shares	5,000	
6% Loan notes	11,000	
Bank loan	3,000	
		19,000
		289,000

The ordinary shares of Dinla Co are currently trading at $4.26 per share on an ex-dividend basis and have a nominal value of $0.25 per share.

Ordinary dividends are expected to grow in the future by 4% per year and a dividend of $0.25 per share has just been paid.

The 5% preference shares have an ex dividend market value of $0.56 per share and a nominal value of $1.00 per share. These shares are irredeemable.

The 6% loan notes of Dinla Co are currently trading at $95.45 per loan note on an ex interest basis and will be redeemed at their nominal value of $100 per loan note in five years' time.

The bank loan has a fixed interest rate of 7% per year.

Dinla Co pays corporation tax at a rate of 25%.

Required:

(a)   Calculate the after-tax weighted average cost of capital of Dinla Co on a market value basis. ▦   **(8 marks)**

(b)   Discuss the connection between the relative costs of sources of finance and the creditor hierarchy. ⌨   **(3 marks)**

(c)   Explain the differences between Islamic finance and other conventional finance. ⌨
                                                                                   (4 marks)

(d)   Discuss the circumstances under which the current weighted average cost of capital of a company could be used in investment appraisal and indicate briefly how its limitations as a discount rate could be overcome. ⌨   **(5 marks)**

                                                                          (Total: 20 marks)

55 TINEP CO (DEC 14 – MODIFIED)

 Question debrief

Tinep Co is planning to raise funds for an expansion of existing business activities (the intention to expand has already been announced to the stock market). In preparation for this, the company has decided to calculate its weighted average cost of capital. Tinep Co has the following capital structure:

	$m	$m
Equity		
Ordinary shares	200	
Reserves	650	
		850
Non-current liabilities		
Loan notes		200
		1,050

The ordinary shares of Tinep Co have a nominal value of 50 cents per share and are currently trading on the stock market on an ex dividend basis at $5.85 per share. Tinep Co has an equity beta of 1.15.

The loan notes have a nominal value of $100 and are currently trading on the stock market on an ex interest basis at $103.50 per loan note. The interest on the loan notes is 6% per year before tax and they will be redeemed in six years' time at a 6% premium to their nominal value.

The risk-free rate of return is 4% per year and the equity risk premium is 6% per year. Tinep Co pays corporation tax at an annual rate of 25% per year.

Required:

(a) **Calculate the market value weighted average cost of capital and the book value weighted average cost of capital of Tinep Co, and comment briefly on any difference between the two values.** ▦ **(9 marks)**

(b) **Discuss the factors to be considered by Tinep Co in choosing to raise funds via a rights issue.** 💻 **(6 marks)**

(c) Tinep Co ultimately decides to finance the business expansion with a new issue of 8% loan notes. The company then announces to the stock market both this financing decision and an expected increase in profit before interest and tax of 20% arising from the business expansion.

Required:

Assuming the stock market is semi-strong form efficient, analyse and discuss the effect of the financing and profitability announcement on the financial risk and share price of Tinep Co. 💻 **(5 marks)**

(Total: 20 marks)

 Calculate your allowed time, allocate the time to the separate parts

56   TUFA CO (SEP/DEC 2017)

The following statement of financial position information relates to Tufa Co, a company listed on a large stock market, which pays corporation tax at a rate of 30%.

	$m	$m
Equity and liabilities		
Share capital	17	
Retained earnings	15	
Total equity		32
Non-current liabilities		
Long-term borrowings	13	
Current liabilities	21	
Total liabilities		34
Total equity and liabilities		66

The share capital of Tufa Co consists of $12m of ordinary shares and $5m of irredeemable preference shares.

The ordinary shares of Tufa Co have a nominal value of $0.50 per share, an ex-dividend market price of $7.07 per share and a cum dividend market price of $7.52 per share. The dividend for 20X7 will be paid in the near future. Dividends paid in recent years have been as follows:

Year	20X6	20X5	20X4	20X3
Dividend ($/share)	0.43	0.41	0.39	0.37

The 5% preference shares of Tufa Co have a nominal value of $0.50 per share and an ex dividend market price of $0.31 per share.

The long-term borrowings of Tufa Co consist of $10m of loan notes and a $3m bank loan. The bank loan has a variable interest rate.

The 7% loan notes have a nominal value of $100 per loan note and a market price of $102.34 per loan note. Annual interest has just been paid and the loan notes are redeemable in four years' time at a 5% premium to nominal value.

Required:

(a)   Calculate the after-tax weighted average cost of capital of Tufa Co on a market value basis. ▦   (11 marks)

(b)   Discuss the circumstances under which it is appropriate to use the current WACC of Tufa Co in appraising an investment project. ▄   (3 marks)

(c)   Discuss THREE advantages to Tufa Co of using convertible loan notes as a source of long-term finance. ▄   (6 marks)

(Total: 20 marks)

57 TIN CO (MAR/JUN 2018)

Tin Co is planning an expansion of its business operations, which will increase profit before interest and tax by 20%. The company is considering whether to use equity or debt finance to raise the $2m needed by the business expansion.

If equity finance is used, a 1 for 5 rights issue will be offered to existing shareholders at a 20% discount to the current ex dividend share price of $5.00 per share. The nominal value of the ordinary shares is $1.00 per share.

If debt finance is used, Tin Co will issue 20,000 8% loan notes with a nominal value of $100 per loan note.

Financial statement information prior to raising new finance:

	$000
Profit before interest and tax	1,597
Finance costs (interest)	(315)
Taxation	(282)
Profit after tax	1,000

	$000
Equity	
Ordinary shares	2,500
Retained earnings	5,488
Long-term liabilities: 7% loan notes	4,500
Total equity and long-term liabilities	12,488

The current price/earnings ratio of Tin Co is 12.5 times. Corporation tax is payable at a rate of 22%.

Companies undertaking the same business as Tin Co have an average debt/equity ratio (book value of debt divided by book value of equity) of 60.5% and an average interest cover of 9 times.

Required:

(a) (i) Calculate the theoretical ex-rights price per share. ⊞ **(2 marks)**

(ii) Assuming equity finance is used, calculate the revised earnings per share after the business expansion. ⊞ **(4 marks)**

(iii) Assuming debt finance is used, calculate the revised earnings per share after the business expansion. ⊞ **(3 marks)**

(iv) Calculate the revised share prices under both financing methods after the business expansion. ⊞ **(1 mark)**

(v) Use calculations to evaluate whether equity finance or debt finance should be used for the planned business expansion. ⊞ **(4 marks)**

(b) Discuss TWO Islamic finance sources which Tin Co could consider as alternatives to a rights issue or a loan note issue. ▦ **(6 marks)**

(Total: 20 marks)

58   CORFE CO (MAR/JUN 2019)

The following information has been taken from the statement of financial position of Corfe Co, a listed company.

	$m	$m
Non-current assets		50
Current assets:		
Cash and cash equivalents	4	
Other current assets	16	20
	———	———
Total assets		70
		———
Equity and reserves:		
Ordinary shares	15	
Reserves	29	44
Non-current liabilities:		
6% preference shares	6	
8% loan notes	8	
Bank loan	5	19
	———	———
Current liabilities		7
		———
Total equity and liabilities		70
		———

The ordinary shares of Corfe Co have a nominal value of $1 per share and a current ex-dividend market price of $6.10 per share. A dividend of $0.90 per share has just been paid.

The 6% preference shares of Corfe Co have a nominal value of $0.75 per share and an ex-dividend market price of $0.64 per share.

The 8% loan notes of Corfe Co have a nominal value of $100 per loan note and a market price of $103.50 per loan note. Annual interest has just been paid and the loan notes are redeemable in five years' time at a 10% premium to nominal value.

The bank loan has a variable interest rate.

The risk-free rate of return is 3.5% per year and the equity risk premium is 6.8% per year. Corfe Co has an equity beta   of 1.25.

Corfe Co pays corporation tax at a rate of 20%.

Investment in facilities

Corfe Co's board is looking to finance investments in facilities over the next three years, forecast to cost up to $25m. The board does not wish to obtain further long-term debt finance and is also unwilling to make an equity issue. This means that investments have to be financed from cash which can be made available internally. Board members have made a number of suggestions about how this can be done:

Director A has suggested that the company does not have a problem with funding new investments, as it has cash available in the reserves of $29m. If extra cash is required soon, Corfe Co could reduce its investment in working capital.

Director B has suggested selling the building which contains the company's headquarters in the capital city for $20m. This will raise a large one-off sum and also save on ongoing property management costs. Head office support functions would be moved to a number of different locations rented outside the capital city.

Director C has commented that although a high dividend has just been paid, dividends could be reduced over the next three years, allowing spare cash for investment.

Required:

(a)   Calculate the after-tax weighted average cost of capital of Corfe Co on a market value basis. ⊞   **(11 marks)**

(b)   Discuss the views expressed by the three directors on how the investment should be financed. 🖥   **(9 marks)**

(Total: 20 marks)

BUSINESS VALUATIONS – PRACTICE QUESTIONS

59   CLOSE CO (DEC 11 MODIFIED)

 *Question debrief*

Recent financial information relating to Close Co, a stock market listed company, is as follows.

	$m
Profit after tax (earnings)	66.6
Dividends	40.0

Statement of financial position information:

	$m	$m
Non-current assets		595
Current assets		125
		——
Total assets		720
		——
Current liabilities		70
Equity		
Ordinary shares ($1 nominal)	80	
Reserves	410	
	——	
		490
Non-current liabilities		
6% Bank loan	40	
8% Bonds ($100 nominal)	120	
	——	
		160
		——
		720
		——

Financial analysts have forecast that the dividends of Close Co will grow in the future at a rate of 4% per year. This is slightly less than the forecast growth rate of the profit after tax (earnings) of the company, which is 5% per year. The finance director of Close Co thinks that, considering the risk associated with expected earnings growth, an earnings yield of 11% per year can be used for valuation purposes.

Close Co has a cost of equity of 10% per year and a before-tax cost of debt of 7% per year. The 8% bonds will be redeemed at nominal value in six years' time. Close Co pays tax at an annual rate of 30% per year and the ex-dividend share price of the company is $8·50 per share.

Required:

(a)   **Calculate the value of Close Co using the following methods:**

   (i)   **net asset value method**

   (ii)   **dividend growth model**

   (iii)   **earnings yield method.** ⊞   **(5 marks)**

(b)   Calculate the weighted average after-tax cost of capital of Close Co using market values where appropriate. ⊞   (8 marks)

(c)   Discuss the circumstances under which the weighted average cost of capital (WACC) can be used as a discount rate in investment appraisal. Briefly indicate alternative approaches that could be adopted when using the WACC is not appropriate. 💻   (7 marks)

(Total: 20 marks)

 Calculate your allowed time, allocate the time to the separate parts

60   NN CO (DEC 10 – MODIFIED)

The following financial information refers to NN Co:

Current statement of financial position

	$m	$m	$m
Assets			
Non-current assets			101
Current assets			
Inventory		11	
Trade receivables		21	
Cash		10	
		——	42
Total assets			143
Equity and liabilities			
Ordinary share capital		50	
Preference share capital		25	
Retained earnings		19	
		——	
Total equity			94
Non-current liabilities			
Long-term borrowings		20	
Current liabilities			
Trade payables	22		
Other payables	7		
	——		
Total current liabilities		29	
Total liabilities			49
			——
Total equity and liabilities			143

NN Co has just paid a dividend of 66 cents per share and has a cost of equity of 12%. The dividends of the company have grown in recent years by an average rate of 3% per year. The ordinary shares of the company have a nominal value of 50 cents per share and an ex div market value of $8.30 per share.

The long-term borrowings of NN Co consist of 7% bonds that are redeemable in six years' time at their nominal value of $100 per bond. The current ex interest market price of the bonds is $103.50.

The preference shares of NN Co have a nominal value of 50 cents per share and pay an annual dividend of 8%. The ex div market value of the preference shares is 67 cents per share.

NN Co pay profit tax at an annual rate of 25% per year.

Required:

(a) Calculate the equity value of NN Co using the following business valuation methods:

    (i)   the dividend growth model

    (ii)   net asset value. ▦   **(5 marks)**

(b) Calculate the after-tax cost of debt of NN Co. ▦   **(4 marks)**

(c) Calculate the weighted average after-tax cost of capital of NN Co. ▦   **(6 marks)**

(d) Explain the concept of market efficiency and distinguish between strong form efficiency and semi-strong form efficiency. ▭   **(5 marks)**

                                                              (Total: 20 marks)

61 CORHIG CO (JUNE 2012 – MODIFIED)

Corhig Co is a company that is listed on a major stock exchange. The company has struggled to maintain profitability in the last two years due to poor economic conditions in its home country and as a consequence it has decided not to pay a dividend in the current year. However, there are now clear signs of economic recovery and Corhig Co is optimistic that payment of dividends can be resumed in the future. Forecast financial information relating to the company is as follows:

Year	1	2	3
Earnings ($000)	3,000	3,600	4,300
Dividends ($000)	nil	500	1,000

The company is optimistic that earnings and dividends will increase after Year 3 at a constant annual rate of 3% per year.

Corhig Co currently has a before-tax cost of debt of 5% per year and an equity beta of 1.6. On a market value basis, the company is currently financed 75% by equity and 25% by debt.

During the course of the last two years, the company acted to reduce its gearing and was able to redeem a large amount of debt. Since there are now clear signs of economic recovery, Corhig Co plans to raise further debt in order to modernise some of its non-current assets and to support the expected growth in earnings. This additional debt would mean that the capital structure of the company would change and it would be financed 60% by equity and 40% by debt on a market value basis. The before-tax cost of debt of Corhig Co would increase to 6% per year and the equity beta of Corhig Co would increase to 2.

The risk-free rate of return is 4% per year and the equity risk premium is 5% per year. In order to stimulate economic activity the government has reduced profit tax rate for all large companies to 20% per year.

The current average price/earnings ratio of listed companies similar to Corhig Co is 5 times.

Required:

(a) Estimate the value of Corhig Co using the price/earnings ratio method and discuss the usefulness of the variables that you have used. ▦ **(4 marks)**

(b) Calculate the current cost of equity of Corhig Co and, using this value, calculate the value of the company using the dividend valuation model. ▦ **(6 marks)**

(c) Calculate the current weighted average after-tax cost of capital of Corhig Co and the weighted average after-tax cost of capital following the new debt issue, and comment on the difference between the two values. ▦ **(6 marks)**

(d) Discuss how the shareholders of Corhig Co can assess the extent to which they face business risk, explaining the nature of the risk being assessed. ▭ **(4 marks)**

(Total: 20 marks)

62 MAT CO

MAT Co operates a chain of stores selling furniture. It has a successful business model and is seeking to raise additional finance in order to grow further. MAT Co is currently listed on AIM (a secondary market) but the shares in the company are only traded infrequently. The following information for 20X6 refers to MAT Co:

Most recent statement of financial position

	$m	$m
Assets		
Non-current assets		71
Current assets		
Inventory	8	
Trade receivables	11	
Cash	15	
		34
Total assets		105
Equity and liabilities		
Ordinary share capital		40
Retained earnings	27	
Total equity		67
Non-current liabilities		
Long-term borrowings		18
Current liabilities		
Trade payables	20	
Total liabilities		38
Total equity and liabilities		105

MAT Co has paid the following dividends in recent years:

20X4 – 4.1 cents

20X5 – 4.3 cents

20X6 – 4.7 cents

Since the most recent statement of financial position, the company has declared a dividend of 5.0 cents for 20X7 and this will be paid shortly. The ordinary shares of the company have a nominal value of 25 cents and a market value of 66 cents per share. The equity beta of the company is estimated to be 1.15.

Prior to considering potential sources of finance, the directors of MAT Co are keen to gain a better understanding of the value of the company.

The return on government bonds is currently 5% and the equity risk premium is 8%.

Required:

(a)   Calculate the total equity value of MAT Co using the dividend growth model. ▦
                                                                (6 marks)

(b)   Comment on the relevance of the total equity value calculated when compared to the total market value of the equity of the company. 💻   (5 marks)

(c)   Explain the factors the directors of MAT Co should take into account when considering how to raise additional finance. 💻   (9 marks)

                                                        (Total: 20 marks)

63   THP CO (JUNE 08 – MODIFIED)   *Walk in the footsteps of a top tutor*

THP Co is planning to buy CRX Co, a company in the same business sector, and is considering paying cash for the shares of the company. The cash would be raised by THP Co through a 1 for 3 rights issue at a 20% discount to its current share price.

The purchase price of the 1 million issued shares of CRX Co would be equal to the rights issue funds raised, less issue costs of $320,000. Earnings per share of CRX Co at the time of acquisition would be 44.8c per share. As a result of acquiring CRX Co, THP Co expects to gain annual after-tax savings of $96,000.

THP Co maintains a payout ratio of 50% and earnings per share are currently 64c per share. Dividend growth of 5% per year is expected for the foreseeable future and the company has a cost of equity of 12% per year.

Information from THP Co's statement of financial position:

Equity and liabilities	$000
Shares ($1 nominal value)	3,000
Reserves	4,300
	———
	7,300
Non-current liabilities	
8% loan notes	5,000
Current liabilities	2,200
	———
Total equity and liabilities	14,500
	———

Further information:

THP Co

THP Co dividend per share = 32c per share

Share price of THP Co = $4.80

Market capitalisation of THP Co = $14.4m

Price earnings ratio of THP Co = 7.5

Required:

(a)   Assuming the rights issue takes place and ignoring the proposed use of the funds raised, calculate:

(i)   the rights issue price per share

(ii)   the cash raised

(iii) the theoretical ex rights price per share; and

(iv)   the market capitalisation of THP Co.   (5 marks)

(b)   Using the price/earnings ratio method, calculate the share price and market capitalisation of CRX Co before the acquisition.   (3 marks)

(c)   Assuming a semi-strong form efficient capital market, calculate and comment on the post-acquisition market capitalisation of THP Co in the following circumstances:

(i)   THP Co does not announce the expected annual after-tax savings; and

(ii)   the expected after-tax savings are made public.   (5 marks)

(d)   Discuss the factors that THP Co should consider, in its circumstances, in choosing between equity finance and debt finance as a source of finance from which to make a cash offer for CRX Co.   (7 marks)

                                                                    (Total: 20 marks)

64   DARTIG CO (DEC 08 – MODIFIED) *Walk in the footsteps of a top tutor*

Dartig Co is a stock-market listed company that manufactures consumer products and it is planning to expand its existing business. The investment cost of $5 million will be met by a 1 for 4 rights issue. The current share price of Dartig Co is $2.50 per share and the rights issue price will be at a 20% discount to this. The finance director of Dartig Co expects that the expansion of existing business will allow the average growth rate of earnings per share over the last four years to be maintained into the foreseeable future.

The earnings per share and dividends paid by Dartig over the last four years are as follows:

	20X3	20X4	20X5	20X6	20X7
Earnings per share (cents)	27.7	29.0	29.0	30.2	32.4
Dividend per share (cents)	12.8	13.5	13.5	14.5	15.0

Dartig Co has a cost of equity of 10%. The price/earnings ratio of Dartig Co has been approximately constant in recent years. Ignore issue costs.

Required:

(a) Calculate the theoretical ex rights price per share prior to investing in the proposed business expansion. **(3 marks)**

(b) Calculate the expected share price following the proposed business expansion using the price/earnings ratio method. **(3 marks)**

(c) Discuss whether the proposed business expansion is an acceptable use of the finance raised by the rights issue, and evaluate the expected effect on the wealth of the shareholders of Dartig Co. **(5 marks)**

(d) At a recent board meeting of Dartig Co, a non-executive director suggested that the company's remuneration committee should consider scrapping the company's current share option scheme, since executive directors could be rewarded by the scheme even when they did not perform well. A second non-executive director disagreed, saying the problem was that even when directors acted in ways which decreased the agency problem, they might not be rewarded by the share option scheme if the stock market were in decline.

Required:

Explain the nature of the agency problem and discuss the use of share option schemes as a way of reducing the agency problem in a stock-market listed company such as Dartig Co. **(9 marks)**

(Total: 20 marks)

65 PHOBIS (DEC 07 – MODIFIED)

> *Question debrief*

(a) Phobis Co is considering a bid for Danoca Co. Both companies are stock market listed and are in the same business sector. Financial information on Danoca Co, which is shortly to pay its annual dividend, is as follows:

Number of ordinary shares	5 million
Ordinary share price (ex div basis)	$3.30
Earnings per share	40.0c
Proposed payout ratio	60%
Dividend per share one year ago	23.3c
Dividend per share two years ago	22.0c
Equity beta	1.4

Other relevant financial information	
Average sector price/earnings ratio	10
Risk-free rate of return	4.6%
Return on the market	10.6%

Required:

Calculate the value of Danoca Co using the following methods:

(i) price/earnings ratio method

(ii) dividend growth model

and discuss the significance, to Phobis Co, of the values you have calculated, in comparison to the current market value of Danoca Co. **(10 marks)**

(b) Phobis Co has in issue 9% bonds, which are redeemable at their nominal value of $100 in five years' time. Alternatively, each bond may be converted on that date into 20 ordinary shares of the company. The current ordinary share price of Phobis Co is $4.45 and this is expected to grow at a rate of 6.5% per year for the foreseeable future. Phobis Co has a cost of debt of 7% per year.

Required:

Calculate the following current values for each $100 convertible bond:

(i)   **market value**

(ii) **floor value**

(iii) **conversion premium.**   **(6 marks)**

(c) **Discuss the significance to a listed company if the stock market on which its shares are traded is shown to be semi-strong form efficient.**   **(4 marks)**

(Total: 20 marks)

> 🕐 *Calculate your allowed time, allocate the time to the separate parts*

RISK MANAGEMENT – PRACTICE QUESTIONS

66   NEDWEN

> 🕐 *Question debrief*

Nedwen Co is a UK-based company that has the following expected transactions.

One month: Expected receipt of $240,000

One month: Expected payment of $140,000

Three months: Expected receipts of $300,000

The finance manager has collected the following information:

Spot rate ($ per £):   1.7820 ± 0.0002

One-month forward rate ($ per £):   1.7829 ± 0.0003

Three months forward rate ($ per £):   1.7846 ± 0.0004

Money market rates for Nedwen Co:

	Borrowing	Deposit
One year sterling interest rate:	4.9%	4.6%
One year dollar interest rate:	5.4%	5.1%

Assume that it is now 1 April.

Required:

(a)   Discuss the differences between transaction risk, translation risk and economic risk.   **(6 marks)**

(b)   Calculate the expected sterling receipts in one month and in three months using the forward market. ⊞   **(3 marks)**

(c)   Calculate the expected sterling receipts in three months using a money market hedge and recommend whether a forward market hedge or a money market hedge should be used. ⊞   **(5 marks)**

(d)   Discuss how sterling currency futures contracts could be used to hedge the three-month dollar receipt.   **(6 marks)**

                                                                                       (Total: 20 marks)

🕐 *Calculate your allowed time, allocate the time to the separate parts*

---

67   EXPORTERS PLC *Walk in the footsteps of a top tutor*

Exporters plc, a UK company, is due to receive 500,000 Northland dollars in 6 months' time for goods supplied. The company decides to hedge its currency exposure by using the forward market. The short-term interest rate in the UK is 12% per annum and the equivalent rate in Northland is 15%. The spot rate of exchange is 2.5 Northland dollars to the pound.

Required:

(a)   Calculate how much Exporters plc actually gains or losses as a result of the hedging transaction if, at the end of the six months, the pound, in relation to the Northland dollar, has:

(1)   gained 4%

(2)   lost 2% or

(3)   remained stable.

You may assume that the forward rate of exchange simply reflects the interest differential in the two countries (i.e. it reflects the Interest Rate Parity analysis of forward rates). ⊞   **(8 marks)**

(b)   Compare a forward market currency hedge with:

(1)   a currency futures hedge

(2)   a currency options hedge.

Indicate in each of the three cases how the hedging facility is actually provided, the nature of the costs and the potential outcomes of the hedge.   **(12 marks)**

                                                                                       (Total: 20 marks)

---

68 CC CO

CC Co is considering launching a new product. Relevant financial information includes:

Selling price (current price terms)	$12 per unit
Variable costs (current price terms)	$7 per unit
Incremental fixed overhead costs	$250,000 per year

General price inflation is expected to average 4.7% per year over the period. However, the selling price is expected to inflate at 5% per annum, the variable costs to inflate by just 4% per annum, and the fixed costs by 6% per year.

Production and sales are expected to be at the following levels:

Year	1	2	3	4
Units	250,000	500,000	400,000	200,000

To manufacture the new product CC Co will need to purchase a new machine. The only suppliers of this machine are located overseas. If the machine was ordered immediately it would cost €1.5m. Payment must be made in Euros and would be due upon delivery of the machine in three months' time.

CC Co will be able to claim tax allowable depreciation on the investment on a straight line basis over the estimated four-year life of the asset. The company pays tax one year in arrears at a rate of 30% and the asset is not expected to have any scrap value at the end of the project.

The real weighted average cost of capital of CC Co is 5.1%.

The spot exchange rate is 0.70 €/$ and the three-month forward exchange rate is 0.698 €/$. CC Co can earn 2.9% per year on short-term euro deposits and can borrow short term in dollars at 5.5%.

Required:

(a) Calculate the expected dollar payment in three months' time using both a forward market hedge and a money market hedge and recommend whether a forward market hedge or a money market hedge should be used to mitigate the exchange risk on the potential purchase of the machine. ⊞ **(6 marks)**

(b) Based on your recommendation in part (a), calculate the net present value of the proposed investment in three months' time and comment on the project's acceptability. ⊞ **(10 marks)**

(c) Discuss the impact inflation has on exchange rates. 🖳 **(4 marks)**

(Total: 20 marks)

69   PLAM CO (MAR 16 – MODIFIED)

The directors of Plam Co expect that interest rates will fall over the next year and they are looking forward to paying less interest on the company's debt finance. The dollar is the domestic currency of Plam Co. The company has a number of different kinds of debt finance, as follows:

	Loan notes	Loan notes	Bank loan	Overdraft
Denomination	Dollar	Peso	Dollar	Dollar
Nominal value	$20m	300m pesos	$4m	$3m
Interest rate	7% per year	10% per year	8% per year	10% per year
Interest type	Fixed rate	Fixed rate	Variable rate	Variable rate
Interest due	6 months' time	6 months' time	6 months' time	monthly
Redemption	8 years' time at nominal value	8 years' time at nominal value	Instalments	Continuing at current level

The 7% loan notes were issued domestically while the 10% loan notes were issued in a foreign country.

The interest rate on the long-term bank loan is reset to bank base rate plus a fixed percentage at the end of each year. The annual payment on the bank loan consists of interest on the year-end balance plus a capital repayment.

Relevant exchange rates are as follows:

	Offer	Bid
Spot rate (pesos/$)	58.335	58.345
Six-month forward rate (pesos/$)	56.585	56.597

Plam Co can place pesos on deposit at 3% per year and borrow dollars at 10% per year. The company has no cash available for hedging purposes.

Required:

(a)   **Evaluate the risk faced by Plam Co on its peso-denominated interest payment in six months' time and advise how this risk might be hedged.** ⊞   **(5 marks)**

(b)   **Identify and discuss the different kinds of interest rate risk faced by Plam Co.** 💻
                                                                                          (5 marks)

(c)   The dollar denominated loan notes each have a nominal value of $1,000 and are convertible. As an alternative to redemption in eight years, the loan note holders could after seven years convert each loan note into 110 ordinary shares of Plam Co. The ordinary shares of Plam Co are currently trading at $6.50 per share on an ex-dividend basis. The current cost of debt of the convertible loan notes is 8%.

Required:

Justifying any assumptions that you make, calculate the current market value of the loan notes of Plam Co, using future share price increases of:

(i)   **4% per year**

(ii)   **6% per year.** ⊞   **(6 marks)**

(d)   **Discuss the limitations of the dividend growth model as a way of valuing the ordinary shares of a company.** 💻   **(4 marks)**

                                                                                    (Total: 20 marks)

Section A

ANSWERS TO OBJECTIVE TEST QUESTIONS

FINANCIAL MANAGEMENT FUNCTION

1   C

The others are secondary objectives that could be used to help achieve the primary objective.

2   Statements 2, 3 and 5 are financial objectives

Achieving market share (a relative measure), or customer satisfaction (a qualitative measure), are non-financial objectives.

3   B, C and D

Financial management aims to ensure that the money is available to finance profitable projects and to select those projects that the company should undertake. Once profits have been made the decision then needs to be made about how much to distribute to the owners and how much to re-invest for the future. Income decisions are really sub-divisions of the investment decision. Appraisal decisions would be sub-divisions of the investment decision and budget decisions would be performed by management accountants.

4   C and E

C – ROCE is a financial objective. E - this is a financial objective that relates to the level of financial risk that the company is prepared to accept. The other objectives are non-financial.

5   C

Value for money relates to economy (value for money on inputs to the organisation), efficiency (vfm on converting inputs to outputs) and effectiveness (vfm on the outputs). Economy relates to keeping costs down without sacrificing quality, efficiency is about effective resource utilisation (such as decreasing waste levels) and effectiveness relates to the overall objectives of the organisation being achieved.

6   D

All the others are common in the role of a financial manager.

---

7   True, True, True

8   A

A review of overtime spending and apportioning overheads to cost units is typically carried out by a member of the management accounting team. Depreciation of non-current assets is typically carried out by a member of the financial accounting team.

9   A and D

B, C and E are examples of connected stakeholders.

10   C

To facilitate effective management of organisations and to make organisations more visibly accountable to a wider range of stakeholders.

11   C

The separation of ownership and control creates a situation where managers act as the agents of the owners (shareholders).

12   Statements 2 and 3 are correct

The three E's in statement 4 should be economy, efficiency and effectiveness.

13   A and C

Efficiency targets aim to make the most efficient use of the resources available. Paying rates for staff of appropriate levels of qualification is an 'economy' target (B). Customer satisfaction rating is an 'effectiveness' target (D).

14   A, B and D

Managerial reward schemes should be clearly defined and impossible to manipulate. Their targets should align with the aims of shareholders so should be focused on both long- and short-term goals.

15   Is a criticism, Is a criticism, Is a criticism

All three statements are typical criticisms of executive share option schemes.

16   B

Invoices are received from suppliers, not any of the other three stakeholders.

17   A

The Code clearly states that the requirement is for independent non-executive directors, but only one member of the committee (as a minimum) needs have recent and relevant financial experience, not all of them.

18   C

Advising on investments in non-current assets is a key role of financial management.

19   False, True, False, True

It is correct that the agency problem means that shareholder wealth is not being maximised and that cum dividend means the buyer of the share is entitled to receive the dividend shortly to be paid. Value for money means economy, efficiency and effectiveness. The dividend payout ratio compares the dividend to the profit before the dividend.

FINANCIAL MANAGEMENT ENVIRONMENT

20   B

Fiscal policy is implemented through the raising and lowering of taxes and through the raising and lowering of government spending. 1 only is not correct because there is another aspect to fiscal policy other than just taxation. 2 and 3 is not correct because government actions to raise or lower the size of the money supply is an aspect of monetary policy, not fiscal policy. 1, 2, and 3 is not correct because government actions to raise or lower the size of the money supply is an aspect of monetary policy, not fiscal policy.

21   Statements 1 and 3 are correct.

A reverse yield gap is where the yield on debt is greater than that of equities. Statement 4 describes cost-push inflation.

22   Both statements are true

23   C

Governments may choose to run a surplus or a deficit as appropriate.

24   B and D

Statements A, C and E relate to monetary policy.

25   A, B and C

Money markets provide short-term (< 1 year) debt financing and investment. Shares are long-term sources of finance.

26   C

Money markets focus on short term financial instruments. A corporate bond is a long-term source of finance, hence is a capital market instrument.

27   A, B and D

28   A

Primary capital markets relate to the sale of new securities, while secondary capital markets are where securities trade after their initial offering.

29   D

Monetary policy that increases the level of domestic interest rates is likely to raise exchange rates as capital is attracted into the country (statement 1). Any restrictions on the stock of money, or restrictions on credit, will raise the cost of borrowing, making fewer investment projects worthwhile and discouraging expansion by companies (statement 2). Periods of credit control and high interest rates reduce consumer demand (statement 3). Monetary policy is often used to control inflation (statement 4).

30   D

Imperfect competition can be addressed by a competition regulator to prevent consumers being taken advantage of, for instance by a firm with monopoly power. Social costs or externalities can be regulated against by imposing fines on firms that create them, for instance where a factory emits too many greenhouse gases. Imperfect information can be legally addressed by ensuring full disclosure, for instance on the launch of a bid for stock market flotation, so as not to disadvantage purchasers of shares.

31   B and C

It is the secondary market, not the primary market, that deals in 'second-hand' securities. Money markets provide short-term rather than long-term debt finance and investment.

32   Both statements are true

33   C

The audit committee should consist of non-executive directors.

34   C

A balanced budget occurs when total expenditure is matched by total taxation.

35   Both statements are true

36   A, C and D

Certificates of deposits are fully negotiable and hence attractive to the depositor since they ensure instant liquidity if required and are tradeable.

37   C

A stock market listing is likely to involve a significant loss of control to a wider circle of investors.

38   C

One of the principal objectives of macroeconomic policy will typically be to achieve balance of payments equilibrium, not a deficit.

39   A, B and C

Local operating units (decentralised treasury function) should have a better feel for local conditions than head office and can respond more quickly to local developments. This is an advantage of decentralisation. Divisional managers would be more motivated if they had more control over their cash resources.

40   B

A funding gap often arises when SMEs want to expand beyond their available funds but are not yet ready for a listing on the stock market.

41   Money market, stock market, money market, money market

Convertible loan notes are long-term finance and are traded on a stock market. The others are short-term and traded on a money market.

42   C

Decreasing taxation and increasing government expenditure would lead to increased aggregate demand. Decreasing interest rates reduces the incentive to save and so would lead to an increase in aggregate demand.

43   C and D

Financial intermediaries transform maturity and risk.

44   False, True, False, False

It is true that a government may intervene to weaken its country's exchange rate in order to eliminate a balance of payments deficit. The other statements are false.

WORKING CAPITAL MANAGEMENT

45   A

B and D are solutions for long-term cash surpluses. C would assist with a short-term shortage of cash, not a surplus.

46   All three statements are correct

Working capital will naturally increase with sales as more inventory is needed to satisfy demand and more credit is offered to more customers. Payables will also increase, reducing working capital but to a lower degree.

Lengthening of the operating cash cycle will lead to cash being out of the business for longer and more funding therefore needed to cover this.

Overtrading (undercapitalisation) is where the business doesn't have enough cash funding to sustain the level of trading activity.

47   D

Taking longer to pay trade payables would shorten the cash cycle as cash stays with company possession for a longer period of time. Lower net operating cash flows and slower inventory turnovers are signs of a lengthening cash cycle. Depreciation expenditure is a non-cash item and does not affect the cash cycle.

48   17 weeks

	Weeks
Raw materials	6
Payables	(7)
Production	2
Finished goods	6
Receivables	10
	───
	17
	───

49   Current ratio: decrease   Quick ratio: increase

The current liabilities figures used as the denominator will stay the same in both cases. The total of the current assets will decrease because the reduction in the inventory value will be greater than the increase in cash. Therefore, the current ratio will decrease. The total of the liquid assets will increase because of the higher cash balance. Therefore, the quick ratio will increase.

50   C

As there is no new capital and all profits are paid out as dividends, the total of the SFP of 1,250 will not change. The cash balance is therefore a balancing figure to maintain this total after the other changes have been put through.

	$000	$000	Next year	$000	$000
Non-current assets		1,000	⟶		1,000
Current assets					
Inventories	200			400	
Receivables	150			300	
Cash	100			Nil	
	450			700	
Current liabilities					
Overdraft				(50)	
Payables		(200)		(400)	
Net current assets		250			250
		1,250			1,250
Capital		1,250			1,250

51   80

The cash operating cycle = receivables days + inventory holding period – payables days.

The receivables days = 365/average receivables turnover or 365/10.5 = 34.76. The inventory holding period = 365/inventory turnover or 365/4 = 91.25. The payables days = 365/payables turnover ratio = 365/8 = 45.63.

Putting it all together: cash operating cycle = 34.76 + 91.25 – 45.63 = 80.38 days or 80 to the nearest day.

52   A

Receivables days plus inventory holding period minus payables days.

53   B

Inventory = 15,000,000 × 60/360 = $2,500,000

Trade receivables = 27,000,000 × 50/360 = $3,750,000

Trade payables = 15,000,000 × 45/360 = $1,875,000

Net investment required = 2,500,000 + 3,750,000 – 1,875,000 = $4,375,000

54 D

	October $	November $	December $
Total receipts	30,000	15,500	20,500
Total payments	(20,600)	(8,250)	(12,700)
Net cash flow	9,400	7,250	5,800
Balance b/f	500	9,900	17,150
Balance c/f	9,900	17,150	24,950

'Credit sales' under 'Receipts' implies receipts from credit customers.

55 A and C

Checking credit limits once a year is too specific and may not be appropriate, for example, if a customer is known to be struggling. Delaying payments to obtain a 'free' source of finance would be a key aspect of a company's accounts payable policy, not accounts receivable.

56 A, B and F

Bad debt write offs, changes in provisions and losses on disposal are non-cash items.

57 C

Closing receivables days = closing receivables balance/sales × 365 days.

58 A

While overtrading can result in higher inventory and receivables (and payables), resulting in the current ratio increasing in the short term, over the longer term the inevitable drain on cash will result in falling liquidity ratios.

59 A

Customer bargaining power increasing is associated with increased receivables days, not payables days.

60 A and C

The system aims to create a flexible production process that is responsive to the customer's requirements, not an inflexible process (B). With a Just in Time system, although inventory holding costs are close to zero, inventory ordering costs are high, not low as more frequent small deliveries of supplies will be needed (D).

61 B and C

62 D

Working capital management may have an impact on dividend policy, but the other areas will be more significant.

63   **10**

Only the fluctuating element of the inventory balance will need to be financed with the overdraft, i.e. the difference between 120 days' worth and 90 days' worth of inventory – 30 days' worth.

$200m × 30/360 × 0.6 = $10m

64   **Decrease, Increase, No change, No change**

Short-term finance is generally cheaper than long-term finance so finance costs should decrease. Pop Co is moving to an aggressive funding strategy that will increase refinancing risk as short-term financing needs to be renewed more frequently. Interest rate risk is seen on both fixed rate (e.g. risk of underlying rate changing to a more favourable one and the company missing out) and variable rate (e.g. risk of rate moving adversely and company suffering) financing. Overcapitalisation relates to the level of funding rather than the type.

65   **D**

Obsolete inventory is minimised under just-in-time inventory management.

66   **A**

Commercial paper will be issued at a discount and then repaid at nominal value on the settlement date. It is short term and traded on the money market.

67   **A**

For every day reduction, 1/365th less working capital will be needed. Receivables will reduce by 8 days, inventory by 10 days and payables by 5 days.

Reduced receivables = 8/365 × $20,500,000 = $449,300

Reduced inventory = 10/365 × $12,800,000 = $350,685

Reduced payables = 5/365 × $12,800,000 = $175,342

Total net working capital effect = –$449,300 – $350,685 + $175,342 = –$624,643 decrease.

68   **D**

If the discount is accepted, the company must pay $2,462.50 at the end of one month.

Alternatively, the company can effectively borrow the $2,462.50 for an additional two months at a cost of $37.50.

The two-month rate of interest is therefore $37.50/$2,462.5 × 100 = 1.5228%

The annual equivalent rate (AER) is therefore:

$(1 + 0.015228)^6 - 1 = 0.0949$ or 9.49%

Alternatively use the formula:

$(1 + \text{discount/amount left to pay})^{12 / \text{months saved}} - 1$

$= (1 + (1.5/98.5))^{12/2} - 1 = 0.0949$ or 9.49%

69   1,140

The buffer inventory is not needed for the EOQ calculation (it would be included as part of the calculation for total inventory costs).

EOQ = √(2 × Co × D / Ch)

Co = $65, D = 300,000, Ch = $2.50 × 12 = $30 (the period of demand and of the holding costs must match, here both calculated as annual figures).

EOQ = √(2 × $65 × 300,000/$30) = 1,140 units

70   A and D

Statement A is true. The Baumol model assumes cash flows are steady and predictable. If cash flows are more erratic, then the Miller Orr model is better suited as a model. Statement B is false – they both assume that cash is held in either a current account or short-term investments and can easily be switched between the two. Statement C is false. It is the lower limit that is set by management. Statement D is true. Statement E is false. The current account balance is only taken back to the return point when either the higher or lower limit is hit. If these limits are not reached, no attempt will be made to adjust the balance.

71 $28,000

Spread = 3 × [3/4 × transaction cost × variance of cash flows/interest rate]$^{1/3}$

Transaction cost = $25

Variance = standard deviation squared = $3,000^2 = $9,000,000 per day

Interest (over a timescale that matches the variance, i.e. days) = 7.3/365 = 0.02% per day

Spread = 3 × [3/4 × $25 × $9,000,000/0.0002]$^{1/3}$ = $28,348 or $28,000 to the nearest $000

72 $4,000,000

Receivables balance calculation = receivables days × sales/360

Customers who don't take the discount (40%)

Receivables = 75 × $30m × 40%/360 = $2,500,000

Customers who take the discount (60%)

Receivables = 30 × $30m × 60% × 99%/360 = $1,485,000

Total new receivables balance = $2,500,000 + $1,485,000 = $3,985,000

If discount is ignored in calculation for those who take the discount:

Receivables = 30 × $30m ×60% / 360 = $1,500,000

Total new receivables balance = $2,500,000 + $1,500,000 = $4,000,000

Under either calculation, balance to the closest hundred thousand is $4,000,000

INVESTMENT APPRAISAL

73 **$152,000**

Time	Flow	DF@10%	PV
0	(125,000)	1	(125,000)
0	(4,000)	1	(4,000)
2	4,000	0.826	3,304
			125,696

Therefore, contract price @ time 2 × 0.826 = 125,696

Price = 125,696/0.826 = $152,174 or $152,000 to the nearest $000.

74 **C and D**

It is the tax saving on the tax allowable depreciation that is the relevant cash flow, not the depreciation itself. The cost of capital is used for asset replacement decisions. The after tax cost of debt would be used in a lease vs buy decision. The profitability index can be used to rank divisible projects. Government restrictions on bank lending would represent hard capital rationing.

75 **A**

The investment is made on 1 January 20X5, so tax-allowable depreciation can first be set off against profits for the accounting period ended 31 December 20X5. The tax cash saving will therefore be at 31 December 20X5. i.e. time 1.

Time	Date	$	Tax saved ($)	Payment time
0	1 January 20X5	2,000,000		
1	Tax-allowable depreciation	(500,000)	@ 30% = 150,000	1
		1,500,000		
2	31 December 20X6	(350,000)		
		1,150,000	@ 30% = 345,000	2

Present value = ($150,000 × 0.870) + ($345,000 × 0.756) = $391,320

76 **$11,100**

EV of PV of year 1 cash flow: $16,000 × 0.15 + $12,000 × 0.6 − $4,000 × 0.25 = $8,600

EV of PV of year 2 cash flow: $20,000 × 0.75 − $2,000 × 0.25 = $14,500

Total PV = ($12,000) + $8,600 + $14,500 = $11,100

77   12%

(1 + money rate) = (1 + real rate) × (1 + inflation rate)

1.21 = (1 + real rate) × 1.08

Real rate= 12%

78   C

In general, it is possible for a project to have up to as many IRRs as there are sign changes in the cash flows. Since the project's cash flows have two sign changes there can be up to two IRRs. The NPV profile could take various forms depending on the relative magnitudes of the cash flows.

79   Payback period: decrease   Internal rate of return: increase

The payback period will decrease and the IRR increase, because the outflow at time 0 is unaffected by inflation.

Consider a simple project.

Time	Cash flow	Inflation at, say, 10%	Revised cash flow
	$		$
0	(100)	1	(100)
1	(100)	1.1	(110)
2	100	1.12	121
3	100	1.13	133
4	100	1.14	146

Payback period 3 years to 2.7 years

IRR = approx. 17% to approx. 30%

80   B

The internal rate of return (C) and the cost of the initial investment (A) are independent of the risk of the project. The lower the risk of the project, the less (not greater) is the required rate of return (D).

81   Year 5

To work out discounted payback, cash flows must first be discounted at the company rate.

Year	Cash flow	Discount factor	Present value	Cumulative present value
	$		$	$
0	(100,000)	1	(100,000)	(100,000)
1	40,000	0.909	36,360	(63,640)
2	20,000	0.826	16,520	(47,120)
3	30,000	0.751	22,530	(24,590)
4	5,000	0.683	3,415	(21,175)
5	40,000	0.621	24,840	3,665

Discounted payback occurs in year 5.

82   A

Net initial investment = $732,000

The IRR is the interest rate at which the NPV of the investment is zero.

PV of perpetuity = $146,400/r

The IRR is where $146,400/r = $732,000

IRR = $146,400/$732,000 × 100% = 20%

If you selected 25% you in fact assumed that the first inflow is coterminous with the initial investment. If you selected 500% you calculated the $732,000 net investment correctly but your final calculation was 'upside-down'. If you selected 400% you made both of these errors.

83   A, B and F

IRR is based on discounted cash flow principles. It therefore considers all of the cash flows in a project (A), does not include notional accounting costs such as depreciation (B) and it considers the time value of money (F). It is not an absolute measure of return, however, as IRR is expressed as a percentage. It is calculated using linear interpolation, which only provides an estimate of the IRR. It is not useful when liquidity is poor as the timings of cash flows are hidden within the calculation. A project can have a high IRR even if the cash flows are weighted towards the end of the project.

84   B

Tax period	Narrative		Tax saved @ 30%	Timing	DF @ 10%	PV
		$	$			$
y/e 31/12/X2	Cost of asset	90,000				
	Tax allowable depreciation	(22,500)	6,750	1	0.909	6,136
		67,500				
y/e 31/12/X3	Tax allowable depreciation	(16,875)	5,063	2	0.826	4,182
		50,625				
y/e 31/12/X4	Tax allowable depreciation	(12,656)	3,797	3	0.751	2,852
		37,969				
y/e 31/12/X5	Disposal	(25,000)				
	Balancing allowance	12,969	3,891	4	0.683	2,658
		NIL				15,828

85   B

	P	Q	R	S
NPV/$ of capital in restricted period	60/20	40/10	80/30	80/40
	= 3	= 4	= 2.67	= 2

The optimal sequence is QPRS.

86   7,785 units

	Cash flow	10% factor	PV
	$000		$
Time 0 machine	(280)	1	(280,000)
Time 1 – 5 contribution	200	3.791	758,200
Time 1 – 5 fixed costs	(95)	3.791	(360,145)
Positive NPV			118,055

PV of contribution must fall by $118,055

Sales volume must fall by $118,055/758,200 = 15.57%

Fall in sales volume   = 0.1557 × 50,000 = 7,785

87   Before, after

The calculation of payback uses all relevant cash flows, so would be calculated before depreciation (not a cash flow) and after taxation.

88   B

As there are different rates of inflation the 'money approach' must be used, i.e. the cash flows must be inflated at their specific rates and discounted at the money cost of capital.

(1 + Money rate) = (1 + Real rate) × (1 + Inflation rate) = 1.1 × 1.08 = 1.188

89   C

Money cost of capital = [(1.08 × 1.12) – 1] × 100 = 20.96%

Time	t0	t1	t2
	$	$	$
Outlay	(18,000)		
Labour		9,000	9,900
Salvage			5,000
			14,900
20.96% discount factor	1	0.8267	0.6835
Present value	(18,000)	7,440	10,184

NPV = $(376) or $(380) to nearest $10

90   C

	$	Discount factor	$
Time 0	(10,000)	1.000	(10,000)
Time 1	(3,000)	0.909	(2,727)
Time 2	(5,000)	0.826	(4,130)
Time 3	(5,000)	0.751	(3,755)
NPV	(20,612)		

Equivalent annual cost = 20,612/2.487 = $8,288

91   B

	Capital needed at time 0	NPV	NPV/£ needed at time 0	Rank	Invested	NPV
	$	$	$		$	$
Project 1	10,000	30,000	3.0	2	10,000	30,000
Project 2	8,000	25,000	3.125	1	8,000	25,000
Project 3	12,000	30,000	2.5	3	12,000	30,000
Project 4	16,000	36,000	2.25	4 (1/8)	2,000	4,500
					32,000	89,500

92   C

The NPV impact of the initial outflow is unaffected.

The revenue flows will be subject to inflation, but then should be discounted at a money rate that includes this inflation. The net effect is no change in the PV.

The sales proceeds represent a flow of money, not affected by inflation, but this will now be discounted at a higher money rate, lowering the net present value of the project.

93   C and D

The true statements are 'the payback method is based on the project's cash flows' and 'a requirement for early payback can increase a company's liquidity'.

The payback method is based on cash flows whereas the ARR method is based on accounting profit. ARR looks at the project's entire cash flows whereas payback may not. Neither method is related to the cost of capital.

94   False, True, False, False

Sensitivity analysis considers the effect of changing one variable at a time (A). Simulation gives more information about the investment decision but does not point to the correct result of assess the likelihood of a variable changing.

95   A

The tighter the distribution, the lower the standard deviation will be (B). The wider the dispersion, the more risky the situation (C). It is the expected value, not the standard deviation, that is the weighted average of all the possible outcomes (D).

96   D

Under a long-term lease, the lessee is responsible for repairs and maintenance of the leased asset.

97   20%

Operating profit/(D + E) = 2,500/(10,000 + 2,500) × 100 = 20%

98   10%

Initial ROCE = average annual profits before interest and tax/initial capital × 100

Profits = operating cash flows before taxation − depreciation

Depreciation over project life = $65,000 − $10,000 = $55,000

Depreciation per annum = $55,000/4 = $13,750

Average annual profits = $20,000 − $13,750 = $6,250 per annum

Initial ROCE = $6,250/$65,000 × 100 = 9.6% or 10% to nearest whole percentage

BUSINESS FINANCE AND COST OF CAPITAL

99   9.2%

Return per CAPM = Rf + beta (Rm − Rf)

Return = 6% + (0.80 × 4%) = 9.2%

Note: market risk premium − (Rm − Rf)

100   B and E

Bonus issues do not raise any cash. Under the M&M no tax theory, the financing decision is irrelevant. (Their 'with tax' theory did conclude that financing was important and that it should be with as much debt as possible). They concluded that the dividend decision is irrelevant as shareholders would be happy with dividends or capital gains. Therefore, the statement is true only of their with tax theory but not as a whole. Managers/directors decide on dividend amounts. An offer for tender should ensure that all shares on offer are taken up but if the majority tender at a lower price than anticipated, a lower amount of cash will be raised than anticipated.

101   C

The companies are identical except for their gearing and the beta factor of equity shares will increase with the gearing level. The beta of B plc (gearing 80%) is therefore higher than the beta for D plc (gearing 60%), i.e. over 1.22. The beta of C plc (gearing 35%) is higher than the beta for A plc (gearing 30%) and below the beta for D plc. It must therefore be in the range 0.89 to 1.22.

102   Statements 1 and 3 are correct.

Statement 4: gross profit is calculated as gross profit divided by revenue.

103   9.1%

$$Kd = \frac{I\,(1-T)}{D} = \frac{12\times(1-0.30)}{92} = 9.1\%$$

104 C

$$\frac{k=0.18\times(24\times2.50)+(8/92)\times6\times0.92+0.125\times(1-0.30)\times8}{24\times2.50+6\times0.92+8}=16.29$$

105 True, True, True

All three statements are true. As the cost of equity increases, it pushes the WACC up. A higher WACC leads to a lower market value (as future cash flows would be discounted at a higher rate). Debt cost is usually lower then preference share cost as the risk of investing in debt is lower than that of investing in preference shares.

106 27.7%

$$\frac{25.6\times1.16}{280-25.6}+0.16=27.7\%$$

107 B and D

Operating gearing = fixed costs divided by variable costs, so a decrease in the gearing ratio implies a lower proportion of fixed costs. Therefore, C is wrong.

Consider the following example.

	Higher gearing $m	Lower gearing $m
Sales	100	100
Variable costs	(20)	(30)
Fixed costs	(30)	(20)
Profit	50	50
Operating gearing ratio	3/2	2/3

Suppose sales volume, and hence variable costs, fall by 20%.

The profits will be affected as follows.

	$m	$m
Sales	80	80
Variable costs	(16)	(24)
Fixed costs	(30)	(20)
Profit	34	36

With the lower gearing ratio, profits are less affected by the change in volume. D is correct.

A is wrong – profitability is unconnected to gearing. B is correct – profits are less risky, as the example shows above.

108 B

The traditional view is that, as an organisation introduces debt into its capital structure, the weighted average cost of capital will fall, because initially the benefit of cheap debt finance more than outweighs any increases in the cost of equity required to compensate equity holders for higher financial risk. As gearing continues to increase, equity holders will ask for progressively higher returns and eventually this increase will start to outweigh the benefit of cheap debt finance, and the weighted average cost of capital will rise.

109 A

It increases the number of shares without affecting the value of the company, so market price per share and earnings per share will fall. The total market value of the shares will be unaffected so the market value gearing would be unaffected.

110 Cost of equity: increases   WACC: decreases   Total MV: increases

In a perfect capital market, the theories of Modigliani & Miller on gearing apply. In the with tax model, WACC decreases with increased gearing and therefore the market value rises.

111 Financial risk: decreases   operating risk: increases

Financial risk is dependent on the debt/equity ratio. The lower the value of debt in the ratio, the lower the financial risk. This is because of lower interest and repayment commitments relative to the level of profits.

Operating risk is dependent on the ratio of variable costs to fixed costs. The lower the proportion of variable costs (and the higher the proportion of fixed costs), the higher the operating risk. This is because fixed costs do not fluctuate with sales levels whereas variable costs do. With a high proportion of fixed costs, profits will fluctuate more with changes in sales levels. More fluctuation means more risk.

112 Security X is overpriced.   Security Y is underpriced

If security Z is correctly priced, its actual return will be the return predicted by CAPM.

$13.2 = 6 + 1.2 (Rm - 6)$

$13.2 - 6 = 1.2 (Rm - 6)$

$7.2/1.2 + 6 = Rm = 12$

Security X has a beta value of 1.6 and should provide a return of $6 + 1.6 (12 - 6) = 15.6\%$

Security Y has a beta value of 0.9 and should provide a return of $6 + 0.9(12 - 6) = 11.4\%$

Security X does not give a high enough return, so is overpriced. Security Y gives too high a return, so is underpriced.

113 A

Gearing = $[(4,000 \times 1.05) + 6,200 + (2,000 \times 0.8)]/(8,000 \times 2 \times 5) = 12,000/80,000 = 15\%$

114 Systematic risk, financial risk

Systematic risk cannot be diversified; it is linked to market factors that influence all shares in a similar way. Gearing up increases financial risk.

115 False, false

Under M&M (implied by the phrase 'perfect capital markets') with no tax, the WACC is unaffected by gearing, but the cost of equity starts to rise immediately gearing is introduced.

116 B and D

High tax rates mean that there is a larger tax shield on interest payments on debt finance, making debt more attractive. Intangible assets being a low proportion of assets. Debt providers are more likely to lend if there are tangible assets to secure the debt against. If few of the assets are intangible, then more are tangible and hence finance providers will be more willing to lend. With more potential debt providers, gearing is more likely to be high.

117 B

Because of the potential for making gains by conversion, investors are willing to accept a lower coupon rate on the debt.

A   The equity component is not a risk imposed on holders.

B   Convertibles keep holders' options open.

C   Additional payments are not required.

D   They don't have to rank after ordinary debt and even if they did, this would increase their servicing cost.

118 D

A is a result of assuming that a perfect capital market exists; it is not a conclusion.

B is the Gordon growth model.

C contradicts the dividend valuation model, which is not disputed by M&M.

The correct answer is D.

119 A

$\beta e > \beta a$; WACC < Cost of equity calculated using βa; WACC < Cost of equity calculated using βe

$\beta e > \beta a$ because gearing increases equity risk.

Tax relief on debt finance always reduces WACC below the ungeared cost of equity and hence below the geared cost of equity.

120 B

If the company were to automate its production line, its level of fixed costs (e.g. maintenance and depreciation) would increase and its variable costs (notably wage) decrease.

Therefore, operating gearing would increase.

121 B

CAPM can be used to predict the cost of equity. Using an asset beta will predict the ungeared cost of equity. Using the equity beta (geared beta) will predict the geared cost of equity.

122 A

The formula for the required return is ke = risk free rate + beta × (market rate − risk free rate).

123 A

Interest cover measures a company's financial risk, gross profit margin measures operating profitability and return on capital employed measures how efficiently the company is using the funds available.

124 Increase current assets by 100 or decrease current liabilities by 50

For the current ratio to equal 2.0, current assets would need to move to $600 (or up by $100) or current liabilities would need to decrease to $250 (or down by $50). Remember that CA − CL = working capital (500 − 300 = 200).

125 Preference shares are a form of <u>equity</u> capital, which carry <u>higher</u> risk than ordinary shares.

Although they share many features in common with loan capital, preference shares give their holders certain ownership rights in the company, which means that their position is legally very different to that of lenders. Risk wise, from the investor point of view, they are lower risk than ordinary shares and higher risk than debt. From the company point of view, they are higher risk than ordinary shares as they carry a requirement to pay dividends that ordinary shares do not.

126 A

It is the interest yield which is the interest or coupon rate expressed as a percentage of the market price and this is a measure of return on investment for the debt holder (B). It is the total shareholder return ratio which measures the returns to the investor by taking account of dividend income and capital growth (C). It is the dividend per share ratio which helps individual shareholders see how much of the overall dividend payout they are entitled to (D).

127 A and D

The lessor does not retain the risks or rewards of ownership. For long-term leases, there is usually one lease that covers the majority of the useful life of the asset, not many.

128 A

As risk rises, the market value of the security will fall to ensure that investors receive an increased yield.

129 B

Value of a right = ((5m x $8 + 1.25m × $6)/6.25 m − $6) = $1.60

This represents the value of the right to buy 1 new share, but it takes 4 existing shares to get this right, so the right per existing share = $1.60/4 shares = $0.4 per share.

130 C

The maturity gap relates to the fact that using its non-current assets an SME may find it easier to secure long-term finance when it may actually need short- or medium-term finance.

131 $9.80

Current share price = $0.5 × 20 = $10 per share

Rights issue price = $10 × 90/100 = $9 per share

Number of shares in issue = $50m/$10 = 5m

Number of shares to be issued = 5m × 1/4 = 1.25m shares

TERP = (5m × $10 + 1.25m × $9)/6.25m = $9.80 per share.

132 Funding gap

The difference between the finance required to operate an SME and the amount obtained is the funding gap.

133 A

TSR = (change in share price over the period + dividend for the period)/share price at start of period × 100

TSR = ($3.00 − $2.50 + $0.15)/$2.50 × 100 = 26%

134 B

Dividend to be paid = $0.80 × 0.55 = $0.44 per share

Retention ratio = 100% − 55% = 45%

Dividend growth rate g = bre = 45% × 20% = 9% per year

P0 = ex div price = $4.60 − $0.44 = $4.16

Ke = D0 ((1 + g)/P0) + g

Ke = (($0.44 × 1.09)/$4.16) + 0.09 = 20.5%

135 1.4 Times

Contribution = $180,000 – ($100,000 × 70%) = $110,000

Operational gearing = contribution/PBIT = $110,000/$80,000 = 1.375 times or 1.4 times to 1 decimal place.

Alternative calculation to give the same answer: % change in EBIT/% change in revenue

Say revenue rises by 10% to $198,000, what % change is there in EBIT?

70% of cost of sales ($70,000) will also rise by 10%, while the remainder ($30,000) will stay the same, giving a new cost of sale of $30,000 + $70,000 × 1.1 = $107,000.

New EBIT = $198,000 – $107,000 = $91,000, a percentage change of ($91,000 – $80,000)/ $80,000 × 100 = 13.75%

Operational gearing is therefore 13.75/10 = 1.375 times

Either method can be used in the exam

BUSINESS VALUATIONS

136 C

The preferred approach is a good spread of shares, as this minimises the risk in the portfolio and should ensure Mr Mays does achieve something approaching the average return for the market. Strong form efficiency means that Mr Mays cannot do anything to guarantee beating the market – even by insider trading, so options A and D are a waste of time.

137 $92.67

MV = (7 × 5.033) + (105 × 0.547) = $92.67

138 $3.50

Monetary value of return = $3.10 × 1.197 = $3.71

Current share price = $3.71 – $0.21 = $3.50

139 A

The new ex-div market value per share = (4 × $4.10 + $2.50)/5 = $3.78

140 C

Technical analysis, or chartism, is where investors study past share price movements in order to try and predict future ones.

141 $1.39

The period 20X1 to 20X5 covers four years of growth, and the average growth rate 'g' can be calculated as follows

$$(1 + g)^4 = \frac{4,236}{2,200}$$

$1 + g = 1.178$

$g = 17.8\%$

Therefore, PO = $\dfrac{4,236 \times 1.178}{0.25 - 0.178}$ = \$69,306,000

Price per share (50 million shares) = \$1.39

142 A

$g = rb = 0.15 \times 0.7 = 0.105$

$$MV = \frac{D_0(1+g)}{K_e - g} = \frac{50,000,000 \times 1.105}{0.25 - 0.105} = \$381,000,000 \text{ rounded}$$

143 B

	$000
Value of Alpha and Beta combined (210 + 900 + 100) × 18	21,780
Value of Beta on its own 900 × 21	(18,900)
Maximum value of Alpha	2,880

144 B and D

A higher P/E ratio valuation may be justified when the target company has higher growth prospects, not when the bid company does. A higher valuation could also be justified when the target is in an industry/country where the normal P/E ratio is higher than in the industry/country of the bidder. Better-quality assets might also be a reason for offering a price that values the target on a higher P/E. Higher gearing ratios are more likely to reduce the P/E ratio than increase it.

145 Weak form efficient

For the investor to make gains consistently from his policy, he must believe that he is 'one step ahead' of the market, i.e. that published information has not already been incorporated into the market price. Thus, the market can be weak-form efficient at best.

146 $1,247,000

$$PO = d0 \; \frac{(1+g)}{(k_e - g)}$$

$$G = rb = 0.4 \times 15\% = 6\%$$

$$PO = \frac{200,000 \times 1.06}{0.23 - 0.06} = \$1,247,000$$

147 Statement 1: false   Statement 2: true

EMH concerns share prices, not whether good projects exist, so statement 1 is false.

In a strong form market, investors would know the reasons behind any change in dividends, so there would not be any new information content in them. Thus, statement 2 is true.

148 B

Number of shares in issue = 400m + 30m = 430m

Earnings = $(120m + 35m + 4m)

= $159m

EPS = $159m/$430m = $0.370

Price per share = $3.00

P/E ratio = 3.0/0.370

= 8.11

149 $3.44

The geometric average dividend growth rate is (36.0/31.1)1/3 − 1 = 5%

The ex div share price = (36.0 × 1.05)/(0.16 − 0.05) = $3.44

150 B

When the company is being bought for the earnings/cash flow that all of its assets can produce in the future, a price/earnings ratio method or a discounted cash flow technique would be useful (A). Asset-based measures using net realisable values help to identify a minimum, not a maximum, price in a takeover (C). When the company has a highly-skilled workforce, this would not be reflected in the value of the assets within the statement of financial position (D). The correct answer is B – asset valuation models are useful in the situation that a company is going to be purchased to be broken up and its assets sold off.

151 A

Answer B = Value per share

Answer C = Earnings yield

Answer D = Price earnings ratio

152 $4.20

Dividend growth rate = 100 × ((33.6/32) – 1) = 5%

MV = 33.6/(0.13 – 0.05) = $4.20

153 D

Expected share price in three years' time = $3.50 × (1.04)3 = $3.94

Conversion value = $3.94 × 30 = $118.20

Compared with redemption at nominal value of $100, conversion will be preferred.

The current market value will be the present value of future interest payments, plus the present value of the conversion value, discounted at the cost of debt of 5% per year.

Market value of each convertible loan note = [($100 × 6%) × 3yr 5% AF] + ($118.20 × 3yr 5% DF)

= ($6 × 2.723) + ($118.20 × 0.864)

= $118.46

154 $14

They should not accept less than NRV: (30m + 18m + 4m – 2m – 12m – 10m)/2m = $14 per share.

155 D

Theoretical value = 2m/0.08 = $25m

156 $83

Conversion value = $3.60 × 1.05^5 × 25 = $114.87

This is higher than the cash redemption value so should be used in the MV calculation.

MV of loan note is the value that would bring the purchase of the loan note and the receipt of interest and the redemption value to an NPV of $0 when discounted at the investors' discount rate (the pre-tax cost of the note) of 10%. In other words, the MV of the loan note will be equal to the PV of the interest receipts and redemption value.

Discounting at 10%, loan note value = ($3 × 3.791) + ($114.87 × 0.621) = $82.71 ($83 to the nearest $)

157 False, False, True, False

It is correct that the price/earnings ratio is the reciprocal of the earnings yield. The other statements are incorrect.

158 D

It is correct that research has shown that, over time, share prices appear to follow a random walk. Because it is true for weak form efficiency, it is also true for semi-strong and strong-form as they both incorporate weak form efficiency.

159 A and D

Herding is where investors buy or sell shares in a company or sector because many other investors have already done so. Noise traders are those who do not base their decisions on fundamental analysis of company performance and prospects.

Fishing is a distractor and simulation is a term relating to investment appraisal. A stock market bubble is the result of herding behaviour rather than a term to explain why irrational decisions were made.

160 D

The market paradox occurs because in order for markets to be inefficient, investors have to believe that they are inefficient. For instance, a profit seeking investor would not feel that it is worth buying shares that are fairly priced in an efficient market as they would not believe that there is an opportunity to make a gain on those shares.

RISK MANAGEMENT

161 B

Matching refers to the balancing of receipts and payments in the same currency.

162 A

The hedge needs to create a peso liability to match the 500,000 peso future income.

6-month peso borrowing rate = 8/2 = 4%

6-month dollar deposit rate = 3/2 = 1.5%

Dollar value of money market hedge = 500,000 × 1.015/(1.04 × 15) = $32,532 or $32,500

163 Would not provide cover, Would provide cover, Would provide cover, Would provide cover

Leading with the payment eliminates the foreign currency exposure by removing the liability. Borrowing short-term in euros to meet the payment obligation in three months' time matches assets and liabilities and provides cover against the exposure. A forward exchange contract is a popular method of hedging against exposure.

164 Statement 1: false   Statement 2: false

Lagging does not guarantee a lowering of risk. If the exchange rate moves in the opposite direction to what is expected, then the business will suffer as a result.

Matching receipts and payments is a method of reducing the risk of transaction exposure, not translation exposure.

165 UK exporter: gain   Swedish importer: no effect

The Swedish importer is unaffected as he is invoiced in local currency; the UK exporter will gain as more pounds will be received for the kroner.

166 2.0383 $/£

The company has to change £ to $ to buy the machine, and will be offered the lower rate for this conversion, 2.0383.

167 1.4379 €/£

Applying interest rate parity:

Invest £1,000 at 5.75% for three months (0.0575/4) = £1,014.375

Convert £1,000 to € at 1.4415 = €1,441.5

Invest that at 4.75% for three months (0.0475/4) = €1,458.62

Implied forward rate is therefore 1,458.62/1,014.375 = 1.4379

Incorrect answers – not converting the annual rate to the three monthly one

£1,000 becoming £1,057.50

€1,441.50 becoming €1,509.97

Forward rate = 1.4279

Applying wrong interest rates (£/€ mixed up)

1,000 × (1 + 0.0475/4) = 1,011.88

1,441.50 × (1 + 0.0575/4) = 1,462.22

Forward rate = 1.4451

1,000 × 1.0475 = 1,047.5

1,441.50 × 1.0575 = 1,524.39

Forward rate = 1.4553

168 The missing word is basis

169 B

Once purchased, the close out date is already set for currency futures. Forward contracts are binding and will not be allowed to lapse by the bank. Options are paid for when they are taken on. They may never be exercised.

170 Exercise, let it lapse

(1) The investor can buy £500,000 for US$950,000 compared to US$975,000 on the spot market.

(2) The investor can sell the £400,000 for S$1,160,000 compared to S$1,180,000 on the spot market.

The call option should be exercised but the put option should not be exercised.

171 Eady plc: loss   Canadian supplier: no effect

The Canadian supplier is unaffected as it invoices in its local currency, the Canadian dollar. It will receive the same number of Canadian $ regardless of any movements of the C$ against the £. Eady plc will have to pay more £ to purchase the C$ payable, so will suffer a loss on the weakening of sterling.

172 True and True

Overseas customers will find the country's goods cheaper, thus boosting exports. On the other hand, imported raw materials will become more expensive resulting in inflationary pressure.

173 A

A contract that gives one party the right to sell a stock at a certain price and the other party an obligation to buy the asset at that price, on or before a specific date in the future, is a put option. A contract that gives one party the right to buy a stock at a certain price and the other party an obligation to sell the asset at that price, on or before a specific date in the future, is a call option.

174 A   Both statements are true

175 B

If you sell a futures contract you have a contract to borrow money (not lend). What you are selling is the contract to make interest payments.

176 C

Flat yield theory does not influence the yield curve.

177 B

The relationship between time to maturity and bond interest rates.

178 B

A put option gives the holder the right to sell currency.

179 B

The normal yield curve slopes upward to reflect increasing compensation to investors for being unable to use their cash now.

180 D

Inflation rates are not relevant to Interest Rate Parity theory (they are relevant to Purchasing Power Parity Theory).

181 C

Basis risk is the possibility that movements in the currency futures price and spot price will be different. It is one of the reasons for an imperfect currency futures hedge.

182 B

1: (1.04 × 1.05/1.02) − 1 = 7.06%

2: 1.5 dinar × 1.02/1.05 = 1.4571 dinar/$

3: Y real rate = (1.04/1.02) − 1 = 1.96%, X real rate = (1.0706/1.05) − 1 = 1.96%

183 1.62

Six-month country Y interest rate = 1%/2 = 0.5%

Six-month country X interest rate = 3%/2 = 1.5%

Forward rate = spot rate × (1 + foreign country interest rate)/(1 + home currency interest rate).

Because the rate is quoted in pesos per $, pesos is the foreign currency and $ is the home currency.

Forward rate = 1.60 × (1.015/1.005) = 1.62 pesos per $

184 Incorrect, Correct, Incorrect, Incorrect

It is correct that the cost of an interest rate floor is higher than the cost of an interest rate collar. The other statements are incorrect.

185 4-9 FRA with a rate fixed at 4.0%

The start date of the FRA should be in 4 months' time when the borrowing will be required and it should end in 9 months when the borrowing will finish. As it is a borrowing, the larger of the spread of rates will be offered by the bank.

186 5,181

The forward rates provided have the counter currency as Japanese yen and the base currency (always the currency stated as a value of 1) of New Zealand dollars. When choosing a rate, it can be useful to work out what the bank is doing with the counter currency, as with this currency it will buy high and sell low.

Here, Plum Co will need to purchase the counter currency, Yen, in order to make the payment in yen. This means the bank is selling the counter currency and will offer the low rate of the spread.

Yen 400,000/77.2 = 5181 New Zealand dollars to the nearest dollar.

Section B

ANSWERS TO OBJECTIVE TEST CASE STUDY QUESTIONS

FINANCIAL MANAGEMENT FUNCTION AND ENVIRONMENT

1   COUNTRY A

    (a)   B and D

        A is false – MM suggested that the pattern of dividends was irrelevant.

        B is true – the fear that many shareholders will view the cut similarly is the clientele effect.

        C is false – residual theory suggests undertaking all investments before paying a dividend.

        D is true – the cut in dividend may signal to shareholders that the company is now higher risk.

    (b)   B

        PPPT suggests that exchange rates will move to compensate for differences in inflation rates.

    (c)   B and D

        A is false – profits have a poor correlation with shareholder value, so it is possible to boost short-term profit at the expense of shareholder wealth.

        B is true.

        C is false – the sackings may generate bad publicity that erodes investor confidence and hence reduces the share price.

        D is true.

    (d)   B

        Statement (i) is true – controlling the money supply has more impact on demand for goods, than, say, the oil price or wage demands.

        Statement (ii) is true – restricting the money supply will reduce the availability of funds and increase the cost of funds.

        Statement (iii) is false – restricting the money supply is part of monetary policy.

(e)   **C**

A is true – this is known as economic inefficiency.

B is true – the lack of competition means monopolies can make excessive profits without having to spend on new products or processes.

C is false – monopolies are more likely to engage in price discrimination to boost profits.

D is true – monopolies may charge high prices to deter entrants.

2   ARKWRIGHT CO

(a)   **8.8%**

$g = (D_0 / D_n)^{1/n} - 1$

$g = (\$0.21/\$0.15)^{1/4} - 1$

$g = 0.0878$ or 8.8%

(b)   **B and D**

Monetary policy aims to control the economy by using interest rates and amending the size of the money supply.

Fiscal policy aims to manage the economy using taxation and government spending.

If inflation is high due to rising aggregate demand then increasing interest rates rather than cutting them is a way of trying to supress and reduce demand (as saving becomes more attractive and borrowing to spend less attractive).

Increased government borrowing leads to increased government spending, meaning less need for business investment. It also raises interest rates, making it harder for businesses to borrow and invest.

(c)   **A**

If the budget deficit is increasing then government spending exceeds government taxation income and if this is the case then government borrowing will also be rising. If government spending is rising more than taxation income then the deficit will be growing.

(d)   **B and F**

EPS uses earnings after taxation and so would fall. ROCE uses profits before interest and taxation so would not initially be affected.

(e)   **B**

Both statements are true. Externalities do not affect the producer or consumer of the product but affect other members of society.

Because it doesn't affect them directly, producers and consumers often ignore externalities and end up producing/buying more of products with external costs and fewer of those with external benefits – a misallocation of resources.

WORKING CAPITAL MANAGEMENT

3   GREEN CO

(a)   Is an assumption, Is not an assumption

Demand has to be constant so that average inventory is half of the order quantity. As long as the lead-time is constant and known, this is sufficient for the EOQ formula to hold; it does not have to be zero.

(b)   40 units

$C_o = \$10$; $D = 4,000$; $C_h = \$2 + 10\%$ of $\$480 = \$50$

$EOQ = \sqrt{(2 \times C_o \times D \div C_h)} = \sqrt{(2 \times 10 \times 4,000 \div 50)} = 40$ units

The alternative answers come from either ignoring the cost of capital tied up in inventory or including the irrelevant chief buyer's salary (or both).

(c)   77 units

The company must be sure that there is sufficient inventory on hand when it places an order to last the weeks' lead-time. It must therefore place an order when there is one weeks' worth of demand in inventory:

i.e. re-order level = $1/52 \times 4,000 =$ **77 units** remaining in inventory.

(d)   B

With deliveries being made on a daily (or more frequent) basis, ordering costs need to be low compared to the benefits of holding inventory. Under the EOQ model, holding costs and ordering costs are balanced off, with the EOQ being at the point where these are equal to each other.

Periodic review means ordering inventory at a fixed and regular time interval. Inventory levels are reviewed at a fixed time. The inventory in hand is then made up to a predetermined level.

Statements (1) and (3) are correct.

(e)   D

One of the earliest American firms to adopt JIT was Hewlett Packard who put forward all of these, based on a study of four of their divisions.

4   HALL CO

(a)   Would influence, Would influence, Would influence, Would not influence

Supplier's terms help determine credit policy in respect of accounts payable, rather than accounts receivable.

(b) $14,400

Sales $1,600,000; business sales = 60% of $1.6m - $960,000

Receivables = $(0.4 \times 1/12 + 0.4 \times 2/12 + 0.2 \times 3/12) \times \$960,000 = \$144,000$

Interest costs = 10% of $144,000 = $14,400

Incorrect answers may come from taking costs of sales into account and reducing the time by which payment has been brought forward by a month.

(c) **A**

Monthly cost = [(100 ÷ 98.5) – 1] × 100 = 1.523%

Bringing payments forward 1 month has an annual cost of $(1.01523^{12} - 1) \times 100 = 19.89\%$

Bringing payments forward 2 months has an annual cost of $(1.01523^{6} - 1) \times 100 = 9.49\%$

Alternative answers come from confusing current receivables periods and reduction of receivables periods and reducing the time by which payment has been brought forward by a month.

Tutorial note

The IRR of a project that involves bringing forward the date of receipt of cash from a customer can be seen by looking at the comparative cash flows.

Time	0	month 1	month 2
No discount	–	–	*100*
With discount	–	*98.5*	–
Subtracting	–	*(98.5)*	*100*

An extra $1.50 is being made on an 'investment' of $98.50 by a customer, a return over the month of 1.523 per month, or 19.89 per annum.

(d) **D**

Under debt factoring the customer will be aware that a factor is being used as the payment details on the invoice will be for the factor. Under invoice discounting this is not the case and the customer will be unaware that invoice discounting is being used.

Invoice discounters lend money using the business's receivables assets as security. Debt factors effectively purchase the receivables assets from the business.

(e) **B**

The list (excluding B) has appeared in a model answer from the ACCA of roles of a credit control department. The second option would be part of the role of a purchase ledger department.

5 **JEEPS CO**

(a) **A**

To calculate the benefit of paying less money, we can use the formula [1 + (discount/amount left to pay)]$^{(360/\text{days earlier payment is made})} - 1$

For the invoices currently paid at 60 days, payment will be made 45 days earlier and the annual saving is $[1 + (2/98)]^{(360/45)} - 1 = 0.175$ or 17.5%

For the invoices currently paid at 90 days, payment will be made 75 days earlier and the annual saving is $[1 + (2/98)]^{(360/75)} - 1 = 0.102$ or 10.2%

These figures need to be compared to the cost of capital, which is 12%.

The benefit of the cash saved on the 60 day payment is 17.5%, but the cost (of the increased funding needed due to the lower payables balance) is 12%. This means the settlement discount should be accepted.

The benefit of the cash saved on the 90 day payment is only 10.2%, which is lower than the cost of extra working capital funding needed at 12%, so this discount would not be worthwhile.

Tutorial note

Marginally different annual returns are reached (17.8% and 10.2%) if the periods of the 'investment' are taken as 1½ months and 2½ months, but the conclusion is the same.

(b)   67 days

Total payables = $2m + $3m × 2 + $4m × 3 = $20m

Total credit purchases = ($2m + $3m + $4m) × 12 = $108m

Payables period = $20m ÷ $108m × 360 = 67 days

Tutorial note

30 days per month = 360 days per year for the calculation.

A weighted average of payables would also give the correct figure of 67.

(c)   B

Increasing shareholder funds suggests a business that is aware of an increasing need for extra capital as it expands and that shareholders understand that need.

(d) $6,300

Monthly rate = $(1.12^{(1/12)} - 1) \times 100 = 0.95\%$

$$\text{PV of instalments} = 75 + \frac{45}{1.0095^1} + \frac{45}{1.0095^2} + \frac{45}{1.0095^3} + \frac{45}{1.0095^4} + \frac{45}{1.0095^5} = \$293,727$$

Paying by instalments will save Jeeps Co $6,273 compared to paying $300,000 immediately (or $6,300 to the nearest $00).

(e)   Aggressive, Aggressive

Aggressive policies make use of short term, risky funding rather than long-term, secure funding. Payables are a source of short-term funding.

6 KING CO

(a) C

Baumol tranche size = √(2 × $500 × $1,000,000 ÷ 0.05) = $141,421

Alternative answers arise from not entering the interest rate as a decimal or using total demand for cash rather than annual demand.

(b) D

Miller-Orr spread = 3 × (¾ × $7,000² × $500 ÷ (0.05/365))^{1/3} = $153,569

Alternative answers come from using standard deviation instead of variance or not calculating a daily interest rate from the annual one given.

(c) $211,200

Month	3	4	5	6	7
Sales volume (000s)	10	11	13	16	20
Sales revenue ($000)	240	264	312	384	480
Cash sales (20%)	48.0	52.8	62.4	76.8	96
Receivables:					
1-month (25% of 80%)	–	48.0	52.8	62.4	76.8
2-month (50% of 80%)	–	–	96.0	105.6	124.8
3-month (25% of 80%)	–	–	–	48.0	52.8
			211.2		

The alternative answers come from not spotting that credit sales are only 80% of total sales and from getting the months muddled.

Tutorial note

The calculations for months other than Month 5 are not essential but tend to reduce the chance of making mistakes (although, without the need for calculations of payments, Months 6 and 7 could be ignored).

(d) Both statements are true.

(e) C

Divisional responsibility for cash will be reduced as the responsibility will be held centrally.

7   GRUMPY CO

(a)   B

$$\text{Receivables period} = \frac{85{,}000}{480{,}000} \times 365 = 65 \text{ days}$$

(b)   52 days

$$\text{Payables period} = \frac{30{,}000}{212{,}000} \times 365 = 52 \text{ days}$$

(c)   B

$$\text{Inventory holding period} = \frac{52{,}000}{226{,}000} \times 365 = 84 \text{ days}$$

The cost of sales of £226,000 is equal to 45,000 + 233,000 – 52,000

(d)   112 days

The start of the cycle is the point at which the supplier is paid. This is on 25/02/15.

The end point of the cycle is the date on which Grumpy receives the payment from the debtor. The goods were delivered 21 days after the order on 07/02/15. They were sold 62 days later on 10/04/15. The debtor then took 68 days to pay (the offered credit is irrelevant) and so Grumpy was paid on 17/06/15.

The number of days between 25/2/15 and 17/6/15 is the operating cycle for cycle X and this is 112 days.

Alternatively, from the delivery (and invoice) date from the supplier on 07/02/15, the payables days (until 25/02/15) comes to 18 days. Add together the inventory days of 62 and the receivables days of 68 and deduct the payables days of 18 to get to the 112 days of the cycle.

(e)   True, True

A period of strong growth when a business has a long operating cycle is a classic example of over trading.

New businesses tend to struggle to get credit from suppliers and often have to give longer credit to customers for fear of breaking a new and fragile relationship with them.

INVESTMENT APPRAISAL

8   BELL CO

(a)   A

Money cost of capital = (1.05 × 1.02) – 1 = 7.1%

(b)   Cash flow = $120,000 × 1.04^3 = $134,984

Present value = $134,984 ÷ 1.08^4 = $99,217

Answer to the nearest thousand dollars is **$99,000**

(c) D

Time	0	1	2	3
	$000	$000	$000	$000
Inflow (in money terms)	–	2,040	3,121	2,122
Outflow (in money terms)	(1,000)	(1,854)	(2,652)	(1,639)
Net cash flow	(1,000)	186	469	483
Present value at 9%	(1,000)	171	395	373

NPV = $(61,000)

Answer A has discounted current cash flows at the rates of inflation rather than at the money cost of capital, answer B has ignored inflation and answer C has only used one year of inflation for the cash flows at times 2 and 3.

Tutorial note

This final mistake is easy to make; anyone who thought C was correct needs to check how the money cash flows in the model answer were calculated (the figures have been rounded to the nearest $'000 in the workings).

(d) B

A is incorrect. There is no decision rule with simulations. B is a clear advantage that simulations have over sensitivity analysis. C is incorrect. The input variables and distributions are estimates. D has some validity potentially, but is not necessarily the case.

(e) The **answer is yes** and the **reason is that it will happen if the rate of inflation exceeds the money cost of capital.**

This was a situation that was highlighted by Brian Carsberg and Tony Hope in the 1970s (a time of high inflation) in their book Business Investment Decisions under Inflation, ICAEW, 1976. With the current state of low interest rates, the situation may be just as relevant today.

Reason A is not correct, the only negative discount rate that makes calculating an NPV tricky is -100%. Tutorial note: You may wish use a spreadsheet to calculate the NPV of a simple project for a range of discount rates from −200% to +200%.

Reason B is not correct since there have been many instances of negative interest rates. The European Central Bank recently introduced negative rates, which have also been seen in Sweden, Denmark and Switzerland.

Reason C is not correct since deflation (negative inflation) is likely to increase the chance of having a positive real discount rate (unless your money cost of capital is even more negative).

9   CARE CO

(a)   **$228,000**

Negative NPV ($000) = ($540 + $47 × 2.487 − ($120 ÷ 1.10^3)) = $566.731

Equivalent annual cost = $566.731 ÷ 2.487 = $227.875, say $228,000

Answers A and C do not find an equivalent annual cost since they do not divide by an annuity factor, merely divide by 3 (or 4). Answers A and B assume the project lasts four years rather than three.

(b)   **Both statements are correct.**

The EAC method assumes that the operating efficiency of the machines will be similar. The method also assumes that the assets will be replaced in perpetuity, or at least into the foreseeable future.

(c)   **C**

Scrap value	Probability		Expected value
$120,000	0.6 × 0.7	= 0.42	50,400
£108,000	0.4 × 0.7 + 0.6 × 0.3	= 0.46	49,680
$96,000	0.4 × 0.3	= 0.12	11,520
		1.00	$111,600

Answers B and D ignore joint probabilities; whereas answers A and B misinterpret the effects of a strong dollar (a strong dollar would make an overseas sale less attractive).

(d)   **Only statement 2 is true.**

Simulation will not eliminate the effects of risk, it will merely help quantify the effects by producing a range of possible NPVs and an idea of the probability distribution of those NPVs.

(e)   **B**

Using the 'lowest common multiple' approach (12 years) is an alternative to simple replacement decisions.

10   EASTER CO

(a)   **False, False, True, False**

Hard rationing is the limit on the amount of finance imposed by the lending institutions. Soft rationing may arise as a means of controlling divisional managers.

(b)   **A and E**

Project	NPV	Investment	NPV/$	Rank
	$000	$000	$	
A	4,900	3,200	1.53	2nd
B	7,400	9,320	0.80	5th
C	5,900	7,300	0.81	4th
D	7,500	5,200	1.44	3rd
E	9,000	5,600	1.61	1st

Total investment required is $30.62m, total available is $10m.

Possible combinations (assuming that will give a higher NPV than any single project):

Project A and D NPV ($000) = 4,900 + 7,500 = 12,400

Projects A and E NPV ($000) = 4,900 + 9,000 = 13,900

These are higher than the NPVs of any single project.

(c) **A**

Based on the workings of the previous question, now the combination A and E is not possible (since they are mutually exclusive). This leaves the highest NPV as combination A and D.

(d) **B**

Using the previous NPV/$ calculations and rankings, the combination accepted must be A plus E plus a portion of D.

Tutorial note

To reach the correct answer to this question, it doesn't matter what proportion of D is required, the answer to the correct option of the four is Option B. The next calculation is therefore unnecessary.

Projects A and E require a total investment of $8.8m, leaving $1.2m to invest in part of Project D. Since Project D requires a total investment of $5.2m, the proportion of that project undertaken can be:

1.2m ÷ 5.2m = 3/13 (as in Option B) or 23.1%

(e) **A and E**

The NPV at a discount rate of zero (the net undiscounted cash flows) is negative at $(30,000), which may cause confusion as the board members may feel that it could therefore never earn a positive NPV.

This project has two 'changes in sign' in the pattern of cash flows, therefore may have two positive IRRs.

The NPV at an infinitely high discount rate (the initial investment) is $(4,000,000).

The NPV at 10% is − $4m + [$8.8m ÷ 1.10] − [$4.83m ÷ 1.10^2], i.e. $8,264, therefore the project can actually earn a positive NPV.

This indicates that there is likely to be an IRR between 0 and 10% and between 10% and infinity. Trial and error, or elementary algebra, can show that the two positive IRRs are 5% and 15%. These are shown on two graphs shown below, one for discount rates over a reasonable range and one for a much larger range of rates, some of which have little practical significance.

Graphs of NPV (in $00,000) against discount rate for a project.

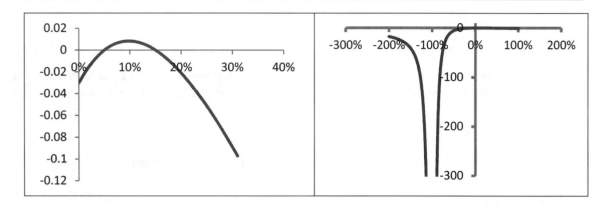

Tutorial note

The second graph shows that strange things happen with a rate of –100%.

These graphs can be compared with those for a conventional project (investing $4m at time 0 and receiving $3m at time 1 and time 2).

11 ACE CO

(a) **B**

NPV of project

Time	Description	CF	DF @ 12%	PV $
0	Loose tools	(6,000)	1	(6,000)
1–4	Contribution	25,000	3.037	75,925
1–4	Allocated overhead	0		0
2–5	Tax on contribution	(6,250)	2.712	(16,950)
	NPV			52,975

The allocated overhead is not a relevant cash flow.

(b) **C**

Statement (1) is true. The pattern of cash flows can affect this decision, for example, for projects where positive cash flows arise first with negative cash flows thereafter then the statement would be false.

(c) **C**

The reported profits are not affected by tax-allowable depreciation. The current NPV is positive and would be made more positive by the extra tax savings so the decision would not alter.

(d)   2.9 months

The payback period is

In the first year the project spends 6,000 but receives 25,000. The tax flow does not arise until the following year. So the payback is (6000/25000) × 12 months = 2.9 months.

(e)   True, True, False

One of payback's problems is the lack of a clear decision criterion.

12   FENCE CO

(a)   2.75 years

Payback period = 2 + (1,200/1,600) = 2.75 years.

(b)   26.0%

Average annual accounting profit = (Total operating cash flows – total depreciation)/ life of project

= (5,880 – 3,800)/4 = $520,000 per year

Average investment = (3,900 + 100)/2 = $2,000,000

ROCE = 100 × 520/2,000 = 26%

(c)   C and D

Risk can be taken into account by shortening the required payback period, meaning that only those cash flows closer to the present (and thus less risky) are considered. Payback period ignores the timing of cash flows within the payback period is correct.

(d)   D

All the statements are correct.

(e)   C

Introducing a share option scheme would help bring directors' objectives in line with shareholders' objectives and linking financial rewards to a target return on capital employed will encourage short-term profitability and discourage capital investment are correct. Executive directors' pay in a listed company should be subject to the recommendations of a remuneration committee made up wholly of independent non-executive directors.

13   LINK CO

(a)   13.2%

$511/$3,880 × 100 = 13.2%

(b)   A

Sensitivity Analysis does not assess the risk of a project (probability analysis does).

(c)   C

Annual operating cash flow = $729,000

Annual depreciation = $1,800,000/4 = $450,000

Annual profit = operating cash flows – depreciation = $729,000 – $450,000 = $279,000

Average investment = $1,800,000/2 = $900,000

ROCE = $279,000/$900,000 × 100 = 31%

(d)   C

A new issue of loan notes takes place in the primary market.

(e)   Correct, Correct, Correct

All three statements are correct.

14   GAIMETT CO

(a)   D

As the projects are divisible, the profitability index (NPV/$ invested) should be calculated to rank the projects and the cash allocated in order of the ranking.

Project	NPV	Investment value	Profitability index	Ranking
	$000	$000		
A	125	375	0.33	2
B	240	800	0.3	3
C	80	400	0.2	5
D	40	50	0.8	1
E	150	600	0.25	4

Of the $1.5 million, cash can be allocated to projects D, A and B in full, with $275,000 left for the fourth ranked project, E.

(275/600) 45.8% of project E can be done with this remaining cash.

(b)   C

The projects are now indivisible so cannot be done in part. The optimum combination can be found by looking at all possible combinations and choosing the one with the highest NPV. For example:

B, C and D would generate $360,000

C, D and E would generate $270,000

B, D and E would generate $430,000

B, C, D and E is not a possible combination as it would use too much investment cash.

(c)   C and D

Soft capital rationing comes from internal decisions, such as managers believing that better quality projects will become available or because they wish to hold onto some cash to provide against unexpected expenditure (the precautionary motive). Answers A, B and E relate to external factors and therefore relate to hard capital rationing.

(d)   A and D

The cash is only available for investment over a 3 month period and will be needed at that point to invest in the new project. This means that long-term investments are unsuitable and high risk investments, where come or all of the cash may be lost, should be avoided. Investments where Gaimett Co may struggle to return the cash should also be avoided.

Certificates of deposit and instant access bank accounts would both be suitable under these circumstances. Listed company shares would be too risky, as the share prices could fall and the entire cash may not be returned. Listed company debt would also suffer from this risk. Unlisted company shares may be difficult to sell, meaning that cash isn't returned back in time. Their value could also fall.

(e)   C

Tax allowable depreciation is not a cash flow and should not be included. All the others do involve payments or receipts of cash, so would be included. Note that any tax savings in relation to the tax allowable depreciation would affect the amount paid for tax and therefore would be included.

BUSINESS FINANCE AND COST OF CAPITAL

15   BRASH CO

(a)   True, False

Leasing companies sometimes pass the obligation for maintenance back to the lessee, as everything is negotiable.

(b)   A and D

Both calculations will discount the relevant cash flows at the post-tax cost of borrowing, which accounts for the cost of any interest payments. This means that to include the interest payments themselves would be double counting, so they would not be included. The saving on maintenance, residual value and tax –allowable depreciation all apply to one option and not the other and so would need to be included to make a comparison between the two options. The cash benefits arising from use of the machinery should be the same under either option so do not need to be considered.

(c)   B

Years 1 – 5 maintenance of $20,000 and years 2 – 6 tax savings on the maintenance costs discounted at 6% discount rate.

Annuity factor 5 years at 6% = 4.212

$(20,000) × 4.212 = $(84,240)

$20,000 × 25% × 4.212 × 0.943 = $19,860

Net PV = $(64,380)

(d) **$145,000**

5 lease payments made at start of year from time period 0 to time period 4. First tax computation at end of year, at time period 1. First tax saving 1 year in arrears at time period 2. Tax savings over 5 years from time period 2 to time period 6.

Years 2 – 6 tax relief of $146,000 × 0.25 = $36,500 discounted at 6% post-tax discount rate.

$36,500 × 4.212 × 0.943 = $144,975

(e) **True, true**

If the PV of leasing is cheaper than the PV of purchasing then a project NPV will increase through the use of a lease as opposed to purchasing an asset, so could potentially rise from negative to positive. The existence of a lease will represent extra risk for shareholders that may be perceived by them, due to the legal commitments for cash payments that come with the lease.

16 KELVIN CO

(a) **$19.60**

The TERP value is calculated as:

$$TERP = \frac{MV \text{ of existing shares} + \text{proceeds from issue}}{\text{Number of shares after issue}}$$

$$TERP = \frac{(4m \times \$20) + (1m \times 20 \times 0.9)}{5m}$$

TERP = $19.60 per share

(b) **C**

Whilst the TERP would fall, it could not do so to the detriment of existing shareholders. In the formula above, the top line would remain the same whilst the number of shares on the bottom line would increase.

(c) **True, True**

Both the statements are true. The discount makes the rights offer appear more attractive but the theory indicates it should make no difference to the accepting shareholder.

(d) **C**

As long as the shareholder takes some form of action they will be better off than doing nothing. The second worst action (by the way) is D as the shareholder will lose out on 50% of the offer.

(e) **A**

Dilution occurs if a shareholders % ownership reduces. This will not happen if a shareholder takes up 100% of the offer.

17 DOMINANCE CO

(a) D

All the other options will involve at least the risk of new shareholders diluting ownership.

(b) D

Option A has no new tax shield at all as preference dividend does not attract it. Option B does contain tax shield but presumably less than C and D given the lower value and interest rate. Option C has less interest on it and hence tax shield than D.

(c) 14.4%

The cost of equity formula is:

$$Ke = \frac{D_1}{P0} + g \quad \text{(where P0 is the ex div price of the shares)}$$

$$Ke = \frac{16 \times 1.10}{420 - 16} + 0.10$$

$$Ke = 14.4\%$$

(d) 3.75%

The cost of debt formula is:

$$Kd = \frac{\text{Interest } (1 - t)}{P0}$$

$$Kd = \frac{4(1 - 0.25)}{80}$$

$$Kd = 3.75\%$$

(e) D

The tax shield is relevant but is minor when one considers the risk premium is approximately 10.4%.

The main driver for risk premium is systematic risk. All the specific risk will be ignored by the well-diversified shareholder.

18 EMPIRE CO

(a) C

Dividend irrelevancy theory states that shareholders wish to increase their wealth but are indifferent as to whether it comes from dividends received or through a rise in the share price. Companies should therefore focus on project value rather than the pattern of dividend payments.

(b) B

The signalling effect is where changes in dividend patterns can affect the investors' view of the business.

(c)   A

Dividend dependency suggests that investors have invested because of the current pattern of dividends and a change in that pattern will upset that and negate their reasons for investing.

(d)   D

Company liquidity issues mean that the company should only pay out what it can afford or offer a non-cash alternative instead.

(e)   False, True

A scrip issue gives more shares to shareholders but since the overall market value is not affected then the share price falls. The shareholder does not gain except for an increased marketability.

19   BANK

(a)   C and E

A bank is rather unusual in that many of the variables that would normally be counted as systematic risks for other businesses are in fact specific risks for the bank. Interest rates and defaults fall into this category. Equally, the bank will compete for loans in the market and so that too is a specific risk.

(b)   C

The rate of return on government securities is an appropriate figure to use as a risk free rate as government securities should be amongst the lowest risk of all. The calculation is from the investor point of view, so the rate should not be adjusted for tax savings by the company.

(c)   "In the CAPM formula $R = Rf + \beta j(Rm - Rf)$ where βj represents the project beta, R represents **the required return on the new project** and the market risk premium is represented by **(Rm – Rf)**."

The CAPM gives you the required return of equity shareholders for the level of risk indicated by the value of the beta used, therefore if the beta is that of the project then the R value is the return required for the project. The market risk premium is represented by Rm – Rf. Rm on its own is the market return.

(d)   16.75%

$R = Rf + \beta j(Rm - Rf)$

$R = 5.2 + 1.52(12.8 - 5.2)$

$R = 16.75\%$

(e)   D

The investment has the same level of systematic risk as the market.

20 FREEDLING CO

(a) **False, False**

Having fixed costs in a cost structure is risky since they have to be paid and are often unavoidable in the short run if the business starts to turn downwards. This has a magnifying effect on the businesses profit for a given volume change.

(b) **D**

Statement (1) is untrue. Debt is riskier for the company but safer for the investor and therefore the investors do not demand as high a return as they would for equity. Statement (2) is true. Increasing the proportion of debt increases the variability of returns (risk) to equity shareholders and they demand a higher return to compensate for the increased risk.

(c) **False, True, True**

Under M&M no tax the WACC would generally not change. M&M argued that the level of gearing was not relevant to a company WACC. With corporation tax introduced into their model a tax benefit tended to pull down the WACC as gearing increased.

Under the traditional theory of gearing modest amounts of debt often went unnoticed by shareholders and this lack of response (in the form of increased demands for higher return) meant the WACC fell.

(d) **D**

It is a common error to think that M&M claimed 'it does not matter how a business raises its finance'. Finance can come with it a host of unpleasant conditions that are best avoided for example. The second statement is what they actually said and the first statement is a rather clumsy paraphrase.

(e) **True, true, true**

All the statements are true.

21 TULIP CO

(a) **10.7%**

k_e (aka $E(r_i)$) = $R_f + \beta_i(E(r_m) - R_f)$

k_e = 2.5 + (1.05 × 7.8) = 10.7%

Note that the 'premium' is represented by $E(r_m) - Rf$. $E(r_m)$ itself would be expressed as the return, not the premium.

(b) **D**

Cost of debt can be calculated as the IRR of the cash flows of owning the debt. Usually, the interest value would need to be a post-tax value, but as no tax is mentioned in the question, no tax adjustment is needed.

Year	$	5% DF	PV	6%DF	PV
0	(100.00)	1.000	(100.00)	1.000	(100.00)
1-5	3.00	4.329	12.99	4.212	12.64
5	115.00	0.784	90.16	0.747	85.91
			3.15		(1.45)

IRR = L + [N_L / ($N_L - N_H$)] × (H − L)

Kd = 5 + [3.15 / (3.15 + 1.45)] × (6 − 5) = 5.7%

(c) **A**

The capital asset pricing model assumes that all shareholders of a company have the same required rate of return. Answers B and D relate to the dividend growth model rather than the CAPM. Answer C is not an assumption made.

(d) **C and E**

Retained earnings are a source of equity finance. Cutting a dividend is a means of using equity finance. Equity finance reserves represent retained profits rather than cash. Cash may not be available even if reserves are large, if the cash has already been spent on projects. Bonus issues are free issues of shares, so cannot be used to raise finance for the company. Preference shares are not generally recognised as equity finance as they have more in common with debt finance.

(e) **B**

Murabaha is similar to trade credit and therefore would not meet Tulip Co's needs. It is correct to state that Mudaraba involves an investing partner and a managing partner.

BUSINESS VALUATIONS

22 KEVIN DUTTON

(a) **C**

Consider a bond with a nominal value of $100

MV = PV of future receipts discounted at Kevin's required return of 30%

MV = (Interest of 5 × 5yr annuity factor @ 30%) + (redemption of 100 × 5yr DF @ 30%)

MV = (5 × 2.436) + (100 × 0.269) = 39.08

Thus total MV = $390,800 or $391,000 to the nearest $1,000.

(b) **8.9%**

An investment of 60 now will result in a cash receipt of 100 in 6 years.

Solving $60 \times (1 + r)^6 = 100$, gives $1 + r = 1.0889$, so r = 8.9%.

(c) **C**

Issue value × $(1.10)^6 = 100$, giving an issue value of 56.447

Thus a discount of at least 43.55%, or 44% must be applied.

(d)   False, True, False

The first statement is false, otherwise no companies would be able to issue deep discounted bonds in the first place. (Note: it is illegal for companies to issue **shares** at a discount.)

The second statement is true – the nature of forestry is that an initial investment is required (planting saplings), followed by no income until the trees are ready to be harvested. The repayment pattern with deep discounted bonds matches this.

The third statement is false – the price investors buy the bonds at reflects the risks and, hence, the required return. Thus, the precise nature of the cash flows associated with a bond (e.g. coupon rate) are not important.

(e)   D and E

A: False: MV = PV of future receipts discounted at the investors' required return. A change in interest rates will affect investors' required returns and hence the bond price.

B: False: MV = PV of future receipts discounted at investors' required return. A change in inflation rates will affect investors' required returns in money terms and hence the bond price.

C: False: the statement is the wrong way round – changes in the required return affect the bond value.

D: True. As rates rise, investors require a higher return, hence the value of the receipts (interest and redemption) falls.

E: Without any market imperfections, the theoretical price should be the market price, but as soon as the assumptions made regarding the perfect market do not hold true, this may not be the case. For example, herding behaviour may push a price above or below its theoretical value.

23   LOKI

(a)   C

The break-up value of the assets normally represents the minimum price which should be accepted for the sale of a business as a going concern, since if the income based valuations give figures lower than the break-up value it is apparent that the owner would be better off by ceasing to trade and selling off all the assets piecemeal.

Replacement cost should provide a measure of the maximum amount that any purchaser should pay for the whole business, since it represents the total cost of forming the business from scratch.

Asset based measures typically ignore non statement of financial position intangible assets e.g. a highly skilled workforce, strong management team and competitive positioning of the company's products.

(b)   0.89

Step 1: 'degear' Q's equity beta to give an asset beta

$$\beta_a = \beta_e \left[\frac{V_E}{V_E + V_D[1-t]} \right] = 1.2 \left[\frac{2}{2 + 1[1-0.3]} \right] = 0.8888... = 0.89$$

This can then be taken as Loki's asset beta as the two companies have similar business activities.

Given Loki is all equity financed, then this is also Loki's equity beta – no 'regearing' is required.

(c)   A

Fair MV = PV of future dividends discounted at the K_e of 14%

Fair MV = $0.14m/(0.14 – 0.04) = $1.4m or $0.70 per share

Note: the dividend of $0.14m is already a t=1 figure so does not need to be multiplied by a factor of 1.04.

However, the issue price will be at a 15% discount, giving $0.70 × 0.85 = $0.595 = $0.60.

(d) $96.53

Consider a bond with a nominal value of $100

MV = PV of future receipts discounted at investor's required return of 6%

MV = (Interest of 5 × 4yr annuity factor) + (redemption of 100 × 4yr DF)

MV = ($5 × 3.465) + ($100 × 0.792) = $96.53

(e)   B and C

A is false – the secured bonds will have the lowest risk.

B is true – the option to convert acts as a sweetener, allowing Loki to pay lower dividends.

C is true – the venture capital company is likely to have well diversified shareholders.

D is false – the family are unlikely to want to lose control of their company.

24   DAVINA MCNABB

(a)   C

Company A is in a very capital intensive business and it is likely that the value of the housing stock is a very close estimate of the value of the company, particularly given recent losses.

Recent and even future losses make it difficult to use earnings (option A) and/or dividend (option B) approaches.

Given it is unquoted, there is no share price to use to estimate market capitalisation (option D).

(b) $125.0 m

MV = next year's earnings/(earnings yield – g)

MV = 12.5 / (0.12 – 0.02) = 12.5/0.10 = 125.0m

(c) **B**

MV = PV of future dividends discounted at the K_e of 14%

MV = 5 × annuity factor for 3 years + value of growing perpetuity × 3yr simple discount factor

MV = 5 × 2.322 + [5 × 1.03/(0.14 − 0.03)] × 0.675

MV = 11.6 + 31.6 = 43.2m

(d) **B**

A: Strong form implies all shares are fairly priced, even taking into account secret information.

B: In a semi strong market, secret information would enable an investor to outperform the market by identifying undervalued companies, so option B is true.

C: A semi-strong market will incorporate all publicly available information in the share price, so Davina will not unearth anything useful looking at such information.

D: Weak form efficiency is sufficient to imply that there are no trends in share prices and hence Davina will not find any useful by her 'chartism'.

(e) **True, False, False**

Statement (i) is true. The shareholders of M Inc. are likely to be well diversified (even M Inc is likely to be well diversified) so will not be interested in attempts to reduce unsystematic risk further.

Statement (ii) is false – Davina should be looking at risk **and** return and try to develop a portfolio where the anticipated return exceeds the CAPM required return.

Statement (iii) is false – only unsystematic risk can be diversified away, by definition.

25 PIKE

(a) **C**

Minimum value to the seller is given by NRV (note: this would have already deducted the value of the loan).

(b) **$50**

MV = P/E × future sustainable earnings

To get an estimate of future earnings we need firstly to inflate the historic figure by 3% and then, secondly adjust for the post-tax salary

Sustainable earnings = (7,000,000 × 1.03) − (100,000 × 0.70) = 7,140,000

MV = 7 × 7,140,000 = 49,980,000, or $50m

(c) **A**

PV of future CFs discounted at the WACC = 6/(0.12 − 0.04) = $75m

However, this gives the value of equity + debt, so the value of the debt must be deducted

MV equity = 75 − 2.5 = $72.5m

(d)   A and B

A is true. The decision by owner/managers how to take funds out of a company is usually made to reduce tax.

B is true. In a service business the goodwill may be tied up with the owner/manager rather than the company.

C is false – in a strong form market the share price will react before information is made public.

D is false – given Pike is listed and a conglomerate, then it is highly likely that its shareholders are well diversified and, hence, only concerned about **systematic** risk.

(e)   B

Statement (i) is true. Minnow operates in a service industry that is not capital intensive.

Statement (ii) is true – DCF approaches are generally seen as superior.

Statement (iii) is false for two reasons – firstly historic dividend shave been artificially high, a trend unlikely to continue and, secondly, DVM is less useful for valuing a majority stake.

26   PREY CO

(a) $185,000

Value = (100 + 170) + (25 – 100) + (40 – 50) = $185,000

Alternatively, value = 400 – 100 + 25 + 40 – 140 – 40 = 185

(b)   C

Value = (100 + 170) + (500 – 100) = $670,000

Alternatively, value = 400 – 100 + 500 + 50 – 140 – 40 = 670

(c)   False, True, False

Statement (i) is false. Despite operating in a capital intensive industry, without an estimate of the value of Prey Ltd.'s brand name, the asset valuation is likely to be far too low.

Statement (ii) is true – Prey Ltd.'s value stems from the quality of its products and its reputation.

Statement (iii) is false – if the statement has said 'net realisable value' rather than 'net book value', then it would have been true.

(d)   B

The P/E ratio of the quoted company will be based on historic eps but value is based on future earnings potential.

MV = 10 × 156 = $1,560,000

There are 200,000 shares, giving a share price of $7.80.

(e)   9.5%

The growth rate used in the DVM should be future growth.

The best indicator of future growth can be calculated using years 20X4 to 20X6 (20X3 was a transition year and the impact of the boost in demand was only partially seen).

Solving $65(1 + g)^2 = 78$, gives g = 0.0954... or 9.5%

27 RING CO

(a) $9.45

Historical dividend growth rate = $100 \times (($0.450/$0.370)^{0.25} - 1) = 5\%$

Share price = ($0.450 \times 1.05) / (0.1 - 0.05) = 9.45

(b) B

MV of loan note is the value that would bring the purchase of loan note and the receipt of interest and the redemption value to an NPV of $0 when discounted at the investors' discount rate (the pre-tax cost of the note) of 4%. In other words, the MV of the loan note will be equal to the PV of the interest receipts and redemption value.

Market value = ($6 \times 6.002) + ($100 \times 0.760) = $36.01 + $76.0 = 112.01

(c) C and D

Total assets should be added together, with total liabilities deducted. This is represented by either:

Non-current assets plus current assets less total liabilities or

Net current assets (current assets − current liabilities) plus non-current assets less long-term liabilities.

(d) C

The dividend valuation model makes the unreasonable assumption that average dividend growth is constant is correct.

The earnings yield method = earnings × 1/yield

The P/E ratio method = earnings × P/E ratio

The equity market value would not include any debt value.

(e) Correct, Incorrect, Correct

Insider information cannot be used to make abnormal gains in a strong form efficient capital market and Ring Co's share price reacts quickly and accurately to newly-released information in a semi-strong form efficient capital market but not in a weak form one.

28 CORAL CO

(a) 221.52

Number of shares in issue = $7.8m/$0.25 = 31.2m shares.

Equity market value = $7.10 \times 31.2m = $221.52m$.

(b) C

Conversion value = $7.10 \times 1.08^6 \times 10 = 112.67 per loan note.

Market value = ($7 \times 5.076) + ($112.67 \times 0.746) = 35.53 + 84.05 = 119.58.

(c) B

If the capital market is semi-strong form efficient, newly-released insider information will quickly and accurately be reflected in share prices.

The other statements are true.

(d) Is an assumption, Is an assumption, Is an assumption

All three are assumptions made by the dividend growth model.

(e) B

A valuation for corporate taxation purposes is not necessary.

29 BLUEBELL CO

(a) C

The net realisable value can be calculated by taking the value of tangible assets (adjusted for any named adjustments), making sure that the intangible goodwill is not included. Then deduct the value of the liabilities.

Net realisable value = 1,350 − (768 − 600) − (192 × 0.1) − 30 − 105 − 662 = $365.8m

(b) $1,875 million

Value = earnings × 1/earnings yield

Earnings yield = 1/PE ratio = 1/12.5 = 0.08 (8%)

Value = 150 × 1/0.08 = $1,875 million

(c) A

Asset-based valuations are useful in asset- stripping acquisitions. Intangible assets aren't included in the valuation, although in real life, some attempt to do this may be made. Asset based valuations don't take into account future incomes or cash flows. Deprival value is the lower of replacement cost and recoverable value, so cannot be said to be replacement cost alone.

(d) C

Market imperfections mean that share prices will not react as they would be expected to if the market were efficient. If the market were efficient, investors would react rationally to news, whether expected or not. Overreaction to unexpected news is therefore an example of a market imperfection. So is the low volume of trading of small company shares. With low trading levels, the market will struggle to come to an efficient equilibrium price for the shares.

(e) B and E

A control premium would be paid on shares when buying a controlling stake. An unlisted company like Dandelion Co would be more difficult to value as there is no market price to use as a guide. Scrip dividends increase the liquidity of shares, as there will be more shares in issue, each with a lower value than prior to the issue. The lower the value, the more tradeable they are. Dandelion Co is unlikely to have a lower cost of equity and higher share value than similar listed companies, as the purchase of shares in an unlisted company is a higher risk investment for equity shareholders (as the shares are less tradeable than those in a listed company), leading to a higher return demanded and therefore a higher cost of equity. In a semi-strong form efficient market, insider trading opportunities occur between the time that new information about the business happens and the time that the news is released to the public.

30   GWW CO

(a) $160 MILLION

Value of ordinary shares in statement of financial position = $20.0 million

Nominal (par) value of ordinary shares = $0.50

Number of ordinary shares of company = $20.0m/$0.5 = 40m shares

Ordinary share price = $4.00 per share

Market capitalisation = share price × number of shares in issue = $4.00 × 40m − $1600 million

(b) $61.7 MILLION

Current net asset value (NAV) = $91.0m + $8.3m − $7.1m − $25.0m = $67.2 million

Decrease in value of non-current assets on liquidation = $86.0m − $91.0m = $5m

Increase in value of inventory on liquidation = $4.2m − $3.8m = $0.4m

Decrease in value of trade receivables = $4.2m × 0.2 = $0.9m

NAV (liquidation basis) = $67.2m − $5m + $0.4m − $0.9m = $61.7m

(c)   C

Valuation = earnings (post-tax profits) × P/E ratio

Historic earnings of GWW Co = $10.1 million

Average price/earnings ratio of GWW Co business sector = 17 times

Valuation = $10.1 million × 17 = $171.7 million

(d) $235 MILLION

Historic dividend growth rate = $(D_0 / D_n)^{(1/n)} - 1$

Growth = $(\$6.0m/\$5.0m)^{(1/3)} - 1 = 0.0627$ (6.27%)

An assumption is then made that future dividend growth is similar to historic dividend growth.

Value using the dividend growth model = $D_0 (1+g)/(r_e + g)$ (from formulae sheet)

Value = $6.0m × 1.0627/(0.09 − 0.0627) = $233.56 million, or $235 million to the nearest $5 million.

NB: Calculations using a more rounded growth rate of 6.3% would give $236.22 million, which is still $235 million to the nearest $5 million.

(e)   B

Gordon's growth approximation estimates the dividend growth rate using $g = br_e$, where b is the retention rate of dividends and r_e is the accounting rate of return on equity.

Using the most recent figures, b = ($10.1m − $6.0m)/$10.1m = 0.4059 or 40.59%

r_e = $10.1m/$67.2m = 0.1503 or 15.03%

growth = 0.4059 × 0.1503 = 0.061 or 6.1%

RISK MANAGEMENT

31 MALLETT CO

(a) **1,174,000 AUD**

Mallett Co will receive 850,000USD in 3 months' time.

The company will (1) borrow the appropriate amount in US dollars now; (2) convert the US dollars to Australian dollars immediately; (3) invest the Australian dollars in an Australian dollar bank account knowing that it will grow over the next three months; (4) use the client's cash (US dollars) to pay off the US dollar borrowing (which will have grown with interest) and close the account; (5) take the Australian dollars out of its account, it will have increased by interest but will be a known amount that can be calculated now.

The amount to borrow now, as in (1), is 850,000 USD ÷ 1.00825 = 843,045 USD.

This will be converted now, as in (2), to 843,045 ÷ 0.7233 AUD = 1,165,554 AUD.

Placed on deposit, as in (3), it grows to 1,165,554 × 1.00725 AUD = 1,174,004 AUD.

(The client's receipt will pay off the US dollar loan which has increased with interest.)

The alternative answers come from ignoring the need to allow for 3-month's interest on the Australian dollar account and from using annual rates instead of quarterly rates.

(b) **A**

The expectation theory suggests that you would earn the same amount by investing in a one-year bond which is then rolled into a second one-year bond as you would by buying a two-year bond today.

(c) **0.7240 US dollars to the Australian dollar**

The ACCA formula sheet tells you that interest rate parity says that: $F_0 = S_0 \times \dfrac{(1+i_c)}{(1+i_b)}$

Using more useful notation for this question: $F_0 = S_0 \times \dfrac{(1+\text{US rate})}{(+\text{Australian rate})}$

Three-month forward rate $= 0.7233 \times \dfrac{(1+0.033 \div 4)}{1+0.029 \div 4)} = 0.7240$ USD to the AUD

(d) **D**

Translation losses can, for example, result from restating the book-value of an overseas branch's assets at the exchange rate at the balance sheet date.

(e) **D**

The option provides you with the right, but not the obligation to exchange currencies.

32 NOON CO

(a) B

Noon needs to pay 3 million Flyland Francs in three months.

Using the 3-month forward rate, these will cost 3m ÷ 6.321 = 474,608 CC.

Alternative answers are arrived at by using the spot rate or using the rate for selling Flyland Francs rather than buying them.

(b) C

Interest rate parity uses the current spot rate combined with the home and foreign currency interest rates to predict the forward rate.

(c) D

Noon needs to pay 3m Flyland Francs in three months.

The company will (1) borrow the appropriate amount in Centreland Colons now; (2) convert the Colons into Flyland Francs immediately; (3) invest the Francs in a Flyland Franc bank account knowing that it will grow to 3 m Francs in three months' time; (4) pay the 3m Francs to the Flyland supplier and close the account; (5) repay the amount borrowed in (1) in Colons which will have increased by interest but will be a known amount that can be calculated now.

The amount to invest in step (3) in Francs at a rate of 13.5% per year or 3.375% over 3 months = 3m Francs ÷ 1.03375 = 2,902,056.

The amount to convert to Francs now in step (2) = 2,902,056 ÷ 6.170 = 470,349 Colons.

The amount that will have to be paid in three months' time to pay off this borrowing in Colons = 470,349 × 1.02025 = 479,874 Colons.

The alternative answers come from using annual rates rather than 3-monthly ones and forgetting that we compare two payments made in three months' time, i.e. forgetting to increase the borrowing in Colons by 3 months' interest.

(d) Correct, Correct, Correct, Correct

All four statements are correct.

(e) 14%

Purchasing power parity formula: $S1 = S0 \times \dfrac{1+h_c}{1+h_b}$

More usefully:

Spot rate in 3 months' time ≈ 3-month forward rate

$= \text{Spot rate} \times \dfrac{(1+\text{overseas inflation rate})}{(1+\text{domestic inflation rate})}$

Using lower of the two exchange rates (as recommended) and using quarterly inflation rates based on the annual rates given.

6.321 = 6.170 × (1 + [annual overseas inflation rate ÷ 4]) ÷ (1 + [0.038 ÷ 4])

1 + [annual overseas rate ÷ 4] = (6.321 ÷ 6.170) ×1.0095 = 1.0342

Annual overseas rate = 3.42 × 4 = 13.682, or 14%

Alternative answers come from getting the original purchasing power parity formula the wrong way up or from not spotting that you need to use quarterly inflation rates (since you have been given a three-month forward exchange rate).

Tutorial note

You get a similar result (13.684%) if you use the higher exchange rate, i.e. no difference when working to the nearest percentage point. Many pieces of information about money markets seem to take annual rates and divide them, by 4 to find quarterly rates or take quarterly rates and quadruple them when one would expect to use fourth roots of indexes or raise them to the power four. It only makes a small difference in this case. An annual inflation rate of 14.3% would be found by raising an index number based on a quarterly rate to the power 4, a perfectly understandable calculation in view of the way inflation operates. It was the reason for asking for an answer to the nearest percent.

33 PZK CO

(a)   A

The foreign exchange risk exposure relates to the value of the receipt for an individual transaction.

(b) $3,521

The current dollar value of the future euro receipt = €1,200,000/4.2080 = $285,171.

If a forward contract is taken out, PZK Co can lock into the six-month forward exchange rate of 4.2606 euros per dollar.

Future dollar value using the forward contract = €1,200,000/4.2606 = $281,650.

Loss using the forward contract = 285,171 – 281,650 = $3,521.

(c)   D

The implied interest rate in the foreign country can be calculated using interest rate parity.

From the formulae sheet, $F_0 = S_0 \times (1 + i_c)/(1 + i_b)$

Hence $4.3132 = 4.2080 \times (1 + i_c)/1.04$

Rearranging, $(1 + i_c) = 4.3132 \times 1.04/4.2080 = 1.066$

The implied annual interest rate in the foreign country is 6.6%.

(d)   C

The forward rates indicate that the dollar will buy more euros in the future.

Given the receipt is in euros, then PZK can expect the $ equivalent value of the receipt to fall as the dollar strengthens.

Thus PZK should consider 'leading' and trying to get the receipt sooner.

(e)   **False, True, True**

Statement (i) is false – PZK may still be exposed to transaction risk on purchases.

Statement (ii) is true – One of the simplest ways for PZK Co to avoiding exchange rate risk is to invoice in its home currency, which passes the exchange rate risk on to the foreign customer, who must effectively find the dollars with which to make the payment.

Statement (iii) is true – This strategy may not be commercially viable, however, since the company's foreign customers will not want to take on the exchange rate risk. They will instead transfer their business to those competitors of PZK Co who invoice in the foreign currency and who therefore shoulder the exchange rate risk.

34   H CO

(a)   **B and D**

A is false – the factory doesn't exist yet so would not be good security on the loan.

B is true – MM with tax concluded that companies should gear up as much as possible.

C is false – some forms of equity, such as cutting a dividend, have very low issue costs.

D is true – the cost of debt will (normally) be lower than the cost of equity, due mainly to lower investor risk and tax relief on interest.

(b)   **C**

Market segmentation theory helps explain any 'wiggle' on the yield curve rather than why it might be normal instead of inverted.

(c)   **$10,000 payment**

The interest payable on the actual loan will be linked to the spot rate of 7.6%.

However, the FRA effectively locks into a reference rate of 7.8% (borrowing so use higher rate).

Thus, F company will have to make a payment of 0.2%.

This equates to $0.2\% \times 10m \times 6/12 = \$10,000$.

(d)   **A, B and C**

A is correct – rounding the number of contracts may result in a mismatch.

B is correct – the futures price and the underlying price may be different on any date other than the contract date, leading to basis risk.

C is correct – the basis may not move as expected.

D is false – unpredictability is why we hedge in the first place!

(e)   **C**

Statements (i) and (iii) are true – the hedge is constructed by borrowing at the market rate and then the FRA/futures position will generate a gain or loss that can be offset against the loss or gain on the associated real world borrowing.

Statement (ii) is false – FRAs are OTC instruments arranged with a bank.

35   F CO

(a)   A and D

The main reason for an inverted curve is when interest rates are high but expected to fall. Historically, yield curves often invert before a major turning point in the business cycle and an economy heads into recession. A good example is when the U.S. Treasury yield curve inverted in 2000 just before the U.S. equity markets collapsed.

(b) $1,250 payment

The interest receivable on the actual deposit will be linked to the spot rate of 5.5%.

However, the FRA effectively locks into a reference rate of 5% (depositing so use the lower of the two quoted rates).

Thus F company will have to make a payment of 0.5%.

This equates to 0.5% × 1m × 3/12 = $1,250.

(c)   A

Interest rate options are the right to buy or sell interest rate futures. The option will only be exercised in order to make a profit on the futures, which will help to mitigate any losses on a loan or deposit due to a rise in interest rates.

Interest rate options do not give entitlement to a loan or deposit. This is taken out independently of the options. An interest rate option does not give the right to an interest rate. It effectively increases deposit receipts when interest rates fall adversely by providing a profit on the futures that have been bought or sold.

(d)   C

An interest rate guarantee allows the company a period of time during which it has the option to buy an FRA at a set price (A). An interest rate future locks the company into an effective interest rate (B). An interest rate swap **does not** involve the exchange of the principal, only the exchange of a floating stream of interest payments for a fixed stream of interest payments and vice versa (D).

(e)   True, False, False

Statement (i) is true – lenders set rates primarily based on risk assessments.

Statement (ii) is false – under swaps there is no exchange of principals.

Statement (iii) is false – F would only be liable for the loan it borrowed.

36   HERD CO

(a)   €1.566 per $1

Six-month forward rate – use 6 monthly simple interest rate.

Domestic rate = 2% × 6/12 = 1%

Foreign rate = 5% × 6/12 = 2.5%

Forward rate = 1.543 × (1.025/1.01) = €1.566 per $1

(b)   A

The euro receipt is subject to transaction risk.

(c)   D and E

A forward rate agreement is used for hedging against interest rate risk rather than foreign exchange risk. A currency swap is not a suitable method for hedging a one-off transaction.

(d)   B

If the dollar nominal interest rate is less than the euro nominal interest rate, interest rate parity indicates that the euro will depreciate against the dollar.

If the dollar inflation rate is less than the euro inflation rate, purchasing power parity indicates that the euro will appreciate against the dollar.

(e)   A and C

In exchange for a premium, Herd Co could hedge its interest rate risk by buying interest rate options is correct.

Floors guarantee a minimum rate – good for deposits but not borrowing.

With a borrowing requirement, futures contracts must be sold initially and bought back on close out.

Matching would only be potentially viable with a floating rate on an asset, not on another liability.

37   PARK CO

(a) $202,000

Borrow dinars for the dinar receipt to pay off, swap the dinars for $ and put the $ on deposit for six months.

Dinar value to borrow at 4% per six months = 12m/1.04 = 11,538,462 dinars.

Sell dinars for $ at spot rate (bank buys high), $ received = 11,538,462/57.52 = $200,599.

Dollar maturity value after six months at 0.5% = $200,599 × 1.005 = $201,602, or $202,000 to the nearest $000.

(b) **Effective, Effective, Effective**

All three hedges will allow Park Co to hedge its foreign currency risk.

Leading should work because, based on the given forward rates between € and $, the $ is due to depreciate and so making payments while the $ is more valuable will mean that fewer $ are needed to buy the € needed.

Forward exchange contracts and tailor made currency options would both provide perfect hedges for the transactions.

(c) **B**

Only the dinar-denominated overdraft will be effective, by matching assets and liabilities.

The long-term euro-denominated loan will increase payments to be made in euros and hence increase foreign currency risk.

(d) **Incorrect, Incorrect**

Purchasing power parity predicts the future spot rate, not the forward exchange rate.

The international Fisher effect does not predict real interest rates.

(e) **A**

If default risk increases with duration, compensation for default risk increases with time and hence the yield curve will slope upwards.

38   PEONY CO

(a) **C**

A kink in the normal yield curve can be due to differing yields in different market segments.

(b) **Payment is made from peony co to the bank of $450,000**

As the forward rate agreement is used for a borrowing, the higher rate of 7.1% is guaranteed under the FRA. As the actual borrowing rate is lower, the company will have to pay the difference to the bank via the FRA.

Company pays bank $100m \times (9/12) \times (7.1 - 6.5)/100 = \$450,000$

(c) **$112.9 million**

12-month forward rate = $5 \times 1.1/1.065 = 5.1643$ pesos per $1

6-month forward rate = $5 \times 1.05/1.0325 = 5.0848$ pesos per $1

Income = $(200/5.0848) + (380/5.1643) = \$112.9$ m

(d) **C**

Both statements are true.

(e) **B**

A borrower can hedge interest rate risk by selling interest rate futures now and buying them back in the future. Interest rate options do not have to be exercised at all, but can be abandoned. Only the interest, not the principal, is exchanged using an interest rate swap. To set up an interest rate collar for borrowing, Peony would have to buy a cap and sell a floor.

Section C

ANSWERS TO CONSTRUCTED RESPONSE (LONG) PRACTICE QUESTIONS

FINANCIAL MANAGEMENT FUNCTION AND ENVIRONMENT

1   UUL CO

Key answer tips

This ratio combines a very examinable area (financial ratios) with the less frequently examined topic of stakeholder objectives and regulation.

Part (a) requires some calculations to be performed. Critically though, you must also comment on these calculations.

To answer parts (b) and (c) you will need to think practically and considering the real world position of water companies should help you generate ideas.

The highlighted words are key phrases that markers are looking for.

(a)   Equivalent annual growth in dividends – $(7.1/4.2)^{0.25} - 1 = 14.0\%$

Equivalent annual growth in earnings – $(41.3/31.6)^{0.25} - 1 = 6.9\%$

Share price – 20X2 – 31.6c × 17 = $5.37

Share price – 20X6 – 41.3c × 22 = $9.09

Equivalent annual growth in share price – $(9.09/5.37)^{0.25} - 1 = 14.1\%$

The chairperson states that the company has delivered above average performance. However, whilst dividend growth has exceeded the water industry average, the growth in earnings and the growth in share price is significantly behind the water industry average. Hence, it is hard to justify the statement made by the chairperson.

Indeed, the shareholders should be concerned that given the growth in earnings, the current dividend growth rate does not seem sustainable.

On the positive side, given the inflation rate during this period, the company has delivered real growth in earnings, dividends and share price. Additionally, the P/E ratio has grown, which indicates the market is increasingly confident about the future of the company.

(b) Three other key stakeholders in UUL Co are the local community in the area that the company operates, the customers of the company and the government.

The local community will be interested in the financial success of the company, as this will potentially generate jobs and wealth in their region. Equally, they will be keen to ensure that the company adheres to best practice in the treatment and disposal of sewage and that the risk of pollution is minimised.

Customers of the company will be keen that their cost for water is minimised. At the same time, they will be keen to make sure that they have a constant, reliable and safe water supply.

The government will be keen to extract tax receipts and will be keen to see the company succeed so that those tax receipts grow. The government will also want to make sure that all the operations of the company comply with the relevant environmental legislation and that all developments by the company, such as the development of a new reservoir, comply with planning laws.

Tutorial note

Sensible references to other stakeholders would have also been acceptable.

(c) The government will be keen to minimise the impact that the likely monopoly position of UUL Co will have on its customers. The monopoly position may itself be tolerated, as the water industry is a natural monopoly where it would be hard to introduce competition and where the economies of scale necessary to justify the infrastructure investment make a monopoly acceptable. Hence, the government is very likely to control price increases and limit the return that the company is able to make in order to make sure that UUL Co does not take advantage of its monopoly position. Equally, the government is likely to impose minimum service standards that UUL Co must provide to its customers, as the customers do not have a choice of provider.

The government will also intervene to make sure that UUL Co is carrying out its operations in a way that will not cause unnecessary environmental damage.

As a public company UUL Co will suffer all the costs associated with making sure that they have, and are seen to have, good corporate governance.

Additionally, UUL Co will suffer interference from government, as water is a strategic commodity and the government have an obligation to make sure that the country's anticipated needs are forecast and planned for.

2   CCC

(a)   The key criteria that need to be considered when objective setting are as follows:

Stakeholder expectations

All organisations need to identify key stakeholders, examine their expectations and try to set objectives to meet them.

For CCC stakeholders include:

- Local residents want to see the provision of quality health and education services and value for money in response to paying local taxes.

- Local businesses who will be interested in local infrastructure when deciding whether to invest in the area. In particular, CCC may be keen to ensure that DDD does not close its local offices, with resulting job losses, and move to the capital city.

- Central Government committees who make funding decisions based on local population and deprivation.

For DDD stakeholders include:

- Shareholders want to see their wealth increased through a mixture of growing dividends and an increasing share price. DDD has reflected this in the objective to increase shareholder wealth by 10% per annum.

- Customers will expect a certain level of quality and value for money, depending on the nature of products sold.

- The local communities affected by DDD will expect them to be good citizens and operate at high levels of corporate social responsibility.

Stakeholder power

All organisations will find conflicts between stakeholders so they need to consider how to prioritise them.

For a company like DDD the expectations of shareholders come first for the following reasons:

- This is usually reflected in companies' legislation where directors have a duty in law to put shareholder interests first. Many governance recommendations focus on protecting shareholder interests.

- Failure to deliver shareholder expectations will result in a falling share price and difficulties raising finance. Ultimately, shareholders have the power to remove directors should they feel dissatisfied.

However, this does not mean that other stakeholders' needs are ignored. Clearly if customers are unhappy then sales will be lost with a resulting fall in profitability and shareholder wealth.

For CCC the problem is more complex:

- It is much more difficult to prioritise stakeholder expectations. For example, given limited funds, should community health care needs come before educational ones?

- Even individual stakeholder groups have multiple conflicting objectives. For example, residents want to pay less tax and have better provision of services. Thus, even if some groups are satisfied, other may still vote for changes in CCC.

- With companies, customers pay directly for the products they receive, ensuring that customer needs are addressed. With CCC, the bulk of its funding comes from central government, not the local community who benefit from CCC's actions. Thus, the needs of the funding body may take priority over locals needs, otherwise funding may be cut (note: this is less likely here as funding is mainly driven by population size).

Measurement issues

For an organisation like DDD, once shareholders have been prioritised, all decisions can be evaluated by reference to financial measures such as profitability. While non-financial targets will be incorporated as well, the 'bottom line' will be seen as key. Thus, financial targets can be set for most objectives.

For CCC it is much more difficult to measure whether it is achieving its stated aims and hence to set targets.

- For example, how do you assess whether somewhere is an 'attractive place to live and work' or whether health and education provision is 'excellent'?

Other issues

All organisations need to ensure that objectives set relate to controllable factors to ensure staff is motivated to meet them.

All organisations need to differentiate between cause and effect and have objectives for both. For example, DDD may have an objective of customer satisfaction, which will need to be translated into objectives for quality, cost, etc.

(b) As described above, companies make decisions with the primary objective of maximising shareholder wealth.

Investment decisions

Potential investments should thus be assessed using NPV or SVA, rather than ROCE to ensure that shareholder wealth is increased.

This should be the case for both MS and DDD, though the former will have more difficulty determining a suitable discount rate, being unquoted.

Dividend decisions

Once shareholder value has been created, the firm needs to decide how to return those gains to shareholders – either as dividends or reinvested to enhance the share price further.

Modigliani and Miller argued that, given certain assumptions, dividend policy was irrelevant to shareholder wealth. If a dividend was cut, for example, shareholders could manufacture dividends by selling shares without any overall loss of wealth. Central to their theory was the idea that shareholders had perfect information and would understand why a dividend policy was changed.

In the case of MS, shareholders are also employees so will have full information regarding any change in dividend policy and will not thus perceive any information content in the dividends themselves. However, should the dividend be cut, shareholders who require income will not be able to sell shares to generate cash as the company is unquoted. MS should thus try to continue the stable dividend policy it has adopted to date, even though historical dividend cover is lower than the 'rule of thumb' of two.

In the case of DDD, major institutional shareholders will have good information from the company but may have tax preferences regarding income and capital gains so DDD should adopt a consistent dividend policy to meet their requirements. DDD will probably have attracted a certain clientele of shareholder based on previous policies.

Financing decisions

Both firms need to raise finance in order to undertake new investments to increase shareholder wealth. The issue here is whether the finance used ultimately affects shareholder wealth as well.

From a theoretical point of view, Modigliani and Miller argued that in the absence of taxation, and certain other assumptions, the choice between debt or equity finance was irrelevant. With corporation tax, they concluded that debt finance was preferable, due to the benefits of the tax shield. With personal taxes, the conclusions depend on the specific circumstances of the company and its shareholders. Incorporating real world factors, many analysts argue that there is an optimal gearing level for each company.

DDD is already at the typical gearing ratio for its industry so it would reasonable to assume that this is their optimal gearing level. Future financing should involve a mixture of debt and equity to maintain this ratio.

MS is all-equity financed at present so it should seek to raise at least some of the $15 million required using debt finance to take advantage of the tax relief and low costs involved.

Interrelationships

All three types of decisions are inter-related, thus the financing decision will affect the cost of capital, and as a consequence, the net benefits obtainable from a particular project, thereby influencing the investment decision, while the financing decision concerning gearing will affect both the other decisions.

The dividend decision, in determining the level of retentions, will affect the cash available for investment, and the extent to which external sources of funds need to be sought in financing to optimise operations.

3   NEIGHBOURING COUNTRIES

Key answer tips

A careful read of the specifics of all parts of the question was needed to ensure you answered the requirement in full and didn't end up discussing areas that wouldn't earn marks. The highlighted words are key phrases that markers are looking for.

(a)   The objectives of the nationalised industry in Country A are likely to be influenced by the government, rather than by financial matters. The major objectives are likely to be the provision of a service to the public, and the provision of electricity for the economic development of the country. This may mean providing electricity at considerable cost to outlying areas, or to areas that the government wishes to develop. The financial objectives will be secondary, and will probably attempt to achieve a target rate of return, although the government may be prepared to accept a negative return in order to achieve its political objectives.

The primary objectives of the private sector companies in Country B will probably be the maximisation of shareholder wealth. The companies' managements will decide the objectives, which may be merely 'satisficing', with other non-financial objectives such as good working conditions for employees, market share and provision of a good service to customers. An important industry such as the provision of electricity will, however, be subject to strong government influences and constraints.

Investment planning and appraisal techniques will differ largely as a result of the differing objectives.

In the nationalised industry, strategic investment planning will be instigated by the government, with the tactical decisions left to the management of the industry. The amount of capital investment involved will be determined by the government, which is responsible for the supply of funds.

Appraisal techniques will be designed to ensure that the government targets are met, e.g. ROCE and budgetary control.

In the private sector, investment will be influenced by market forces, with managements attempting to maximise shareholder wealth, or at least satisfy their shareholders while meeting other objectives. Managements will be responsible for both strategic and tactical decisions.

Appraisal techniques will be introduced to ensure that the objectives are met, and will almost certainly include DCF and budgetary control. Failure to meet the objectives may have serious consequences on the share price, with the risk of take-over and possible job losses.

In conclusion, it may be that both the nationalised industry and the privately controlled industry use the same evaluation techniques. It will be the objectives that are likely to be different, with the consequences of failure being more serious in the private sector.

(b) **(i)** **Responding to various stakeholder groups**

If a company has a single objective in terms of maximising profitability then it is only responding to one stakeholder group, namely shareholders. However, companies can no longer fail to respond to the interests and concerns of a wider range of groups, particularly with respect to those who may have a non-financial interest in the organisation. Stakeholder groups with a non-financial interest can therefore generate for companies non-financial objectives and place constraints on their operations to the extent that the company is prepared to respond to such groups.

Various stakeholder groupings can emerge. The following represents examples of likely groups, their non-financial objectives and/or the constraints they may place on a business:

Stakeholder	Objective	Constraints
Employees	Employee welfare	Maximum hours worked
Community	Responding to community concerns	Limits on activities
Customers	Product or service levels	Minimum quality standards
Suppliers	Good trading relationships	
Government	Protecting the consumer	Minimum standards on products or services
Trade bodies	Protecting professional reputation	Minimum standards on products or services

(ii) The difficulties associated with managing organisations with multiple objectives.

To the extent that an organisation faces a range of stakeholders, then they also face multiple objectives. This would not particularly be a problem if the multiple objectives were congruent, but they normally are not. There are a number of difficulties:

- Multiple stakeholders imply multiple objectives. To the extent that they conflict then compromises must be made. This will lead potentially to opportunity costs in that maximisation of profitability will potentially be reduced.

- Responding to stakeholders other than shareholders involves costs, either in management time or in directly responding to their needs.

- Some objectives are not clearly defined, for example what is actually meant by 'protecting the consumer'? It will therefore not always be clear to the organisation that they have met the needs of all of their stakeholders.

- Some of the objectives may actually be conflicting where compromise is not possible. Prioritisation and ranking will then have to take place. Questions then arise as to who is the most important stakeholder or what ranking should be assigned?

- New stakeholder groups often emerge. This can create a problem of longer-term strategic management in that plans can be diverted if new pressures arise. For example, environmental issues were not so important 20 years ago.

- Management of the organisation becomes complex when multiple objectives have to be satisfied. Each managerial decision is likely to face many constraints.

4   RZP CO

Key answer tips

Part (a) required a large volume of albeit, relatively straightforward calculations. You must be careful not to spend too much time on the numbers at the expense of the commentary. Parts (b) and (c) were more straightforward. The highlighted words are key phrases that markers are looking for.

(a)   Analysis of data provided

Year	20X4	20X3	20X2	20X1	20X0
Dividend per share	2.8¢	2.3¢	2.2¢	2.2¢	1.7¢
Annual dividend growth	21.7%	4.5%	Nil	29.4%	
Earnings per share	19.04¢	14.95¢	11.22¢	15.84¢	13.43¢
Annual earnings growth	27.3%	33.2%	−29.2%	17.9%	
Year	20X4	20X3	20X2	20X1	20X0
Price/earnings ratio	22.0	33.5	25.5	17.2	15.2
Share price P/E×EPS	418.9¢	500.8¢	286.1¢	272.4¢	204.1¢
Annual share price growth	−16.3%	75.0%	5.0%	33.5%	
Dividend per share	2.8¢	2.3¢	2.2¢	2.2¢	1.7¢
General price index	117	113	110	105	100
Real dividend per share	2.4¢	2.0¢	2.0¢	2.1¢	1.7¢
Annual dividend growth	20.0%	Nil	−4.8%	23.5%	

Average dividend growth:

Arithmetic mean = (21.7 + 4.5 + 0 + 29.4)/4 = 55.6/4 = 13.9%
Equivalent annual growth rate = $[(2.8/1.7)^{0.25} - 1] \times 100 = 13.3\%$

Average earnings per share growth:

Arithmetic mean = (27.3 + 33.2 − 29.2 + 17.9)/4 = 49.2/4 = 12.3%
Equivalent annual growth rate = $[(19.04/13.43)^{0.25} - 1] \times 100 = 9.1\%$

Average share price growth:

Arithmetic mean = (−16.3 + 75.0 + 5.0 + 33.5)/4 = 97.2/4 = 24.3%
Equivalent annual growth rate = $[(418.9/204.1)^{0.25} - 1] \times 100 = 19.7\%$

Average real dividend growth:

Arithmetic mean = (20.0 + 0 − 4.8 + 23.5)/4 = 38.7/4 = 9.7%
Equivalent annual growth rate = $[(2.4/1.7)^{0.25} - 1] \times 100 = 9.0\%$

Discussion of analysis and views expressed by chairperson

The chairperson's statement claims that RZP Co has delivered growth in every year in dividends, earnings and ordinary share price, apart from 20X2. Analysis shows that the chairperson is correct in excluding 20X2, when no growth occurred in dividends, earnings fell by 29.2%, and real dividends fell by 4.8%. Analysis also shows that no growth in real dividends occurred in 20X3 and that the company's share price fell by 16.3% in 20X4. It is possible the chairperson may not have been referring to real dividend growth, in which case his statement could be amended. However, shareholders will be aware of the decline in share price in 20X4 or could calculate the decline from the information provided, so the chairperson cannot claim that RZP Co has delivered share price growth in 20X4. In fact, the statement could explain the reasons for the decline in share price in order to reassure shareholders. It also possible for the five-year summary to be extended to include annual share price data, such as maximum, minimum and average share price, so that shareholders have this information readily available.

The chairperson's statement claims that RZP Co has consistently delivered above-average performance. The company may have delivered above- or below-average performance in individual years but without further information in the form of sector averages for individual years, it is not possible to reach a conclusion on this point. The average growth rates for the sector cannot therefore be used to comment on the performance of RZP Co in individual years. If the company has consistently delivered above-average performance, however, the company's average annual growth rates should be greater than the sector averages.

The growth rates can be compared as follows:

	Arithmetic mean	Equivalent annual rate	Sector
Nominal dividends	13.9%	13.3%	10%
Real dividends	9.7%	9.0%	9%
Earnings per share	12.3%	9.1%	10%
Share price	24.3%	19.7%	20%

It can be seen that if the sector average growth rates are arithmetic mean growth rates, the chairperson's statement is correct. If the sector average growth rates are equivalent annual growth rates, however, only the nominal dividend growth rate is greater than the sector average. The basis on which the sector average growth rates have been prepared should therefore be clarified in order to determine whether the chairperson's statement is correct.

(b) The dividend yield and capital growth for 20X4 must be calculated with reference to the 20X3 end-of-year share price. The dividend yield is 0.56% (100 × 2.8/500.8) and the capital growth is −16.35% (100 × (418.9 − 500.8)/500.8), so the total shareholder return is −15.79% or −15.8% (0.56 − 16.35). A negative return of 15.8% looks even worse when it is noted that annual inflation for 20X4 was 3.5% (117/113).

While the negative total shareholder return is at odds with the chairperson's claim to have delivered growth in dividends and share price in 20X4, a different view might have emerged if average share prices had been used, since the return calculation ignores share price volatility. The chairperson should also be aware that share prices may be affected by other factors than corporate activity, so a good performance in share price terms may not be due to managerial excellence. It also possible that the negative return may represent a good performance when compared to the sector as a whole in 20X4: further information is needed to assess this.

Note that total shareholder return can also be found as (100 × (2.8 + 418.9 − 500.8)/500.8).

(c) The objectives of managers may conflict with the objectives of shareholders, particularly with the objective of maximisation of shareholder wealth. Management remuneration package are one way in which goal congruence between managers and shareholders may be increased. Such packages should motivate managers while supporting the achievement of shareholder wealth maximisation. The following factors should be considered when deciding on a remuneration package intended to encourage directors to act in ways that maximise shareholder wealth.

Clarity and transparency

The terms of the remuneration package should be clear and transparent so that directors and shareholders are in no doubt as to when rewards have been earned or the basis on which rewards have been calculated.

Appropriate performance measure

The managerial performance measure selected for use in the remuneration package should support the achievement of shareholder wealth maximisation. It is therefore likely that the performance measure could be linked to share price changes.

Quantitative performance measure

The managerial performance measure should be quantitative and the manner in which it is to be calculated should be specified. The managerial performance measure should ideally be linked to a benchmark comparing the company's performance with that of its peers. The managerial performance measure should not be open to manipulation by management.

Time horizon

The remuneration package should have a time horizon that is linked to that of shareholders. If shareholders desire long-term capital growth, for example, the remuneration package should discourage decisions whose objective is to maximise short-term profits at the expense of long-term growth.

Impartiality

In recent years, there has been an increased emphasis on decisions about managerial remuneration packages being removed from the control of managers who benefit from them. The use of remuneration committees in listed companies is an example of this. The impartial decisions of non-executive directors, it is believed, will eliminate or reduce managerial self-interest and encourage remuneration packages that support the achievement of shareholder rather than managerial goals.

5   JJG CO

Key answer tips

This question may cause problems for some students, especially regarding the level of depth to go into on part (a).

Part (a) requires an evaluation of the performance of JJG. The provision of information on industry averages gives some clear indications of the ratios that any analysis should focus on.

Part (b) is a relatively straightforward calculation of the impact of a rights issue.

Part (c) gives plenty of opportunity to gain easy marks although the final words "for the expansion" means comments must be specific to the scenario presented.

The highlighted words are key phrases that markers are looking for.

(a)   Financial analysis

	20X8	20X7	20X6	20X5
Revenue ($m)	28.0	24.0	19.1	16.8
Revenue growth	17%	26%	14%	
Geometric average growth: 18.6%				
Profit before interest and tax ($m)	9.8	8.5	7.5	6.8
PBIT growth	15%	13%	10%	
Geometric average growth: 13.0%				
Earnings ($m)	5.5	4.7	4.1	3.6
Earnings per share (cents)	100	85	75	66
EPS growth	18%	13%	14%	
Geometric average growth: 14.9%				

	20X8	20X7	20X6	20X5
Dividends ($m)	2.2	1.9	1.6	1.6
Dividends per share (cents)	40	35	29	29
DPS growth	14%	21%	nil	
Geometric average growth: 11.3%				
Ordinary shares ($m)	5.5	5.5	5.5	5.5
Reserves ($m)	13.7	10.4	7.6	5.1
	——	——	——	——
Shareholders' funds ($)	19.2	15.9	13.1	10.6
8% Bonds, redeemable 20Y5 ($m)	20	20	20	20
	——	——	——	——

Capital employed ($m)	39.2	35.9	33.1	30.6
Profit before interest and tax ($m)	9.8	8.5	7.5	6.8
Return on capital employed	25%	24%	23%	22%
Earnings ($m)	5.5	4.7	4.1	3.6
Return on shareholders' funds	29%	30%	31%	34%
8% Bonds, redeemable 20Y5 ($m)	20	20	20	20
Market value of equity ($m)	47.5	31.6	18.4	14.7
Debt/equity ratio (market value)	42%	63%	109%	136%
Share price (cents)	864	574	335	267
Dividends per share (cents)	40	35	29	29
Total shareholder return	58%	82%	36%	

Achievement of corporate objectives

JJG Co has shareholder wealth maximisation as an objective. The wealth of shareholders is increased by dividends received and capital gains on shares owned. Total shareholder return compares the sum of the dividend received and the capital gain with the opening share price. The shareholders of JJG Co had a return of 58% in 20X8, compared with a return predicted by the capital asset pricing model of 14%. The lowest return shareholders have received was 36% and the highest return was 82%. On this basis, the shareholders of the company have experienced a significant increase in wealth. It is debatable whether this has been as a result of the actions of the company, however. Share prices may increase irrespective of the actions and decisions of managers, or even despite them. In fact, looking at the dividend per share history of the company, there was one year (20X6) where dividends were constant, even though earnings per share increased. It is also difficult to know when wealth has been maximised.

Another objective of the company was to achieve a continuous increase in earnings per share. Analysis shows that earnings per share increased every year, with an average increase of 14.9%. This objective appears to have been achieved.

Comment on financial performance

Return on capital employed (ROCE) has been growing towards the sector average of 25% on a year-by-year basis from 22% in 20X5. This steady growth in the primary accounting ratio can be contrasted with irregular growth in revenue, the reasons for which are unknown.

Return on shareholders' funds has been consistently higher than the average for the sector. This may be due more to the capital structure of JJG Co than to good performance by the company, however, in the sense that shareholders' funds are smaller on a book value basis than the long-term debt capital. In every previous year but 20X8 the gearing of the company was higher than the sector average.

(b) The current debt/equity ratio of JJG Co is 42% (20/47.5). Although this is less than the sector average value of 50%, it is more useful from a financial risk perspective to look at the extent to which interest payments are covered by profits.

	20X8	20X7	20X6	20X5
Profit before interest and tax ($m)	9.8	8.5	7.5	6.8
Bond interest ($m)	1.6	1.6	1.6	1.6
Interest coverage ratio (times)	6.1	5.3	4.7	4.3

The interest on the bond issue is $1.6 million (8% of $20m), giving an interest coverage ratio of 6.1 times. If JJG Co has overdraft finance, the interest coverage ratio will be lower than this, but there is insufficient information to determine if an overdraft exists. The interest coverage ratio is not only below the sector average, it is also low enough to be a cause for concern. While the ratio shows an upward trend over the period under consideration, it still indicates that an issue of further debt would be unwise.

A placing, or any issue of new shares such as a rights issue or a public offer, would decrease gearing. If the expansion of business results in an increase in profit before interest and tax, the interest coverage ratio will increase and financial risk will fall. Given the current financial position of JJG Co, a decrease in financial risk is certainly preferable to an increase.

A placing will dilute ownership and control, providing the new equity issue is taken up by new institutional shareholders, while a rights issue will not dilute ownership and control, providing existing shareholders take up their rights. A bond issue does not have ownership and control implications, although restrictive or negative covenants in bond issue documents can limit the actions of a company and its managers.

All three financing choices are long-term sources of finance and so are appropriate for a long-term investment such as the proposed expansion of existing business.

Equity issues such as a placing and a rights issue do not require security. No information is provided on the non-current assets of JJG Co, but it is likely that the existing bond issue is secured. If a new bond issue was being considered, JJG Co would need to consider whether it had sufficient non-current assets to offer as security, although it is likely that new non-current assets would be bought as part of the business expansion.

ACCA marking scheme		Marks
(a)	Relevant financial analysis	6 – 7
	Shareholder wealth discussion	2 – 3
	Earnings per share discussion	2 – 3
	Comment on financial performance	1 – 2
	Maximum	13
(b)	Financial analysis	1 – 2
	Discussion of rights issue and placing	2 – 3
	Discussion of bond issue	2 – 3
	Maximum	7
Total		20

Examiner's comments

This question provided historical information relating to a company and average values for its business sector.

In part (a), candidates were required to evaluate the financial performance of the company and to discuss the extent to which it had achieved its objectives of maximising shareholder wealth and continuous growth in earnings per share (EPS).

Many candidates had difficulty in calculating accounting ratios to compare with the sector averages provided. Accounting ratios have standard names and standard definitions and candidates should know these. Some candidates calculated profit after tax, even though the question gave annual earnings for each of four years. Some candidates averaged the four years of data provided, simply because the question provided average sector data. Some candidates calculated ratios for one year only and ignored the three other years.

Many candidates did not understand the significance of the inclusion in the question of an average sector value for the return predicted by the capital asset pricing model (CAPM). This value (14%) provided a way to assess whether the company had achieved its objective of maximising the wealth of shareholders. If the return that shareholders had received each year, in the form of capital gains and dividend, exceeded the return predicted by the CAPM, it could be argued that the objective had been achieved, since the company had outperformed the business sector as a whole. Since total shareholder return was 36%, 82% and 58%, this certainly seemed to be the case here. Some candidates argued that this objective had been achieved on the basis of inappropriate analysis, such as that the amount of reserves or the return on capital employed had increased each year.

It could be demonstrated that the objective of achieving continuous growth in EPS had been achieved by calculating the EPS figure for each year.

Part (b) asked for an analysis and discussion of the relative merits of a rights issue, a placing and an issue of bonds as ways of raising the $15 million of finance needed. Better answers started with analysis and used this as the basis for discussion. The effect of raising the $15 million of finance on gearing and interest cover, for example, had to be assessed before an informed answer could be offered.

Many answers had little or no analysis and compared the three financing methods in general terms, for example looking at ownership and control, increase or decrease in gearing and financial risk, issue costs, servicing costs and maturity.

6   NEWS FOR YOU

Key answer tips

To score well on part (a), you must ensure you apply your basic knowledge of economics to the specifics of News For You's situation. In part (b) the majority of marks are available for the justifications you provide as opposed to the conclusion you reach. The highlighted words are key phrases that markers are looking for.

(a)   Economic opinion on the effect of an **interest rate change** on News For You might vary. Keynesian economists argue that if base rate (and other interest rates) fall, this will lead to an increase in consumer demand (i.e. consumer spending). Unfortunately, however, even if the recent drop in the base rate increases consumer demand, it is unlikely to have any significant impact on the particular business of News For You. Sales are likely to remain unchanged, because newspapers and small confectionery items are low cost purchases, often bought on impulse. Interest rate movements will not make such items suddenly affordable where before they were not.

News For You needs to think about other ways in which the interest rate change might affect its business, and particularly its impact on business costs. If the company has an overdraft facility, its cost of borrowing will have been reduced. At the same time, the expansion plans require the business to raise $2 million, and changes in interest rates affect the cost of all types of capital, both loans and equity. Corporate borrowing rates are generally linked to the prevailing base rate or inter-bank lending rate, with companies paying a premium above base or interbank rate for their loans. The drop in interest rates will therefore affect the required return on the finance needed to fund the proposed expansion. If News For You uses Discounted Cash Flow analysis for investment appraisals, the fall in the cost of capital resulting from the drop in the base rate will mean that a lower discount rate can be applied to the investment evaluation. A lower rate of discount will result in a higher Net Present Value for any given proposal.

Keynesian economists, however, do not agree that changes in interest rates affect corporate investment decisions. They argue that investments are more dependent on the level of business confidence. It might be possible to suggest that News For You will see the fall in the base rate as stimulating general economic confidence. If so, it will be more confident about the future of its business, and so regardless of any changes in the cost of capital, it might be more willing to undertake the expansionary investment. (On the other hand, a fall in interest rates could be a response to a deterioration in the economy, and a loss of business confidence.)

The **inflation figures** are useful to News For You because they can directly affect profit and cash flow forecasts. The impact of inflation on cash flows and profit will be dependent to a large degree on the relative rates of increase in wages, the cost of wholesale supplies for the shop, and the prices that News For You can charge its customers. The quoted rate of inflation is very low at just over 1% per year and, although the rate is not expected to fall any further, its current level is unlikely to have a dramatic effect on the ability of the business to trade profitably. The greater risk for the business might come from the problem that, because inflation is so low, customers are not prepared to tolerate any price rises at all.

If so, News For You might become more vulnerable to loss of business to the large food stores, which can draw away customers via price cutting campaigns.

Personal and corporation tax rates are relevant to the owners of News For You because they will affect the net gain to the business that may be generated by expansion. As with interest rates, tax rates can affect personal spending patterns and therefore affect the sales revenue of a particular business. News For You, however, is unlikely to have a business that is sensitive to tax rates, because its products are basic essentials and low cost items. Nonetheless, the information that tax rates will remain unchanged is useful because it allows the business to be certain of the amount of tax relief that may be available on loan finance, and the relief that equity investors may claim for investing in a small unquoted company. This information might be useful in deciding whether or not to go ahead with the expansion, because it may affect the relative cost and availability of capital.

The **changes in taxes on tobacco** might be expected to have had a significant effect on News For You because it is one of the relatively high value products sold by the stores. The question indicates that tobacco sales have been falling, but it is unclear whether this drop is linked to the 10% rise in tax over the last twelve months, or simply a result of the population becoming more health conscious and so buying fewer cigarettes. If customers are price-sensitive in their purchasing of tobacco, News For You might once again find itself vulnerable to competition from the food retailers that can exercise greater buying power and sell similar products at lower prices. The high cost of these items also means that inventory holding costs are high, and if inventory turnover is reduced because of tax increase, then the amount of working capital required by News For You will rise.

The **investigation into the food sector** might prove detrimental to News For You if it serves to initiate a price war amongst the retailers, all of whom will be anxious to prove that they look after their customers. The business grew very quickly between 20X2 and 20X6, but since then sales revenue has increased by just 2% per year, and the owners must be concerned that further growth potential is limited, at least within the existing outlets. Moving into the sale of basic foodstuffs has been used as a strategy to compensate for loss of sales in other products such as tobacco, but in many countries a large proportion of people do their food shopping in large retail outlets. By expanding their product range, News For You has also created for itself another set of competitors in the form of food retailers. The only way in which the business might gain from this investigation is if it also covers food wholesaling, and the result is a drop in the prices that News For You have to pay for their inventory.

(b) **Arguments in favour of the expansion include the following:**

- The sales revenue figures suggest that there is only limited opportunity for the business to continue to grow organically. The business is seeking to replace sales of tobacco and newspapers with sales of foods, but as suggested in answer to (a), the potential of this side of the business may be limited. News For You may be advised to try to grow sales revenue by means of acquiring new outlets instead.

- If News For You is being forced into paying relatively high prices for supplies from a local wholesaler, then expansion may allow it to gain more bargaining power, and purchase at reduced rates from a national wholesale chain. Increased size will offer the opportunity to take advantage of possible economies of scale via bulk ordering. In this way, margins could be widened and the overall business made more profitable.

- With a larger number of stores covering a wider geographic area, News For You will be able to broaden the nature of their business base, so that it will be less vulnerable to regional economic trends.

Arguments against any expansion include the following:

- The potential to increase sales substantially via food sales is very limited. The majority of people purchase most of their food from larger stores, and will only use a local shop for small low cost items, for which it is not worthwhile making a special car journey to the supermarket. It is unlikely a profitable business can be created based on this type of sale.

- The widespread ownership of televisions and access to differing forms of mass media communications is likely to mean that fewer people will purchase newspapers on a daily basis. This is particularly true of those papers that are also published in electronic form. Many newsagents are dependent for the bulk of their sales on customers who come into the shop to buy a newspaper and then purchase additional items at the same time. If customers do not come in for a newspaper, then the associated sales income will also be lost. Expanding a business where there is such a risk of demand falling away may be regarded as very risky.

- The information in the question suggests that the competitive environment for News For You is becoming much tougher on a number of different fronts simultaneously, with rising excise duties, powerful food retailers and a reduction in tobacco and newspaper purchases. Expansion usually occurs because a business is very confident of the future, but in this case it is questionable whether News For You has much about which to be confident.

It would therefore seem advisable for News For You to postpone its expansion plans, and perhaps look at ways of using its existing outlets to sell very different products, thereby 're-inventing' their business, perhaps by moving completely away from confectionery and into, for example, video rental.

WORKING CAPITAL MANAGEMENT

7   GORWA CO

Key answer tips

In part (a) students may go into more depth about how to hedge interest rate risk and miss marks for analysing the effects of an increase in interest rates on the company concerned. Although the model answer presents a number of calculations that could be performed, there are only 1 – 2 marks available for the financial analysis. This is another reminder that the FM exam is far from wholly numerical.

In part (b), again a huge range of calculations are possible. If students only manage a selection of those presented in the model answer, they should still be able to score highly. The weighting between calculations and discussion is 50:50 and the discussion provided in the model answer demonstrates the style the examiner is hoping for.

(a)   **Financial analysis**

Fixed interest debt proportion (20X6) = 100 × 2,425/(2,425 + 1,600) = 60%

Fixed interest debt proportion (20X7) = 100 × 2,425/(2,425 + 3,225) = 43%

Fixed interest payments = 2,425 × 0.08 = $194,000

Variable interest payments (20X6) = 274 – 194 = $80,000 or 29%

Variable interest payments (20X7) = 355 – 194 = $161,000 or 45%

(Alternatively, considering the overdraft amounts and the average variable overdraft interest rate of 5% per year:

Variable interest payments (20X6) = 1.6m × 0.05 = $80,000 or 29%

Variable interest payments (20X7) = 3.225m × 0.05 = $161,250 or 45%)

Interest coverage ratio (20X6) = 2,939/274 = 10.7 times

Interest coverage ratio (20X7) = 2,992/355 = 8.4 times

Debt/equity ratio (20X6) = 100 × 2,425/11,325 = 21%

Debt/equity ratio (20X7) = 100 × 2,425/12,432 = 20%

Total debt/equity ratio (20X6) = 100 × (2,425 + 1,600)/11,325 = 35%

Total debt/equity ratio (20X7) = 100 × (2,425 + 3,225)/12,432 = 45%

Discussion

Gorwa Co has both fixed interest debt and variable interest rate debt amongst its sources of finance. The fixed interest bonds have ten years to go before they need to be redeemed and they therefore offer Gorwa Co long-term protection against an increase in interest rates.

In 20X6, 60% of the company's debt was fixed interest in nature, but in 20X7 this had fallen to 43%. The floating-rate proportion of the company's debt therefore increased from 40% in 20X6 to 57% in 20X7. The interest coverage ratio fell from 10.7 times in 20X6 to 8.4 times in 20X7, a decrease which will be a cause for concern to the company if it were to continue. The debt/equity ratio (including the overdraft due to its size) increased over the same period from 35% to 45% (if the overdraft is excluded, the debt/equity ratio declines slightly from 21% to 20%). From the perspective of an increase in interest rates, the financial risk of Gorwa Co has increased and may continue to increase if the company does not take action to halt the growth of its variable interest rate overdraft. The proportion of interest payments linked to floating rate debt has increased from 29% in 20X6 to 45% in 20X7. An increase in interest rates will further reduce profit before taxation, which is lower in 20X7 than in 20X6, despite a 40% increase in revenue.

One way to hedge against an increase in interest rates is to exchange some or all of the variable-rate overdraft into long-term fixed-rate debt. There is likely to be an increase in interest payments because long-term debt is usually more expensive than short-term debt. Gorwa would also be unable to benefit from falling interest rates if most of its debt paid fixed rather than floating rate interest.

Interest rate options and interest rate futures may be of use in the short term, depending on the company's plans to deal with its increasing overdraft.

For the longer term, Gorwa Co could consider raising a variable-rate bank loan, linked to a variable rate-fixed interest rate swap.

(b) **Financial analysis**

		20X7	20X6
Inventory days	(365 × 2,400)/23,781		37 days
	(365 × 4,600)/34,408	49 days	
Receivables days	(365 × 2,200)/26,720		30 days
	(365 × 4,600)/37,400	45 days	
Payables days	(365 × 2,000)/23,781		31 days
	(365 × 4,750)/34,408	51 days	
Current ratio	4,600/3,600		1.3 times
	9,200/7,975	1.15 times	
Quick ratio	2,200/3,600		0.61 times
	4,600/7,975	0.58 times	
Sales/net working capital	26,720/1,000		26.7 times
	37,400/1,225	30.5 times	
Revenue increase	37,400/26,720	40%	
Non-current assets increase	13,632/12,750	7%	
Inventory increase	4,600/2,400	92%	
Receivables increase	4,600/2,200	109%	
Payables increase	4,750/2,000	138%	
Overdraft increase	3,225/1,600	102%	

Discussion

Overtrading or undercapitalisation arises when a company has too small a capital base to support its level of business activity. Difficulties with liquidity may arise as an overtrading company may have insufficient capital to meet its liabilities as they fall due. Overtrading is often associated with a rapid increase in revenue and Gorwa Co has experienced a 40% increase in revenue over the last year. Investment in working capital has not matched the increase in sales, however, since the sales/net working capital ratio has increased from 26.7 times to 30.5 times.

Overtrading could be indicated by a deterioration in inventory days. Here, inventory days have increased from 37 days to 49 days, while inventory has increased by 92% compared to the 40% increase in revenue. It is possible that inventory has been stockpiled in anticipation of a further increase in revenue, leading to an increase in operating costs.

Overtrading could also be indicated by deterioration in receivables days. In this case, receivables have increased by 109% compared to the 40% increase in revenue. The increase in revenue may have been fuelled in part by a relaxation of credit terms.

As the liquidity problem associated with overtrading deepens, the overtrading company increases its reliance on short-term sources of finance, including overdraft, trade payables and leasing. The overdraft of Gorwa Co has more than doubled in size to $3.225 million, while trade payables have increased by $2.74 million or 137%. Both increases are much greater than the 40% increase in revenue. There is evidence here of an increased reliance on short-term finance sources.

Overtrading can also be indicated by decreases in the current ratio and the quick ratio. The current ratio of Gorwa Co has fallen from 1.3 times to 1.15 times, while its quick ratio has fallen from 0.61 times to 0.58 times.

There are clear indications that Gorwa Co is experiencing the kinds of symptoms usually associated with overtrading. A more complete and meaningful analysis could be undertaken if appropriate benchmarks were available, such as key ratios from comparable companies in the same industry sector, or additional financial information from prior years so as to establish trends in key ratios.

ACCA marking scheme			
			Marks
(a)	Discussion of effects of interest rate increase	3 – 4	
	Relevant financial analysis	1 – 2	
	Interest rate hedging	2 – 3	
		———	
			Max 9
(b)	Financial analysis	5 – 6	
	Discussion of overtrading	4 – 5	
	Conclusion as to overtrading	1	
		———	
			Max 11
			———
Total			**20**
			———

Examiner's comments

Part (a) asked for a discussion, with supporting calculations, of the possible effects on a company of an increase in interest rates, and advice on how to protect against interest rate risk.

Some candidates were not aware of the difference between interest rate and interest payment, and consequently discussed how the company's finance costs (interest payments) had increased from one year to the next. Analysis would have shown that the increase in the finance cost was due to the increase in the overdraft and that the interest rate applied to the overdraft was 5% in each year, i.e. the interest rate had not changed. The bonds were fixed-rate in nature, as they were given in the statement of financial position as 8% bonds. As the question asked about hedging interest rate risk, looking at the balance between fixed rate debt (bonds) and floating rate debt (overdraft) was also relevant here, as was a consideration of gearing and interest cover.

The question was, in fact, very open in nature, and a discussion of the effects of an increase in interest rates could look at an increase in financial risk, a decrease in sales due to a fall in demand, an increase in operating costs and a cutting back of investment plans.

Many answers offered a number of ways of protecting (hedging) against interest rate risk, including matching and smoothing: using forward rate agreements, interest rate futures, interest rate options and interest rates swaps; and taking steps to decrease the dependency on variable-rate overdraft finance and hence the exposure to interest rate increases, for example by improving working capital management.

In part (b), the requirement was to discuss, with supporting calculations, whether a company was overtrading (undercapitalised). Relevant financial analysis, including ratio analysis, therefore needed to look at the level of business activity and the area of working capital management.

Better answers calculated a series of accounting ratios, perhaps adding some growth rates and changes in financial statement entries, and used this analysis to look at the increasing dependence of the company on short-term sources of finance while sales were expanding at a high rate. Some answers noted that short-term finance had been used to acquire additional non-current assets, that inventory growth exceeded sales growth, and so on. Weaker answers often did little more than repeat in words the financial ratios that had been already calculated, without explaining how or why the identified changes supported the idea that the company was overtrading.

8   FLG CO

Key answer tips

Parts (a) and (b) are both standard textbook material. In part (a), for six marks you should discuss at least three factors. Don't forget the requirement is to "discuss" not "state" so you must give some commentary: 'the length of the working capital cycle' will not get the full marks available.

In part (b) the requirement is again to "discuss". Given the emphasis is on how both factoring and invoice discounting can assist in the **management** of accounts receivable, there should be more discussion on factoring than invoice discounting (the latter being a tool for managing cash flow rather than managing accounts receivable). Don't forget to define each of the terms to collect some easy marks.

The calculation in part (c) requires some "out of the box" thinking in order to see how the brief information provided can be used to work out the size of the overdraft.

Not only does it involve re-arranging the usual working capital ratios we're used to seeing, it also requires a disaggregation of the operating cycle to reveal the inventory holding period.

In contrast, part (d) is a fairly straightforward application of the EOQ model that shouldn't pose many difficulties. The highlighted words are key phrases that markers are looking for.

(a)   There are a number of factors that determine the level of investment in current assets and their relative importance varies from company to company.

Length of working capital cycle

The working capital cycle or operating cycle is the period of time between when a company settles its accounts payable and when it receives cash from its accounts receivable. Operating activities during this period need to be financed and as the operating period lengthens, the amount of finance needed increases. Companies with comparatively longer operating cycles than others in the same industry sector, will therefore require comparatively higher levels of investment in current assets.

Terms of trade

These determine the period of credit extended to customers, any discounts offered for early settlement or bulk purchases, and any penalties for late payment. A company whose terms of trade are more generous than another company in the same industry sector will therefore need a comparatively higher investment in current assets.

Policy on level of investment in current assets

Even within the same industry sector, companies will have different policies regarding the level of investment in current assets, depending on their attitude to risk. A company with a comparatively conservative approach to the level of investment in current assets would maintain higher levels of inventory, offer more generous credit terms and have higher levels of cash in reserve than a company with a comparatively aggressive approach. While the more aggressive approach would be more profitable because of the lower level of investment in current assets, it would also be more risky, for example in terms of running out of inventory in periods of fluctuating demand, of failing to have the particular goods required by a customer, of failing to retain customers who migrate to more generous credit terms elsewhere, and of being less able to meet unexpected demands for payment.

Industry in which organisation operates

Another factor that influences the level of investment in current assets is the industry within which an organisation operates. Some industries, such as aircraft construction, will have long operating cycles due to the length of time needed to manufacture finished goods and so will have comparatively higher levels of investment in current assets than industries such as supermarket chains, where goods are bought in for resale with minimal additional processing and where many goods have short shelf lives.

(b) Factoring involves a company turning over administration of its sales ledger to a factor, which is a financial institution with expertise in this area. The factor will assess the creditworthiness of new customers, record sales, send out statements and reminders, collect payment, identify late payers and chase them for settlement, and take appropriate legal action to recover debts where necessary.

The factor will also offer finance to a company based on invoices raised for goods sold or services provided. This is usually up to 80% of the face value of invoices raised. The finance is repaid from the settled invoices, with the balance being passed to the issuing company after deduction of a fee equivalent to an interest charge on cash advanced.

If factoring is without recourse, the factor rather than the company will carry the cost of any bad debts that arise on overdue accounts. Factoring without recourse therefore offers credit protection to the selling company, although the factor's fee (a percentage of credit sales) will be comparatively higher than with non-recourse factoring to reflect the cost of the insurance offered.

(c) **Calculation of size of overdraft**

Inventory period = operating cycle + payables period − receivables period = 3 + 1 − 2 = 2 months

Inventory = 1.89m × 2/12 = $315,000

Accounts receivable = 4.2m × 2/12 = $700,000

Current assets = 315,000 + 700,000 = $1,015,000

Current liabilities = current assets/current ratio = 1,015,000/1.4 = $725,000

Accounts payable = 1.89m × 1/12 = $157,500

Overdraft = 725,000 − 157,500 = $567,500

Net working capital = current assets − current liabilities = 1,015,000 − 725,000 = $290,000

Short-term financing cost = 567,500 × 0.07 = $39,725

Long-term financing cost = 290,000 × 0.11 = $31,900

Total cost of financing current assets = 39,725 + 31,900 = $71,625

(d) (i) Economic order quantity = $\sqrt{(2 \times 6 \times 60,000/0.5)}$ = 1,200 units

Number of orders = 60,000/1,200 = 50 order per year

Annual ordering cost = 50 × 6 = $300 per year

Average inventory = 1,200/2 = 600 units

Annual holding cost = 600 × 0.5 = $300 per year

Inventory cost = 60,000 × 12 = $720,000

Total cost of inventory with EOQ policy = 720,000 + 300 + 300 = $720,600 per year

(ii) Order size for bulk discounts = 10,000 units

Number of orders = 60,000/10,000 = 6 orders per year

Annual ordering cost = 6 × 6 = $36 per year

Average inventory = 10,000/2 =5,000 units

Annual holding cost = 5,000 × 2 = $10,000 per year

Discounted material cost = 12 × 0.99 = $11.88 per unit

Inventory cost = 60,000 × 11.88 = $712,800

Total cost of inventory with discount = 712,800 + 36 + 10,000 = $722,836 per year

The EOQ approach results in a slightly lower total inventory cost

ACCA marking scheme				Marks
(a)	Discussion of key factors		Maximum	4
(b)	Discussion of factoring		Maximum	3
(c)	Value of inventory			1
	Accounts receivable and accounts payable			1
	Current liabilities			1
	Size of overdraft			1
	Net working capital			1
	Total cost of financing working capital			1
				6
(d)	(i)	Economic order quantity		1
		Ordering cost and holding cost under EOQ		1
		Inventory cost under EOQ		1
		Total cost of inventory with EOQ policy		1
				4
	(ii)	Ordering cost and holding cost with discount		1
		Inventory cost with discount		1
		Total cost of inventory with bulk purchase discount		1
		Conclusion		1
	Maximum			3
Total				20

Examiner's comments

Part (a) asked for a discussion of the factors which determine the level of investment in current assets. Although this topic is clearly identified in the FM Study Guide (C3a), answers often referred incorrectly to working capital funding strategies (C3b). The suggested answer to this question refers to factors mentioned in the FM Study Guide, such as length of working capital cycle, terms of trade, working capital policy and so on. Answers that discussed these or similar factors gained high marks.

Part (b) asked for a discussion of the ways in which factoring could help in managing accounts receivable. Many candidates discussed relevant points in relation to factoring and received credit accordingly.

In part (c), candidates were asked to calculate the size of an overdraft, the net working capital, and the total cost of financing current assets.

The variable quality of the answers indicates a need for candidates to ensure, not only that they are familiar with accounting ratios, but also that they are familiar with the accounting items to which the ratios relate, in this case sales, cost of sales, inventory, trade receivables, trade payables and so on. Many candidates were unable to calculate the inventory turnover period, given the operating cycle, the average collection period and the average payable period. Many candidates were also unable to work backwards from the provided ratios, for example to calculate the level of receivables given the average collection period and the amount of credit sales. Some candidates omitted the overdraft when calculating net working capital, indicating unfamiliarity with the structure of the statement of financial position.

Part (d) asked candidates to calculate the total cost of inventory using the economic order quantity model (EOQ) and to evaluate a discount offered by a supplier. Many candidates gained high marks here by offering a comprehensive answer. Candidates who did not gain high marks appeared to be unsure of the meaning of the variables in the EOQ, even though the units of each were clearly specified in the question.

9   PKA CO   *Walk in the footsteps of a top tutor*

Key answer tips

This question combines elements from throughout the working capital management area of the syllabus with the foreign currency risk section. It is a good reflection of the examiner's style. The highlighted words are key phrases that markers are looking for.

Tutor's top tips

Part (a) will require some thought. This is a fairly common exam question but the complexity of it can change depending on the information given. Your starting point should be to work out the economic order quantity (EOQ). We're given the formula in the exam so it's really just a case of finding the three pieces of information required, all of which are clearly stated in the scenario. Having calculated the EOQ, you are now equipped to work out the relative costs of the current policy compared to a potential new policy based on the EOQ. You will need to calculate:

– *Total order costs (using annual demand, order size and cost per order)*

– *Total holding costs (using the cost of holding one unit and the average level of inventory).*

Four of these five things are given to us in the scenario or have already been calculated. The tricky one is the average level of inventory as we need to consider not only the size of the order but also the level of buffer stocks held. You would be forgiven for thinking the buffer stock is 35,000 units, however you would be wrong. Some of these units would in fact be used in the two weeks it takes for the order to arrive. The information provided on annual demand will enable us to calculate how many units would be used in those two weeks, from which we can work out the level of inventory just prior to the order being delivered. This is by far the trickiest part of this question and it's important to keep it in context. Had you not spotted this, you would only have lost 2 marks. Don't forget, the requirement asks for the saving – be sure that you specifically calculate this to get all the marks.

(a) **Cost of current ordering policy of PKA Co**

Ordering cost = €250 × (625,000/100,000) = €1,563 per year

Weekly demand = 625,000/50 = 12,500 units per week

Consumption during 2 weeks lead time = 12,500 × 2 = 25,000 units

Buffer stock = re-order level less usage during lead time = 35,000 – 25,000 = 10,000 units

Average stock held during the year = 10,000 + (100,000/2) = 60,000 units

Holding cost = 60,000 × €0.50 = €30,000 per year

Total cost = ordering cost plus holding cost = €1,563 + €30,000 = €31,563 per year

Economic order quantity = √(2 × 250 × 625,000/0.5) = 25,000 units

Number of orders per year = 625,000/25,000 = 25 per year

Ordering cost = €250 × 25 = €6,250 per year

Holding cost (ignoring buffer stock) = €0.50 × (25,000/2) = €0.50 × 12,500 = €6,250 per year

Holding cost (including buffer stock) = €0.50 × (10,000 + 12,500) = €11,250 per year

Total cost of EOQ-based ordering policy = €6,250 + €11,250 = €17,500 per year

Saving for PKA Co by using EOQ-based ordering policy = €31,563 – €17,500 = €14,063 per year

Tutor's top tips

A quick read of the scenario for accounts receivable management gives us some ideas for sub-headings to use to answer part (b); accounts receivable period and bad debts. For 5 marks you should be aiming for a couple of points under each heading.

(b) The information gathered by the Financial Manager of PKA Co indicates that two areas of concern in the management of domestic accounts receivable are the increasing level of bad debts as a percentage of credit sales and the excessive credit period being taken by credit customers.

Reducing bad debts

The incidence of bad debts, which has increased from 5% to 8% of credit sales in the last year, can be reduced by assessing the creditworthiness of new customers before offering them credit and PKA Co needs to introduce a policy detailing how this should be done, or review its existing policy, if it has one, since it is clearly not working very well. In order to do this, information about the solvency, character and credit history of new clients is needed. This information can come from a variety of sources, such as bank references, trade references and credit reports from credit reference agencies. Whether credit is offered to the new customer and the terms of the credit offered can then be based on an explicit and informed assessment of default risk.

Reduction of average accounts receivable period

Customers have taken an average of 75 days credit over the last year rather than the 30 days offered by PKA Co, i.e. more than twice the agreed credit period.

As a result, PKA Co will be incurring a substantial opportunity cost, either from the additional interest cost on the short-term financing of accounts receivable or from the incremental profit lost by not investing the additional finance tied up by the longer average accounts receivable period. PKA Co needs to find ways to encourage accounts receivable to be settled closer to the agreed date.

Assuming that the credit period offered by PKA Co is in line with that of its competitors, the company should determine whether they too are suffering from similar difficulties with late payers. If they are not, PKA Co should determine in what way its own terms differ from those of its competitors and consider whether offering the same trade terms would have an impact on its accounts receivable. For example, its competitors may offer a discount for early settlement while PKA Co does not and introducing a discount may achieve the desired reduction in the average accounts receivable period. If its competitors are experiencing a similar accounts receivable problem, PKA Co could take the initiative by introducing more favourable early settlement terms and perhaps generate increased business as well as reducing the average accounts receivable period.

PKA Co should also investigate the efficiency with which accounts receivable are managed. Are statements sent regularly to customers? Is an aged accounts receivable analysis produced at the end of each month? Are outstanding accounts receivable contacted regularly to encourage payment? Is credit denied to any overdue accounts seeking further business? Is interest charged on overdue accounts? These are all matters that could be included by PKA Co in a revised policy on accounts receivable management.

Tutor's top tips

Finally, in part (c), you must be very clear on the scenario before your start. PKA has a foreign supplier so to settle their debts PKA will need to buy Dollars. If PKA is buying, the bank will be selling (remember the rhyme – the bank will always sell low (sounds like hello) and buy high (sounds like bye bye)!) We therefore know the appropriate spot rate is 1.998 – 0.002 = $1.996:€ and the appropriate forward rate is 1.979 – 0.004 = $1.975:€.

Once you're happy on which rates are to be used, you can calculate the Euros payable under the forward market hedge (don't let this term confuse you – it simply means a forward exchange contract) using the forward rate. You can also start the calculation for the lead payment using the spot rate. Finish this by thinking about the interest payable on the required loan. Since this is a Euro loan, you need half of the one year Euro borrowing rate.

Lastly, you can work on the money market hedge. Start by drawing out a diagram of the process, remembering the purpose is to eliminate the exchange risk by doing the translation now but then making sure that money continues to work for us by investing it in a Dollar bank account to earn interest.

(c)   Money market hedge

PKA Co should place sufficient dollars on deposit now so that, with accumulated interest, the six-month liability of $250,000 can be met. Since the company has no surplus cash at the present time, the cost of these dollars must be met by a short-term euro loan.

Six-month dollar deposit rate = 3.5/2 = 1.75%

Current spot selling rate = 1.998 – 0.002 = $1.996 per euro

Six-month euro borrowing rate = 6.1/2 = 3.05%

Dollars deposited now = 250,000/1.0175 = $245,700

Cost of these dollars at spot = 245,700/1.996 = 123,096 euros

Euro value of loan in six months' time = 123,096 × 1.0305 = 126,850 euros

Forward market hedge

Six months forward selling rate = 1.979 – 0.004 = $1.975 per euro

Euro cost using forward market hedge = 250,000/1.975 = 126,582 euros

Lead payment

Since the dollar is appreciating against the euro, a lead payment may be worthwhile.

Euro cost now = 250,000/1.996 = 125,251 euros

This cost must be met by a short-term loan at a six-month interest rate of 3.05%

Euro value of loan in six months' time = 125,251 × 1.0305 = 129,071 euros

Evaluation of hedges

The relative costs of the three hedges can be compared since they have been referenced to the same point in time, i.e. six months in the future. The most expensive hedge is the lead payment, while the cheapest is the forward market hedge. Using the forward market to hedge the account payable currency risk can therefore be recommended.

Tutor's top tips

The key learning points from this question are the importance of doing the easy parts of the question first and making sure you maintain good time discipline to ensure you don't get bogged down in one part of the question at the expense of another part.

Examiner's comments

In part (a) candidates were asked to calculate the cost of a company's current ordering policy and to determine the saving that could be made by using the economic order quantity (EOQ) model. Many candidates gained high marks for their answers to this part of question 4, calculating correctly the ordering costs of both the current and the EOQ policies, and comparing the total costs of each policy to show the saving arising from adoption of the EOQ policy. Many of these comparisons, however, were based on incorrect calculations of the holding costs of each policy.

Some candidates failed to consider the buffer inventory in calculating holding costs. Others used the re-order inventory level as the buffer level, failing to reduce inventory by consumption during the lead-time it took for orders to arrive after being placed. Others added the re-order level to order quantity before dividing by two to calculate average inventory level, when only the order quantity is averaged.

Part (b) required candidates to discuss the ways in which a company could improve the management of domestic accounts receivable and many gained full marks here. Candidates failing to gain high marks tended to offer a limited number of possible methods, for example by focussing at length on factoring to the exclusion of internal accounts receivables management methods. Despite the requirement to discuss domestic accounts receivable, some candidates discussed export factoring and exchange rate hedging.

In part (c) candidates were required to evaluate whether a money market hedge, a forward market hedge or a lead payment should be used to hedge a foreign account payable. Some candidates offered discursive answers, for which they gained little credit since the question asked for an evaluation of hedging methods.

Many candidates were unable to calculate correctly the spot and forward exchange rates from the information provided. Many candidates failed to compare all three hedges from a common time horizon perspective, i.e. either from the current time or from three months hence.

Since it was a foreign currency account payable that was being hedged (a liability), the money market hedge involved creating a foreign currency asset (a deposit). The hedging company therefore needed to borrow euros, exchange them into dollars and place these dollars on deposit. Some candidates offered the opposite hedge, i.e. borrowing dollars and exchanging them into euros.

10   KXP CO

Key answer tips

Part (a) draws heavily upon knowledge of financial ratios and how various figures in the financial statements relate to each other.

Part (b) is a fairly common requirement but does require students to work methodically through the information and lay out their working clearly in order for their thought process to be followed.

It is important to make sure the requirement in part (c) is read carefully to ensure students do not go off on a tangent. The words "working capital" and "policy" must not be ignored and discussion should not focus on investment and financing in detail.

The highlighted words are key phrases that markers are looking for.

(a)   **Calculation of net cost/benefit**

Current receivables = $2,466,000

Receivables paying within 30 days = 15m × 0.5 × 30/365 = $616,438

Receivables paying within 45 days = 15m × 0.3 × 45/365 = $554,795

Receivables paying within 60 days = 15m × 0.2 × 60/365 = $493,151

Revised receivables = 616,438 + 554,795 + 493,151 = $1,664,384

Reduction in receivables = 2,466,000 – 1,664,384 = $801,616

Reduction in financing cost = 801,616 × 0.06 = $48,097

Cost of discount = 15m × 0.5 × 0.01 = $75,000

Net cost of proposed changes in receivables policy = 75,000 – 48,097 = $26,903

Alternative approach to calculation of net cost/benefit

Current receivables days = (2,466/15,000) × 365 = 60 days

Revised receivables days = (30 × 0.5) + (45 × 0.3) + (60 × 0.2) = 40.5 days

Decrease in receivables days = 60 − 40.5 = 19.5 days

Decrease in receivables = 15m × 19.5/365 = $801,370

(The slight difference compared to the earlier answer is due to rounding)

Decrease in financing cost = 801,370 × 0.06 = $48,082

Net cost of proposed changes in receivables policy = 75,000 − 48,082 = $26,918

Comment

The proposed changes in trade receivables policy are not financially acceptable. However, if the trade terms offered are comparable with those of its competitors, KXP Co needs to investigate the reasons for the (on average) late payment of current customers. This analysis also assumes constant sales and no bad debts, which is unlikely to be the case in reality.

(b) **Cost of current inventory policy**

Cost of materials = $540,000 per year

Annual ordering cost = 12 × 150 = $1,800 per year

Annual holding cost = 0.24 × (15,000/2) = $1,800 per year

Total cost of current inventory policy = 540,000 + 1,800 + 1,800 = $543,600 per year

Cost of inventory policy after bulk purchase discount

Cost of materials after bulk purchase discount = 540,000 × 0.98 = $529,200 per year

Annual demand = 12 × 15,000 = 180,000 units per year

KXP Co will need to increase its order size to 30,000 units to gain the bulk discount

Revised number of orders = 180,000/30,000 = 6 orders per year

Revised ordering cost = 6 × 150 = $900 per year

Revised holding cost = 0.24 × (30,000/2) = $3,600 per year

Revised total cost of inventory policy = 529,200 + 900 + 3,600 = $533,700 per year

Evaluation of offer of bulk purchase discount

Net benefit of taking bulk purchase discount = 543,600 − 533,700 = $9,900 per year

The bulk purchase discount looks to be financially acceptable. However, this evaluation is based on a number of unrealistic assumptions. For example, the ordering cost and the holding cost are assumed to be constant, which is unlikely to be true in reality. Annual demand is assumed to be constant, whereas in practice seasonal and other changes in demand are likely.

(c) Working capital investment policy is concerned with the level of investment in current assets, with one company being compared with another. Working capital financing policy is concerned with the relative proportions of short-term and long-term finance used by a company. While working capital investment policy is therefore assessed on an inter-company comparative basis, assessment of working capital financing policy involves analysis of financial information for one company alone.

Working capital financing policy uses an analysis of current assets into permanent current assets and fluctuating current assets. Working capital investment policy does not require this analysis. Permanent current assets represent the core level of investment in current assets that supports a given level of business activity.

Fluctuating current assets represent the changes in the level of current assets that arise through, for example, the unpredictability of business operations, such as the level of trade receivables increasing due to some customers paying late or the level of inventory increasing due to demand being less than predicted.

Working capital financing policy relies on the matching principle, which is not used by working capital investment policy. The matching principle holds that long-term assets should be financed from a long-term source of finance. Non-current assets and permanent current assets should therefore be financed from a long-term source, such as equity finance or loan note finance, while fluctuating current assets should be financed from a short-term source, such as an overdraft or a short-term bank loan.

Both working capital investment policy and working capital financing policy use the terms conservative, moderate and aggressive. In investment policy, the terms are used to indicate the comparative level of investment in current assets on an inter-company basis.

One company has a more aggressive approach compared to another company if it has a lower level of investment in current assets, and *vice versa* for a conservative approach to working capital investment policy.

In working capital financing policy, the terms are used to indicate the way in which fluctuating current assets and permanent current assets are matched to short-term and long-term finance sources.

An aggressive financing policy means that fluctuating current assets and a portion of permanent current assets are financed from a short-term finance source. A conservative financing policy means that permanent current assets and a portion of fluctuating current assets are financed from a long-term source.

An aggressive financing policy will be more profitable than a conservative financing policy because short-term finance is cheaper than long-term finance, as indicated for debt finance by the normal yield curve (term structure of interest rates).

However, an aggressive financing policy will be riskier than a conservative financing policy because short-term finance is riskier than long-term finance. For example, an overdraft is repayable on demand, while a short-term loan may be renewed on less favourable terms than an existing loan.

Provided interest payments are made, however, long-term debt will not lead to any pressure on a company and equity finance is permanent capital.

Overall, therefore, it can be said that while working capital investment policy and working capital financing policy use similar terminology, the two policies are very different in terms of their meaning and application. It is even possible, for example, for a company to have a conservative working capital investment policy while following an aggressive working capital financing policy.

ACCA marking scheme			
			Marks
(a)	Revised trade receivables		1
	Reduction in trade receivables		1
	Reduction in financing cost		1
	Cost of early settlement discount		1
	Net cost of change in receivables policy		1
	Comment on findings		1
			—
		Maximum	6
			—
(b)	Current annual ordering cost		0.5
	Current holding cost		0.5
	Total cost of current inventory policy		1
	Revised cost of materials		0.5
	Revised number of orders		0.5
	Revised ordering cost		0.5
	Revised holding cost		0.5
	Net benefit of bulk purchase discount		1
	Comment on assumptions		1
			—
		Maximum	6
			—
(c)	Working capital investment policy		3–4
	Working capital financing policy		5–6
			—
		Maximum	8
			—
Total			20
			—

Examiner's comments

Part (a) asked students to calculate the net benefit or cost of proposed changes in receivables policy, commenting on findings. The cost of an early settlement discount had to be calculated, as well as the decrease in financing cost arising from a reduction in the trade receivables balance.

Candidates were expected to recognise that although current trade terms allowed credit customers to pay after 30 days, they were in fact paying on average after 60 days, as shown by a comparison between credit sales and the level of trade receivables. The average trade receivables period after introducing the proposed changes in receivables policy was 40.5 days, leading to a lower level of trade receivables and a lower financing cost.

Weaker answers showed a lack of understanding of how the receivables days' ratio links credit sales for a period with the trade receivables balance at the end of the period. Some answers, for example, tried to calculate the revised trade receivables balance by applying changed receivables days ratios to current receivables, instead of applying them to credit sales.

In part (b) candidates were asked here to calculate whether an offered bulk purchase discount was financially acceptable, commenting on assumptions made by the calculation.

Perhaps because information on holding cost and order cost was provided in the question, many candidates calculated the economic order quantity (EOQ). The question made no reference to the EOQ and an EOQ calculation was not necessary. In fact, what was needed was a comparison between the current ordering policy and the ordering policy employing the bulk discount. Candidates who wasted time calculating the EOQ found that the company was already using an EOQ approach to ordering inventory.

Some answers did not gain full credit because they did not comment on the assumptions made by their calculations. Credit was also lost by candidates who could not calculate order cost, or holding cost, or both.

The requirement in part (c) was to discuss the similarities and differences between working capital investment policy and working capital financing policy. Many answers struggled to gain good marks with this question, and yet the topics of working capital investment policy (the level of investment in current assets) and working capital financing policy (the balance between short-term and long-term funds in financing current assets) have been examined a number of times in recent years.

Some answers ignored the words "working capital" and "policy", and discussed investment and financing in some detail. These answers did not offer what was being looked for and, for example, discussed investment appraisal techniques (investment) and equity, bonds and leasing (financing). If you look at the question as a whole, you will see that it focuses on that part of the syllabus relating to working capital.

While many answers showed good understanding of working capital financing policy, fewer answers showed understanding of working capital investment policy, and fewer answers still could discuss the similarities and differences between the two policy areas. Both policies are characterised by an assessment of their risk (conservative, moderate or matching, and aggressive), but working capital investment policy is comparative (one company is conservative or aggressive compared to another), while working capital financing policy looks only at the long-term/short-term finance balance in a given company (for example, using mainly short-term financing for permanent current assets is an aggressive policy).

Many answers seemed to be unaware that it is possible for an aggressive working capital investment policy to occur in a given company at the same time as a conservative working capital financing policy, and vice versa. These answers assumed that a company was either aggressive in both kinds of policy, or not, for example.

11   ULNAD

Key answer tips

This question covers two of the key elements within the working capital management section of the syllabus. Part (a) requires a methodical approach, working though the impact of the proposed change. Part (b) is more straightforward given that the Miller Orr formula is provided in the exam; don't neglect to explain the relevance of the values though. Part (c) covers common discursive areas and should give an opportunity to just learn and churn. The highlighted words are key phrases that markers are looking for.

(a)   Evaluation of change in credit policy

Current average collection period = 30 + 10 = 40 days

Current accounts receivable = 6m × 40/365 = $657,534

Average collection period under new policy = (0.3 × 15) + (0.7 × 60) = 46.5 days

New level of credit sales = $6.3 million

Accounts receivable after policy change = 6.3 × 46.5/ 365 = $802,603

Increase in financing cost = (802,603 – 657,534) × 0.07 = $10,155

	$
Increase in financing cost	10,155
Incremental costs = 6.3m × 0.005 =	31,500
Cost of discount = 6.3m × 0.015 × 0.3 =	28,350
Increase in costs	70,005
Contribution from increased sales = 6m × 0.05 × 0.6 =	180,000
Net benefit of policy change	109,995

The proposed policy change will increase the profitability of Ulnad Co

(b)   Determination of spread:

Daily interest rate = 5.11/365 = 0.014% per day

Variance of cash flows = 1,000 × 1,000 = $1,000,000 per day

Transaction cost = $18 per transaction

Spread $= 3 \times ((0.75 \times \text{transaction cost} \times \text{variance})/\text{interest rate})^{1/3}$

$= 3 \times ((0.75 \times 18 \times 1,000,000)/0.00014)^{1/3} = 3 \times 4,585.7 = \$13,757$

Lower limit (set by Renpec Co) = $7,500

Upper limit = 7,500 + 13,757 =$21,257

Return point = 7,500 + (13,757/3) = $12,086

The Miller-Orr model takes account of uncertainty in relation to receipts and payment. The cash balance of Renpec Co is allowed to vary between the lower and upper limits calculated by the model. If the lower limit is reached, an amount of cash equal to the difference between the return point and the lower limit is raised by selling short-term investments. If the upper limit is reached an amount of cash equal to the difference between the upper limit and the return point is used to buy short-term investments. The model therefore helps Renpec Co to decrease the risk of running out of cash, while avoiding the loss of profit caused by having unnecessarily high cash balances.

**(c)   **When considering how working capital is financed, it is useful to divide assets into non-current assets, permanent current assets and fluctuating current assets. Permanent current assets represent the core level of working capital investment needed to support a given level of sales. As sales increase, this core level of working capital also increases. Fluctuating current assets represent the changes in working capital that arise in the normal course of business operations, for example when some accounts receivable are settled later than expected, or when inventory moves more slowly than planned.

The matching principle suggests that long-term finance should be used for long-term assets. Under a matching working capital funding policy, therefore, long-term finance is used for both permanent current assets and non-current assets. Short-term finance is used to cover the short-term changes in current assets represented by fluctuating current assets.

Long-term debt has a higher cost than short-term debt in normal circumstances, for example because lenders require higher compensation for lending for longer periods, or because the risk of default increases with longer lending periods. However, long-term debt is more secure from a company point of view than short-term debt since, provided interest payments are made when due and the requirements of restrictive covenants are met, terms are fixed to maturity. Short-term debt is riskier than long-term debt because, for example, an overdraft is repayable on demand and short-term debt may be renewed on less favourable terms.

A conservative working capital funding policy will use a higher proportion of long-term finance than a matching policy, thereby financing some of the fluctuating current assets from a long-term source. This will be less risky and less profitable than a matching policy, and will give rise to occasional short-term cash surpluses.

An aggressive working capital funding policy will use a lower proportion of long-term finance than a matching policy, financing some of the permanent current assets from a short-term source such as an overdraft. This will be more risky and more profitable than a matching policy.

Other factors that influence a working capital funding policy include management attitudes to risk, previous funding decisions, and organisation size. Management attitudes to risk will determine whether there is a preference for a conservative, an aggressive or a matching approach. Previous funding decisions will determine the current position being considered in policy formulation. The size of the organisation will influence its ability to access different sources of finance. A small company, for example, may be forced to adopt an aggressive working capital funding policy because it is unable to raise additional long-term finance, whether equity of debt.

	ACCA marking scheme		
			Marks
(a)	Increase in financing cost	2 marks	
	Incremental costs	1 mark	
	Cost of discount	1 mark	
	Contribution from increased sales	1 mark	
	Conclusion	1 mark	
			6
(b)	Calculation of spread	2 marks	
	Calculation of upper limit	1 mark	
	Calculation of return point	1 mark	
	Explanation of findings	2 marks	
			6
(c)	Analysis of assets	1–2 marks	
	Short-term and long-term debt	2–3 marks	
	Discussion of policies	2–3 marks	
	Other factors	1–2 marks	
	Maximum		8
Total			20

12 APX CO

Key answer tips

This question approaches the topic of working capital management from a less frequently examined angle; providing a series of accounting ratios and asking students to work back to a forecast statement of profit or loss and statement of financial position. What makes this question tough is that parts (b) and (c) cannot be attempted without some stab at an answer to part (a). This means there are very few obvious "easy" marks on this question. The highlighted words are key phrases that markers are looking for.

(a) Forecast statement of profit or loss

	$m
Revenue = 16.00m × 1.084 =	17.344
Cost of sales = 17.344m − 5.203m =	12.141
	———
Gross profit = 17.344m × 30% =	5.203
Other expenses = 5.203m − 3.469m =	1.734
	———
Net profit = 17.344m × 20% =	3.469
Interest = (10m × 0.08) + 0.140m =	0.940
	———
Profit before tax	2.529
Profit before tax	2.529
Tax = 2.529m × 0.3 =	0.759
	———
Profit after tax	1.770
Dividends = 1.770m × 50% =	0.885
	———
Retained profit	0.885
	———

Tutor's top tips

The best way to approach this part of the requirement is to work through the statement of profit or loss and statement of financial position line by line, recognising that the overdraft will be your balancing figure.

Forecast statement of financial position

	$m	$m
Non-current assets		22.00
Current assets		
Inventory	3.66	
Trade receivables	3.09	
	———	
		6.75
	———	
Total assets		28.75
		———
Equity finance:		
Ordinary shares	5.00	
Reserves	8.39	
	———	
		13.39
Bank loan		10.00
		———
		23.39
Current liabilities		
Trade payables	2.49	
Overdraft	2.87	
	———	
		5.36
		———
Total liabilities		28.75
		———

Workings

Inventory = 12.141m × (110/365) = $3.66m

Trade receivables = 17.344m × (65/365) = $3.09m

Trade payables = 12.141m × (75/365) = $2.49m

Reserves = 7.5m + 0.885m = $8.39m

Overdraft = 28.75m – 23.39m – 2.49 = $2.87m (balancing figure)

(b) Working capital financing policies can be classified into conservative, moderate (or matching) and aggressive, depending on the extent to which fluctuating current assets and permanent current assets are financed by short-term sources of finance. Permanent current assets are the core level of investment in current assets needed to support a given level of business activity or revenue, while fluctuating current assets are the changes in the levels of current assets arising from the unpredictable nature of some aspects of business activity.

A conservative working capital financing policy uses long-term funds to finance non-current assets and permanent current assets, as well as a proportion of fluctuating current assets. This policy is less risky and less profitable than an aggressive working capital financing policy, which uses short-term funds to finance fluctuating current assets and a proportion of permanent current assets as well. Between these two extremes lies the moderate (or matching) policy, which uses long-term funds to finance long-term assets (non-current assets and permanent current assets) and short-term funds to finance short-term assets (fluctuating current assets).

The current statement of financial position shows that APX Co uses trade payables and an overdraft as sources of short-term finance. In terms of the balance between short- and long-term finance, 89% of current assets (100 × 4.1/4.6) are financed from short-term sources and only 11% are financed from long-term sources. Since a high proportion of current assets are permanent in nature, this appears to be a very aggressive working capital financing policy, which carries significant risk. If the overdraft were called in, for example, APX Co might have to turn to more expensive short-term financing.

The forecast statement of financial position shows a lower reliance on short-term finance, since 79% of current assets (100 × 5.36/6.75) are financed from short-term sources and 21% are financed from long-term sources. This decreased reliance on an aggressive financing policy is sensible, although with a forecast interest coverage ratio of only 3.7 times (3.469/0.94), APX Co has little scope for taking on more long-term debt. An increase in equity funding to decrease reliance on short-term finance could be considered.

(c) **Working capital management**

Financial analysis shows deterioration in key working capital ratios. The inventory turnover period is expected to increase from 81 days to 110 days, the trade receivables period is expected to increase from 50 days to 65 days and the trade payables period is expected to increase from 64 days to 75 days. It is also a cause for concern here that the values of these working capital ratios for the next year are forecast, i.e. APX Co appears to be anticipating a worsening in its working capital position. The current and forecast values could be compared to average or sector values in order to confirm whether this is in fact the case.

Because current assets are expected to increase by more than current liabilities, the current ratio and the quick ratio are both expected to increase in the next year, the current ratio from 1.12 times to 1.26 times and the quick ratio from 0.54 times to 0.58 times. Again, comparison with sector average values for these ratios would be useful in making an assessment of the working capital management of APX Co. The balance between trade payables and overdraft finance is approximately the same in both years (trade payables are 46% of current liabilities in the current statement of financial position and 47% of current liabilities in the forecast statement of financial position), although reliance on short-term finance is expected to fall slightly in the next year.

The deteriorating working capital position may be linked to an expected deterioration in the overall financial performance of APX Co. For example, the forecast gross profit margin (30%) and net profit margin (20%) are both less than the current values of these ratios (32% and 23% respectively), and despite the increase in revenue, return on capital employed (ROCE) is expected to fall from 16.35% to 14.83%.

Analysis

Extracts from current statement of profit or loss:

	$m
Revenue	16.00
Cost of sales	10.88
Gross profit	5.12
Other expenses	1.44
Net profit	3.68

		Current	Forecast
Gross profit margin (100 × 5.12/16.00)		32%	
			30%
Net profit margin (100 × 3.68/16.00)		23%	
			20%
ROCE (100 × 3.68/22.5)		16.35%	
(100 × 3.469/23.39)			14.83%
Inventory period (365 × 2.4/10.88)		81 days	
			110 days
Receivables period (365 × 2.2/16.00)		50 days	
			65 days
Payables period (365 × 1.9/10.88)		64 days	
			75 days
Current ratio	(4.6/4.1)	1.12 times	
	(6.75/5.36)		1.26 times
Quick ratio	(2.2/4.1)	0.54 times	
	(3.09/5.36)		0.58 times

ACCA marking scheme			Marks
(a)	Gross profit		1.0
	Net profit		1.0
	Profit before tax		1.0
	Retained profit		1.0
	Inventory		1.0
	Trade receivables		1.0
	Trade payables		1.0
	Reserves		1.0
	Overdraft		1.0
	Layout and format		1.0
		Maximum	9.0
(b)	Working capital financing policies		2–3
	Financial analysis		1–2
	Working capital financing policy of company		2–3
		Maximum	6.0
(c)	Discussion of working capital management		3–4
	Financial analysis		2–4
		Maximum	5.0
Total			**20**

Examiner's comments

Candidates often gained high marks in part (a) of this question, but answers to parts (b) and (c) lacked focus.

Part (a) required candidates to prepare a forecast statement of profit or loss and a forecast statement of financial position. Many answers were of a very good standard and gained full marks.

Some candidates ignored the forecast financial ratios and applied the expected revenue growth rate to cost of sales and other expenses. Other candidates showed a lack of knowledge of the structure of the statement of profit or loss by calculating the tax liability before subtracting the interest payments. Candidates should recognise that a good understanding of accounting ratios is needed if they expect to achieve a pass standard and they are advised to study the suggested answer carefully in comparison to the question set.

Part (b) asked for an analysis and discussion of the working capital financing policy of the company in the question. Many students were not aware of the conservative, aggressive and matching approaches to working capital financing policy, and so were ill prepared for this question.

Analysis of the statement of financial position shows that 89% of the current assets of the company are financed from a short-term source, while only 11% are financed from a long-term source. Noting this, good answers discussed the aggressive nature of the company's working capital financing policy and the risks to which it gave rise.

Weaker answers discussed conservative and aggressive approaches to the level of investment in working capital, or focused on the cash conversion cycle (operating cycle) of the company, or combined part (b) with part (c).

Part (c) asked for a discussion of the forecast financial performance of the company in terms of working capital management. Comparing the current position with the forecast position showed that a deterioration in financial performance was expected. Better answers recognised this and made appropriate comments. Weaker answers failed to focus on working capital ratios (for example by calculating and discussing ratios such as interest coverage, debt/equity ratio and dividend per share), or offered only general discussions of areas of working capital management (such as explaining ways in which inventory control or credit management could be improved).

13   HGR CO

Key answer tips

The generic requirement of part (a), to "discuss the working capital financing strategy of HGR" can result in a lack of direction and focus in your answer. This sort of question highlights the importance of good exam preparation that includes practising as many past exam questions as possible as requirements such as this are not unusual.

Part (b) may overwhelm some students as the initial perception is that many calculations need to be made. However, this is not the case. Part (i) (for 2 marks) involves simply plugging in the numbers provided before doing a quick calculation of overdraft interest. In part (ii), (for 5 marks) you need to evaluate the impact of the finance director's proposals surrounding both accounts receivable and inventory management. Both calculations involve a manipulation of the standard working capital cycle formulae that students should be familiar, although this might not be obvious to some students. The model answer shows the most efficient way of laying out the answer. Of the 9 marks available for part (b), up to 3 are available for commenting on the forecast position and making suitable recommendations. This could easily be overlooked if you're not careful.

Finally, part (c) gives a good opportunity to pick up some easier marks. This part of the question should be attempted first. The highlighted words are key phrases that markers are looking for.

(a)   When considering the financing of working capital, it is useful to divide current assets into fluctuating current assets and permanent current assets. Fluctuating current assets represent changes in the level of current assets due to the unpredictability of business activity. Permanent current assets represent the core level of investment in current assets needed to support a given level of revenue or business activity. As revenue or level of business activity increases, the level of permanent current assets will also increase. This relationship can be measured by the ratio of revenue to net current assets.

The financing choice as far as working capital is concerned is between short-term and long-term finance. Short-term finance is more flexible than long-term finance: an overdraft, for example, is used by a business organisation as the need arises and variable interest is charged on the outstanding balance. Short-term finance is also more risky than long-term finance: an overdraft facility may be withdrawn, or a short-term loan may be renewed on less favourable terms. In terms of cost, the term structure of interest rates suggests that short-term debt finance has a lower cost than long-term debt finance.

The matching principle suggests that long-term finance should be used for long-term investment. Applying this principle to working capital financing, long-term finance should be matched with permanent current assets and non-current assets. A financing policy with this objective is called a 'matching policy'. HGR Co is not using this financing policy, since of the $16,935,000 of current assets, $14,000,000 or 83% is financed from short-term sources (overdraft and trade payables) and only $2,935,000 or 17% is financed from a long-term source, in this case equity finance (shareholders' funds) or traded bonds.

The financing policy or approach taken by HGR Co towards the financing of working capital, where short-term finance is preferred, is called an aggressive policy. Reliance on short-term finance makes this riskier than a matching approach, but also more profitable due to the lower cost of short-term finance. Following an aggressive approach to financing can lead to overtrading (undercapitalisation) and the possibility of liquidity problems.

(b) Bank balance in three months' time if no action is taken:

Month	1	2	3
	$000	$000	$000
Receipts	4,220	4,350	3,808
Payments	(3,950)	(4,100)	(3,750)
Interest on bonds		(200)	
Overdraft interest	(19)	(18)	(18)
Capital investment			(2,000)
Net cash flow	251	32	(1,960)
Opening balance	(3,800)	(3,549)	(3,517)
Closing balance	(3,549)	(3,517)	(5,477)

Bank balance in three months' time if the finance director's proposals are implemented:

Month	1	2	3
	$000	$000	$000
Receipts	4,220	4,350	3,808
Payments	(3,950)	(4,100)	(3,750)
Interest on bonds		(200)	
Overdraft interest	(19)	(15)	(13)
Capital investment			(2,000)
Accounts receivable	270	270	270
Inventory	204	204	204
Net cash flow	725	509	(1,481)
Opening balance	(3,800)	(3,075)	(2,566)
Closing balance	(3,075)	(2,566)	(4,047)

Workings:

Reduction in accounts receivable days

Current accounts receivable days = (8,775/49,275) × 365 = 65 days

Reduction in days over six months = 65 – 53 = 12 days

Monthly reduction = 12/6 = 2 days

Each receivables day is equivalent to 8,775,000/65 =$135,000 (Alternatively, each receivables day is equivalent to 49,275,000/365 =$135,000)

Monthly reduction in accounts receivable = 2 × 135,000 = $270,000

Reduction in inventory days

Current inventory days = (8,160/37,230) × 365 = 80 days

Each inventory day is equivalent to 8,160,000/80 = $102,000 (Alternatively, each inventory day = 37,230,000/365 = $102,000)

Monthly reduction in inventory = 102,000 × 2 = $204,000

Overdraft interest calculations

Monthly overdraft interest rate = $(1.0617)^{1/12}$ = 1.005 or 0.5%

If no action is taken:

Period 1 interest = 3,800,000 × 0.005 = $19,000

Period 2 interest = 3,549,000 × 0.005 = $17,745 or $18,000

Period 3 interest = 3,517,000 × 0.005 = $17,585 or $18,000

If action is taken:

Period 1 interest = 3,800,000 × 0.005 = $19,000

Period 2 interest = 3,075,000 × 0.005 = $15,375 or $15,000

Period 3 interest = 2,566,000 × 0.005 = $12,830 or $13,000

Discussion

If no action is taken, the cash flow forecast shows that HGR Co will exceed its overdraft limit of $4 million by $1.48 million in three months' time. If the finance director's proposals are implemented, there is a positive effect on the bank balance, but the overdraft limit is still exceeded in three months' time, although only by $47,000 rather than by $1.47 million.

In each of the three months following that, the continuing reduction in accounts receivable days will improve the bank balance by $270,000 per month. Without further information on operating receipts and payments, it cannot be forecast whether the bank balance will return to less than the limit, or even continue to improve.

The main reason for the problem with the bank balance is the $2 million capital expenditure. Purchase of non-current assets should not be financed by an overdraft, but a long-term source of finance such as equity or bonds. If the capital expenditure were removed from the area of working capital management, the overdraft balance at the end of three months would be $3.48 million if no action were taken and $2.05 million if the finance director's proposals were implemented. Given that HGR Co has almost $50 million of non-current assets that could possibly be used as security, raising long-term debt through either a bank loan or a bond issue appears to be sensible. Assuming a bond interest rate of 10% per year, current long-term debt in the form of traded bonds is approximately ($200m × 2)/0.1 = $4m, which is much less than the amount of noncurrent assets.

A suitable course of action for HGR Co to follow would therefore be, firstly, to implement the finance director's proposals and, secondly, to finance the capital expenditure from a long-term source. Consideration could also be given to using some long-term debt finance to reduce the overdraft and to reduce the level of accounts payable, currently standing at 100 days.

(c) When credit is granted to foreign customers, two problems may become especially significant. First, the longer distances over which trade takes place and the more complex nature of trade transactions and their elements means foreign accounts receivable need more investment than their domestic counterparts. Longer transaction times increase accounts receivable balances and hence the level of financing and financing costs. Second, the risk of bad debts is higher with foreign accounts receivable than with their domestic counterparts. In order to manage and reduce credit risks, therefore, exporters seek to reduce the risk of bad debts and to reduce the level of investment in foreign accounts receivable.

Many foreign transactions are on 'open account', which is an agreement to settle the amount outstanding on a predetermined date. Open account reflects a good business relationship between importer and exporter. It also carries the highest risk of non-payment.

One way to reduce investment in foreign accounts receivable is to agree early payment with an importer, for example by payment in advance, payment on shipment, or cash on delivery. These terms of trade are unlikely to be competitive, however, and it is more likely that an exporter will seek to receive cash in advance of payment being made by the customer.

One way to accelerate cash receipts is to use bill finance. Bills of exchange with a signed agreement to pay the exporter on an agreed future date, supported by a documentary letter of credit, can be discounted by a bank to give immediate funds. This discounting is without recourse if bills of exchange have been countersigned by the importer's bank.

Documentary letters of credit are a payment guarantee backed by one or more banks. They carry almost no risk, provided the exporter complies with the terms and conditions contained in the letter of credit. The exporter must present the documents stated in the letter, such as bills of lading, shipping documents, bills of exchange, and so on, when seeking payment. As each supporting document relates to a key aspect of the overall transaction, letters of credit give security to the importer as well as the exporter.

Companies can also manage and reduce risk by gathering appropriate information with which to assess the creditworthiness of new customers, such as bank references and credit reports.

Insurance can also be used to cover some of the risks associated with giving credit to foreign customers. This would avoid the cost of seeking to recover cash due from foreign accounts receivable through a foreign legal system, where the exporter could be at a disadvantage due to a lack of local or specialist knowledge.

Export factoring can also be considered, where the exporter pays for the specialist expertise of the factor as a way of reducing investment in foreign accounts receivable and reducing the incidence of bad debts.

ACCA marking scheme			
			Marks
(a)	Analysis of current assets	1 – 2	
	Short-term and long-term finance	2 – 3	
	Matching principle	1 – 2	
	Financing approach used by company	1 – 2	
		Maximum	6
(b)	Bank balance if no action is taken	2	
	Bank balance if action is taken	5	
	Working capital management implications	1 – 2	
	Advice on course of action	1 – 2	
		Maximum	9
(c)	Relevant discussion		5
Total			**20**

Examiner's comments

Part (a) required candidates to discuss the working capital financing strategy of a company. Some candidates ignored the word 'financing' and discussed working capital strategy in general. Other candidates took 'working capital financing strategy' to mean the proposals in the question to reduce the level of account receivables and inventory by operational improvements.

The question gave extracts from a statement of financial position which showed that the company was financing 83% of its current assets from short-term sources, namely a bank overdraft and trade receivables. This is an aggressive rather than a conservative financing strategy and better answers recognised this, discussing how current assets could be divided into fluctuating and permanent current assets, and linking this analysis of current assets via the matching principle to the use of short-term and long-term finance.

Part (b) asked candidates to calculate the bank balance in three months' time if no action were taken, and if the proposals were implemented. Many candidates had great difficulty in rolling forward the current cash balance (the overdraft of $3.8 million) using the receipts and payments given in the question, while allowing for one month's interest on the balance of the account at the start of each month. Common errors included failing to recognise that the opening balance was the overdraft and therefore having no opening balance: calculating annual interest rather than monthly interest; and including cash flows other than those given in the question (for example from the credit sales and cost of sales figures given in the question). All candidates are expected to be able to prepare cash flow forecasts and the general standard of answers to this question showed that many candidates need further preparation in this important area.

Part (c) required candidates to discuss how risks arising from granting credit to foreign customers could be managed and reduced. Many candidates gave answers of a good standard, although some answers were one-sided, concentrating on exchange rate risk rather than on credit risk. Since the question referred to foreign customers, it was inappropriate to limit answers to a discussion of domestic receivables management.

14   ANJO

Key answer tips

This is a fairly straightforward question. The highlighted words are key phrases that markers are looking for.

(a)   Calculation of ratios

Inventory days	20X6:	$(3,000/9,300) \times 365$	= 118 days
	20X5:	$(1,300/6,600) \times 365$	= 72 days
		Sector average: 90 days	

Receivables days	20X6:	$(3,800/15,600) \times 365$	= 89 days
	20X5:	$(1,850/11,100) \times 365$	= 61 days
		Sector average: 60 days	

Payables days	20X6:	$(2,870/9,300 \times 0.95) \times 365$	= 119 days
	20X5:	$(1,600/6,600 \times 0.95) \times 365$	= 93 days
		Sector average: 80 days	

In each case, the ratio in 20X6 is higher than the ratio in 20X5, indicating that deterioration has occurred in the management of inventories, receivables and payables in 20X6.

Inventory days have increased by 46 days or 64%, moving from below the sector average to 28 days – one month – more than it. Given the rapid increase in sales revenue (40%) in 20X6, Anjo Inc may be expecting a continuing increase in the future and may have built up inventories in preparation for this, i.e. inventory levels reflect future sales rather than past sales. Accounting statements from several previous years and sales forecasts for the next period would help to clarify this point.

Receivables days have increased by 28 days or 46% in 20X6 and are now 29 days above the sector average. It is possible that more generous credit terms have been offered in order to stimulate sales. The increased sales revenue does not appear to be due to offering lower prices, since both gross profit margin (40%) and net profit margin (34%) are unchanged.

In 20X5, only management of payables was a cause for concern, with Anjo Inc taking 13 more days on average to settle liabilities with trade payables than the sector. This has increased to 39 days more than the sector in 20X6. This could lead to difficulties between the company and its suppliers if it is exceeding the credit periods they have specified. Anjo Inc has no long-term debt and the statement of financial position indicates an increased reliance on short-term finance, since cash has reduced by $780,000 or 87% and the overdraft has increased by $850,000 to $1 million.

Perhaps the company should investigate whether it is undercapitalised (overtrading). It is unusual for a company of this size to have no long-term debt.

(b)   Cash operating cycle (20X5) = 72 + 61 – 93 = 40 days

       Cash operating cycle (20X6) = 118 + 89 – 119 = 88 days

       The cash operating cycle or working capital cycle gives the average time it takes for the company to receive payment from receivables after it has paid its trade payables. This represents the period of time for which payables require financing. The cash operating cycle of Anjo Inc has lengthened by 48 days in 20X6 compared with 20X5. This represents an increase in working capital requirement of approximately $15,600,000 × 48/365 = $2.05 million.

(c)   Use of factor costs 0.5% of credit sales of $15.6 million = $78,000 cost

       Admin savings 2% of $1 million = $20,000 saving

       Factor promises to reduce receivables balance by 30%.

       Current receivables funding cost: $3.8m × 8% = $304,000

       New receivables balance = $3.8m × 70% = $2.66m

       The factor will advance 80% of this and charge a fee of (8 + 1) 9%

       The remaining 20% will still need to be funded using the overdraft at a rate of 8%

       $2.66m × 80% × 9% = $191,520 factor funding cost

       $2.66m × 20% × 8% = $42,560 overdraft funding cost

       Total new funding cost = $191,520 + $42,560 = $234,080

       Saving in funding costs = $304,000 – $234,080 = $69,920

       Total net position: $(78,000) + £20,000 + $69,920 = $11,920 net saving

       Although the terms of the factor's offer are financially acceptable, suggesting a net financial benefit of $11,920, this benefit is small compared with annual sales revenue of $15.6 million. Other benefits, such as the application of the factor's expertise to the receivables management of Anjo Inc, might also be influential in the decision on whether to accept the offer.

15   ZSE CO

Key answer tips

This question combines the key area of working capital management with the slightly less examined area of probability analysis and expected values. The calculations required in part (a) are fairly straightforward. However, the unusual combination of these two syllabus areas may confuse some students. Parts (b) and (c) require a 'learn and churn' type discussion so students should feel more comfortable with this. The highlighted words are key phrases that markers are looking for.

(a) **(i)** **Period 1 closing balance**

Opening balance	Cash flow	Closing balance	Probability	Expected value
$000	$000	$000	$000	$000
(500)	8,000	7,500	0.1	750
(500)	4,000	3,500	0.6	2,100
(500)	(2,000)	(2,500)	0.3	(750)
				————
				2,100
				————

The expected value of the period 1 closing balance is $2,100,000.

Tutorial note

An alternative approach to this part of the question is to calculate the expected value of the cash flow in period 1, and then add this to the opening balance. This could be achieved as follows:

(8,000 × 0.1) + (4,000 × 0.6) – (2,000 × 0.3) = 2,600

(500) + 2,600 = $2,100k

(ii) **Period 2 closing balance**

Period 1 closing balance	Probability	Period 2 cash flow	Probability	Period 2 closing balance	Joint probability	Expected value
$000		$000		$000		$000
7,500	0.1	7,000	0.3	14,500	0.03	435
		3,000	0.5	10,500	0.05	525
		(9,000)	0.2	(1,500)	0.02	(30)
3,500	0.6	7,000	0.3	10,500	0.18	1,890
		3,000	0.5	6,500	0.30	1,950
		(9,000)	0.2	(5,500)	0.12	(660)
(2,500)	0.3	7,000	0.3	4,500	0.09	405
		3,000	0.5	500	0.15	75
		(9,000)	0.2	(11,500)	0.06	(690)
						————
						3,900
						————

The expected value of the period 2 closing balance is $3,900,000.

(iii)

Tutorial note

The key to answering parts (iii) and (iv) is to consider the net effect of the flows. For part (iii), if the period 2 cash flow was ($9,000,000) then it wouldn't matter what the period 1 cash flow was, the balance would be negative at the end of period 2. With any of the other two possibilities, the balance would be positive, regardless of what cash flow arose in period 1. The answer is therefore the probability of the $9,000,000 cash outflow in period 2, which is 20%.

For part (iv), the same thought process can be used, except this time you're not looking at whether the balance is above or below zero; your benchmark changes to the overdraft limit of $2m.

The probability of a negative cash balance at the end of period 2 = 0.02 + 0.12 + 0.06 = 20%

(iv) The probability of exceeding the overdraft limit in period 2 is 0.12 + 0.06 = 18%.

Tutor's top tips

Ensure you cover off all parts of the requirement. In part (a) it is easy to drop marks by failing to discuss whether your analysis can assist the company in managing its cash flows.

Discussion

The expected value analysis has shown that, on an average basis, ZSE Co will have a positive cash balance at the end of period 1 of $2.1 million and a positive cash balance at the end of period 2 of $3.9 million. However, the cash balances that are expected to occur are the specific balances that have been averaged, rather than the average values themselves.

There could be serious consequences for ZSE Co if it exceeds its overdraft limit. For example, the overdraft facility could be withdrawn. There is a 30% chance that the overdraft limit will be exceeded in period 1 and a lower probability, 18%, that the overdraft limit will be exceeded in period 2. To guard against exceeding its overdraft limit in period 1, ZSE Co must find additional finance of $0.5 million ($2.5m – $2.0m). However, to guard against exceeding its overdraft limit in period 2, the company could need up to $9.5 million ($11.5m – $2.0m). Renegotiating the overdraft limit in period 1 would therefore be only a short-term solution.

One strategy is to find now additional finance of $0.5 million and then to re-evaluate the cash flow forecasts at the end of period 1. If the most likely outcome occurs in period 1, the need for additional finance in period 2 to guard against exceeding the overdraft limit is much lower.

The expected value analysis has been useful in illustrating the cash flow risks faced by ZSE Co. Although the cash flow forecasting model has been built with the aid of a firm of financial consultants, the assumptions used in the model must be reviewed before decisions are made based on the forecast cash flows and their associated probabilities.

Expected values are more useful for repeat decisions rather than one-off activities, as they are based on averages. They illustrate what the average outcome would be if an activity was repeated a large number of times. In fact, each period and its cash flows will occur only once and the expected values of the closing balances are not closing balances that are forecast to arise in practice. In period 1, for example, the expected value closing balance of $2.1 million is not forecast to occur, while a closing balance of $3.5 million is likely to occur.

(b) The factors to be considered in formulating a policy to manage the trade receivables of ZSE Co will relate to the key areas of credit assessment or analysis, credit control and collection procedures. A key factor is the turbulence in the company's business environment and the way it affects the company's customers.

Credit analysis

The main objective of credit analysis is to ensure that credit is granted to customers who will settle their account at regular intervals in accordance with the agreed terms of sale. The risk of bad debts must be minimised as much as possible.

Key factors to consider here are the source and quality of the information used by ZSE Co to assess customer creditworthiness. The information sources could include bank references, trade references, public information such as published accounts, credit reference agencies and personal experience. The quality of the information needs to be confirmed as part of the credit analysis process. Some organisations have developed credit-scoring systems to assist in the assessment of creditworthiness.

Credit control

Once credit has been granted, it is essential to ensure that agreed terms and conditions are adhered to while the credit is outstanding. This can be achieved by careful monitoring of customer accounts and the periodic preparation of aged debtor analyses. A key factor here is the quality of the staff involved with credit control and the systems and procedures they use to maintain regular contact with customers, for example invoices, statements, reminders, letters and telephone contacts.

ZSE Co has been experiencing difficulties in collecting amounts due because its customers have been experiencing difficult trading conditions. Close contact with customers is essential here in order to determine where revised terms can be negotiated when payment is proving hard, and perhaps to provide advance warning of serious customer liquidity or going concern problems.

Collection procedures

The objective here is to ensure timely and secure transfer of funds when they are due, whether by physical means or by electronic means. A key factor here is the need to ensure that the terms of trade are clearly understood by the customer from the point at which credit is granted. Offering credit represents a cost to the seller and ensuring that payment occurs as agreed prevents this cost from exceeding budgeted expectations.

Procedures for chasing late payers should be clearly formulated and trained personnel must be made responsible for ensuring that these procedures are followed. Legal action should only be considered as a last resort, since it often represents the termination of the business relationship with a customer.

(c) Profitability and liquidity are usually cited as the twin objectives of working capital management. The profitability objective reflects the primary financial management objective of maximising shareholder wealth, while liquidity is needed in order to ensure that financial claims on an organisation can be settled as they become liable for payment.

The two objectives are in conflict because liquid assets such as bank accounts earn very little return or no return, so liquid assets decrease profitability. Liquid assets in fact incur an opportunity cost equivalent either to the cost of short-term finance or to the profit lost by not investing in profitable projects.

Whether profitability is a more important objective than liquidity depends in part on the particular circumstances of an organisation. Liquidity may be the more important objective when short-term finance is hard to find, while profitability may become a more important objective when cash management has become too conservative. In short, both objectives are important and neither can be neglected.

ACCA marking scheme		
		Marks
(a)	Expected value of period 1 closing balance	2
	Expected value of period 2 closing balance	5
	Probability of negative cash balance	1
	Probability of exceeding overdraft limit	2
	Discussion of expected value analysis	3
		———
	Maximum	12
(b)	Credit analysis	2–3
	Credit control	2–3
	Collection procedures	2–3
		———
	Maximum	5
(c)	Relevant discussion	3
		———
Total		**20**
		———

Examiner's comments

This part (a) required candidates to calculate expected values and probabilities from data given in the question, and to discuss the usefulness of expected value analysis.

A number of candidates lost marks by calculating the expected values of the cash flows for period 1 and period 2, but not calculating the closing balances for period 1 and period 2, which is what the question had asked for. There is clearly a difference between cash flow and closing balance.

Candidates were expected to calculate the closing balances using a probability table approach, but many candidates calculated the closing balances using an average cash flow approach. While this provided correct values for the closing balances and hence was given full credit, it did not help with calculating the probability of a negative closing balance in period 2, and it did not help with calculating the probability of exceeding the overdraft limit at the end of period 2. Many candidates were unable to calculate these probabilities because they did appreciate the importance of the joint probabilities used in a probability table.

Candidates were then asked to discuss whether the expected value analysis could assist the company to manage its cash flows. Many candidates tended to discuss ways in which the company could manage cash flows in general, even in some cases discussing cash management models, rather than discussing the usefulness of an expected value analysis. Better answers discussed the benefits and limitations of the analysis that had been undertaken.

In part (b), candidates were asked to identify and discuss factors relevant to formulating a trade receivables management policy. While many candidates gained good marks here, there was a very strong tendency for answers to be framed around lists of ways of improving trade receivables management (a question that has been asked in the past), rather than around factors influencing trade receivables policy. Fortunately, a strong relationship exists between the two areas, and it was possible to give credit for knowledge about the management of trade receivables.

Part (c) asked candidates to discuss whether profitability or liquidity was the primary objective of working capital management. Many candidates answered appropriately that both profitability and liquidity were important: profitability because it related to the overall objective of wealth maximisation and liquidity because of the need to meet liabilities as they became due for settlement.

16   PNP PLC

Key answer tips

Part (a) requires the usual comparison of the costs and benefits of implementing a discount. The complexity of the question means there are a large number of elements to consider and key to tackling the calculations is to recognise that the average payment period per class of receivable will equal the receivables days. Remember, each individual calculation will earn marks so you don't need to have identified all of them to score well. Both parts (a) and (b) of this question require a significant amount of workings. Laying your workings out neatly and clearly cross referencing them to your answer will ensure you have the best chance of scoring well. When laying out your answer to part (c), use plenty of sub-headings to clearly indicate to your marker the points you are making. The highlighted words are key phrases that markers are looking for.

(a)   **Effect on profitability of implementing the proposal**

	£	£
Benefits:		
Increased contribution (W1)	200,000	
Decrease in irrecoverable debts (W2)	6,300	
		206,300
Costs		
Increase in current Class 1 discount (W3)	12,167	
Discount from transferring Class 2 receivables (W4)	11,498	
Discount from new Class 1 receivables (W5)	3,750	
Increase in irrecoverable debts, new Class 2 receivables (W6)	2,055	
Increase in financing cost from new receivables (W7)	4,932	34,402
Net benefit of implementing the proposal		171,898

The proposed change appears to be financially acceptable and so may be recommended. Uncertainty with respect to some of the assumptions underlying the financial evaluation would be unlikely to change the favourable recommendation.

Workings

Contribution/sales ratio = $100 \times (5,242 - 3,145)/5,242 = 40\%$

Irrecoverable debts ratio for Class 2 receivables = $100 \times (12,600/252,000) = 5\%$

Increase in Class 1 receivables from new business = $250,000 \times 30/365 = £20,548$

Increase in Class 2 receivables from new business = $250,000 \times 60/365 = £41,096$

(W1) Contribution from increased business = $500,000 \times 40\% = £200,000$

(W2) Decrease in irrecoverable debts for transferring current Class 2 receivables = $12,600 \times 0.5 = £6,300$

   (Note that other assumptions regarding irrecoverable debts are possible here)

(W3) Current sales of Class 1 receivables = $200,000 \times (365/30) = £2,433,333$

   Rise in discount cost for current Class 1 receivables = $2,433,333 \times 0.005 = £12,167$

(W4) Current sales of Class 2 receivables = $252,000 \times (365/60) = £1,533,000$

   Discount cost of transferring Class 2 receivables = $1,533,000 \times 0.5 \times 0.015 = £11,498$

(W5) Discount cost for new Class 1 receivables = $250,000 \times 0.015 = £3,750$

(W6) Irrecoverable debts arising from new Class 2 receivables = $41,096 \times 0.05 = £2,055$

   (Note that other assumptions regarding irrecoverable debts are possible here)

(W7) Increase in financing cost from new receivables = $(20,548 + 41,096) \times 0.08 = £4,932$

   (**Note** that it could be assumed that transferring receivables pay after 30 days rather than 60 days.)

   Examiner's Note: because of the various assumptions that could be made regarding irrecoverable debts and payment period, other approaches to a solution are also acceptable.

Tutorial note:

An alternative approach to this part of the question is to lay out all of the calculations regarding the current and revised position before getting into the detail. This can often allow a clearer thought process and a more time efficient approach to the question.

You know from your studies that the main costs and benefits to consider when deciding on a level of discount to offer are:

—   *The cost of the discount itself (for this you will need to know the value of sales for each class)*

—   *The benefit of reduced financing costs (for this you will need to know the level of receivables under the current strategy and the proposed strategy*

—   *The benefit of reduced irrecoverable debts (for this you will need to know the new level of receivables by class together with the typical ratio of bad debts).*

In this particular case, we will also need to consider the contribution that will be earned on the additional sales resulting from the revised policy.

Now we know the information we will require, we can set about obtaining it.

	Current level of discount		Revised level of discount	
		£000		£000
Class 1 sales	£200k × 365/30	2,433.3	£2,433.3k + £250k (being half of the new sales) + £766.5k (being half of the previous class 2 receivables)	3,449.8
Class 1 receivables	Per question	200	£3,449.8k × 30/365	283.5
Cost of financing class 1 receivables	£200k × 8%	16	£283.5k × 8%	22.7
Class 2 sales	£252k × 365/60	1,533	£1,533k/2 + £250k	1,016.5
Class 2 receivables	Per question	252	£1,016.5k × 60/365	167
Cost of financing class 2 receivables	£252k × 8%	20.2	£167k × 8%	13.4

The other pieces of information required were shown at the beginning of this answer; the contribution/sales ratio of 40% and the irrecoverable debts ratio for class 2 receivables of 5%.

Having gathered all of the information, it is quite a simple job to detail out the costs and benefits.

Costs

Additional discount

Remember this will need to reflect both the additional 0.5% payable on existing class 1 sales as well as the full 1.5% payable on all new sales and the previous class 2 sales that will now pay promptly.

£2,433.3k × 0.5%	*= £12.2k*
(£3,449.8k – £2,433.3k) × 1.5%	*= £15.2k*
Total cost	***= £27.4k***
Benefits	
Additional contribution	
£500k × 40%	*= £200k*
Reduction in irrecoverable debts	
(£167k – £252k) × 5%	*= £4.2k*
Reduction in financing costs	
(£16k + £20.2k) – (£22.7k + £13.4k)	*= £0.1k*
Total benefit	***= £204.3k***
Net benefit	***= £176.9k***

Note: *this answer differs from that presented above due to the approach taken. It would however, score in full.*

(b) Current cash operating cycle:

Inventory days = (603/3,145) × 365 = 70 days

Payables days = (574.5/3,145) × 365 = 67 days

Average receivables days = (744.5/5,242) × 365 = 52 days

Cash operating cycle = 70 + 52 – 67 = 55 days

After implementation of the proposal, it is reasonable to assume that inventory days and payables days remain unchanged. Total receivables have increased by £61,644 to £806,144 and sales revenue has increased to £5.742m. Average receivables days are now 365 × (806/5,742) = 51 days. The cash operating cycle has marginally decreased by one day to 54 days (70 + 51 – 67).

(c) The key elements of a receivables management system may be described as establishing a credit policy, credit assessment, credit control and collection of amounts due.

Establishing credit policy

The credit policy provides the overall framework within which the receivables management system of PNP plc operates and will cover key issues such as the procedures to be followed when granting credit, the usual credit period offered, the maximum credit period that may be granted, any discounts for early settlement, whether interest is charged on overdue balances, and actions to be taken with accounts that have not been settled in the agreed credit period. These terms of trade will depend to a considerable extent on the terms offered by competitors to PNP plc, but they will also depend on the ability of the company to finance its receivables (financing costs), the need to meet the costs of administering the system (administrative costs) and the risk of irrecoverable debts.

Credit assessment

In order to minimise the risk of irrecoverable debts, PNP plc should assess potential customers as to their creditworthiness before offering them credit. The depth of the credit check depends on the amount of business being considered, the size of the client and the potential for repeat business. The credit assessment requires information about the customer, whether from a third party as in a trade reference, a bank reference or a credit report, or from PNP itself through, for example, its analysis of a client's published accounts. The benefits of granting credit must always be greater than the cost involved. There is no point, therefore, in PNP plc paying for a detailed credit report from a credit reference agency for a small credit sale.

Credit control

Once PNP plc has granted credit to a customer, it should monitor the account at regular intervals to make sure that the agreed terms are being followed. An aged receivables analysis is useful in this respect since it helps the company focus on those clients who are the most cause for concern. Customers should be reminded of their debts by prompt despatch of invoices and regular statements of account. Customers in arrears should not be allowed to take further goods on credit.

Collection of amounts due

The customers of PNP plc should ideally settle their accounts within the agreed credit period. There is no indication as to what this might be, but the company clearly feels that a segmental analysis of its clients is possible given their payment histories, their potential for irrecoverable debts and their geographical origin. Clear guidelines are needed over the action to take when customers are late in settling their accounts or become irrecoverable debts, for example indicating at what stage legal action should be initiated.

17 PLOT CO

Key answer tips

Care must be taken in parts (a) and (b) due to the number of calculations necessary to fulfil the various requirements. A clear and methodical approach to the **Workings** is vital.

Part (c) should be a straight forward repetition of knowledge in this small syllabus area.

The highlighted words are key phrases that markers are looking for.

(a) (i) Cost of current ordering policy

Ordering cost = 12 × 267 = $3,204 per year

Monthly order = monthly demand = 300,000/12 = 25,000 units

Buffer inventory = 25,000 × 0.4 = 10,000 units

Average inventory excluding buffer inventory = 25,000/2 = 12,500 units

Average inventory including buffer inventory = 12,500 + 10,000 = 22,500 units

Holding cost = 22,500 × 0.1 = $2,250 per year

Total cost = 3,204 + 2,250 = $5,454 per year

(ii) **Cost of ordering policy using economic order quantity (EOQ)**

EOQ = √(2 × 267 × 300,000/0.10) = 40,025 or 40,000 units per order

Number of orders per year = 300,000/40,000 = 7.5 orders per year

Order cost = 7.5 × 267 = $2,003

Average inventory excluding buffer inventory = 40,000/2 = 20,000 units

Average inventory including buffer inventory = 20,000 + 10,000 = 30,000 units

Holding cost = 30,000 × 0.1 = $3,000 per year

Total cost = $2,003 + $3,000 = $5,003 per year

(iii) Saving from introducing EOQ ordering policy = 5,454 – 5,003 = $451 per year

(b) Product Q trade payables at end of year = 456,000 × 1 × 60/365 = $74,959

Product Q trade payables after discount = 456,000 × 1 × 0.99 × 30/365 = $37,105

Decrease in Product Q trade payables = 74,959 – 37,105 = $37,854

Increase in financing cost = 37,854 × 0.05 = $1,893

Value of discount = 456,000 × 0.01 = $4,560

Net value of offer of discount = 4,560 – 1,893 = $2,667

(c) The objectives of working capital management are usually taken to be profitability and liquidity. Profitability is allied to the financial objective of maximising shareholder wealth, while liquidity is needed in order to settle liabilities as they fall due. A company must have sufficient cash to meet its liabilities, since otherwise it may fail.

However, these two objectives are in conflict, since liquid resources have no return or low levels of return and hence decrease profitability. A conservative approach to working capital management will decrease the risk of running out of cash, favouring liquidity over profitability and decreasing risk. Conversely, an aggressive approach to working capital management will emphasise profitability over liquidity, increasing the risk of running out of cash while increasing profitability.

Working capital management is central to financial management for several reasons.

First, cash is the life-blood of a company's business activities and without enough cash to meet short-term liabilities, a company would fail.

Second, current assets can account for more than half of a company's assets, and so must be carefully managed. Poor management of current assets can lead to loss of profitability and decreased returns to shareholders.

Third, for SMEs current liabilities are a major source of finance and must be carefully managed in order to ensure continuing availability of such finance.

ACCA marking scheme				
				Marks
(a)	(i)	Current ordering cost		
		Ordering cost		0.5
		Monthly demand		0.5
		Buffer inventory		0.5
		Average inventory		0.5
		Holding cost		0.5
		Total cost		0.5
				———
			Maximum	3
				———
	(ii)	Economic order quantity		1
		EOQ order cost		1
		Holding cost		0.5
		Total cost		0.5
				———
			Maximum	3
				———
	(iii)	Saving from EOQ ordering policy		1
(b)		Current trade payables		1
		Trade payables after discount		1
		Increase in finance costs		1
		Value of discount		1
		Net value of discount offer		1
				———
			Maximum	5
				———
(c)		Objectives of working capital management		3–4
		Role of working capital management		3–4
				———
			Maximum	8
				———
Total				**20**
				———

Examiner's comments

Part (a) asked candidates to calculate the total cost of the current ordering policy, the total cost of an ordering policy using the economic order quantity (EOQ), and the net cost or saving of introducing an ordering policy using the EOQ. Many answers gained good marks here. Where candidates made calculation errors, these showed a lack of understanding of the calculation process, for example including only half of buffer inventory in average inventory, or using annual demand as average inventory, or omitting holding cost completely.

Almost all candidates who calculated the two total costs also calculated the net cost or saving of introducing an ordering policy using the EOQ.

In part (b) candidates had to calculate the purchase cost saving if the early settlement discount were accepted and the increase in finance cost due to paying the supplier 30 days earlier. Some candidates ran into difficulties because they included total purchase costs in a comparison of current and revised costs, but only incremental costs and benefits are relevant here, so there was no need to include total purchase costs.

Errors that were made included:

- Treating the reduction in trade payables as a benefit
- Comparing annual benefit with monthly cost, and vice versa
- Including only a benefit, or including only a cost
- Calculating an annual percentage cost, when the question asked for net value in dollars.

Some candidates, having calculated net value of the early settlement discount, went on to discuss whether it should be accepted. No credit was given to such a discussion, however, as the question asked only for calculation.

In part (c) better answers identified profitability and liquidity as the main objectives of working capital management, perhaps briefly explaining the conflict between the two, before focusing on a discussion of the central role of working capital management in financial management, referring perhaps to the importance of cash and cash management, the importance of currents assets to a company, the importance of current liabilities as a source of finance, especially for SMEs, the need to have policies relating to the elements of working capital such as trade receivables and inventory, and so on.

18 WQZ CO

Key answer tips

This question covers two popular areas of working capital management: inventory and accounts receivable management. The calculations in part (a) give some early chances to pick up some relatively easy marks. Part (b) and (d) are both discursive requirements that should also prove relatively straightforward. The trickiest element is part (c) although the requirement to calculate the maximum early settlement discount that could be offered is only worth one mark: don't let this put you off gathering the marks for the earlier parts of the process. The highlighted words are key phrases that markers are looking for.

(a) Cost of the current ordering policy

Order size = 10% of 160,000 = 16,000 units per order

Number of orders per year = 160,000/16,000 = 10 orders per year

Annual ordering cost = 10 × 400 = $4,000 per year

Holding cost ignoring buffer stock = 5.12 × (16,000/2) = $40,960 per year

Holding cost of buffer inventory = 5.12 × 5,000 = $25,600 per year

Total cost of current policy = 4,000 + 40,960 + 25,600 = $70,560 per year

Cost of the ordering policy using the EOQ model

Order size = $\sqrt{(2 \times 400 \times 160,000/5.12)}$ = 5,000 units per order

Number of orders per year = 160,000/5,000 = 32 orders per year

Annual ordering cost = 32 × 400 = $12,800 per year

Holding cost ignoring buffer stock = 5.12 × (5,000/2) = $12,800 per year

Holding cost of buffer inventory = 5.12 × 5,000 = $25,600 per year

Total cost of current policy = 12,800 + 12,800 + 25,600 = $51,200 per year

Change in costs of inventory management by using EOQ model

Decrease in costs = 70,560 – 51,200 = $19,360

Tutorial note

Since the buffer inventory is the same in both scenarios, its holding costs do not need to be included in calculating the change in inventory management costs.

(b) Holding costs can be reduced by reducing the level of inventory held by a company. Holding costs can be reduced to a minimum if a company orders supplies only when it needs them, avoiding the need to have any inventory at all of inputs to the production process. This approach to inventory management is called just-in-time (JIT) procurement.

The benefits of a JIT procurement policy include a lower level of investment in working capital, since inventory levels have been minimised: a reduction in inventory holding costs; a reduction in materials handling costs, due to improved materials flow through the production process; an improved relationship with suppliers, since supplier and customer need to work closely together in order to make JIT procurement a success; improved operating efficiency, due to the need to streamline production methods in order to eliminate inventory between different stages of the production process; and lower reworking costs due to the increased emphasis on the quality of supplies, since hold-ups in production must be avoided when inventory between production stages has been eliminated.

(c) **Evaluation of changes in receivables management**

Tutor's top tips

When asked to evaluate a proposed change in policy you should always focus on quantifying the additional costs and benefits. Start by listing them out, and then begin with the easier calculations first. You don't need to complete the evaluation in order to score reasonable marks.

The current level of receivables days = (18/87.6) × 365 = 75 days

Since 25% of credit customers will take the discount, 75% will not be doing so.

The revised level of receivables days = (0.25 × 30) + (0.75 × 60) = 52.5 days

Current level of trade receivables = $18m

Revised level of trade receivables = 87.6 × (52.5/365) = $12.6m

Reduction level of trade receivables = 18 – 12.6 = $5.4m

Cost of short-term finance = 5.5%

Reduction in financing cost = 5.4m × 0.055 = $297,000

Administration and operating cost savings = $753,000

Total benefits = 297,000 + 753,000 = $1,050,000

Cost of early settlement discount = 87.6m × 0.25 × 0.01 = $219,000

Net benefit of early settlement discount = 1,050,000 – 219,000 = $831,000

The proposed changes in receivables management are therefore financially acceptable, although they depend heavily on the forecast savings in administration and operating costs.

Maximum early settlement discount

Tutor's top tips

To calculate this you must start with the awareness that the maximum discount that could be offered is one where the cost equals the benefit. Anything above this, and it wouldn't be worth offering the discount.

You've already calculated the value of the benefit, so all that remains is to convert this figure into a percentage of sales revenue, remembering that only 25% of customers are expected to take up the offer.

Comparing the total benefits of $1,050,000 with 25% of annual credit sales of $87,600,000, which is $21,900,000, the maximum early settlement discount that could be offered is 4.8% (100 × (1.050k/21.9m)).

(d) Factors that should be considered when formulating working capital policy on the management of trade receivables include the following:

The level of investment in trade receivables

If the amount of finance tied up in trade receivables is substantial, receivables management policy may be formulated with the intention of reducing the level of investment by tighter control over the way in which credit is granted and improved methods of assessing client creditworthiness.

The cost of financing trade credit

If the cost of financing trade credit is high, there will be pressure to reduce the amount of credit offered and to reduce the period for which credit is offered.

The terms of trade offered by competitors

In order to compete effectively, a company will need to match the terms offered by its competitors, otherwise customers will migrate to competitors, unless there are other factors that will encourage them to be loyal, such as better quality products or a more valuable after-sales service.

The level of risk acceptable to the company

Some companies may feel that more relaxed trade credit terms will increase the volume of business to an extent that compensates for a higher risk of bad debts. The level of risk of bad debts that is acceptable will vary from company to company. Some companies may seek to reduce this risk through a policy of insuring against non-payment by clients.

The need for liquidity

Where the need for liquidity is relatively high, a company may choose to accelerate cash inflow from credit customers by using invoice discounting or by factoring.

The expertise available within the company

Where expertise in the assessment of creditworthiness and the monitoring of customer accounts is not to a sufficiently high standard, a company may choose to outsource its receivables management to a third party, i.e. a factor.

ACCA marking scheme			
			Marks
(a)	Current policy:		
	Annual ordering cost		1
	Annual holding cost		1
	Total annual cost		1
	EOQ policy:		
	Annual order size		1
	Annual ordering cost and holding cost		1
	Change in inventory management cost		1
			―――
		Maximum	6
(b)	Benefits of JIT procurement policy		3
(c)	Reduction in trade receivables		2
	Financing cost saving		1
	Cost of early settlement discount		1
	Comment on net benefit		1
	Maximum early settlement discount		1
			―――
		Maximum	6
(d)	Relevant discussion		5
			―――
Total			**20**
			―――

Examiner's comments

Many candidates gained full marks in answering part (a), picked up reasonable marks on parts (b) and (d), but in many cases gave poor answers to part (c).

Part (a) required candidates to calculate the cost of a current inventory ordering policy, and the change in inventory management costs when the economic ordering quantity (EOQ) model was used to find the optimum order size.

A number of answers failed to gain full marks because they did not calculate the change in inventory management costs, even after correctly calculating these costs under the current ordering policy and after applying the EOQ model.

Poorer answers showed a lack of understanding of the relationship between ordering costs and holding costs, and an inability to calculate these costs.

In part (b), candidates were required to describe briefly the benefits of a just-in-time (JIT) procurement policy. No credit was given for discussing the disadvantages of such a policy, as these were not required. Many answers gave a short list of benefits, rather than a description of the benefits, and so were not able to gain full marks.

Part (c) asked candidates to calculate and comment on whether a proposed change in receivables management (offering an early settlement discount) was acceptable, and to calculate the maximum discount that could be offered.

Some candidates gained full marks for calculating correctly the reduction in financing cost, the cost of the discount and the net benefit of offering the discount. The reduction in financing cost and the cost of the discount were both based on credit sales for the year of $87.6 million.

Poorer answers based their calculations on current trade receivables of $18 million, even though the question stated that the early settlement discount would be offered to 25% of credit customers. Comparing current trade receivables and current credit sales showed that current receivables paid on average after 75 days, a credit period that would be reduced to 60 days through improved operational procedures. Some candidates assumed incorrectly that the current trade receivables period was 60 days and made incorrect calculations as a result.

The maximum discount that could be offered would be equal to the benefit gained from the discount, i.e. the saving in administration and operating costs added to the reduction in financing cost.

Feedback from markers indicated that some answers to this part of question 3 were disorganised, with unlabelled calculations and a lack of explanation. It is important to help the marking process by labelling calculations, explaining workings and using correct notation, e.g. '$ per year', '$m', 'days' and so on.

Part (d) required candidates to discuss the factors that should be considered in formulating working capital policy on the management of trade receivables.

Poorer answers offered a list of actions that could be met in trade receivables management, such as "send out letters to trade receivables", "call customers on the telephone", "produce an aged receivables analysis regularly". Working capital policy on trade receivables management should consider what period of credit to offer, how to determine the amount of credit offered, when creditworthiness needs to be assessed and to what extent, and so on, and it is often informed by the trade receivables management policies of competitors. The policy should provide the framework within which the actions referred to above would be undertaken.

19   FLIT CO

Key answer tips

Part (a) is relatively simple but needs a methodical approach and should not be rushed. Part (b) is a simple calculation. Parts (c) and (e) are stand-alone knowledge regurgitation questions. Part (d) is the most complex, requiring an understanding that if early settlement speeds up payment from customers, the receivables balance and therefore the cost of financing receivables will be affected along with an understanding of all the other elements that will be affected such as bad debts, more profit from extra sales, etc. The highlighted words are key phrases that markers are looking for.

(a)   Cash balances at the end of each month:

	December	January	February	March	April
Sales (units)	1,200	1,250	1,300	1,400	1,500
Selling price ($/unit)	800	800	840	840	
Sales ($000)	960	1,000	1,092	1,176	
Month received	January	February	March	April	

	December	January	February	March
Production (units)	1,250	1,300	1,400	1,500
Raw materials (units)	2,500	2,600	2,800	3,000
Raw materials ($000)	500	520	560	600
Month payable	January	February	March	April

	December	January	February	March
Production (units)	1,250	1,300	1,400	1,500
Variable costs ($000)	125	130	140	150
Month payable	December	January	February	March

Monthly cash balances:

	January $000	February $000	March $000
Receivables	960	1,000	1,092
Loan			300
Income:	960	1,000	1,392
Raw materials	500	520	560
Variable costs	130	140	150
Machine			400
Expenditure:	630	660	1,110
Opening balance	40	370	710
Net cash flow	330	340	282
Closing balance	370	710	992

(b) **Calculation of current ratio**

Inventory at the end of the three-month period:

This will be the finished goods for April sales of 1,500 units, which can be assumed to be valued at the cost of production of $400 per unit for materials and $100 per unit for variable overheads and wages. The value of the inventory is therefore 1,500 × 500 = $750,000.

Trade receivables at the end of the three-month period:

These will be March sales of 1,400 × 800 × 1.05 = $1,176,000.

Cash balance at the end of the three-month period:

This was forecast to be $992,000.

Trade payables at the end of the three-month period:

This will be the cash owed for March raw materials of $600,000.

Forecast current ratio

Assuming that current liabilities consist of trade payables alone:

Current ratio = (750,000 + 1,176,000 + 992,000)/600,000 = 4.9 times

(c) If Flit Co generates a short-term cash surplus, the cash may be needed again in the near future. In order to increase profitability, the short-term cash surplus could be invested, for example, in a bank deposit. However, the investment selected would normally not be expected to carry any risk of capital loss. Shares traded on a large stock market carry a significant risk of capital loss, and hence are rarely suitable for investing short-term cash surpluses.

(d) Current credit sales income = $30,000,000 × 0.8 = $24,000,000

Credit sales income after introducing discount = $24,000,000 × 1.2 = $28,800,000
Increase in income by introducing discount = $24,000,000 × 0.2 = $4,800,000
Increase in net profit (profit before interest and tax) = $4,800,000 × 0.1 = $480,000

Current level of bad debts = $24,000,000 × 0.005 = $120,000 per year
Revised level of bad debts = $28,800,000 × 0.00375 = $108,000 per year
This would be a benefit of $120,000 – $108,000 = $12,000 per year

	$000
Trade receivables taking discount = $28,800,000 × 0.75 × 30/360 =	1,800
Trade receivables not taking discount = $28,800,000 × 0.25 × 51/360 =	1,020

Revised level of trade receivables	2,820
Current trade receivables = $24,000,000 × 51/360 =	3,400

Reduction in trade receivables	580

	$	$
Benefits		
Reduction in financing costs = 580,000 × 0.04 =	23,200	
Increase in net profit =	480,000	
Reduction in bad debts =	12,000	

		515,200
Costs		
Increase in administration costs	35,000	
Cost of discount = $28,800,000 × 0.005 × 0.75 =	108,000	

		143,000

Net benefit of proposed early settlement discount =		372,200

(e) A company could reduce the risk associated with foreign accounts receivable, such as export credit risk, by reducing the level of investment in them, for example, by using bills of exchange.

If payment by the foreign customer is linked to bills of exchange, these can either be discounted or negotiated by a company with its bank. Discounting means that the trade bills (term bills) are sold to the bank at a discount to their face value. The company gets cash when the bills are discounted, thereby decreasing the outstanding level of trade receivables. Negotiation means that the bank makes an advance of cash to the company, with the debt being settled when the bills of exchange (sight bills) are paid.

Advances against collection means that the bank handling the collection of payment on behalf of the selling company could be prepared to make a cash advance of up to 90% of the face value of the payment instrument, for example, bills of exchange. Again, this would reduce the level of investment in foreign accounts receivable.

The risk of non-payment by foreign accounts receivable can be reduced by raising an international letter of credit (documentary credit) linked to the contract for the sale of goods. This could be confirmed (guaranteed) by a bank in the foreign customer's country.

The exporting company could also arrange for export credit insurance (export credit cover) against the risk of non-payment, which could occur for reasons outside the control of the foreign customer.

The risk of foreign accounts receivable becoming bad debts can be reduced by performing the same creditworthiness assessment processes on foreign credit customers as those used with domestic credit customers, such as seeking credit references and bank references.

Examiner's note: Only TWO methods were required to be discussed.

ACCA marking scheme		Marks
(a)	Monthly receivables	1
	Loan	0.5
	Raw materials	1
	Variable costs	1
	Machine	0.5
	Closing balances	1
	Maximum	5
(b)	Closing finished goods inventory	0.5
	Closing trade receivables	0.5
	Closing trade payables	0.5
	Current ratio	0.5
	Maximum	2
(c)	Temporary nature of short-term cash surplus	1
	Investment should have no risk of capital loss	1
	Shares are not suitable for investment	1
	Maximum	3
(d)	Increase in net profit	1
	Benefit of reduction in bad debts	1
	Reduction in trade receivables	1
	Reduction in financing costs	1
	Cost of discount	1
	Evaluation of early settlement discount	1
		6
(e)	First method of reducing risk	2
	Second method of reducing risk	2
		4
Total		**20**

Examiner's comments

Part (a). Candidates were required to calculate the cash balance at the end of each month in a three-month period. Most candidates did well on this question. Some answers made timing errors, while others overlooked that each unit produced required two units (not one unit) of raw material. Some answers lost marks because they wrongly believed that net cash flow was the same as cash balance, or because they located the January opening cash balance in December.

Part (b). Candidates were asked to calculate the forecast current ratio at the end of the three-month period, which could be calculated here as:

(Inventory + Trade Receivables + Cash)/Trade Payables

Surprisingly, most answers did not gain full marks. One reason for this was that many answers, without explanation, omitted one or more of the elements indicated above. While the question stated that no raw materials inventory was held, finished goods inventory had to be calculated, as production of finished goods took place one month before sales. Another reason why most answers did not gain full marks was including elements that were not current assets or current liabilities, such as a newly purchased machine or a new long-term loan. Some answers did not explain the figures that were being used to calculate the current ratio, giving markers no guidance as to the working capital elements that the candidate believed were being used.

Part (c). Candidates were asked here to assume that the company expected to have a short-term cash surplus in the three-month period, and to discuss whether this short-term cash surplus should be invested in shares listed on a large stock market.

Some answers discussed, occasionally at length, how the company could decide if it had a cash surplus, even though they were told to assume this. Such answers might for example discuss one or more reasons for holding cash (transaction, precautionary and speculative), or recommend using the Miller-Orr model to clarify the size of the cash surplus.

Other answers discussed, occasionally at length, working capital financing policy, and said that the investment decision depended on whether this policy was conservative, matching or aggressive. Financing policy is not relevant to an investment decision.

The key learning point here is that a short-term cash surplus must be invested with no risk of capital loss, as the cash will be needed again. Shares on a stock market, even a large stock market, can fall in value very quickly and so are not a suitable way of investing a short-term cash surplus. Satisfactory answers recognised this key point, in some cases suggesting appropriate ways of investing the short-term cash surplus.

Part (d) asked for an evaluation of an early settlement discount. Answers to this question demonstrated the importance of reading the question carefully, for example:

- candidates were told to assume that there were 360 days in each year, yet some answers used 365 days

- credit sales were stated to be 80% of total income of $30 million, yet some answers used $30 million as credit sales

- income from credit sales was stated to increase by 20% as a result of offering the early settlement discount, yet some answers did not increase credit sales income.

Answers to this question also demonstrated the importance of labelling all calculations or workings, as some answers offered a sea of calculations with no indication of what each calculation related to. It is up to candidates to communicate clearly what they are doing in their answers, as markers cannot be expected to guess what unlabelled calculations are trying to achieve.

Candidates who adopted a methodical approach to working through the information provided in the question gained high marks.

Part (e) asked candidates to discuss TWO ways in which a company could reduce the risk associated with foreign accounts receivable. The block capitals were in the original question and they emphasise that only two ways were required to be discussed. Answers that discussed more than two ways were therefore wasting valuable time, as marks would only be awarded to the first two ways discussed in an answer.

Some answers discussed foreign currency risk in addition to or as well as the export credit risk and default risk discussed in the suggested answer, and full credit was given to such answers.

20   NESUD CO

Key answer tips

Part (a) relies on an understanding that if a settlement discount is received from a supplier it reduces the amount paid but increases the amount of funding needed for payables. While the calculations are similar to those for a receivables discount, the benefits and costs are the other way round. In part (b) you're asked to evaluate whether the EOQ model should be adopted. This means looking at whether the total of holding and ordering costs will reduce. For 6 marks it isn't enough to just say that the EOQ will optimise the costs – calculations are needed. Part (c) is a stand-alone knowledge regurgitation question. You will need to have a good knowledge of this area to be able to write enough for 10 marks. The highlighted words are key phrases that markers are looking for.

(a)   Relevant trade payables before discount = 1,500,000 × 60/360 = $250,000

Relevant trade payables after discount = 1,500,000 × 30/360 = $125,000

Reduction in trade payables = 250,000 – 125,000 = $125,000

More quickly, reduction in trade payables = 1,500,000 × (60 – 30)/360 = $125,000

The finance needed to reduce the trade payables will increase the overdraft.

Increase in finance cost = 125,000 × 0.04 = $5,000

Administration cost increase = $500

Discount from supplier = $1,500,000 × 0.005 = $7,500

Net benefit of discount = 7,500 – 5,000 – 500 = $2,000 per year

On financial grounds, Nesud Co should accept the supplier's early settlement discount offer.

(b)   Annual demand = 2,400,000/5 = 480,000 units per year

Each month, Nesud Co orders 480,000/12 = 40,000 units

Current ordering cost = 12 × 248.44 = $2,981 per year

Average inventory of Component K = 40,000/2 = 20,000 units

Current holding cost = 20,000 × 1.06 = $21,200 per year

Total cost of current ordering policy = 2,981 + 21,200 = $24,181

Economic order quantity = (2 × 248.44 × 480,000/1.06)0.5 = 15,000 units per order

Number of orders per year = 480,000/15,000 = 32 orders per year

Ordering cost = 32 x 248.44 = $7,950 per year

Average inventory of Component K = 15,000/2 = 7,500 units

Holding cost = 7,500 × 1.06 = $7,950 per year

Total cost of EOQ ordering policy = 7,950 + 7,950 = $15,900

On financial grounds, Nesud Co should adopt an EOQ approach to ordering Component K as there is a reduction in cost of $8,281.

(c)   Management of trade receivables can be improved by considering credit analysis, credit control and collection of amounts owing. Management of trade receivables can also be outsourced to a factoring company, rather than being managed in-house.

Credit analysis

Offering credit to customers exposes a company to the risk of bad debts and this should be minimised through credit analysis or assessing creditworthiness. This can be done through collecting and analysing information about potential credit customers. Relevant information includes bank references, trade references, reports from credit reference agencies, records of previous transactions with potential customers, annual reports, and so on.

A company might set up its own credit scoring system in order to assess the creditworthiness of potential customers. Where the expected volume of trade justifies it, a visit to a company can be made to gain a better understanding of its business and prospects.

Credit control

The accounts of customers who have been granted credit must be monitored regularly to ensure that agreed trade terms are being followed and that accounts are not getting into arrears.

An important monitoring device here is an aged trade receivables analysis, identifying accounts and amounts in arrears, and the extent to which amounts are overdue.

A credit utilisation report can assist management in understanding the extent to which credit is being used, identifying customers who may benefit from increased credit, and assessing the extent and nature of a company's exposure to trade receivables.

Collection of amounts owed

A company should ensure that its trade receivables are kept informed about their accounts, amounts outstanding and amounts becoming due, and the terms of trade they have accepted. An invoice should be raised when a sale is made. Regular statements should be sent, for example, on a monthly basis. Customers should be encouraged to settle their accounts on time and not become overdue. Offering a discount for early settlement could help to achieve this.

Overdue accounts should be chased using procedures contained within a company's trade receivables management policy. Reminders of payment due should be sent, leading to a final demand if necessary. Telephone calls or personal visits could be made to a contact within the company. Taking legal action or employing a specialised debt collection agency could be considered as a last resort. A clear understanding of the costs involved is important here, as the costs incurred should never exceed the benefit of collecting the overdue amount.

Factoring of trade receivables

Some companies choose to outsource management of trade receivables to a factoring company, which can bring expertise and specialist knowledge to the tasks of credit analysis, credit control, and collection of amounts owed. In exchange, the factoring company will charge a fee, typically a percentage of annual credit sales. The factoring company can also offer an advance of up to 80% of trade receivables, in exchange for interest.

ACCA Marking scheme		Marks
(a)	Change in trade payables	1
	Increase in finance cost	1
	Administration cost increase	0.5
	Early settlement discount	0.5
	Comment on financial acceptability	1
		4
(b)	Annual demand	1
	Current ordering cost	1
	Current holding cost	1
	Economic order quantity	1
	EOQ ordering cost	0.5
	EOQ holding cost	0.5
	Comment on adopting EOQ approach to ordering	1
		6
(c)	Credit analysis	2
	Credit control	2
	Collection of amounts owed	2
	Factoring of trade receivables	2
	Other relevant discussion	2
		10
Total		**20**

21 OSCAR CO

Key answer tips

For part (a), remember that a reduction in receivables' days means less financing is needed for receivables and financing costs will fall. This is often the most complex part of calculations on this topic. Don't forget to include the easier costs and benefits in your totals. For part (b) you are only asked for benefits, so disadvantages of factoring will not score marks. For part (c) make sure that your answer focuses on working capital investment policy rather than working capital financing policy. Make sure you're able to distinguish between these two topics in the exam. DO not present more than three factors as any extra will not be marked.

The highlighted words are key phrases that markers are looking for.

(a)

Option 1

	$	$
Current trade receivables	5,370,000	
Revised trade receivables (28,000,000 × 30/365)	2,301,370	
Reduction in receivables	3,068,630	
	$	$
Reduction in financing cost (3,068,630 × 0.07)	214,804	
Reduction in admin costs	30,000	
Benefits		244,804
Factor's fee (28,000,000 × 0.005)		(140,000)
Net benefit		104,804

Option 2

	$	$
Reduction in financing cost (3,068,630 × 0.07)	214,804	
Reduction in admin costs	30,000	
Bad debts saved (28,000,000 × 0.02)	560,000	
Benefits		804,804
Increase in finance cost (2,301,370 × 0.8 × 0.02)	36,822	
Factor's fee (28,000,000 × 0.015)	420,000	
Costs		(456,822)
Net benefit		347,982

Both options are financially acceptable to Oscar Co, with Option 2 offering the greatest benefit and therefore it should be accepted.

(b)   Oscar Co may benefit from the services offered by the factoring company for a number of different reasons, as follows:

Economies of specialisation

Factors specialise in trade receivables management and therefore can offer 'economies of specialisation'. They are experts at getting customers to pay promptly and may be able to achieve payment periods and bad debt levels which clients could not achieve themselves. The factor may be able to persuade the large multinational companies which Oscar Co supplies to pay on time.

Scale economies

In addition, because of the scale of their operations, factors are often able to do this more cheaply than clients such as Oscar Co could do on their own. Factor fees, even after allowing for the factor's profit margin, can be less than the clients' own receivables administration cost.

Free up management time

Factoring can free up management time and allow them to focus on more important tasks. This could be a major benefit for Oscar Co, where directors are currently spending a large amount of time attempting to persuade customers to pay on time.

Bad debts insurance

The insurance against bad debts shields clients from non-payment by customers; although this comes at a cost, it can be particularly attractive to small companies who may not be able to stand the financial shock of a large bad debt. This could well be the case for Oscar Co. As a small company which supplies much larger car manufacturing companies, it is particularly exposed to default by customers. On the other hand, it could be argued that large multinational companies are financially secure and default is unlikely, rendering bad debt insurance unnecessary.

Accelerate cash inflow

Factor finance can be useful to companies who have exhausted other sources of finance. This could be useful to Oscar Co if it cannot negotiate an increase in its overdraft limit.

Finance through growth

Although factor finance is generally more expensive than a bank overdraft, the funding level is linked to the company's volume of sales. This can help to finance expansion and protects the company against overtrading. In a rapid growth company such as Oscar Co, this could be a major advantage of factor finance.

(c)   A company's working capital investment is equal to the sum of its inventories and its accounts receivable, less its accounts payable.

The following factors will determine the level of a company's investment in working capital:

The nature of the industry and the length of the working capital cycle

Some businesses have long production processes which inevitably lead to long working capital cycles and large investments in working capital. Housebuilding, for example, requires the building company to acquire land, gain government permission to build, build houses and when complete, sell them to customers. This process can often take more than a year and require large investment in work-in-progress and therefore in working capital.

Other industries, such as supermarkets, buy goods on long credit terms, have rapid inventory turnover and sell to customers for cash. They often receive payment from customers before they need to pay suppliers and therefore have little (or negative) investment in working capital.

Working capital investment policy

Some companies take a conservative approach to working capital investment, offering long periods of credit to customers (to promote sales), carrying high levels of inventory (to protect against stock-outs), and paying suppliers promptly (to maintain good relationships). This approach offers many benefits, but it necessitates a large investment in working capital.

Others take a more aggressive approach offering minimal credit, carrying low levels of inventory and delaying payments to suppliers. This will result in a low level of working capital investment.

Efficiency of management and terms of trade

If management of the components of working capital is neglected, then investment in working capital can increase. For example, a failure to apply credit control procedures such as warning letters or stop lists can result in high levels of accounts receivable. Failure to control inventory by using the EOQ model, or JIT inventory management principles, can lead to high levels of inventory.

ACCA marking scheme		Marks
(a)	Revised trade receivables	1
	Finance cost reduction	1
	Admin savings	1
	Factor fee Option 1	1
	Bad debt saving	1
	Finance cost increase	1
	Factor fee Option 2	1
	Comment	1
		8
(b)	Benefits	3
	Oscar Co link	3
		6
(c)	First factor	2
	Second factor	2
	Third factor	2
		6
Total		**20**

Examiner's comments

Part (a)

This question required candidates to calculate the costs and benefits of two options offered to Oscar Co by a factoring company and to comment on the findings.

The net benefit of Option 1 was often precisely calculated, with many candidates arriving at $104,804.

There were fewer totally correct answers in the computation of the net benefit of option 2. The most frequently occurring error here was a failure to recognise that the factor's advance would bring about an increase in the cost of the financing of the revised trade receivables. In other words, 80% of the trade receivables would be financed at 9%, rather than at 7%.

Other errors included:

*   Using trade receivables as the basis for calculating factor fees or even, via trade receivables days of 30, credit sales revenue

*   Putting bad debt savings in both options

*   Basing bad debt savings on trade receivables and not credit sales revenue

*   Failing to calculate the effect on financing costs of the respective options

*   Basing the increased financial cost in option 2 on current trade receivables, or on current credit sales revenue

*   Confusing the nature of items, such as mixing capital and revenue items, so, for example, the value of the factor's advance is incorrectly included as a cost, rather than the impact of its financing cost.

Candidates sitting this examination in the future should be aware that having the use of spreadsheet functionality does not abdicate responsibility for showing the build-up of how a figure has been arrived at. A supporting working can be shown inside a single cell. Hence the increase in finance cost referred to above could be built up in the following way:

$28,000,000 \times 30/365 \times 0.80 \times 0.02 = \$36,822$.

Some candidates did not make a comment on their findings, which should simply be about which option to choose and why, thereby failing to gain a relatively straightforward mark.

Part (b)

Here candidates were required to discuss the reasons why Oscar Co may benefit from the services offered by the factoring company. There are two important points about the stated requirement which are worth emphasising here. Firstly, the requirement is clear in asking for reasons other than costs and benefits already calculated. Secondly, the requirement asks for reasons why Oscar Co may benefit from the factoring company.

Whilst there were good responses here that discussed valid reasons, such as those outlined in the suggested solution, and were able to relate these reasons to the circumstances outlined in the case scenario, there were a disappointing number of responses which were too brief for the marks available. In a requirement asking for a discussion and attracting six marks, it is insufficient to offer short phrases or bullet points lacking in detail.

As already noted, the requirement was for discussion of reasons other than costs or benefits already calculated. Sadly, many answers discussed these already-calculated costs and benefits, such as the reduction in administrative costs or the bad debt savings.

Furthermore, some answers simply made no link to Oscar Co, even though this was a question requirement. Candidates sitting in the future are encouraged to read the requirement carefully and, where asked for, relate their answers to the company in question. This should be done in a meaningful way by, for example, discussing the factor's expertise and contrasting this with the lack of business administration skills of the four founders of the company. Simply mentioning Oscar Co several times in a response, but not actually discussing the company's characteristics and circumstances, does not qualify as linking reasons to the company.

Part (c)

This question required candidates to discuss three factors which determine the level of a company's investment in working capital.

Firstly, a discussion is asked for. If six marks are offered for discussing three factors, then assuming that two marks are offered for each factor is reasonable. The grid now seen in Computer Based Examinations should prove useful in organising candidates' answers. That said, it is worth reiterating, a 'bullet point' or short phrase is rarely, if ever, going to be sufficient to attract the two marks available for each factor.

It is worth commenting that answers to this question were disappointing. Many answers did not appear to understand the question requirement, even though this was taken directly from the Financial Management syllabus.

Common errors in candidates' responses included:

- Discussing (or simply listing) elements of working capital, without relating answers to the question requirement

- Discussing working capital financing policy, when the requirement said working capital investment policy

- Interpreting 'factors determining the level of working capital investment' as 'accounting ratios', such as current ratio or quick ratio

- Stating a factor, but then with no accompanying discussion e.g. the 'nature of the industry', but without explaining why the industry affected working capital or giving examples.

As sometimes happens, candidates offered responses based upon what they would have liked to have been asked about working capital management, rather than to the actual question asked in the examination. For example, some candidates' entire answers to this part (c) were wholly about 'liquidity versus profitability' or about permanent and fluctuating assets, and conservative, aggressive and moderate policies.

INVESTMENT APPRAISAL

22 ARMCLIFF CO

Key answer tips

In part (a) the first part of the data in the question relates to current operations – try to think why the examiner has given you this. The requirement is to determine whether the proposed project is attractive to *Armcliff* – not the parent company. Presumably, what will make a project attractive to a division's management is one that will improve their current performance measure. Thus, it is useful to know what the current level of ARR being achieved. This can then be compared with the project ARR.

Remember that the ARR is a financial accounting based measure – returns are in terms of accounting profits, and investments valued at statement of financial position amounts – you must try to put all 'relevant cost' principles to the back of your mind. Whilst there are various possible definitions of the ARR (a point that can be raised in (b)) here you are given precise directions, so make sure you follow them. Both average profits and average investment need to be ascertained.

Don't forget to conclude by comparison with both current and required rates of return.

In part (b) the question requires you to show both theoretical and practical knowledge about investment appraisal methods.

In part (c), even though this is a examining a general area of credit management, try wherever you can to relate your points to the business in the question – it is stated that Armcliff intends to extend its credit to improve sales. Again, make sure that you explain points enough to get the marks available, whilst still offering sufficient variety. Note that it is not enough simply to say that the advantage of ARR is its simplicity. With spreadsheets, this is hardly going to be a consideration. Show instead that you appreciate that mangers are influenced by the methods used for their performance measurement – both internally and externally. The highlighted words are key phrases that markers are looking for.

(a) **Current return on capital employed**

= Operating profit/capital employed

= $20m/($75m + $25m) = $20m/$100m = 20%.

Analysis of the project

Project capital requirements are $14 million fixed capital plus $0.5 million inventory. The annual depreciation charge (straight line) is:

($14m – expected residual value of $2m)/4 = $3 million per annum.

Profit profile ($m)

Year	1	2	3	4
Sales revenue	(5.00 × 2m) = 10.00	(4.50 × 1.8m) = 8.10	(4.00 × 1.6m) = 6.40	(3.50 × 1.6m) = 5.60
Operating costs	(2.00)	(1.80)	(1.60)	(1.60)
Fixed costs	(1.50)	(1.35)	(1.20)	(1.20)
Depreciation	(3.00)	(3.00)	(3.00)	(3.00)
Profit	3.50	1.95	0.60	(0.20)

Total profit over four years = $5.85 million.

Capital employed (start-of-year):

Non-current assets	14.00	11.00	8.00	5.00
Inventories	0.50	0.50	0.50	0.50
	14.50	11.50	8.50	5.50

Average capital employed = (14.50 + 11.50 + 8.50 + 5.50)/4 = $10 million.

$$\text{Average rate of return} = \frac{\text{Average profit}}{\text{Average capital employed}} = \frac{\$5.85m/4}{\$10.0m} = \frac{\$1.46m}{\$10.0m}$$

= 14.6%

Note: If receivables were to be included in the definition of capital employed, this would reduce the calculated rate of return, while the inclusion of payables would have an offsetting effect. However, using the ARR criterion as defined, the proposal has an expected return above the minimum stipulated by Shevin Inc. It is unlikely that the managers of Armcliff will propose projects that offer a rate of return below the present 20% even where the expected return exceeds the minimum of 10%. To undertake projects with returns in this range will depress the overall divisional return and cast managerial performance in a weaker light.

However, it is unlikely that the senior managers of the Armcliff subsidiary would want to undertake the project.

(b) (i) The **ARR can be expressed in a variety of ways**, and is therefore susceptible to manipulation. Although the question specifies average profit to average capital employed, many other variants are possible, such as average profit to initial capital, which would raise the computed rate of return.

It is also **susceptible to variation in accounting policy** by the same firm over time, or as between different firms at a point in time. For example, different methods of depreciation produce different profit figures and hence different rates of return.

Perhaps, most fundamentally, it is **based on accounting profits expressed net of deduction for depreciation provisions, rather than cash flows**. This effectively results in double counting for the initial outlay i.e. the capital cost is allowed for twice over, both in the numerator of the ARR calculation and also in the denominator. This is likely to depress the measured profitability of a project and result in rejection of some worthwhile investment.

Finally, because it simply averages the profits, it **makes no allowance for the timing of the returns** from the project.

(ii)   The continuing use of the ARR method can by explained largely by its utilisation of statement of financial position and statement of profit or loss magnitudes familiar to managers, namely 'profit' and 'capital employed'. In addition, the impact of the project on a company's financial statements can also be specified. Return on capital employed is still the commonest way in which business unit performance is measured and evaluated, and is certainly the most visible to shareholders. It is thus not surprising that some managers may be happiest in expressing project attractiveness in the same terms in which their performance will be reported to shareholders, and according to which they will be evaluated and rewarded.

(c)   Armcliff intends to achieve a sales increase by extending its receivables collection period. This policy carries several dangers. It implies that credit will be extended to customers for whom credit is an important determinant of supplier selection, hinting at financial instability on their part. Consequently, the risk of later than expected, or even no payment, is likely to increase. Although losses due to default are limited to the incremental costs of making these sales rather than the invoiced value, Armcliff should recognise that there is an opportunity cost involved in tying up capital for lengthy periods. In addition, companies which are slow payers often attempt to claim discounts to which they are not entitled. Armcliff may then face the difficult choice between acquiescence to such demands versus rejection, in which case, it may lose repeat sales.

23   WARDEN CO

Key answer tips

Tackling this question requires a methodical and logical approach. The requirements must be attempted in the order given. It is an excellent test of your understanding on the key investment appraisal topic.

The highlighted words are key phrases that markers are looking for.

(a) **Calculation of net present value (NPV)**

Year	1	2	3	4	5	6
	$000	$000	$000	$000	$000	$000
Sales revenue	1,600	1,600	1,600	1,600	1,600	
Variable costs	(1,100)	(1,100)	(1,100)	(1,100)	(1,100)	
Contribution	500	500	500	500	500	
Fixed costs	(160)	(160)	(160)	(160)	(160)	
Taxable cash flow	340	340	340	340	340	
Tax liabilities		(102)	(102)	(102)	(102)	(102)
After-tax cash flow	340	238	238	238	238	(102)
Working capital					90	
Scrap value					40	
Net cash flow	340	238	238	238	368	(102)
Discount factors	0.901	0.812	0.731	0.659	0.593	0.535
Present values	306	193	174	157	218	(55)

	$000
Present value of cash inflows	993
Working capital investment	(90)
Cost of machine	(800)
NPV	103

Since the investment has a positive NPV, it is financially acceptable.

Alternative layout of NPV calculation

	$000
PV of sales revenue = 100,000 × 16 × 3·696 =	5,914
PV of variable costs = 100,000 × 11 × 3·696 =	(4,066)
PV of contribution	1,848
PV of fixed costs = 160,000 × 3·696 =	(591)
PV of taxable cash flow	1,257
PV of tax liabilities = (340,000 × 0·3 × 3·696) × 0·901 =	(340)
	917
PV of working capital recovered = 90,000 × 0·593 =	53
PV of scrap value = 800,000 × 0·05 × 0·593 =	24
PV of cash inflows	994
Initial working capital investment	(90)
Initial purchase cost of new machine	(800)
Net present value	104

(b)   Calculation of internal rate of return (IRR)

NPV at 11% was found to be $103,000

NPV at 17%:

Net cash flow	340	238	238	238	368	(102)
Discount factors	0.855	0.731	0.624	0.534	0.456	0.390
Present values	291	174	149	127	168	(40)

	$000
Present value of cash inflows	869
Working capital investment	(90)
Cost of machine	(800)
NPV	(21)

IRR = 11 + (((17 − 11) × 103,000)/(103,000 + 21,000)) = 11 + 5.0 = 16.0%

Since the internal rate of return of the investment (16%) is greater than the cost of capital of Warden Co, the investment is financially acceptable.

Examiner's note: although the value of the calculated IRR will depend on the two discount rates used in linear interpolation, other discount rate choices should produce values close to 16%.

(c)   (i)   Sensitivity

Sensitivity analysis indicates which project variable is the key or critical variable, i.e. the variable where the smallest relative change makes the net present value (NPV) zero. Sensitivity analysis can show where management should focus attention in order to make an investment project successful, or where underlying assumptions should be checked for robustness.

The sensitivity of an investment project to a change in a given project variable can be calculated as the ratio of the NPV to the present value (PV) of the project variable. This gives directly the relative change in the variable needed to make the NPV of the project zero.

(ii)   Selling price sensitivity

The PV of sales revenue = 100,000 × 16 × 3.696 = $5,913,600

The tax liability associated with sales revenue needs be considered, as the NPV is on an after-tax basis.

Tax liability arising from sales revenue = 100,000 × 16 × 0.3 = $480,000 per year

The PV of the tax liability without lagging = 480,000 × 3.696 = $1,774,080

(Alternatively, PV of tax liability without lagging = 5,913,600 × 0.3 = $1,774,080)

Lagging by one year, PV of tax liability = 1,774,080 × 0.901 = $1,598,446 After-tax PV of sales revenue = 5,913,600 − 1,598,446 = $4,315,154

Sensitivity = 100 × 103,000/4,315,154 = 2.4%

Discount rate sensitivity

The breakeven discount rate is the IRR calculated in part (b).

Increase in discount rate needed to make NPV zero = 16 − 11 = 5%

Relative change in discount rate needed to make NPV zero = 100 × 5/11 = 45%

Conclusion

Of the two variables, the key or critical variable is selling price, since the investment is more sensitive to a change in this variable (2.4%) than it is to a change in discount rate (45%).

ACCA marking scheme		
		Marks
(a)	Sales income	0.5
	Variable costs	0.5
	Fixed costs	0.5
	Tax liabilities	1
	Working capital recovered	0.5
	Scrap value	0.5
	Initial working capital investment	0.5
	Initial investment	0.5
	Discount factors	0.5
	Net present value	1
	Comment on financial acceptability	1
	Maximum	7
(b)	Calculation of revised NPV	1
	Calculation of IRR	2
	Comment on financial acceptability	1
	Maximum	4

(c)	(i)	Explanation of sensitivity analysis		2
	(ii)	After-tax present value of sales revenue		2
		Selling price sensitivity		2
		Discount rate sensitivity		1
		Comment on findings		2
			Maximum	7
Total				**20**

Examiner's comments

Part (a) asked for a calculation of (NPV. Many answers scored full marks here. Some answers lost marks because they left something out (error of omission). These answers, for example, did not include incremental fixed costs, or working capital investment, or working capital recovery, or scrap value, or even in some cases one whole year of income and costs (the evaluation was over five years). Other answers lost marks because there was a mistake in the way that NPV was calculated (error of principle). Such mistakes included treating working capital recovery or scrap value as tax-allowable deductions, and calculated tax liability on sales or on contribution, rather than on net taxable cash flow.

Part (b) asked students to calculate the internal rate of return (IRR) of an investment and many answers gained full marks. Some answers lost marks due to calculation errors, while as in previous examinations, there were a small number of answers that calculated ARR (accounting rate of return or return on capital employed) instead of IRR. Some candidates did not understand the IRR decision rule, claiming wrongly that the investment was not acceptable because the IRR was greater than the cost of capital of the investing company.

Part (c)(i) asked for an explanation of sensitivity analysis. Weaker answers did not refer to investment appraisal, or suggested that project variables were sensitive to NPV, rather than NPV being sensitive to project variables.

In part (c) (ii) candidates were asked here to calculate the sensitivity to a change in selling price and discount rate, and comment on the findings. Many candidates had difficulty with the brief calculations required here. Looking first at selling price, many answers noted correctly that sensitivity could be found by dividing NPV by the present value (PV) of the relevant project variable. Many answers calculated correctly the PV of sales income, but did not adjust this for tax liability. Weaker answers used the PV of selling price, or the PV of total sales income, or did not use a present value at all.

Some answers used an algebraic version of the NPV calculation, with selling price as the unknown variable. While this is an acceptable alternative to the simpler method of dividing NPV by PV of relevant project variable, answers often contained calculation errors, or incorrect adjustments for tax liability, or omitted some of the one-off project cash flows.

Turning to the discount rate sensitivity, what was needed was a simple comparison of the IRR with the company's discount rate. Many candidates seemed unaware of this and wasted valuable time with calculations that had no merit at all.

Sensitivity analysis can also be undertaken by changing a project variable by a set amount and calculating the change in the NPV. Some answers used this method correctly and gained credit. Since only one variable at a time is changed in sensitivity analysis, answers that changed simultaneously both selling price and discount showed a lack of understanding and gained little credit.

24 INVESTMENT APPRAISAL

Key answer tips

Parts (a) and (b)(i) should present an opportunity to gain some easy marks by outlining some basic areas of the syllabus. The calculations in part (b) (ii) were relatively straightforward. Make sure you don't neglect the final part of the requirement – to identify other factors that the company should take into account when deciding of the optimal cycle. The highlighted words are key phrases that markers are looking for.

(a) Accounting rate of return (ARR) is a measure of the return on an investment where the annual profit before interest and tax is expressed as a percentage of the capital sum invested.

There are a number of alternative formulae that can be used to calculate ARR, which differ in the way in which they define capital cost. The more common alternative measures available are:

- average annual profit to initial capital invested, and

- average annual profit to average capital invested.

The method selected will affect the resulting ARR figure, and for this reason it is important to recognise that the measure might be subject to manipulation by managers seeking approval for their investment proposals. The value for average annual profit is calculated after allowances for depreciation, as shown in the example below:

Suppose ARR is defined as: $\dfrac{\text{Average profit (after depreciation)}}{\text{Initial capital invested}} \times 100\%$

A project costing $5 million, and yielding average profits of $1,250,000 per year after depreciation charges of $500,000 per year, would give an ARR of:

1,250,000/5,000,000 × 100% = 25%

If the depreciation charged were to be increased to $750,000 per year, for example as a result of technological changes reducing the expected life of an asset, the ARR becomes:

1,000,000/5,000,000 × 100% = 20%

The attraction of using ARR as a method of investment appraisal lies in its simplicity and the ease with which it can be used to specify the impact of a project on a company's statement of profit or loss. The measure is easily understood and can be directly linked to the use of ROCE as a performance measure. Nonetheless, ARR has been criticised for a number of major drawbacks, perhaps the most important of which is that it uses accounting profits after depreciation rather than cash flows in order to measure return. This means that the capital cost is over-stated in the calculation, via both the numerator and the denominator. In the numerator, the capital cost is taken into account via the depreciation charges used to derive accounting profit, but capital cost is also the denominator. The practical effect of this is to reduce the ARR and thus make projects appear less profitable. This might in turn result in some worthwhile projects being rejected. Note, however, that this problem does not arise where ARR is calculated as average annual profit as a percentage of average capital invested.

The most important criticism of ARR is that it takes no account of the time value of money. A second limitation of ARR, already suggested, is that its value is dependent on accounting policies and this can make comparison of ARR figures across different investments very difficult. A further difficulty with the use of ARR is that it does not give a clear decision rule. The ARR on any particular investment needs to be compared with the current returns being earned within a business, and so unlike NPV for example, it is impossible to say 'all investments with an ARR of x or below will always be rejected.

The payback method of investment appraisal is used widely in industry – generally in addition to other measures. Like ARR, it is easily calculated and understood. The payback approach simply measures the time required for cumulative cash flows from an investment to sum to the original capital invested.

Example

Original investment $100,000

Cash flow profile: Years 1–3 $25,000 p.a.

Years 4 – 5 $50,000 p.a.

Year 6 $5,000

The cumulative cash flows are therefore:

End Year 1	$25,000
End Year 2	$50,000
End Year 3	$75,000
End Year 4	$125,000
End Year 5	$175,000
End Year 6	$180,000

The original sum invested is returned via cash flows some time during the course of Year 4. If cash flows are assumed to be even throughout the year, the cumulative cash flow of $100,000 will have been earned halfway through year 4. The payback period for the investment is thus 3 years and 6 months.

The payback approach to investment appraisal is useful for companies that are seeking to claw back cash from investments as quickly as possible. At the same time, the concept is intuitively appealing as many businesspersons will be concerned about how long they may have to wait to get their money back, because they believe that rapid repayment reduces risks. This means that the payback approach is commonly used for initial screening of investment alternatives.

The disadvantages of the payback approach are as follows:

(i)   Payback ignores the overall profitability of a project by ignoring cash flows after payback is reached. In the example above, the cash flows between 3–4 years and the end of the project total $80,000. To ignore such substantial cash flows would be naïve. As a consequence, the payback method is biased in favour of fast-return investments. This can result in rejecting investments that generate cash flows more slowly in the early years, but which are overall more profitable.

(ii)   As with ARR, the payback method ignores the time value of money.

(iii)   The payback method, in the same way as ARR, offers no objective measure of what is the desirable return, as measured by the length of the payback period.

(b)   **(i)**   Discounted cash flow analysis is a technique whereby the value of future cash flows is discounted back to a present value, so that the monetary values of all cash flows are equivalent, regardless of their timing. The logic for discounting is that the value of money declines over time because of individual time preferences and the impact of inflation in eroding spending power. People value money received sooner rather than later because as soon as cash is received they can increase consumption, or re-invest the capital.

NPV uses discounting to calculate the present value of all cash flows associated with a project. The present value of cash outflows is then compared with the present value of cash inflows, to obtain a net present value (NPV). If the present value (PV) of cash outflows exceeds the PV of cash inflows, then the NPV will be negative. If the present value (PV) of cash inflows exceeds the PV of cash outflows, then the NPV will be positive. The size of the NPV is dependent on the cash flow pattern and the rate of discount that is applied. The general rule is that a company will discount the forecast cash flows at a rate equal to its cost of capital. The reason for this is that if a company has an overall cost of capital of, for example, 12%, it is essential that the rate of return exceeds 12% or the funding costs will not be covered. Hence, if the cash flows are discounted at the cost of capital and the project yields a positive NPV, this implies that the return exceeds the cost of capital. When using NPV for investment appraisal then a simple rule is applied: invest if NPV is positive, and do not invest if it is negative.

IRR uses discounting in a slightly different way to determine the profitability of an investment. The Internal Rate of Return is defined as the discount rate at which the net present value equals zero. For example, an investment may yield a forecast NPV of $15,000 when the cash flows are discounted at 10%. If the rate of discount is increased, the net present value will fall, and the IRR represents the effective, break-even discount rate for the investment. Suppose, for example, that the IRR is 15%, this figure can then be used to establish a decision rule for investments. An IRR of 15% means that if the cost of capital exceeds 15% then the investment would generate a negative NPV. If the company is currently having to pay 12% on its investment funds, then it knows that it can afford to see its cost of capital rise by 3% before the investment will become financially non-viable. As long as the IRR exceeds the cost of capital, then the company should invest and so, as a general rule, the higher the IRR the better.

NPV and IRR measures may sometimes contradict one another when used in relation to mutually exclusive investments. An example of the ambiguity which can occur when choosing between mutually exclusive decisions is when one of the investments has a higher NPV than the other, and so is preferable on that basis, but at the same time it has a lower IRR. When IRR and NPV give conflicting results, the preferred alternative is the project with the highest NPV.

In conclusion, although both NPV and IRR use discounted cash flows as a method of arriving at an investment decision, the results that they generate need to be interpreted with care, and they do not always yield the same investment decisions. NPV is the preferred criterion for selecting between two or more mutually exclusive investments, where the two approaches give differing recommendations.

(ii) If the laptops are replaced every year:

NPV of one year replacement cycle

Year	Cash flow $	DF at 14%	PV $
0	(2,400)	1.000	(2,400.0)
1	1,200	0.877	1,052.4
			————
			(1,347.6)
			————

Equivalent annual cost = PV of cost of one replacement cycle/Cumulative discount factor

= $1,347.6/0.877 = $1,536.6

NPV of two-year replacement cycle

Year	Cash flow $	DF at 14%	PV $
0	(2,400)	1.000	(2,400.0)
1	(75)	0.877	(65.8)
2	800	0.769	615.2
			————
			(1,850.6)
			————

EAC = $1,850.6/1.647 = $1,123.6

NPV of three-year replacement cycle

Year	Cash flow $	DF at 14%	PV $
0	(2,400)	1.000	(2,400.0)
1	(75)	0.877	(65.8)
2	(150)	0.769	(115.4)
3	300	0.675	202.5
			————
			(2,378.7)
			————

EAC = $2,378.7/2.322 = $1,024.4

Conclusion

The optimal cycle for replacement is every three years, because this has the lowest equivalent annual cost. Other factors which need to be taken into account are the non-financial aspects of the alternative cycle choices. For example, computer technology and the associated software is changing very rapidly and this could mean that failure to replace annually would leave the salesmen unable to utilise the most up to date systems for recording, monitoring and implementing their sales. This could have an impact on the company's competitive position. The company needs to consider also the compatibility of the software used by the laptops with that used by the in-house computers and mainframe. If system upgrades are made within the main business that render the two computers incompatible, then rapid replacement of the laptops to regain compatibility is essential.

25 CHARM INC

Key answer tips

In part (a) the NPV calculation is reasonably straightforward provided you read the information carefully. The calculation of fixed costs is an easy number to get wrong if you didn't carefully read that the financial information presented on 'Fingo' was for the first year of production.

In part (b) ensure you compare with NPV with other appraisal methods rather than just stating the benefits of NPV. The highlighted words are key phrases that markers are looking for.

(a)   Calculation of NPV of 'Fingo' investment project

Year	1	2	3	4
	$000	$000	$000	$000
Sales revenue	3,750	1,680	1,380	1,320
Direct materials	(810)	(378)	(324)	(324)
Variable production	(900)	(420)	(360)	(360)
Advertising	(650)	(100)		
Fixed costs (W1)	(600)	(600)	(600)	(600)
Taxable cash flow	790	182	96	36
Taxation	(237)	(55)	(29)	(11)
	553	127	67	25
CA tax benefits (W2)	60	45	34	101
Net cash flow	613	172	101	126
Discount at 10%	0.909	0.826	0.751	0.683
Present values	557.2	142.1	75.9	86.1

	$000
Present value of future benefits	861.3
Initial investment	800.0
Net present value	61.3

Workings

(W1) Fixed costs in year 1 = $150,000 × 4 = $600,000 and since these represent a one-off increase in fixed production overheads, these are the fixed costs in subsequent years as well.

(W2) **Tax allowable depreciation tax benefits**

Year	TA depreciation ($)		Tax benefit ($)	
1	200,000	(800,000 × 0.25)	60,000	(0.3 × 200,000)
2	150,000	(600,000 × 0.25)	45,000	(0.3 × 150,000)
3	112,500	(450,000 × 0.25)	33,750	(0.3 × 112,500)
	———			
	462,500			
	nil	(scrap value)		
	———			
	462,500			
4	337,500	(by difference)	101,250	(0.3 × 337,500)
	———			
	800,000			
	———			

Comment

The net present value of $61,300 is positive and the investment can therefore be recommended on financial grounds. However, it should be noted that the positive net present value depends heavily on sales in the first year. In fact, sensitivity analysis shows that a decrease of 5% in first year sales will result in a zero net present value. (Note: you are not expected to conduct a sensitivity analysis.)

(b) There are many reasons that could be discussed in support of the view that net present value (NPV) is superior to other investment appraisal methods.

NPV considers cash flows

This is the reason why NPV is preferred to return on capital employed (ROCE), since ROCE compares average annual accounting profit with initial or average capital invested. Financial management always prefers cash flows to accounting profit, since profit is seen as being open to manipulation. Furthermore, only cash flows are capable of adding to the wealth of shareholders in the form of increased dividends. Both internal rate of return (IRR) and Payback also consider cash flows.

NPV considers the whole of an investment project

In this respect NPV is superior to Payback, which measures the time it takes for an investment project to repay the initial capital invested. Payback therefore considers cash flows within the payback period and ignores cash flows outside of the payback period. If Payback is used as an investment appraisal method, projects yielding high returns outside of the payback period will be wrongly rejected. In practice, however, it is unlikely that Payback will be used alone as an investment appraisal method.

NPV considers the time value of money

NPV and IRR are both discounted cash flow (DCF) models that consider the time value of money, whereas ROCE and Payback do not. Although Discounted Payback can be used to appraise investment projects, this method still suffers from the criticism that it ignores cash flows outside of the payback period. Considering the time value of money is essential, since otherwise cash flows occurring at different times cannot be distinguished from each other in terms of value from the perspective of the present time.

NPV is an absolute measure of return

NPV is seen as being superior to investment appraisal methods that offer a relative measure of return, such as IRR and ROCE, and which therefore fail to reflect the amount of the initial investment or the absolute increase in corporate value. Defenders of IRR and ROCE respond that these methods offer a measure of return that is understandable by managers and which can be intuitively compared with economic variables such as interest rates and inflation rates.

NPV links directly to the objective of maximising shareholders' wealth

The NPV of an investment project represents the change in total market value that will occur if the investment project is accepted. The increase in wealth of each shareholder can therefore be measured by the increase in the value of their shareholding as a percentage of the overall issued share capital of the company. Other investment appraisal methods do not have this direct link with the primary financial management objective of the company.

NPV always offers the correct investment advice

With respect to mutually exclusive projects, NPV always indicates which project should be selected in order to achieve the maximum increase on corporate value. This is not true of IRR, which offers incorrect advice at discount rates that are less than the internal rate of return of the incremental cash flows. This problem can be overcome by using the incremental yield approach.

NPV can accommodate changes in the discount rate

While NPV can easily accommodate changes in the discount rate, IRR simply ignores them, since the calculated internal rate of return is independent of the cost of capital in all time periods.

NPV has a sensible re-investment assumption

NPV assumes that intermediate cash flows are re-invested at the company's cost of capital, which is a reasonable assumption as the company's cost of capital represents the average opportunity cost of the company's providers of finance, i.e. it represents a rate of return that exists in the real world. By contrast, IRR assumes that intermediate cash flows are reinvested at the internal rate of return, which is not an investment rate available in practice.

NPV can accommodate non-conventional cash flows

Non-conventional cash flows exist when negative cash flows arise during the life of the project. For each change in sign, there is potentially one additional internal rate of return. With non-conventional cash flows, therefore, IRR can suffer from the technical problem of giving multiple internal rates of return.

26 PLAY CO

Key answer tips

This is a fairly typical NPV with tax and inflation question. The key to picking up the easy marks in the calculative part (a) is to take a methodical approach that you show clearly in a series of workings.

Parts (b) and (c) are more discursive and require you to demonstrate your knowledge in the context of this scenario. Try to think broadly and ensure you go into sufficient depth in your answer to score highly.

The highlighted words in the written sections are key phrases that markers are looking for.

(a)

Year	1	2	3	4	5
	$000	$000	$000	$000	$000
Costs saved (W1)	350	385	455	560	
Variable costs (W2)	(82)	(94)	(113)	(144)	
Maintenance costs	(42)	(44)	(46)	(49)	
Fixed costs (W3)	(66)	(68)	(69)	(70)	
	―――	―――	―――	―――	
Taxable cash flow	160	180	227	297	
Taxation		(48)	(54)	(68)	(89)
CA tax benefits (W4)		30	23	17	36
Scrap value				50	
	―――	―――	―――	―――	―――
After-tax cash flows	160	162	196	296	(53)
Discount at 15%	0.870	0.756	0.658	0.572	0.497
	―――	―――	―――	―――	―――
Present values	139	122	129	169	(26)
	―――	―――	―――	―――	―――

	$000
Present value of benefits	533
Initial investment	400
Early termination fine	150
	―――
Net present value	(18)
	―――

The net present value is negative and so the investment is not financially acceptable.

Workings

(W1) Costs saved

Year	1	2	3	4
Demand (tonnes/yr)	100,000	110,000	130,000	160,000
Cost ($/tonne)	3.50	3.50	3.50	3.50
	―――	―――	―――	―――
Contribution ($/yr)	350,000	385,000	455,000	560,000
	―――	―――	―――	―――

(W2) Variable costs incurred

Year	1	2	3	4
Demand (tonnes/yr)	100,000	110,000	130,000	160,000
Cost ($/tonne) – 3% inflation	0.82	0.85	0.87	0.90
Contribution ($/yr)	82,000	93,500	113,100	144,000

(W3) Fixed costs incurred

Annual depreciation = ($400,000 – $50,000) ÷ 4 = $87,500

Other fixed costs = $192,500 – $87,500 – $40,000 = $65,000

Inflating at 2% per annum

(W4) Tax allowable depreciation tax benefits

Year	TA depreciation ($)		Tax benefit ($)	
1	100,000	(400,000 × 0.25)	30,000	(0.3 × 100,000)
2	75,000	(300,000 × 0.25)	22,500	(0.3 × 75,000)
3	56,250	(225,000 × 0.25)	16,875	(0.3 × 56,250)
	231,250			
	50,000	(scrap value)		
	281,250			
4	118,750	(by difference)	35,625	(0.3 × 118,750)
	400,000			

(b)

Tutorial note

There are more points noted below than would be needed to earn full marks, however, they do reflect the full range of limitations that could be discussed.

NPV is a commonly used technique employed in investment appraisal, but it is subject to a number of restrictive assumptions and limitations that call into question its general relevance. Nonetheless, if the assumptions and limitations are understood then its application is less likely to be undertaken in error.

Some of the difficulties with NPV are listed below:

(i) NPV assumes that firms pursue an objective of maximising the wealth of their shareholders. This is questionable given the wider range of stakeholders who might have conflicting interests to those of the shareholders. NPV is largely redundant if organisations are not wealth maximising. For example, public sector organisations may wish to invest in capital assets but will use non-profit objectives as part of their assessment.

(ii) NPV is potentially a difficult method to apply in the context of having to estimate what is the correct discount rate to use. This is particularly so when questions arise as to the incorporation of risk premia in the discount rate, since an evaluation of the riskiness of the business, or of the project in particular, will have to be made but may be difficult to discern. In this instance, the additional fixed costs will increase the risk profile of the business and this will need to be factored in.

(iii) NPV can most easily cope with cash flows arising at period ends and is not a technique that is used easily when complicated, mid-period cash flows are present.

(iv) NPV is not universally employed, especially in a small business environment. The available evidence suggests that businesses assess projects in a variety of ways (payback, IRR, accounting rate of return). The fact that such methods are used which are theoretically inferior to NPV calls into question the practical benefits of NPV, and therefore hints at certain practical limitations.

(v) The conclusion from NPV analysis is the present value of the surplus cash generated from a project. If reported profits are important to businesses, then it is possible that there may be a conflict between undertaking a positive NPV project and potentially adverse consequences on reported profits. This will particularly be the case for projects with long time horizons, large initial investment and very delayed cash inflows. In such circumstances, businesses may prefer to use accounting measures of investment appraisal.

(vi) Managerial incentive schemes may not be consistent with NPV, particularly when long time horizons are involved. Thus, managers may be rewarded on the basis of accounting profits in the short term and may be incentivised to act in accordance with these objectives, and thus ignore positive NPV projects. This may be a problem of the incentive schemes and not of NPV; nonetheless, a potential conflict exists and represents a difficulty for NPV.

(vii) NPV treats all time periods equally, with the exception of discounting far cash flows more than near cash flows. In other words, NPV only accounts for the time value of money. To many businesses, distant horizons are less important than near horizons, if only because that is the environment in which they work. Other factors besides applying higher discount rates may work to reduce the impact of distant years. For example, in the long term, nearly all aspects of the business may change and hence a too-narrow focus on discounting means that NPV is of limited value and more so the further the time horizon considered.

(viii) NPV is of limited use in the face of non-quantifiable benefits or costs. NPV does not take account of non-financial information, which may even be relevant to shareholders who want their wealth maximised. For example, issues of strategic or environmental benefit may arise against which it is difficult to immediately quantify the benefits but for which there are immediate costs. NPV would treat such a situation as an additional cost since it could not incorporate the indiscernible benefit.

(c)

Tutor's top tips

Start by identifying the range of stakeholders affected before considering the impact this proposal will have on them. Make sure you include the details given in the scenario to ensure you give a tailored answer.

The project should affect the different stakeholders of Play Co as follows:

Stakeholder	Impact
Shareholders	• Wealth would decrease by the negative NPV of the project – i.e. $18,000 • Risks will increase due the higher fixed costs (increased operational gearing)
Society	• More tyres will be recycled, protecting the environment
Customers	• Customers may perceive the quality of the product to increase because it is more environmentally friendly
Suppliers	• Existing suppliers of particles will lose business (although they will receive the $150,000 early termination fine)
Potential investors	• Play Co will become more attractive to "green chip" investors, possibly making future financing easier

27   DUO CO *Walk in the footsteps of a top tutor*

Key answer tips

Given the generic nature of part (b) and the significant number of marks available, it would be sensible to tackle this part of the requirement first. You can then follow on with the calculations in part (a).

The key learning point from this question is the importance of being efficient when reading the scenario to cut down on the amount of time wasted trying to locate information. By forming an expectation of what you'll be given and considering the significance of information that you read, you can easily complete the question in the time allocated. The highlighted words are key phrases that markers are looking for.

(a)   Net present value evaluation of investment

Tutor's top tips

An NPV calculation in part (a) followed by an IRR calculation in part (b) is a fairly common exam question. Clearly, it is more logical to tackle part (a) first. One important aspect to note from the requirement is to work to the nearest $1,000. This can help to save a significant amount of time when performing the calculations and noting your workings.

Knowing that you must calculate an NPV, you should carefully read the scenario, looking for details on:

—   *Relevant cash flows*

—   *Tax payments (1 year time lag or not)*

—   *Capital expenditure and scrap values*

—   *Timescales and length of the project*

—   *Working capital*

—   *Inflation*

—   *Discount rate.*

Whenever you read any details, make a note in the margin on what that section provides you information on. This will help prevent you having to re-read the scenario several times to find the bit of information you require.

From reading this scenario, you should have noted that:

—   *Relevant cash flows will be the incremental contribution and fixed costs only*

—   *Incremental contribution will be calculated based on the excess of demand over current production capacity (one million kilograms)*

—   *The maximum output of the new machine is 600,000 kg meaning that even with the new machine, Duo will be unable to produce more that 1.6 million kg*

—   *The tax rate is 30% and there is a one year time lag*

—   *The cost of the machine is $800,000 and it will be scrapped in four years' time for $30,000*

—   *The length of the project is four years*

—   *You are not given any information on working capital requirements or inflation. These can therefore be ignored*

—   *You have not been told what discount rate to use. Instead, you've been given information on the cost of equity and the cost of debt, together with the capital structure (ratio of equity to debt) in the company.*

Having gleaned this information, you should start by setting up your proforma NPV calculation based on 5 periods (4 years of the project + 1 year time lag for tax). Next, you should enter in any easy numbers that require little or no calculation. This would include the asset purchase and scrap and the incremental fixed costs.

Now you can move on to calculating some of the more complex numbers. All of these calculations should be performed using workings that should be clearly cross-referenced to your main NPV calculation. You should end up with workings for contribution (make sure you clearly show how many extra units will be sold), the tax effect of tax allowable depreciation and the weighted average cost of capital/discount factors. As you complete each working, transfer the numbers into your main calculation and add anything extra that you can now complete (for example, once you have calculated contribution, you can enter the tax charge at 30%). When all of your workings are complete, discount the cash flow in each year and work out the net present value. Don't forget that the requirement is to calculate and advise. There will always be marks available for reaching a conclusion and stating whether the project should be accepted or not. Note the examiner's comment (below) about explaining your decision.

After-tax weighted average cost of capital = $(11 \times 0.8) + (8.6 \times (1 - 0.3) \times 0.2) = 10\%$

Year	1	2	3	4	5
	$000	$000	$000	$000	$000
Contribution	440	550	660	660	
Fixed costs	(240)	(260)	(280)	(300)	
Taxable cash flow	200	290	380	360	
Taxation		(60)	(87)	(114)	(108)
CA tax benefits		60	45	34	92
Scrap value				30	
After-tax cash flows	200	290	338	310	(16)
Discount at 10%	0.909	0.826	0.751	0.683	0.621
Present values	182	240	254	212	(10)

	$000
Present value of benefits	878
Initial investment	800
Net present value	78

The net present value is positive and so the investment is financially acceptable. However, demand becomes greater than production capacity in the fourth year of operation and so further investment in new machinery may be needed after three years. The new machine will itself need replacing after four years if production capacity is to be maintained at an increased level. It may be necessary to include these expansion and replacement considerations for a more complete appraisal of the proposed investment.

A more complete appraisal of the investment could address issues such as the assumption of constant selling price and variable cost per kilogram and the absence of any consideration of inflation, the linear increase in fixed costs of production over time and the linear increase in demand over time. If these issues are not addressed, the appraisal of investing in the new machine is likely to possess a significant degree of uncertainty.

Workings

Annual contribution

Year	1	2	3	4
Excess demand (kg/yr)	400,000	500,000	600,000	700,000
New machine output (kg/yr)	400,000	500,000	600,000	600,000
Contribution ($/kg)	1.1	1.1	1.1	1.1
Contribution ($/yr)	440,000	550,000	660,000	660,000

Tax allowable depreciation tax benefits

Year	TA depreciation ($)		Tax benefit ($)	
1	200,000	(800,000 × 0.25)	60,000	(0.3 × 200,000)
2	150,000	(600,000 × 0.25)	45,000	(0.3 × 150,000)
3	112,500	(450,000 × 0.25)	33,750	(0.3 × 112,500)
	462,500			
	30,000	(scrap value)		
	492,500			
4	307,500	(by difference)	92,250	(0.3 × 307,500)
	800,000			

Tutor's top tips

A careful read of the requirement shows that part (b) is essentially three requirements rolled into one:

(i)   Explain the difference between risk and uncertainty

(ii)   Describe how sensitivity analysis can be used to incorporate risk into investment appraisal

(iii)   Describe how probability analysis can be used to incorporate risk into investment appraisal.

Given the verbs being used (both 'explain' and 'describe' imply much more that merely 'stating') we can expect between 2 & 3 marks for each section, with 2 or 3 relevant comments picking up those marks.

Don't forget, there are often marks available for defining terms. So in part (i), a definition should be given of both risk and uncertainty before the differences between the two are explained. Similarly, in parts (ii) & (iii), you could define both sensitivity analysis and probability analysis before describing how they incorporate risk into the appraisal process.

Finally, you could touch on the common problems with the two techniques although be careful not to spend too much time on this as it wasn't specifically mentioned in the requirement. Now you can move on to the numerical aspects of the question.

(b) Risk refers to the situation where probabilities can be assigned to a range of expected outcomes arising from an investment project and the likelihood of each outcome occurring can therefore be quantified. Uncertainty refers to the situation where probabilities cannot be assigned to expected outcomes. Investment project risk therefore increases with increasing variability of returns, while uncertainty increases with increasing project life. The two terms are often used interchangeably in financial management, but the distinction between them is a useful one.

Sensitivity analysis assesses how the net present value of an investment project is affected by changes in project variables. Considering each project variable in turn, the change in the variable required to make the net present value zero is determined, or alternatively the change in net present value arising from a fixed change in the given project variable. In this way, the key or critical project variables are determined. However, sensitivity analysis does not assess the probability of changes in project variables and so is often dismissed as a way of incorporating risk into the investment appraisal process.

Probability analysis refers to the assessment of the separate probabilities of a number of specified outcomes of an investment project. For example, a range of expected market conditions could be formulated and the probability of each market condition arising in each of several future years could be assessed. The net present values arising from combinations of future economic conditions could then be assessed and linked to the joint probabilities of those combinations. The expected net present value (ENPV) could be calculated, together with the probability of the worst-case scenario and the probability of a negative net present value. In this way, the downside risk of the investment could be determined and incorporated into the investment decision.

ACCA marking scheme		
		Marks
(a)	After-tax weighted average cost of capital	2
	Annual contribution	2
	Fixed costs	1
	Taxation	1
	TAX depreciation tax benefits	3
	Scrap value	1
	Discount factors	1
	Net present value	1
	Comment	1–2
		13
(b)	Risk and uncertainty	2–3
	Discussion of sensitivity analysis	2–3
	Discussion of probability analysis	2–3
		7
Total		**20**

Examiner's comments

Part (a) of this question asked candidates to calculate the net present value (NPV) of buying a new machine and to advise on its acceptability. Many candidates gained very high marks here.

Common errors (where there were errors) included failing to calculate correctly the weighted average cost of capital of the investing company (for example using the before-tax rather than the after-tax cost of debt in the calculation): failing to use incremental demand as the production volume of the new machine; failing to recognise the cap on production in Year 4 compared to demand; failing to lag tax liability by one year; including scrap value or tax benefits of tax allowable depreciation with taxable income; incorrect calculation of balancing allowance; treating initial investment as a Year 1 rather than a Year 0 cash flow; and using annuity factors rather than discount factors in calculating NPV.

A number of candidates lost straightforward marks by failing to comment on the calculated NPV, or by simply saying 'accept' without referring to the NPV decision rule. The reason for accepting an investment project must be clearly explained.

Candidates were asked in part (b) to explain the difference between risk and uncertainty in the context of investment appraisal, and to describe how sensitivity analysis and probability analysis could be used to incorporate risk and uncertainty into investment appraisal. Answers here tended to be weaker than answers to parts (a).

Many candidates were not able to explain the difference between risk and uncertainty in investment appraisal, offering answers that were founded on interpretations of the words 'risk' and 'uncertainty', or which discussed the various kinds of risk to be found in financial management. The key point is to recognise that risk can be quantified (probabilities can be assigned and outcomes can be predicted) while uncertainty cannot be quantified. Answers that offered numerical examples of sensitivity analysis or probability analysis gained credit, although candidates should note that sensitivity analysis is not a method of measuring or predicting risk.

28 OKM CO

Key answer tips

The style of this question is not something we've seen regularly from the examiner. Based on the core topic of investment appraisal, students should easily be able to spot the mistakes in the appraisal presented and, having done that, should not encountered many problems preparing a revised calculation. The highlighted words are key phrases that markers are looking for.

(a) **Errors in the original investment appraisal**

Inflation was incorrectly applied to selling prices and variable costs in calculating contribution, since only one year's inflation was allowed for in each year of operation.

The fixed costs were correctly inflated, but included $200,000 per year before inflation that was not a relevant cost. Only relevant costs should be included in investment appraisal.

Straight-line accounting depreciation had been used in the calculation, but this depreciation method is not acceptable to the tax authorities. The approved method using 25% reducing balance tax allowable depreciation should be used.

Interest payments have been included in the investment appraisal, but these are allowed for by the discount rate used in calculating the net present value.

The interest rate on the debt finance has been used as the discount rate, when the nominal weighted average cost of capital should have been used to discount the calculated nominal after-tax cash flows.

(b)   Nominal weighted average cost of capital = $1.07 \times 1.047 = 1.12$, i.e. 12% per year

Year	1	2	3	4	5
	$000	$000	$000	$000	$000
Contribution	1,330	2,264	3,010	1,600	
Fixed costs	(318)	(337)	(357)	(379)	
Taxable cash flow	1,012	1,927	2,653	1,221	
Taxation		(304)	(578)	(796)	(366)
CA tax benefits		150	112	84	178
After-tax cash flow	1,012	1,773	2,187	509	(188)
Scrap value				250	
After-tax cash flows	1,012	1,773	2,187	759	(188)
Discount at 12%	0.893	0.797	0.712	0.635	0.567
Present values	904	1,413	1,557	482	(107)

	$000
Present value of future cash flows	4,249
Initial investment	2,000
Net present value	2,249

The net present value is positive and so the investment is financially acceptable.

Alternative NPV calculation using taxable profit calculation

Year	1	2	3	4	5
	$000	$000	$000	$000	$000
Contribution	1,330	2,264	3,010	1,600	
Fixed costs	(318)	(337)	(357)	(379)	
Taxable cash flow	1,012	1,927	2,653	1,221	
TA depreciation	(500)	(375)	(281)	(594)	
Taxable profit	512	1,552	2,372	627	
Taxation	(154)	(466)	(712)	(188)	
Profit after tax	512	1,398	1,906	(85)	(188)
TA depreciation	500	375	281	594	
After-tax cash flow	1,012	1,773	2,187	509	(188)
Scrap value				250	
After-tax cash flows	1,012	1,773	2,187	759	(188)
Discount at 12%	0.893	0.797	0.712	0.635	0.567
Present values	904	1,413	1,557	482	(107)

	$000
Present value of future cash flows	4,249
Initial investment	2,000
Net present value	2,249

Workings

Annual contribution

Year	1	2	3	4
Sales volume (units/yr)	250,000	400,000	500,000	250,000
Selling price ($/unit)	12.60	13.23	13.89	14.59
Variable cost ($/unit)	7.28	7.57	7.87	8.19
Contribution ($/unit)	5.32	5.66	6.02	6.40
Contribution ($/yr)	1,330,000	2,264,000	3,010,000	1,600,000

Tax allowable depreciation tax benefits

Year	TA depreciation ($)	Tax benefit ($)
1	500,000	150,000
2	375,000	112,500
3	281,250	84,375
4	593,750	178,125
Scrap value	250,000	
	2,000,000	

(c) **(i)** **Multiple internal rates of return**

An investment project may have multiple internal rates of return if it has unconventional cash flows, that is, cash flows that change sign over the life of the project. A mining operation, for example, may have initial investment (cash outflow) followed by many years of successful operation (cash inflow) before decommissioning and environmental repair (cash outflow). This technical difficulty makes it difficult to use the internal rate of return (IRR) investment appraisal method to offer investment advice.

One solution is to use the net present value (NPV) investment appraisal method instead of IRR, since the non-conventional cash flows are easily accommodated by NPV. This is one area where NPV is considered to be superior to IRR.

(ii) **Projects with significantly different business risk to current operations**

Where a proposed investment project has business risk that is significantly different from current operations, it is no longer appropriate to use the weighted average cost of capital (WACC) as the discount rate in calculating the net present value of the project. WACC can only be used as a discount rate where business risk and financial risk are not significantly affected by undertaking an investment project.

Where business risk changes significantly, the capital asset pricing model should be used to calculate a project-specific discount rate that takes account of the systematic risk of a proposed investment project.

ACCA marking scheme			
			Marks
(a)	Identification of errors in the evaluation		
		Maximum	5
(b)	Nominal weighted average cost of capital		1
	Inflated selling prices		1
	Inflated variable costs		1
	Inflated contribution		1
	Inflated fixed costs		1
	TA depreciation and/or related tax benefits		3
	Scrap value		1
	Discount factors		1
	Net present value		1
	Comment		1–2
		Maximum	10
(c)	Discussion of projects with several IRR		2
	Discussion of projects with different business risk		3
		Maximum	5
Total			**20**

Examiner's comments

Many students did well on parts (a) and (b) of this question, while finding part (c) to be more challenging.

In part (a), candidates were asked to identify and comment on any errors in an investment appraisal prepared by a trainee accountant. Candidates who did not gain full marks failed to identify clearly the errors they had identified, or did not comment on these errors, or identified errors that did not exist.

Part (b) required candidates to prepare a revised calculation of the NPV of an investment project and to comment on its acceptability.

Many candidates did well here, using the template of the NPV calculation provided in the question to prepare a corrected calculation. The contribution had to be inflated correctly, the fixed costs had to be calculated correctly, the depreciation and interest payments had to be stripped out, the tax effect of tax allowable depreciation needed to be calculated and included, and the correct discount rate had to be used.

Candidates who did not amend the provided contribution figures were not aware that inflation must be applied every year and not just in the first year. The development costs had to be excluded from the fixed costs in the investment appraisal because they had already been incurred, i.e. they were not relevant costs. Depreciation had to be stripped out because it is not a cash flow, and NPV is an investment appraisal method that uses cash flows. Interest payments had to be excluded because they would be taken account of by the discount rate.

The tax effect of tax allowable depreciation could be included by any one of three methods: by using the correctly timed tax benefits of each tax allowable depreciation; by subtracting the tax allowable depreciation from taxable cash flow to give taxable profit and then adding them back after calculating the tax liability; and by carrying out a separate tax calculation.

Within the investment appraisal, cash flows had been inflated by specific inflation rates and so the evaluation was a nominal terms (or money terms) evaluation, requiring a nominal discount rate. The real discount rate was provided in the question, together with the general rate of inflation, and the nominal discount rate could be calculated from these two pieces of information using the Fisher equation.

Part (c) tested candidates' understanding of different aspects of investment appraisal by asking what problems were faced, and how these problems could be overcome, in three different investment appraisal areas.

The first investment appraisal area related to multiple internal rates of return, a technical problem associated with non-conventional cash flows that is not experienced by NPV.

The second investment appraisal area related to investments with a different level of business risk than the investing company. Many candidates identified correctly here that the capital asset pricing model could be used to calculate a project-specific discount rate that reflected project risk.

29   BRT CO

Key answer tips

It is reasonable to expect a good mark to be achieved for part (a) as this is a commonly tested area with nothing out of the ordinary. It is important not to ignore the stated requirement to use a nominal terms approach.

Part (b) should also have been straightforward, being essentially bookwork.

The highlighted words are key phrases that markers are looking for.

(a)   Net present value evaluation of new confectionery investment

Year	1	2	3	4	5
	$000	$000	$000	$000	$000
Sales	3,605	8,488	11,474	16,884	
Variable cost	(2,019)	(5,093)	(6,884)	(10,299)	
Fixed costs	(1,030)	(1,910)	(3,060)	(4,277)	
Taxable cash flow	556	1,485	1,530	2,308	
Taxation		(167)	(446)	(459)	(692)
CA tax benefits		150	113	84	253
Working capital	(23)	(23)	(24)	820	
After-tax cash flows	533	1,445	1,173	2,753	(439)
Discount at 12%	0.893	0.797	0.712	0.636	0.567
Present values	476	1,152	835	1,751	(249)

	$000
Sum of present values	3,965
Working capital	(750)
Initial investment	(2,000)
Net present value	1,215

Comment:

The proposed investment in the new product is financially acceptable, as the NPV is positive.

Examiner's note:

Including tax-allowable depreciation tax benefits by subtracting tax-allowable depreciation, calculating tax liability and then adding back the tax-allowable depreciation is also acceptable.

Workings

Year	1	2	3	4
Sales volume (boxes)	700,000	1,600,000	2,100,000	3,000,000
Inflated selling price ($/box)	5.150	5.305	5.464	5.628
Sales ($000/yr)	3,605	8,488	11,474	16,884

Year	1	2	3	4
Sales volume (boxes)	700,000	1,600,000	2,100,000	3,000,000
Variable cost ($/box)	2.80	3.00	3.00	3.05
Inflated variable cost ($/box)	2.884	3.183	3.278	3.433
Variable cost ($000/yr)	2,019	5,093	6,884	10,299

Year	1	2	3	4
Sales volume (boxes)	700,000	1,600,000	2,100,000	3,000,000
Fixed costs ($000)	1,000	1,800	2,800	3,800
Inflated fixed costs ($000)	1,030	1,910	3,060	4,277

Year	1	2	3	4
	$	$	$	$
Tax-allowable depreciation	500,000	375,000	281,250	843,750
Tax benefit (30%)	150,000	112,500	84,375	253,125

Year	0	1	2	3	4
	$	$	$	$	$
Working capital	750,000	772,500	795,675	819,545	
Incremental		22,500	23,175	23,870	(819,545)

(b) **Examiner note: only THREE ways of incorporating risk into investment appraisal were required to be discussed.**

Risk and uncertainty

Risk in investment appraisal refers to the attachment of probabilities to the possible outcomes from an investment project and therefore represents a quantified assessment of the variability of expected returns.

Uncertainty cannot be quantified by attaching probabilities and although the terms are often used interchangeably, the difference is important in investment appraisal.

Sensitivity analysis

This assesses the sensitivity of project NPV to changes in project variables. It calculates the relative change in a project variable required to make the NPV zero, or the relative change in NPV for a fixed change in a project variable. Only one variable is considered at a time. When the sensitivities for each variable have been calculated, the key or critical variables can be identified. These show where assumptions may need to be checked and where managers could focus their attention in order to increase the likelihood that the project will deliver its calculated benefits. However, since sensitivity analysis does not incorporate probabilities, it cannot be described as a way of incorporating risk into investment appraisal, although it is often described as such.

Probability analysis

This approach involves assigning probabilities to each outcome of an investment project, or assigning probabilities to different values of project variables. The range of net present values that can result from an investment project is then calculated, together with the joint probability of each outcome. The net present values and their joint probabilities can be used to calculate the mean or average NPV (the expected NPV or ENPV) which would arise if the investment project could be repeated a large number of times. Other useful information that could be provided by the probability analysis includes the worst outcome and its probability, the probability of a negative NPV, the best outcome and its probability, and the most likely outcome. Managers could then make a decision on the investment that took account more explicitly of its risk profile.

Risk-adjusted discount rate

It appears to be intuitively correct to add a risk premium to the 'normal' discount rate to assess a project with greater than normal risk. The theoretical approach here would be to use the capital asset pricing model (CAPM) to determine a project-specific discount rate that reflected the systematic risk of an investment project. This can be achieved by selecting proxy companies whose business activities are the same as the proposed investment project: removing the effect of their financial risk by ungearing their equity betas to give an average asset beta; regearing the asset beta to give an equity beta reflecting the financial risk of the investing company; and using the CAPM to calculate a project-specific cost of equity for the investment project.

Adjusted payback

Payback can be adjusted for risk, if uncertainty is considered to be the same as risk, by shortening the payback period. The logic here is that as uncertainty (risk) increases with the life of the investment project, shortening the payback period for a project that is relatively risky will require it to pay back sooner, putting the focus on cash flows that are more certain (less risky) because they are nearer in time.

Payback can also be adjusted for risk by discounting future cash flows with a risk-adjusted discount rate, i.e. by using the discounted payback method. The normal payback period target can be applied to the discounted cash flows, which will have decreased in value due to discounting, so that the overall effect is similar to reducing the payback period with undiscounted cash flows.

ACCA marking scheme		Marks
(a)	Inflated selling price per box	1
	Sales	1
	Inflated variable cost per box	1
	Variable cost	1
	Inflated fixed costs	1
	Tax payable	1
	TA depreciation tax benefits	1
	Balancing allowance	1
	Timing of tax payments or benefits	1
	Initial working capital investment	1
	Incremental working capital investment	1
	Working capital recovery	1
	Discount factors	1
	Net present value	1
	Comment on acceptability	1
	Maximum	13
(b)	Discussion of three methods, 2–3 marks per method	7
	Maximum	7
Total		**20**

Examiner's comments

Part (a) asked candidates to calculate the net present value (NPV) of a new confectionary line using a nominal terms approach, allowing for inflation and taxation.

Some candidates said that, because the same rate of inflation was applied to selling price, variable cost and fixed cost, inflation could be ignored and their answers used a real terms approach. This ignores the stated requirement to use a nominal terms approach and is also not correct in this case, as profit tax was payable in arrears. A nominal terms approach discounts nominal (inflated) cash flows with a nominal cost of capital, which was given in the question. Some answers made the mistake of either inflating or deflating the provided nominal cost of capital.

Some answers did not defer the tax liabilities, or the tax benefits on the tax-allowable depreciation available on the cost of equipment, or both, although the question required this. Although the question said that a balancing allowance would be claimed in the fourth year of production, some candidates did not calculate this.

Almost all answers correctly located the discount factors from the tables provided in the examination, although as mentioned earlier a few answers used a discount rate that was different from the one provided in the question. In a very small number of answers, annuity factors were used instead of discount factors.

Almost all answers calculated a net present value. Although the question required that the candidate advise on the financial acceptability of the proposed investment, some answers did not do this, or made a casual comment that did not gain full marks.

In part (c), candidates were required to discuss three ways of incorporating risk into the investment appraisal process. Many candidates lost marks by not reading the question correctly and discussing the nature of different kinds of risk, rather than how risk could be incorporated in the investment appraisal process. Better answers discussed ways of incorporating risk into investment appraisal that were covered in the syllabus, such as sensitivity analysis, probability analysis, and the capital asset pricing model.

30   BASRIL

Key answer tips

Students who score badly on this question do so because they get bogged down in the numerical calculations in part (a). The best way to avoid this trap is to tackle the wordy parts of the requirement first. The highlighted words are key phrases that markers are looking for.

(a) **(i)** **Analysis of projects assuming they are divisible**

	Discount factor at 12%	Project 1 Cash flow	PV	Project 3 Cash flow	PV
		$	$	$	$
Initial investment	1.000	(300,000)	(300,000)	(400,000)	(400,000)
Year 1	0.893	85,000	75,905	124,320	111,018
Year 2	0.797	90,000	71,730	128,795	102,650
Year 3	0.712	95,000	67,640	133,432	95,004
Year 4	0.636	100,000	63,600	138,236	87,918
Year 5	0.567	95,000	53,865	143,212	81,201
PV of savings			332,740		477,791
NPV			32,740		77,791
Profitability index		32,740/300,000 = 0.11		77,791/400,000 = 0.19	

	Discount factor at 12%	Project 2 Cash flow	PV
		$	$
Initial investment	1.000	(450,000)	(450,000)
Annual cash flows, years 1 – 5	3.605	140,800	507,584
Net present value			57,584
Profitability index	57,584/450,000		= 0.13

Order of preference (in order of profitability index) = Project 3 then Project 2 then Project 1.

Project	Profitability index	Ranking	Investment	NPV	
			$	$	
3	0.19	1st	400,000	77,791	
2	0.13	2nd	400,000	51,186	(= 57,584 × 400/450)
			800,000	128,977	

(ii)   **Analysis of projects assuming they are indivisible**

If the projects are assumed to be indivisible, the total NPV of combinations of projects must be considered.

Projects	Investment	NPV	
	$	$	
1 and 2	750,000	90,324	£(32,740 + 57,584)
1 and 3	700,000	110,531	£(32,740 + 77,791)
2 and 3	850,000	not feasible, too much investment	

The optimum combination is now projects 1 and 3.

(b)   The NPV decision rule requires that a company invest in all projects that have a positive net present value. This assumes that sufficient funds are available for all incremental projects, which is only true in a perfect capital market. When insufficient funds are available, that is when capital is rationed, projects cannot be selected by ranking by absolute NPV. Choosing a project with a large NPV may mean not choosing smaller projects that, in combination, give a higher NPV. Instead, if projects are divisible, they can be ranked using the profitability index in order make the optimum selection. If projects are not divisible, different combinations of available projects must be evaluated to select the combination with the highest NPV.

(c)   The NPV decision rule, to accept all projects with a positive net present value, requires the existence of a perfect capital market where access to funds for capital investment is not restricted. In practice, companies are likely to find that funds available for capital investment are restricted or rationed.

Hard capital rationing is the term applied when the restrictions on raising funds are due to causes external to the company. For example, potential providers of debt finance may refuse to provide further funding because they regard a company as too risky. This may be in terms of financial risk, for example if the company's gearing is too high or its interest cover is too low, or in terms of business risk if they see the company's business prospects as poor or its operating cash flows as too variable. In practice, large established companies seeking long-term finance for capital investment are usually able to find it, but small and medium-sized enterprises will find raising such funds more difficult.

Soft capital rationing refers to restrictions on the availability of funds that arise within a company and are imposed by managers. There are several reasons why managers might restrict available funds for capital investment. Managers may prefer slower organic growth to a sudden increase in size arising from accepting several large investment projects. This reason might apply in a family-owned business that wishes to avoid hiring new managers. Managers may wish to avoid raising further equity finance if this will dilute the control of existing shareholders. Managers may wish to avoid issuing new debt if their expectations of future economic conditions are such as to suggest that an increased commitment to fixed interest payments would be unwise.

One of the main reasons suggested for soft capital rationing is that managers wish to create an internal market for investment funds. It is suggested that requiring investment projects to compete for funds means that weaker or marginal projects, with only a small chance of success, are avoided. This allows a company to focus on more robust investment projects where the chance of success is higher. This cause of soft capital rationing can be seen as a way of reducing the risk and uncertainty associated with investment projects, as it leads to accepting projects with greater margins of safety.

31 ASOP CO

Key answer tips

This question encompasses two of the more fringe topics within the investment appraisal part of the syllabus; lease v buy and equivalent annual costs. It is a fair question, which well prepared students (those who have studied the syllabus in detail) should handle well.

The highlighted words are key phrases that markers are looking for.

(a) After-tax cost of borrowing = 8.6 × (1 – 0.3) = 6% per year

Evaluation of leasing

Year	Cash flow	Amount ($)	6% Discount factors	Present value ($)
0–3	Lease rentals	(380,000)	1.000 + 2.673 = 3.673	(1,395,740)
2–5	Tax savings	114,000	3.465 × 0.943 = 3.267	372,438
				(1,023,302)

Present value of cost of leasing = $1,023,074

Evaluation of borrowing to buy

Year	Capital	Licence fee	Tax benefits	Net cash flow	6% discount factors	Present value
	$	$	$	$	$	$
0	(1,000,000)			(1,000,000)	1.000	(1,000,000)
1		(104,000)		(104,000)	0.943	(98,072)
2		(108,160)	106,200	(1,960)	0.890	(1,744)
3		(112,486)	88,698	(23,788)	0.840	(19,982)
4	100,000	(116,986)	75,934	58,948	0.792	46,687
5			131,659	131,659	0.747	98,349
						(974,762)

Present value of cost of borrowing to buy = $974,762

Workings

Year	TA depreciation	Tax benefits	Licence fee tax benefits	Total
	$	$	$	$
2	1,000,000 × 0.25 = 250,000	75,000	31,200	106,200
3	750,000 × 0.25 = 187,500	56,250	32,448	88,698
4	562,500 × 0.25 =140,625	42,188	33,746	75,934
5	421,875 – 100,000 = 321,875	96,563	35,096	131,659

ASOP Co should buy the new technology, since the present cost of borrowing to buy is lower than the present cost of leasing.

(b) Nominal terms net present value analysis

Year	1	2	3	4	5
	$	$	$	$	$
Cost savings	365,400	479,250	637,450	564,000	
Tax liabilities		(109,620)	(143,775)	(191,235)	(169,200)
Net cash flow	365,400	369,630	493,675	372,765	(169,200)
Discount at 11%	0.901	0.812	0.731	0.659	0.593
Present values	329,225	300,140	360,876	245,652	(100,336)

Present value of benefits	1,135,557
Present cost of financing	(974,762)
Net present value	160,795

The investment in new technology is acceptable on financial grounds, as it has a positive net present value of $160,795.

Workings

Year	1	2	3	4
	$	$	$	$
Operating cost saving ($/unit)	6.09	6.39	6.71	7.05
Production (units/year)	60,000	75,000	95,000	80,000
Operating cost savings ($/year)	365,400	479,250	637,450	564,000
Tax liabilities at 30% ($/year)	109,620	143,775	191,235	169,200

(Examiner's note: Including the financing cash flows in the NPV evaluation and discounting them by the WACC of 11% is also acceptable.)

(c) The equivalent annual cost or benefit method can be used to calculate the equal annual amount of cost or benefit which, when discounted at the appropriate cost of capital, produces the same present value of cost or net present value as a set of varying annual costs or benefits.

For example, the net present value (NPV) of investing in the new technology of $160,795 in part (b) was calculated using a weighted average cost of capital (WACC) of 11% over an expected life of four years. The annuity factor for 11% and four years is 3.102. The equivalent annual benefit (EAB) is therefore 160,795/3.102 = $51,835.9 per year. This can be checked by multiplying the EAB by the annuity factor, i.e. 51,835.9 × 3.102 = $160,795.

If an alternative investment in similar technology over five years had a lower EAB, the four-year investment would be preferred as it has the higher EAB.

	ACCA marking scheme		Marks
(a)	Present value of lease rentals	2	
	Present value of lease rental tax benefits	1	
	Present value of cost of leasing	1	
	Investment and scrap values	1	
	Licence fee	1	
	TA depreciation tax benefits	2	
	Licence fee tax benefits	1	
	Present value of cost of borrowing to buy	1	
	Appropriate decision on leasing versus buying	1	
			11
(b)	Inflated cost savings	2	
	Tax liabilities	1	
	Present values of net cash flows	1	
	Net present value	1	
	Advice on acceptability of investment	1	
			6
(c)	Definition of equivalent cost or benefit	1	
	Relevant discussion	1	
	Appropriate illustration	1	
			3
Total			**20**

Examiner's comments

Many students were able to do well in this question, especially in part (b).

In part (a), candidates were asked to calculate and determine whether a company should lease or buy new technology. Since this was a financing decision, candidates were instructed to use only financing cash flows. The lease versus borrowing to buy decision is covered in the Study Texts that support students studying FM.

From a leasing perspective, candidates needed to calculate the present value of correctly timed annual lease rental payments and their tax benefits, discounted by the after-tax cost of debt.

From a buying perspective, candidates needed to calculate the present value of the purchase price of the new technology and related tax allowable depreciation tax benefits, and the annual licence fees and their associated tax benefits, discounted by the after-tax cost of debt.

Many candidates did not follow the instruction to use financing cash flows only and included in their evaluation the reduced operating costs arising from using the new technology.

Common errors were splitting the licence fee out of the lease rental payments: using the weighted average cost of capital of the company as the discount rate, rather than the after-tax cost of debt; including interest payments in the evaluation, when these are taken account of by the discount rate: omitting the tax benefit arising on lease rental payments; incorrect timing of lease rental payments or tax benefits; including loan repayments or repayment of principal; and not using a present value approach to comparing the two financing choices. The correct approach can be found in the suggested answers to this examination.

Part (b) required calculating the net present value of buying the new technology using a nominal terms approach, and offering advice on the acceptability of the investment.

The net present value calculation included the nominal value of the operating cost reductions and their associated tax benefits, discounted by the weighted average cost of capital of the company, less the present value of the financing cash flows. Some candidates used the Fisher equation and the inflation rate of the costs savings to calculate a 'nominal' discount rate, but specific inflation cannot be used in this way and no other inflation rate was given in the question. The weighted average cost of capital could therefore be assumed to be in nominal terms.

While some answers included the net present value calculation with the financing evaluation by combining parts (a) and (b) of the question, many answers to this part of question one were of a good standard.

Part (c) asked candidates to discuss and illustrate how equivalent annual cost or equivalent annual benefit could be used to choose between technologies with different expected lives. Candidates who had studied the equivalent annual cost method were able to gain full marks on this part of question one.

Weaker answers discussed new technology or the need for cost-benefit analysis rather than meeting the requirement of the question.

While many answers gave a suitable illustration, such as dividing the net present value calculated in part (b) by a suitable annuity factor, some answers provided illustrations that were much longer than necessary and therefore wasted valuable time, given that this part of question 1 was worth only three marks.

32   DEGNIS CO

Key answer tips

Parts (a) and (b) link together to perform the calculation of a project that will last into the foreseeable future. Part (a) looks at the standalone NPV of the first few years of a project and part (b) puts it into the context of a perpetuity. You'll have to use some of the figures from part (a) in your calculation for (b). If your calculations for the first part are wrong, this won't affect your marks in (b) as long as you use your numbers correctly. The trickiest part will be realising that the benefits of the tax allowable depreciation will not be a perpetuity – they are an annuity that will end after 10 years of the project. Parts (c) and (d) should be relatively easy on which to pick up marks on if you have revised the subject areas. The highlighted words are key phrases that markers are looking for.

(a)   Calculation of NPV over four years

Tutorial note

*The question asks for the **expected** NPV. This means that you shouldn't prepare three different NPV calculations for the three different motorhome types, but use probability analysis to calculate an expected value of selling price and conversion cost to be included in a single NPV calculation. Do be aware though of the limitations of doing this. The NPV calculated will be an average result.*

Year	1	2	3	4
	$000	$000	$000	$000
Sales income	12,525	15,030	22,545	22,545
Conversion cost	(7,913)	(9,495)	(14,243)	(14,243)
Contribution	4,612	5,535	8,302	8,302
Fixed costs	(4,000)	(5,000)	(5,500)	(5,500)
Before-tax cash flow	612	535	2,802	2,802
Tax liability at 28%	(171)	(150)	(785)	(785)
Tax allowable depreciation benefits	112	112	112	112
After-tax cash flow	553	497	2,129	2,129
Discount at 11%	0.901	0.812	0.731	0.659
Present values	498	404	1,556	1,403

	$000
Sum of present values	3,861
Initial investment	4,000
NPV	(139)

Workings

Average selling price = (30,000 × 0.20) + (42,000 × 0.45) + (72,000 × 0.35) = $50,100 per unit

Average conversion cost = (23,000 × 0.20) + (29,000 × 0.45) + (40,000 × 0.35) = $31,650 per unit

Year	1	2	3	4
Sales volume (units/year)	250	300	450	450
Average selling price ($/unit)	50,100	50,100	50,100	50,100
Sales income ($000/year)	12,525	15,030	22,545	22,545

Year	1	2	3	4
Sales volume (units/year)	250	300	450	450
Average conversion cost ($/unit)	31,650	31,650	31,650	31,650
Conversion cost ($000/year)	7,913	9,495	14,243	14,243

Contribution may be calculated directly, with small rounding differences. Average contribution = 50,100 − 31,650 = $18,450 per unit.

Year	1	2	3	4
Sales volume (units/year)	250	300	450	450
Average contribution ($/unit)	18,450	18,450	18,450	18,450
Contribution ($000/year)	4,613	5,535	8,303	8,303

Tax allowable depreciation = 4,000,000/10 = $400,000 per year.

Benefit of tax allowable depreciation = 400,000 × 0.28 = $112,000 per year.

(b) Ignoring tax allowable depreciation, after-tax cash flow from year five onwards into perpetuity will be: 2,802,000 − 785,000 = $2,017,000 per year.

Present value of this cash flow in perpetuity = (2,017,000/0.11) × 0.659 = $12,083,664

There would be a further six years of tax benefits from tax allowable depreciation. The present value of these annuity cash flows would be 112,000 × 4.231 × 0.659 = $312,282.

Increase in NPV of production and sales continuing beyond the first four years would be 12,083,664 + 312,282 = $12,395,946 or approximately $12.4 million.

If only the first four years of operation are considered, the NPV of the planned investment is negative and so it would not be financially acceptable. If production and sales beyond the first four years are considered, the NPV is strongly positive and so the planned investment is financially acceptable. In fact, the NPV of the planned investment becomes positive if only one further year of operation is considered:

NPV = (2,129,000 × 0.593) − 139,000 = 1,262,497 − 139,000 = $1,123,497

(c) Risk in investment appraisal refers to a range of outcomes whose probability of occurrence can be quantified. Risk can therefore be distinguished from uncertainty in investment appraisal, where the likelihood of particular outcomes occurring cannot be quantified.

As regards incorporating risk into investment appraisal, probability analysis can be used to calculate the values of possible outcomes and their probability distribution, the value of the worst possible outcome and its probability, the probability that an investment will generate a positive NPV, the standard deviation of the possible outcomes and the expected value (mean value) of the NPV. Standard deviation is a measure of risk in financial management.

One difficulty with probability analysis is its assumption that an investment can be repeated a large number of times. The expected value of the NPV, for example, is a mean or average value of a number of possible NPVs, while standard deviation is a measure of dispersal of possible NPVs about the expected (mean) NPV. In reality, many investment projects cannot be repeated and so only one of the possible outcomes will actually occur. The expected (mean) value will not actually occur, causing difficulties in applying and interpreting the NPV decision rule when using probability analysis.

Another difficulty with probability analysis is the question of how the probabilities of possible outcomes are assessed and calculated. One method of determining probabilities is by considering and analysing the outcomes of similar investment projects from the past. However, this approach relies on the weak assumption that the past is an acceptable guide to the future. Assessing probabilities this way is also likely to be a very subjective process.

(d) Theoretically, a company should invest in all projects with a positive net present value in order to maximise shareholder wealth. If a company has attractive investment opportunities available to it, with positive net present values, it will not be able to maximise shareholder wealth if it does not invest in them, for example, because investment finance is limited or rationed.

If investment finance is limited for reasons outside a company, it is called 'hard capital rationing'. This may arise because a company is seen as too risky by potential investors, for example, because its level of gearing is so high that it is believed it may struggle to deliver adequate returns on invested funds. Hard capital rationing could also arise if a company wants to raise debt finance for investment purposes, but lacks sufficient assets to offer as security, leading again to a risk-related problem.

During a time of financial crisis, investors may seek to reduce risk by limiting the amount of funds they are prepared to invest and by choosing to invest only in low-risk projects. It is also true to say that companies could struggle to secure investment when the capital markets are depressed, or when economic prospects are poor, for example, during a recession.

If investment funds are limited for reasons within a company, the term 'soft capital rationing' is used. Investing in all projects with a positive net present value could mean that a company increases in size quite dramatically, which incumbent managers and directors may wish to avoid in favour of a strategy of controlled growth, limiting the investment finance available as a consequence. Managers and directors may limit investment finance in order to avoid some consequences of external financing, such as an increased commitment to fixed interest payments if new debt finance were raised, or potential dilution of earnings per share if new equity finance were raised, whether from existing or new shareholders.

Investment finance may also be limited internally in order to require investment projects to compete with each other for funds. Only robust investment projects will gain access to funds, it is argued, while marginal projects with low net present values will be rejected. In this way, companies can increase the likelihood of taking on investment projects which will actually produce positive net present values when they are undertaken, reducing the uncertainty associated with making investment decisions based on financial forecasts.

ACCA Marking scheme			Marks
(a)	Sales income		1
	Conversion cost		1
	Before-tax cash flow		1
	Tax liability		1
	Tax allowable depreciation benefits		1
	After-tax cash flow		1
	Calculation of NPV		1
		Maximum	7
(b)	PV of future cash flows ignoring tax allowable depreciation		1
	PV of tax allowable depreciation benefits		1
	Comment on financial acceptability		1
		Maximum	3
(c)	Risk and uncertainty		1
	Explanation of probability analysis		1–2
	Repeatability assumption		1–2
	Difficulty in determining probabilities		1–2
		Maximum	5
(d)	Reasons for hard capital rationing		1–4
	Reasons for soft capital rationing		1–4
		Maximum	5
Total			**20**

Examiner's comments

This longer-form question was from the investment appraisal part of the syllabus.

Many candidates did very well on part (a), which required them to calculate the expected net present value (ENPV) of a planned investment over 4 years. They calculated correctly the mean values of selling price per unit and conversion cost per unit, and the expected values of sales income and conversion cost. Some candidates incorrectly treated annual fixed costs as fixed costs per unit.

Investment appraisal calculations must be correct as to the timing of tax-allowable depreciation (TAD) and tax cash flows. The question said corporation tax was payable in the year in which it arose. Some candidates incorrectly had tax liabilities and/ or TAD benefits payable one year in arrears. Timing errors can easily be avoided if the requirements of the question are understood and followed. Although the question required candidates to use straight-line TAD, some answers used 25% reducing balance TAD instead, or straight-line TAD over 4 years instead of the 10 years specified in the question.

Part (b) asked candidates to calculate the effect on the ENPV of continuing production and sales beyond the first four years and to comment on the financial acceptability of the planned investment. Many candidates calculated the present value of additional years of production, some stopping after 10 years because this was end of the period over which the cost of the initial investment was depreciated, while others adopted a perpetuity approach. Having carried out calculations on the effect on the ENPV, some candidates failed to comment on the financial acceptability of the planned investment.

Part (c) asked candidates to critically discuss using probability analysis in incorporating risk into investment appraisal and this question was often not answered well. Some candidates were not clear about the difference between risk and uncertainty in the context of investment appraisal, namely that risk can be quantified whereas uncertainty cannot. It is essential to understand this difference. In a critical discussion of probability analysis, these two terms must be used very carefully. Risk can be quantified by assigning probabilities to project variables and project outcomes. Probability analysis leads to calculating the ENPV of a planned investment, calculating the probability of the worst outcome, calculating the probability of a negative NPV and so on. Probability analysis has a much wider scope than an expected value analysis, such as was carried out in question part (a).

Part (d) asked for a discussion of the reasons why investment finance might be limited, even when a company had attractive investment opportunities available to it. Better answers based their discussion in the area of capital rationing, discussing hard and soft capital rationing, and their causes. Some answers discussed the difficulties faced by SME in gaining access to investment finance. Unsatisfactory answers adopted a very broad or general approach to discussing why investment finance might be limited, offering few if any clearly explained reasons.

33 HRAXIN CO

Key answer tips

Part (a) is a fairly standard NPV calculation, albeit with the inclusion of probabilities. Do be conscious that it asks for **expected** NPV. Part (b) requires an understanding not just of sensitivity analysis but how it is different to probability analysis and is the trickiest section of the question. Only a couple of marks are available for describing what sensitivity analysis is. Don't go into too much detail on part (c). Think about the main things you would need to know in order to do the calculations. The highlighted words are key phrases that markers are looking for.

(a) **Calculation of expected net present value**

	1	2	3	4
	$000	$000	$000	$000
Revenue	4,524	7,843	13,048	10,179
Variable cost	(2,385)	(4,200)	(7,080)	(5,730)
Contribution	2,139	3,643	5,968	4,449
Overhead	(440)	(484)	(532)	(586)
Cash flow before tax	1,699	3,159	5,436	3,863
Tax	(510)	(948)	(1,631)	(1,159)
Depreciation benefits	338	338	338	338
Cash flow after tax	1,527	2,549	4,143	3,042
Scrap value				500
Project cash flow	1,527	2,549	4,143	3,542
Discount at 11%	0.901	0.812	0.731	0.659
Present values	1,376	2,070	3,029	2,334

	$000
PV of future cash flows	8,809
Initial investment	(5,000)
Expected net present value (ENPV)	3,809

The investment project has a positive ENPV of $3,809,000. This is a mean or average NPV that will result from the project being repeated many times. However, as the project is not being repeated, the NPVs associated with each future economic state must be calculated as it is one of these NPVs that is expected to occur. The decision by management on the financial acceptability of the project will be based on these NPVs and the risk associated with each one.

Workings

Mean or average selling price = (25 × 0.35) + (30 × 0.5) + (35 × 0.15) = $29 per unit

Year	1	2	3	4
Inflated selling price ($ per unit)	30.16	31.37	32.62	33.93
Sales volume (units/year)	150,000	250,000	400,000	300,000
Sales revenue ($000/year)	4,524	7,843	13,048	10,179

Year	1	2	3	4
Inflated overhead ($000/year)	440	484	532	586

Total tax-allowable depreciation = 5,000,000 − 500,000 = $4,500,000

Annual tax-allowable depreciation = 4,500,000/4 = $1,125,000 per year

Annual cash flow from tax-allowable depreciation = 1,125,000 × 0.3 = $337,500 per year.

(b) Sensitivity analysis assesses the extent to which the net present value (NPV) of an investment project responds to changes in project variables. Two methods are commonly used: one method determines the percentage change in a project variable which results in a negative NPV, while the other method determines the percentage change in NPV which results from a fixed percentage change (for example, 5%) in each project variable in turn. Whichever method is used, the key or critical project variables are identified as those to which the NPV is most sensitive, for example, those where the smallest percentage change results in a negative NPV. Sensitivity analysis is therefore concerned with calculating relative changes in project variables.

When discussing risk in the context of investment appraisal, it is important to note that, unlike uncertainty, risk can be quantified and measured. The probabilities of the occurrence of particular future outcomes can be assessed, for example, and used to evaluate the volatility of future cash flows, for example, by calculating their standard deviation. The probabilities of the future economic states in the assessment of the investment project of Hraxin Co are an example of probability analysis and these probabilities can lead to an assessment of project risk.

Sensitivity analysis is usually studied in investment appraisal in relation to understanding how risk can be incorporated in the investment appraisal process. While sensitivity analysis can indicate the critical variables of an investment project, however, sensitivity analysis does not give any indication of the probability of a change in any critical variable. Selling price may be a critical variable, for example, but sensitivity analysis is not able to say whether a change in selling price is likely to occur. In the appraisal of the investment project of Hraxin Co, the probabilities of different selling prices arising with related economic states have come from probability analysis, not from sensitivity analysis.

Sensitivity analysis will not therefore directly assist Hraxin Co in assessing the risk of the investment project. However, it does provide useful information which helps management to gain a deeper understanding of the investment project and which focuses management attention on aspects of the investment project where problems may arise.

(c) When considering whether to lease or buy an asset, because the cash flows of leasing and buying generally last over the life of the project, discounted cash flow techniques should be used. This will mean that the time value of money is taken into account, the cash flows are all expressed in present value terms and the two options will be directly comparable.

The cash flows related to leasing and those to buying should be compared, discounted at the post tax cost of borrowing. This makes the assumption that the asset is either being leased or purchased with the use of financing – hence the discount rate used for both options is the borrowing cost.

The cash flows of the lease that will be relevant are the lease payments themselves and the tax savings that these lease payments will lead to. This is on the assumption that the business is making enough profits overall to benefit from the reduced tax bill seen from offsetting the lease payments against profits.

The cash flows of the purchase option will be those of the purchase itself, any scrap value and the tax savings from any tax allowable depreciation available. Interest cash flows on any borrowing used for the purchase will not be included as these are accounted for within the cost of capital used for discounting.

Cash flows that are common to both options can be ignored as it's the differences between the two options that will determine which is chosen.

Once the two sets of discounted cash flows have been calculated, they are compared and the lowest cost option is chosen.

ACCA Marking scheme		Marks
(a)	Mean selling price per unit	0.5
	Inflated selling price per unit	1
	Inflated revenue	1
	Inflated overhead	1
	Tax liabilities	1
	Timing of tax liabilities	1
	Tax-allowable depreciation benefits	1
	Scrap value	0.5
	Present values of future cash flows	1
	Comment on financial acceptability	1
		9
(b)	Explanation of sensitivity analysis	1–3
	Explanation of risk in investment appraisal	1–2
	Discussion of sensitivity analysis and risk	1–3
	Maximum	6
(c)	Discounted cash flows should be used	1
	Post tax cost of borrowing should be used	1
	Lease cash flows	1
	Purchase cash flows	1
	Ignore common cash flows	1
	Interest cash flows on financing are part of cost of capital	1
	Make comparison and choose lowest cost option	1
	Maximum	5
Total		**20**

Examiner's comments

Candidates were required here to calculate the expected net present value (ENPV) of an investment project and to comment on its financial acceptability. Most answers gained good marks.

The selling price was forecasted to depend on the future state of the economy and most answers correctly used the probabilities of the future economic states to calculate an average selling price. Some answers, however, wasted valuable time by calculating an NPV for each the economic states.

The question gave the forecast total nominal variable costs, which some candidates incorrectly inflated. Nominal values, of course, include inflation.

Although the question stated that tax liabilities were paid in the year they arose, some answers incorrectly deferred the tax liabilities by one year.

Credit was given for tax benefits arising from tax-allowable depreciation whether the effect of the scrap value was accounted for in the final year of operation or on an average basis over the life of the investment project (the method used in the suggested answer), provided a straight-line approach was adopted. Some answers incorrectly used a 25% reducing balance approach to tax-allowable depreciation.

While the suggested answer uses tax benefits arising from tax-allowable depreciation, credit was also given where tax-allowable depreciation was subtracted to give taxable profit, then added back after the tax liability had been calculated. The after-tax cash flow would be the same irrespective of which approach were adopted. Some answers incorrectly treated tax-allowable depreciation as a positive cash flow.

Credit was given for including the scrap value whether it was placed in the fourth year or the fifth year, although the question did say that it was expected to arise at the end of four years.

Even though the question required candidates to calculate the ENPV, many answers commented on financial acceptability by stating that the NPV of the investment project was positive and therefore it was financially acceptable. This ignores the fact that the ENPV is an average NPV which is not expected to occur in practice. An average NPV might also include a negative NPV in its calculation.

A key learning point here is the need to read the question carefully, not just in order to clearly understand the question requirement, but also to understand the information provided by the question.

In part (b) the requirement here was to critically discuss if sensitivity analysis would assist a company in assessing the risk of an investment project. Many answers were not able to gain high marks, for several reasons.

Many answers were able to explain that sensitivity analysis considered the relative change in a project variable needed to make the NPV zero, or the change in the NPV arising from a specified change in a given project variable. Some answers discussed the idea of the key or critical variable, which was the project variable where the smallest relative change resulted in a zero NPV. The limitation of only changing one variable at a time in sensitivity analysis was often mentioned, with better answers pointing out that in reality project variables are often interrelated to a greater or lesser extent.

A key point in providing a good answer to this question was recognising that risk could be quantified using probabilities, unlike uncertainty. Having recognised this, better answers pointed out that, as sensitivity analysis did not consider probabilities, it could not assist a company in assessing the risk of an investment project.

Even though the requirement was for a critical discussion, many answers attempted to calculate sensitivities of project variables. No credit was given for these calculations because they were not required.

34 HEBAC CO

Key answer tips

Part (a) is a straightforward NV calculation including inflation, tax and working capital. For part (b), note in the question that the project is to be launched in a new market outside its current operations. This is the indicator that the CAPM may be useful here, to deal with the changed risk of this new project in comparison to its current business. If you spot this then the question lends itself nicely to discussion of risk levels and proxy beta factors that may need to be de-geared and re-geared. The highlighted words are key phrases that markers are looking for.

(a)

Year	1	2	3	4
	$000	$000	$000	$000
Sales revenue	3,120	15,576	22,275	10,296
Variable cost	(1,890)	(7,936)	(9,378)	(4,376)
Contribution	1,230	7,640	12,897	5,920
Fixed cost	(540)	(583)	(630)	(680)
Taxable cash flow	690	7,057	12,267	5,240
Taxation	(138)	(1,411)	(2,453)	(1,048)
TAD tax benefits	125	94	70	186
After-tax cash flow	677	5,740	9,884	4,378
Scrap value				125
Working capital	(90)	(95)	(102)	1,787
Net cash flows	587	5,645	9,782	6,290
Discount at 12%	0.893	0.797	0.712	0.636
Present values	524	4,499	6,965	4,000

	$000	
PV of future cash flows	15,988	
Initial investment	4,000	(2.5m + 1.5m)
N PV	11,988	

The NPV is strongly positive and so the project is financially acceptable.

Workings

Sales revenue

Year	1	2	3	4
Selling price ($/unit)	15	18	22	22
Inflated at 4% per year	15.60	19.47	24.75	25.74
Sales volume (000 units/year)	200	800	900	400
Sales revenue ($000/year)	3,120	15,576	22,275	10,296

Variable cost

Year	1	2	3	4
Variable cost ($/unit)	9	9	9	9
Inflated at 5% per year	9.45	9.92	10.42	10.94
Sales volume (000 units/year)	200	800	900	400
Variable cost ($000/year)	1,890	7,936	9,378	4,376

Tax benefits of tax-allowable depreciation

Year	1	2	3	4
	$000	$000	$000	$000
Tax-allowable depreciation	625	469	352	929
Tax benefit	125	94	70	186*

*((2,500 – 125) × 0.2) –-125 – 94 – 70 = $186,000

Working capital

Year	0	1	2	3	4
	$000	$000	$000	$000	$000
Working capital	1,500				
Inflated at 6%	1,590	1,685	1,787		
Incremental	90	95	102	1,787	

Alternative calculation of after-tax cash flow

Year	1	2	3	4
	$000	$000	$000	$000
Taxable cash flow	690	7,057	12,267	5,240
Tax-allowable depreciation	(625)	(469)	(352)	(929)
Taxable profit	65	6,588	11,915	4,311
Taxation	(13)	(1,318)	(2,383)	(862)
After-tax profit	52	5,270	9,532	3,449
Add back TAD	625	469	352	929
After-tax cash flow	677	5,739	9,884	4,378

(b) A company can use its weighted average cost of capital (WACC) as the discount rate in appraising an investment project as long as the project's business risk and financial risk are similar to the business and financial risk of existing business operations. Where the business risk of the investment project differs significantly from the business risk of existing business operations, a project-specific discount rate is needed.

The capital asset pricing model (CAPM) can provide a project-specific discount rate. The equity beta of a company whose business operations are similar to those of the investment project (a proxy company) will reflect the systematic business risk of the project. If the proxy company is geared, the proxy equity beta will additionally reflect the systematic financial risk of the proxy company.

The proxy equity beta is ungeared to remove the effect of the proxy company's systematic financial risk to give an asset beta that solely reflects the business risk of the investment project.

This asset beta is re-geared to give an equity beta that reflects the systematic financial risk of the investing company.

The re-geared equity beta can then be inserted into the CAPM formula to provide a project-specific cost of equity. If this cost of capital is used as the discount rate for the investment project, it will indicate the minimum return required to compensate shareholders for the systematic risk of the project. The project-specific cost of equity can also be included in a project-specific WACC. Using the project-specific WACC in appraising an investment project will lead to a better investment decision than using the current WACC as the discount rate, as the current WACC does not reflect the risk of the investment project.

ACCA Marking scheme		
		Marks
(a)	Inflated selling price per unit	1
	Sales revenue	1
	Inflated variable cost	1
	Inflated fixed costs	1
	Tax liabilities	1
	Tax-allowable depreciation benefits years 1–3	1
	Tax allowable depreciation benefits year 4	1
	Incremental working capital and recovery	2
	Calculation of present values	1
	Correct initial investment	1
	Comment on financial acceptability	1
		———
		12
		———
(b)	Business risk, financial risk and WACC	2
	Using a proxy company	1
	Systematic risk, business risk and financial risk	1
	Ungearing the equity beta	1
	Regearing the asset beta	1
	Project-specific cost of equity and WACC	2
		———
		8
		———
Total		20
		———

35 VYXYN CO

Key answer tips

The NPV calculation in part (b) is straightforward. Students just need to be methodical about their numbers, particularly when applying inflation.

Part (a) relies on textbook knowledge for the marks, while there is more leeway in part (c).

Consider what would make you more confident about an investment decision where there is a potential spread of returns. There are various techniques in the textbook and a couple of points per technique will be enough to pick up the marks.

The highlighted words are key phrases that markers are looking for.

(a) The terms risk and uncertainty are often used interchangeably in everyday discussion. However, there is a clear difference between them in relation to investment appraisal.

Risk refers to the situation where an investment project has several outcomes, all of which are known and to which probabilities can be attached, for example, on the basis of past experience. Risk can therefore be quantified and measured by the variability of returns of an investment project.

Uncertainty refers to the situation where an investment project has several possible outcomes but it is not possible to assign probabilities to their occurrence. It is therefore not possible to say which outcomes are likely to occur.

The difference between risk and uncertainty, therefore, is that risk can be quantified whereas uncertainty cannot be quantified. Risk increases with the variability of returns, while uncertainty increases with project life.

(b) **NPV calculation**

Year	1	2	3	4	5
	$000	$000	$000	$000	$000
Sales income	12,069	16,791	23,947	11,936	
Variable cost	(5,491)	(7,139)	(9,720)	(5,616)	
Contribution	6,578	9,652	14,227	6,320	
Fixed cost	(1,100)	(1,121)	(1,155)	(1,200)	
Taxable cash flow	5,478	8,531	13,072	5,120	
Taxation at 28%		(1,534)	(2,389)	(3,660)	(1,434)
TAD tax benefits		1,400	1,050	788	2,362
After-tax cash flow	5,478	8,397	11,733	2,248	928
Discount at 10%	0.909	0.826	0.751	0.683	0.621
Present values	4,980	6,936	8,812	1,535	576

	$000
PV of future cash flows	22,839
Initial investment	(20,000)
ENPV	2,839

Comment

The probability that variable cost per unit will be $12.00 per unit or less is 80% and so the probability of a positive NPV is therefore at least 80%. However, the effect on the NPV of the variable cost increasing to $14.70 per unit must be investigated, as this may result in a negative NPV. The expected NPV is positive and so the investment project is likely to be acceptable on financial grounds.

Workings

Sales revenue

Year	1	2	3	4
Selling price ($/unit)	26.50	28.50	30.00	26.00
Inflated at 3.5% per year	27.43	30.53	33.26	29.84
Sales volume (000 units/year)	440	550	720	400
Sales income ($000/year)	12,069	16,791	23,947	11,936

Variable cost

Mean variable cost = ($10.80 × 0.45) + ($12.00 × 0.35) + ($14.70 × 0.20) = $12.00 per unit

Year	1	2	3	4
Variable cost ($/unit)	12.00	12.00	12.00	12.00
Inflated at 4% per year	12.48	12.98	13.50	14.04
Sales volume (000 units/year)	440	550	720	400
Variable cost ($000/year)	5,491	7,139	9,720	5,616

Year	1	2	3	4
TAD ($000)	5,000	3,750	2,813	8,437
Tax benefits at 28% ($000)	1,400	1,050	788	2,362*

* ($20m × 0.28) − 1,400 − 1,050 − 788 = $2,362,000

Alternative calculation of after-tax cash flow

Year	1	2	3	4	5
	$000	$000	$000	$000	$000
Taxable cash flow	5,478	8,531	13,072	5,120	
TAD ($000)	(5,000)	(3,750)	(2,813)	(8,437)	
Taxable profit	478	4,781	10,259	(3,317)	
Taxation at 28%		(134)	(1,339)	(2,873)	929
After-tax profit	478	4,647	8,920	(6,190)	929
Add back TAD	5,000	3,750	2,813	8,437	
After-tax cash flow	5,478	8,397	11,733	2,247	929

(c) There are several ways of considering risk in the investment appraisal process.

Sensitivity analysis

This technique looks at the effect on the NPV of an investment project of changes in project variables, such as selling price per unit, variable cost per unit and sales volume. There are two approaches which are used. The first approach calculates the relative (percentage) change in a given project variable which is needed to make the NPV zero. The second approach calculates the relative (percentage) change in project NPV that results from a given change in the value of a project variable (e.g. 5%).

Sensitivity analysis considers each project variable individually. Once the sensitivities for each project variable have been calculated, the next step is to identify the key or critical variables. These are the project variables where the smallest relative change makes the NPV zero, or where the biggest change in NPV results from a given change in the value of a project variable. The key or critical project variables indicate where underlying assumptions may need to be checked or where managers may need to focus their attention in order to make an investment project successful. However, as sensitivity analysis does not consider risk as measured by probabilities, it can be argued that it is not really a way of considering risk in investment appraisal at all, even though it is often described as such.

Probability analysis

This technique requires that probabilities for each project outcome be assessed and assigned. Alternatively, probabilities for different values of project variables can be assessed and assigned. A range of project NPVs can then be calculated, as well as the mean NPV (the expected NPV or ENPV) associated with repeating the investment project many times. The worst and best outcomes and their probabilities, the most likely outcome and its probability and the probability of a negative NPV can also be calculated. Investment decisions could then be based on the risk profile of the investment project, rather than simply on the NPV decision rule.

Risk-adjusted discount rate

It is often said that 'the higher the risk, the higher the return'. Investment projects with higher risk should therefore be discounted with a higher discount rate than lower risk investment projects. Better still, the discount rate should reflect the risk of the investment project.

Theoretically, the capital asset pricing model (CAPM) can be used to determine a project-specific discount rate that reflects an investment project's systematic risk. This means selecting a proxy company with similar business activities to a proposed investment project, ungearing the proxy company equity beta to give an asset beta which does not reflect the proxy company financial risk, regearing the asset beta to give an equity beta which reflects the financial risk of the investing company, and using the CAPM to calculate a project-specific cost of equity for the investment project.

Adjusted payback

If uncertainty and risk are seen as being the same, payback can consider risk by shortening the payback period. Because uncertainty (risk) increases with project life, shortening the payback period will require a risky project to pay back sooner, thereby focusing on cash flows which are nearer in time (less uncertain) and so less risky.

Discounted payback can also be seen as considering risk because future cash flows can be converted into present values using a risk-adjusted discount rate. The target payback period normally used by a company can then be applied to the discounted cash flows. Overall, the effect is likely to be similar to shortening the payback period with undiscounted cash flows.

ACCA marking scheme		Marks
(a)	Explain risk	1
	Explain uncertainty	1
	Discuss difference	1
		3
(b)	Inflated revenue	1
	Mean variable cost	1
	Inflated variable cost	1
	Tax liabilities	1
	TAD benefits	1
	Timing of tax flows	1
	Calculation of PVs	1
	Comment on variable cost	1
	Comment on NPV	1
		9
(c)	Sensitivity analysis	2
	Probability analysis	2
	Risk-adjusted rate	2
	Adjusted payback	2
		8
Total		20

Examiner's comments

Part (a)

Candidates were asked here to discuss the difference between risk and uncertainty in relation to investment appraisal. Risk relates to the variability of returns and it can be measured by the probability of different returns being achieved by an investment project, that is, by attaching probabilities to different possible investment project outcomes. Risk can therefore be measured or quantified, whereas uncertainty cannot. Many answers showed little understanding of the link to variability of returns, tending to focus on quantifiable versus unquantifiable aspects.

Part (b)

This question asked candidates to calculate the NPV of an investment project and comment on its financial acceptability, considering taxation, inflation and a probability forecast of variable cost.

In questions relating to allowing for inflation and taxation in DCF techniques such as NPV, it is essential to understand and apply the information provided. Many errors arose from not following this advice, for example, using straight-line tax-allowable depreciation (TAD) when the question specified 25% reducing balance TAD, or charging tax liabilities in the year they arose when the question specified one year in arrears. Some answers placed tax liabilities one year in arrears, yet inconsistently placed TAD tax benefits in the year the TAD arose.

Other answers based tax liabilities on sales income, or on contribution, rather than on taxable cash flow.

Candidates would do well to remember that TAD is not a cash flow, as some answers treated TAD as an increase to taxable cash flow, resulting in TAD being taxed. Some answers omitted to incorporate a balancing allowance in their TAD calculation.

In relation to inflation, it was surprising to find some answers replacing inflation with deflation. An error made too frequently was applying one year's inflation to all years: candidates should remember that inflation is cumulative in its effect, like discounting.

Some answers used incorrect discount rates, indicating a lack of understanding in relation to the need to discount nominal cash flows with a nominal discount rate.

Some answers incorrectly placed the initial investment at the end of year 1, rather than year 0.

Some NPV calculations were incomplete, with unfinished present value calculations, missing years, or unjustified acceptability comments, such as 'Accept! Good project!'

In making the NPV calculation, candidates needed to calculate the expected value of variable cost as a step in calculating total variable cost. In addition to calculating the NPV of the investment project and commenting on its financial acceptability, candidates were asked to comment on the risk relating to variable cost. Many candidates were not able to see that the expected value calculation gave them the percentage chance of the investment project having a positive NPV.

Part (c)

Candidates were asked here to critically discuss how risk could be considered in the investment appraisal process. Four techniques that could be discussed are listed in the F9 study guide: sensitivity analysis, probability analysis, risk-adjusted discount rates and adjusted payback. Simulation could have been discussed as well, as part of probability analysis. While sensitivity analysis is not technically a technique that considers risk, which depends on probabilities, it is usually included in a discussion of risk in investment appraisal, perhaps because it is commonly seen as a method of assessing project risk. Emphasising the need to read the question carefully, answers were often not focussed on the question requirement, but discussed instead different kinds of risk, such as systematic risk, unsystematic risk, business risk, financial risk and exchange rate risk.

In some cases, even excellent NPV calculations were associated with a lack of understanding of the role played by the discount rate in building risk into investment appraisal.

36   DYSXA CO

Key answer tips

Part (a) is a straightforward NPV calculation. Be methodical to avoid making unnecessary areas in a question that should pick you up some good marks. Don't forget to comment on the result.

Make sure in part (b) that you pick up that the projects are divisible rather than indivisible due to the different approaches needed for each type.

For students who have revised the theory, part (c) should also provide some relatively easy marks. Make sure you at least know the difference between the two types.

In part (d), try to focus on risk rather than uncertainty. Probability analysis deals with risk by using probabilities to weight the different outcomes and the CAPM is a really good example of adjusting equity returns (and subsequently the WACC) to compensate for changes in risk.

The highlighted words are key phrases that markers are looking for.

(a)   NPV calculation

Year	1	2	3	4	5
$000	$000	$000	$000	$000	
Sales revenue	2,712	2,797	2,882	2,967	
Variable costs	(995)	(1,054)	(1,114)	(1,182)	
Contribution	**1,717**	**1,743**	**1,768**	**1,785**	
Fixed costs	(110)	(205)	(330)	(330)	
Taxable cash flow	**1,607**	**1,538**	**1,438**	**1,455**	
Taxation at 20%		(321)	(308)	(288)	(291)
TAD tax benefits		160	120	90	270
After-tax cash flows	**1,607**	**1,377**	**1,250**	**1,257**	**(21)**
Discount at 10%	0.909	0.826	0.751	0.683	0.621
Present values	**1,461**	**1,137**	**939**	**859**	**(13)**

	$000
PV of future cash flows	4,383
Initial investment	(3,200)
NPV	**1,183**

Comment

The NPV is positive and so the investment project is financially acceptable.

Workings

Sales revenue

Year	1	2	3	4
Selling price ($/unit)	3.10	3.10	3.10	3.10
Inflated at 3% per year	3.19	3.29	3.39	3.49
Sales volume (000 units/year)	850	850	850	850
Sales revenue ($000/year)	**2,712**	**2,797**	**2,882**	**2,967**

Variable cost

Year	1	2	3	4
Variable cost ($/unit)	1.10	1.10	1.10	1.10
Inflated at 6% per year	1.17	1.24	1.31	1.39
Sales volume (000 units/year)	850	850	850	850
Variable cost ($000/year)	**995**	**1,054**	**1,114**	**1,182**

Year	1	2	3	4
TAD ($000)	800	600	450	1,350
Tax benefits ($000)	160	120	90	270*

*($3,200 × 0.2) – 160 – 120 – 90 = $270,000

Alternative calculation of after-tax cash flow

Year	1	2	3	4	5
	$000	$000	$000	$000	$000
Taxable cash flow	1,607	1,538	1,438	1,455	
TAD	(800)	(600)	(450)	(1,350)	
Taxable profit	**807**	**938**	**988**	**105**	
Taxation at 20%		(161)	(188)	(198)	(21)
After-tax profit	**807**	**777**	**800**	**(93)**	**(21)**
Add back TAD	800	600	450	1,350	
After-tax cash flows	**1,607**	**1,377**	**1,250**	**1,257**	**(21)**

(b) **Analysis of profitability indexes**

Project	Initial investment	Net present value	Profitability index*	Rank
A	$3,000,000	$6,000,000	2.0	2nd
B	$2,000,000	$3,200,000	1.6	4th
C	$1,000,000	$1,700,000	1.7	Excluded
D	$1,000,000	$2,100,000	2.1	1st
E	$2,000,000	$3,600,000	1.8	3rd

*NPV divided by initial investment

Optimum investment schedule

Project	Initial investment	Rank	Net present value	
D	$1,000,000	1st	$2,100,000	
A	$3,000,000	2nd	$6,000,000	
E	$2,000,000	3rd	$3,600,000	
B	$1,000,000	4th	$1,600,000	($3.2m × $1m/$2m)
	$7,000,000		**$13,300,000**	

The NPV of the optimum investment schedule for Delta division is $13.3 million.

(c) Capital rationing can be divided into hard capital rationing, which is externally imposed, or soft capital rationing, which is internally imposed.

Soft capital rationing

Investment capital may be limited internally because a company does not want to take on a commitment to increased fixed interest payments, for example, if it expects future profitability to be poor. A company may wish to avoid diluting existing earnings per share or changing existing patterns of ownership and control by issuing new equity. A company may limit investment funds because it wishes to pursue controlled growth rather than rapid growth. Given the uncertainty associated with forecasting future cash flows, a company may limit investment funds in order to create an internal market where investment projects compete for finance, with only the best investment projects being granted approval.

Hard capital rationing

External reasons for capital rationing can be related to risk and to availability of finance. Providers of finance may see a company as too risky to invest in, perhaps because it is highly geared or because it has a poor record or poor prospects in terms of profitability or cash flow. Long-term finance for capital investment may have limited availability because of the poor economic state of the economy, or because there is a banking crisis.

(d) The risk of an investment project could be assessed by using probability analysis or by using the capital asset pricing model (CAPM).

Probability analysis

Project risk can be assessed or quantified by attaching probabilities to expected investment project outcomes. At an overall level, this could be as simple as attaching probabilities to two or more expected scenarios, for example, associated with different economic states. Key project variables might then take different values depending on the economic state.

At the level of individual project variables, probability distributions of values could be found through expert analysis, and the probability distributions and relationships between variables then built into a simulation model. This model could then be used to generate a probability distribution of expected project outcomes in terms of net present values. Project risk could then be measured by the standard deviation of the expected net present value.

CAPM

The systematic business risk of an investment project can be assessed by identifying a proxy company in a similar line of business. The equity beta of the proxy company can then be ungeared to give the asset beta of the company, which reflects systematic business risk alone as the effect of the systematic financial risk of the proxy company is removed by the ungearing process. The asset beta can then be regeared to reflect the systematic financial risk of the investing company, giving an equity beta that reflects the systematic risk of the investment project.

	ACCA marking scheme	
		Marks
(a)	Inflated sales revenue	1
	Inflated variable cost	1
	Tax liabilities	1
	Tax-allowable depreciation benefits years 1–3	1
	Tax-allowable depreciation benefits year 4	1
	Timing of tax liabilities and depreciation benefits	1
	Calculation of present values	1
	Comment on financial acceptability	1
		8
(b)	Calculating profitability indexes	1
	Formulating optimum investment schedule	1
	NPV of optimum investment schedule	1
		3
(c)	Soft capital rationing	2
	Hard capital rationing	2
	Additional detail	1
		5
(d)	Risk assessment method 1	2
	Risk assessment method 2	2
		4
Total		**20**

Examiner's comments

This longer-form question was from the investment appraisal part of the syllabus and comprised four parts, totalling 20 marks.

Part (a) asked candidates to calculate the NPV of a project and comment on its financial acceptability. This was generally done well, with many candidates scoring full marks. Common errors arise due to not reading the information in the question properly, such as that regarding the timing of the cash flow associated with taxation or when the initial investment is made. Also, where inflation is stated as being per year, this means that the inflation accumulates year upon year so that, for example, a year 4 variable cost per unit needs to be inflated by four years' worth of inflation.

As already stated, candidates need to say more than "accept" or "reject" in order to meet the criteria for a comment about financial acceptability.

Part (b) asked candidates to determine an optimum investment schedule given limited capital investment funds and divisible projects, two of which were mutually exclusive. Whilst there were many correct answers, too many incorrect answers were seen. Common errors included taking the trial and error approach associated with indivisible projects, calculating the profitability indices for the projects but then not knowing what to do with them and providing schedules which included both of the mutually exclusive projects, the latter of which seems to suggest a lack of understanding of the term 'mutually exclusive' (some candidates were even treating such items as complimentary pair and not as substitutes).

In part (c), the reasons for hard and soft capital rationing occurring needed to be discussed. There was a mixed bag of answers here. There were many good answers, but also answers lacking in detail.

Most candidates understood the notion of hard rationing being associated with external factors and soft rationing associated with internal factors. This statement, though, needs to be precise. Stating that hard rationing is the use of external finance and soft rationing being the use of retained earnings is not correct.

Also, precision in discussing the reasons is required. When stating that hard capital rationing is due to banks being unwilling to lend, a discussion should follow incorporating the reasons for this, such as government imposed bank lending restrictions or that the bank views the company as too risky due to its existing level of indebtedness.

Part (d) produced the weakest candidates' responses in Section C. The requirement was to discuss the ways in which the risk of an investment project can be assessed. Whilst some candidates correctly identified probability analysis and CAPM as suitable ways in which to do this, even these responses often neglected to discuss the ways correctly and in sufficient depth.

The weakest outcomes here simply misinterpreted the requirement and seemed to ignore the risk factor, instead writing in general terms about simply how to assess projects with detailed, irrelevant discussions about ARR, payback and NPV. IRR also featured often, yet incorrectly, as a method with which risk can be assessed.

The most common error was to discuss sensitivity analysis as a way in which risk can be assessed. This is not the case. Sensitivity analysis is a method of analysing the uncertainty surrounding a project. Future candidates should be fully aware that risk and uncertainty, whilst studied together, are distinct from each other. Risk uses past relevant experience such as assigning probabilities to outcomes, whilst uncertainty is where there is little past experience and, as such, it is difficult to assign probabilities to outcomes.

37   PELTA CO

Key answer tips

Part (a) (i) is a relatively straightforward net present value calculation, although with an element (the use of the terminal value) that is different to what you will have practised before. Follow the instructions and you should pick up good marks here. For part (a) (ii) discounted payback uses the annual present values that you have already calculated and looks at them cumulatively for 2 marks. In part (b) you should refer back to your calculations in your answer and remember that NPV is always the superior method if it clashes with other methods used. The key to part (c) is restricting your answer to what is specifically asked for – a critique of the directors' views. Answers that don't fit into this remit will not pick up marks.

The highlighted words are key phrases that markers are looking for.

(a) (i)

Year	1	2	3	4	5
	$000	$000	$000	$000	$000
Sales income	16,224	20,248	24,196	27,655	
Variable costs	(5,356)	(6,752)	(8,313)	(9,694)	
Contribution	10,868	13,495	15,883	17,962	
Fixed costs	(700)	(735)	(779)	(841)	
Cash flow before tax	10,168	12,760	15,104	17,121	
Corporation tax		(3,050)	(3,828)	(4,531)	(5,136)
TAD tax benefits		1,875	1,406	1,055	2,789
After-tax cash flow	10,168	11,585	12,682	16,644	(2,347)
Terminal value				1,250	
Project cash flow	10,168	11,585	12,682	14,894	(2,347)
Discount at 12%	0.893	0.797	0.712	0.636	0.567
Present values	9,080	9,233	9,030	9,473	(1,331)

PV of future cash flows ($000)	35,485
Initial investment ($000)	(25,000)
NPV	10,485

Workings

Year	1	2	3	4
Sales volume (units/year)	520,000	624,000	717,000	788,000
Selling price ($/unit)	30.00	30.00	30.00	30.00
Inflated by 4% per year	31.20	32.45	33.75	35.10
Income ($000/year)	16,224	20,248	24,196	27,655

Year	1	2	3	4
Sales volume (units/year)	520,000	624,000	717,000	788,000
Variable costs ($/unit)	10.00	10.20	10.61	10.93
Inflated by 3% per year	10.30	10.82	11.59	12.30
Variable costs ($000/year)	5,356	6,752	8,313	9,694

Year	1	2	3	4
Fixed costs ($000/year)	700	735	779	841
Year	1	2	3	4
TAD ($000 per year)	6,250	4,688	3,516	9,297
TAD benefits ($000/year)	1,875	1,406	1,055	2,789

(ii)

Year	1	2	3	4	5
	$000	$000	$000	$000	$000
Present values	9,080	9,233	9,030	9,473	(1,331)
Cumulative NPV	(15,920)	(6,687)	2,343	11,815	10,485
Discounted payback (years)		2.7			

(b) The investment project is financially acceptable under the NPV decision rule because it has a substantial positive NPV.

The discounted payback period of 2.7 years is greater than the maximum target discounted payback period of two years and so from this perspective the investment project is not financially acceptable.

The correct advice is given by the NPV method, however, and so the investment project is financially acceptable.

(c) The views of the directors on investment appraisal can be discussed from several perspectives.

Evaluation period

Sales are expected to continue beyond year 4 and so the view of the directors that all investment projects must be evaluated over four years of operations does not seem sensible. The investment appraisal would be more accurate if the cash flows from further years of operation were considered.

Assumed terminal value

The view of the directors that a terminal value of 5% of the initial investment should be assumed has no factual or analytical basis to it. Terminal values for individual projects could be higher or lower than 5% of the initial investment and in fact may have no relationship to the initial investment at all.

A more accurate approach would be to calculate a year 4 terminal value based on the expected value of future sales.

Discounted payback method

The directors need to explain their view that an investment project's discounted payback must be no greater than two years. Perhaps they think that an earlier payback will indicate an investment project with a lower level of risk. Although the discounted payback method does overcome the failure of simple payback to take account of the time value of money, it still fails to consider cash flows outside the payback period. Theoretically, Pelta Co should rely on the NPV investment appraisal method.

ACCA marking scheme			Marks
(a) (i)	Inflated sales		1
	Inflated VC/unit		1
	Inflated total VC		1
	Tax liabilities		1
	TAD benefits years 1-3		1
	TAD benefits year 4		1
	Timing of tax flows		1
	Terminal value		1
	Calculate PVs		1
			9
(ii)	Cumulative NPV		1
	Discounted payback		1
			2
(b)	Acceptability – NPV		1
	Acceptability – payback		1
	Correct advice		1
			3
(c)	Evaluation period		2
	terminal value		2
	Discounted payback		2
			6
Total			**20**

Examiner's comments

Part (a) (i)

This question asked candidates to calculate the NPV of an investment project, considering taxation and inflation.

Candidates have continued to do well on investment appraisal questions requiring NPV calculations, with candidates gaining good marks here, including many with full marks.

That said, a recurring error in the cash flow workings is a failure to apply a 'per year inflation rate' correctly. If an inflation rate of 3% per year needs to be applied to a variable cost per unit, then by the end of year 3, the given variable cost per unit needs to be inflated three times i.e. by 1.03^3.

A number of answers to this question used an incorrect discount rate, usually the real discount rate, to discount the nominal values already calculated.

Other errors seen quite often included:

* incorrectly placing initial investment at year 1 rather than year 0
* incorrectly placing the terminal value at year 5 rather than year 4, or not including it altogether
* not placing tax-related cash flows one year in arrears
* omitting the tax-related cash flows in year 5
* not calculating a balancing allowance, or calculating a balancing allowance but not adjusting it for the scrap value of the asset.

Part (a) (ii)

This requirement to calculate the discounted payback period of the project was done well, with many candidates scoring the two marks on offer.

Where errors were made, they included a recalculation of the present values from (a) (i) by erroneously using the real discount rate or using cash flows before tax.

Even on a two-mark part question such as this, in Section C it is still good examination technique for candidates to show all workings, such as the calculation of cumulative NPV and how the part year element of the discounted payback period has been calculated.

Part (b)

Here candidates were asked to discuss the financial acceptability of the investment project. Three marks were available.

Most candidates were able to refer to the decision rules relevant to net present value and discounted payback, but do need to justify financial acceptability comments. Standalone comments such as 'Accept' or alternatively 'Positive NPV' should be explained as should 'more than 2 years' in respect of the discounted payback period.

In this question, there was a conflict between the two methods regarding acceptability, therefore candidates needed to refer to the respective investment appraisal methods and conclude by asserting the superiority of one method (NPV) over the other (discounted payback).

Weaker responses simply referred to the positive NPV calculated in (a) (i), which is insufficient for a part question worth three marks.

Part (c)

This question asked candidates to critically discuss the views of the directors in respect of the company's investment appraisal. These views were concerned with the evaluation period of projects, an assumed terminal value and the investment appraisal techniques to be used, including a strict two-year discounted payback period (DPB).

Responses demonstrated that, whilst candidates can produce very good NPV computations and calculate (discounted) payback periods correctly, improvement is required when it comes to discussion.

This question asked candidates to critically discuss viewpoints. It is rarely sufficient to simply list a few points. A critical discussion should involve looking at a viewpoint or a statement in more than one way, for instance by looking at both its good aspects and those aspects which could be criticised.

Many candidates simply ignored the directors' view on terminal value. Other errors included saying that NPV considered the whole life of an investment project, even though the directors had limited NPV's application to four years. Also, too many answers said that payback failed to take account of the time value of money, even though the directors required DPB to be used.

Some answers assumed that the investment project ended after four years, when in fact the directors simply required that only the first four years be evaluated using NPV.

Too many answers failed to directly address the question requirement, often offering a discussion of investment appraisal in general rather than the directors' views specifically, whilst poor answers did not address the question requirement by discussing only forecasting problems, such as difficulties in forecasting cash flows, inflation rate, changes in the cost of capital etc.

38 COPPER CO

Key answer tips

All elements of part (a) can be addressed using the joint probability table. The key here is to remember that the probability of one thing and another thing happening can be found by multiplying the probabilities of the individual events together, whereas the probability of one thing or another thing happening can be found by adding the probabilities of the individual events together.

The joint probabilities here refer to the probabilities of a particular cash flow occurring in year 1 and then a particular cash flow occurring in year 2.

Once the table has been put together, the questions can then be addressed. For instance the probability of a negative NPV happening is the probabilities of each of the negative outcomes added together as the NPV will be negative if one of these events OR any of the others occurs.

Added complexity came from having to apply discounting to the cash flows before including them in the table.

Part (b)'s marks should have been simpler to achieve, although make sure that only two methods were discussed – discussion of the third one would not pick up marks.

The highlighted words are key phrases that markers are looking for.

(a)   (i)   ENPV calculation

Year	PV of Y1 CF	prob	PV of Y2 CF	prob	Total PV	joint prob	PV × JP	NPV
	$000		$000		$000		$000	$000
PV of c/f 1	893	0.1	1,594	0.3	2,487	0.03	74.6	(1,013)
			2,391	0.6	3,284	0.06	197.0	(216)
			3,985	0.1	4,878	0.01	48.8	1,378
PV of c/f 2	1,786	0.5	1,594	0.3	3,380	0.15	507.0	(120)
			2,391	0.6	4,177	0.30	1,253.1	677
			3,985	0.1	5,771	0.05	288.6	2,271
PV of c/f 3	2,679	0.4	1,594	0.3	4,273	0.12	512.8	773
			2,391	0.6	5,070	0.24	1,216.8	1,570
			3,985	0.1	6,664	0.04	266.6	3,164

Sum of PV	4,365
Investment	(3,500)
ENPV	865

Workings

Year	Yr 1	factor	PV	Yr 2	factor	PV
Cash flow 1	1,000	0.893	893	2,000	0.797	1,594
Cash flow 2	2,000	0.893	1,786	3,000	0.797	2,391
Cash flow 3	3,000	0.893	2,679	5,000	0.797	3,985

(ii)   **Negative NPV probability**   24%   Sum of joint probabilities with negative NPVs

(iii)   **Most likely outcome ($000)** 677.0 Highest joint probability

(iv)   **Comment**

The mean (expected) NPV is positive and so it might be thought that the proposed investment is financially acceptable. However, the mean (expected) NPV is not a value expected to occur because of undertaking the proposed investment, but a mean value from undertaking it many times. There is no clear decision rule associated with the mean (expected) NPV.

A decision on financial acceptability must also consider the risk (probability) of a negative NPV being generated by the investment. At 24%, this might appear too high a risk to be acceptable. The risk preferences of the directors of Copper Co will inform the decision on financial acceptability; there is no decision rule to be followed here.

(b)   Simulation

Simulation is a computer-based method of evaluating an investment project whereby the probability distributions associated with individual project variables and interdependencies between project variables are incorporated.

Random numbers are assigned to a range of different values of a project variable to reflect its probability distribution. Each simulation run randomly selects values of project variables using random numbers and calculates a mean (expected) NPV.

A picture of the probability distribution of the mean (expected) NPV is built up from the results of repeated simulation runs. The project risk can be assessed from the probability distribution as the standard deviation of the expected returns, together with the most likely outcome and the probability of a negative NPV.

Adjusted payback

If risk and uncertainty are considered to be the same, payback can be used to adjust for risk and uncertainty in investment appraisal.

As uncertainty (risk) increases, the payback period can be shortened to increase the emphasis on cash flows that are nearer to the present time and hence less uncertain. Conversely, as uncertainty (risk) decreases, the payback period can be lengthened to decrease the emphasis on cash flows that are nearer to the present time.

Discounted payback adjusts for risk in investment appraisal in that risk is reflected by the discount rate employed. Discounted payback can therefore be seen as an adjusted payback method.

Risk-adjusted discount rates

The risk associated with an investment project can be incorporated into the discount rate as a risk premium over the risk free rate of return.

The risk premium can be determined on a subjective basis, for example, by recognising that launching a new product is intrinsically riskier that replacing an existing machine or a small expansion of existing operations.

The risk premium can be determined theoretically by using the capital asset pricing model in an investment appraisal context. A proxy company equity beta can be ungeared and the resulting asset beta can be regeared to reflect the financial risk of the investing company, giving a project-specific equity beta that can be used to find a project-specific cost of equity or a project-specific discount rate.

(Examiner note: Only two methods were required to be discussed.)

ACCA marking scheme				Marks
(a)	(i)	Initial PVs		1
		Total PVs		2
		CF1 joint prob		1
		CF2 joint prob		1
		CF3 joint prob		1
		ENPV		2
				8
	(ii)	Negative NPV prob		1
	(iii)	Most likely NPV		1
	(iv)	Comment on ENPV		1
		Comment on risk		1
				2
(b)		First method		4
		Second method		4
				8
Total				**20**

Examiner's comments

Part (a) (i)

This question required candidates to calculate the mean (expected) NPV of an investment project. Candidates were required to use a joint probability table.

Some candidates chose not to use a joint probability table and calculated the ENPV from the average annual cash flows instead. Perhaps these candidates decided that only the value of the ENPV was important, or perhaps they did not know what a joint probability table was, or perhaps they thought they were saving time. Because using a joint probability statement was a requirement, candidates who did not satisfy this requirement could not obtain all of the marks. Candidates must meet the requirements of a question if they wish to gain marks.

Some candidates made errors because they did not understand clearly that probabilities are multiplied together to produce joint probabilities, while cash flows are added together to produce total cash flows. With three probabilities applied to year one cash flows and three probabilities applied to year two cash flows, there were nine different total cash flows and NPVs over the two-year period, with nine associated joint probabilities. Three of the NPVs were negative. Some candidates made the mistake of multiplying cash flows by their associated probabilities within each year before adding these to give total cash flow. Some candidates wrongly treated initial investment as a year one cash flow before discounting it.

Some candidates thought that using probabilities meant that discounting was not needed and labelled their calculated cash flows as NPVs or PVs (present values) when they were in future value terms, not present value terms.

Part (a) (ii)

This question required candidates to calculate the probability of a negative NPV.

As mentioned earlier, three of the NPVs in the joint probability table were negative so the probability of a negative NPV could be found by adding the joint probabilities of these three NPVs. Some candidates made the surprising error of calculating the sensitivity of the project ENPV to a change in year one cash flow and called this the probability of a negative NPV. Some candidates did not understand that a probability is a percentage value and calculated a monetary value, which they called the probability of a negative NPV.

Part (a) (iii)

This question required candidates to calculate the NPV of the most likely outcome.

The NPV of the most likely outcome could be found from the joint probability table by selecting the NPV with the highest joint probability. A number of candidates who had not prepared a joint probability table in calculating the ENPV were able to work their way to the correct answer by considering the cash flows associated with the highest probabilities in each year.

Part (b)

Here candidates were required to discuss TWO out three named methods of adjusting for risk and uncertainty in investment appraisal.

As the requirement was for TWO methods of adjusting for risk and uncertainty in investment appraisal to be discussed, candidates who discussed a third method were just wasting valuable examination time. Eight marks were on offer, hence it is reasonable to assume that four marks were offered for each of two methods discussed. Better answers maintained their focus on the requirement of the question and were not diverted into, for example, discussing the difference between systematic risk and unsystematic risk, or the difficulty of finding the value of the equity risk premium when using the capital asset pricing model.

39   MELANIE CO

Key answer tips

The calculations for part (a) are made easier by the absence of taxation, making this a straightforward question. The key is getting the correct cash flows in the correct time periods and where you would use the post-tax cost of borrowing normally to evaluate the cash flows, the simple cost of borrowing can be used as there is no tax. For part (b) it is essential to know the equivalent annual cost calculation formula, which is not given on the formula sheet. Also remember that you are evaluating costs and are looking for the cheapest option. The requirement to 'critically discuss' in part (c) means that just stating reasons why NPV is superior will not be enough to pick up full marks. There has to be a discussion element to your answer. Also remember to limit yourself to four reasons – any extra will not be marked.

The highlighted words are key phrases that markers are looking for.

(a)   (i)

Year	Year 0	Year 1	Year 2	Year 3
	$	$	$	$
Lease				
Lease payment	(55,000)	(55,000)	(55,000)	
PV factor at 8%	1	0.926	0.857	
Present value	(55,000)	(50,930)	(47,135)	
Present value cost	(153,065)			
Borrow and buy				
Initial cost	(160,000)			
Residual value				40,000
Maintenance		(8,000)	(8,000)	(8,000)
Total	(160,000)	(8,000)	(8,000)	32,000
PV factor at 8%	1	0.926	0.857	0.794
Present value	(160,000)	(7,408)	(6,856)	25,408
Present value cost	(148,856)			

As borrow and buy offers the cheapest present value cost the machine should be financed by borrowing.

(ii)

3-year replacement cycle	Year 0	Year 1	Year 2	Year 3	Year 4
	$	$	$	$	$
Initial cost	(160,000)				
Residual value				40,000	
Maintenance		(8,000)	(8,000)	(8,000)	
Total	(160,000)	(8,000)	(8,000)	32,000	
PV factor at 10%	1	0.909	0.826	0.751	
Present value	(160,000)	(7,272)	(6,608)	24,032	
Present value cost	(149,848)				

EAC 3 year cycle	=PV cost/Annuity factor 3 years at 10%
EAC	$(149,848)/2.487 = $(60,253)

4-year replacement cycle	Year 0	Year 1	Year 2	Year 3	Year 4
	$	$	$	$	$
Initial cost	(160,000)				
Residual value					11,000
Maintenance		(12,000)	(12,000)	(12,000)	(12,000)
Total	(160,000)	(12,000)	(12,000)	(12,000)	(1,000)
PV factor at 10%	1	0.909	0.826	0.751	0.683
Present value	(160,000)	(10,908)	(9,912)	(9,012)	(683)
Present value cost	(190,515)				

EAC 4 year cycle	=PV cost/Annuity factor 4 years at 10%
EAC	$(190,515)/3.170 = $(60,099)

Recommendation

The machine should be replaced every four years as the equivalent annual cost is lower.

(b) In most simple accept or reject decisions, IRR and NPV will select the same project. However, NPV has certain advantages over IRR as an investment appraisal technique.

NPV and shareholder wealth

The NPV of a proposed project, if calculated at an appropriate cost of capital, is equal to the increase in shareholder wealth which the project offers. In this way NPV is directly linked to the assumed financial objective of the company, the maximisation of shareholder wealth. IRR calculates the rate of return on projects, and although this can show the attractiveness of the project to shareholders, it does not measure the absolute increase in wealth which the project offers.

Absolute measure

NPV looks at absolute increases in wealth and thus can be used to compare projects of different sizes. IRR looks at relative rates of return and in doing so ignores the relative size of the compared investment projects.

Non-conventional cash flows

In situations involving multiple reversals in project cash flows, it is possible that the IRR method may produce multiple IRRs (that is, there can be more than one interest rate which would produce an NPV of zero). If decision-makers are aware of the existence of multiple IRRs, it is still possible for them to make the correct decision using IRR, but if unaware they could make the wrong decision.

Mutually-exclusive projects

In situations of mutually-exclusive projects, it is possible that the IRR method will (incorrectly) rank projects in a different order to the NPV method. This is due to the inbuilt reinvestment assumption of the IRR method. The IRR method assumes that any net cash inflows generated during the life of the project will be reinvested at the project's IRR. NPV on the other hand assumes a reinvestment rate equal to the cost of capital. Generally NPV's assumed reinvestment rate is more realistic and hence it ranks projects correctly.

Changes in cost of capital

NPV can be used in situations where the cost of capital changes from year to year. Although IRR can be calculated in these circumstances, it can be difficult to make accept or reject decisions as it is difficult to know which cost of capital to compare it with.

Note: Only four reasons were required to be discussed.

ACCA marking scheme			
			Marks
(a)	(i)	Lease timing	1
		PV leasing	1
		Maintenance cost	1
		Purchase cost	0.5
		Residual value	0.5
		PV buy	1
		Decision	1
			⎯⎯
			6
			⎯⎯
	(ii)	3-year PV cost	1
		3-year EAC	1
		Maintenance 4-year	0.5
		Residual value 4-year	0.5
		4-year PV cost	1
		4-year EAC	1
		Decision	1
			⎯⎯
			6
			⎯⎯
(b)		First reason	2
		Second reason	2
		Third reason	2
		Fourth reason	2
			⎯⎯
			8
			⎯⎯
Total			20
			⎯⎯

Examiner's comments

Part (a) (i)

This question asked candidates to evaluate whether the company should use leasing or borrowing as a source of finance.

There were some very good complete answers here.

The two marks available for the present value of the leasing option were often gained. Errors here mainly occurred where the lease rental payments were mistimed (treated as year-end cash flows and not, as the question stated, cash flows in advance), or where discounting the cash flows was not performed at all, thereby ignoring the fundamental principle of the time value of money.

In terms of the borrowing option, a fundamental error kept reoccurring which displayed a lack of understanding of the very nature of discounted cash flow. This error, seen far too often, was the inclusion of interest payments within the computation of net cash flow. The cost of capital which should be used to discount the net cash flows in this case is the cost of the debt finance being used (taxation being ignored in this question), and hence the inclusion of interest payments in the cash flow schedule means that such interest payments are effectively being double counted.

Some errors were also seen in the timing of the relevant cash flows, namely the purchase cost, the maintenance costs and the residual value. Some candidates also erroneously decided to use the 10% discount rate, which was not presented until it became relevant in part (a)(ii).

Lastly, the requirement asked candidates to evaluate the source of finance to be used, hence it is expected that a recommendation would be made based upon the figures calculated.

Failure to do this meant that a relatively straightforward mark was not gained.

Part (a) (ii)

The requirement here was to calculate the equivalent annual cost (EAC) of operating both a three-year and a four-year replacement cycle, and to make a recommendation.

There were many fully correct answers here.

Where candidates had made the error noted above in part (a)(i), namely including interest payments in their cash flow schedules, it was usually repeated in these computations. The other common error here was a failure to know how to arrive at an EAC, with the division of NPV simply by the number of years being an often seen mistake, as well as a simple comparison of NPVs computed in order to make a judgement. Some responses lacked an appreciation of the role of annuity factors.

Some other mistakes made included a failure to use the different maintenance costs and residual value in the four-year option, as well as unnecessary computation of the EAC of the leasing option (sic) or the EACs of other replacement cycles.

As has been discussed in respect of other requirements, a mark could have been scored by making the required recommendation. This was disappointingly missed by some candidates.

Part (b)

Here candidates were asked to critically discuss four reasons why net present value (NPV) is regarded as superior to internal rate of return (IRR) as an investment appraisal technique.

Eight marks were available, with two marks being available for each of the four reasons. The grid available to candidates in the CBE environment is useful in helping to organise candidates' answers, although some responses were too brief and some offered fewer than the four reasons required by the question.

Whilst some of the reasons outlined in the suggested solution were seen quite often in candidates' answers, weaker responses simply described what NPV and IRR are and how their respective calculations are performed. Furthermore, many answers gained very few marks because they did not adopt a comparative approach to addressing the requirement, for example, by making a statement about NPV without referring to IRR and so not discussing the superiority of NPV over IRR.

Other errors seen included:

- Stating that IRR is inferior to NPV because IRR ignores the time value of money

- Arguing that IRR is inferior to NPV because different choices for discount rates give different values of IRR. However, manual calculation of IRR is a first approximation for the actual value of IRR, which can be found quickly using a spreadsheet function, as indeed can NPV

- Making very general and brief points such as quick, easy, simple to understand

- Suggesting that one technique or the other is more easily understood by managers, without any justification.

40 PINKS CO

Key answer tips

In part (a) (i) the nominal NPV calculation is relatively straightforward. Apply inflation to the cash flows and use the nominal cost of capital. You may come unstuck on part (a) (ii). The real terms appraisal in theory should be done from scratch using uninflated values for all numbers, but for only four marks, an approximation can be found by taking the pre-tax nominal cash flows and deflating them by the general rate of inflation, before taxing them and discounting the total at the real cost of capital. Limit your answer to part (b) to only four ways. This part of the syllabus will rarely be tested in section C but the examiner has reserved the right to do so by using the word 'mainly' in his description of which syllabus sections are valid for testing in section C. Don't let this put you off. Make sure you revise all areas of the syllabus thoroughly.

The highlighted words are key phrases that markers are looking for.

(a) (i) Nominal terms appraisal of the investment project

Year	1	2	3	4
	$000	$000	$000	$000
Sales revenue	39,375	58,765	85,087	32,089
Variable cost	(22,047)	(31,185)	(41,328)	(17,923)
Contribution	17,328	27,580	43,759	14,166
Fixed costs	(3,180)	(3,483)	(3,811)	(3,787)
Cash flows before tax	14,148	24,097	39,948	10,379
Tax at 26%	(3,679)	(6,265)	(10,387)	(2,699)
TAD tax benefits	1,300	975	731	2,194
Cash flows after tax	11,769	18,807	30,292	9,874
Discount at 12%	0.893	0.797	0.712	0.636
Present values	10,510	14,989	21,568	6,280

	$000
Sum of PV of future cash flows	53,347
Initial investment	(20,000)
NPV	33,347

Workings

Year	1	2	3	4
Selling price ($/unit)	125	130	140	120
Inflated by 5%/year	131.25	143.33	162.07	145.86
Sales volume (units)	300,000	410,000	525,000	220,000
Sales revenue ($000)	39,375	58,765	85,087	32,089

Year	1	2	3	4
Variable costs ($/unit)	71	71	71	71
Inflated by 3.5%/year	73.49	76.06	78.72	81.47
Sales volume (units)	300,000	410,000	525,000	220,000
Variable costs ($000) ($000/year)	22,047	31,185	41,328	17,923

Year	1	2	3	4
Fixed costs ($000) ($000/year)	3,000	3,100	3,200	3,000
Inflated by 6%/year	3,180	3,483	3,811	3,787
TAD ($000)	5,000	3,750	2,813	8,437
TAD benefits ($000/year)	1,300	975	731	2,194

(ii)   Real terms appraisal of the investment project

Year	1	2	3	4
	$000	$000	$000	$000
Nominal cash flows before tax	14,148	24,097	39,948	10,379
Real cash flows before tax	13,643	22,408	35,823	8,975
Tax at 26%	(3,547)	(5,826)	(9,314)	(2,334)
TAD tax benefits	1,300	975	731	2,194
Cash flows after tax	11,396	17,557	27,240	8,835
Discount at 8%	0.926	0.857	0.794	0.735
Present values	10,553	15,046	21,629	6,494

	$000
Sum of PV of future cash flows	53,722
Initial investment	(20,000)
NPV	33,722

Note: the real cash flows before tax are found by taking the nominal cash flows and deflating by the **general** rate of inflation, 3.7%:

Year 1 14,147/1.037 = 13,643

Year 2 24,097/1.037^2 = 22,408

Year 3 39,948/1.037^3 = 35,823

Year 4 10,379/1.037^4 = 8,975

Comment: The real terms appraisal gives almost the same positive NPV as the nominal terms appraisal, the difference being due to the different discount rate being applied to the same TAD benefits. As the NPV is positive, the investment project is financially acceptable.

(b)   The achievement of stakeholder objectives by managers can be encouraged by managerial reward schemes, for example, share option schemes and performance-related pay (PRP), and by regulatory requirements, such as corporate governance codes of best practice and stock exchange listing regulations.

Share option schemes

The agency problem arises due to the separation of ownership and control, and managers pursuing their own objectives, rather than the objectives of shareholders, specifically the objective of maximising shareholder wealth. Managers can be encouraged to achieve stakeholder objectives by bringing their own objectives more in line with the objectives of stakeholders such as shareholders. This increased goal congruence can be achieved by turning the managers into shareholders through share option schemes, although the criteria by which shares are awarded need very careful consideration.

Performance-related pay

Part of the remuneration of managers can be made conditional upon their achieving specified performance targets, so that achieving these performance targets assists in achieving stakeholder objectives. Achieving a specified increase in earnings per share, for example, could be consistent with the objective of maximising shareholder wealth. Achieving a specified improvement in the quality of emissions could be consistent with a government objective of meeting international environmental targets.

However, PRP performance objectives need very careful consideration if they are to be effective in encouraging managers to achieve stakeholder targets. In recent times, long-term incentive plans (LTIPs) have been accepted as more effective than PRP, especially where a company's performance is benchmarked against that of its competitors.

Corporate governance codes of best practice

Codes of best practice have developed over time into recognised methods of encouraging managers to achieve stakeholder objectives, applying best practice to many key areas of corporate governance relating to executive remuneration, risk assessment and risk management, auditing, internal control, executive responsibility and board accountability. Codes of best practice have emphasised and supported the key role played by non-executive directors in supporting independent judgement and in following the spirit of corporate governance regulations.

Stock exchange listing regulations

These regulations seek to ensure a fair and efficient market for trading company securities such as shares and loan notes.

They encourage disclosure of price-sensitive information in supporting pricing efficiency and help to decrease information asymmetry, one of the causes of the agency problem between shareholders and managers. Decreasing information asymmetry encourages managers to achieve stakeholder objectives as the quality and quantity of information available to stakeholders gives them a clearer picture of the extent to which managers are attending to their objectives.

Monitoring

One theoretical way of encouraging managers to achieve stakeholder objectives is to reduce information asymmetry by monitoring the decisions and performance of managers. One form of monitoring is auditing the financial statements of a company to confirm the quality and validity of the information provided to stakeholders.

Note: Only four ways to encourage the achievement of stakeholder objectives were required to be discussed.

		ACCA marking scheme	
			Marks
(a)	(i)	Sales nominal	1
		VC nominal	1
		FC nominal	1
		Tax liability	1
		TAD	1
		TAD benefits	1
		Tax timing	1
		PVs and nominal NPV	1
			8
	(ii)	Real CF before tax	1
		Tax treatment	1
		PVs and real NPV	1
		Comment	1
			4
(b)		First way	2
		Second way	2
		Third way	2
		Fourth way	2
			8
Total			**20**

Examiner's comments

Part (a) (i)

Candidates were required here to calculate the nominal net present value (NPV) of an investment project, incorporating inflation and taxation into the calculation. Many answers gained good marks here.

In relation to inflation, one error which occurred was inflating each year by one year only, when inflation has a compounding effect. A small number of candidates used an inflation rate of 50% instead of 5% in relation to selling price inflation, and 35% instead of 3.5% for variable cost inflation. There were occasionally magnitude errors when calculating inflated incremental fixed costs, such as using $3,180 instead of $3,180,000. Forecast fixed costs were different in the second and third years to those in the first year, but some candidates incorrectly inflated the first-year value throughout the four-year period. Surprisingly, some candidates, having applied specific inflation correctly to selling prices, variable costs and fixed costs, then applied the general rate of inflation as well.

In general, most candidates did quite well in relation to taxation calculations, where the most frequent error was omitting a balancing allowance from the fourth-year calculation of tax-allowable depreciation (TAD). Although the question stated that the tax liability was settled in the year in which it arose, some candidates incorrectly placed tax cash flows one year in arrears. Some candidates also incorrectly used a taxation rate which was different from the 26% figure provided in the question.

Some candidates incorrectly located the initial investment at the end of the first year when, as an initial investment, it should have been located at year 0.

Although the question provided a nominal after-tax cost of capital, some candidates calculated and applied a different figure by putting values into the Fisher equation.

(a)(ii)

The requirement here was for candidates to calculate the real NPV of the investment project.

The correct approach to calculating the real before-tax cash flows was to deflate the nominal before-tax cash flows using the general rate of inflation. These cash flows could then be adjusted for taxation and discounted using the real cost of capital. Many candidates did not adopt the correct approach. One incorrect approach adopted by some candidates was to use the nominal after-tax cash flows, without considering deflation, discounted by the real cost of capital.

Using nominal cash flows as real cash flows in this way shows a lack of understanding of the difference between the real terms and nominal terms approaches to investment appraisal. Another approach adopted by some candidates was to calculate the before-tax cash flows ignoring inflation and then adjust for taxation, before discounting by the real cost of capital. It must be emphasised that real cash flows are found by inflating using specific inflation and then deflating by the general rate of inflation. Only when there is no specific inflation, which was not the case here, can general inflation be ignored.

Candidates were also required to comment on their findings and many comments were limited to saying whether the investment project was financially acceptable. Many candidates were not aware that the nominal terms approach and the real terms approach should give the same NPV, and discussed, sometimes at length, the reasons for the differences in value between their nominal and real NPVs.

Part (b)

This part of the question required candidates to discuss four ways by which managers might be encouraged to achieve stakeholder objectives.

Since eight marks were offered for discussing four ways of encouraging managers, it seems a reasonable deduction that two marks were offered for each way discussed. Good examination technique suggests discussing four ways and spending an equal amount of time on each way.

Marks would clearly be lost if candidates discussed fewer than four ways.

Many candidates correctly discussed performance-related pay (PRP) as a way of encouraging managers to achieve stakeholder objectives, linking performance to specific stakeholders, suggesting, for example, that a PRP target such as EPS could be linked to shareholder objectives, while an emissions-related PRP target could be linked to government objectives.

Many candidates correctly discussed share option schemes, perhaps linking these to addressing the agency problem between shareholders and managers, and indicating the corporate and shareholder benefits which might arise if managers saw themselves as shareholders.

Other ways of encouraging managers to achieve stakeholder objectives, such as the application of corporate governance, are discussed in the suggested solution.

Some candidates did not gain marks because they did not focus on the question requirement in relation to encouraging managers. For example, some candidates discussed the need to separate the roles of CEO and MD, but did not explain how this separation might encourage managers to achieve stakeholder objectives. Similarly, some candidates suggested that managers should receive a bonus, but did not suggest what that bonus might be for.

Some candidates lost marks by offering answers which were too brief for the marks available, lacking the discussion which was part of the question requirement. For example, 'offer them company shares' gains no marks because it is not discussion. Explanation is needed as to why this might encourage managers to seek to achieve objectives of stakeholders. Other candidates lost marks by discussing topics outside the requirement of the question, such as the origins of the agency problem, or the shortcomings of EPS as a managerial performance target, or the need for managers to use DCF investment appraisal techniques.

BUSINESS FINANCE AND COST OF CAPITAL

41   FENCE CO

Key answer tips

A well-rehearsed candidate should not struggle with the calculations here but layout is key so the marker can follow the method used.

Part (c) is standard textbook knowledge where some easy marks could be gained.

The highlighted words in the written sections are key phrases that markers are looking for.

(a)   Cost of equity

The current cost of equity can be calculated using the capital asset pricing model.

Equity or market risk premium = 11 − 4 = 7%

Cost of equity = 4 + (0.9 × 7) = 4 + 6.3 = 10.3%

After-tax cost of debt

After-tax interest payment = 100 × 0.07 × (1 − 0.2) = $5.60 per bond

Year	Cash flow	$	5% discount	PV ($)	4% discount	PV ($)
0	market value	(107.14)	1.000	(107.14)	1.000	(107.14)
1 − 7	interest	5.60	5.786	32.40	6.002	33.61
7	redemption	100.00	0.711	71.10	0.760	76.00
				(3.64)		2.47

After-tax cost of debt = IRR = 4 + ((5 − 4) × 2.47)/(2.47 + 3.64) = 4 + 0.4 = 4.4%

Market value of equity = 10,000,000 × 7.50 = $75 million

Market value of Fence Co debt = 14 million × 107.14/100 = $15 million

Total market value of company = 75 + 15 = $90 million

WACC = [Ve/(Ve + Vd)] × ke + [Vd/(Ve + Vd)] × kd

WACC = [75/90] × 10.3 + [15/90] × 4.4 = 9.3%

(b) Since the investment project is different to business operations, its business risk is different to that of existing operations. A cost of equity for appraising it can be therefore be found using the capital asset pricing model.

Ungearing proxy company equity beta

Asset beta = 1.2 × 54/(54 + (12 × 0.8)) = 1.2 × 54/63.6 = 1.019

Regearing asset beta

Market value of debt = $15m (calculated in part (a))

Regeared asset beta = 1.019 × (75 + (15 × 0.8))/75 = 1.019 × 87/75 = 1.182

Using the CAPM

Equity or market risk premium = 11 − 4 = 7%

Cost of equity = 4 + (1.182 × 7) = 4 + 8.3 = 12.3%

(c) Portfolio theory suggests that the total risk of a portfolio of investments can be reduced by diversifying the investments held in the portfolio, e.g. by investing capital in a number of different shares rather than buying shares in only one or two companies.

Even when a portfolio has been well-diversified over a number of different investments, there is a limit to the risk-reduction effect, so that there is a level of risk which cannot be diversified away. This undiversifiable risk is the risk of the financial system as a whole, and so is referred to as systematic risk or market risk. Diversifiable risk, which is the element of total risk which can be reduced or minimised by portfolio diversification, is referred to as unsystematic risk or specific risk, since it relates to individual or specific companies rather than to the financial system as a whole.

Portfolio theory is concerned with total risk, which is the sum of systematic risk and unsystematic risk. The capital asset pricing model assumes that investors hold diversified portfolios, and so is concerned with systematic risk alone.

(d) Capital market efficiency is concerned with pricing efficiency when weak form, semi-strong form and strong form efficiency are being discussed.

In relation to pricing efficiency, the efficient markets hypothesis (EMH) suggests that share prices fully and fairly reflect all relevant and available information. Relevant and available information can be divided into past information, public information and private information.

Significance of EMH to financial managers

If the EMH is correct and share prices are fair, there is no point in financial managers seeking to mislead the capital market, because such attempts will be unsuccessful. Window-dressing financial statements, for example, in order to show a company's performance and position in a favourable light, will be seen through by financial analysts as the capital market digests the financial statement information in pricing the company's shares.

Another consequence of the EMH for financial managers is that there is no particular time which is best for issuing new shares, as share prices on the stock market are always fair.

Because share prices are always fair, there are no bargains to be found on the stock market, i.e. companies whose shares are undervalued. An acquisition strategy which seeks to identify and exploit such stock market bargains is pointless if the EMH is correct.

It should be noted, however, that if real-world capital markets are semi-strong form efficient rather than strong form efficient, insider information may undermine the strength of the points made above. For example, a company which is valued fairly by the stock market may be undervalued or overvalued if private or insider information is taken into account.

	ACCA marking scheme		
			Marks
(a)	Calculation of equity risk premium		1
	Calculation of cost of equity		1
	After-tax interest payment		1
	Setting up IRR calculation		1
	Calculating after-tax cost of debt		1
	Market value of equity		0.5
	Market value of debt		0.5
	Calculating WACC		1
		Maximum	7
(b)	Ungearing proxy company equity beta		2
	Regearing equity beta		1
	Calculation of cost of equity		1
		Maximum	4
(c)	Risk diversification		1–2
	Systematic risk		1–2
	Unsystematic risk		1–2
	Portfolio theory and the CAPM		1–2
		Maximum	4
(d)	Nature of capital market efficiency		1–2
	Significance of EMH for financial manager		2–3
		Maximum	5
Total			**20**

Examiner's comments

Part (a) of this question asked candidates to calculate the weighted average cost of capital of a company. Many answers gained very good marks here. Some candidates wrongly used the average return on the market (11%) as the equity or market risk premium in calculating the cost of equity using the capital asset pricing model (CAPM). More common were errors in calculating the after-tax cost of debt of the 7% bond, including:

- taking incorrect values from the discount and annuity tables
- using nominal value as market value
- using market value as nominal value
- calculating the after-tax interest payment with an incorrect corporation tax rate
- employing the before-tax interest payment in calculating the after-tax cost of debt
- making calculation errors when using the internal rate of return formula. It should be mentioned that candidates, when calculating the after-tax cost of debt, should be seeking to make their answers reasonably accurate. Consequently, if the first estimate of the cost of debt produces a negative NPV when interpolating the internal rate of return, the second estimate of the cost of debt should be lower, as the first estimate was too high.

Choosing a higher rate rather than a lower rate indicates an intention to extrapolate rather than interpolate, and to seek inaccuracy rather than accuracy. Having a wide spread between the estimated costs of debt also increases inaccuracy, so choosing 1% and 20% indicates an unwillingness to think about what the value of the after-tax cost of debt might roughly be. A bond approximation model (correctly used) can provide an initial estimate of the cost of debt as a guide to selecting discount rates for linear interpolation.

Part (b) required candidates to calculate a project-specific cost of equity. First, the beta of a proxy company had to be ungeared to give an asset beta. Second, the asset beta had to be regeared to give a project-specific equity beta. Finally, the project-specific cost of equity could be calculated using the CAPM.

Many candidates gained very good marks here. One error that some candidates made was to omit the tax effect from the calculation, which was surprising, as the equation required was given in the formulae sheet.

Part (c) asked to explain the difference between systematic and unsystematic risk in relation to portfolio theory and the capital asset pricing model (CAPM). Many answers struggled to gain good marks, essentially due to a lack of knowledge.

Systematic risk cannot be reduced by portfolio diversification, while unsystematic risk can be reduced by portfolio diversification. Some candidates got this the wrong way round and said that systematic risk could be reduced by portfolio diversification.

Systematic risk includes both business risk and financial risk (as illustrated by the equity beta in the CAPM), however some candidates wrongly identified systematic risk with business risk and unsystematic risk with financial risk.

Investors can reduce risk by portfolio diversification and the CAPM assumes that investors have diversified portfolios, yet many answers suggested that companies should reduce unsystematic risk by diversifying business operations.

Some candidates discussed unnecessary material in their answers, for example the process whereby a proxy equity beta can be ungeared and regeared in calculating a project-specific cost of equity or a project-specific weighted average cost of capital.

42 BAR CO

Key answer tips

This question presents a fairly unusual way of testing this syllabus area. The answers to parts (a) and (c) should be easily achieved. Part (b) however required a mix of both calculations and discussion, combined with a fair amount of forethought in order to answer the requirement. Students who struggle in this area should pay particular attention to the calculations shown in the marking guide that are necessary to generate a relevant discussion.

The highlighted words are key phrases that markers are looking for.

(a) **Theoretical ex rights price**

Rights issue price = 7.50 × 0.8 = $6.00 per share

Number of shares issued = $90m/6.00 = 15 million shares

Number of shares currently in issue = 60 million shares

The rights issue is on a 1 for 4 basis.

Theoretical ex rights price = ((4 × 7.50) + (1 × 6.00))/5 = $7.20 per share

Alternatively, theoretical ex rights price = ((60m × 7.50) + (15m × 6.00))/75m = $7.20 per share, where 75 million is the number of shares after the rights issue.

(b) **Financial acceptability to shareholders of buying back loan notes**

The financial acceptability to shareholders of the proposal to buy back loan notes can be assessed by calculating whether shareholder wealth is increased or decreased as a result.

The loan notes are being bought back by Bar Co at their market value of $112.50 per loan note, rather than their nominal value of $100 per loan note. The total nominal value of the loan notes redeemed will therefore be less than the $90 million spent redeeming them.

Nominal value of loan notes redeemed = 90m × (100/112.50) = $80 million

Interest saved by redeeming loan notes = 80m × 0.08 = $6.4 million per year

Earnings per share will be affected by the redemption of the loan notes and the issue of new shares.

Revised profit before tax = 49m − (10m − 6.4m) = $45.4 million

Revised profit after tax (earnings) = 45.4m × 0.7 = $31.78 million

Revised earnings per share = 100 × (31.78m/75m) = 42.37 cents per share

Current earnings per share = 100 × (27m/60m) = 45 cents per share

Current price/earnings ratio = 750/45 = 16.7 times

The revised earnings per share can be used to calculate a revised share price if the price/earnings ratio is assumed to be constant.

Revised share price = 16.7 × 42.37 cents = 708 cents or $7.08 per share

This share price is less than the theoretical ex rights price per share ($7.20) and so the effect of using the rights issue funds to redeem the loan notes is to decrease shareholder wealth. From a shareholder perspective, therefore, this use of the funds cannot be recommended.

However, this conclusion depends heavily on the assumption that the price/earnings ratio remains constant, as this ratio was used to calculate the revised share price from the revised earning per share. In reality, the share price after the redemption of loan notes will be set by the capital market and it is this market-determined share price that will determine the price/earnings ratio, rather than the price/earnings ratio determining the share price. Since the financial risk of Bar Co has decreased following the redemption of loan notes, the cost of equity is likely to fall and the share price is likely to rise, leading to a higher price/earnings ratio. If the share price increases to above the theoretical ex rights price per share, corresponding to an increase in the price/earnings ratio to more than 17 times (720/42.37), shareholders will experience a capital gain and so using the cash raised by the rights issue to buy back loan notes will become financially acceptable from their perspective.

(c) A key financial objective for a stock exchange listed company is to maximise the wealth of shareholders. This objective is usually replaced by the objective of maximising the company's share price, since maximising the market value of the company represents the maximum capital gain over a given period. The need for dividends can be met by recognising that share prices can be seen as the sum of the present values of future dividends.

Maximising the company's share price is the same as maximising the equity market value of the company, since equity market value (market capitalisation) is equal to number of issued shares multiplied by share price. Maximising equity market value can be achieved by maximising net corporate cash income and the expected growth in that income, while minimising the corporate cost of capital. Listed companies therefore have maximising net cash income as a key financial objective.

Not-for-profit (NFP) organisations seek to provide services to the public and this requires cash income. Maximising net cash income is therefore a key financial objective for NFP organisations as well as listed companies. A large charity seeks to raise as much funds as possible in order to achieve its charitable objectives, which are non-financial in nature.

Both listed companies and NFP organisations need to control the use of cash within a given financial period, and both types of organisations therefore use budgets. Another key financial objective for both organisations is therefore to keep spending within budget.

The objective of value for money (VFM) is often identified in connection with NFP organisations. This objective refers to a focus on economy, efficiency and effectiveness. These three terms can be linked to input (economy refers to securing resources as economically as possible), process (resources need to be employed efficiently within the organisation) and output (the effective use of resources in achieving the organisation's objectives).

Described in these terms, it is clear that a listed company also seeks to achieve value for money in its business operations. There is a difference in emphasis, however, which merits careful consideration. A listed company has a profit motive, and so VFM for a listed company can be related to performance measures linked to output, e.g. maximising the equity market value of the company. An NFP organisation has service-related outputs that are difficult to measure in quantitative terms and so it focuses on performance measures linked to input, e.g. minimising the input cost for a given level of output.

Both listed companies and NFP organisations can use a variety of accounting ratios in the context of financial objectives. For example, both types of organisation may use a target return on capital employed, or a target level of income per employee, or a target current ratio.

Comparing and contrasting the financial objectives of a stock exchange listed company and a not-for-profit organisation, therefore, shows that while significant differences can be found, there is a considerable amount of common ground in terms of financial objectives.

ACCA marking scheme			
			Marks
(a)	Rights issue price		1
	Theoretical ex rights price		2
			___
		Maximum	3
			___
(b)	Nominal value of bonds redeemed		1
	Interest saved on redeemed bonds		1
	Earnings per share after redemption		1
	Current price/earnings ratio		1
	Revised share price		1
	Comment on acceptability to shareholders		1–2
	Comment on constant price/earnings ratio		1–2
			___
		Maximum	7
			___
(c)	Maximising shareholder wealth		2–3
	Maximising cash income		2–3
	Controlling spending with budgets		2–3
	Value for money		2–3
	Other relevant discussion		2–3
			___
		Maximum	10
			___
Total			**20**
			___

Examiner's comments

There were a number of points that could have been discussed, including the finance director's view that the dividend per share 'should be increased by 20% in order to make the company more attractive to equity investors'. Increases in dividends usually lag behind increases in earnings and depend on the dividend policy of a company. It is debatable whether increasing the dividend per share makes a company more attractive to investors. It could be argued, for example, that its existing dividend clientele are satisfied by its current dividend policy. It could also be argued that making a dividend decision without also considering investment and financing needs is foolish.

Candidates were asked in part (a) to calculate the theoretical ex rights price per share and most answers did this correctly.

Part (b) required candidates to calculate and discuss whether using the rights issue cash to buy back loan notes was acceptable to shareholders, commenting on the belief that the price/earnings ratio would remain constant. Good answers calculated the current price/earnings ratio: the nominal value of the loan notes redeemed ($80 million); the nominal value of the loan notes remaining in the statement of financial position ($45 million); the reduction in the interest payable each year (down from $10 million to $3.6 million); the revised earnings and earnings per share values; and the revised share price (by multiplying the revised earnings per share by the current price/earnings ratio). The revised share price could then be compared with the theoretical ex rights price per share to assess the effect on shareholder wealth (a capital loss).

Answers lost marks to the extent that they did not achieve the elements described above. Answers that did not calculate the effect of redeeming $80 million of loan notes could discuss in general terms only whether buying back loan notes would be acceptable to shareholders. Many answers used the assumption of a constant price/earnings ratio, together with the theoretical ex rights price per share, to calculate implied earnings per share figure, but this serves no purpose and does not take account of buying back loan notes. Although the question said that the company planned to use the rights issue funds to pay off some of its debt, some answers assumed incorrectly that all of the loan notes were to be bought (using reserves to finance the difference, even though these are not cash).

Some answers calculated a revised price/earnings ratio using the theoretical ex rights price per share, but the statement that the price/earnings ratio was expected to remain constant meant that a revised share price could be calculated from the revised earnings per share. The theoretical ex rights price per share is the share price before the rights issue funds are used: once these funds are used, the share price will change, so the theoretical ex rights price per share cannot be used to calculate a revised price/earnings ratio.

Part (c) asked candidates to compare and contrast the financial objectives of a stock exchange listed company and a not-for-profit (NFP) organisation. In general, the answers to this part of question 4 were often quite weak. One reason for this is that many answers spent a lot of time discussing non-financial objectives, even though the question asked clearly for a discussion of financial objectives. A second reason for this is that many answered showed a general lack of awareness of financial objectives as such: some answers were not able to offer much more than shareholder wealth maximisation and increasing profit as financial objectives. A third reason is that some answers picked up on "compare and contrast" while ignoring financial objectives, and therefore offered a general comparison of the key features or decision areas of the two organisations. For example, the functional areas of the organisations might be compared and contrasted, or their stakeholders, or their personnel. This is not what the question was looking for.

43 NUGFER

Key answer tips

This question combines business finance with financial ratios, interest rates and market efficiency. It is an excellent example of the current examiner's style, especially part (a) where the requirement is deliberately left fairly open. The highlighted words are key phrases that markers are looking for.

(a)

Tutor's top tips

Before starting to answer this section you should think about what sources of finance you can think of, and what might be the deciding factors regarding whether they would be suitable or not. Key to this will be the current financial position of the company (existing gearing levels in particular) and how the company has performed recently. Take your steer from the information provided in the scenario – for every item consider why the examiner might have told you that, and how you can use this in your answer.

Nugfer Co is looking to raise $200m in cash in order to acquire a competitor. Any recommendation as to the source of finance to be used by the company must take account of the recent financial performance of the company, its current financial position and its expected financial performance in the future, presumably after the acquisition has occurred.

Recent financial performance

The recent financial performance of Nugfer Co will be taken into account by potential providers of finance because it will help them to form an opinion as to the quality of the management running the company and the financial problems the company may be facing. Analysis of the recent performance of Nugfer Co gives the following information:

Year	20X3	20X4	20X5	20X6
Operating profit	$41.7m	$43.3m	$50.1m	$56.7m
Net profit margin	34%	34%	32%	30%
Interest coverage ratio	7 times	7 times	4 times	3 times
Revenue growth		3.8%	23.0%	20.9%
Operating profit growth		3.8%	15.7%	13.2%
Finance charges growth		3.3%	101.6%	50.4%
Profit after tax growth		4.0%	1.2%	0.8%

Geometric average growth in revenue = $(189.3/122.6)^{0.33} - 1 = 15.6\%$

Geometric average operating profit growth = $(56.7/41.7)^{0.33} - 1 = 10.8\%$

One positive feature indicated by this analysis is the growth in revenue, which grew by 23% in 20X5 and by 21% in 20X6. Slightly less positive is the growth in operating profit, which was 16% in 20X5 and 13% in 20X6. Both years were significantly better in revenue growth and operating profit growth than 20X4. One query here is why growth in operating profit is so much lower than growth in revenue. Better control of operating and other costs might improve operating profit substantially and decrease the financial risk of Nugfer Co.

The growing financial risk of the company is a clear cause for concern. The interest coverage ratio has declined each year in the period under review and has reached a dangerous level in 20X6. The increase in operating profit each year has clearly been less than the increase in finance charges, which have tripled over the period under review. The reason for the large increase in debt is not known, but the high level of financial risk must be considered in selecting an appropriate source of finance to provide the $200m in cash that is needed.

Current financial position

The current financial position of Nugfer Co will be considered by potential providers of finance in their assessment of the financial risk of the company. Analysis of the current financial position of Nugfer Co shows the following:

Debt/equity ratio = long-term debt/total equity = 100 × (100/221) = 45%

Debt equity/ratio including short-term borrowings = 100 × ((100 + 160)/221) = 118%

The debt/equity ratio based on long-term debt is not particularly high. However, the interest coverage ratio indicated a high level of financial risk and it is clear from the financial position statement that the short-term borrowings of $160m are greater than the long-term borrowings of $100m. In fact, short-term borrowings account for 62% of the debt burden of Nugfer Co. If we include the short-term borrowings, the debt/equity ratio increases to 118%, which is certainly high enough to be a cause for concern. The short-term borrowings are also at a higher interest rate (8%) than the long-term borrowings (6%) and as a result, interest on short-term borrowings account for 68% of the finance charges in the statement of profit or loss.

It should also be noted that the long-term borrowings are bonds that are repayable in 20X8. Nugfer Co needs therefore to plan for the redemption and refinancing of $100m of debt in two years' time, a factor that cannot be ignored when selecting a suitable source of finance to provide the $200m of cash needed.

Recommendation of suitable financing method

There are strong indications that it would be unwise for Nugfer Co to raise the $200m of cash required by means of debt finance, for example the low interest coverage ratio and the high level of gearing.

If no further debt is raised, the interest coverage ratio would improve after the acquisition due to the increased level of operating profit, i.e. (56.7m + 28m)/18.8 = 4.5 times. Assuming that $200m of 8% debt is raised, the interest coverage ratio would fall to ((84.7/(18.8 + 16)) = 2.4 times and the debt/equity ratio would increase to 100 × (260 + 200)/221 = 208%.

If convertible debt were used, the increase in gearing and the decrease in interest coverage would continue only until conversion occurred, assuming that the company's share price increased sufficiently for conversion to be attractive to bondholders. Once conversion occurred, the debt capacity of the company would increase due both to the liquidation of the convertible debt and to the issuing of new ordinary shares to bond holders. In the period until conversion, however, the financial risk of the company as measured by gearing and interest coverage would remain at a very high level.

If Nugfer Co were able to use equity finance, the interest coverage ratio would increase to 4.5 times and the debt/equity ratio would fall to $100 \times (260/(221 + 200))$ = 62%. Although the debt/equity ratio is still on the high side, this would fall if some of the short-term borrowings were able to be paid off, although the recent financial performance of Nugfer Co indicates that this may not be easy to do. The problem of redeeming the current long-term bonds in two years also remains to be solved.

However, since the company has not paid any dividend for at least four years, it is unlikely that current shareholders would be receptive to a rights issue, unless they were persuaded that dividends would be forthcoming in the near future. Acquisition of the competitor may be the only way of generating the cash flows needed to support dividend payments.

A similar negative view could be taken by new shareholders if Nugfer Co were to seek to raise equity finance via a placing or a public issue.

Sale and leaseback of non-current assets could be considered, although the nature and quality of the non-current assets is not known. The financial position statement indicates that Nugfer Co has $300m of non-current assets, $100m of long-term borrowings and $160m of short-term borrowings. Since its borrowings are likely to be secured on some of the existing non-current assets, there appears to be limited scope for sale and leaseback.

Venture capital could also be considered, but it is unlikely that such finance would be available for an acquisition and no business case has been provided for the proposed acquisition.

While combinations of finance could also be proposed, the overall impression is that Nugfer Co is in poor financial health and, despite its best efforts, it may not be able to raise the $200m in cash that it needs to acquire its competitor.

(b) When a new issue of bonds is made by a company, the interest rate on the bonds will be influenced by factors that are specific to the company, and by factors that relate to the economic environment as a whole.

Company-specific factors

The interest rate charged on a new issue of bonds will depend upon such factors as the risk associated with the company and any security offered.

The risk associated with the company will be assessed by considering the ability of the company to meet interest payments in the future, and hence its future cash flows and profitability, as well as its ability to redeem the bond issue on maturity.

Where an issue of new bonds is backed by security, the interest rate charged on the issue will be lower than for an unsecured bond issue. A bond issue will be secured on specific non-current assets such as land or buildings, and as such is referred to as a fixed-charge security.

Economic environment factors

As far as the duration of a new issue of bonds is concerned, the term structure of interest rates suggests that short-term debt is usually cheaper than long-term debt, so that the yield curve slopes upwards with increasing term to maturity. The longer the duration of an issue of new bonds, therefore, the higher will be the interest rate charged. The shape of the yield curve, which can be explained by reference to liquidity preference theory, expectations theory and market segmentation theory, will be independent of any specific company.

The rate of interest charged on a new issue of bonds will also depend on the general level of interest rates in the financial system. This is influenced by the general level of economic activity in a given country, such as whether the economy is in recession (when interest rates tend to fall) or experiencing rapid economic growth (when interest rates are rising as capital availability is decreasing). The general level of interest rates is also influenced by monetary policy decisions taken by the government or the central bank. For example, interest rates may be increased in order to exert downward pressure on demand and hence decrease inflationary pressures in an economy.

Tutorial note

The above answer is longer than would be expected from a candidate under examination conditions.

ACCA marking scheme		
		Marks
(a)	Analysis of recent financial performance	1–3
	Discussion of recent financial performance	1–3
	Analysis of current financial position	1–3
	Discussion of current financial position	1–2
	Consideration of suitable sources of finance	4–6
	Recommendation of suitable source of finance	1
	Maximum	16
(b)	Company-specific factors	2–3
	Economic environment factors	2–3
	Maximum	4
Total		**20**

Examiner's comments

Many students gained good marks on part (b) of this question, while not doing very well on part (a).

In part (a) of this question, candidates were provided with financial information for a company and asked to evaluate suitable methods for it to raise $200 million, using both analysis and critical discussion. Many answers struggled to gain good marks for reasons such as poor understanding of sources of finance, a lack of analysis or errors in analysis, misunderstanding of the financial position and performance of the company, and a shortage of discussion.

The question said that the current assets of the company did not include any cash, but many answers suggested that $121 million of the $200 million needed could be provided from $121 million of retained earnings in the statement of financial position. As the company had no cash, this was of course not possible and shows a misunderstanding of the nature of retained earnings.

Some answers suggested asking the bank to increase the $160 million overdraft to $360 million in order to provide the finance for the $200 million acquisition. Since the acquisition was a long-term investment, short-term finance could not be used under the matching principle. Suggestions of using lease finance were also not appropriate, although discussion of the sale and leaseback of the company's non-current assets was relevant. Some answers discussed business angels, government grants and venture capital, but these sources of finance are not relevant to a $200 million acquisition.

Analysis of the financial information given in the question was needed to support any critical discussion of ways of raising the $200 million required. Some answers gave no analysis or very little analysis and so were quite general in nature, outlining for example the differences between equity finance and debt finance. Errors in ratio calculations were common, highlighting the need for candidates to understand accounting ratio definitions. Four years of profitability information was provided, allowing trends and growth rates to be calculated, although some answers considered only information from the first year and the last year. The information, when analysed, gave a very gloomy picture and indicated that the company would have difficulty raising the cash it needed, whether from debt finance or equity finance. Taking on more debt would cause gearing, interest cover and financial risk to rise to dangerous levels, while existing and potential shareholders would not look favourably on a company that had not paid dividends for four years, especially one whose growth in profitability was on a downward trend.

Part (b) asked candidates to briefly explain the factors that influence the interest rate charged on a new issue of bonds, i.e. traded debt. Good answers discussed such factors as the period to redemption, the risk of the issuing company, the general level of interest rates in the economy, expectations of future inflation, redemption value and so on, and easily gained full marks. Poorer answers did not show understanding of the relationship for a bond between market value, interest rate, period to redemption, redemption value and cost of debt.

44   SPOT CO

Key answer tips

Students should be well equipped with the tools required for the evaluation in part (a). Care needs to be taken when choosing relevant numbers from the scenario to use in the **Workings**.

Part (b) should provide some easy marks for straightforward knowledge on this relatively new part of the syllabus.

(a) In order to evaluate whether Spot Co should use leasing or borrowing, the present value of the cost of leasing is compared with the present value of the cost of borrowing.

Leasing

The lease payments should be discounted using the cost of borrowing of Spot Co. Since taxation must be ignored, the before-tax cost of borrowing must be used. The 7% interest rate of the bank loan can be used here.

The five lease payments will begin at year 0 and the last lease payment will be at the start of year 5, i.e. at the end of year 4. The appropriate annuity factor to use will therefore be 4.387 (1.000 + 3.387).

Present value of cost of leasing = 155,000 × 4.387= $679,985

Borrowing

The purchase cost and the present value of maintenance payments will be offset by the present value of the future scrap value. The appropriate discount rate is again the before-tax cost of borrowing of 7%.

Year	Cash flow	$	7% Discount factor	Present value ($)
0	Purchase	(750,000)	1.000	(750,000)
1 – 5	Maintenance	(20,000)	4.100	(82,000)
5	Scrap value	75,000	0.713	53,475

Present value of cost of borrowing = 750,000 + 82,000 – 53,475 = $778,525

The cheaper source of financing is leasing, since the present value of the cost of leasing is $98,540 less than the present value of the cost of borrowing.

(b) Leasing can act as either a source of short-term or long-term finance.

Short-term leasing offers a solution to the obsolescence problem, whereby rapidly aging assets can decrease competitive advantage. Where keeping up-to-date with the latest technology is essential for business operations, short-term leasing provides equipment on short-term contracts that can usually be cancelled without penalty to the lessee. Short-term leasing can also provide access to skilled maintenance, which might otherwise need to be bought in by the lessee, although there will be a charge for this service.

Long-term leasing spreads the cost of an asset over the majority of the useful life of that asset and means that the business doesn't have to source separate finance to cover the purchase of the asset.

Both short-term and long-term leasing provide access to non-current assets in cases where borrowing may be difficult or even not possible for a company. For example, the company may lack assets to offer as security, or it may be seen as too risky to lend to. Since ownership of the leased asset remains with the lessor, it can be retrieved if lease rental payments are not forthcoming.

(c) Interest (riba) is the predetermined amount received by a provider of finance, over and above the principal amount of finance provided. Riba is absolutely forbidden in Islamic finance. Riba can be seen as unfair from the perspective of the borrower, the lender and the economy. For the borrower, riba can turn a profit into a loss when profitability is low. For the lender, riba can provide an inadequate return when unanticipated inflation arises. In the economy, riba can lead to allocational inefficiency, directing economic resources to sub-optimal investments.

Islamic financial instruments require that an active role be played by the provider of funds, so that the risks and rewards of ownership are shared. In a Mudaraba contract, for example, profits are shared between the partners in the proportions agreed in the contract, while losses are borne by the provider of finance. In a Musharaka contract, profits are shared between the partners in the proportions agreed in the contract, while losses are shared between the partners according to their capital contributions. With Sukuk, certificates are issued which are linked to an underlying tangible asset and which also transfer the risk and rewards of ownership. The underlying asset is managed on behalf of the Sukuk holders.

In a Murabaha contract, payment by the buyer is made on a deferred or instalment basis. Returns are made by the supplier as a mark-up is paid by the buyer in exchange for the right to pay after the delivery date. In an Ijara contract, which is equivalent to a lease agreement, returns are made through the payment of fixed or variable lease rental payments.

ACCA marking scheme			Marks
(a)	Timing of lease payments		1
	Present value of cost of leasing		1
	Present value of maintenance costs		1
	Present value of salvage value		1
	Present value of cost of borrowing		2
	Evaluation of financing choice		1
	Explanation of evaluation of financing method		3
		Maximum	10
(b)	Attractions of leasing as short-term finance source		2–3
	Attractions of leasing as long-term finance source		2–3
		Maximum	5
(c)	Explanation of interest (riba)		1–2
	Explanation of returns on Islamic financial instruments		3–4
		Maximum	5
Total			**20**

45 ECHO CO *Walk in the footsteps of a top tutor*

Key answer tips

The key learning points from this question are the benefits of answering requirements in an order that best suits you as well as the need to take guidance from the specific words used in both the scenario and the requirement itself. The highlighted words are key phrases that markers are looking for.

Tutor's top tips

Start by reading the requirement. Having a good understanding of what is expected from you will allow you to read the scenario more effectively, processing the information as you go. Scribble you thoughts in the margins on what each piece of information could be used for in relation to the requirements.

The first thing that should strike you is this question has 3, very independent requirements. This means you can pick the order in which to tackle them to suit your strengths. The question is very generic and requires little more than regurgitation of knowledge from the syllabus.

Part (c) has the most guidance on the structure and content of your answer. These therefore represent the easiest marks. The layout of the scenario means you can immediately re-read the information on proposal C and then consider what additional information you will need.

The slightly different requirements in part (a) and part (b) is reflected in the mark allocation. In part (a) the requirement is to 'analyse' and 'discuss' compared to 'evaluate' and 'discuss' in part (b). Part (b) will therefore require some further calculations.

In part (a) you need to link back to the scenario where we're told the aim of proposal A is to make the company more attractive to equity investors. A sensible approach is to consider what makes a share attractive. You should immediately highlight the dividend payment, discussion of which would lead on to Modigliani & Miller's theories on dividend policy and efficient markets hypothesis.

(a) Echo Co paid a total dividend of $2 million or 20c per share according to the statement of profit or loss information. An increase of 20% would make this $2.4 million or 24c per share and would reduce dividend cover from 3 times to 2.5 times. It is debatable whether this increase in the current dividend would make the company more attractive to equity investors, who use a variety of factors to inform their investment decisions, not expected dividends alone. For example, they will consider the business and financial risk associated with a company when deciding on their required rate of return.

It is also unclear what objective the finance director had in mind when suggesting a dividend increase. The primary financial management objective is the maximisation of shareholder wealth and if Echo Co is following this objective, the dividend will already be set at an optimal level. From this perspective, a dividend increase should arise from increased maintainable profitability, not from a desire to 'make the company more attractive'. Increasing the dividend will not generate any additional capital for Echo Co, since existing shares are traded on the secondary market.

Furthermore, Miller and Modigliani have shown that, in a perfect capital market, share prices are independent of the level of dividend paid. The value of the company depends upon its income from operations and not on the amount of this income that is paid out as dividends. Increasing the dividend would not make the company more attractive to equity investors, but would attract equity investors who desired the new level of dividend being offered. Current shareholders who were satisfied by the current dividend policy could transfer their investment to a different company if their utility had been decreased.

The proposal to increase the dividend should therefore be rejected, perhaps in favour of a dividend increase in line with current dividend policy.

Tutor's top tips

In part (b), the scenario directs us towards the differences between short term and long-term interest rates. As in part (c) the impact on gearing and interest cover can be highlighted and the lack of any investment opportunity should by highlighted as a problem.

(b) The proposal to raise $15 million of additional debt finance does not appear to be a sensible one, given the current financial position of Echo Co. The company is very highly geared if financial gearing measured on a book value basis is considered. The debt/equity ratio of 150% is almost twice the average of companies similar to Echo Co. This negative view of the financial risk of the company is reinforced by the interest coverage ratio, which at only four times is half that of companies similar to Echo Co.

Raising additional debt would only worsen these indicators of financial risk. The debt/equity ratio would rise to 225% on a book value basis and the interest coverage ratio would fall to 2.7 times, suggesting that Echo Co would experience difficulty in making interest payments.

The proposed use to which the newly-raised funds would be put merits further investigation. Additional finance should be raised when it is needed, rather than being held for speculative purposes. Until a suitable investment opportunity comes along, Echo Co will be paying an opportunity cost on the new finance equal to the difference between the interest rate on the new debt (10%) and the interest paid on short-term investments. This opportunity cost would decrease shareholder wealth. Even if an investment opportunity arises, it is very unlikely that the funds needed would be exactly equal to $15m.

The interest charge in the statement of profit or loss information is $3m while the interest payable on the 8% loan notes is $2.4m (30 × 0.08). It is reasonable to assume that $0.6m of interest is due to an overdraft. Assuming a short-term interest rate lower than the 8% loan note rate – say 6% – implies an overdraft of approximately $10m (0.6/0.06), which is one-third of the amount of the long-term debt. The debt/equity ratio calculated did not include this significant amount of short-term debt and therefore underestimates the financial risk of Echo Co.

The bond issue would be repayable in eight years' time, which is five years after the redemption date of the current loan note issue. The need to redeem the current $30m loan note issue cannot be ignored in the financial planning of the company. The proposal to raise £15m of long-term debt finance should arise from a considered strategic review of the long-term and short-term financing needs of Echo Co, which must also consider redemption or refinancing of the current loan note issue and, perhaps, reduction of the sizeable overdraft, which may be close to, or in excess of, its agreed limit.

In light of the concerns and considerations discussed, the proposal to raise additional debt finance cannot be recommended.

Analysis

Current gearing (debt/equity ratio using book values) = 30/20 = 150%

Revised gearing (debt/equity ratio using book values) = (30 + 15)/20 = 225%

Current interest coverage ratio = 12/3 = 4 times

Additional interest following debt issue = 15m × 0.1 = $1.5m

Revised interest coverage ratio = 12/(3 + 1.5) = 2.7 times

Tutorial note

The industry gearing has been calculated as debt/equity. You must ensure your calculation is consistent with this otherwise an effective comparison could not be made.

Tutor's top tips

To calculate the theoretical ex-rights price (TERP), you will need the current share price, the subscription price and the basis of the issue. All are contained in the paragraph labelled 'Proposal C'. To calculate the amount of finance that would be raised, you also need to know the number of shares to be issued. This can be worked out based on the current number of shares in issue given in the Statement of financial position information. Be careful to read this carefully. There is $5m of share capital but as the nominal value of each share is 50c, this means there are 10m in issue.

Both of these are simple calculations and will most likely attract 1 mark each. This therefore leaves 5 marks for your evaluation and discussion of the proposal. A requirement to 'evaluate' implies some further calculations will be needed, this time relating to gearing and financial risk. Start by reviewing the information given in the scenario and consider what calculations would be both possible and useful. You should identify:

- *Gearing calculations. Whilst you have market values for equity, you only have the book value of debt. To be consistent you should therefore use book values of both to calculate gearing. In order to discuss the proposal, you will need to know the existing gearing and the new gearing under the proposal. Both can be usefully compared to the industry average.*

- *You have also been provided with average data on interest cover. This signals that calculation of current and projected interest cover will be a source of further marks. Some further calculations need to be done by assuming the proceeds from the rights issue are able to earn the same rate of return as existing funds. This will therefore give an estimate of the new level of profitability. These calculations might not seem obvious and are not essential to passing the question.*

When discussing the impact of the proposal on gearing and financial risk it is essential to highlight that there doesn't appear to be a need to raise this finance as there is no plan on how it will be spent.

(c) **Analysis**

Rights issue price = 2.30 × 0.8 = $1.84

Theoretical ex rights price = (1.84 + (2.30 × 4))/5 = $2.21 per share

Number of new shares issued = (5/0.5)/4 = 2.5 million

Cash raised = 1.84 × 2.5m = $4.6 million

Number of shares in issue after rights issue = 10 + 2.5 = 12.5 million

Current gearing (debt/equity ratio using book values) = 30/20 = 150%

Revised gearing (debt/equity ratio using book values) = 30/24.6 = 122%

Current interest coverage ratio = 12/3 = 4 times

Current return on equity (ROE) = 6/20 = 30%

In the absence of any indication as to the return expected on the new funds, we can assume the rate of return will be the same as on existing equity, an assumption consistent with the calculated theoretical ex rights price. After-tax return on the new funds = 4.6m × 0.3 = $1.38 million Before-tax return on new funds = 1.38m × (9/6) = $2.07 million Revised interest coverage ratio = (12 + 2.07)/3 = 4.7 times

The current debt/equity and interest coverage ratios suggest that there is a need to reduce the financial risk of Echo Co. A rights issue would reduce the debt/equity ratio of the company from 150% to 122% on a book value basis, which is 50% higher than the average debt/equity ratio of similar companies. After the rights issue, financial gearing is still therefore high enough to be a cause for concern.

The interest coverage ratio would increase from 4 times to 4.7 times, again assuming that the new funds will earn the same return as existing equity funds. This is still much lower than the average interest coverage ratio of similar companies, which is 8 times. While 4.7 times is a safer level of interest coverage, it is still somewhat on the low side.

No explanation has been offered for the amount to be raised by the rights issue. Why has the Finance Director proposed that $4.6m be raised? If the proposal is to reduce financial risk, what level of financial gearing and interest coverage would be seen as safe by shareholders and other stakeholders? What use would be made of the funds raised? If they are used to redeem debt they will not have a great impact on the financial position of the company, in fact it appears likely that the overdraft is twice as big as the amount proposed to be raised by the rights issue. The refinancing need therefore appears to be much greater than $4.6m. If the funds are to be used for investment purposes, further details of the investment project, its expected return and its level of risk should be considered.

There seems to be no convincing rationale for the proposed rights issue and it cannot therefore be recommended, at least on financial grounds.

ACCA marking scheme		
		Marks
(a)	Discussion of proposal to increase dividend	
		___
		5
		___
(b)	Evaluation of debt finance proposal	3–4
	Discussion of debt finance proposal	4–5
		___
		8
		___
(c)	Theoretical ex rights price per share	1
	Amount of finance raised	1
	Evaluation of rights issue proposal	2–3
	Discussion of rights issue proposal	3–4
		___
		7
		___
Total		**20**
		___

Examiner's comments

Part (a) asked candidates to analyse and discuss a proposal to increase dividend per share. Many candidates calculated correctly the increased dividend per share and then offered very little by way of discussion in order to gain any further marks.

There were a number of points that could have been discussed, including the finance director's view that the dividend per share 'should be increased by 20% in order to make the company more attractive to equity investors'. Increases in dividends usually lag behind increases in earnings and depend on the dividend policy of a company. It is debatable whether increasing the dividend per share makes a company more attractive to investors. It could be argued, for example, that its existing dividend clientele are satisfied by its current dividend policy. It could also be argued that making a dividend decision without also considering investment and financing needs is foolish: paying an increased dividend and then borrowing to meet investment plans is not advisable for a company as highly geared as the one under consideration here. Other points are discussed in the suggested answer to this question.

Part (b) asked for evaluation and discussion of a proposal to make a $15m bond issue and to invest the funds raised on a short-term basis until a suitable investment opportunity arose. Candidates were expected to be aware that finance should be raised in order to meet a specific need and that investing long-term funds on a short-term basis would incur an unnecessary net interest cost. In this case, a highly-geared company would be choosing to increase its gearing and financial risk, without the prospect of investing the funds in a project offering returns greater than the increased financing cost.

The sector average debt/equity ratio (D/E) was provided, but many candidates chose to calculate capital gearing (D/(D + E)) in the mistaken belief that this was the debt to equity ratio. Comparison with the sector average gearing was therefore pointless, since the gearing ratios were on a different basis. Some candidates also calculated incorrectly the interest coverage, dividing interest into profit before tax or profit after tax, rather than into profit before interest and tax.

There were some lucid discussions of the dangers attached to the proposal to make a bond issue and these gained high marks.

It was surprising to see many candidates attempting to calculate the cost of debt (internal rate of return) of the bond issue. The bonds were to be issued and redeemed at nominal value and so their cost of debt was the same as their interest rate, as these unnecessary calculations confirmed (where they were made correctly).

In part (c), candidates were asked to calculate the theoretical ex rights price per share and the amount of finance to be raised by a proposed rights issue, which was intended to reduce gearing and financial risk.

Many candidates were able to calculate the theoretical ex rights price and the finance raised, and went on to calculate the effect of the rights issue on the gearing of the company. Some candidates mistakenly assumed that the proceeds of the right issue would be used to redeem some of the existing debt, but the question did not specify this and in practice this might not be possible. Very few candidates recognised that, just as with the proposal to make a bond issue, there had been no evaluation of the funding needs of the company. Why raise $4.6m? Why not $10m? What were the rights issue funds going to be used for? A more concrete plan than raising cash to reduce gearing was needed if shareholder wealth was going to be maximised.

46 PAVLON

Key answer tips

This is a difficult question that requires some imaginative thinking in order to tackle efficiently. The idea of calculating the dividend payout ratio for part (a) is one which seems logical when you review the answer but might not necessarily have occurred to you when attempting the question under timed conditions.

Part (b) is a more clear cut application of the dividend valuation model with the change in growth rate being the only complication. The highlighted words are key phrases that markers are looking for.

(a) **(i)** The first step is to try to determine exactly what is Pavlon's current dividend policy.

Year prior to listing	Number of shares	EPS	Growth over previous year	Dividend per share	Payout ratio
5	21,333,333	8.44¢	–	3.6¢	42.7%
4	21,333,333 (Note 2)	11.25¢	33%	4.8¢	42.7%
3	26,666,667	14.44¢	28%	6.16¢	42.7%
2	26,666,667	15.38¢	6%	6.56¢	42.7%
1	26,666,667 (Note 1)	16.69¢	8.5%	7.12¢	42.7%
Current	40,000,000	13.75¢ (est)	–18%	5.5¢ (proposed)	40%

Note 1 $\dfrac{40,000,000}{1.5} = 26,666,667$

Note 2 $\dfrac{26,666,667}{1.25} = 21,333,333$

Pavlon appears to be adopting a policy of a fixed payout ratio of 42.7% pa over the five year period. In general, such a policy can lead to wide variations in dividends per share. In Pavlon's case over the last five years earnings have been rising and a continual (though declining) growth in dividend has resulted.

If it is believed that share price is affected by dividend policy then these fluctuations in dividends and the decline in growth could depress equity value.

Most listed companies attempt to adopt a stable or rising level of dividend per share even in the face of fluctuating earnings. This approach is taken in order to maintain investor confidence. If Pavlon were to continue with its present policy and earnings were to decline the resultant dividend could have serious repercussions for share price.

(ii)   The proposed final dividend gives a total for the year of 5.5¢. This is a significant fall in dividend per share and a small decline in the dividend payout ratio. In the absence of market imperfections such as taxation and transaction costs, it could be argued that dividend policy has no impact on shareholder wealth. It is the firm's future earnings stream that is of importance, not the way in which it is split between dividend and retentions.

However, once market imperfections are introduced dividend policy can be shown to have an impact on investor wealth.

Private individuals may pay income tax at a higher rate than capital gains tax due to available CGT annual exemptions. They would therefore prefer retentions to distributions. Any income required could be generated by selling shares to manufacture 'home made' dividends (note however the problem of transaction costs).

If the reduction in dividend payout were carefully explained it might therefore be acceptable to wealthy individuals.

The tax position of institutional shareholders varies and so therefore will their attitude to dividend policy. Most, however, require a steady flow of income to meet their day-to-day obligations (pensions, insurance claims etc.) and may not wish (or be able) to generate homemade dividends.

It could be argued that new investors have bought shares in Pavlon with full knowledge of its dividend policy and should therefore not be surprised if it sticks to a policy of a 40% payout. However, many shareholders might expect it to change its policy now that it has obtained a listing.

A further factor to consider is the informational content of dividends. The proposed dividend cut might be seen as a signal of poor earnings in the future and lead to investors of either group selling shares.

Overall, there is no conclusive evidence on what makes for an optimal dividend policy. Pavlon should however consider the tax position of its investors and the potential reaction of the market to a cut in dividend.

(b) If the company's profits and dividends are expected to increase initially by 15% pa then investors will expect this year's dividend to be 7.12¢ × 1.15 = 8.188¢.

Value of first three years' dividend

Year	Dividend			PV factor 12%	Present value
Current	7.12 × 1.15	=	8.188	0.893	7.312
2	8.188 × 1.15	=	9.416	0.797	7.505
3	9.416 × 1.15	=	10.829	0.712	7.710
					–––––––
					22.527
					–––––––

Note for simplicity we assume that the current dividend is one year hence.

Value of dividends years 4 – ∞

$$= \frac{d(1 + g)}{i - g} = \frac{10.829(1.08)}{0.12 - 0.08} = 292.383$$

This gives the value of the perpetuity as at year 3. To obtain year 0 values we must discount back.

292.383 × 0.712 = 208.2

Value of share at time 0 = 22.527 + 208.2 = 231¢

Since the current market value of Pavlon's shares is $78m/40m = $1.95 the share appears to be undervalued.

47 ARWIN

Key answer tips

Part (a) should be straightforward, except that you need to be careful with the calculation of the fixed costs in the cost of sales. These are not expected to rise next year, and so should be calculated using the current year figures. For part (b), the question does not state how financial gearing or operational gearing should be measured: there are different methods of calculation. Make clear the method of calculation you are using. (The solution here gives two methods of measuring financial gearing and three methods of measuring operational gearing, but your answer only needs one of each.) For part (c), you need to consider the link between operating gearing and financial gearing as measures of risk. The highlighted words are key phrases that markers are looking for.

(a) The forecast statements of profit or loss are as follows:

	Debt finance $000	Equity finance $000
Sales revenue (50,000 × 1.12)	56,000	56,000
Variable cost of sales (85% × sales)	28,560	28,560
Fixed cost of sales (15% × 30,000)	4,500	4,500
Gross profit	22,940	22,940
Administration costs (14,000 × 1.05)	14,700	14,700
Profit before interest and tax	8,240	8,240
Interest (see working)	800	300
Profit before tax	7,440	7,940
Taxation at 30%	2,232	2,382
Profit after tax	5,208	5,558
Note: Dividends paid (60%)	3,125	3,335
Net change in equity (retained profit)	2,083	2,223

Working

Interest under debt financing = $300,000 + ($5,000,000 × 0.10) = $800,000.

(b) Financial gearing

If financial gearing is measured as the debt: equity ratio:

Using debt/equity ratio:	Current	Debt finance	Equity finance
Debt	2,500	7,500	2,500
Share capital and reserves	22,560	24,643	29,783
Debt/equity ratio (%)	11.1	30.4	8.4

Workings:

Share capital and reserves (debt finance) = 22,560 + 2,083 = $24,643

Share capital and reserves (equity finance) = 22,560 + 5,000 + 2,223 = $29,783.

If financial gearing is measured as the ratio of debt capital to total capital:

Using capital (total) gearing:	Current	Debt finance	Equity finance
Debt	2,500	7,500	2,500
Total long-term capital	25,060	32,143	32,283
Capital (total) gearing (%)	10.0	23.3	7.7

Operational gearing:

If operational gearing is measured as the ratio of fixed costs to total costs:

Using fixed costs/total costs:	Current	Debt finance	Equity finance
Fixed costs	18,500	19,200	19,200
Total costs	44,000	47,760	47,760
Operational gearing (%)	42.0%	40.2%	40.2%

Total costs are assumed to consist of cost of sales plus administration costs.

If operational gearing is measured as the ratio of fixed costs to variable costs:

Using fixed costs/variable costs:	Current	Debt finance	Equity finance
Fixed costs	18,500	19,200	19,200
Variable costs	25,500	28,560	28,560
Operational gearing (%)	0.73	0.67	0.67

If operational gearing is measured as the ratio of contribution to profit before interest and tax (PBIT):

Using contribution/PBIT	Current	Debt finance	Equity finance
Contribution	24,500	27,440	27,440
PBIT	6,000	8,240	8,240
Operational gearing	4.1	3.3	3.3

Contribution is sales revenue minus the variable cost of sales.

Interest cover:

	Current	Debt finance	Equity finance
Profit before interest and tax	6,000	8,240	8,240
Debt interest	300	800	300
Interest cover	20	10.3	27.5

Earnings per share:

	Current	Debt finance	Equity finance
Profit after tax	3,990	5,208	5,558
Number of shares	10,000	10,000	11,250
Earnings per share (cents)	39.9	52.1	49.4

Comment:

The debt finance proposal leads to the largest increase in earnings per share, but results in an increase in financial gearing and a decrease in interest cover. Whether these changes in financial gearing and interest cover are acceptable depends on the attitude of both investors and managers to the new level of financial risk; a comparison with sector averages would be helpful in this context. The equity finance proposal leads to a decrease in financial gearing and an increase in interest cover. The expansion leads to a decrease in operational gearing, whichever measure of operational gearing is used, indicating that fixed costs have decreased as a proportion of total costs.

(c)   As operational gearing increases, a business becomes more sensitive to changes in sales revenue and the general level of economic activity, and profit before interest becomes more volatile. From this perspective, operational gearing is a measure of business risk.

Financial risk in the context of this question can be described as the possibility of a company experiencing changes in the level of its distributable earnings as a result of the need to make interest payments on debt finance. The earnings volatility of companies in the same business will therefore depend not only on business risk, but also on the proportion of debt finance each company has in its capital structure.

It is likely that a business with high operational gearing will have low financial gearing, and a business with high financial gearing will have low operational gearing. This is because managers will be concerned to avoid excessive levels of total risk, i.e. the sum of business risk and financial risk. A business with a combination of high operational gearing and high financial gearing clearly runs an increased risk of experiencing liquidity problems, making losses and becoming insolvent.

48   AMH CO

Key answer tip

Part (a) requires some standard WACC Workings but care needs to be taken to give a clear layout as there are several stages involved. Similarly, the key to answering part (b) is to set out the steps clearly and logically. This part of the question involves no application so could have been attempted first for some easier marks. It is important to be guided by the mark allocation as to the length of your discussion.

The highlighted words are key phrases that markers are looking for.

(a)   Cost of equity

The geometric average dividend growth rate in recent years:

$(D_0/D_{n \text{ years ago}})^{1/n} - 1$

$(36.3/30.9)^{1/4} - 1 = 1.041 - 1 = 0.041$ or 4.1% per year

Using the dividend growth model:

$Ke = D_0 (1 + g)/P_0 + g$

$Ke = [(36.3 \times 1.041)/470] + 0.041 = 0.080 + 0.041 = 0.121$ or 12.1%

Cost of preference shares

As the preference shares are not redeemable:

$Kp = D_0/P_0$

$Kp = 0.04/0.40 = 0.1 = 10\%$

Cost of debt of loan notes

The annual after-tax interest payment is $7 \times 0.7 = \$4.9$ per loan note.

Using linear interpolation:

Year	Cash flow	$	5% DF	PV ($)	4% DF	PV ($)
0	Market price	(104.50)	1.000	(104.50)	1.000	(104.5)
1 – 6	Interest	4.9	5.076	24.87	5.242	25.69
6	Redemption	105	0.746	78.33	0.790	82.95
				(1.30)		4.14

After-tax cost of debt = $4 + [((5 - 4) \times 4.14)/(4.14 + 1.30)] = 4 + 0.76 = 4.8\%$

Cost of debt of bank loan

If the bank loan is assumed to be perpetual (irredeemable), the after-tax cost of debt of the bank loan will be its after-tax interest rate, i.e. $4\% \times 0.7 = 2.8\%$ per year.

Market values

Number of ordinary shares = $4,000,000/$0.5 = 8 million shares

	$000
Equity: 8m × 4.70 =	37,600
Preference shares: 3m × 0.4 =	1,200
Redeemable loan notes: 3m × 104.5/100 =	3,135
Bank loan (book value used)	1,000
Total value of AMH Co	42,935

WACC calculation

WACC = [Ve/(Ve + Vd + Vp)] × ke + [Vp/(Ve + Vd + Vp)] × kp + [Vd/(Ve + Vd + Vp)] × kd

WACC = [37,600/42,935] × 12.1 + [1,200/42,935] × 10 + [3,135/42,935] × 4.8 + [1,000/42,935] × 2.8 = 11.3%

(b) The capital asset pricing model (CAPM) assumes that investors hold diversified portfolios, so that unsystematic risk has been diversified away. Companies using the CAPM to calculate a project-specific discount rate are therefore concerned only with determining the minimum return that must be generated by an investment project as compensation for its systematic risk.

The CAPM is useful where the business risk of an investment project is different from the business risk of the investing company's existing business operations. In such a situation, one or more proxy companies are identified that have similar business risk to the investment project. The equity beta of the proxy company represents the systematic risk of the proxy company, and reflects both the business risk of the proxy company's business operations and the financial risk arising from the proxy company's capital structure.

Since the investing company is only interested in the business risk of the proxy company, the proxy company's equity beta is 'ungeared' to remove the effect of its capital structure. 'Ungearing' converts the proxy company's equity beta into an asset beta, which represents business risk alone. The asset betas of several proxy companies can be averaged in order to remove any small differences in business operations.

The asset beta can then be 'regeared', giving an equity beta whose systematic risk takes account of the financial risk of the investing company as well as the business risk of an investment project. Both ungearing and regearing use the weighted average beta formula, which equates the asset beta with the weighted average of the equity beta and the debt beta.

The project-specific equity beta resulting from the regearing process can then be used to calculate a project-specific cost of equity using the CAPM. This can be used as the discount rate when evaluating the investment project with a discounted cash (DCF) flow investment appraisal method such as net present value or internal rate of return. Alternatively, the project-specific cost of equity can be used in calculating a project-specific weighted average cost of capital, which can also be used in a DCF evaluation.

ACCA marking scheme		
		Marks
(a)	Calculation of historic dividend growth rate	1
	Calculation of cost of equity using DGM	2
	Calculation of cost of preference shares	1
	Calculation of after-tax interest payment on bond	1
	Setting up linear interpolation calculation	1
	Calculation of after-tax cost of debt of bond	1
	Calculation of after-tax cost of debt of bank loan	1
	Calculation of market values	2
	Calculation of WACC	2
	Maximum	12
(b)	Ungearing proxy company equity beta	1–2
	Averaging and regearing asset betas	1–2
	Project-specific cost of equity using CAPM	1–2
	Project-specific WACC	1–2
	Appropriate reference to business risk	1
	Appropriate reference to financial risk	1
	Maximum	8
Total		20

Examiner's comments

Candidates were asked here to calculate the market value weighted average cost of capital (WACC) of a company. Most candidates did well on this question.

As the question asked for market values to be used, no marks were given to using book values as weights. Most candidates calculated market values correctly for ordinary shares, preference shares and loan notes, although some candidates forgot that the loan note market price related to a nominal value per loan note of $100.

Some candidates incorrectly omitted the long-term bank loan from the WACC calculation. Although the bank loan had no market value, its book value could be used instead and due to its significance as a long-term source of finance in this case, it had to be included in the WACC calculation.

The historical dividend growth rate needed to be calculated for use in the dividend growth model (DGM) and some candidates had difficulty here, using either the wrong dividend or the wrong base period. Most candidates were able to calculate the cost of equity using the DGM and where this was not the case, a lack of understanding was usually in evidence.

Most candidates calculated the cost of preference shares correctly, although some candidates lost marks by making it an after-tax value. Since preference shares pay a dividend, which is a distribution of after-tax profit, there is no tax effect to consider.

Most candidates calculated the cost of debt of the loan notes either correctly or reasonably well. Errors that were made in the internal rate of return calculation included:

– Redemption at nominal value rather than at a 5% premium to nominal value.

– Using nominal value as the purchase price of the loan note rather than market value.

– Treating the purchase price as income and interest and redemption value as expenditure.

- Using the before-tax interest payment in the calculation instead of the after-tax interest payment.

- Interpolating when the calculated net present values called for extrapolation.

Some candidates used the before-tax interest rate on the bank loan as its cost of debt, when the after-tax interest rate should have been used. Alternatively (with explanation), the after-tax cost of debt of the loan notes could have been used as the cost of debt of the bank loan.

Part (b) asked candidates to discuss how the capital asset pricing model (CAPM) could be used to calculate a project-specific cost of capital. The requirement gave a strong hint as to how this might be done by requiring the discussion to refer to systematic risk, business risk and financial risk.

Answers to this question were of variable quality. The key concept here is risk and better answers addressed the following points.

- Related project risk to the business risk of the proxy company.

- Discussed the need to un-gear the equity beta of the proxy company to an asset beta, in order to remove the effect of its financial risk element.

- Discussed the need to re-gear the asset beta to an equity beta, in order to reflect the financial risk of the investing company.

- Noted the need to use the CAPM to calculate a project-specific cost of equity.

- Discussed how the final step would be in calculating a project-specific WACC.

Weaker answers limited themselves to saying something about each of the three kinds of risk mentioned in the question requirement, and saying little about how to calculate a project-specific cost of capital.

Definitions of business risk and financial risk were often quite vague. In the context of the question, both business risk and financial risk relate the variability of returns to the shareholder, since the CAPM calculates the cost of equity. Business risk relates to the variability of shareholder returns due to operational factors, which are factors that influence profit before interest and tax (PBIT). Financial risk relates to the variability of shareholder returns due to how a company finances its operations, which affects the relationship between profit before tax and PBIT. Business risk can be measured by operational gearing, while financial risk can be measured by statement of financial position gearing or by interest cover. When risk is seen from this perspective, the CAPM makes much more sense as a way of calculating the cost of equity.

49 **GTK INC** *Walk in the footsteps of a top tutor*

Key answer tip

Both parts (a) and (b) are relatively straightforward investment appraisal calculations that shouldn't pose many problems. In part (c) it is essential that you read the requirement carefully. As you have to make a recommendation you must ensure any advantages or disadvantages you note are relevant to the scenario given. The highlighted words are key phrases that markers are looking for.

(a)   Expected net present value of Proposed 1

Tutor's top tips

It's worthwhile giving some quick consideration to the best way to layout your answer to this part of the requirement. A columnar format, like that presented here, will often be the most efficient and will reduce the amount of information you need to write more than once. This is particularly important here since your answer to part (i) will naturally lead into your answer to part (ii).

Don't forget the requirement to comment on your findings. In situation involving expected values, your comments should generally focus on the reliability of the probability estimates and the risk involved (look at the variability between the best result and the worst).

	Scenario 1	Scenario 2	Scenario 3
Number of sunny days	100	125	150
Saving ($/day)	700	700	700
Annual saving ($)	70,000	87,500	105,000
Costs	(24,000)	(24,000)	(24,000)
Net annual savings	46,000	63,500	81,000
Present value of net savings at 10%	460,000	635,000	810,000
Investment	500,000	500,000	500,000
Net present value	(40,000)	135,000	310,000
Probability	30%	60%	10%

Expected net present value = (−40,000 × 0.3) + (135,000 × 0.6) + (310,000 × 0.1) = $100,000

The ENPV is $100,000 so if the investment is evaluated on this basis, it is financially acceptable. In reaching a decision, however, the company should consider that there is a 30% chance of making a loss. This may be seen as an unacceptably high risk. Furthermore, the number of sunny days each year will not be constant, as assumed here, and may or may not be exactly 100, 125 or 150 days. It is possible the net present values of Scenarios 1 and 3 represent extremes in terms of expectations, and that the net present value of Scenario 2 may be most useful as representing the most likely outcome, even on a joint probability basis. It is also worth noting that inflation has not been taken into account and that the ever-increasing cost of energy may make the proposed investment much more financially attractive if it were factored into the analysis.

Workings

Present values must be calculated with the before-tax cost of capital of 10%, since before-tax cash flows are being evaluated here. The present value of a perpetuity is found by dividing the constant annual cash flow by the cost of capital.

Present value of net savings, Scenario 1 = 46,000/0.10 = $460,000

Present value of net savings, Scenario 2 = 63,500/0.10 = $635,000

Present value of net savings, Scenario 3 = 81,000/0.10 = $810,000

Tutor's top tips

You are asked how equity finance or traded debt might be raised and will therefore need to discuss the different methods of issuing shares (rights issue, and placing being the most suitable here) and different things to consider when issuing debt.

(b) GTK Inc is a company with a small overdraft and no long-term debt. The $1.1 million could be raised as follows:

Equity finance

The equity financing choices available to GTK Inc are a rights issue or a placing.

Rights issue

In this method of raising new equity finance, new shares are offered to existing shareholders pro rata to their existing shareholdings, meeting the requirements of company law in terms of shareholders' pre-emptive rights. Since GTK Inc has several million dollars of shareholders' funds, it may be able to raise $1.1 million through a rights issue, but further investigation will be needed to determine if this is possible. Factors to consider in reaching a decision will include

- the number of shareholders, the type of shareholders (institutional shareholders may be more willing to subscribe than small shareholders)
- whether a recent rights issue has been made
- the recent and expected financial performance of GTK Inc, and
- the effect of a rights issue on the company's cost of capital.

A rights issue would not necessarily disturb the existing balance of ownership and control between shareholders. Approximately half of the finance needed is for a permanent investment and the permanent nature of equity finance would match this.

Placing

This way of raising equity finance involves allocating large amounts of ordinary shares with a small number of institutional investors. Existing shareholders will need to agree to waive their pre-emptive rights for a placing to occur, as it entails issuing new shares to new shareholders. The existing balance of ownership and control will therefore be changed by a placing. Since GTK Inc is a listed company, it is likely that a significant percentage of its issued ordinary share capital will be in public hands and the effect of a placing on this fraction will need to be considered. There may be a change in shareholder expectations after the placing, depending on the extent to which institutional investors are currently represented among existing shareholders, but since the company is listed there is likely to be a significant institutional representation.

Traded debt

A new issue of traded debt could be redeemable or irredeemable, secured or unsecured, fixed rate or floating rate, and may perhaps be convertible. Deep discount bonds and zero coupon bond are also a possibility, but much rarer. The effect of an issue of debt on the company's cost of capital should also be considered.

Security

Bonds may be secured on assets in order to reduce the risk of the bond from an investor point of view. Fixed charge debt is secured on specified non-current assets, such as land or buildings, while floating charge debt is secured on all assets or on a particular class of assets. In the event of default, holders of secured debt can take action to recover their investment, for example by appointing a receiver or by enforcing the sale of particular assets.

Redemption

Irredeemable corporate debt is very rare and a new issue of traded debt by GTK Inc would be redeemable, i.e. repayable on a specified future date. The project life of two of the proposed capital investments suggests that medium-term debt would be appropriate.

Fixed rate and floating rate

Fixed rate debt gives a predictable annual interest payment and, in terms of financial risk, makes the company immune to changes in the general level of interest rates. If interest rates are currently low, GTK Inc could lock into these low rates until its new debt issue needs to be redeemed. Conversely, if interest rates are currently high and expected to fall in the future, GTK Inc could issue floating rate debt rather than fixed rate debt, in the expectation that its interest payments would decrease as interest rates fell.

Cost of capital

GTK Inc has no long-term debt and only a small overdraft. Since debt is cheaper than equity in cost of capital terms, the company could reduce its overall cost of capital by issuing traded debt. A decrease in the overall cost of capital could benefit the shareholders in terms of an increase in the market value of the company, and an increase in the number of financially acceptable investment projects.

50 TFR

Key answer tips

Provided you have carefully read the details of the scenario, the calculations in part (a) should be relatively uncomplicated. Part (b) requires you to be more practical. The key element in part (b) is the implications for cash flow. An estimate of this would therefore be useful. The highlighted words are key phrases that markers are looking for.

(a) **Statement of profit or loss for TFR for the five-year period**

Year	Current	Year 1	Year 2	Year 3	Year 4	Year 5
	$	$	$	$	$	$
Sales revenue	210,000	255,000	300,000	345,000	390,000	390,000
Expenses	168,000	204,000	240,000	276,000	312,000	312,000
Net profit	42,000	51,000	60,000	69,000	78,000	78,000
Interest	2,000	11,000	8,750	6,500	4,250	2,000
Profit before tax	40,000	40,000	51,250	62,500	73,750	76,000
Tax	10,000	10,000	12,813	15,625	18,438	19,000
Profit after tax	30,000	30,000	38,438	46,875	55,313	57,000
Finance						
Dividend	15,000	15,000	19,219	23,438	27,656	28,500
Retained profit	15,000	15,000	19,219	23,438	27,656	28,500
Equity finance	200,000	215,000	234,219	257,656	285,313	313,813
Debt finance	Nil	75,000	50,000	25,000	Nil	Nil
Ratios						
Interest cover (times)	21.0	4.6	6.9	10.6	18.4	39
Debt/equity (%)	Nil	35	21	10	Nil	Nil
ROE (%)	15	14	16	18	19	18
ROCE (%)	21	18	21	24	27	25
ROCE (%)*	19	16	20	23	26	23

*Including the existing and continuing overdraft in capital employed.

Workings

Annual interest (assuming the continuing overdraft is maintained at the current level)

Year 1 interest payment = 100,000 × 0.09 = 9,000 + 2,000 = $11,000

Year 2 interest payment = 75,000 × 0.09 = 6,750 + 2,000 = $8,750

Year 3 interest payment = 50,000 × 0.09 = 4,500 + 2,000 = $5,500

Year 4 interest payment = 25,000 × 0.09 = 2,250 + 2,000 = $4,250

Year 5 interest payment = $2,000

Note: in year 5, we have assumed that no further growth in sales revenue occurs after the fourth year.

(b)   Financial implications for TFR of accepting bank loan

Cash flow

A key consideration is whether TFR will be able to meet the annual payments of interest and capital. It is assumed, in preparing a cash flow forecast, that there is no difference between profit and cash, and that inflation can be ignored. The annual cash surplus after meeting interest and tax payments is therefore assumed to be equal to retained profit.

Year	1	2	3	4
Net change in equity (retained profit)	15,000	19,219	23,438	27,656
Capital repayment	25,000	25,000	25,000	25,000
Net cash flow	(10,000)	(5,781)	(1,563)	2,656

TFR is clearly not able to meet the annual capital repayments as things stand.

Dividend policy

One way to try to address this would be to change the dividend policy.

It appears that TFR have maintained a policy of paying out a constant proportion of profit after tax as dividends. One possible course of action is to cut its dividend now and then increase it in the future as profitability allows. Since TFR is owner-managed, a change in dividend policy may be possible, depending of course on the extent to which the owner or owners rely on dividend income.

The annual cash flow shortfall is less than the annual dividend payment, so a change in dividend policy would probably allow the loan to be accepted.

Year	1	2	3	4
Profit after tax	30,000	38,438	46,875	55,313
Capital repayment	25,000	25,000	25,000	25,000
Available funds	5,000	13,438	21,875	30,313

It is useful to consider key financial information after the loan has been paid off.

Financial risk

The effect on financial risk of taking on the loan can be examined. If the interest and capital payments are kept up, financial risk will be lower than its current level at the end of four years, all things being equal. Interest cover increases from its current level after five years, from 21 times to 39 times, but is on the low side at the end of the first year (4.6 times), although an improved level is reached at the end of the second year (6.9 times), with further increases in subsequent years. The debt/equity ratio peaks at 35% at the end of the first year and falls rapidly thereafter, at no time looking dangerous, and TFR returns to its current ungeared position after five years. The bank, as provider of debt finance, would be interested in the trend in these ratios, as well as in the ongoing cash flow position.

Both return on equity (ROE) and return on capital employed (ROCE) improve with growth in sales revenue, but are lower than current levels in the first and second years following taking on the loan. At the end of five years ROE has improved to 18% from 15% and ROCE from 19% to 23%. Interest and capital payments would not increase with inflation.

Provided TFR can meet the interest and capital repayments, business expansion using debt finance may be financially feasible. However, this analysis has ignored any potential pressure for reduction or repayment of the overdraft. An average overdraft of $20,000 is quite large for a company with an annual sales revenue of $210,000 and therefore cannot be ignored in any assessment of financial risk. TFR may therefore consider asking for a longer repayment period, with lower annual capital repayments, if it plans to reduce the size of the overdraft or if it is concerned about future cash flow problems.

51   GXG CO

Key answer tips

This is a nice, relatively simple business finance question. It is vital to note that the first two requirements ask the student to comment on their findings.

The highlighted words are key phrases that markers are looking for.

(a)   The dividend growth model can give a value of GXG Co at the end of the second year of not paying dividends, based on the dividends paid from the end of the third year onwards. The company has 10 million shares in issue ($5 million/50 cents nominal value) and so the total dividend proposed at the end of the third year will be $2.5 million (25 cents per share × 10m). If these dividends increase by 4% per year in subsequent years, their capital value at the end of the second year will be:

2.5/(0.09 – 0.04) = $50 million

The dividend valuation model value (the capital value of the dividends at year 0) will be:

Using the discount factor $(1 + r)^{-n}$

50×1.09^{-2} = $42.1 million

The current present value of dividends to shareholders, using the existing 3% dividend growth rate:

(1.6 × 1.03)/(0.09 – 0.03) = $27.5 million

The proposal will increase shareholder wealth by 42.1 – 27.5 = $14.6 million and so is likely to be acceptable to shareholders.

Examiner note:

Calculations on a per share basis could also be used to evaluate the effect of the proposal on shareholder wealth).

(b)   Increase in before-tax income = 0.18 × 3.2m = $576,000

Revised operating profit = 576,000 + 3,450,000 = $4,026,000

Interest on new debt = 3,200,000 × 0.06 = $192,000

Revised interest = 192,000 + 200,000 = $392,000

Revised profit before tax = 4,026,000 − 392,000 = $3,634,000

Revised profit after tax = 3,634,000 × 0.8 = $2,907,200

Revised earnings per share = 100 × (2,907,200/10,000,000) = 29.1 cents per share

Earnings per share would increase by 3.1 cents per share.

Current interest cover = 3,450,000/200,000 = 17 times

Revised interest cover = 4,026,000/392,000 = 10 times

The increase in earnings per share would be welcomed by shareholders, but further information on the future of the company following the investment in research and development would be needed for a more comprehensive answer. The decrease in interest cover is not serious and the increase in financial risk is unlikely to upset shareholders.

(c)   Traded bonds are debt securities issued onto the capital market in exchange for cash received by the issuing company. The cash raised must be repaid on the redemption date, usually between five and fifteen years after issue. Bonds are usually secured on non-current assets of the issuing company, which reduces the risk to the lender. In the event of default on interest payments by the borrower, the bond holders can appoint a receiver to sell the assets and recover their investment. Interest paid on the bonds is tax-deductible, which reduces the cost of debt to the issuing company. Provided the borrower continues to pay the interest, however, bond finance is a low risk financing choice by the issuer.

There are a number of differences between bond finance and a new equity issue via a placing that will influence the choice between them. Equity finance does not need to be redeemed, since ordinary shares are truly permanent finance. While bond interest is usually fixed, the return to shareholders in the form of dividends depends on the dividend decision made by the directors of a company, and so these returns can increase, decrease or be passed. Furthermore, since dividends are a distribution of after-tax profit, they are not tax-deductible like interest payments, and so equity finance is not tax-efficient like debt finance.

Venture capital is found in specific financing situations, i.e. where risk finance is needed, for example, in a management buyout. Both equity and debt finance can be part of a venture capital financing package, but the return expected on venture capital is very high because of the level of risk faced by the investor.

			Marks
(a)	Value of company at end of two years using DGM		2
	Value of company at year zero		1
	Current value of company using Dividend Valuation Model		2
	Acceptability of option 1 to shareholders		1
	Comment on findings		1
			———
		Maximum	6
			———
(b)	Revised operating profit		0.5
	Revised interest		0.5
	Revised profit after tax		0.5
	Revised earnings per share		0.5
	Current interest cover		0.5
	Revised interest cover		0.5
	Comment on earnings per share		1
	Comment on findings		1
	Comment on findings		1
			———
		Maximum	5
			———
(c)	Discussion of bond finance		3–4
	Discussion of equity finance via placing		3–4
	Discussion of venture capital		3–4
	Comment on findings		1
			———
		Maximum	9
			———
Total			**20**
			———

ACCA marking scheme

Examiner's comments

Candidates tended to struggle with part (a), although some scored full marks. In this question, the proposal was to suspend dividends for two years, before paying higher dividends at a higher growth rate than the current one from the third year onwards. The DGM could be used to calculate a share price (the present value of future dividends from the third year onwards) at the end of the second year. This share price could then be discounted for two years to give a current share price. Some candidates adopted a different, but equally valid, approach of discounting the year 3 dividend to the end of year 1 or to year 0, and then applying the DGM. How then would we know if the proposal was acceptable? By comparing the share price for the proposal to the current share price, calculated using the current dividend, the current dividend growth rate and the DGM.

General comments about whether shareholders would accept a two-year dividend suspensions, for example from the perspective of dividend relevance or irrelevance theory, were give some credit in the marking process. However, the expectation was that the comment on acceptability would refer to the comparison of the values discussed above.

The requirement in part (b) was to calculate the effect on earnings per share and interest cover of a proposal to raise finance by a loan note issue, commenting on the findings. The key points here were:

– Investing the funds at 18% before tax would increase operating profit

– Financing the investment with debt would result in an increase in interest payments

– Financing the investment with debt meant that the number of issued shares would not change.

Some answers calculated correctly the interest on the new debt, but ignored interest payable on the current debt when calculating interest cover. Another error was ignoring the return on the new funds invested, so that both current and revised interest cover were calculated using the same operating profit. Some answers calculated interest cover using profit before tax, or profit after tax, indicating a lack of understanding of accounting ratios. Credit was given for sensible comments on findings, even where the findings contained errors.

Answers to part (c) were of variable quality, indicating that some candidates were lacking on knowledge in this area of the syllabus. A number of answers, for example, showed limited understanding of placing venture capital. Some answers limited themselves to discussing each source of finance separately, without addressing the requirement to discuss the factors to be considered in choosing between them, and so could not be awarded full marks. At the other extreme, some answers discussed a number of factors, but related these very loosely, if at all, to the three sources of finance to which the question referred. For example, saying that a company should consider maturity, without indicating how maturity is a feature of the three sources of finance, does not help in choosing between them. A balanced discussion was therefore needed for full marks.

52 ILL COLLEAGUE

Key answer tips

A solid understanding of the basics of calculating the weighted average cost of capital will be sufficient to answer part (a). Part (b) represents more of a challenge and requires you to be competent in gearing and ungearing betas. Part (c) could have been attempted first as it gave an opportunity to gain some easy marks.

(a) (i) Dividend valuation model

If we assume a constant growth in dividends, we may estimate the cost of equity by using:

$$K(e) = \frac{Do(1+g)}{Po} + g$$

where: D_0 = \$2.14m/10m shares = 21.4c

P_0 = 321c

g = 11%

Therefore:

K(e) = (21.4c × 1.11/321c) + 0.11 = 0.184, or 18.4%

Kd(1-t)

As the question tells us to assume that 'corporate debt is risk-free', we can therefore assume that the cost of debt equals the risk free rate:

Kd (1-t) = 12% × (1 − 0.35) = 7.8%

The weighted average cost of capital (WACC) is therefore:

WACC = 18.4% × $\frac{2}{3}$ + 7.8% × $\frac{1}{3}$

= 14.87%

(ii)   Capital asset pricing model

R SHARES $= R_f + \beta SHARES \times [R_m - R_f]$

Beta $= 1.4$

R_f $= 12\%$

R_m $= 16\%$

Therefore:

R SHARES $= 12\% + [16\% - 12\%] \times 1.40 = 17.6\%$

Kd $= 7.8\%$ as in part (i)

WACC $= 17.6\% \times \frac{2}{3} + 7.8\% \times \frac{1}{3}$

$= 14.33\%$

The cost of equity may be estimated using either the dividend valuation model or the capital asset pricing model. In theory the two models should provide the same estimate of the cost of equity. In many instances, because of market imperfections and problems in the estimation of an appropriate growth rate in the dividend valuation model, the two models often give different results. CAPM is normally considered to be the better alternative. However, this model also has theoretical weaknesses and there may be problems in obtaining data to input into the model.

(b)   A major diversification into a new industry is likely to involve a different level of systematic risk from that of the company's existing investment portfolio. In these circumstances a project specific discount rate should be estimated, and the company's weighted average cost of capital is not appropriate. The project specific discount rate will need to reflect both the systematic risk (business risk) of operating cash flows and the financial gearing (financial risk) of the company as a whole.

A pragmatic way of identifying the systematic business risk is to use the published equity beta coefficients of other companies within the industry. These equity betas are considered to reflect the systematic risk of our company's major investment in the industry. However, if the average gearing level of the companies in the industry differs from our company's gearing, the beta will need to be adjusted (degeared and regeared) to reflect the gearing level (financial risk) of our company.

The β equity of the industry is 1.50.

Using β asset $= \beta \text{ equity } \dfrac{E}{E+D(1-t)} + \beta \text{ debt } \dfrac{D(1-t)}{E+D(1-t)}$

As β debt is 0.

β asset $= 1.50 \times \dfrac{3}{3+1(1-0.35)} + 0$

β asset $(= \beta$ equity for an ungeared project$) = 1.23$

Adjustment for the company's gearing level may be achieved by 're-gearing' the β asset.

Asset beta $= \text{Equity beta} \times \dfrac{E}{E+D(1-t)}$

1.23 $= \text{Equity beta} \times \dfrac{2}{2+1(1-0.35)}$

Equity beta $= 1.23/0.75 = 1.64$

Project E(r equity) $= 12 + (16 - 12) \times 1.64$

$= 18.56\%$

(c)   **Practical problems estimating data inputs for the CAPM**

The CAPM is an ex-ante model. It is difficult, if not impossible, to forecast accurate future returns of the company, project, or market. For practical purposes, ex-post data is normally used in the CAPM.

Even if the use of ex-post data is considered to be acceptable, it is difficult to estimate the appropriate data inputs:

Rf – What is the appropriate risk-free rate? A short-term government bill? A long-term government stock?

Rm – What is the market return? Do returns on companies comprising the FTSE All Share Index (or similar) provide a satisfactory estimate of returns on the market as a whole?

Beta – The use of an historical beta assumes that future risk is the same as past risk. Evidence for individual companies suggests that this is not the case.

Timescales – Over what period should historic data be considered? How frequently should returns be calculated?

53   CARD CO

Key answer tips

Parts (a) and (c) require the use of models that students should feel comfortable with. Care must be taken to extract the relevant information from the scenario and a clear layout must be used in order for marks to be allocated where due.

Part (d) is standard fare in terms of a discussion about the impact of changing capital structure on the value of the company. Students must be well prepared for this common requirement.

The highlighted words are key phrases that markers are looking for.

(a)   **Cost of equity of Card Co using DGM**

The average dividend growth rate in recent years is 4%:

$(62.0/55.1)^{0.333} - 1 = 1.040 - 1 = 0.04$ or 4% per year

Using the dividend growth model:

Ke = $[(62 \times 1.04)/716] + 0.04 = 0.09 + 0.04 = 0.13$ or 13%

(b)   The dividend growth model calculates the apparent cost of equity in the capital market, provided that the current market price of the share, the current dividend and the future dividend growth rate are known. While the current market price and the current dividend are readily available, it is very difficult to find an accurate value for the future dividend growth rate. A common approach to finding the future dividend growth rate is to calculate the average historic dividend growth rate and then to assume that the future dividend growth rate will be similar. There is no reason why this assumption should be true.

The capital asset pricing model tends to be preferred to the dividend growth model as a way of calculating the cost of equity as it has a sound theoretical basis, relating the cost of equity or required return of well-diversified shareholders to the systematic risk they face through owning the shares of a company. However, finding suitable values for the variables used by the capital asset pricing model (risk-free rate of return, equity beta and equity risk premium) can be difficult.

(c)   First, the proxy company equity beta must be ungeared:

Asset beta = $(1.038 \times 0.75)/(0.75 + (0.25 \times 0.7)) = 0.842$

The asset beta must then be regeared to reflect the financial risk of Card Co:

Equity beta = $0.842 \times (57,280 + (5,171 \times 0.7))/57,280 = 0.895$

Project-specific cost of equity = $4 + (0.895 \times 5) = 8.5\%$

Workings

Market values

	$000
Equity: 8m × 7.16 =	57,280
Loan notes: 5m × 103.42/100 =	5,171
Total value of Card Co	62,451

(d)   The value of a company can be expressed as the present value of its future cash flows, discounted at its weighted average cost of capital (WACC). The value of a company can therefore theoretically be maximised by minimising its WACC. If the WACC depends on the capital structure of a company, i.e. on the balance between debt and equity, then the minimum WACC will arise when the capital structure is optimal.

The idea of an optimal capital structure has been debated for many years. The traditional view of capital structure suggests that the WACC decreases as debt is introduced at low levels of gearing, before reaching a minimum and then increasing as the cost of equity responds to increasing financial risk.

Miller and Modigliani originally argued that the WACC is independent of a company's capital structure, depending only on its business risk rather than on its financial risk. This suggestion that it is not possible to minimise the WACC, and hence that it is not possible to maximise the value of a company by selecting a particular capital structure, depends on the assumption of a perfect capital market with no corporate taxation.

However, real world capital markets are not perfect and companies pay taxes on profit. Since interest is a tax-allowable deduction in calculating taxable profit, debt is a tax-efficient source of finance and replacing equity with debt will decrease the WACC of a company. In the real world, therefore, increasing gearing will decrease the WACC of a company and hence increase its value.

At high levels of gearing, the WACC of a company will increase due, for example, to increasing bankruptcy risk. Therefore, it can be argued that use of debt in a company's capital structure can reduce its WACC and increase its value, provided that gearing is kept to an acceptable level.

ACCA marking scheme			
			Marks
(a)	Calculation of historic dividend growth rate		1
	Calculation of cost of equity using DGM		2

		Maximum	3

(b)	Dividend growth model discussion		2–3
	Capital asset pricing model discussion		2–3

		Maximum	5

(c)	Ungearing proxy company equity beta		1
	Regearing asset beta		1
	Project-specific cost of equity using CAPM		2

		Maximum	4

(d)	Traditional view of capital structure		1–2
	Miller and Modigliani views of capital structure		3–4
	Market imperfections view of capital structure		2–3
	Other relevant discussion		1–2

		Maximum	8

Total			**20**
			---

54   DINLA CO

Key answer tips

Part (a) is a standard WACC calculation. As with any WACC calculation care should be taken to ensure that all elements of long term funding are identified and then a cost and value calculated for each. Don't forget to then include all of these in the WACC calculation itself. Don't let the term 'creditor hierarchy' in part (b) put you off. It's simply to do with that fact that some funders come higher in priority for pay-outs than others. Part (c) is a standard way of testing the syllabus area of Islamic finance. Make sure you're well versed on this area before the exam to pick up relatively easy marks if it comes up. Note the emphasis in the question for part (d). It isn't to talk through the methods for adjusting WACC – it's to discuss the circumstances under which it is useful or otherwise. Only briefly should you go into the method of adjusting it. The highlighted words are key phrases that markers are looking for.

(a)   Cost of equity

The dividend growth model can be used to calculate the cost of equity.

$K_e = ((0.25 \times 1.04)/4.26) + 0.04 = 10.1\%$

Cost of preference shares

$K_p = (0.05 \times 1.00)/0.56 = 8.9\%$

Cost of debt of loan notes

After-tax annual interest payment = 6 × (1 – 0.25) = 6 × 0.75 = $4.50 per year.

Year ($)	Cash Flow ($)	5% discount	PV ($)	6% discount	PV ($)
0	(95.45)	1.000	(95.45)	1.000	(95.45)
1–5	4.50	4.329	19.48	4.212	18.95
5	100.00	0.784	78.40	0.747	74.70
			2.43		(1.80)

After-tax cost of debt of loan notes = Kd = 5 + (2.43) / (2.43 + 1.80) × (6 – 5) = 5 + 0.57 = 5.6%.

Cost of debt of bank loan

The after-tax fixed interest rate of the bank loan can be used as its cost of debt. This will be 5.25% (7 × 0.75). Alternatively, the after-tax cost of debt of the loan notes can be used as a substitute for the after-tax cost of debt of the bank loan.

Market values

	$000
Equity: 4.26 × (23,000,000/0.25) =	391,920
Preference shares: 0.56 × (5,000,000/1.00) =	2,800
Loan notes: 95.45 × (11,000,000/100) =	10,500
Bank loan	3,000
	408,220

After-tax weighted average cost of capital

[391,920/408,220] × 10.1 + [2,800/408,220] × 8.9 + [10,500/408,220] × 5.6 + [3,000/408,220] × 5.25 = 9.9%

(b) The creditor hierarchy refers to the order in which financial claims against a company are settled when the company is liquidated. The hierarchy, in order of decreasing priority, is secured creditors, unsecured creditors, preference shareholders and ordinary shareholders. The risk of not receiving any cash in a liquidation increases as priority decreases. Secured creditors (secured debt) therefore face the lowest risk as providers of finance and ordinary shareholders face the highest risk.

The return required by a provider of finance is related to the risk faced by that provider of finance. Secured creditors therefore have the lowest required rate of return and ordinary shareholders have the highest required rate of return. The cost of debt should be less than the cost of preference shares, which should be less than the cost of equity.

(c) Wealth creation in Islamic finance requires that risk and reward, in terms of economic benefit, are shared between the provider of finance and the user of finance. Economic benefit includes wider economic goals such as increasing employment and social welfare.

Conventional finance, which refers to finance which is not based on Islamic principles and which has historically been used in the financial system, does not require the sharing of risks and rewards between the provider of finance (the investor) and the user of finance.

Interest (*riba*) is absolutely forbidden in Islamic finance and is seen as immoral. This can be contrasted with debt in conventional finance, where interest is seen as the main form of return to the debt holder, and with the attention paid to interest rates in the conventional financial system, where interest is the reward for depositing funds and the cost of borrowing funds.

Islamic finance can only support business activities which are acceptable under Sharia law.

Murabaha and sukuk are forms of Islamic finance that can be compared to conventional debt finance. Unlike conventional debt finance, however, murabaha and sukuk must have a direct link with underlying tangible assets.

(d) The current weighted average cost of capital (WACC) of a company reflects the required returns of existing providers of finance, such as the cost of equity of shareholders and the cost of debt of providers of debt finance, for example, banks and loan note holders.

The cost of equity and the cost of debt depend on particular elements of the existing risk profile of the company, such as business risk and financial risk. Providing the business risk and financial risk of a company remain unchanged, the cost of equity and the cost of debt, and hence the WACC, should remain unchanged.

Turning to investment appraisal, the WACC could be used as the discount rate in calculating the present values of investment project cash flows. Since the discount rate used should reflect the risk of investment project cash flows, using the WACC as the discount rate will only be appropriate if the investment project does not result in a change in the business risk and financial risk of the investing company.

One of the circumstances which is likely to leave business risk unchanged is if the investment project were an expansion of existing business activities. WACC could therefore be used as the discount rate in appraising an investment project that looked to expand existing business operations.

However, business risk depends on the size and scope of business operations as well as on their nature, and so an investment project that expands existing business operations should be small in relation to the size of the existing business.

Financial risk will remain unchanged if the investment project is financed in such a way that the relative weighting of existing sources of finance is unchanged, leaving the existing capital structure of the investing company unchanged.

While this is unlikely in practice, a company may finance investment projects with a target capital structure in mind, about which small fluctuations are permitted.

If business risk changes as a result of an investment project, so that using the WACC of a company in investment appraisal is not appropriate, a project-specific discount rate should be calculated. The capital asset pricing model (CAPM) can be used to calculate a project-specific cost of equity and this can be used in calculating a project-specific WACC.

ACCA Marking scheme

			Marks
(a)	Cost of equity		1
	Cost of preference shares		1
	After-tax loan note interest payment		1
	Setting up loan note cost of debt calculation		1
	After-tax cost of debt of loan notes		1
	After-tax cost of debt of bank loan		1
	Market values		1
	After-tax weighted average cost of capital		1
		Maximum	8
(b)	Explanation of creditor hierarchy		1
	Relative risks and costs of sources of finance		2
		Maximum	3
(c)	Sharing of risk and reward		1–2
	Forbidding of riba		1–2
	Other relevant discussion		1–2
		Maximum	4
(d)	WACC and business risk		2
	WACC and financial risk		2
	CAPM and project-specific WACC		1
			5
Total			**20**

Examiner's comments

Part (a) asked candidates to calculate the after-tax weighted average cost of capital (WACC) of a company on a market value basis. The company had four sources of finance.

Most candidates were able to calculate correctly the cost of equity using the dividend growth model. The question gave all the information needed and no subsidiary calculations were needed.

Most candidates were able to calculate correctly the cost of capital of the irredeemable preference shares, although some candidates mistakenly calculated the cost of capital on an after-tax basis.

Although irredeemable preference shares are included with debt as prior charge capital, they pay a dividend, not interest, and so are not tax-efficient.

Many candidates were able to calculate correctly the after-tax cost of debt of the redeemable loan notes using linear interpolation, based on sensible cost of debt estimates, although some candidates had difficulty laying out the interpolation calculation.

Many candidates correctly used the after-tax interest cost of the bank loan as an approximation for its after-tax cost of debt. As the bank loan was a non-current liability, it could not be ignored in calculating the WACC, although some candidates did this.

Candidates were required to use market value when calculating WACC and many were able to calculate these. Some candidates incorrectly included the value of reserves when calculating the market value of equity.

The majority of candidates were able to make a reasonable attempt at a WACC calculation, although some candidates, having laid out the calculation, did not calculate the WACC.

Part (b) required candidates to discuss the connection between the relative costs of sources of finance and the creditor hierarchy. Some candidates incorrectly discussed pecking order theory instead of the creditor hierarchy.

The creditor hierarchy refers to the order in which financial claims are settled when a company goes into liquidation. Some candidates discussed the relative costs of different sources of finance but did not explain the creditor hierarchy or discuss any connection with it.

Part (c) asked candidates to explain the differences between Islamic finance and other conventional finance. Better answers referred to the sharing of risk and reward, the forbidding of riba and only supporting business activities that are acceptable under Sharia law. Weaker answers offered a list of various forms of Islamic finance, without explaining any differences compared to other conventional finance.

Question 4b required a discussion about the weighted average cost of capital and the circumstances under which it could be used in investment appraisal. Lots of candidates made only a generic statement such as 'when the business and financial risk remain unchanged'. A better discussion of each of the risks and, also, as to how a project specific discount rate could be found when business risk does change, would have scored more marks.

Some candidates drifted into irrelevant discussion (e.g. M&M theory, time value of money), which scored no marks, and they spent valuable time doing so.

55 TINEP CO

Key answer tips

In part (a) remember than when using book values for a WACC calculation (or for a gearing one), reserves are included in the value of equity. Also, as beta figures, risk free premium and the equity risk premium are given and no information on dividends, the cost of equity must be calculated using the CAPM rather than the dividend valuation model. Part (b) is standard textbook knowledge. In part (c) not only do you need to understand the theory behind the efficient market hypothesis but to earn good marks you have to apply it to Tinep's situation, particularly the fact that part of the information about the project has already been released and the rest is about to be released. The highlighted words are key phrases that markers are looking for.

(a) Cost of equity

Tutorial note

Be careful when using the CAPM. The question has given you the equity risk premium rather than the equity risk return. The return itself would give you a value for $E(r_m)$ but the premium is the difference between the equity return and the risk free return. In other words the question has given you directly the value of $(E(r_m) - R_f)$.

Using the capital asset pricing model, $K_e = 4 + (1.15 \times 6) = 10.9\%$

Cost of debt of loan notes

After-tax annual interest payment = $6 \times 0.75 = \$4.50$ per loan note.

Year	$	5% discount	PV ($)	4% discount	PV ($)
0	(103.50)	1.000	(103.50)	1.000	(103.50)
1–6	4.50	5.076	22.84	5.242	23.59
6	106.00	0.746	79.08	0.790	83.74
			(1.58)		3.83

$K_d = 4 + [(1 \times 3.83)/(3.83 + 1.58)] = 4 + 0.7 = 4.7\%$ per year

Market values of equity and debt

Number of ordinary shares = 200m/0.5 = 400 million shares

Market value of ordinary shares = 400m × 5.85 = $2,340 million

Market value of loan notes = 200m × 103.5/100 = $207 million

Total market value = 2,340 + 207 = $2,547 million

Market value WACC

$K_0 = [2,340/2,547] \times 10.9 + [207/2,547] \times 4.7 = 10.4\%$

Book value WACC

$K_0 = [850/1,050] \times 10.9 + [200/1,050] \times 4.7 = 9.7\%$

Comment

Market values of financial securities reflect current market conditions and current required rates of return. Market values should therefore always be used in calculating the weighted average cost of capital (WACC) when they are available. If book values are used, the WACC is likely to be understated, since the nominal values of ordinary shares are much less than their market values. The contribution of the cost of equity is reduced if book values are used, leading to a lower WACC, as evidenced by the book value WACC (9.7%) and the market value WACC (10.4%) of Tinep Co.

(b) A rights issue raises equity finance by offering new shares to existing shareholders in proportion to the number of shares they currently hold. Existing shareholders have the right to be offered new shares (the pre-emptive right) before they are offered to new investors, hence the term 'rights issue'. There are a number of factors that Tinep Co should consider.

Issue price

Rights issues shares are offered at a discount to the market value. It can be difficult to judge what the amount of the discount should be.

Relative cost

Rights issues are cheaper than other methods of raising finance by issuing new equity, such as an initial public offer (IPO) or a placing, due to the lower transactions costs associated with rights issues.

Ownership and control

As the new shares are being offered to existing shareholders, there is no dilution of ownership and control, providing shareholders take up their rights.

Gearing and financial risk

Increasing the weighting of equity finance in the capital structure of Tinep Co can decrease its gearing and its financial risk. The shareholders of the company may see this as a positive move, depending on their individual risk preference positions.

(c)   If the stock market on which Tinep Co is listed is semi-strong form efficient, share prices on the stock market will quickly and accurately react to the release of new information. The stock market will have already factored the information about the proposed business expansion into the share price of the company. The announcement that the business expansion will be financed by an issue of 8% loan stock is new information, as is the announcement of the expected increase in profit before interest and tax (PBIT). The effect of the announcements on the share price of Tinep Co will depend on how the stock market interprets this new information.

Interest cover

The information about the financing choice indicates that annual interest will increase. The stock market will already know Tinep Co's current interest cover levels and will look at the effect on this figure to see if it reaches a worryingly low level.

Debt/equity ratio

The total market value of debt would increase. Tinep currently has a capital structure comprised of 8.1% debt (based on market values $207m/$2,547m). An increase to this figure should not overly concern investors as it is relatively low.

Share price of Tinep Co

Of course, the debt/equity ratio on a market value basis of Tinep Co depends on the ordinary share price of the company. With both interest cover and gearing levels rising, the shareholders of Tinep Co will experience an increase in financial risk. The cost of equity of the company is therefore likely to increase. This will exert a downward pressure on the share price of Tinep Co, leading to a further increase in the market value basis debt/equity ratio. The announcements of the financing decision and the expected increase in PBIT could therefore lead to a fall in the share price of Tinep Co. The extent to which this happens will depend on the shareholders' view of the level of extra risk they are experiencing.

On the positive side, the increase in PBIT may lead to more cash being available to pay dividends. If the company were to make an announcement about increased future dividends, this would exert an upward pressure on the share price of Tinep Co, and this could counteract the downward pressure due to the increase in financial risk.

ACCA marking scheme		
		Marks
(a)	Cost of equity	1
	After-tax interest payment	1
	Setting up IRR calculation	1
	After-tax cost of debt of loan notes	1
	Market values	1
	Market value WACC	1
	Book value WACC	1
	Comment on difference	2
	Maximum	9
(b)	Issue price	1–2
	Relative cost	1–2
	Ownership and control	1–2
	Gearing and financial risk	1–2
	Maximum	6
(c)	Semi-strong form market and new information	1
	Interest cover discussion	1
	Gearing discussion	1
	Discussion of effect on share price	1
	Any other relevant points	1
	Maximum	5
Total		20

Examiner's comments

In part (a) most answers were able to correctly calculate the cost of equity using the capital asset pricing model. One error that arose occasionally was to treat the equity risk premium as though it were the return on the market.

Calculations of the after-tax cost of debt of the loan notes using linear interpolation were often correct. Some answers used extreme estimates of discount rates, such as 1% and 20%, which diminished the accuracy of their estimates of the after-tax cost of debt. Another error that was occasionally made was to substitute the nominal value of the loan notes ($100) for either the current market value ($103.50) or the redemption value ($106), or for both. A more common error was to use the before-tax interest payment ($6.00) rather than the after-tax interest payment ($4.50) in the interpolation calculation.

The majority of answers calculated correctly the market values of the equity and debt. A very common error, surprisingly, was using the value of the ordinary share account ($200m) as the book value of equity, when the correct value was $850m, which is the sum of the ordinary share account and the reserves.

Comment on the difference between the two WACC values was often limited to stating that there was a difference and this difference was due to a difference in the weights that were used in the WACC calculations.

Better answers emphasised the importance of using market value weights in calculating WACC in order to take account of the risks and returns present in the current business environment of a company, and referred to the possibility of making sub-optimal investment decisions if the book value were to be used in investment appraisal.

In part (b) the requirement was to discuss the factors to be considered by the company in the question (Tinep Co) in choosing to raise funds via a rights issue.

Many answers lacked a focus on the question asked, often discussing equity finance versus debt finance in general terms. For example, some answers suggested that a rights issue could be used to reduce high gearing, failing to recognise the Tinep Co had low gearing. Other answers discussed, sometimes at great length, pecking order theory or the views of Miller and Modigliani on capital structure.

Many answers gave a list of characteristics of a rights issue, rather than factors to discuss.

Part (c) asked candidates to analyse and discuss the effect of new information being given by an announcement in a semi-strong form efficient stock market. Analysis would show an increase in the debt/equity ratio and a decrease in interest cover, both indicating an increase in financial risk and downward pressure on the company's share price.

56 TUFA CO

Key answer tips

In part (a) the only information given about the bank loan is its nominal value and that it has a variable rate, which isn't enough to calculate a cost of debt. Don't let this put you off – if there is not enough information given then put in something appropriate so that you can carry on with the question and gain the remaining marks. Parts (b) and (c) require careful reading of the question to ensure that you are answering specifically what has been asked.

The highlighted words are key phrases that markers are looking for.

(a) **Cost of equity**

$ke = D_0 (1 + g)/P_0 + g$

D_0 – cum div price – ex div price = $7.52 – $7.07 = $0.45

$g = [D_0/D_n]^{1/n} – 1 = [$0.45/0.37]^{1/4} – 1 = 0.050$ or 5%

$ke = $0.45 × 1.05/$7.07 + 0.05 = 0.117$ or 11.7%

Cost of preference shares

$kp = D / P_0$

D = nominal value × % rate = $0.50 × 5% = $0.025

$kp = $0.025/$0.31 = 0.0806$ or 8.06%

Cost of redeemable debt

Interest rate of loan notes (%)	7
Nominal value of loan notes ($)	100.00
Market price of loan notes ($)	102.34
Time to redemption (years)	4
Redemption premium (%)	5
Tax rate (%)	30

Year	Item	%	5% DF	PV ($)	6% DF	PV ($)
0	MV	(102.34)	1.000	(102.34)	1.000	(102.34)
1-4	Interest	4.90	3.546	17.38	3.465	16.98
4	Redeem	105.00	0.823	86.42	0.792	83.16
			NPV	1.45	NPV	(2.20)

IRR (%) (5 + (1.45 / (1.45 + 2.20))) × (6 – 5) = 5.40
Cost of bank loan (%) = 5.40

Market values and WACC calculation

	BV($000)	Nominal	MV	MV($000)	Cost (%)	WACC
Ordinary shares	12,000	0.50	7.07	169,680	11.7	10.67
Preference shares	5,000	0.50	0.31	3,100	8.06	0.13
Loan notes	10,000	100.00	102.34	10,234	5.40	0.30
Bank loan	3,000			3,000	5.40	0.09
				186,014		11.19

(b) The current WACC of Tufa Co represents the mean return required by the company's investors, given the current levels of business risk and financial risk faced by the company.

The current WACC can be used as the discount rate in appraising an investment project of the company provided that undertaking the investment project does not change the current levels of business risk and financial risk faced by the company.

The current WACC can therefore be used as the discount rate in appraising an investment project of Tufa Co in the same business area as current operations, for example, an expansion of current business, as business risk is likely to be unchanged in these circumstances.

Similarly, the current WACC can be used as the discount rate in appraising an investment project of Tufa Co if the project is financed in a way that mirrors the current capital structure of the company, as financial risk is then likely to be unchanged.

The required return of the company's investors is likely to change if the investment project is large compared to the size of the company, so the WACC is likely to be an appropriate discount rate providing the investment is small in size relative to Tufa Co.

(c) The following advantages of using convertible loan notes as a source of long-term finance could be discussed.

Conversion rather than redemption

If the holders of convertible loan notes judge that conversion into ordinary shares will increase their wealth, conversion of the loan notes will occur on the conversion date and Tufa Co will not need to find the cash needed to redeem the loan notes. This is sometimes referred to as 'self-liquidation'.

Lower interest rate

The option to convert into ordinary shares has value for investors as ordinary shares normally offer a higher return than debt. Investors in convertible loan notes will therefore accept a lower interest rate than on ordinary loan notes, decreasing the finance costs for the issuing company.

Debt capacity

If Tufa Co issued convertible loan notes, its gearing and financial risk will increase and its debt capacity will decrease. When conversion occurs, its gearing and financial risk will decrease and its debt capacity will increase because of the elimination of the loan notes from its capital structure. There will be a further increase in debt capacity due to the issue of new ordinary shares in order to facilitate conversion.

Attractive to investors

Tufa Co may be able to issue convertible loan notes to raise long-term finance even when investors might not be attracted by an issue of ordinary loan notes, because of the attraction of the option to convert into ordinary shares in the future.

Facilitates planning

It has been suggested than an issue of fixed-interest debt such as convertible loan notes can be attractive to a company as the fixed nature of future interest payments facilitates financial planning.

ACCA marking scheme		Marks
(a)	Dividend for 20X7	1
	Dividend growth rate	1
	Cost of equity	1
	Cost of pref. shares	1
	After-tax interest	1
	kd calculation setup	1
	Calculating kd	1
	Cost of bank loan	0.5
	MV ordinary shares	0.5
	MV pref. shares	0.5
	MV loan notes	0.5
	WACC calculations	2
		___
		11
		___
(b)	Business risk	1
	Financial risk	1
	Size of investment	1
		___
		3
		___
(c)	First advantage	2
	Second advantage	2
	Third advantage	2
		___
		6
		___
Total		20
		___

Examiner's comments

Part (a)This question required candidates to calculate the after-tax weighted average cost of capital (WACC) of the company, where there were four distinct sources of finance. Hence, all four elements needed to be considered, and a separate cost and value calculated for each.

Attempts at calculating the cost of equity and the value of ordinary shares were generally good. Some candidates were not able to calculate the current dividend as the difference between the cum div and ex div share prices, nor were they able to recognise that there were four years of dividend growth. Most candidates were, however, able to perform correctly a dividend growth rate computation.

Correct calculations of the cost of capital of preference shares were disappointingly low in number. Too many candidates made errors such as using an 'after tax' preference dividend or appeared to be simply guessing at the combination of figures that needed to be used.

Using an IRR approach to calculate the after tax cost of loan notes was generally done well. Errors in calculation included not using after tax interest in the IRR calculation, not including the redemption value of the loan note at its stated premium and/or using nominal value as the purchase price of loan notes rather than market value.

Omissions of the cost of the bank loan, and indeed its value, due to it 'having a variable rate' were common, but in error. The bank loan was part of the total finance of the company and needed to be included by using an appropriate substitute value for its cost, such as the after- tax cost of debt of the loan notes or the after-tax interest rate of the loan notes.

Good examination technique here was for candidates to present the cost and value of the four sources of finance as four separate workings and then to calculate the WACC by clearly showing its four elements. Some candidates were combining sources of finance and this led to errors. Examples of this were treating preference shares as ordinary shares and treating the bank loan as loan notes.

The question asked for the WACC on a market value basis, hence using book values instead of market values as weightings is simply incorrect.

Part (b)

Here candidates were required to discuss the circumstances where it is appropriate to use the WACC in appraising an investment project. Some candidates discussed all three of the required circumstances, including an explanation of what is meant by business risk and financial risk. However, too many responses simply said "the WACC can be used if business risk and financial risk are unchanged" without further development. Whilst correct, the statement needs further discussion. A minority of responses made the point about the new investment needing to be small in relation to the company.

The key to answering a question such as this is to focus clearly on the requirement. Indeed, a common mistake in this question at this diet was to discuss circumstances under which it was not appropriate to use the current WACC and how WACC could be amended to address these circumstances. This was not what was asked.

Some answers were not even related to the requirement, discussing instead capital structure theory, or the creditor hierarchy, or pecking order theory, to name just some. There were also a disappointing number of candidates marking no attempt at this part question.

Part (c). This question required candidates to discuss three advantages to the company of using convertible loan notes as a source of long-term finance.

Better candidates broke down this requirement and addressed its component parts.

Firstly, a discussion is asked for. If six marks are offered for discussing three advantages, then assuming that two marks are offered for each advantage is reasonable. A 'bullet point' or short phrase is rarely, if ever, going to be sufficient to attract the two marks available for an advantage.

Secondly, if three advantages are required, then discussing a fourth or even fifth advantage is both poor examination technique and poor time management.

Thirdly, the question was clearly asked from the viewpoint of the user of the finance, which was a company listed on a large stock exchange, and not the providers of the finance. Better responses understood this important difference of viewpoint.

Fourthly, when answering a question like this, there is a tendency for candidates to write all they know about the topic or to write in general terms about one of the areas, without focusing precisely on the specific requirements of the question. Here the requirement was about a specific type of debt finance, convertible loan notes, and the candidate's answer should have addressed that type of finance precisely.

Weaker responses ignored the possibility of conversion and were related only to the debt or non-equity nature of the loan notes e.g. debt is cheaper than equity or interest on debt is tax deductible. Some answers thought that conversion was a choice exercised by the company, rather than the investor and other answers assumed that conversion was automatic, rather than a wealth-maximising decision made by investors.

57   TIN CO

Key answer tips

Parts (a) (i) to (a) (iv) are relatively straightforward and should be calculations that you are familiar with by the time you take the exam. In part (v) you need to think harder about what kind of information the finance providers would be interested in. The question scenario mentions gearing and interest cover which has not yet been calculated, so it's worth doing these calculations. Calculations alone will only earn part of the marks. You must discuss the numbers from the point of view of the investors to earn full marks.

In part (b) you are asked to discuss two sources of Islamic finance. Marks will be restricted to discussion of only two sources, so mentioning a third or fourth will not earn marks. A lack of knowledge here will be very detrimental as the question specifically asks for one source to be an alternative to a rights issue and the other to debt finance, so if you're not aware that mudaraba is closest to equity finance and sukuk or ijara are closest to debt finance you will struggle.

The highlighted words are key phrases that markers are looking for.

(a) (i)

Financial statement data

	$000
Profit before interest and tax	1,597
Finance costs (interest)	(315)
Taxation	(282)
Profit after tax	1,000

	$000
Equity	
Ordinary shares	2,500
Retained earnings	5,488
Long-term liabilities	
7% loan notes	4,500
Total equity and long-term liabilities	12,488

Other information

Current share price ($/share)	5.00
Rights issue discount (%)	20
Current EPS ($/share) (given)	0.40
Current PER (times) (given)	12.5

Rights issue price (S/share)	4.00	
TERP ($/share)	**4.83**	[(5 × $5) + (1 × $4)]/6

(ii)

	$000	
Increased PBIT	1,916	
Finance costs (interest)	(315)	
Revised profit before tax	1,601	
Taxation at 22%	(352)	
Revised profit after tax	1,249	
Increased number of shares	3,000,000	
Revised EPS ($/share) using equity	**0.42**	(1,249/3,000)

(iii)

	$000	
Increased PBIT	1,916	
Finance costs (interest)	(475)	(= 315 + 160)
Revised profit before tax	1,441	
Taxation at 22%	(317)	
Revised profit after tax	1,124	
Current number of shares	2,500,000	
Revised EPS ($/share) using debt	**0.45**	(1,124/2,500)

(iv)   **Revised share prices ($/share)**

Using equity = 12.5 × 0.42   5.25

Using debt = 12.5 × 0.45   5.63

(v)   **Discussion**

Gearing

Current D/E using BV = 4,500/(2,500 + 5,488) = 4,500/7,988 = 56.3%

Equity finance D/E using BV = 4,500/(7,988 + 2,000) = 4,500/9,988 = 45.1%

Debt finance D/E using BV = (4,500 + 2,000)/7,988 = 6,500/7,988 = 81.4%

Sector average D/E using BV = 60.5%

The gearing of Tin Co at 56.3% is just below the sector average gearing of 60.5%. If equity finance were used, gearing would fall even further below the sector average at 45.1%. If debt finance were used, gearing would increase above the sector average to 81.4%.

Interest cover

Current interest cover = 1,597/315 = 5.1 times

Interest cover using equity finance = 1,916/315 = 6.1 times

Interest cover using debt finance = 1,916/475 = 4.0 times

Sector average interest cover = 9 times

Interest cover calculations show that raising equity finance would make the interest cover of Tin Co look much safer. Interest cover of 4 times under debt finance looks quite risky.

Share price changes

The shareholders of Tin Co experience a capital gain of $0.63 per share ($5.63 – $5.00) if debt finance is used, compared to a capital gain of $0.42 per share ($5.25 – $4.83) if equity finance is used. Although using debt finance looks more attractive, it comes at a price in terms of increased financial risk. It might be decided, on balance, that using equity finance looks to be the better choice.

(b)   The forms of Islamic finance equivalent to a rights issue and a loan note are mudaraba and sukuk respectively. Musharaka is similar to venture capital and hence is not seen as equivalent to a rights issue, which is made to existing shareholders. Ijara, which is similar to lease finance, might be an alternative to a loan note issue, depending on the nature of the planned business expansion.

Mudaraba

A mudaraba contract is between a capital partner (rab al mal) and an expertise partner (mudarab) for the undertaking of business operations. The business operations must be compliant with Sharia 'a law and are run on a day to day basis by the mudarab. The rab al mal has no role in relation to the day-to-day operations of the business.

Profits from the business operations are shared between the partners in a proportion agreed in the contract. Losses are borne by the rab al mal alone, as provider of the finance, up to the limit of the capital provided.

Sukuk

Conventional loan notes are not allowed under Sharia 'a law because there must be a link to an underlying tangible asset and because interest (riba) is forbidden by the Quran. Sukuk are linked to an underlying tangible asset, ownership of which is passed to the sukuk holders, and do not pay interest.

Since the sukuk holders take on the risks and rewards of ownership, sukuk also has an equity aspect. As owners, sukuk holders will bear any losses or risk from the underlying asset. In terms of rewards, sukuk holders have a right to receive the income generated by the underlying asset and have a right to dismiss the manager of the underlying asset, if this is felt to be necessary.

Ijara

In this form of Islamic finance, the lessee uses a tangible asset in exchange for a regular rental payment to the lessor, who retains ownership throughout the period of the lease contract. The contract may allow for ownership to be transferred from the lessor to the lessee at the end of the lease period.

Major maintenance and insurance are the responsibility of the lessor, while minor day to day maintenance is the responsibility of the lessee. The lessor may choose to appoint the lessee as their agent to undertake all maintenance, both major and minor.

ACCA marking scheme		Marks
(a) (i)	Rights issue price	1
	TERP	1
		2
(ii)	Increased PBIT	0.5
	Revised PBT	0.5
	Revised PAT	1
	Number of shares	1
	Revised EPS	1
		4
(iii)	Increased interest	1
	Revised PAT	1
	Revised EPS	1
		3
(iv)	Equity share price	0.5
	Debt share price	0.5
		1
(v)	Financial analysis	1
	Gearing	1
	Interest cover	1
	Share price effects	1
		4
(b)	First finance source	2
	Second finance source	2
	Additional detail	2
		6
Total		**20**

Examiner's comments

Part (a) (i)

The scenario was that a company needed to evaluate equity finance from a rights issue and debt finance from a loan note issue as financing sources for a planned business expansion. The five parts of this question are the successive stage of this evaluation. This first question asked candidates to calculate the theoretical ex rights price per share (TERPS).

Some candidates made errors with respect to the form of the rights issue, for example using 'five for one' rather than the 'one for five' form given in the question. Some candidates could not calculate the rights issue price correctly. Some candidates wasted valuable time by calculating values that had not been requested, such as the monetary value of the rights per existing share.

Part (a) (ii)

This question asked candidates to calculate the revised earnings per share (EPS) if equity finance were used.

Better candidates understood how to calculate the revised profit after tax (PAT) for the business expansion by calculating revised figures for profit before interest and tax (PBIT), and for tax, then dividing PAT by the revised number of shares.

Errors that were made included:

- Not recalculating the tax, even after increasing PBIT, with interest unchanged

- Not increasing PBIT for the business expansion

- Miscalculating the revised number of shares.

One error that was particularly surprising was where candidates used retained earnings from the statement of financial position instead of PBIT from the statement of profit or loss as the basis for their calculations, suggesting a poor understanding of financial statements. FM candidates are expected to have a good applied knowledge of ratio analysis and financial statement analysis, and candidates should review their understanding of all financial ratios in preparing for the examination.

Part (a) (iii)

This question asked candidates to calculate the revised earnings per share (EPS) if debt finance were used.

Better candidates understood the need to calculate the increased PBIT, subtract from this figure the increased interest charge (on both existing debt and new debt) to give a revised PBT, calculate revised tax and revised PAT, then divide by the current number of shares.

Errors made by candidates, mirroring those in the previous question, included:

- Miscalculating the increased interest charge

- Not recalculating tax having increased PBIT

- Using the number of shares for a rights issue instead of the current number of shares.

Part (a) (iv)

This question required candidates to calculate revised share prices under the two financing choices.

Candidates could reasonably assume that the price/earnings ratio (PER) of the company would be constant since the expansion was of existing business operations and so the company's business risk would not change. Candidates could then multiply the already calculated EPS figures by the existing PER to give the revised share prices.

Candidates in general were able to calculate the revised share prices, although some candidates only calculated one share price and some candidates calculated net asset value (NAV) per share in the belief that was the required share price.

A general point about the first four questions is that the required calculations could all be practised in revising for the examination.

Part (a) (v)

This question required candidates to use calculations to evaluate whether equity or debt finance should be selected.

The first point to note here is the requirement to use calculations. A general discussion about the different features of equity and debt would get very little, if any, reward here because the requirement is for calculations.

What calculations should be used though? The question scenario gives average debt/equity ratios and interest cover ratios for similar companies, so calculating these ratios on a before and-after basis under the two financing choices was sensible. Many candidates correctly calculated relevant interest cover ratios. The debt/equity ratio under debt financing was often calculated correctly, while the ratio where most errors occurred was the debt/equity ratio under equity financing.

Many candidates in evaluating the two financing choices did not consider adequately the objective of shareholder wealth maximisation. Capital gains could be calculated under both financing choices, the equity finance comparison being between the TERPS and the related PER-revised share price, and the debt finance comparison being between the current share price and the related PER-revised share price. Candidates' comments in this area tended to consider share prices or EPS figures rather than capital gains, and the TERPS was often not mentioned at all.

While calculations can be revised and practised through repetition, the thinking behind this kind of evaluation is more difficult to prepare for. One guiding principle that can be a real help is the relationship between risk and return. Debt financing carries the higher risk here (financial risk, measured by gearing and interest cover) and offers the higher return to the shareholder, while equity finance offers the lower risk and the lower return.

Part (b)

This question required candidates to discuss TWO Islamic finance sources that could be considered as alternatives to a rights issue and a loan note issue.

The first point to note is that only TWO sources were to be discussed, so the third choice and beyond would not gain any additional marks, while wasting valuable time in the exam.

The second point to note is the requirement to discuss Islamic sources of finance. Those candidates who lacked knowledge of Islamic finance choices, for example who discussed overdraft finance or the nature of an initial public offering, were unlikely to gain any marks here. Candidates needed to discuss Islamic finance sources covered in the syllabus, such as Mudaraba and Sukuk.

The third point to note is that the requirement referred to a rights issue and a loan note issue. These are long-term sources of finance and so the Islamic finance sources discussed also needed to be long term, which excluded Murabaha.

Overall, answers to this question were sometimes confused, discussing general principles such as forbidding riba or prescribed business activities, rather than discussing clearly the features of individual Islamic finance sources.

58   CORFE CO

Key answer tips

In part (a) the only information given about the bank loan is its nominal value and that it has a variable rate, which isn't enough to calculate a cost of debt. Don't let this put you off – if there is not enough information given then put in something appropriate so that you can carry on with the question and gain the remaining marks. Otherwise this is a conventional WACC calculation. Part (b) requires you to relate your answer specifically to what each directors has said. To 'discuss' their views means you need to give both pros and cons regarding their comments.

The highlighted words are key phrases that markers are looking for.

(a)

$k_e = 3.5\% + (1.25 \times 6.8\%) = 12.00\%$

$k_p = (0.06 \times 0.75) / 0.64 = 7.03\%$

Loan notes

After tax interest payment	$8\% \times (1 - 0.2) = 6.4\%$
Nominal value of loan notes	$100.00
Market value of loan notes	$103.50
Time to redemption (years)	5
Redemption premium (5%)	10

Year	Item	%	5% DF	PV ($)	10% DF	PV ($)
0	MV	(103.50)	1.000	(103.50)	1.000	(103.50)
1–5	Interest	6.40	4.329	27.71	3.791	24.26
5	Redeem	110.00	0.784	86.24	0.621	68.31
			NPV	10.45	NPV	(10.93)

$$IRR = N_L + [N_L / (N_L - N_H)] \times (H - L)$$

$$IRR = 5 + [10.45/(10.45 + 10.93)] \times (10 - 5) = 7.44\%$$

This figure can also be used for the cost of debt of the bank loan

Market values and WACC calculation:

	BV($m)	Nominal	MV	MV($m)	Cost (%)	MV× cost (%)
Equity shares	15	1.00	6.10	91.50	12.00	1,098.00
Preference shares	6	0.75	0.64	5.12	7.03	35.99
Loan notes	8	100.00	103.50	8.28	7.44	61.60
Bank loan	5			5.00	7.44	37.20
				109.90		1,232.79

$$WACC = 1,232.79/109.90 \times 100 = 11.22\%$$

(b)   Director A

Director A is incorrect in saying that $29m of cash reserves are available. Reserves are $29m, but this figure represents backing for all Corfe Co's assets and not just cash.

Corfe Co has $4m of cash. Some of this could be used for investment, although the company will need a minimum balance of cash to maintain liquidity for its day-to-day operations.

Corfe Co's current ratio is (20/7) = 2.86. This may be a high figure (depending on the industry Corfe Co is in), so Corfe Co may have scope to generate some extra cash by reducing working capital. Inventory levels could be reduced by just-in-time policies, trade receivables reduced by tighter credit control and payments delayed to suppliers. All of these have possible drawbacks. Just-in-time policies may result in running out of inventory, and tighter policies for trade receivables and payables may worsen relations with customers and suppliers. Again also, Corfe Co would have to maintain minimum levels of each element of working capital, so it seems unlikely that it could raise the maximum $25m solely by doing what Director A suggests.

Director B

Selling the headquarters would raise most of the sum required for investment, assuming that Director B's assessment of sales price is accurate. However, Corfe Co would lose the benefit of the value of the site increasing in future, which may happen if the headquarters is in a prime location in the capital city. Being able to sell the headquarters would be subject to the agreement of lenders if the property had been used as security for a loan. Even if it has not been used as security, the sale could reduce the borrowing capacity of the company by reducing the availability of assets to offer as security.

An ongoing commitment to property management costs of an owned site would be replaced by a commitment to pay rent, which might also include some responsibility for property costs for the locations rented. It is possible that good deals for renting are available outside the capital city. However, in the longer term, the rent may become more expensive if there are frequent rent reviews.

There may also be visible and invisible costs attached to moving and splitting up the functions. There will be one-off costs of moving and disruption to work around the time of the move. Staff replacement costs may increase if staff are moved to a location which is not convenient for them and then leave. Senior managers may find it more difficult to manage functions which are in different locations rather than the same place. There may be a loss of synergies through staff in different functions not being able to communicate easily face-to-face any more.

Director C

The dividend just paid of $13.5m seems a large amount compared with total reserves. If a similar level of funds is available for distribution over the next two years, not paying a dividend would fund the forecast expenditure.

However, shareholders may well expect a consistent or steadily growing dividend. A cut in dividend may represent a significant loss of income for them. If this is so, shareholders may be unhappy about seeing dividends cut or not paid, particularly if they have doubts about the directors' future investment plans. They may see this as a signal that the company has poor prospects, particularly if they are unsure about why the directors are not seeking finance from external sources.

The directors' dividend policy may also be questioned if the dividend just paid was a one-off, high payment. Such a payment is normally made if a company has surplus cash and does not have plans to use it. However, the directors are planning investments, and shareholders may wonder why a high dividend was paid when the directors need money for investments.

ACCA marking scheme		Marks
(a)	Ke setup	1
	Ke calculation	1
	Kp calculation	1
	Interest after tax	1
	Kd setup	1
	Kd calculation	1
	Kd bank loan	1
	MV equity shares	0.5
	MV pref shares	0.5
	MV loan notes	0.5
	MV bank loan	0.5
	WACC calculation	2
		11
(b)	Director A	3
	Director B	3
	Director C	3
		9
Total		**20**

Examiner's comments

Part (a)

The requirement here was for candidates to calculate the after-tax weighted average cost of capital (WACC) of a company on a market value basis. Many answers gained good marks here.

The question provided information which allowed the capital asset pricing model (CAPM) to be used to calculate the cost of equity and most candidates were able to calculate this correctly. The CAPM formula is provided in the Financial Management formulae sheet. Some candidates incorrectly used the equity risk premium as the return on the market, when the equity risk premium is the difference between the return on the market and the risk-free rate of return.

Some answers incorrectly attempted to use the dividend growth model (DGM) to calculate the cost of equity, but the question did not give information which allowed the DGM to be used, for example, the future dividend growth rate was not known.

Most candidates were able to calculate correctly the cost of capital of the preference shares.

One potential source of error was using $1.00 as the nominal value of the shares, rather than $0.75 as given in the question, leading to miscalculation of the preference dividend. Another source of error was not recognising that preference shares pay a dividend, which is a distribution of after-tax profit, and treating the preference dividend as though it were interest by including a tax effect.

Most candidates correctly calculated the after-tax interest payment for including in a linear interpolation calculation of the after-tax cost of debt of the 8% loan notes. Errors were sometimes made by using an incorrect value for the current ex interest market value of the loan notes, for example, using nominal value, or by using an incorrect value for the redemption value of the loan notes, again, for example, using the nominal value.

Some spreadsheet calculations of the after-tax cost of debt of the 8% loan notes lost marks by incorrectly applying the spreadsheet IRR function to three cash flows (such as −103.5, +6.4, +110), when it had to be applied to cash flows for each of six years (−103.5, +6.4, +6.4, +6.4, +6.4, +116.4).

Some candidates ignored the cost of debt of the bank loan, even though it was identified in the question as a non-current liability. Because the bank loan had a variable interest rate, a justified value for inclusion in the WACC calculation had to be provided. Some candidates correctly identified the after-tax cost of debt of the loan notes as an appropriate proxy value, while other argued for the after-tax interest rate on the loan notes. Some candidates used a value without providing an explanation for their choice. Whatever approach was adopted, the bank loan could not be ignored. Surprisingly, some candidates used the cost of equity, calculated using the CAPM, as the cost of debt of the bank loan.

In calculating the WACC itself, it was surprising to see some candidates using book values as weights when the explicit requirement was for a market value basis. Most candidates who calculated market values did so correctly. Some candidates included a tax effect in the WACC calculation when their calculated cost of debt was already on an after-tax basis. Some candidates unbalanced their weights by including the book value of the bank loan in the denominator while excluding the term for the cost of debt of the bank loan from the numerator.

Part (b)

Candidates were required here to discuss three suggestions on how an investment project costing $25m could be funded from internal finance sources. The first suggestion was to use reserves and a reduced investment in working capital. The second suggestion was to use the proceeds from selling the company's headquarters and relocating head office functions to several locations outside of the capital city. The third suggestion was to use cash released from a three-year reduction in dividends.

The problem with the first suggestion was that while the company had reserves of $29m, it only had $4m of cash and cash equivalents. Surprisingly, many candidates incorrectly believed that the company's equity reserves were cash which could be invested and discussed, sometimes at length, how the reserves represented an attractive source of finance which provided the full amount of cash needed. As for reducing investment in working capital, many candidates correctly discussed some of the difficulties which might arise in undertaking such a change in working capital investment strategy.

Discussion of the second suggestion was frequently of a good standard, with candidates correctly noting that while the full amount of the required finance could be delivered by the proposed sale, it might not be an immediate source of finance and its availability depended on whether the building was being used as security for debt finance. Some candidates queried the relocation costs which might arise, and the disruption to head office operations, and employee travel and working patterns, which might result, as well as the cost of renting or leasing accommodation outside the capital city.

Discussion of the third suggestion tended to focus on the reaction of shareholders to a cut in dividends, the existence of a dividend clientele, and arguments relating to dividend relevance or irrelevance in determining company value. Many candidates did not quantify the finance which might be available from a dividend cut, even though information which allowed such a calculation was given in the question.

BUSINESS VALUATIONS

59   CLOSE CO

Key answer tips

It is important to take note of how succinctly the model answer arrives at the answers for each element of part (a) as time can easily be wasted with more long-winded approaches.

Part (c) is a standalone requirement that could have been attempted first to gain some easy marks relatively quickly.

The highlighted words are key phrases that markers are looking for.

(a)   Net asset valuation

In the absence of any information about realisable values and replacement costs, net asset value is on a book value basis. It is the sum of non-current assets and net current assets, less long-term debt, i.e. 595 + 125 – 70 – 160 = $490 million.

Dividend growth model

$P_0 = D_0 (1 + g)/(r_e - g)$

Total dividends of $40 million are expected to grow at 4% per year and Close Co has a cost of equity of 10%. Value of company = (40m × 1.04)/(0.1 – 0.04) = $693 million.

Earnings yield method

Profit after tax (earnings) is $66.6 million and the finance director of Close Co thinks that an earnings yield of 11% per year can be used for valuation purposes.

Ignoring growth, value of company = 66.6m/0.11 = $606 million

Alternatively, profit after tax (earnings) is expected to grow at an annual rate of 5% per year and earnings growth can be incorporated into the earnings yield method using the growth model. Value of company = (66.6m × 1.05)/(0.11 – 0.05) = $1,166 million.

> **Examiner's note:** full credit would be gained whether or not growth is incorporated in the earnings yield method.

(b)   Market value of equity

Close Co has 80 million shares in issue and each share is worth $8.50 per share. The market value of equity is therefore 80 × 8.50 = $680 million.

Cost of equity

This is given as 10% per year.

Market value of 8% bonds

The market value of each bond will be the present value of the expected future cash flows (interest and principal) that arise from owning the bond. Annual interest is 8% per year and the bonds will be redeemed at their nominal value of $100 per bond in six years' time. The before-tax cost of debt is given as 7% per year and this is used as a discount rate.

Present value of future interest = (8 × 4.767) = $38.14

Present value of future principal payment = (100 × 0.666) = $66.60

Ex interest bond value = 38.14 + 66.60 = $104.74 per bond

Market value of bonds = 120m × (104.74/100) = $125.7 million

After-tax cost of debt of 8% bonds

The before-tax cost of debt of the bonds is given as 7% per year.

After-tax cost of debt of bonds = 7 × (1 − 0.3) = 7 × 0.7 = 4.9% per year

Value of the 6% bank loan

The bank loan has no market value and so its book value of $40 million is used in calculating the weighted average cost of capital.

After-tax cost of debt of 6% bank loan

The interest rate of the bank loan can be used as its before-tax cost of debt. After-tax cost of debt of bank loan = 6 × (1 − 0.3) = 6 × 0.7 = 4.2% per year.

Calculation of weighted average after-tax cost of capital (WACC)

Total value of company = 680m + 125.7m + 40m = $845.7m

After-tax WACC = [680/845.7] × 10 + [125.7/845.7] × 4.9 + [40/845.7] × 4.2 = 9.0 % per year.

> **Examiner's note:** the after-tax cost of debt of the 8% bonds could have been calculated using linear interpolation, although the result would be close to 4.9%.

(c) The weighted average cost of capital (WACC) is the average return required by current providers of finance. The WACC therefore reflects the current risk of a company's business operations (business risk) and way in which the company is currently financed (financial risk). When the WACC is used as discount rate to appraise an investment project, an assumption is being made that the project's business risk and financial risk are the same as those currently faced by the investing company. If this is not the case, a marginal cost of capital or a project-specific discount rate must be used to assess the acceptability of an investment project.

The business risk of an investment project will be the same as current business operations if the project is an extension of existing business operations, and if it is small in comparison with current business operations. If this is the case, existing providers of finance will not change their current required rates of return. If these conditions are not met, a project-specific discount rate should be calculated, for example by using the capital asset pricing model.

The financial risk of an investment project will be the same as the financial risk currently faced by a company if debt and equity are raised in the same proportions as currently used, thus preserving the existing capital structure. If this is the case, the current WACC can be used to appraise a new investment project. It may still be appropriate to use the current WACC as a discount rate even when the incremental finance raised does not preserve the existing capital structure, providing that the existing capital structure is preserved on an average basis over time via subsequent finance-raising decisions.

Where the capital structure is changed by finance raised for an investment project, it may be appropriate to use the marginal cost of capital rather than the WACC.

ACCA marking scheme			
			Marks
(a)	Net asset value		1
	Dividend growth model value		2
	Earnings yield method		2
			___
		Maximum	5
			___
(b)	Market value of equity		1
	Market value per bond		2
	Market value of bonds		1
	After-tax cost of debt		1
	After-tax cost of bank loan		1
	Weighted average cost of capital		2
			___
		Maximum	8
			___
(c)	Business risk		2–3
	Financial risk		2–3
	Project-specific discount rate		1–2
	Marginal cost of capital		1–2
			___
		Maximum	7
			___
Total			**20**
			___

Examiner's comments

Candidates were asked here to calculate the value of a company using net asset value, the dividend growth model and the earnings yield method.

It was surprising how many answers struggled to calculate net asset value from the statement of financial position figures provided in the question. This calculation is a relatively straightforward one.

Most candidates were able to calculate correctly the value of the company using the dividend growth model. Some answers wasted time calculating the value per share, but the question did not ask for this, rather it asked for the value of the company.

Fewer candidates were able to calculate correctly the value of the company using the earnings yield method, whether without earnings growth (earnings divided by earnings yield) or with earnings growth (using the growth model). Some answers converted the earnings yield figure given in the question into a price/earnings ratio (the one is the reciprocal of the other), but the price/earnings ratio valuation method was not asked for here. Some answers substituted the cost of equity for the earnings yield, or incorrectly used dividends rather than earnings.

The requirement in part (c) was to calculate the weighted average cost of capital (WACC) of a company. The cost of equity and the before-tax cost of debt were given in the question.

Some answers seemed to follow a learned routine for calculating WACC, without noting the information given by the question. This is the only reason I can offer to explain why some answers calculated the cost of equity, even though this was stated to be 10%. In order to calculate the WACC, the market values of equity and the 8% bonds were needed. Most answers calculated correctly the market value of equity. Many answers then assumed that the market value of the bonds was $120 million, but this was in fact the nominal (par) value of the bonds in the statement of financial position. The information needed to calculate the market value per bond was given in the question: interest rate, redemption value, maturity and cost of debt. Some answers calculated the market value using the after-tax interest payments, when the interest payments should have been before tax.

The after-tax cost of debt could be calculated by multiplying the before-tax cost of debt by one minus the tax rate, or by linear interpolation. Many answers used linear interpolation, but if the market value of the bonds had not been calculated, the interpolation calculation had no purpose. Candidates should be aware that if a bond is trading at nominal value ($100) and is to be redeemed at nominal value ($100), then the interest rate is the same as the cost of debt. A linear interpolation calculation using these values to find the cost of debt simply goes round in a circle back to the interest rate.

While some answers ignored the bank loan, other answers correctly included it using the after-tax interest cost as its cost of debt, or explaining why it could be costed using the after-tax cost of debt of the 8% bonds.

A small number of answers added reserves to the market value of equity, but reserves are only of significance when using book values as weights.

Part (d) asked for a discussion of the circumstances under which WACC could be used as the discount rate in investment appraisal, together with a brief indication of alternative approaches that could be used where WACC was not appropriate.

Good answers identified and discussed the link between business risk, financial risk and WACC, along the lines covered by the suggested answer. Essentially, WACC can be used as the discount rate in investment appraisal if business risk and financial risk do not change. Some answers ignored the requirement to indicate briefly alternative approaches that could be adopted and discussed at length the use of the capital asset pricing model in investment appraisal.

60   NN CO

Key answer tips

A fairly straightforward question for this key syllabus area. The calculations in parts (a) to (c) shouldn't present many problems and the discursive part (d) on market efficiency was also straightforward. The highlighted words are key phrases that markers are looking for.

(a)   Using the dividend growth model, the share price of NN Co will be the present value of its expected future dividends, i.e. $(66 \times 1.03)/(0.12 - 0.03)$ = 755 cents per share or $7.55 per share

Number of ordinary shares = 50/0.5 = 100m shares

Value of NN Co = 100m × 7.55 = $755m

Net asset value of NN Co = total assets less total liabilities = 143 − 29 − 20 − 25 = $69m

In calculating net asset value, preference share capital is included with long-term liabilities, as it is considered to be prior charge capital.

Tutorial note

Don't forget that you're trying to get back to the value of the company for the owners – meaning the ordinary shareholders. This is why you need to also deduct the value of preference shares, even though they are not shown as liabilities on the statement of financial position.

(b)   The after-tax cost of debt of NN Co can be found by linear interpolation

The annual after-tax interest payment = $7 \times (1 - 0.25)$ = 7 × 0.75 = $5.25 per year

Year	Cash flow ($)	5% Discount factor	Present value ($)
0	(103.50)	1.000	(103.50)
1–6	5.25	5.076	26.65
6	100	0.746	74.60
			─────
			(2.25)
			─────

Year	Cash flow ($)	4% Discount factor	Present value ($)
0	(103.50)	1.000	(103.50)
1–6	5.25	5.242	27.52
6	100	0.790	79.00
			3.02

After-tax cost of debt = 4 + [(1 × 3.02)/(3.02 + 2.25)] = 4 + 0.57 = 4.6%

Tutorial note

The calculated value of the after-tax cost of debt will be influenced by the choice of discount rates used in the linear interpolation calculation and so other values would also gain credit here.

(c) Annual preference dividend = 8% × 50 cents = 4 cents per share

Cost of preference shares = 100 × (4/67) = 6%

Number of ordinary shares = 50/0.5 = 100m shares

Market value of equity = V_e = 100m shares × 8.30 = $830m

Number of preference shares = 25/0.5 = 50m shares

Market value of preference shares = V_p = 0.67 × 50m = $33.5m

Market value of long-term borrowings = V_d = 20 × 103.50/100 = $20.7m

Total market value of company = (V_e + V_d + V_p) = (830 + 33.5 + 20.7) = $884.2m

WACC = [Ve/(Ve + Vd + Vp)] × ke + [Vp/(Ve + Vd + Vp)] × kp + [Vd/(Ve + Vd + Vp)] × kd

WACC = [830/884.2] × 12 + [33.5/884.2] × 6 + [20.7/884.2] × 4.6 = 11.6%

(d) Market efficiency is usually taken to refer to the way in which ordinary share prices reflect information. Fama defined an efficient market as one in which share prices fully and fairly reflect all available information.

A semi-strong form efficient market is one where share prices reflect all publicly available information, such as past share price movements, published company annual reports and analysts' reports in the financial press.

A strong form market is one where share prices reflect all information, whether publicly available or not. Share prices would reflect, for example, takeover decisions made at private board meetings.

	ACCA marking scheme		
			Marks
(a)	Share price using dividend growth model		2
	Value of company using dividend growth model		1
	Net asset value of company		2

		Maximum	5
(b)	Correct use of taxation		1
	Calculation of after-tax cost of debt		3

		Maximum	4
(c)	Cost of preference shares		1
	Market value of equity		1
	Market value of preference shares		1
	Market value of debt		1
	Weighted average cost of capital		2

		Maximum	6
(d)	Explanation of "efficiency"		1–2
	Semi-strong form		1–2
	Strong form		1–2

		Maximum	5
Total			**20**

Examiner's comments

Many candidates did well in parts (a)(i), (b) and (c), while doing poorly in part (a)(ii) and struggling to remain focused on the question asked in part (d).

In part (a) candidates were required to calculate the equity value of a company using the dividend growth model (DGM) and then the net asset value.

Many candidates calculated correctly the share price of the company using the DGM, although some candidates failed to multiply this share price by the number of shares to give the equity value of the company. Poorer answers re-arranged the DGM in order to calculate a cost of equity using the current share price, but this was unnecessary, as the cost of equity was given in the question.

The net asset value calculated by many candidates showed that they were uncertain as to the meaning of 'net asset value'. Some candidates gave a net asset value of $94 million, a figure which fails to treat preference share capital as prior charge capital and hence include it with long-term liabilities.

Part (b) asked candidates to calculate the after-tax cost of debt of a company. Many candidates gained full marks by calculating the after-tax interest payment, using two discount rates to calculate two net present values for investing in the bond, and using linear interpolation to calculate the after-tax cost of debt. Answers that did not gain full marks contained errors such as using the wrong tax rate (it was 25%), addition or multiplication errors, using the before-tax interest payment, or putting incorrect values to variables in the linear interpolation calculation.

Some answers calculated the cost of capital of preference shares in addition to calculating the after-tax cost of debt, and then attempted to average the two costs of capital. While preference shares are classed as prior charge capital, they pay a dividend, not interest, and preference shares are not debt.

In part (c), candidates were required to calculate the weighted average cost of capital (WACC) of a company. Candidates therefore needed to calculate the market values of ordinary shares, preference shares and bonds, and the preference share cost of capital, having already calculated the after-tax cost of debt and being given the cost of equity by the question.

The most common reason for not gaining full marks was calculating incorrectly the cost of capital of the preference shares. This can be found by dividing the preference dividend by the market price of the preference share, but many candidates used the dividend rate of the preference shares (8% per year) as the dividend, instead of calculating the preference dividend from the nominal value (par value), i.e. 8% of 50 cents giving a dividend of 4 cents per share.

Other reasons for losing marks included aggregating the market values of ordinary shares and preference shares, before applying the cost of equity to both: omitting the preference share capital from the WACC calculation; multiplying the after-tax cost of debt by $(1 - t)$ (one minus the tax rate); and calculating a new cost of equity, even though the cost of equity was given in the question.

61 CORHIG CO

Key answer tips

To answer this question effectively you need a logical approach and an awareness of the calculations behind the valuation methods. A look down the formulae sheet will help to reveal the correct path.

The highlighted words are key phrases that markers are looking for.

(a)

Tutorial note

On the face of it, the price/earnings ratio valuation method is simple. Find an earnings figure, or earnings per share (EPS) figure, multiply by a price/earnings ratio and you have either the value of the company (if you used earnings) or a share price (if you used EPS). The number of issued shares of Corhig Co was not given in the question and some answers invented a figure, but as the requirement was to calculate the value of the company, the number of shares was not needed.

Price/earnings ratio valuation

The value of the company using this valuation method is found by multiplying future earnings by a price/earnings ratio. Using the earnings of Corhig Co in Year 1 and the price/earnings ratio of similar listed companies gives a value of 3,000,000 × 5 = $15,000,000.

Using the current average price/earnings ratio of similar listed companies as the basis for the valuation rests on two questionable assumptions. First, in terms of similarity, the valuation assumes similar business operations, similar capital structures, similar earnings growth prospects, and so on. In reality, no two companies are identical. Second, in terms of using an average price/earnings ratio, this may derive from companies that are large and small, successful and failing, low-geared and high-geared, and domestic or international in terms of markets served. The calculated company value therefore has a large degree of uncertainty attached to it.

The earnings figure used in the valuation does not include expected earnings growth. If average forecast earnings over the next three years are used ($3.63 million), the price/earnings ratio value increases by 21% to $18.15 million (3.63 × 5). Although earnings growth beyond the third year is still ignored, $18.15 million is likely to be a better estimate of the value of the company than $15 million because it recognises that earnings are expected to increase by almost 50% in the next three years.

(b)

Tutorial note

A useful point to remember with questions such as this is that it is essential to pin down the amount and the timing of future cash flows when calculating present values.

Value of company using the dividend valuation model

The current cost of equity using the capital asset pricing model = 4 + (1.6 × 5) = 12%

Since a dividend will not be paid in Year 1, the dividend growth model cannot be applied straight away. However, dividends after Year 3 are expected to grow at a constant annual rate of 3% per year and so the dividend growth model can be applied to these dividends. The present value of these dividends is a Year 3 present value, which will need discounting back to year 0. The market value of the company can then be found by adding this to the present value of the forecast dividends in Years 2 and 3.

PV of year 2 dividend = $500,000/1.12^2$ = $398,597

PV of year 3 dividend = $1,000,000/1.12^3$ = $711,780

Year 3 PV of dividends after year 3 = (1,000,000 × 1.03)/(0.12 – 0.03) = $11,444,444

Year 0 PV of these dividends = $11,444,444/1.12^3$ = $8,145,929

Market value from dividend valuation model = 398,597 + 711,780 + 8,145,929 = $9,256,306 or approximately $9.3 million.

Alternative calculation of dividend valuation method market value

The year 3 dividend of $1m can be treated as D1 from the perspective of year 2

The year 2 value of future dividends using the dividend growth model will then be:

$1,000,000/(0.12 − 0.03) = $11,111,111

Year 0 PV of these dividends = 11,111,111/1.122 = $8,857,710

Adding the PV of the year 2 dividend gives a market value of 8,857,710 + 398,597 = $9,256,308 which, allowing for rounding, is the same as the earlier calculated value.

(c) **Current weighted average after-tax cost of capital**

Current cost of equity using the capital asset pricing model = 12%

After-tax cost of debt = 5 × (1 − 0.2) = 5 × 0.8 = 4%

Current after-tax WACC = (12 × 0.75) + (4 × 0.25) = 10% per year

Weighted average after-tax cost of capital after new debt issue

Revised cost of equity = K_e = 4 + (2.0 × 5) = 14%

Revised after-tax cost of debt = 6 × (1 − 0.2) = 6 × 0.8 = 4.8%

Revised after-tax WACC = (14 × 0.6) + (4.8 × 0.4) = 10.32% per year

Comment

The after-tax WACC has increased slightly from 10% to 10.32%. This change is a result of the increases in the cost of equity and the after-tax cost of debt, coupled with the change in gearing. Although the cost of equity has increased, the effect of the increase has been reduced because the proportion of equity finance has fallen from 75% to 60% of the long-term capital employed. Although the after-tax cost of debt has increased, the cost of debt is less than the cost of equity and the proportion of cheaper debt finance has increased from 25% to 40% of the long-term capital employed.

(d) **Nature and assessment of business risk**

Business risk arises due to the nature of a company's business operations, which determines the business sector into which it is classified, and to the way in which a company conducts its business operations. It is the variability in shareholder returns that arises as a result of business operations.

Business risk can therefore be related to the way in which profit before interest and tax (PBIT or operating profit) changes as revenue changes. This can be assessed from a shareholder perspective by calculating operational gearing, which essentially looks at the relative proportions of fixed operating costs to variable operating costs.

Another measure of operational gearing that can be used is (100 × contribution/PBIT), although other measures are also used.

	ACCA marking scheme		
			Marks
(a)	Price/earnings value using year 1 earnings		1
	Price/earnings value using average earnings		1
	Discussion of variables		2
			___
		Maximum	4
			___
(b)	Calculation of current cost of equity using CAPM		1
	PV of year 2 dividends		0.5
	PV of year 3 dividends		0.5
	Year 3 DGM value		2
	Year 0 PV of year 3 DGM value		1
	Company value using dividend valuation model		1
			___
		Maximum	6
			___
(c)	After-tax cost of debt		1
	After-tax WACC		1
	Revised cost of equity using CAPM		2
	Revised after-tax WACC		1
	Comment on change in WACC		1
			___
		Maximum	6
			___
(d)	Nature of business risk		1–2
	Assessment of business risk		1–2
			___
		Maximum	4
			___
Total			**20**
			___

> **Examiner's comments**
>
> In part (a) the requirement was to calculate the value of a company (Corhig Co) using the price/earnings ratio (PER) method, discussing the usefulness of the variables used. Many students struggled with this question.
>
> In reality, the PER method presents a number of problems, and this was illustrated by the question, which provided forecast earnings for the end of year 1, the end of year 2 and the end of year 3. What earnings figure should be used to give a PER value? It is better to use future earnings than past earnings and as the question shows, a value for future earnings should not be selected mechanically, but after careful thought.
>
> Part (b) asked for a calculation of the current cost of equity of Corhig Co, and an estimate of the value of the company using the dividend valuation model.
>
> Most answers correctly calculated the current cost of equity using the capital asset pricing model, although some answers confused the equity risk premium of 5% given in the question with the return on the market. Most answers struggled to use the dividend valuation model to value the company. Simply put, the dividend valuation model holds that the value of a company is equal to the present value of its future dividend. Most answers limited their valuation attempt to using the dividend growth model, ignoring the dividend expected in year 2. The dividend growth model can be used to provide a year 3 present value of the dividend stream expected after year 3. This year 2 present value then needed to be discounted back to year 0, and added to the present values of the dividend from years 2 and 3, to give the value of the company.

Part (c) asked candidates to calculate the current weighted average cost of capital (WACC) of Corhig Co, and then the revised WACC following a debt issue, commenting on the difference between the two values. Many answers gained high marks here, although some answers failed to offer a comment.

Many answers to part (d) showed the need to think about the nature of the risk faced by shareholders. Better answers gave evidence of an understanding of underlying concepts and used key terms.

62   MAT CO

Key answer tips

To answer part (a) effectively you need a logical approach and an awareness of the calculations behind the valuation methods. A look down the formulae sheet will help to reveal the correct path for part (a) (i).

This question is an excellent example of how calculations alone will not get you through this exam. Part (b) requires you to understand the meaning of the calculations so you can comment sensibly on your results. Finally, part (c) gives you an opportunity to demonstrate your knowledge about raising finance. If you are to score well on this section, you must apply your comments to the specific scenario presented.

(a)   Dividend growth model

From the formulae sheet – $P_0 = \dfrac{Do(1 + g)}{(r_e - g)}$

Tutorial note

From the formulae sheet, you can directly see that to calculate the share price (P_0) using the growth model, you will need three pieces of information: the dividend (D_0), the growth rate in dividends (g) and the cost of equity (r_e). Now you can look into the scenario and see how this information can be obtained.

1   You're told the dividend about to be paid is 5.0 cents.

2   You've been provided with information on the dividends paid in recent years. This means you can calculate the historic growth rate and assume this will continue in the future. Since we don't have any information on profitability, this will be only method of estimating dividend growth in this question.

3   You've been told that the return on government bonds (i.e. the risk free rate of return) is 5% and that the equity risk premium ($R_m - R_f$) is 8%. These pieces of information should trigger you to realise that CAPM can be used to calculate the cost of equity. In the formulae sheet you're given the correct formula to use.

To calculate the cost of equity (r_e) using CAPM, we have the formula (from the sheet)

$E(r)_j = R_f + \beta_j (E(r_m) - R_f)$

$r_e = 5\% + (1.15 \times 8\%) = 14.2\%$

Annual dividend growth (g) = $\sqrt[n]{\dfrac{\text{current dividend}}{\text{dividend n years ago}}} - 1$

$g = \sqrt[3]{\dfrac{5.0}{4.1}} - 1 = 0.0684$

Value per share = $\dfrac{5.0 \times 1.0684}{0.142 - 0.0684}$ = 72.6c

Total number of shares – $40m ÷ 0.25 = 160 million

Total equity value (ex div) – 160m × $0.726 = $116.16m

(b)

Summary of equity values:

Dividend growth model (from (a)(i) above)	$116.16m
Total market value of equity (ex div) (from the scenario): 160m × ($0.66 – $0.05) =	$97.6m

Tutor's top tips

To score well on this sort of requirement you must look at each number in turn and outline the arguments for and against the value as a basis. Remember, business valuation is not a precise science and many of the theories presented can be challenged when faced with reality.

Comments:

The dividend growth model value is just under $20m higher than the current market value.

A market value is often considered a highly relevant value but the current market value of MAT Co could be understated because the market is a secondary market and hence may not be so efficient and may not properly reflect the value of MAT Co. The market value may also be understated because the shares in the company are only traded infrequently and hence are not very liquid.

The dividend growth model could be incorrect and hence less relevant as it is very sensitive to changes in the inputs. For instance, the forecast dividend growth rate is just based on recent growth and could prove wrong. The growth rate forecast of 6.84% does seem high given recent economic circumstances and could well prove unsustainable. Equally, the cost of equity used is based on an estimate of the equity beta. This estimate could be incorrect.

(c)

Tutor's top tips

Key to scoring well on this requirement is to relate your comments back to the scenario given. Simply writing a list of generic factors that any company should consider will not score highly.

The directors of MAT Co should take the following factors into account when considering how to raise additional finance:

Cost – Debt finance is cheaper and hence if the company has the capacity to raise more debt it could be advantageous. Indeed, given the property value in the company of $65m and the long-term debt of only $18m the company would seem capable of raising more debt.

Cash flows – Prior to raising more debt the company must forecast future cash flows to ensure sufficient cash will be generated to service any debt raised. Given the current cash balances the company does seem to be cash generative.

Risk – Prior to raising finance, the directors must consider the risk of the company. For instance if future expansion is going to increase the business risk of the company they may be more wary of taking on more debt and increasing the financial risk. Equally, the directors should consider the gearing/financial risk of similar companies and the appetite for risk of the shareholders.

Availability – The directors must consider the likely availability of finance.

As the shares do not seem very liquid raising new equity from new investors may be difficult. Equally, they should question whether the existing shareholders have the ability to support a rights issue. Given the recent dividend growth and dividend yield they may be happy to invest more in the company.

More debt finance is likely to be available if the company can show good cash flow forecasts as plenty of security seems available.

Security and Covenants – The directors must be aware that additional debt finance is likely to require security and may require covenants. The directors must ensure they are happy to give any such guarantees before raising additional debt.

Control – The directors must consider that raising equity from new investors could have an impact upon the control of the company.

Duration – The directors must consider the term of any proposed finance and make sure it is appropriate given the nature of what it is to be invested in. Furthermore, the investors should ensure that any new debt finance does not become repayable at the same time as the existing long term liability as this could put a large cash flow strain on the company.

Economic outlook – Prior to raising finance the directors should ensure that they have considered the outlook for the economy and the impact this could have on the trade of the company and the cost of finance. In particular, the outlook for interest rates should be considered if debt finance is to be raised.

63   THP CO *Walk in the footsteps of a top tutor*

Key answer tips

The key learning point from this question is the importance of making sure your marker can follow your answer. This will often involve explaining your thought process, including commenting on why the calculation you've performed is the right approach. The highlighted words are key phrases that markers are looking for.

Tutor's top tips

In the 15 minutes reading time you should aim to have skim read the scenario, getting a feeling for the information you've been provided with and paying particular attention to names and dates. You should also have skim read the requirement, underlining the models referred to and noted the calculations that are being asked for. Look for any part of the question that relies purely on knowledge of the syllabus (i.e. no calculations) and flag these as a good place to start. Part (e) of this question falls into this category.

Once you've completed part (e) you should look at the other requirements. Is there a specific order you will need to do them in or can you choose your strongest area to do first. Here we'll need to tackle the requirements in order as you need the output of part (a) to answer part (b).

Tutor's top tips

In part (a) you should follow the order presented in the requirement. It is leading you through the process. All the information is stated in the scenario or can be calculated without many complications. Part (iv) is the area most likely to cause problems (although you might not realise it at the time). The majority of situations the market capitalisation after an issue would be the TERP × new number of shares in issue. However, in this scenario, we've been told of some issue costs which must be deducted. Don't worry if you didn't spot this, it will only have been worth 2 marks (maximum). However, this does show the benefits of querying every piece of information provided by the examiner and asking "why has he told me that?"

(a)   Rights issue price

This is at a 20% discount to the current share price = 4.80 × 0.8 = $3.84 per share

New shares issued = 3m/3 = 1m

Cash raised = 1m × 3.84 = $3,840,000

Theoretical ex rights price = [(3 × 4.80) + 3.84]/4 = $4.56 per share

Market capitalisation after rights issue = 14.4m + 3.84m = $18.24 – 0.32m = $17.92m

This is equivalent to a share price of 17.92/4 = $4.48 per share

The issue costs result in a decrease in the market value of the company and therefore a decrease in the wealth of shareholders equivalent to 8c per share.

Tutor's top tips

The key to part (b) is recognising that since CRX is in the same business sector as THP, you can use THP's P/E ratio as a proxy for CRX. Whilst you're not specifically told this, you do have the information to work it out. Make sure your answer explains what you're doing and why this is an acceptable approach.

(b) **Price/earnings ratio valuation**

Price/earnings ratio of THP Co = 480/64 = 7.5

Earnings per share of CRX Co = 44.8c per share

Using the price earnings ratio method, share price of CRX Co = (44.8 × 7.5)/100 = $3.36

Market capitalisation of CRX Co = 3.36 × 1m = $3,360,000

(Alternatively, earnings of CRX Co = 1m × 0.448 = $448,000 × 7.5 = $3,360,000)

Tutor's top tips

Part (c) starts by asking you to assume a semi-strong form efficient market. Your first thought should be to consider the implications of this, which is that only publicly available information will be reflected in the share price. Again, you should note down your thought process. Next, you will need to identify what will affect the market capitalisation post acquisition. You should conclude this will be the market capitalisation of THP plus the market capitalisation of CRX less the price paid for CRX (since this cash has left the business). All of this information is available, either as a result of your previous calculations or given in the scenario. Only in part (ii) will we need to factor in the additional savings since this information has now been made public.

(c) In a semi-strong form efficient capital market, share prices reflect past and public information. If the expected annual after-tax savings are not announced, this information will not therefore be reflected in the share price of THP Co. In this case, the post acquisition market capitalisation of THP Co will be the market capitalisation after the rights issue, plus the market capitalisation of the acquired company (CRX Co), less the price paid for the shares of CRX Co, since this cash has left the company in exchange for purchased shares. It is assumed that the market capitalisations calculated in earlier parts of this question are fair values, including the value of CRX Co calculated by the price/earnings ratio method.

Price paid for CRX Co = 3.84m – 0.32m = $3.52m

Market capitalisation = 17.92m + 3.36m − 3.52m = $17.76m

This is equivalent to a share price of 17.76/4 = $4.44 per share

The market capitalisation has decreased from the value following the rights issue because THP Co has paid $3.52m for a company apparently worth $3.36m. This is a further decrease in the wealth of shareholders, following on from the issue costs of the rights issue.

If the annual after-tax savings are announced, this information will be reflected quickly and accurately in the share price of THP Co since the capital market is semi-strong form efficient. The savings can be valued using the price/earnings ratio method as having a present value of $720,000 (7.5 × 96,000). The revised market capitalisation of THP Co is therefore $18.48m (17.76m + 0.72m), equivalent to a share price of $4.62 per share (18.48/4). This makes the acquisition of CRX Co attractive to the shareholders of THP Co, since it offers a higher market capitalisation than the one following the rights issue. Each shareholder of THP Co would experience a capital gain of 14c per share (4.62 − 4.48).

In practice, the capital market is likely to anticipate the annual after-tax savings before they are announced by THP Co.

Tutor's top tips

Part (d) is an opportunity to score an easy 8 marks by discussing the relative things to consider when deciding between debt and equity. Be careful though, the requirement does specify that your points should be relevant to THP. So for example, don't just talk about the impact on gearing, work it out using the information provided. To ensure you don't spend too much time on this part of the question, you should think about the mark allocation. For 8 marks where you are being asked to 'discuss' you should be spend no more than 14 minutes (8 × 1.8 mins per mark) talking about 4 factors THP should consider. Contrast this with a requirement to 'state' or 'list' which is more likely to attract only 1 mark per relevant point.

(d) There are a number of factors that should be considered by THP Co, including the following:

Gearing and financial risk

Equity finance will decrease gearing and financial risk, while debt finance will increase them. Gearing for THP Co is currently 68.5% and this will decrease to 45% if equity finance is used, or rise to 121% if debt finance is used. There may also be some acquired debt finance in the capital structure of CRX Co. THP Co needs to consider what level of financial risk is desirable, from both a corporate and a stakeholder perspective.

Target capital structure

THP Co needs to compare its capital structure after the acquisition with its target capital structure. If its primary financial objective is to maximise the wealth of shareholders, it should seek to minimise its weighted average cost of capital (WACC). In practical terms this can be achieved by having some debt in its capital structure, since debt is relatively cheaper than equity, while avoiding the extremes of too little gearing (WACC can be decreased further) or too much gearing (the company suffers from the costs of financial distress).

Availability of security

Debt will usually need to be secured on assets by either a fixed charge (on specific assets) or a floating charge (on a specified class of assets). The amount of finance needed to buy CRX CO would need to be secured by a fixed charge to specific fixed assets of THP Co. Information on these fixed assets and on the secured status of the existing 8% loan notes has not been provided.

Economic expectations

If THP Co expects buoyant economic conditions and increasing profitability in the future, it will be more prepared to take on fixed interest debt commitments than if it believes difficult trading conditions lie ahead.

Control issues

A rights issue will not dilute existing patterns of ownership and control, unlike an issue of shares to new investors. The choice between offering new shares to existing shareholders and to new shareholders will depend in part on the amount of finance that is needed, with rights issues being used for medium-sized issues and issues to new shareholders being used for large issues. Issuing traded debt also has control implications however, since restrictive or negative covenants are usually written into the bond issue documents.

Workings

Current gearing (debt/equity, book value basis) = 100 × 5,000/7,300 = 68.5%

Gearing if equity finance is used = 100 × 5,000/(7,300 + 3,840) = 45%

Gearing if debt finance is used = 100 × (5,000 + 3,840)/7,300 = 121%

ACCA marking scheme			
			Marks
(a)		Rights issue price	1
		Cash raised	1
		Theoretical ex rights price per share	1
		Market capitalisation	2
			—
			5
(b)		Calculation of price/earnings ratio	1
		Price/earnings ratio valuation	2
			—
			3
(c)		Calculations of market capitalisation	2–3
		Comment	3–4
			—
		Maximum	5
(d)		Relevant discussion	6–7
		Links to scenario in question	2–3
			—
		Maximum	7
			—
Total			**20**
			—

Examiner's comments

In part (a) candidates were asked to calculate the rights issue price per share, the cash raised by the rights issue, the theoretical ex rights price per share and the market capitalisation after the rights issue.

A significant number of candidates showed that they were unfamiliar with this part of the syllabus and gave answers that gained little credit. Candidates should be aware that rights issues will not be made at a discount to nominal value.

Part (b) required the use of the price/earnings ratio method to calculate a share price and market capitalisation. Answers to this part of question 2 were often incomplete or adopted an incorrect methodology, for example calculating the price/earnings ratio of the target company when the question did not give the information needed for this. The correct approach is to multiply an earnings per share figure (or total earnings) by a suitable price/earnings ratio (in this case that of the acquirer).

Part (c) asked candidates to calculate and comment on market capitalisation before and after an announcement of expected annual after-tax cost savings, assuming a semi-strong form efficient market. The key thing to remember here is that in such a market, share prices fully and fairly reflect all relevant past and public information. The market capitalisation after the announcement would include the present value of the expected savings, calculated for example by the price/earnings method or by the dividend growth model. Before the announcement, the market capitalisation would not include this information and would be the market capitalisation immediately after the rights issue had taken place, adjusted for issue costs and the market value of the company acquired. Many candidates did not offer any calculations to support their discussion here, or offered calculations that did not relate to the question asked. Please refer to the suggested answer to this question for more detailed information on appropriate discussion and calculations.

Part (d) asked for a discussion of the factors that should be considered in choosing between equity and debt, with the answer being related to the circumstances of the acquirer and its proposed cash offer. Good answers focused on the circumstances of the company, considered its current capital structure, and discussed such factors as financial risk, current and expected interest rates, security and servicing costs, while weak answers offered a brief list of points with no discussion.

64   DARTIG CO *Walk in the footsteps of a top tutor*

Key answer tips

This question has a few trickier elements that may unnerve some students.

Part (e) gives the easiest opportunity to grab marks. A straightforward explanation of the agency problem as well as how share options could be used to reduce the issue should allow most students to score highly. Being unrelated to the other parts, it should be tackled first.

The other four parts to the question all require some degree of calculations. Part (a) is also straightforward, and should result in full marks for most candidates.

Part (d) should be reasonable for most candidates. The highlighted words are key phrases that markers are looking for.

(a)   Rights issue price = 2.5 × 0.8 = $2.00 per share

Theoretical ex rights price = ((2.50 × 4) + (1 × 2.00)/5=$2.40 per share

(Alternatively, number of rights shares issued = $5m/$2.00 = 2.5m shares

Existing number of shares = 4 × 2.5m = 10m shares

Theoretical ex rights price per share = ((10m × 2.50) + (2.5m × 2.00))/12.5m = $2.40).

Tutor's top tips

In parts (b) and (c), students may be thrown by the assertion that "the expansion of existing business will allow the average growth rate of earnings per share over the last four years to be maintained". A rights issue would normally result in a fall in EPS due to the higher number of shares in issue. In this case though, the new finance from the rights issue will be invested and will earn a sufficiently high return to avoid the usual reduction. Indeed, growth of 4% is being predicted.

Some background calculations may help to illustrate this further:

$$\frac{\$5m}{\$2.50 \times 80\%} = 2.5 \text{ million new shares to be issued.}$$

A 1 for 4 rights issue therefore implies the company must have 10 million shares in issue at present and will have 12.5 million after the rights issue.

Current EPS = 32.4 cents. Total earnings is therefore 0.324 × 10 million = $3.24 million

New total earnings will be 12.5 million × $0.324 × 1.04 = $4.21 million.

In the cold light of day, it is not unreasonable to expect the finance raised to increase earnings by this amount (an annual return of just under 20%). However, such rational thought often escapes candidates within the pressure of the exam hall.

(b)   Current price/earnings ratio = 250/32.4 = 7.7 times

Average growth rate of earnings per share = $100 \times ((32.4/27.7)^{0.25} - 1) = 4.0\%$

Earnings per share following expansion = $32.4 \times 1.04 = 33.7$ cents per share

Share price predicted by price/earnings ratio method = $33.7 \times 7.7 = \$2.60$

Since the price/earnings ratio of Dartig Co has remained constant in recent years and the expansion is of existing business, it seems reasonable to apply the existing price/earnings ratio to the revised earnings per share value.

(c)   The proposed business expansion will be an acceptable use of the rights issue funds if it increases the wealth of the shareholders. The share price predicted by the price/earnings ratio method is \$2.60. This is greater than the current share price of \$2.50, but this is not a valid comparison, since it ignores the effect of the rights issue on the share price. The rights issue has a neutral effect on shareholder wealth, but the cum rights price is changed by the increase in the number of shares and by the transformation of cash wealth into security wealth from a shareholder point of view. The correct comparison is with the theoretical ex rights price, which was found earlier to be \$2.40. Dartig Co shareholders will experience a capital gain due to the business expansion of $\$2.60 - 2.40 = 20$ cents per share. However, these share prices are one year apart and hence not directly comparable.

If the dividend yield remains at 6% per year ($100 \times 15.0/250$), the dividend per share for 20X8 will be 15.6 cents (other estimates of the 20X8 dividend per share are possible). Adding this to the capital gain of 20 cents gives a total shareholder return of 35.6 cents or 14.24% ($100 \times 35.6/240$). This is greater than the cost of equity of 10% and so shareholder wealth has increased.

Tutor's top tips

The model answer for both parts (b) and (c) both illustrate an approach to the question set but it is doubtful that many students actually produced the results presented, especially regarding the total shareholder return. However, even if you have difficulties getting your head around the situation, it is still possible to gather many of the marks. Method marks are available for any students who demonstrate a logical approach and utilise the basic price/earnings ratio method.

(d)   The primary financial management objective of a company is usually taken to be the maximisation of shareholder wealth. In practice, the managers of a company acting as agents for the principals (the shareholders) may act in ways which do not lead to shareholder wealth maximisation. The failure of managers to maximise shareholder wealth is referred to as the agency problem.

Shareholder wealth increases through payment of dividends and through appreciation of share prices. Since share prices reflect the value placed by buyers on the right to receive future dividends, analysis of changes in shareholder wealth focuses on changes in share prices. The objective of maximising share prices is commonly used as a substitute objective for that of maximising shareholder wealth.

The agency problem arises because the objectives of managers differ from those of shareholders: because there is a divorce or separation of ownership from control in modern companies; and because there is an asymmetry of information between shareholders and managers that prevents shareholders being aware of most managerial decisions.

One way to encourage managers to act in ways that increase shareholder wealth is to offer them share options. These are rights to buy shares on a future date at a price which is fixed when the share options are issued. Share options will encourage managers to make decisions that are likely to lead to share price increases (such as investing in projects with positive net present values), since this will increase the rewards they receive from share options. The higher the share price in the market when the share options are exercised, the greater will be the capital gain that could be made by managers owning the options.

Share options therefore go some way towards reducing the differences between the objectives of shareholders and managers. However, it is possible that managers may be rewarded for poor performance if share prices in general are increasing. It is also possible that managers may not be rewarded for good performance if share prices in general are falling. It is difficult to decide on a share option exercise price and a share option exercise date that will encourage managers to focus on increasing shareholder wealth while still remaining challenging, rather than being easily achievable.

ACCA marking scheme			Marks
(a)	Rights issue price	1	
	Theoretical ex rights price per share	2	
			3
(b)	Existing price/earnings ratio	1	
	Revised earnings per share	1	
	Share price using price/earnings method	1	
			3
(c)	Discussion of share price comparisons	3 – 4	
	Calculation of capital gain and comment	1 – 2	
			Max 5
(d)	Discussion of agency problem	4 – 5	
	Discussion of share option schemes	4 – 5	
			Max 9
Total			20

Examiner's comments

In part (a), candidates were asked to calculate a theoretical ex rights price per share. Many candidates gained full marks for their calculations. Weaker answers made errors as regards the form of the issue (it was 1 for 4, not 4 for 1), or thought the theoretical ex rights price was the rights issue price, or calculated the value of the rights.

Part (b) required the calculation of the share price after the business expansion, using the price/earnings ratio method. The first step was to calculate the current price/earnings ratio. The second step was to calculate the earnings per share (EPS) after the proposed business expansion. The final step was to calculate the future share price by multiplying the two together.

A number of candidates were not able to calculate the price/earnings ratio by dividing the current share price by the current EPS. Calculating the EPS after the expansion by multiplying the current EPS by the average historic EPS growth rate was also a problem for some candidates, who were unable to calculate average historic growth rate, or who applied the growth rate to the average EPS rather than the current EPS.

Some students were also unfamiliar with the PER valuation method, even though this is discussed in the study texts.

Part (c) asked for a discussion of whether the business expansion was an acceptable use of the rights issue funds, and an evaluation of the effect of the expansion on the wealth of shareholders. The two parts of the question are linked, since the question of whether the use made of the finance is acceptable depends on the effect on the wealth of shareholders.

If shareholder wealth increases, the proposed use of the finance is acceptable. Better answers therefore looked to compare the theoretical rights price per share (the share price before the rights issue funds were invested) with the share price after the investment had taken place (for example the share price calculated in part (b)), or to compare the return from the investment (for example, total shareholder return, which is the sum of capital gain and divided yield) with the cost of equity.

Part (d) required candidates to explain the nature of the agency problem and to discuss using share option schemes to reduce it in a stock-market listed company. The agency problem is that managers may act in ways that do not lead to the maximisation of shareholder wealth. Shareholder wealth increases through receiving dividends and through capital gains in share prices, and is usually assessed through changes in share prices. Better answers referred to these key financial management concepts.

Share option schemes, in making managers into shareholders, lead to convergence of objectives, if only on a shared focus on increased wealth through increasing share prices. Unfortunately, while share prices increases can arise from good managerial decisions, share price changes can arise for other reasons as well. There was scope here for candidates to discuss a range of issues relating to the difficulty of designing a share option scheme that rewarded managers for good performance, but not for poor performance.

65 PHOBIS

Key answer tips

This question has three discrete requirements that are of varying difficulty. To score well you must ensure you capture the easy marks quickly and don't get bogged down on one particular area meaning you run out of time, or worse still, run over time and limit your ability to get all marks on later questions. Part (b) is the most difficult of the three requirements. This should have been tackled last. The highlighted words are key phrases that markers are looking for.

(a) **(i)** **Price/earnings ratio method valuation**

Earnings per share of Danoca Co = 40c

Average sector price/earnings ratio = 10

Implied value of ordinary share of Danoca Co = 40 × 10 = $4.00

Number of ordinary shares = 5 million

Value of Danoca Co = 4.00 × 5m = $20 million

(ii) **Dividend growth model**

Earnings per share of Danoca Co = 40c

Proposed payout ratio = 60%

Proposed dividend of Danoca Co is therefore = 40 × 0.6 = 24c

If the future dividend growth rate is expected to continue the historical trend in dividends per share, the historic dividend growth rate can be used as a substitute for the expected future dividend growth rate in the dividend growth model. Average geometric dividend growth rate over the last two years = (24/22)1/2 = 1.045 or 4.5% (Alternatively, dividend growth rates over the last two years were 3% (24/23.3) and 6% (23.3/22), with an arithmetic average of (6 + 3)/2 = 4.5%).

Cost of equity of Danoca Co using the capital asset pricing model (CAPM)

= 4.6 + 1.4 × (10.6 − 4.6) = 4.6 + (1.4 × 6) = 13%

Value of ordinary share from dividend growth model = (24 × 1.045)/(0.13 − 0.045) = $2.95

Value of Danoca Co = 2.95 × 5m = $14.75 million

The current market capitalisation of Danoca Co is $16.5m ($3.30 × 5m). The price/earnings ratio value of Danoca Co is higher than this at $20m, using the average price/earnings ratio used for the sector. Danoca's own price/earnings ratio is 8.25. The difference between the two price/earnings ratios may indicate that there is scope for improving the financial performance of Danoca Co following the acquisition. If Phobis Co has the managerial skills to effect this improvement, the company and its shareholders may be able to benefit as a result of the acquisition.

The dividend growth model value is lower than the current market capitalisation at $14.75m. This represents a minimum value that Danoca shareholders will accept if Phobis Co makes an offer to buy their shares. In reality they would want more than this as an inducement to sell. The current market capitalisation of Danoca Co of $16.5m may reflect the belief of the stock market that a takeover bid for the company is imminent and, depending on its efficiency, may indicate a fair price for Danoca's shares, at least on a marginal trading basis. Alternatively, either the cost of equity or the expected dividend growth rate used in the dividend growth model calculation could be inaccurate, or the difference between the two values may be due to a degree of inefficiency in the stock market.

(b) **Calculation of market value of each convertible bond**

Expected share price in five years' time = $4.45 \times 1.065^5 = \$6.10$

Conversion value = $6.10 \times 20 = \$122$

Compared with redemption at nominal value of $100, conversion will be preferred

The current market value will be the present value of future interest payments, plus the present value of the conversion value, discounted at the cost of debt of 7% per year.

Market value of each convertible bond = $(9 \times 4.100) + (122 \times 0.713) = \$123.89$

Calculation of floor value of each convertible bond

The current floor value will be the present value of future interest payments, plus the present value of the redemption value, discounted at the cost of debt of 7% per year.

Floor value of each convertible bond = $(9 \times 4.100) + (100 \times 0.713) = \$108.20$

Calculation of conversion premium of each convertible bond

Current conversion value = $4.45 \times 20 = \$89.00$

Conversion premium = $\$123.89 - 89.00 = \$34.89$

This is often expressed on a per share basis, i.e. 34.89/20 = $1.75 per share

(c) Stock market efficiency usually refers to the way in which the prices of traded financial securities reflect relevant information.

When research indicates that share prices fully and fairly reflect public information as well as past information, a stock market is described as semi-strong form efficient.

The significance to a listed company of its shares being traded on a stock market which is found to be semi-strong form efficient is that any information relating to the company is quickly and accurately reflected in its share price. Managers will not be able to deceive the market by the timing or presentation of new information, such as annual reports or analysts' briefings, since the market processes the information quickly and accurately to produce fair prices. Managers should therefore simply concentrate on making financial decisions that increase the wealth of shareholders.

ACCA marking scheme		
		Marks
(a)	Price/earnings ratio value of company	2
	Proposed dividend per share	1
	Average dividend growth rate	1
	Cost of equity using CAPM	1
	Dividend growth model value of company	2
	Discussion	4
		──
		10
		──
(b)	Conversion value	1
	Market value	2
	Floor value	2
	Conversion premium	1
		──
		6
		──
(c)	Definition of Semi-strong form efficiency	1–2
	Significance of semi-strong form efficiency	2–3
		──
		4
		──
Total		**20**
		──

Examiner's comments

In part (a), candidates were asked to calculate the value of a company using the price/earnings ratio method and the dividend growth model, and to discuss the significance of calculated values, in comparison to the current market value of the company, to a potential buyer. Answers to this part of question 1 often failed to gain many marks, mainly because candidates did not calculate company values.

The prices/earnings ratio method calculates the value of a company by multiplying earnings per share figure by a price/earnings ratio, and then multiplying by the number of issued shares. Alternatively, total earnings can be multiplied by a price/earnings ratio. Although the question provided an average sector price/earnings ratio to use in this context, many candidates simply calculated the current price/earnings ratio of the company and compared this with the sector value. Calculating a price/earnings ratio is not the same as calculating the value of a company. Candidates should also note that the price/earnings ratio is a multiple and neither a percentage nor a monetary amount.

The dividend growth model (DGM) formula is given in the formulae sheet in the examination. Many candidates rearranged the DGM formula in order to calculate a cost of equity, even though what was needed was to calculate a share price by inserting values for the current dividend, the cost of equity and the dividend growth rate into the DGM formula provided. The cost of equity could be calculated from the capital asset pricing model, using the formula given in the formulae sheet. The current dividend could be calculated using the dividend payout ratio and the current earnings per share value provided in the question. The future dividend growth rate could be calculated on an historical average basis, although there were many errors in its calculation. A number of candidates were unable to distinguish between some of the variables given in the question, for example confusing dividend per share with earnings per share, return on the market with cost of equity, and equity beta with retention ratio.

Even though the current market value of the company (number of shares multiplied by share price) was needed, a number of candidates failed to calculate it. The level of discussion was often limited, although some candidates demonstrated that they were aware of the weaknesses of the valuation models used.

Part (b) asked candidates to calculate the market value, floor value and conversion value of a $100 convertible bond. Many candidates either failed to answer this part of question 1, or showed in their answers that they did not understand how to calculate the present value of a stream of future cash flows (which is what the market value of a bond is equivalent to).

Candidates needed to calculate the present value of future interest payments plus the present value of the future conversion value (the market value, since conversion was financially preferable to redemption), and the present value of future interest payments plus the present value of the future redemption at par value (the floor value, since this stream of future cash flows is guaranteed). Some candidates were able to calculate the floor value, but called it the market value. Some candidates were able to calculate the current conversion value, but were not aware that this was used in calculating the conversion premium.

A number of candidates were not aware of the difference between interest rate, cost of debt and share price growth rate and used their values interchangeably. Some candidates introduced an assumed tax rate, when the question made no reference to taxation at all. There were indications of candidates learning a computation method, without acquiring an understanding of the concepts underlying it. Candidates must understand the importance, in financial management, of discounting future values in order to obtain present values, since this is used in investment appraisal, bond valuation, share valuation and company valuation.

Part (c) required candidates to discuss the significance to a listed company of its shares being traded on a semi-strong form efficient stock market.

A number of candidates did not understand and could not discuss market efficiency, and very few correctly discussed the significance of semi-strong market efficiency to a company. Overall, many answers were not of a pass standard.

RISK MANAGEMENT

66 NEDWEN

Key answer tips

This is a fairly straightforward question that has a good balance of discursive and mathematical elements. Parts (a) and (b) offer a chance to pick up some easy marks for simple 'learn and churn' type answers. To score well in parts (c) and (d) you need to be clear on the spot and forward rates provided to ensure you select the right ones The highlighted words are key phrases that markers are looking for.

(a)   Transaction risk

This is the risk arising on short-term foreign currency transactions that the actual income or cost may be different from the income or cost expected when the transaction was agreed. For example, a sale worth $10,000 when the exchange rate is $1.79 per £ has an expected sterling value is $5,587. If the dollar has depreciated against sterling to $1.84 per £ when the transaction is settled, the sterling receipt will have fallen to $5,435. Transaction risk therefore affects cash flows and for this reason most companies choose to hedge or protect themselves against transaction risk.

Translation risk

This risk arises on consolidation of financial statements prior to reporting financial results and for this reason is also known as accounting exposure. Consider an asset worth €14 million, acquired when the exchange rate was €1.4 per $. One year later, when financial statements are being prepared, the exchange rate has moved to €1.5 per $ and the statement of financial position value of the asset has changed from $10 million to $9.3 million, resulting an unrealised (paper) loss of $0.7 million. Translation risk does not involve cash flows and so does not directly affect shareholder wealth. However, investor perception may be affected by the changing values of assets and liabilities, and so a company may choose to hedge translation risk through, for example, matching the currency of assets and liabilities (e.g. a euro-denominated asset financed by a euro-denominated loan).

Economic risk

Transaction risk is seen as the short-term manifestation of economic risk, which could be defined as the risk of the present value of a company's expected future cash flows being affected by exchange rate movements over time. It is difficult to measure economic risk, although its effects can be described, and it is also difficult to hedge against it.

(b)   **Forward market evaluation**

Net receipt in 1 month = $240,000 – $140,000 = $100,000

Nedwen Co needs to sell dollars at an exchange rate of 1.7829 + 0.003 = $1.7832 per £

Sterling value of net receipt = $100,000/1.7832 = £56,079

Receipt in 3 months = $300,000

Nedwen Co needs to sell dollars at an exchange rate of 1.7846 + 0.004 = $1.7850 per £

Sterling value of receipt in 3 months = $300,000/1.7850 = £168,067

(c)   **Evaluation of money-market hedge**

Expected receipt after 3 months = $300,000

Dollar interest rate over three months = 5.4/4 = 1.35%

Dollars to borrow now to have $300,000 liability after 3 months = 300,000/1.0135 = $296,004

Spot rate for selling dollars = 1.7820 + 0.0002 = $1.7822 per £

Sterling deposit from borrowed dollars at spot = $296,004/1.7822 = £166,089

Sterling interest rate over three months = 4.6/4 = 1.15%

Value in 3 months of sterling deposit = £166,089 × 1.0115 = £167,999

The forward market is marginally preferable to the money market hedge for the dollar receipt expected after 3 months.

(d)   A currency futures contract is a standardised contract for the buying or selling of a specified quantity of foreign currency. It is traded on a futures exchange and settlement takes place in three-monthly cycles ending in March, June, September and December, i.e. a company can buy or sell September futures, December futures and so on. The price of a currency futures contract is the exchange rate for the currencies specified in the contract.

When a currency futures contract is bought or sold, the buyer or seller is required to deposit a sum of money with the exchange, called initial margin. If losses are incurred as exchange rates and hence the prices of currency futures contracts change, the buyer or seller may be called on to deposit additional funds (variation margin) with the exchange. Equally, profits are credited to the margin account on a daily basis as the contract is 'marked to market'.

Most currency futures contracts are closed out before their settlement dates by undertaking the opposite transaction to the initial futures transaction, i.e. if buying currency futures was the initial transaction, it is closed out by selling currency futures. A gain made on the futures transactions will offset a loss made on the currency markets and vice versa.

Nedwen Co expects to receive $300,000 in three months' time and so is concerned that sterling may appreciate (strengthen) against the dollar, since this would result in a lower sterling receipt. The company can hedge the receipt using sterling futures contracts as follows. As Nedwen will be buying sterling in June with the dollars it receives from its customer, it will also want to sell June sterling futures contracts at the same time (or as close as possible) so that any movement in exchange rates is offset by the two opposite transactions. This means that Nedwen would have to buy the futures contracts now in order to be able to sell them in June.

ACCA marking scheme			
			Marks
(a)	Transaction risk	2 marks	
	Translation risk	2 marks	
	Economic risk	2 marks	
			6
(b)	Netting	1 mark	
	Sterling value of 3-month receipt	1 mark	
	Sterling value of 1-year receipt	1 mark	
			3
(c)	Evaluation of money market hedge	4 marks	
	Comment	1 mark	
			5
(d)	Definition of currency futures contract	1–2 marks	
	Initial margin and variation margin	1–2 marks	
	Buying and selling of contracts	1–2 marks	
	Hedging the three-month receipt	1–2 marks	
	Maximum		6
Total			**20**

67 EXPORTERS PLC *Walk in the footsteps of a top tutor*

Key answer tips

Another fairly standard question that combines knowledge with application. The highlighted words are key phrases that markers are looking for.

Tutor's top tips

Don't feel you have to tackle the different parts of the requirement in order. Part (b) gives the best opportunities for some easy marks so is the best place to start.

(a) Exporters plc

Tutor's top tips

This first thing to appreciate about this part of the requirement is that it's asking a question that rarely gets asked in reality – what if we hadn't entered into that hedge? Remember, the purpose of hedging a transaction is to eliminate risk, and so it isn't often someone would bother looking back to calculate what would have happened if they hadn't bothered!

That said, to perform the calculation you need to keep in mind the following things:

1   *Forward rates will be determined by interest differentials (the question doesn't specify the forward rate the company is locking in to. It does however, give you the interest differentials that will allow you to work the forward rate out.*

2   *What does happen to interest rates in the future will be determined by many different factors – the rate that does occur in the future is unlikely to be the same as the future rate that was contacted. This will give rise to a gain or loss on the transaction.*

3   *If the £ gains in value (appreciates), you will get more Northland dollars for each £. Equally, if it losses value (depreciates or weakens) it will buy less Northland dollars.*

UK interest rates over 6 months are $\frac{1}{2} \times 12\% = 6\%$.

Northland interest rates over 6 months are $\frac{1}{2} \times 15\% = 7.5\%$

Implied forward rate for the £ after 6 months = $\dfrac{1.075}{1.06} \times 2.5 = 2.5354$.

Tutorial note

If you calculated your forward rate using the annual interest rates, you would only lose one mark. All further calculations will be based on the 'own figure rule' which means that, provided you used the right technique, your answer would be marked as correct, even though you have a different answer to that shown here.

(1)   If the £ has gained 4%, N's actual rate is 2.5 × 1.04 = 2.6 to the £.

Hedged receipt = $\dfrac{\$500{,}000}{2.5354} = £197{,}208$

Unhedged receipt = $\dfrac{\$500{,}000}{2.6} = £192{,}308$

∴ Gain from hedging = £197,208 – £192,308 = £4,900.

(2)   If the £ has lost 2%, N's actual rate is 2.5 × 0.98 = 2.45 to the £

Unhedged receipt = $\dfrac{\$500{,}000}{2.45} = £204{,}082$

∴ Loss from hedging = £204,082 – £197,208 = £6,874.

(3)   If the £ has remained stable, N's actual rate is still 2.5 to the £.

Unhedged receipt = $\dfrac{\$500{,}000}{2.5} = £200{,}000$

∴ Loss from hedging = £200,000 – £197,208 = £2,792.

(b)   **Forward market currency hedge**

A company can use the foreign exchange markets to hedge exactly as shown in the question. A company due to receive foreign currency in 6 months' time can sell that currency forward, i.e. agree an exchange rate now at which that amount of foreign currency will be exchanged into sterling. The cost involved will be paid to the bank arranging the transaction and will usually be built into the contract's exchange rate so that the foreign currency is quoted net. The benefits are peace of mind to the company that they have laid off the risks of exchange rate movements between the contract date and the date when the foreign currency will be paid or received. Part (a) illustrates a range of possible gains and losses on a forward market currency hedge depending on the actual currency movements before the contract matures.

Currency futures hedge

Currency futures contracts are traded on separate exchanges such as the London International Financial Futures and Options Exchange (LIFFE). Each contract provides a simultaneous right and obligation to buy or sell on a specific future date a standard amount of a particular currency at a price that is known at the time of entering the contract. Since the contracts are sold in standard amounts and have a limited number of maturity dates each year, they are highly standardised and a liquid market has developed to trade them.

A UK exporting company due to receive 500,000 Northland dollars in six months' time could only hedge its currency exposure by means of currency futures if contracts are available between Northland dollars and sterling, and then only could it create an exact hedge if 500,000 dollars happened to be a multiple of the standard contract size. But assuming that both these conditions are fulfilled, the company can buy contracts to sell Northland dollars into sterling at the required future time.

Currency options hedge

A call/put option gives the buyer of that option the right, but not the obligation, to buy/sell currency in the future at a particular exchange rate. A UK company which uses a forward or futures position avoids losing from adverse movements on currencies but also fails to gain from favourable movements. A currency option is suitable for a UK company which believes it knows the direction of future exchange rate movements, but is not sure and wishes to minimise the loss arising in the event of being proved incorrect.

The company in the question anticipates dollars receivable in six months' time. It can pay an option premium to buy sterling call options. These enable the company to benefit from the anticipated appreciating dollar while providing protection against the opposite movement.

68   CC CO

Key answer tips

Part (c) can easily be attempted in isolation and could be tackled first to capture the knowledge level marks early within your allotted time.

Part (b) is dependent on your answer to part (a) although the own figure rule will apply when part (b) is marked. A methodical approach should yield some easy marks.

The highlighted words in the written sections are key phrases that markers are looking for.

(a)   **Using a forward market hedge**

Dollar value of payment = €1.5m/0.698 = $2.149m

Using a money market hedge

Expected payment after 3 months = €1.5m

Euro interest rate over three months = 2.9/4 = 0.725%

Euros to invest now to have €1.5m asset after 3 months = €1.5m/1.00725 = €1.4892m

Spot rate for buying Euros = 0.70 €/$

Dollar loan needed for Euros deposited = €1.4892/0.7 = $2.127m

Dollar interest rate over three months = 5.5/4 = 1.375%

Value in 3 months of dollar loan = €2.127 × 1.01375 = $2.1567

The forward market is marginally preferable to the money market hedge for the Euro payment expected after 3 months.

(b)

Year	0	1	2	3	4	5
		$000	$000	$000	$000	$000
Contribution (W1)		1,330	2,830	2,408	1,280	
Fixed costs (W2)		(265)	(281)	(298)	(316)	
		———	———	———	———	———
Taxable cash flow		1,065	2,549	2,110	964	
Taxation			(320)	(765)	(633)	(289)
Initial investment	(2,149)					
CA tax benefits (W3)			161	161	161	161
		———	———	———	———	———
After-tax cash flow	(2,149)	1,065	2,390	1,506	492	(128)
Discount at 10% (W4)	1	0.909	0.826	0.751	0.683	0.621
	———	———	———	———	———	———
Present values	(2,149)	968	1,974	1,131	336	(79)
	———	———	———	———	———	———

Net present value = $2,181,000. The net present value is positive and so the investment is financially acceptable.

Workings

(W1) Annual contribution

Year	0	1	2	3	4
Sales volume (units/yr)		250,000	500,000	400,000	200,000
Selling price ($/unit)		12.60	13.23	13.89	14.59
Variable cost ($/unit)		7.28	7.57	7.87	8.19
Contribution ($/unit)		5.32	5.66	6.02	6.40
Contribution ($/yr)		1,330,000	2,830,000	2,408,000	1,280,000

(W2) Fixed costs

$250,000 inflating at 6% p.a. = $265,000 in T1 etc

(W3) Tax allowable depreciation tax benefits

Tax allowable depreciation is on a straight-line basis over the four-year life of the asset.

$2.149m ÷ 4 years = $537,250 per annum

Tax benefit = $537,250 × 30% = $161,175

(W4) Discount factor

$(1 + i) = (1 + r) \times (1 + h)$

$(1 + i) = (1 + 0.051) \times (1 + 0.047)$

$(1 + i) = 1.1004$

$i = 10\%$

(c) A key effect of inflation on companies is the role it plays in determining exchange rates. Purchasing power parity theory (PPPT) claims that the rate of exchange between two currencies depends on the relative inflation rates within the respective countries. PPPT is based on 'the law of one price'. In equilibrium, identical goods must cost the same, regardless of the currency in which they are sold.

The main function of an exchange rate is to provide a means of translating prices expressed in one currency into another currency. The implication is that the exchange rate will be determined in some way by the relationship between these prices. This arises from the law of one price.

The law of one price states that in a free market with no barriers to trade and no transport or transactions costs, the competitive process will ensure that there will only be one price for any given good. If price differences occurred they would be removed by arbitrage; entrepreneurs would buy in the low market and resell in the high market. This would eradicate the price difference.

If this law is applied to international transactions, it suggests that exchange rates will always adjust to ensure that only one price exists between countries where there is relatively free trade.

An estimate of expected future spot rates can be made using the formula:

$$S_1 = S_0 \times \frac{(1+h_c)}{(1+h_b)}$$

Where:

S_0 = current spot rate

S_1 = expected future spot rate

h_b = inflation rate in country for which the spot is quoted (base currency)

h_c = inflation rate in the other country (counter currency)

Thus, a high level of inflation in an economy, relative to the inflation rates overseas will result in a depreciation of the currency. As a result of the currency fluctuation imports will cost more but it may be easier to export since goods will appear cheaper to overseas purchasers.

69   PLAM CO

Key answer tips

In part (a) the interest payment is on a fixed rate loan so the risk the question is asking you to evaluate is currency risk. Use the numbers given in the question to make your evaluation. There is also enough information given on interest rate to do the calculations for a money market hedge. For part (c) look at each type of borrowing to analyse its risk and remember that risk can be faced on fixed rate debt as well as floating, in that there is the potential to miss out on lower interest payments if rates fall. In part (c), finding the value of convertible loan notes is one of the more difficult determinations of market value that you will have to do, but is certainly not a niche topic. In part (d) you should be able to pick up some easy marks and you could do this part first if you wish. The highlighted words are key phrases that markers are looking for.

(a)   Plam Co needs to make an interest payment of 30 million pesos in six months' time. The current dollar cost of this interest payment is 30/58.335 = $514,271. In six months' time the dollar cost of the interest payment will be 30/56.585 = $530,176. This is an increase in cost of $15,905.

Plam Co could lock into the six-month forward exchange rate of 56.585 pesos/$ by entering into a forward exchange contract with a bank. This would fix the cost of the interest payment at $530,176 and protect Plam Co against any unexpected deterioration in the exchange rate. However, Plam Co could not benefit if the future spot were more favourable than the current forward exchange rate.

Plam Co could use a money market hedge by placing pesos on deposit now, financed by borrowing dollars for repayment in six months' time. The six-month interest rate for placing pesos on deposit is 1.5% (3%/2) and the six-month interest rate for borrowing dollars is 5% (10%/2). The dollar cost of hedging the peso interest payment would be $532,005:

30m pesos/1.015 = 29,556,650 pesos to be deposited now.

$ cost of buying pesos = 29,556,650/58.335 = $506,671 to borrow now.

$ borrowing to pay off after 6 months = $506,671 × 1.05 = $532,005.

On financial grounds, the forward market hedge would be recommended.

(b) Interest rate risk is concerned with the sensitivity of profit and cash flows to changes in interest rates.

Fixed rate debt and floating rate debt

Plam Co has both fixed rate debt and floating rate debt. Analysis shows that floating rate debt contributes 21.7% of nominal value of debt and 24.3% of annual interest payments. Plam Co expects interest rates to fall over the next year and its high proportion of fixed rate debt would lead to the company losing competitive advantage compared to a company with a higher proportion of floating rate debt. Plam Co will continue to be disadvantaged by its fixed interest debt for a long time, if interest rates continue to fall, since its fixed rate debt cannot be redeemed for another eight years.

Gap exposure and basis risk

Gap exposure considers groups of interest-sensitive assets and liabilities with similar maturities and determines whether liabilities exceed assets (a negative gap) or assets exceed liabilities (a positive gap), in evaluating sensitivity to interest rate increases and decreases.

Even if interest-sensitive assets and liabilities are matched, interest rate risk can arise if variable interest rates on assets and liabilities are determined on different bases (basis risk).

There is no information indicating that Plam Co has interest-bearing assets and on this basis gap exposure and basis risk are not relevant.

Workings

Interest on dollar-denominated loan notes = $20m × 0.07 = $1,400,000

Interest on dollar-denominated bank loan = $4m × 0.08 = $320,000

Interest on dollar-denominated overdraft = $3m × 0.1 = $300,000

Interest on peso-denominated loan notes = 300m pesos × 0.1/56.585 = $530,176

Total interest payment = $1,400,000 + $320,000 + $300,000 + $530,176 = $2,550,176

Percentage of floating rate interest = 100 × ($320,000 + $300,000)/$2,550,176 = 24.3%

Debt nominal value = $20m + $4m + $3m + $5.3m* = $32.3 million

Percentage of floating rate debt = 100 × $7m/$32.3m = 21.7%

*$530,176/0.1 or 300m pesos/56.585

Key answer tips

It's easy to miss that while redemption occurs on these loan notes in eight years' time, conversion would happen after seven years. This means that the conversion value of the shares cannot be directly compared to the redemption value as they happen at different time periods.

In order to make a valid comparison, you must look at the cash flows associated with holding onto the loan note for one more year after the conversion date and discount them back one year to give a value as at the conversion date. This can then be compared directly to the conversion value to see which the loan note holder would prefer.

(c) If share prices increase by 4% per year, the share price in seven years' time will be $8.55 per share ($6.50 × 1.04^7) and the conversion value will be $940 per loan note ($8.55 × 110).

This conversion value is less than the nominal value of $1,000 per loan note and less than the expected market value of $990.82 per loan note at the end of seven years (0.926 × $1,070 (redemption value and interest received in 8th year discounted back at the cost of debt of 8% to the 7th year to give an equivalent value to the conversion value in 7 years)). On financial grounds, holders of the loan notes are likely to hold them until redemption after eight years.

The current market value of the loan notes (when anticipated to be redeemed in 8 years, using the cost of debt of 8%) will be ($70 × 5.747) + ($1,000 × 0.540) = $402.29 + $540.00 = $942.29 per loan note. This is also referred to as the floor value of the loan notes.

If share prices increase by 6% per year, the share price in seven years' time will be $9.77 per share ($6.50 × 1.06^7) and the conversion value will be $1,075 per loan note ($9.77 × 110). Holders of the loan notes are likely to prefer conversion, as the conversion value is now greater than nominal value of $1,000 per loan note and the expected market value of $990.82 per loan note at the end of seven years.

The current market value of the loan notes (when anticipated to be converted in 7 years, using the cost of debt of 8%) will be ($70 × 5.206) + ($1,075 × 0.583) = $364.42 + $626.73 = $991.15 per loan note.

(d) The dividend growth model (DGM) values the ordinary shares of a company as the present value of its expected future dividends and the model makes the assumption that these future dividends increase at a constant annual rate.

The main problem with the DGM is that while predictions can be made of future dividends, future dividends cannot be known with certainty. In fact, experience shows that directors take many factors into account when making dividend decisions and dividends do not increase at a constant annual rate in the real world. It is therefore extremely unlikely that future dividends will increase at a constant annual rate in perpetuity.

The DGM also assumes that the cost of equity is constant. In reality, the cost of equity will change as economic circumstances change. The capital asset pricing model suggests that the cost of equity will vary with changes in systematic risk, whether business risk or financial risk. It is therefore unrealistic to expect that the cost of equity will remain constant in the future.

Dividends are of great importance to many shareholders, however, and the value placed on shares will often reflect the value of expected future dividend income. The DGM offers shareholders a way of estimating the value of future dividend income, provided that the assumptions of the model are accepted.

ACCA Marking scheme			
			Marks
(a)	Increased dollar cost of interest payment		1
	Six-month forward market hedge		1
	Six-month interest rates		1
	Six-month money market hedge		1
	Six-month hedging recommendation		1
		Maximum	5
(b)	Fixed interest rate and floating interest rate discussion		1–4
	Analysis of fixed and floating rate interest		1
	Analysis of fixed and floating rate nominal value		1
	Gap exposure and basis risk		1
		Maximum	5
(c)	Conversion value using 4% share price growth		1
	Justification for valuation calculation		1
	Market value using 4% share price growth		1
	Conversion value using 6% share price growth		1
	Justification for valuation calculation		1
	Market value using 6% share price growth		1
		Maximum	6
(d)	Assumption of constant dividend growth rate		1–2
	Assumption of constant cost of equity		1–2
	Other relevant discussion		1–2
		Maximum	4
Total			**20**

Examiner's comments

A number of candidates left parts (a) and (b) of the question until last, perhaps leaving insufficient time for preparing an adequate answer, and perhaps also indicating that they were lacking in preparation in relation to this part of the syllabus.

This suggestion is supported by those answers that discussed foreign currency risk in part (b), which asked for a discussion of interest rate risk. Most answers tended to gain higher marks on (a) compared to (b).

Part (a) required candidates to evaluate the risk faced by a company that had a foreign currency-denominated fixed interest payment to make in six months' time and to advise how this risk might be hedged. Answers that did not evaluate the risk faced by the company could not receive full marks as that part of the question requirement had not been met.

The exchange rates provided in the question indicated an expected depreciation of the dollar, the home currency, against the peso, the foreign currency. The company therefore faced the risk that its peso fixed interest payment would cost more in dollars in six months' time than at present. The best indication of the likely increase in cost could be found by comparing the dollar value of the interest payment using the spot exchange rate and the six-month forward exchange rate, on an offer basis (the company had to buy pesos). Better answers indicated an understanding of the risk faced by the company arising from a depreciation of its home currency, the dollar.

The information provided in the question suggested a forward exchange contract or a money market hedge as possible hedging methods and many answers evaluated these. A lead payment was also a possibility that could be evaluated, as some candidates demonstrated.

Credit was also given to suggestions that the risk faced by the company might be hedged using derivatives such as currency futures or currency options.

Part (b) asked candidates to identify and discuss the different kinds of interest rate risk faced by the company and the question provide details of four different kinds of debt that it had.

Some answers received no credit because they discussed exchange rate risk, for example they discussed transaction risk, translation risk and economic risk.

The main interest rate risk faced by the company related to fixed rate and variable rate debt. The expectation was for interest rates to fall over the next year and the company would benefit quickly from this via its overdraft. Interest on its variable rate bank loan, however, was reset annually and so the benefit here would be slower in arriving. As for its fixed rate dollar loan notes, the problem here was that the company would be locked into its fixed rate for a further eight years and the company would therefore be at a commercial disadvantage as interest rates fell. It is worth noting that interest on this debt was lower than on the three other kinds of debt. Many candidates were able to say something about fixed rate and variable rate debt.

Answers to part (c) were very variable in quality, while answers to part (d) sometimes needed more academic content.

Part (c) asked candidates to calculate the market value of a convertible loan note under two different share price growth rate assumptions. The market value of the loan note is equal to the sum of the present values of the future cash flows accruing to it. If redeemed, the market value of the loan note is equal to the sum of the present value of the interest payments over eight years, plus the present value of the redemption value after eight years. This would be the 'floor value' of the loan note. If converted, the market value of the loan note is equal to the sum of the present value of the interest payments over seven years, plus the present value of the conversion value after seven years.

A decision about whether conversion was likely was therefore needed in order to determine the relevant cash flows to discount to provide the market value. A key step in this valuation was calculating the conversion value of the loan notes. Many candidates were able to make progress towards calculating one or more conversion values. Errors encountered here were applying only one year of share price growth rather than seven years, and applying eight years of share price growth when conversion was after seven years.

A common error when deciding whether conversion was likely was to compare a conversion value with the loan note nominal value. As these values existed at different points in time, they could not be compared directly. One approach was to compare the conversion value with the expected market value of the loan note at the end of seven years, assuming redemption, as in the suggested solution.

A general point in relation to calculating market values of the loan note is that a number of students did not calculate the interest payment by multiplying the interest rate by the nominal value of the loan.

Part (d) required candidates to discuss the limitations of the dividend growth model as a way of valuing the ordinary shares of a company. Many students were able to make one or two points relating to assumptions made by the model, for example about constant future dividend growth or about a constant cost of equity.

Section 7

SPECIMEN EXAM QUESTIONS

F9 Financial Management - Specimen Exam

Exam Summary

Time allowed: This specimen exam is not timed.

This exam is divided into three sections:

Section A

- 15 objective test (OT) questions, each worth 2 marks.
- 30 marks in total.

Section B

- Three OT cases, each containing a scenario which relates to five OT questions, each worth 2 marks.
- 30 marks in total.

Section C

- Two constructed response questions, each containing a scenario which relates to one or more requirement(s).
- Each constructed response question is worth 20 marks in total.
- 40 marks in total.

Please note that the live exam is worth a total of 110 marks, 10 marks of which are for questions that do not count towards your final result and are included for quality assurance purposes. This specimen exam is worth a total of 100 marks, reflecting the element of the live exam on which your result will be based.

All questions are compulsory.

Click **Next** to start your exam.

F9 Financial Management - Specimen Exam

Section A

This section of the exam contains **15 objective test (OT) questions**.

Each question is worth **2 marks** and is compulsory.

This exam section is worth **30 marks** in total.

Select **Next** to continue.

Q1

The home currency of Acaba Co is the dollar ($) and it trades with a company in a foreign country whose home currency is the Dinar. The following information is available:

	Home country	Foreign country
Spot rate	20.00 Dinar per $	
Interest rate	3% per year	7% per year
Inflation rate	2% per year	5% per year

What is the six-month forward exchange rate?

- 20.39 Dinar per $
- 20.30 Dinar per $
- 20.59 Dinar per $
- 20.78 Dinar per $

Q2

The following financial information relates to an investment project:

	$'000
Present value of sales revenue	50,025
Present value of variable costs	(25,475)
Present value of contribution	24,550
Present value of fixed costs	(18,250)
Present value of operating income	6,300
Initial investment	(5,000)
NPV	1,300

What is the sensitivity of the NPV to a change in sales volume?

- 7.1%
- 2.6%
- 5.1%
- 5.3%

Q3

Gurdip plots the historic movements of share prices and uses this analysis to make her investment decisions.

Oliver believes that share prices reflect all relevant information at all times.

Match the level of capital markets efficiency that best reflects each of Gurdip and Oliver's beliefs.

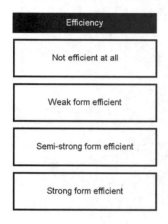

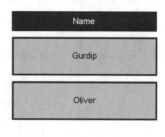

Q4

Which of the following statements concerning capital structure theory is correct?

○ In the traditional view, there is a linear relationship between the cost of equity and financial risk

○ Modigliani and Miller said that, in the absence of tax, the cost of equity would remain constant

○ Pecking order theory indicates that preference shares are preferred to convertible debt as a source of finance

○ Business risk is assumed to be constant as the capital structure changes

Q5

Which of the following actions is LEAST likely to increase shareholder wealth?

○ The weighted average cost of capital is decreased by a recent financing decision

○ The financial rewards of directors are linked to increasing earnings per share

○ The board of directors decides to invest in a project with a positive net present value

○ The annual report declares full compliance with the corporate governance code

Q6

Which TWO of the following statements are features of money market instruments?

☐ A negotiable instrument can be sold before maturity

☐ The yield on commercial paper is usually lower than that on treasury bills

☐ Discount instruments trade at less than face value

☐ Commercial paper is often issued by companies to fund long-term expenditure

Q7

The following are extracts from the statement of profit or loss of Gohar Co:

	$'000
Sales income	60,000
Cost of sales	(50,000)
Profit before interest and tax	10,000
Interest	(4,000)
Profit before tax	6,000
Tax	(4,500)
Profit after tax	**1,500**

60% of the cost of sales is variable costs.

What is the operational gearing of Gohar Co?

◉ 5.0 times

◉ 2.0 times

◉ 0.5 times

◉ 3.0 times

Q8

The management of Lamara Co has annual credit sales of $20m and accounts receivable of $4m. Working capital is financed by an overdraft at 12% interest per year. Assume 365 days in a year.

Calculate the annual finance cost saving if management reduces the collection period to 60 days (to the nearest dollar).

$ [   ]

Q9

Identify, by clicking on the relevant box, whether each of the following statements concerning financial management is true or false.

It is concerned with investment decisions, financing decisions and dividend decisions	TRUE	FALSE
It is concerned with financial planning and financial control	TRUE	FALSE
It considers the management of risk	TRUE	FALSE
It is concerned with providing information about past plans and decisions	TRUE	FALSE

Q10

Skava Co has paid the following dividends per share in recent years:

Year	20X4	20X3	20X2	20X1
Dividend ($ per share)	0.360	0.338	0.328	0.311

The dividend for 20X4 has just been paid and Skava Co has a cost of equity of 12%.

Using the geometric average historical growth rate and the dividend growth model, what is the market price of a Skava Co share on an ex-dividend basis?

○ $4.67

○ $5.14

○ $5.40

○ $6.97

Q11

'There is a risk that the value of our foreign currency-denominated assets and liabilities will change when we prepare our accounts'.

To which risk does the above statement refer?

○ Translation

○ Economic

○ Transaction

○ Interest rate

Q12

The following information has been calculated for Asani Co:

Trade receivables collection period	52 days
Raw material inventory turnover period	42 days
Work in progress inventory turnover period	30 days
Trade payables payment period	66 days
Finished goods inventory turnover period	45 days

Calculate the length of the working capital cycle.

[   ] days

Q13

Which of the following are usually seen as benefits of financial intermediation?

(1) Interest rate fixing
(2) Risk pooling
(3) Maturity transformation

○ 1 and 2 only

○ 1 and 3 only

○ 2 and 3 only

○ 1, 2 and 3

Q14

Which TWO of the following statements concerning working capital management are correct?

☐ The twin objectives of working capital management are profitability and liquidity

☐ A conservative approach to working capital investment will increase profitability

☐ Working capital management is a key factor in a company's long-term success

☐ The current ratio is a measure of profitability

Q15

Governments have a number of economic targets as part of their monetary policy.

Which TWO of the following targets relate predominantly to monetary policy?

☐ Increasing tax revenue

☐ Controlling the growth in the size of the money supply

☐ Reducing public expenditure

☐ Keeping interest rates low

Section B

This section of the exam contains **three OT cases**.

Each OT case contains a scenario which relates to **five OT questions**.

Each question is worth **2 marks** and is compulsory.

This exam section is worth **30 marks** in total.

Select **Next** to continue.

Par Co currently has the following long-term capital structure:

	$m	$m
Equity finance		
Ordinary shares	30.0	
Reserves	38.4	
		68.4
Non-current liabilities		
Bank loans	15.0	
8% convertible loan notes	40.0	
5% redeemable preference shares	15.0	
		70.0
Total equity and liabilities		138.4

The 8% loan notes are convertible into eight ordinary shares per loan note in seven years' time. If not converted, the loan notes can be redeemed on the same future date at their nominal value of $100. Par Co has a cost of debt of 9% per year.

The ordinary shares of Par Co have a nominal value of $1 per share. The current ex-dividend share price of the company is $10.90 per share and share prices are expected to grow by 6% per year for the foreseeable future. The equity beta of Par Co is 1.2.

Q16

The loan notes are secured on non-current assets of Par Co and the bank loan is secured by a floating charge on the current assets of the company.

Arrange the following sources of finance of Par Co in order of the risk to the investor with the riskiest first.

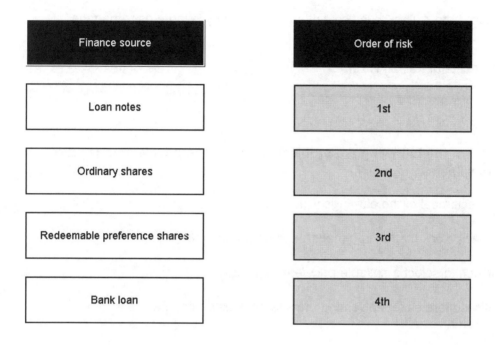

Finance source	Order of risk
Loan notes	1st
Ordinary shares	2nd
Redeemable preference shares	3rd
Bank loan	4th

Q17

Calculate the conversion value of the 8% loan notes of Par Co after seven years (to two decimal places).

$ [   ]

Q18

Assuming the conversion value after seven years is $126.15, what is the current market value of the 8% loan notes of Par Co?

- $115.20
- $109.26
- $94.93
- $69.00

Q19

Which of the following statements relating to the capital asset pricing model is correct?

- The equity beta of Par Co considers only business risk

- The capital asset pricing model considers systematic risk and unsystematic risk

- The equity beta of Par Co indicates that the company is more risky than the market as a whole

- The debt beta of Par Co is zero

Q20

Which TWO of the following are problems in using the price/earnings ratio method to value a company?

- It is the reciprocal of the earnings yield

- It combines stock market information and corporate information

- It is difficult to select a suitable price/earnings ratio

- The ratio is more suited to valuing the shares of listed companies

Zarona Co, whose home currency is the dollar, took out a fixed-interest peso bank loan several years ago when peso interest rates were relatively cheap compared to dollar interest rates. Zarona Co does not have any income in pesos. Economic difficulties have now increased peso interest rates while dollar interest rates have remained relatively stable.

Zarona Co must pay interest on the dates set by the bank. A payment of five million pesos is due in six months' time. The following information is available:

	Pesos per $
Spot rate	12.500 - 12.582
Six-month forward rate	12.805 - 12.889

Interest rates which can be used by Zarona Co:

	Borrow	Deposit
Peso interest rates	10.0% per year	7.5% per year
Dollar interest rates	4.5% per year	3.5% per year

Q21

Calculate the dollar cost of a forward market hedge (to the nearest dollar).

$ [   ]

Q22

Indicate, by clicking on the relevant box, whether each of the following statements relate to interest rate parity only, to purchasing power parity only or to both.

The currency of the country with the higher inflation rate will weaken against the other currency	Interest rate parity only	Purchasing power parity only	Both interest rate and purchasing power parity
The theory holds in the long term rather than the short term	Interest rate parity only	Purchasing power parity only	Both interest rate and purchasing power parity
The exchange rate reflects the different cost of living in two countries	Interest rate parity only	Purchasing power parity only	Both interest rate and purchasing power parity

Q23

What are the appropriate six-month interest rates for Zarona Co to use if it hedges the peso payment using a money market hedge?

Interest rate options	
10.0%	3.75%
7.5%	1.75%
5.0%	3.5%
2.25%	4.5%

Interest rate to be used for:	
Borrowing rate	Deposit rate

Q24

Which TWO of the following are possible ways for Zarona Co to hedge its current foreign currency risk?

☐ Matching receipts and payments

☐ Currency swaps

☐ Leading or lagging

☐ Currency futures

SPECIMEN EXAM : QUESTIONS

Q25

Zarona Co also trades with companies in Europe which use the euro as their home currency. In three months' time Zarona Co will receive €300,000 from a customer.

Which of the following is the correct procedure for hedging this receipt using a money market hedge?

- ○ Step 1   Borrow an appropriate amount in euros now
  - Step 2   Convert the euro amount into dollars
  - Step 3   Place the dollars on deposit
  - Step 4   Use the customer payment to repay the loan

- ○ Step 1   Borrow an appropriate amount in dollars now
  - Step 2   Place the dollars on deposit now
  - Step 3   Convert the dollars into euros in three months' time
  - Step 4   Use the customer payment to repay the loan

- ○ Step 1   Borrow an appropriate amount in dollars now
  - Step 2   Convert the dollar amount into euros
  - Step 3   Place the euros on deposit
  - Step 4   Use the customer payment to repay the loan

- ○ Step 1   Borrow an appropriate amount in euros now
  - Step 2   Place the euros on deposit now
  - Step 3   Convert the euros into dollars in three months' time
  - Step 4   Use the customer payment to repay the loan

Ridag Co operates in an industry which has recently been deregulated as the government seeks to increase competition in the industry.

Ridag Co plans to replace an existing machine and must choose between two machines. Machine 1 has an initial cost of $200,000 and will have a scrap value of $25,000 after four years. Machine 2 has an initial cost of $225,000 and will have a scrap value of $50,000 after three years. Annual maintenance costs of the two machines are as follows:

Year	1	2	3	4
Machine 1 ($ per year)	25,000	29,000	32,000	35,000
Machine 2 ($ per year)	15,000	20,000	25,000	

Where relevant, all information relating to this project has already been adjusted to include expected future inflation. Taxation and tax allowable depreciation must be ignored in relation to machine 1 and machine 2.

Ridag Co has a nominal before-tax weighted average cost of capital of 12% and a nominal after-tax weighted average cost of capital of 7%.

Q26

In relation to Ridag Co, which TWO of the following statements about competition and deregulation are true?

☐ Increased competition should encourage Ridag Co to reduce costs

☐ Deregulation will lead to an increase in administrative and compliance costs for Ridag Co

☐ Deregulation should mean an increase in economies of scale for Ridag Co

☐ Deregulation could lead to a decrease in the quality of Ridag Co's products

Q27

What is the equivalent annual cost of machine 1?

◉ $90,412

◉ $68,646

◉ $83,388

◉ $70,609

Q28

Is each of the following statements, about Ridag Co's use of the equivalent annual cost method, true or false?

Ridag Co cannot use the equivalent annual cost method to compare machine 1 and machine 2 as they have different useful lives	TRUE	FALSE
The machine which has the lowest total present value of costs should be selected by Ridag Co	TRUE	FALSE

Q29

Doubt has been cast over the accuracy of the year 2 and year 3 maintenance costs for machine 2. On further investigation it was found that the following potential cash flows are now predicted:

Year	Cash flow ($)	Probability
2	18,000	0.30
2	25,000	0.70
3	23,000	0.20
3	24,000	0.35
3	30,000	0.45

Calculate the expected present value of the maintenance costs for year 3 (to the nearest dollar).

$ [   ]

Q30

Ridag Co is appraising a different project, with a positive NPV. It is concerned about the risk and uncertainty associated with this other project.

Which of the following statements about risk, uncertainty and the project is true?

○ Sensitivity analysis takes into account the interrelationship between project variables

○ Probability analysis can be used to assess the uncertainty associated with the project

○ Uncertainty can be said to increase with project life, while risk increases with the variability of returns

○ A discount rate of 5% could be used to lessen the effect of later cash flows on the decision

Section C

This section of the exam contains **two constructed response questions**

Each question contains a scenario which relates to one or more requirement(s) which may be split over multiple question screens.

Each question is worth **20 marks** and is compulsory.

This exam section is worth **40 marks** in total.

Important: In your live exam please show all notes/workings that you want the marker to see within the spreadsheet or word processing answer areas. Remember, any notes/workings made on the Scratch Pad or on your workings paper will not be marked.

Select **Next** to continue.

This scenario relates to three requirements.

Vip Co, a large stock-exchange listed company, is evaluating an investment proposal to manufacture Product W33, which has performed well in test marketing trials conducted recently by the company's research and development division. Product W33 will be manufactured using a fully-automated process which would significantly increase noise levels from Vip Co's factory. The following information relating to this investment proposal has now been prepared:

Initial investment	$2 million
Selling price (current price terms)	$20 per unit
Expected selling price inflation	3% per year
Variable operating costs (current price terms)	$8 per unit
Fixed operating costs (current price terms)	$170,000 per year
Expected operating cost inflation	4% per year

The research and development division has prepared the following demand forecast as a result of its test marketing trials. The forecast reflects expected technological change and its effect on the anticipated life-cycle of Product W33.

Year	1	2	3	4
Demand (units)	60,000	70,000	120,000	45,000

It is expected that all units of Product W33 produced will be sold, in line with the company's policy of keeping no inventory of finished goods. No terminal value or machinery scrap value is expected at the end of four years, when production of Product W33 is planned to end. For investment appraisal purposes, Vip Co uses a nominal (money) discount rate of 10% per year and a target return on capital employed of 30% per year. Ignore taxation.

Q31

(a) Calculate the following values for the investment proposal:

(i) net present value;

(5 marks)

(ii) internal rate of return;

(3 marks)

(iii) return on capital employed (accounting rate of return) based on average investment.

(3 marks)

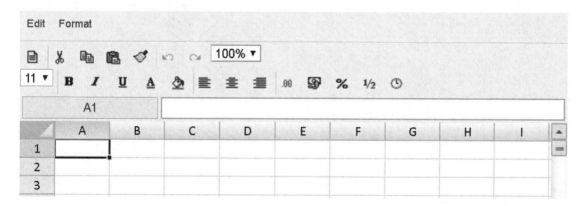

Q32

(b) Briefly discuss your findings in each section of (a) previously and advise whether the investment proposal is financially acceptable.

(4 marks)

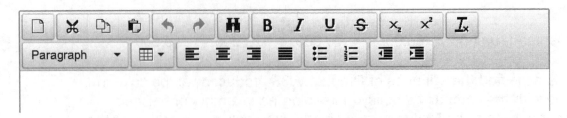

Q33

(c) Discuss how the objectives of Vip Co's stakeholders may be in conflict if the project is undertaken.

(5 marks)

(20 marks)

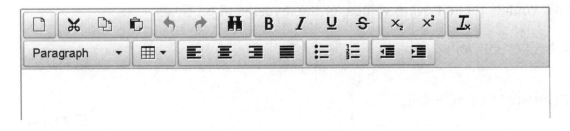

This scenario relates to three requirements.

Froste Co has a dividend payout ratio of 40% and has maintained this payout ratio for several years. The current dividend per share of the company is $0.50 per share and it expects that its next dividend per share, payable in one year's time, will be $0.52 per share.

The capital structure of the company is as follows:

	$m	$m
Equity		
Ordinary shares (nominal value $1 per share)	25	
Reserves	35	
		60
Debt		
Bond A (nominal value $100)	20	
Bond B (nominal value $100)	10	
		30
		90

Bond A will be redeemed at nominal value in ten years' time and pays annual interest of 9%. The cost of debt of this bond is 9·83% per year. The current ex interest market price of the bond is $95·08. Bond B will be redeemed at nominal value in four years' time and pays annual interest of 8%. The cost of debt of this bond is 7·82% per year. The current ex interest market price of the bond is $102·01. Froste Co has a cost of equity of 12·4%. Ignore taxation.

Q34

(a) Calculate the following values for Froste Co:

(i) ex dividend share price, using the dividend growth model;

(3 marks)

(ii) capital gearing (debt divided by debt plus equity) using market values;

(2 marks)

(iii) market value weighted average cost of capital.

(2 marks)

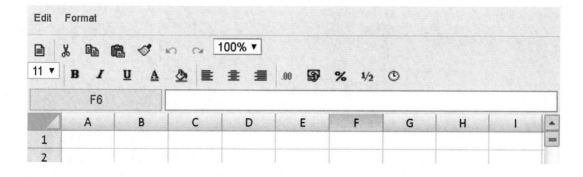

Q35

(b) Discuss whether a change in dividend policy will affect the share price of Froste Co.

(8 marks)

Q36

(c) Explain why Froste Co's capital instruments have different levels of risk and return.

(5 marks)

(20 marks)

Section 8

ANSWERS TO SPECIMEN EXAM QUESTIONS

SECTION A

1

20 x (1·035/1·015) = 20·39 Dinar per $

2

Sensitivity to a change in sales volume = 100 x 1,300/24,550 = 5·3%

3

Gurdip is basing her investment decisions on technical analysis, which means that she believes the stock market is not efficient at all, not even weak form efficient.

Oliver believes markets are strong form efficient

4

Only the statement about business risk is correct.

5

Increases in shareholder wealth will depend on increases in cash flow, rather than increases in earnings per share, i.e. increases in profit. If the financial rewards of directors are linked to increasing earnings per share, for example, through a performance-related reward scheme, there is an incentive to increasing short-term profit at the expense of longer growth in cash flows and hence shareholder wealth.

6

Negotiable instruments can be sold before maturity.
Discount instruments are traded at less than their face value.

7

Contribution = 60,000,000 − (50,000,000 x 0.6) = $30,000,000
Operational gearing = Contribution/ PBIT = $30m/ $10m = 3 times

8

Current collection period is 73 days (4/20 x 365 = 73).
Therefore a reduction to 60 days would be a reduction of 13 days.
13/365 x $20m = $712,329. $712,329 x 0.12 = $85,479

9

Financial management is concerned with investment decisions, financing decisions and dividend decisions as well as financial planning and financial control. It also considers the management of risk.
Information about past plans and decisions is a function of financial reporting, not financial management.

10

The geometric average dividend growth rate is $(36 \cdot 0/31 \cdot 1)^{1/3} - 1 = 5\%$
The ex div share price = $(36 \cdot 0 \times 1 \cdot 05)/(0 \cdot 12 - 0 \cdot 05) = \$5 \cdot 40$

11

The statement refers to translation risk.

12

The length of the operating cycle is 52 + 42 + 30 − 66 + 45 = 103 days.

13

Risk pooling and maturity transformation are always included in a list of benefits of financial intermediation.

14

The true statements are:
The twin objectives of working capital management are profitability and liquidity
Working capital management is a key factor in a company's long-term success

The current ratio is a measure of **liquidity**.
Adopting a conservative approach to working capital management will **decrease** profitability.

15

The two targets relating predominantly to monetary policy are controlling the growth in the size of the money supply and keeping interest rates low.

SECTION B

16

The secured loan notes are safer than the bank loan, which is secured on a floating charge. The redeemable preference shares are above debt in the creditor hierarchy. Ordinary shares are higher in the creditor hierarchy than preference shares.

17

Future share price after 7 years = 10.90×1.06^7 = $16.39 per share
Conversion value of each loan note = 16.39×8 = $131.12 per loan note

18

Market value of each loan note = $(8 \times 5.033) + (126.15 \times 0.547)$ = $40.26 + 69.00$ = $109.26

19

An equity beta of greater than 1 indicates that the security is more risky than the market as a whole.

20

It is correct that the price/earnings ratio is more suited to valuing the shares of listed companies, and it is also true that it is difficult to find a suitable price earnings ratio for the valuation.

21

Interest payment = 5,000,000 pesos
Six-month forward rate for buying pesos = 12.805 pesos per $
Dollar cost of peso interest using forward market = 5,000,000/12.805 = $390,472

22

Exchange rates reflecting the different cost of living between two countries is stated by the theory of purchasing power parity.
Both theories hold in the long term rather than the short term.
The currency of the country with the higher inflation rate will be forecast to weaken against the currency of the country with the lower inflation rate in purchasing power parity.

23

Dollars will be borrowed now for 6 months at $4.5 \times 6/12$ = 2.25%
Pesos will be deposited now for 6 months at $7.5 \times 6/12$ = 3.75%

24

Currency futures and swaps could both be used.
As payment must be made on the date set by the bank leading or lagging are not appropriate.
Matching is also inappropriate as the are no peso income streams.

25

The correct procedure is to: Borrow euro now, convert the euro into dollars and place the dollars on deposit for three months, use the customer receipt to pay back the euro loan.

26

Deregulation to increase competition should mean managers act to reduce costs in order to be competitive. The need to reduce costs may mean that quality of products declines.

27

Since taxation and capital allowances are to be ignored, and where relevant all information relating to project 2 has already been adjusted to include future inflation, the correct discount rate to use here is the nominal before-tax weighted average cost of capital of 12%.

	0	1	2	3	4
Maintenance costs		(25,000)	(29,000)	(32,000)	(35,000)
Investment and scrap	(200,000)				25,000
Net cash flow	(200,000)	(25,000)	(29,000)	(32,000)	10,000
Discount at 12%	1.000	0.893	0.797	0.712	0.636
Present values	(200,000)	(22,325)	(23,113)	(22,784)	(6,360)

Present value of cash flows ($274,582)
Cumulative present value factor 3.037
Equivalent annual cost = 274,582/3.037 = $90,412

28

Both statements are false. The machine with the lowest equivalent annual cost should be purchased not the present value of future cash flows alone.
The lives of the two machines are different and the equivalent annual cost method allows this to be taken into consideration.

29

EV of year 3 cash flow = (23,000 x 0·2) + (24,000 x 0·35) + (30,000 x 0·45) = $26,500
PV discounted at 12% = 26,500 x 0·712 = $18,868

30

The statement about uncertainty increasing with project life is true.

SECTION C

31

Calculation of NPV

Year	0	1	2	3	4
	$	$	$	$	$
Investment	-2,000,000				
Income		1,236,000	1,485,400	2,622,000	1,012,950
Operating costs		-676,000	-789,372	-1,271,227	-620,076
Net cash flow	-2,000,000	560,000	696,028	1,350,773	392,874
Discount at 10%	1	0.909	0.826	0.751	0.683
Present values	-2,000,000	509,040	574,919	1,014,431	268,333

Net present value: **366,723**

Workings

Calculation of income

Year	1	2	3	4
Inflated selling price ($/unit)	20.6	21.22	21.85	22.51
Demand (units/year)	60,000	70,000	120,000	45,000
Income ($/year)	1,236,000	1,485,400	2,622,000	1,012,950

Calculation of operating costs

Year	1	2	3	4
Inflated variable cost ($/unit)	8.32	8.65	9	9.36
Demand (units/year)	60,000	70,000	120,000	45,000
Variable costs ($/year)	499,200	605,500	1,080,000	421,200
Inflated fixed costs ($/year)	176,800	183,872	191,227	198,876
Operating costs ($/year)	676,000	789,372	1,271,227	620,076

Alternative calculation of operating costs

Year	1	2	3	4
Variable cost ($/unit)	8	**8**	8	**8**
Demand (units/year)	60,000	70,000	120,000	45,000
Variable costs ($/year)	480,000	560,000	960,000	360,000
Fixed costs ($/year)	170,000	170,000	170,000	170,000
Operating costs ($/year)	650,000	730,000	1,130,000	530,000
Inflated costs ($/year)	676,000	789,568	1,271,096	620,025

Calculation of internal rate of return

Year	0	1	2	3	4
	$	$	$	$	$
Net cash flow	**-2,000,000**	**560,000**	**696,028**	**1,350,773**	**392,874**
Discount at 20%	1	0.833	0.694	0.579	0.482
Present values	-2,000,000	466,480	483,043	782,098	189,365

Net present value   **-79,014**

Internal rate of return   **18.2**

Calcualtion of ROCE

Total cash inflow	2,999,675
Total depreciation and initial investment are same, as there is no scrap value	
Total accounting profit	999,675
Average annual accounting profit	249,918.75
Average investment	1,000,000
Return on capital employed	25.0%

Marking scheme

			Marks
(a)	i	Inflated income	2
	i	Inflated operating costs	2
	i	Net present value	1
(a)	ii	IRR	3
(a)	iii	ROCE	3
			11

32

The investment proposal has a positive net present value (NPV) of $366,722 and is therefore financially acceptable. The results of the other investment appraisal methods do not alter this financial acceptability, as the NPV decision rule will always offer the correct investment advice.

The internal rate of return (IRR) method also recommends accepting the investment proposal, since the IRR of 18·2% is greater than the 10% return required by Vip Co. If the advice offered by the IRR method differed from that offered by the NPV method, the advice offered by the NPV method would be preferred.

The calculated return on capital employed of 25% is less than the target return of 30%, but as indicated earlier, the investment proposal is financially acceptable as it has a positive NPV. The reason why Vip Co has a target return on capital employed of 30% should be investigated. This may be an out-of-date hurdle rate which has not been updated for changed economic circumstances.

Marking Scheme:

		Marks
(b)	Discussion of findings	3
	Advice on acceptability	1
		4

33

As a large listed company, Vip Co's primary financial objective is assumed to be the maximisation of shareholder wealth. In order to pursue this objective, Vip Co should undertake projects, such as this one, which have a positive NPV and generate additional value for shareholders.

However, not all of Vip Co's stakeholders have the same objectives and the acceptance of this project may create conflict between the different objectives.

Due to Product W33 being produced using an automated production process, it will not meet employees' objectives of continuity or security in their employment. It could also mean employees will be paid less than they currently earn. If this move is part of a longer-term move away from manual processes, it could also conflict with government objectives of having a low rate of unemployment.

The additional noise created by the production of Product W33 will affect the local community and may conflict with objectives relating to healthy living. This may also conflict with objectives from environmental pressure groups and government standards on noise levels as well.

Marking Scheme:

		Marks
(c)	Maximisation of shareholder wealth	2
	Conflict from automation of production process	2
	Conflict from additional noise	1
		5

34

(i)

Dividend growth rate	4	% per year
Share price using DGM	619.05	in cents

(ii)

		$
Number of ordinary shares	25	million
MV of equity	154.75	million
MV of Bond A issue	19.016	million
MV of Bond B issue	10.201	million
MV of debt	29.217	million
MV of capital employed	183.967	million

Capital gearing	15.9	%

(iii)

WACC	11.9	%

Marking scheme

			Marks
(a)	i	Dividend growth rate	1
(a)	i	Share price using DGM	2
(a)	ii	Capital gearing	2
(a)	iii	WACC	2
			7

35

Miller and Modigliani showed that, in a perfect capital market, the value of a company depended on its investment decision alone, and not on its dividend or financing decisions. In such a market, a change in dividend policy by Froste Co would not affect its share price or its market capitalisation. They showed that the value of a company was maximised if it invested in all projects with a positive net present value (its optimal investment schedule). The company could pay any level of dividend and if it had insufficient finance, make up the shortfall by issuing new equity. Since investors had perfect information, they were indifferent between dividends and capital gains. Shareholders who were unhappy with the level of dividend declared by a company could gain a 'home-made dividend' by selling some of their shares. This was possible since there are no transaction costs in a perfect capital market.

Against this view are several arguments for a link between dividend policy and share prices. For example, it has been argued that investors prefer certain dividends now rather than uncertain capital gains in the future (the 'bird-in-the-hand' argument).

It has also been argued that real-world capital markets are not perfect, but semi-strong form efficient. Since perfect information is therefore not available, it is possible for information asymmetry to exist between shareholders and the managers of a company. Dividend announcements may give new information to shareholders and as a result, in a semi-strong form efficient market, share prices may change. The size and direction of the share price change will depend on the difference between the dividend announcement and the expectations of shareholders. This is referred to as the 'signalling properties of dividends'.

It has been found that shareholders are attracted to particular companies as a result of being satisfied by their dividend policies. This is referred to as the 'clientele effect'. A company with an established dividend policy is therefore likely to have an established dividend clientele. The existence of this dividend clientele implies that the share price may change if there is a change in the dividend policy of the company, as shareholders sell their shares in order to reinvest in another company with a more satisfactory dividend policy. In a perfect capital market, the existence of dividend clienteles is irrelevant, since substituting one company for another will not incur any transaction costs. Since real-world capital markets are not perfect, however, the existence of dividend clienteles suggests that if Froste Co changes its dividend policy, its share price could be affected.

Marking Scheme:

		Marks
(b)	Dividend irrelevance	4
	Dividend relevance	4
		8

36

There is a trade-off between risk and return on Froste Co's capital instruments. Investors in riskier assets require a higher return in compensation for this additional risk. In the case of ordinary shares, investors rank behind all other sources of finance in the event of a liquidation so are the most risky capital instrument to invest in. This is partly why Froste Co's cost of equity is more expensive than its debt financing.

Similarly for debt financing, higher-risk borrowers must pay higher rates of interest on their borrowing to compensate lenders for the greater risk involved. Froste Co has two bonds, with Bond A having the higher interest rate and therefore the higher risk. Since both bonds were issued at the same time, business risk is not a factor in the higher level of risk.

Instead, this additional risk is likely to be due to the fact that Bond A has a greater time until maturity, meaning that its cash flows are more uncertain than Bond B. In particular where interest rates are expected to increase in the future, longer-term debt will have a higher rate of interest to compensate investors for investing for a longer period.

A further factor is that the total nominal value (book value) of Bond A is twice as large as Bond B and therefore may be perceived to be riskier.

Marking Scheme:

		Marks
(c)	Discussion of equity	1
	Debt and recognising business risk is not relevant	1
	Time until maturity of bonds	1
	Different value of bonds	1
	Other relevant discussion	1
		5